# The Science of Wealth

This study clarifies the character of 'political economy' as a distinct and separable intellectual discipline in the generic sense, in the texts of Adam Smith. It focuses upon the scope and fundamental conceptualizations of the new science. Smith's conceptualization of economic analysis is shown to constitute a unified intellectual piece for understanding economic society and its dynamics. Smith's fundamental economic language is exhaustively examined, in all his texts, with a view to clarifying the meaning of the basic concepts of his system. As well, the 'prehistories' of those concepts, in literature prior to Smith, back to the earliest times, are quite comprehensively treated, thereby placing his political economy in its larger historical context and conveying a rich sense of the history of these ideas over the whole course of our civilization.

A quite complete account of Smith's economics as a whole is also entailed by this undertaking: his key substantive economic doctrines are thoroughly considered as well, and all the elements of his economic theory receive attention. To that extent, notwithstanding the focus on concepts, an interpretation of the substance of Smith's political economy is also provided. This focus is partly motivated by the view that Smith's intellectual triumph in the history of social science is not so much about the success of specific doctrines. His more considerable theoretical success is at a deeper level: gaining a wide and long-lasting acquiescence in the conceptual universe framed by the fundamental structures of his system, for a newly emerging discipline. Those who subsequently contested Smithian doctrine did so within Smith's framework; they did so 'on his terms'. While the book's primary purpose is to reconstruct the character of Smith's political economy as a distinct intellectual enterprise, it also addresses its relevance to modern economics, and to policy and practice in contemporary liberal society.

This book will be of interest to students and researchers engaged with the history of economic and social thought, as well as philosophy and politics.

**Tony Aspromourgos** is Professor of Economics at the University of Sydney and is the author of *On the Origins of Classical Economics: Distribution and Value from William Petty to Adam Smith*, also published by Routledge.

## Routledge studies in the history of economics

1 **Economics as Literature**
*Willie Henderson*

2 **Socialism and Marginalism in Economics 1870–1930**
*Edited by Ian Steedman*

3 **Hayek's Political Economy**
The socio-economics of order
*Steve Fleetwood*

4 **On the Origins of Classical Economics**
Distribution and value from William Petty to Adam Smith
*Tony Aspromourgos*

5 **The Economics of Joan Robinson**
*Edited by Maria Cristina Marcuzzo, Luigi Pasinetti and Alesandro Roncaglia*

6 **The Evolutionist Economics of Léon Walras**
*Albert Jolink*

7 **Keynes and the 'Classics'**
A study in language, epistemology and mistaken identities
*Michel Verdon*

8 **The History of Game Theory, Vol 1**
From the beginnings to 1945
*Robert W. Dimand and Mary Ann Dimand*

9 **The Economics of W. S. Jevons**
*Sandra Peart*

10 **Gandhi's Economic Thought**
*Ajit K. Dasgupta*

11 **Equilibrium and Economic Theory**
*Edited by Giovanni Caravale*

12 **Austrian Economics in Debate**
*Edited by Willem Keizer, Bert Tieben and Rudy van Zijp*

13 **Ancient Economic Thought**
*Edited by B. B. Price*

14 **The Political Economy of Social Credit and Guild Socialism**
*Frances Hutchinson and Brian Burkitt*

15 **Economic Careers**
Economics and economists in Britain 1930–1970
*Keith Tribe*

16 **Understanding 'Classical' Economics**
Studies in the long-period theory
*Heinz Kurz and Neri Salvadori*

17 **History of Environmental Economic Thought**
*E. Kula*

18 **Economic Thought in Communist and Post-Communist Europe**
*Edited by Hans-Jürgen Wagener*

19 **Studies in the History of French Political Economy**
From Bodin to Walras
*Edited by Gilbert Faccarello*

20 **The Economics of John Rae**
*Edited by O. F. Hamouda, C. Lee and D. Mair*

21 **Keynes and the Neoclassical Synthesis**
Einsteinian versus Newtonian macroeconomics
*Teodoro Dario Togati*

22 **Historical Perspectives on Macroeconomics**
Sixty years after the 'General Theory'
*Edited by Philippe Fontaine and Albert Jolink*

23 **The Founding of Institutional Economics**
The leisure class and sovereignty
*Edited by Warren J. Samuels*

24 **Evolution of Austrian Economics**
From Menger to Lachmann
*Sandye Gloria*

25 **Marx's Concept of Money**
The God of commodities
*Anitra Nelson*

26 **The Economics of James Steuart**
*Edited by Ramón Tortajada*

27 **The Development of Economics in Europe since 1945**
*Edited by A. W. Bob Coats*

28 **The Canon in the History of Economics**
Critical essays
*Edited by Michalis Psalidopoulos*

29 **Money and Growth**
Selected papers of Allyn Abbott Young
*Edited by Perry G. Mehrling and Roger J. Sandilands*

30 **The Social Economics of Jean-Baptiste Say**
Markets and virtue
*Evelyn L. Forget*

31 **The Foundations of Laissez-Faire**
The economics of Pierre de Boisguilbert
*Gilbert Faccarello*

32 **John Ruskin's Political Economy**
*Willie Henderson*

33 **Contributions to the History of Economic Thought**
Essays in honour of R. D. C. Black
*Edited by Antoin E. Murphy and Renee Prendergast*

34 **Towards an Unknown Marx**
A commentary on the manuscripts of 1861–63
*Enrique Dussel*

35 **Economics and Interdisciplinary Exchange**
*Edited by Guido Erreygers*

36 **Economics as the Art of Thought**
Essays in memory of G. L. S. Shackle
*Edited by Stephen F. Frowen and Peter Earl*

37 **The Decline of Ricardian Economics**
Politics and economics in post-Ricardian theory
*Susan Pashkoff*

38 **Piero Sraffa**
His life, thought and cultural heritage
*Alessandro Roncaglia*

39 **Equilibrium and Disequilibrium in Economic Theory**
The Marshall–Walras divide
*Michel de Vroey*

40 **The German Historical School**
The historical and ethical approach to economics
*Edited by Yuichi Shionoya*

41 **Reflections on the Classical Canon in Economics**
Essays in honour of Samuel Hollander
*Edited by Sandra Peart and Evelyn Forget*

42 **Piero Sraffa's Political Economy**
A centenary estimate
*Edited by Terenzio Cozzi and Roberto Marchionatti*

43 **The Contribution of Joseph Schumpeter to Economics**
Economic development and institutional change
*Richard Arena and Cecile Dangel*

44 **On the Development of Long-Run Neo-Classical Theory**
*Tom Kompas*

45 **F. A. Hayek as a Political Economist**
Economic analysis and values
*Edited by Jack Birner, Pierre Garrouste and Thierry Aimar*

46 **Pareto, Economics and Society**
The mechanical analogy
*Michael McLure*

47 **The Cambridge Controversies in Capital Theory**
A study in the logic of theory development
*Jack Birner*

48 **Economics Broadly Considered**
Essays in honour of Warren J. Samuels
*Edited by Steven G. Medema, Jeff Biddle and John B. Davis*

49 **Physicians and Political Economy**
Six studies of the work of doctor-economists
*Edited by Peter Groenewegen*

50 **The Spread of Political Economy and the Professionalisation of Economists**
Economic societies in Europe, America and Japan in the nineteenth century
*Massimo Augello and Marco Guidi*

51 **Historians of Economics and Economic Thought**
The construction of disciplinary memory
*Steven G. Medema and Warren J. Samuels*

52 **Competing Economic Theories**
Essays in memory of Giovanni Caravale
*Edited by Sergio Nisticò and Domenico Tosato*

53 **Economic Thought and Policy in Less Developed Europe**
The nineteenth century
*Edited by Michalis Psalidopoulos and Maria-Eugenia Almedia Mata*

54 **Family Fictions and Family Facts**
Harriet Martineau, Adolphe Quetelet and the population question in England 1798–1859
*Brian Cooper*

55 **Eighteeth-Century Economics**
*Peter Groenewegen*

56 **The Rise of Political Economy in the Scottish Enlightenment**
*Edited by Tatsuya Sakamoto and Hideo Tanaka*

57 **Classics and Moderns in Economics, Volume I**
Essays on nineteenth and twentieth century economic thought
*Edited by Peter Groenewegen*

58 **Classics and Moderns in Economics, Volume II**
Essays on nineteenth and twentieth century economic thought
*Edited by Peter Groenewegen*

59 **Marshall's Evolutionary Economics**
*Tiziano Raffaelli*

60 **Money, Time and Rationality in Max Weber**
Austrian connections
*Stephen D. Parsons*

61 **Classical Macroeconomics**
Some modern variations and distortions
*James C. W. Ahiakpor*

62 **The Historical School of Economics in England and Japan**
*Tamotsu Nishizawa*

63 **Classical Economics and Modern Theory**
Studies in long-period analysis
*Heinz D. Kurz and Neri Salvadori*

64 **A Bibliography of Female Economic Thought to 1940**
*Kirsten K. Madden, Janet A. Sietz and Michele Pujol*

**65 Economics, Economists and Expectations**
From microfoundations to macroeconomics
*Warren Young, Robert Leeson and William Darity Jnr.*

**66 The Political Economy of Public Finance in Britain, 1767–1873**
*Takuo Dome*

**67 Essays in the History of Economics**
*Warren J. Samuels, Willie Henderson, Kirk D. Johnson and Marianne Johnson*

**68 History and Political Economy**
Essays in honour of P. D. Groenewegen
*Edited by Tony Aspromourgos and John Lodewijks*

**69 The Tradition of Free Trade**
*Lars Magnusson*

**70 Evolution of the Market Process**
Austrian and Swedish economics
*Edited by Michel Bellet, Sandye Gloria-Palermo and Abdallah Zouache*

**71 Consumption as an Investment**
The fear of goods from Hesiod to Adam Smith
*Cosimo Perrotta*

**72 Jean-Baptiste Say and the Classical Canon in Economics**
The British connection in French classicism
*Samuel Hollander*

**73 Knut Wicksell on Poverty**
No place is too exalted
*Knut Wicksell*

**74 Economists in Cambridge**
A study through their correspondence 1907–1946
*Edited by M. C. Marcuzzo and A. Rosselli*

**75 The Experiment in the History of Economics**
*Edited by Philippe Fontaine and Robert Leonard*

**76 At the Origins of Mathematical Economics**
The Economics of A. N. Isnard (1748–1803)
*Richard van den Berg*

**77 Money and Exchange**
Folktales and reality
*Sasan Fayazmanesh*

**78 Economic Development and Social Change**
Historical roots and modern perspectives
*George Stathakis and Gianni Vaggi*

**79 Ethical Codes and Income Distribution**
A study of John Bates Clark and Thorstein Veblen
*Guglielmo Forges Davanzati*

**80 Evaluating Adam Smith**
Creating the wealth of nations
*Willie Henderson*

81 **Civil Happiness**
Economics and human flourishing in historical perspective
*Luigino Bruni*

82 **New Voices on Adam Smith**
*Edited by Leonidas Montes and Eric Schliesser*

83 **Making Chicago Price Theory**
Milton Friedman–George Stigler correspondence, 1945–1957
*Edited by J. Daniel Hammond and Claire H. Hammond*

84 **William Stanley Jevons and the Cutting Edge of Economics**
*Bert Mosselmans*

85 **A History of Econometrics in France**
From nature to models
*Philippe Le Gall*

86 **Money and Markets**
A doctrinal approach
*Edited by Alberto Giacomin and Maria Cristina Marcuzzo*

87 **Considerations on the Fundamental Principles of Pure Political Economy**
*Vilfredo Pareto (Edited by Roberto Marchionatti and Fiorenzo Mornati)*

88 **The Years of High Econometrics**
A short history of the generation that reinvented economics
*Francisco Louçã*

89 **David Hume's Political Economy**
*Edited by Carl Wennerlind and Margaret Schabas*

90 **Interpreting Classical Economics**
Studies in long-period analysis
*Heinz D. Kurz and Neri Salvadori*

91 **Keynes's Vision**
Why the Great Depression did not return
*John Philip Jones*

92 **Monetary Theory in Retrospect**
The selected essays of Filippo Cesarano
*Filippo Cesarano*

93 **Keynes's Theoretical Development**
From the tract to the general theory
*Toshiaki Hirai*

94 **Leading Contemporary Economists**
Economics at the cutting edge
*Edited by Steven Pressman*

95 **The Science of Wealth**
Adam Smith and the framing of political economy
*Tony Aspromourgos*

# The Science of Wealth

## Adam Smith and the framing of political economy

**Tony Aspromourgos**

Routledge
Taylor & Francis Group
LONDON AND NEW YORK

First published 2009
by Routledge
2 Park Square, Milton Park, Abingdon, Oxon OX14 4RN

Simultaneously published in the USA and Canada
by Routledge
270 Madison Ave, New York, NY 10016

*Routledge is an imprint of the Taylor & Francis Group, an informa business*



Typeset in Times by Wearset Ltd, Boldon, Tyne and Wear
Printed and bound in Great Britain by TJI Digital, Padstow, Cornwall



*British Library Cataloguing in Publication Data*
A catalogue record for this book is available from the British Library

*Library of Congress Cataloging in Publication Data*
Aspromourgos, Tony, 1957–
The science of wealth: Adam Smith and the framing of political economy/Tony Aspromourgos.
p. cm. – (Routledge studies in the history of economics; 95)
Includes bibliographical references and index.
1. Smith, Adam, 1723–1790. 2. Classical school of economics. 3. Economics–History. I. Title.
HB103.S6A87 2008
330.15′3–dc22 2008016277

ISBN10: 0-415-46385-8 (hbk)
ISBN10: 0-203-88957-6 (ebk)

ISBN13: 978-0-415-46385-0 (hbk)
ISBN13: 978-0-203-88957-2 (ebk)

**wealth** … **1.** The condition of being happy and prosperous; well-being. *Obs.* … **2.** Spiritual well-being. … *Obs.* … **3. a.** Prosperity consisting in abundance of possessions; 'worldly goods', valuable possessions, esp. in great abundance: riches, affluence.… **d.** Abundance of possessions or of valuable products, as characteristic of a people, country, or region; the collective riches of a people or country. The phrase *the wealth of nations* had some currency before it was adopted by Adam Smith in the title of his famous work; but its early history is obscure.…

*Oxford English Dictionary*

**framing** … The action, method, or process of constructing, making, or shaping anything whether material or immaterial.…

*Oxford English Dictionary*

# Contents

# Preface

In a striking example of excessive editorial intrusiveness, Yen Fu, the first translator of the *Wealth of Nations* into Chinese, was moved to insert the following note in his edition of Smith's book: 'When I read the text, in some places it is so moving that I cannot keep from crying. Alas! how touching Smith's sentences are!' (as translated in Lai 1989: 378; p. 22 in the 2000 reprint). I could say that Smith's words have almost moved me to tears at times too, but perhaps for somewhat different reasons. I am therefore very grateful to all those who provided me with advice, comment and other intellectual support during the course of the research culminating in this book.

I am particularly indebted to Matthew Smith and Sarah Jones, who worked on the project as Research Associates, in 2003–4 and 2006–8 respectively. James Duffy and Daniel Rees also provided research assistance in 2005, and Anwar Anaid in 2007–8. James Duffy returned to the project in 2007–8, in the process, reading and scrutinizing the entire text. Beyond these, my greatest debt is to Peter Groenewegen. The extent of that debt is due to the happy coincidence of two factors (happy for me at least): his enormous knowledge and judgement concerning the history of economics and his being in very close proximity to me, at the University of Sydney, during these years. He also read the entire text, much of it more than once. Others who gave of their time, knowledge or judgement, in various forms, include J. Argyrou, G. Brennan, G. Brinsmead, J.L. Cardoso, W. Coleman, S. Cremaschi, R.J. Dixon, P. Docherty, G. Fishburn, P. Garegnani, G. Gill, L. Hill, W.P. Hogan, J.E. King, H.D. Kurz, S.G. Medema, G. Mongiovi, N. Naldi, Rod O'Donnell, C. Panico, J. Pullen, A. Roncaglia, J. Shearmur, A.S. Skinner, A. Stirati, N.J. Theocarakis, V. Varathan, F. Vianello, G.K. White, M.V. White and S. Zamagni. I thank them all and apologize if anyone has been overlooked. Almost needless to say, I have not taken all the advice I was given, and I am alone responsible for the final product. In addition, I thank the Australian Research Council which generously supported my research with a grant for the years 2003 to 2007, and Alan Walker for preparing the index.

I may add that in a sense my greatest debt really is to the editors who have given us the Glasgow Edition of the Works and Correspondence of Adam Smith. While their editorial apparatus is acknowledged at some points below, altogether, these acknowledgements do not do justice to the benefit my work has gained from their remarkable achievement of scholarship. Perhaps only someone who has utilized the edition as I have for what follows can fully appreciate its quality. The Glasgow Edition is quoted with permission of Oxford University Press. Full citations for the six volumes are provided in the Note on Citation Practice immediately below. Chapter 3, not including section 3.5, has been previously published in a considerably abbreviated version in *History of Economic Ideas* (Aspromourgos 2007).

*Tony Aspromourgos*
*Sydney*
*April 2008*

# A note on citation practice

In citations of Smith's writings from the Glasgow Edition, the following abbreviations are used throughout. (In addition, *LJ* is sometimes employed to refer to the lectures on jurisprudence as such, or to *LJA* and *LJB* together.) For the sake of compactness, only page citations are provided, rather than following what has been the more usual practice of citing, for example, book, chapter and paragraph numbers. The Glasgow Edition has now been extant for a sufficiently long time that it may safely be regarded as the widely available standard text. In quotations, not all editorial interventions in the Glasgow Edition texts are preserved (in particular, editorial note numbers, and note letters in relation to text variants). There were six editions of *TMS* authorized by Smith, 1759–90, and six editions of *WN*, 1776–91; but there will be hardly any need to distinguish between editions of either text, for our purposes. (Smith died in 1790.) The *Oxford English Dictionary* is also cited in abbreviated form throughout (*OED*, together with the relevant headword). A second edition of the *Correspondence* incorporates, in a new appendix, eighteen letters discovered subsequent to the first edition (Mossner and Ross 1987: x, 413–34). It has not proven necessary, in anything that follows, to quote or cite any of the additional material in the second edition.

*Corr* E.C. Mossner and I.S. Ross (eds) (1977) *The Correspondence of Adam Smith* (Glasgow Edition of the Works and Correspondence of Adam Smith, vol. 6), Oxford: Clarendon.

*edWN* 'Early Draft of Part of *The Wealth of Nations*', in R.L. Meek, D.D. Raphael and P.G. Stein (eds) (1978) *Adam Smith. Lectures on Jurisprudence* (Glasgow Edition of the Works and Correspondence of Adam Smith, vol. 5), Oxford: Clarendon, pp. 562–81.

*EPS* W.P.D. Wightman, J.C. Bryce and I.S. Ross (eds) (1980) *Adam Smith. Essays on Philosophical Subjects* (Glasgow Edition of the Works and Correspondence of Adam Smith, vol. 3), Oxford: Clarendon.

*fA* 'First Fragment on the Division of Labour', in Meek, Raphael and Stein (eds) op. cit., pp. 582–4.

*fB* 'Second Fragment on the Division of Labour', in Meek, Raphael and Stein (eds) op. cit., pp. 585–6.

*LJA* 'Lectures on Jurisprudence: Report of 1762–3', in Meek, Raphael and Stein (eds) op. cit., pp. 1–394.

*LJB* 'Lectures on Jurisprudence: Report Dated 1766', in Meek, Raphael and Stein (eds) op. cit., pp. 395–558.

*LRB* J.C. Bryce (ed.) (1983) *Adam Smith. Lectures on Rhetoric and Belles Lettres* (Glasgow Edition of the Works and Correspondence of Adam Smith, vol. 4), Oxford: Clarendon.

*TMS* D.D. Raphael and A.L. Macfie (eds) (1976) *Adam Smith. The Theory of Moral Sentiments* (Glasgow Edition of the Works and Correspondence of Adam Smith, vol. 1), Oxford: Clarendon.

*WN* R.H. Campbell, A.S. Skinner and W.B. Todd (eds) (1976) *Adam Smith. An Inquiry into the Nature and Causes of the Wealth of Nations* (Glasgow Edition of the Works and Correspondence of Adam Smith, vol. 2), 2 vols, Oxford: Clarendon.

# 1 Introduction

> It is terrific to contemplate the abysmal gulf of incomprehension that has opened itself between us and the classical economists. Only one century separates us from them: ...*I say a century; but even ½ a century after, in 1870, they did not understand it*.... The classical economists said things which were perfectly true, even according to our standards of truth: they expressed them very clearly, in terse and unambiguous language, as is proved by the fact that they perfectly understood each other. We don't understand a word of what they said: has their language been lost? Obviously not, as the English of Adam Smith is what people talk today in this country. What has happened then?
>
> *Piero Sraffa*, 1927[1]

The latter-day image of Adam Smith has long turned upon his role as a crucial figure – indeed, commonly regarded as the *key* figure – in the formation of political economy as a distinct social science. Perhaps even more, at least in the popular imagination, he has been widely viewed as providing one of the most substantial intellectual cases for liberal capitalism as the best possible system for arranging human society. These are two very different claims to fame, unless economic science itself can be thought of as favouring capitalism, an idea almost too absurd to take seriously. In any case, in the last few decades these beliefs about Smith have been much questioned. The publication from 1976 to 1983 of the Glasgow Edition of Smith's extant writings and related documents (in particular, lecture notes) undoubtedly provided impetus to renewed interest in Smith's intellectual work as a whole, naturally encouraging a more holistic approach to interpreting his thought. The resulting research endeavours, and much of their outcome, were certainly to be welcomed, and remain so. However, there is also a danger that something important about Smith's intellectual achievement might be lost in this orientation towards his thought. There are a number of particular ideas for which Smith is perceived as famous – perhaps most notably, at least in the last half century or so, the 'invisible hand'. Another is the benefits of 'division of labour'. But Smith also regards the *intellectual* division of labour between the various sciences and arts as one of the dimensions of that beneficial process of specialization. In short, prefiguring one of the conclusions of this study, however much he has an all-encompassing and unified conception of science as such, or of the social sciences in particular, Smith has also an understanding of political economy as a separable science, though not thereby an autonomous one.

Certainly the meaning of that for which Smith's standing as a thinker has most endured, his political economy, is better understood by considering *WN* in the context of Smith's entire *oeuvre*, seeing it in the light of his thought as a whole. Like any immensely intelligent person, Smith aims for – and has considerable success in achieving – a consistent, coherent and unified set of views across the range of issues which concern him. We therefore do not fully understand his thought if we do not see that larger frame of reference. But it cannot be inferred from this that the political economy is not a separable intellectual 'discipline'. To be sure, everything depends on everything else, in the end; but the progress of science has always been a result of the segmentation of phenomena, and associated intellectual specialization. Smith certainly endorses this latter proposition. One explicit illustration by him of science proceeding by way of separable branches occurs close to the beginning of *WN*, in relation to division of labour, which Smith argues arises from the human 'propensity to truck, barter, and exchange'. He raises the question of whether this propensity is 'one of those original principles in human nature', or derives from more fundamental human faculties. Smith favours the latter view, but then leaves the issue aside – 'it belongs not to our present subject to enquire' (*WN*: 25). Inquiry into how the propensity to exchange derives from more fundamental human faculties can be pursued; but for the purposes of political economy, that propensity can simply be taken as a given. So it is, we shall see, with other postulates of the political economy, in particular, self-regard and the desire of bettering one's condition.

Our purpose in what follows is to uncover the character and fundamental structures of that particular intellectual project – the 'shape' and 'contours' of the mode of social science inquiry, the intellectual 'discipline' in the generic sense, that Smith conceived of as 'political economy'. In our subtitle the historical development of the conceptualization of that science, both by Smith and by others before him, is described as the 'framing' of political economy. That somewhat awkward term – 'making' or 'invention' would flow more easily off the tongue – is chosen with premeditation. The concern in what follows is not so much with all the myriad detail of Smith's economics, or of the detail of the economic thought of others before him, nor with all the substantive economic doctrines. It is rather with the overall character of the science: its scope and fundamental conceptualizations; the 'frame' of this 'machine' for understanding society.[2] Smith himself is rather keen on the analogy of the world as a machine, and of science as a machine for producing understanding (e.g. *TMS*: 19; *EPS*: 66).

These terms to describe our focus in what follows – 'character', 'fundamental structures', 'shape', 'contours', 'frame', 'machine' – may appear rather vague. The short response to that possible reproach is that the proof of the pudding must be in the eating. But before briefly indicating here, positively, the 'ingredients' in what follows, it may further clarify the object of our inquiry to give a couple of instances of what we will *not* be concerned with. The theory of land-rents is a good example of a particular substantive Smithian doctrine with which we have almost no interest in what follows. Smith's treatment of this subject is a mess and, perhaps not coincidentally, few who have ventured into Smith interpretation have been keen to tread there. But our reason for largely ignoring it is rather that, whatever the extent to which his explanations of the determination of land-rents have any validity, this does not touch upon his 'framing' of political economy, as to its boundaries or fundamental structures. A further instance is Smith's substantive theory of natural price determination. This is more connected than rent theory with what we treat as Smith's fundamental structures in what follows; but even here, what is really fundamental is the conception of natural prices as the 'anchor' for the behaviour of market prices. That his understanding of the determinants of natural prices is unsatisfactory does not compromise the more fundamental conception of the dynamics of competition and market prices in relation to natural prices. Or at least, it does not *necessarily* compromise that conception: on this matter, there are complications which will have to be entered into (in essence, the question of the autonomy of natural prices with respect to the ebb and flow of supply and demand).

It has been suggested above that the proof of the pudding should be in the eating, not least because it is rather tedious in an introductory chapter to elaborately rehearse the arguments which are shortly to follow. But to turn briefly to the positive side – to what *will* actually be offered for consumption below – twelve fundamental elements constitutive of Smith's political economy are examined, three in each of the four subsequent chapters (with key terms in italic):

- Chapter 2: *political economy* as the science of wealth; *wealth* as national product; *nature* as a norm.
- Chapter 3: convergence of market prices towards natural *prices*; *supply and demand*; price as necessary *cost*.
- Chapter 4: *division of labour* and labour productivity; *gross revenue and net revenue*; *capital* and *productive labour*.
- Chapter 5: the progress of *opulence*; the system of natural *liberty*; *policy* and theory.

These elements making up, in our judgement, the fundamental structures of Smith's economics are not examined merely as separate and disparate ideas. By the end, they are shown to constitute a unified intellectual piece, an engine for understanding economic society in general and liberal capitalism (not Smith's term) in particular, a fundamental frame of reference for economic analysis and social theory.[3] Smith's use of these key terms will be very exhaustively examined in the subsequent chapters – as will a small number of other important, related terms he uses (e.g. 'scarcity', 'free' and variants, 'theory'). As well, their 'prehistories' in literature prior to Smith will be rather comprehensively treated; that is to say, the history of the concepts prior to Smith. The systematic examination of these prehistories is with a view to further clarifying his conceptualization of political economy, by placing it in its larger historical context.[4] Smith's political economy will also be engaged with latter-day economics at a number of points in Chapters 2 to 5, or perhaps we should say, contemporary economics will be confronted with Smith's project. This aspect of what follows proceeds from a belief that we still now have something to learn from him about how the social sciences should go about their business. The Epilogue reflects upon the fate of political economy and economics subsequent to Smith, and the lessons one might learn from his project, in a more comprehensive manner.

With regard to those chosen twelve or so concepts and key terms, which are treated as capturing the fundamental structures of Smith's political economy, there is no need for us to dogmatically assert that no different choices could reasonably have been made. If one were to ask a representative sample of informed persons, what are the twelve most important concepts making up the fundamental structures of Smith's political economy, it would be a considerable surprise if the responses turned out to be more or less identical. (One may suggest that the most likely additional candidate over and above our nominations might indeed be the 'invisible hand'.) The inevitable scope for differences of judgement is placed in perspective by keeping in mind that the purpose of the choices is to capture the basic elements of Smith's system. There is no doubt more than one set of choices that can achieve this. In the end, a quite comprehensive account of his economics is entailed by an exercise such as this, so that important concepts which are not key concepts in this study nevertheless find a place in the narrative (including that Smithian 'hand', which has so fascinated in later times). Furthermore, Smith's substantive doctrines are not at all ignored in what follows: all the significant elements of his theory make an appearance. To that extent, notwithstanding the focus of this study, it also conveys an interpretation of the substance of Smith's political economy. As to the choice of the *number* of fundamental concepts for consideration, this is an outcome of resolving the trade-off between breadth and depth. One needs to go broad enough to capture the overall shape of the political economy. At the same time, one must be able to go deep enough to convey a rich sense of the history of these ideas over the whole course of our civilization, from the earliest times to 1776, the *Wealth of Nations* being the key foundational text for the new science of political economy.[5]

The very close attention paid to fundamental aspects of Smith's economic language in this study raises the question, what are we ultimately interested in, his language or his concepts? The answer, fairly emphatically, is the latter. But the discipline of a complete and careful consideration of Smith's use of fundamental terms better enables one to grasp his conceptualizations, free of misreadings arising from the intrusion of latter-day concepts which are associated with the same terms – the meaning of 'supply' and 'demand' offers the most striking example. (We speak somewhat qualifiedly – '*fairly* emphatically' the interest is in Smith's concepts – because the actual historical development of language and of concepts involves dependence and causation, from one to the other, in both directions.[6]) In the chapters which follow, each subsection first considers one (sometimes two) of the twelve or so particular Smithian concepts and exhaustively examines his uses of the particular associated key terms (in all his writings[7]), and then proceeds also to account for the prehistory of those terms and their associated concepts prior to Smith. The exception to this rule is Chapter 3, where the prehistories of the key terms and associated concepts are best considered together, in a single subsection (sec. 3.5), because they are all so closely intertwined, both conceptually and historically. The exhaustiveness of the examination of Smith's language use in relation to key terms is rendered practicable by the advent of a reliable machine-searchable electronic text of the Glasgow Edition.[8] But for the interpretation of a thinker like Smith, good old-fashioned reading is not rendered obsolete by such technology. The research for this study included reading his texts the way he intended them to be read; or perhaps we should say, certainly for the case of so large a book as *WN*, the way Smith at least *hoped* they would be read: from beginning to end.

It is of course impossible for us to devote the same close attention to language use prior to Smith, except with regard to certain particular key instances. Nevertheless, taking language seriously guides the exploration of the prehistory of Smith's concepts as well. The sheer scale of the material potentially relevant to the prehistory means that while a great body of primary sources has been investigated, there is inevitably also reliance on secondary literature, with regard to pre-Smithian thought. The concepts and terms that are the object of our investigation in Smith's texts constitute a finite, well-defined and manageable domain of inquiry; in earlier literature, they do not. The histories we create are always partial, not only because they are from particular standpoints, the usual complaint or affirmation. They are partial also because the raw materials for those histories are commonly so vast (though, still, generally incomplete) as to make it impossible for a single mind to absorb all that is relevant to any 'big picture'. There is much we do not know. With regard to Smith, there is very little need to rely upon secondary sources in what follows. Furthermore, no attempt is made to detail every instance of disagreement (let alone of agreement) between our findings and interpretation, and the very large secondary literature on Smith's political economy. Apart from of course fully documenting any instances of reliance upon secondary literature, we also indicate by reference to key works how our findings stand in relation to other major lines of Smith interpretation. Beyond that, agreements and disagreements are indicated, between this study and those of others, on a range of particular issues. The narrative does not give space to more or less mercilessly pursuing others who take a different view of Smith. I do not share the belief that the best way of advancing one's scholarship is to tear down the efforts of others in the field. The thing to be advanced is the understanding of Adam Smith's texts – and perhaps via that, the understanding of our societies and ourselves.

It may be added that in the course of Chapter 4, recourse will be had to some small instances of 'rational reconstruction', in a precise and limited sense: 'the application of formal models designed to accurately capture the *intentions* or ideas of an earlier author or text, while going beyond the actual analytical or formal *execution* of the writer' (Aspromourgos 1997: 418). I immediately added after this definition: '[t]his is an interpretive method which may enable a clearer grasp of the logical coherence (or otherwise) and implications of a system'. As to otherwise-than-coherent, so it will also be here: formal statement of some aspects of Smith's thinking will clarify certain limitations of his ideas. There has been some adverse reaction to rational reconstruction, though understood in a rather more expansive sense of the term, from some quarters (also discussed in Chapter 4). It is a large part of the primary purpose of this study to take very seriously the language in which Smith articulates the fundamental structures of his economics. That does not oblige a refusal to avail one's self of latter-day methods of analysis; that purpose is not compromised by recourse to some simple, mathematical formulations of certain of Smith's ideas, with a view to better grasping their meaning and limitations. Of course, one must proceed with care and remain alive to the difference between a mathematical statement of a Smithian proposition, and a mathematical inference from it which he did not grasp. So long as such care is taken, no reasonable principle of exegesis and interpretation is violated. Engagement with intellectual history is a messy and difficult business, for which no simple, mechanical rules of procedure – or simple, mechanical rules for *prohibiting* procedures – are legitimately available. Use of a little algebra may assist, and need not cause harm.

Insofar as it presupposes that *WN* is a decisive plateau in the development of political economy, what partly motivates this study is the view that Smith's intellectual triumph, the influence of his book in the history of science, is not so much about the success of his specific theoretical *doctrines*. (His influence in the history of liberal capitalism is another matter.) Smith's most considerable theoretical success is at a deeper level: it is in gaining a wide and long-lasting acquiescence in the conceptual universe, constituted or framed by the fundamental structures of his system, for a newly emerging intellectual discipline. This deeper success meant that those who subsequently contested Smithian doctrine did so within Smith's conceptual universe; they did so, indeed, 'on his terms'. The terrain upon which economic doctrine would be developed and fought over would be the terrain established by that book, for at least a century, and in some important and fundamental respects, well beyond a century. David Ricardo's analytical advances, for example, are entirely within the conceptual universe laid out by Smith. To take another example, the concept of competitive equilibrium prices, which endures in economic theory to this day, is clearly conceptualized, *almost* for the first time, by Smith. (The qualification is due to Anne Robert Jacques Turgot.) There is a deeper success here, a profounder achievement, than merely gaining assent to specific doctrines: a constituting of the more fundamental frames of thought within which particular doctrine subsequently would be articulated, worked out, debated, and perhaps even sometimes resolved.

In our view, this dimension of Smith's intellectual lifework – the conceptual universe he fashioned for a considerable and important part of science of human society – is his most enduringly important contribution. It is more important than the specific economic doctrines, and more important than his prescriptive doctrines concerning the right constitution of polity, society and economy. To tie Smith's significance in particular to the latter prescriptive doctrines, is to tie him to one particular viewpoint in the ongoing human debate about liberal capitalism, an argument which is unlikely soon to end. (It is as well a matter of some controversy as to what, precisely, his particular viewpoint on that matter was!) Smith's contribution at the level of conceptualizing political economy is worthy of, and susceptible of, wider acceptance than any particular ethical view of liberal capitalism. And by approaching his political economy in what follows as a culmination of earlier strands of thought – rather than as the *beginning* of an 'economics' which culminates in the modern marginalist theoretical approach – we may hope to see it more clearly.[9] This stance is not at all inconsistent with also engaging Smith's economics, at least at certain key points, with subsequent developments; and no such engagement is really possible without first grasping the character of his thought, free of misreadings from recourse to latter-day concepts alien to it. This enables assessment of the continuing relevance of Smith's system as a framework for understanding economic society. The conclusions arrived at on that issue are rather positive, though of course there have been many very considerable theoretical advances since 1776.

One reason for studying the history of economics is that an understanding of its past may place its current situation in a clearer light. And it may be hoped that a historical study of Smith which culminates with his work, rather than starting with his work, will naturally be rather less prone to *ex post facto* assimilation of Smith's intellectual project into later, and to some degree or other alien, conceptual and theoretical frameworks. The primary reason for all the attention devoted to Smith since the eighteenth century is of course the sheer importance of his work for the formation of political economy as a distinct intellectual discipline or mode of social science inquiry. That is our primary reason for what follows as well. But it is more particularly motivated by the aim of seeking to retrieve Smith's thought from misreadings through the lens of latter-day forms of thought, in particular, the theories of 1871 and after. To thereby retrieve the conceptual framework of a pivotal work in the history of our civilization is valuable for the role it can play as a source of self-examination, for later intellectual disciplines in the human sciences (most obviously, economics), as well as for our societies.

This is to be preferred to treating intellectual history as a place to which we go, merely to find comforting reflections of our own beliefs – the use of intellectual history as little more than cultural decoration for the ingrained beliefs or prejudices of our own age. The danger to be escaped here is that of remaining trapped in our own latter-day frames of thought, and hence, looking into Smith's texts, seeing only a mirage: 'ourselves' reflected back. (The opposite danger is that we draw from them only a litany of errors.) There is a real political economy of Adam Smith 'out there', which we are capable of discovering or recovering. But from that proposition does not follow the pretence that there is a single, uniquely correct interpretation of its character, meaning and significance. This study is a small contribution to the larger cultural and intellectual project of advancing the understanding of our civilization. But the object of such endeavours is not a stationary outcome; it inevitably depends upon standpoint, and changes as successive generations contemplate and rethink what matters to us as humans. The proposition that each generation makes its own history is not relativism. It is just that the significance of even agreed facts about the intellectual past changes with time.

# 2 The science of wealth

*political economy as the science of wealth*
*wealth as national product*
*nature as a norm*

> ... I do really think, that your book ... might become an institute, containing the *principia* of those laws of motion, by which the system of the human community is framed and doth act, AN INSTITUTE *of political œconomy*, such as I could heartily wish ... that some understanding Tutor in our Universities would take up, as a basis of lectures on this subject.
>
> *Thomas Pownall*, 1776 (*Corr*: 375)

The commonplace latter-day notion that Smith is the founder of political economy is of course false, at least if taken literally. Neither the term 'political economy', nor the concept, originates with him. Nevertheless, he may rightly be conceived of as the founder of the discipline, in a certain particular sense, as we shall see. The first section below clarifies how the notion of a political economy is constituted by Smith. This also requires some consideration of his conception of 'science'. The emergence of various concepts of political economy before Smith is then examined. The second section explores the meaning in his texts of 'wealth', which is the central object of political economy in his understanding of the science. For the purposes of political economy, the critical notion of wealth is as the national product or 'annual produce'. The subsequent examination of the history of the notion of 'wealth' in that section reveals something significant about the transition to modernity. The emergence of modern political economy, both in Smith's thought and that of others, is in this regard an important expression of that transition. These two investigations are preliminary to a consideration of those fundamental structures of Smith's economics, indicated in Chapter 1 and to be explored in subsequent chapters.

Smith's recourse to 'nature' and the 'natural' is also examined here, as a prelude to the more narrowly economic focus of subsequent chapters. Why here? 'Nature' and variants thereof constitute perhaps *the* most pervasive substantive term throughout all Smith's writings. The penultimate section considers Smith's use of *nature* and *natural*, in particular, conceived of as in some sense establishing a norm for social life, and for social theory. It also considers the history of the notion of nature in general, and especially, some aspects of that history particularly pertinent to Smith's political economy. The key element which inescapably grounds Smith's economics in nature is that the claims for political economy as a general or universal science ultimately must rest upon a claim to knowing human nature. Specific elements of his language and concepts pertaining to nature and economics, and their prehistory, are further examined in subsequent chapters (notably, 'natural price'). In summary, what follows here explores and clarifies Smith's conception of political economy as the science of wealth – wealth being understood as national product, with a view to human consumption – together with the earlier history of these two concepts and the associated terms. The contours of this 'new' intellectual discipline, most particularly its fundamental conceptual machinery, will emerge in the subsequent chapters. Political economy will then appear as the legislative or policy science which has as its explanatory or descriptive object, the production, distribution and growth of wealth – and has as its normative or prescriptive purpose, the growth of consumption per capita, for the bulk of the population. The creation of the idea of the very *possibility* of such a science, an important historical transition, which should not be lost sight of (but easily can be), is considered, by way of a summing up, in the concluding section.

## 2.1 Political œconomy and science

### *2.1.1 Smith on 'political economy'*

Following two instances in the table of 'Contents', one in the prefatory 'Introduction and Plan of the Work' and two further passing references, the most eye-catching appearance of *political œconomy* in *WN* makes it a branch of science:

> POLITICAL œconomy, considered as a branch of the science of a statesman or legislator, proposes two distinct objects; first, to provide a plentiful revenue or subsistence for the people, or more properly to enable them to provide such a revenue or subsistence for themselves; and secondly, to supply the state or commonwealth with a revenue sufficient for the publick services. It proposes to enrich both the people and the sovereign.
>
> (*WN*: 428)

This is the opening paragraph of Book IV, 'Of Systems of political Oeconomy'; hence the instances in the Contents: apart from the title of Book IV itself, the title of the ninth chapter of that book, on Physiocracy, also refers to 'Systems of political Oeconomy'.[1] The purpose of that book is to appraise what Smith perceives as the two 'systems of political œconomy, with regard to enriching the people' (*WN*: 428). In this sense, political economy for Smith can refer to a branch of science or knowledge; *or* to a 'policy regime' (our term), as it does in Stewart (1811: 310–12, discussed below); or sometimes simultaneously to both.

In Smith's introduction these systems are described as 'theories of political œconomy' (*WN*: 11; cf. *LJA*: 235).[2] Twice further in Book IV political economy is treated as a science. The first is implicit: discussing tit-for-tat national policies of trade restriction, he allows that retaliation may be 'good policy' in some circumstances, but importantly adds:

> To judge ... does not, perhaps, belong so much to the science of a legislator, whose deliberations ought to be governed by general principles which are always the same, as to the skill of that insidious and crafty animal, vulgarly called a statesman or politician, whose councils are directed by the momentary fluctuations of affairs.
>
> (*WN*: 468; cf. *TMS*: 231–4)

The second is considered below, in relation to a statement of J.-B. Say (*WN*: 678; sec. 2.1.7). Continuing his discussion of the Physiocrats there, Smith comments that their writings 'treat not only of what is properly called Political Oeconomy, or of the nature and causes of the wealth of nations, but of every other branch of the system of civil government' (*WN*: 678–9). This is not merely a descriptive, but is a prescriptive definition – 'properly' (note also the recurrence of the 'branch' metaphor). Consistent with this, at least once Smith's notion of 'wealth' is grasped (sec. 2.2.1), he elsewhere refers to 'cheapness of consumption and ... encouragement ... to production' as 'precisely the two effects which it is the great business of political œconomy to promote' (*WN*: 748). There can be no doubt therefore that Smith regarded *WN* as a contribution to the science of political economy.

Before proceeding more deeply into his notion of political economy, all other uses of *economy* (and variants) may be detailed. The term is employed as a synonym for frugality, including in relation to the State (*TMS*: 173, 209, 304; *WN*: 162, 412, 781, 818, 907, 946; *LJB*: 514). So at one point, a landlord engaged in positive saving is called 'an œconomist', in contrast to those whose revenue is less than or equal to their expenses (*WN*: 385). In a related but wider sense, *economy* is used to refer to the pattern of expenditure (sometimes in relation to income), of an individual or class, a material mode of living (*TMS*: 50, 183–4; *WN*: 98, 346; *LRB*: 228). In the same vein, there is the notion of corporate modes of economic organization: 'rural œconomy'; 'the usual œconomy of ... sovereigns of ... Europe' (*WN*: 242, 399). This sense has kinship with the notion of political economy as policy regime (see n. 2 above). It bears also an affinity with a deeper notion, the 'oeconomy of nature' (discussed further in sec. 2.3.4), by which Smith intends the idea of a structure and design of the world, or nature (including human nature), so ordered as to provide the most efficient means to achieve its definite ends (in particular, preservation of the species), without superfluity:

> The oeconomy of nature is in this respect [i.e. with regard to moral approbation] exactly of a piece with what it is upon many other occasions. With

> regard to all those ends which, upon account of their peculiar importance, may be regarded, if such an expression is allowable, as the favourite ends of nature, she has constantly in this manner not only endowed mankind with an appetite for the end which she proposes, but likewise with an appetite for the means by which alone this end can be brought about, for their own sakes, and independent of their tendency to produce it.
>
> (*TMS*: 77)

> Nature ... acts ... in all ... cases, with the strictest oeconomy, and produces a multitude of effects from one and the same cause....
>
> (*TMS*: 321; also *TMS*: 87, quoted in sec. 2.3.1; *edWN*: 571)

The latter quotation is representing the views of David Hume (see *TMS*: 327). The notion of nature as providing efficient means also appears in *EPS* (163), though without actual reference to 'economy'.

The analogous sense of economy as an efficient or fitting organization, ordering and utilization of means to achieve an end, or just good (or bad) management, is deployed in *WN*:

> In an extensive corn country ... the scantiest crop, if managed with frugality and œconomy, will maintain, through the year, the same number of people that are commonly fed in a more affluent manner by one of moderate plenty.
>
> (*WN*: 526; also 719, 723, 727; *EPS*: 249; *LJB*: 421; *Corr*: 60 with 37, 245, 249)

At *TMS* (183) the means are identified with 'the system, the machine or oeconomy'. In some instances it is not clear whether the frugality or wider good management sense is intended. Finally, following French nomenclature, François Quesnay's *Tableau* is called 'the Oeconomical Table' (see Kuczynski and Meek 1972), and Quesnay and his followers, 'the œconomists' (*WN*: 672, 678–9, 830). It is also worth noting that outside *WN* (and the dozen or so references in *TMS*), there are very few references to *economy* in any of its variants, in the remainder of Smith's texts (in fact, they are all instances of *economy*, not variants): one in the *EPS* volume, in a 1756 letter to the *Edinburgh Review* (and none in the essays themselves); one in the *LRB* volume, but from a 1791 report of Smith's oral comments (not the lectures themselves); twice in *LJB*, and also an entry in the original manuscript index to *LJB* (none in *LJA*); one in *edWN*; and just three in *Corr* (*EPS*: 249; *LRB*: 228; *LJB*: 421, 514, 557; *edWN*: 571; *Corr*: 60, 245, 249).

Returning to Smith's notion of political economy as a branch of a legislative science, does this locate the former in any more definite manner among the sciences? The foundations of law belong to a particularly important science in Smith's view. The civil and criminal laws of states have as their purpose to restrain individuals from infringing upon the happiness of each other: 'The principles upon which those rules either are, or ought to be founded, are the subject of a particular science, of all sciences by far the most important, but hitherto, perhaps, the least cultivated, that of natural jurisprudence' (*TMS*: 218). It considers 'the obligations of the general rules of justice' (*TMS*: 333). The opening sentences of *LJB* closely parallel text in the very last paragraph of *TMS*:

> Jurisprudence is that science which inquires into the general principles which ought to be the foundation of the laws of all nations. [Hugo] Grotius seems to have been the first who attempted to give the world any thing like a regular system of natural jurisprudence, and his treatise on the laws of war and peace, with all its imperfections, is perhaps at this day the most compleat work on this subject.
>
> (*LJB*: 397)

Is political economy then a branch of jurisprudence? Stewart (1811: 310–12n) makes it appear so. He reiterates the above definition of jurisprudence, as the principles underpinning right law, and goes on to argue that 'the great aim' of Smith in *WN* is

> [t]o direct the policy of nations with respect to one most important class of its laws, those which form its system of political economy .... And he has unquestionably had the merit of presenting to the world, the most comprehensive and perfect work that has yet appeared, on the general principles of any branch of legislation.... [T]he precise aim of the political speculations ... of which he ... published so valuable a part in his Wealth of Nations, was to ascertain the general principles of justice and of expediency, which ought to guide the institutions of legislators ....

(The middle sentence here is surely an allusion to Smith's definition at the opening of *WN*, Book IV.) This seems to make jurisprudence that science of the legislator, of which political economy is a branch. Stewart also perceives *WN* as an exemplar of an element of Francis Bacon's programme for science:

> 'The science of such matters [aimed at enabling citizens to live happily] ... belongs ... to the province of men who ... have been led to take a comprehensive survey of the social order; of the interests of the community at large; of the rules of natural equity; of the manners of nations; of the different forms of government; and who are thus prepared to reason concerning the wisdom of laws, both from considerations of justice and of policy. The great desideratum, accordingly, is, by investigating the principles of *natural justice*, and those of *political expediency*, to exhibit a theoretical model of legislation, which, while it serves as a standard for estimating the comparative excellence of municipal codes, may suggest hints for their correction and improvement ....[3]'

But a summary of the content and character of Smith's overall intellectual achievement by John Millar, reproduced by Stewart (1811: 274–5) earlier in his text, and employing the same terms, 'justice' and 'expediency', he draws from Bacon, appears to place rather a different complexion on the relation between jurisprudence and political economy. Smith's lectures as Professor of Moral Philosophy, Millar tells us, were in four parts: natural theology; ethics ('the doctrines which he afterwards published in his Theory of Moral Sentiments'); and third, 'he treated at more length of that branch of morality which relates to *justice*'. Elaborating on the third, Millar says that Smith seemed to be inspired by Charles-Louis de Secondat Montesquieu, in considering 'the gradual progress of jurisprudence … from the rudest to the most refined ages, and … the effects of those arts which contribute to subsistence, and to the accumulation of property, in producing correspondent improvements or alterations in law and government'. Millar adds that Smith did not fulfill his intention of publishing this material (but an editorial note points out that these subjects are treated in *WN*, Books III and V, as well as *LJ*). Fourth and finally, Smith

> examined those political regulations which are founded, not upon the principle of *justice*, but that of *expediency*, and which are calculated to increase the riches, the power, and the prosperity of a State. Under this view, he considered the political institutions relating to commerce, to finances, to ecclesiastical and military establishments. What he delivered on these subjects contained the substance of the work he afterwards published under the title of … the Wealth of Nations.

This would be a surprising way of summarizing the contents of *WN*, and seems to intend a narrower domain than Smith's definition of political economy (*WN*: 428), which gives priority to enriching the people. In any case, this apparent[4] assigning of political economy to the realm of 'expediency' does not sit comfortably with Smith's comments from *WN* (468) quoted at the beginning of this section. It may be concluded that in Smith's understanding, political economy, as a species of science or knowledge, rather than in the sense of policy regime, is indeed a branch of jurisprudence (cf. pp. 147, 203–5, esp. n. 1, below, and sec. 5.2.2).

### *2.1.2 Smith on 'science'*

What then is Smith's concept of science in general? Wightman (1980: 12, cf. 8) comments on his indiscriminate use of *science*, *philosophy* and *art(s)*, interchangeably, and this is certainly true with regard to science and arts. A considerable variety of intellectual disciplines are characterized as sciences in Smith's writings: there are 'the abstruser sciences', most notably 'the higher parts of mathematics', not primarily admired for their 'utility' (*TMS*: 189; cf. *Corr*: 310); 'Ethics' is a science, albeit inexact, of the rules of morality (*TMS*: 329); 'the art of war' at least becomes a 'very intricate and complicated science' (*WN*: 695); logic is 'the science of the general principles of good and bad reasoning' (*WN*: 770; cf. *EPS*: 119–20); there are 'the abstract sciences', evidently mathematical

(*EPS*: 43, 249; *LRB*: 57), but also 'the abstract science of human nature' (*TMS*: 319); politics and morality or ethics are properly more 'Practicall [than "Speculative"] Sciences' (*LRB*: 41); music and oratory are both sciences and arts (*LRB*: 138–9). Casuistry (*TMS*: 333), rhetoric (*WN*: 150, 777; *LRB*: 181–2, 193), 'fortification' (*WN*: 739), metaphysics (*WN*: 770–1; *EPS*: 119–20), law (*WN*: 778), optics (*EPS*: 148, 185, 245), medicine, chemistry, astronomy, mathematics (*EPS*: 67–9, 243; *LJB*: 495; *WN*: 786), 'natural history' (*EPS*: 248) and botany (*Corr*: 252) are also sciences. There are also references to variants of the 'arts and sciences' together (*TMS*: 183, 213, 229; *WN*: 763, 780; *EPS*: 246–8; *LJA*: 223, 231, 265, 337–40; *LJB*: 409), including the significant suggestion (which has a bearing on the relation between division of labour and invention) that 'allmost the whole of the arts and sciences' arise out of the pursuit of human material subsistence and comfort (*LJA*: 337–40; cf. *LJB*: 488–90; *TMS*: 183). Analogous to (as well as interconnected with) the impact of division of labour on labour productivity in ordinary production, philosophy or science is advanced by division of intellectual labour (*WN*: 21–2; *LJA*: 347; *LJB*: 492; *edWN*: 570, 574).

As to the identification of *science* and *philosophy*, this is not an unfortunate or confusing conflation in Smith's language use, so much as his sharing the identification of the two, in most contexts, which was the common understanding in the seventeenth and eighteenth centuries. Hence in an extended discussion at *WN* (766–72), physics (synonymous with natural philosophy), ethics (synonymous with moral philosophy) and logic are identified as the tripartite ancient division of the sciences (cf. *LRB*: 181), subsequently replaced in Europe with a demarcation into the five sciences of logic, ontology, pneumatology, moral philosophy and physics. Elsewhere, natural philosophy, again identified with physics, is described as 'the science of nature' (*EPS*: 119–20, 244; also *LRB*: 144). Philosophy is 'the science of the connecting principles of nature' (*EPS*: 45 – and on the following page is also called an art); 'that science which pretends to lay open the concealed connections that unite the various appearances of nature' (*EPS*: 51; cf. 119). So by extension, the same core notion, in the course of human intellectual history, progressively extends to moral phenomena:

> The maxims of common life were arranged in some methodical order, and connected together by a few common principles, in the same manner as … the phenomena of nature. The science which pretends to investigate and explain those connecting principles, is what is properly called moral philosophy.
>
> (*WN*: 769)

Hence science is unified explanation. The development of science gives rise to the conception of the universe 'as a complete machine, as a coherent system, governed by general laws' (*EPS*: 113–14); 'the great machine of the universe … with the secret wheels and springs which produce' its 'various appearances' (*TMS*: 19; also 289); '[h]uman society … appears like a great, an immense machine … [a] beautiful and noble machine that was the production of human art' (*TMS*: 316).

Hence Smith speaks also of 'a propensity, which is natural to all men, but which philosophers in particular are apt to cultivate with a peculiar fondness,… the propensity to account for all appearances from as few principles as possible' (*TMS*: 299). Further:

> in Nat<urall> Phil<osophy> or any other Science of that Sort … we may lay down certain principles known or proved in the beginning, from whence we account for the severall Phenomena, connecting all together by the same Chain. – This … which we may call the Newtonian method is undoubtedly the most Philosophical, and in every scien<c>e w<h>ether of Moralls or Nat<urall> phi<losophy> etc., is vastly more ingenious …. It gives us a pleasure to see the phaenomena which we reckoned the most unaccountable all deduced from some principle (commonly a wellknown one) and all united in one chain ….
>
> (*LRB*: 145–6; also *TMS*: 289–90 – and *EPS*: 41–5, 50, 58, 66, 91–2, 105, 113–14, for the 'chain' metaphor)

He argues more than once that human 'wonder' or 'curiosity' in response to observed phenomena was the historical origin of, and is the impetus for, science (e.g. *WN*: 767; *EPS*: 42–3, 53–4; *LRB*: 93): 'Wonder … and not any expectation of advantage from its discoveries, is the first principle which prompts mankind to the study of Philosophy' (*EPS*: 51).[5] The beginning of science, on this account, is perplexity (cf. *EPS*: 51, n. 8). There is at least some tension between this proposition and the statement from *LJA* (337) quoted above (and the similar sentiment at *TMS*: 183), that the development of the sciences and arts has a material impetus (discussed further in section 2.4).[6]

What significance then attaches to political economy being a science in Smith's view? In truth his notion has a rather minimal significance, but perhaps for that reason is commendable. The evident somewhat indiscriminate designation of sciences by Smith – the implied 'soft' definition, somewhat disdained by one of the Glasgow editors of *EPS* (Wightman 1980: 12) – is a good thing. A science is understood merely as an organized, and preferably unified, body of knowledge, even more, a *system* of explanation, covering some definite subject matter, and generally with a view to application or policy for the benefit of humanity. Skinner (1996: 259 and esp. n. 6) draws attention to the notion of 'system' also in the economics of Smith's contemporary, James Steuart, as derivative from D'Alembert's design for the French *Encyclopédie* of the mid-eighteenth century: the systematic intellectual temper is a central element of the Enlightenment aspiration. Smith shares this commitment, with the system of political economy itself conceived of as part of a larger system of science (see sec. 5.2.2), but this is not to be confused with the 'spirit of system' (see sec. 5.3.2). Indeed, Dugald Stewart (1811: 322–3) veers in the direction of the view, which later becomes rather widely accepted, that

Smith's contribution is more as systematizer of extant economic ideas, than as an original genius:

> perhaps the merit of such a work as Mr Smith's is to be estimated less from the novelty of the principles it contains, than from the reasonings employed to support these principles, and from the scientific manner in which they are unfolded in their proper order and connection.... [I]n questions of so complicated a nature as occur in political economy, the credit ... belongs ... to the author who first established their solidity, and followed them out to their remote consequences; not to him who, by a fortunate accident, first stumbled on the truth.
>
> Besides the principles which Mr Smith considered as more peculiarly his own, his Inquiry exhibits a systematical view of the most important articles of political economy, so as to serve the purpose of an elementary treatise on that very extensive and difficult science. The skill and the comprehensiveness of mind displayed in his arrangement, can be judged of by those alone who have compared it with that adopted by his immediate predecessors. And perhaps, in point of utility, the labour he has employed in connecting and methodizing their scattered ideas, is not less valuable than the results of his own original speculations....

Smith's endorsement of Newton as the exemplar of science in fact has quite limited prescriptive content: what is embraced as Newtonian is merely the notion of unified explanation. While Pownall's praise of Smith's system by allusion to Newton's *Principia Mathematica* (1687), quoted as the epigraph to this chapter, might be deserved, the genuine analogies between the two are only at the most general level. Nevertheless, when Smith speaks of philosophy as the science which aims – or 'pretends' (more on this in sec. 2.4) – to reveal 'the concealed connections' that explain 'the various appearances of nature' (*EPS*: 51), one cannot help but think of the political economy which renders visible the workings of the 'invisible hand' (cf. Campbell and Skinner 1976: 2–3).[7]

### *2.1.3 Genesis of modern political economy*

Strictly speaking the history of the notion of political economy before Smith takes one back to ancient Greek thought, which is the original source of the two terms making up the phrase. The roots of 'economy' are Greek terms for stewardship or management of a household, in turn derived from the terms for 'house' (*oikos*) and 'to manage, control' or 'law' (*nomos*) (*OED*: 'economy'). The associated sense of economics as household management, in particular, households in the sense of large estates, can be seen in Xenophon's *Oeconomicus* (Marchant and Todd 1923: 362–73), though there is evidently more going on in this dialogue than merely consideration of wise resource management. This conception persisted right through until the eighteenth century. It is evident, for example, in Francis Hutcheson (1747: 255–6), Smith's teacher, in terms of rights and obligations within the family. But as a matter of fact, the all-embracing significance of the *polis*-State in ancient Greece means that *oikonomia* as the art of household management is applied there also to the State. Hence in a discussion of different modes of subsistence, Aristotle comments that hunting

> is naturally a part of the art of household management. It is a form of acquisition which the manager of a household must either find ready to hand, or himself provide and arrange, because it ensures a supply of objects, necessary for life and useful to the association of the polis or the household, which are capable of being stored.
>
> (Barker 1946: 21)[8]

The Greek entered classical Latin as *œconomus* but apparently was reintroduced into medieval Latin with phonetic spelling (*yconomus*), and hence in early French and English uses (the latter, from the sixteenth century) appears as *yconomie*. There are earlier, also English variants of 'economic', almost certainly derived from French (*OED*). In Latin, 'economy' followed the sense of estate management but, importantly, extended it into a generic notion of management and organization, with a wide variety of applications. This notion was transferred to the French, *économie* and, combined with *politique*, became a concept of public administration or management of the affairs of state (Groenewegen 1987c). The terms 'politics' and 'political' derive from the Greek *politicos* (pertaining to citizens or the civic), *ta politica* (affairs of state), in turn from *politis* (citizen) and *polis* (city, State), and subsequently the Latin, *politicus*. It first entered English in the French form – 'politike', 'politique' and similar spellings – in the fifteenth and sixteenth centuries. 'Politics', in various spellings, was in use as a term for the science or art of government from the sixteenth century (and an instance of 'politicien', 1588), though it had a number of other shades of meaning as well (*OED*: 'politic').[9]

It can be conjectured therefore that 'political economy' has its genesis in the imperatives of modern – in particular, French and English – nation-state building, as an intellectual instrument in support of that process. That is to say, at its inception, political economy is a transposition of, or an analogy from, the art of estate management, to the management of political society, though this was in fact already implied in ancient Greek use. Here it is worth noting that if politics is understood as the art and/or science of government, and economy as the art and/or science of resource management, then political economy emerges as the art or science of managing the material resources of the State. This can further be conceived of as management of the *entire* material resources of a society (including its labour force), either on the basis that all such resources are ultimately the State's resources (in political societies with more or less tenuous individual property rights), or on the basis that the State takes some measure of responsibility for the conditions under which all of society's material resources are used, even if property rights limit the State's direct control over all those resources. (Smith's position is a variant of the latter.) King (1948) traces first French uses to Louis de Mayerne-Turquet (1611) and Antoine de Montchrétien (1615), and thinks it 'quite probable' that the term was then already current in French use.[10]

Probably two further developments informed and gave impetus to the formation of the concept, from the early seventeenth century to the arrival of Smith's conception 150 years later. First, there is the rise of a certain temper of 'economism', in the sense of an inclination to reduce politics and human welfare to material questions, which can be read as an important element of the Enlightenment heritage from Francis Bacon's seminal contributions.[11] This can be seen clearly in the English literature, in the transition from Bacon to Thomas Hobbes to William Petty (Aspromourgos 1996: 55–7, 60–3, 69–72). Second, the emergence of widespread, decentralized, market economic organization, in a sense created for the first time a substantial object for economic analysis. It created a phenomenon worthy of, and requiring, a substantial intellectual or scientific effort in order to understand the mode of its operation, giving further impetus to the formation of political economy as a mode of social science inquiry. From this point of view, it becomes intelligible why mercantilism provides the first large-scale and systematic economic literature, of an explanatory kind: the preoccupation with *international* trade and financial flows can be read as partly a reflection of the relatively early development of integrated international economic relationships, as compared with the slower development of integrated domestic economic systems. The needs (or wants) of States for money stocks, combined with the absence of domestic silver and gold mines (and apart from recourse to conquest of lands with such mineral deposits), also gave political impetus to those mercantilist preoccupations.

The second of these two developments can also be given a larger interpretation. For a 'command economy' along feudal or pre-modern lines – an economic organization in which structure, behaviour and outcomes are more or less dictated by direct order of a ruling class – there is no need of an explanatory economic theory of how the system works. A 'theory' of how that economic system works requires little more than a knowledge of the will of the rulers. It is the emergence of a social economy of decentralized production and market exchange, which up to a point has no planned order imposed upon it, which first constitutes an object that genuinely requires a theory, for grasping 'the how and the why' of its systematic characteristics as to structure, behaviour and outcomes. The resulting systematic understanding, reducing the phenomena to theory or science, can also offer itself in the service a new nation-statecraft of economic management. This transforms the basis of policy, from being grounded primarily in just general prescriptive principles, to reliance upon also a systematic body of causal knowledge. Interpretation of the formation of political economy along these lines can lead on to the Marxian view that political economy is coeval with capitalism, as argued by Lunghini (1998: 203–5; cf. Meek 1962: 370–2; McNally 1988: 1–84). This is an intrinsically difficult proposition to demonstrate or refute, being contingent upon how 'political economy' and 'capitalism' are defined. (Certainly there are definitions of those terms which will *make* this proposition true.) I have not been prepared to go so far, writing in particular reference to the theory of surplus and income distribution (see secs. 4.2.2, 4.2.4, 4.4.2):

> Economic understanding only become problematic as economic organization comes to involve complex integrated systems (economic *systems* in the generic sense); so that a scientific effort is required in order to grasp their mode of operation. This renders explicable why so much of early economic explanation was so concerned with money and foreign trade: in a real sense there was an international 'economy' (integrated and interdependent economic relations) *before* there were national economies. In the seventeenth century London was more economically integrated with Amsterdam than it was with large parts of England. From one vantage point, Cantillon's analysis of circulation between city and country [see Aspromourgos 1996: 80] can be understood as an intellectual expression of the historical economic integration of city and country within the nation state – and, in particular, the dissolution of rural production as a self-contained (vertically integrated) economic organization. Of course, the same applies, with even greater force, to the more thoroughgoing intersectoral relations captured in Quesnay's *Tableau*. With regard to the theory of surplus, in a world of self-subsisting village societies, for example, the economics of surplus may well be more or less trivial, though not necessarily its sociology or politics. Similarly, in social systems in which extraction of surplus is via explicit and direct forms of coercion, untutored perception may suffice to render visible the mode of its operation. It is only when economies become more complex systems that a systematic intellectual or scientific effort is required in order to render their operation transparent. It may be that economic theory is in large part, though in a rough and ready way, coeval with capitalism because capitalism is coeval with the emergence of such systems (cf. Roncaglia 1988: 163–5). But the coincidence seems far from complete ....
>
> (Aspromourgos 1996: 124)[12]

### *2.1.4 Enlightenment and political economy*

The influence of Enlightenment economism in shaping the emergence of the modern concept of political economy in the eighteenth century is evident in the articulation of the science by the Physiocrats, *les économistes* as they were known, who take the decisive step in the eighteenth-century conceptualization of political economy. *Philosophie Rurale*[13] describes 'politics' as 'the art of making men useful', implying that the population or labour force is in some sense part of the resources of State, and continues:

> we must consider the common weal in terms of its essence, and humanity as a whole in terms of its root, *subsistence*. All the moral and physical parts of

> which society is constituted derive from this and are subordinate to it. It is upon subsistence, upon the means of subsistence, that all the branches of the political order depend. Religion, in a sense, is purely and simply spiritual, but natural law inspires us and also tells us about duties relative to our needs; the civil laws, which originally are nothing more than rules for the allocation of subsistence; virtues and vices, which are only obedience to or revolt against natural or civil law; government, the sciences, the liberal and mechanical arts, agriculture, trade, industry – all are subordinate to the means of subsistence.
>
> (Meek 1962: 57)

Hence, echoing Petty's rhetoric a century earlier (see below), Mirabeau has 'population … [as] a leading and especially important branch of the speculations of political economy [*la politique économique*]'. He proceeds to make clear that this is to be understood in terms of production and reproduction of subsistence, as the foundation of human preservation, and of the sustainability and expansion of population, concluding:

> Subsistence, or consumption, is therefore at the heart of the matter which we are now discussing, and is the essence of population. Let us seek in the ways of nature and in the lessons of experience for the best methods of enabling the human race to subsist and increase.

This is then linked back to the characterization of politics: 'the art of making men useful … the first of whose cares must be to procure subsistence for them' (Meek 1962: 58–9).

As one might expect, the aim intended here is not mere survival. The 'main purpose' of government in an agricultural society is 'securing the prosperity of agriculture, which is the source of all the wealth of the state and that of all its citizens'. Government, and 'the general science of government', properly aim 'to provide for the security of all and to attain to the greatest degree of prosperity possible for the society' (Meek 1962: 231). The 'circular' character of the production of subsistence and prosperity – which is rendered so strikingly visible in Quesnay's *Tableau* (Kuczynski and Meek 1972), and similarly visible in *agricultural* reproduction in particular – is made explicit immediately following: 'the growth of wealth ensures the growth of the population; *men and wealth* cause agriculture to prosper, expand trade, stimulate industry, and *increase and perpetuate wealth*' (Meek 1962: 232; emphasis added).[14] This is not far from Smith's brief for political economy (albeit with an agricultural bias), as Meek (1962: 367–70) suggests; he also rightly emphasizes the Physiocratic concern with growth, or more truly, economic development: growth involving qualitative change, in particular, technical progress. Meek (1962: 370) is also right to emphasize the self-conscious use of theory by Quesnay and his confrères, though it is not quite so unprecedented as Meek suggests. (At minimum, Cantillon deserves to be honoured in this regard, but also probably others.)

> [L]et us ... salute the achievement of the Physiocrats in recognizing that the formulation of a theoretical model of the economy was a necessary prerequisite to the solution of such problems as these [i.e. economic development]. With the Physiocrats, for the first time in the history of economic thought, we find a firm appreciation of the fact that the 'areas of decision' open to policy-makers in the economic sphere have certain limits, and that a theoretical model of the economy is necessary in order to define these limits.... [Understanding becomes possible] only if we use the methods of simplification, selection, and generalization in our analysis .... It was in their recognition of this vital fact that the Physiocrats took the decisive step leading from politics to political economy.

Whether or not a sense of the limits of policy is so central to it, which is debatable, this consciousness of the necessity of abstraction is very clear in the following commentary from 'Dialogue on the Work of Artisans' (1766), by Quesnay:

> in nature everything is intertwined, everything runs through circular courses which are interlaced with one another. The fact that these different movements are necessarily interconnected means that things can be understood, differentiated, and examined only through the medium of abstract ideas .... It is only through the medium of such abstractions that we can examine and appraise the mutual relations between ... different classes of men and work in the social order, and give them the designations which conform most closely to their functions, in order to express ourselves in exact terms in the detailed working-out of economic science.
>
> (Meek 1962: 204)

The Milanese administrator, Pietro Verri, evidently much influenced by French (and English) economic and wider literature, including the *économistes* (Groenewegen 1986: xx–xxiii), employed the term *political economy* in the title of his little 1771 Italian treatise. However different (and inferior) the substantive content of his political economy *vis-à-vis* that of Quesnay and Smith, Verri shared the belief that a science was coming into being, at least partly driven by statist imperatives. In the Preface to the 1772 Livorno edition of the *Meditazioni*, he comments on the European situation in the aftermath of Columbus's discovery of the Americas:

> Everyone knows what changes have occurred in both minds and customs since that time. New relationships have emerged between States; the wealth of kingdoms is calculated to better know their level of security and prosperity; trade has come to be considered a public objective, and finance part of the law; reason is occupied with illuminating these matters, whose importance and influence on the happiness of human kind is generally known, and a body of knowledge called *Political Economy* is created.

> At the beginning of the work, we have isolated facts and information relating to different States. Then come the universal theories to which the human mind rises once a long series of facts are well known; next, there emerge those who link theories harmoniously together, and gradually by imperceptible degrees, lead our attention firmly from ordinary notions to those more remote and most important: this is the story of every science, and the genesis of every truth.
>
> Political economy, it seems to me, is close to becoming a science; all that is lacking is the method and organisation of theorems to give it form, and it would not be so difficult today to fill the gaps and turn them into a succession of even, comfortable steps.
>
> (transl. in Groenewegen 1986: 2–3; cf. Verri 1986 [1771]: 106–7)

As to the scope or purpose of political economy, the text provides a clear and quite singular answer: 'to increase annual reproduction and push it as far as possible, unleashing and invigorating human activity – this is the sole aim of political economy'; '[i]ncreased annual reproduction must be the aim of political economy' (Verri 1986 [1771]: 81, 19; also 21, 36, 71, 82, 115). That is to say, as with Quesnay and Smith, economic growth is the ultimate objective. There is also a concept of technical efficiency or technical progress incorporated in this aim:

> The problem facing political economy is: *to increase annual reproduction as much as possible with the least possible labour*; in other words, given the *amount of reproduction*, to achieve it with the *minimum of labour*; given the *amount of labour*, to achieve *maximum reproduction*; to increase labour as much as possible and obtain the maximum effect from it in terms of *reproduction*.
>
> (Verri 1771: 66; cf. 77)

Verri commonly articulates the goal of policy in terms of increasing annual production relative to annual consumption. This might appear at first glance to point to the importance of capital accumulation, as also vitally important in Quesnay and Smith. But it is very evident that what Verri (1771: 5, 57–8, 61, 79, 101) has in mind is the balance of foreign trade, not saving and accumulation: concepts of the latter are nowhere to be found in his commentary. To that extent, he remains partly in the framework of the older mercantilist economic literature, the concerns of which Smith will do so much to destroy in *WN*. Verri's common and frequent use of the term, 'annual reproduction', might also seem evocative of the circular approach to production of the Physiocrats (as well as Petty and Cantillon), so crucial to the formation of the new economic science; but the term has no more significance for Verri than as a synonym for annual production or output. Along with 'political economy', he also speaks of 'public economy' (*economia pubblica*), clearly intended as a synonym for the former:

> the object of public economy is to raise annual reproduction to the highest possible level.... The ... minister of public economy ... will release activity in the people by all those means we have seen, and as a result, population will increase, cultivation spread, and all the arts be refined.
>
> (Verri 1771: 112–13; also 2n, 106, 117)

### *2.1.5 Hobbes, Petty, Steuart*

All this strongly supports the conclusion that the term and notion of political economy entered English (as well as Italian) literature from the French eighteenth-century sources. (The absence of the term from *LJ* is surely significant in this regard, given Smith's time in France between his presentation of those lectures and the publication of *WN* – see n. 32 below.) Nevertheless, there are some slight traces of its crossing over into English earlier. In particular, Petty twice uses the term, or at least something very close to it. The first occurs in the context of one instance of his vexed attempt to derive a form of parity between land and labour, understood as the two ultimate inputs to production of commodities (see Aspromourgos 1996: 89–102). Petty (1691a: 181; written much earlier) describes this making of 'a *Par* and *Equation* between Lands and Labour' as 'the most important Consideration in Political Oeconomies'. Notice the plural, which appears strangely awkward compared with the later eighteenth-century use. This perhaps is an expression of the novelty of Petty's early English articulation here, pointing to the possibility that he was independently coining it himself, either from French or Latin. In any case, in a later, short writing devoted primarily to estimating population change, Petty (1683b: 481) draws inferences from a set of data, which he describes as being: 'all digested into the one *Table* or Sheet annexed, consisting of Three Parts, markt *A*, *B*, *C*; being indeed the *A*, *B*, *C*, of *Publick Oeconony*, and even of that *Policy* which tends to Peace and Plenty'.[15] That Petty would imply in this manner that population is the foundation of political economy, and of national policy aimed at prosperity, is fitting, since labour and population are at the centre of his economics of production. The twofold State objective of 'peace' and 'plenty' was then a standard formula for expressing the purposes of statecraft. Petty spent early years in France and Holland acquiring an education, and might have been exposed to the French form of the term there. There is also the possibility of a direct crossover from Latin to English: the young Petty was closely involved with Samuel Hartlib, an important figure in the English scientific revolution of the seventeenth century. In the very large archive of writings and correspondence of Hartlib and his circle, variants of *economy* appear frequently, most commonly in Latin form, but also in English, though not *political* economy.[16] It is also possibly not coincidental that Hobbes (1651: 157), who also was in France for a considerable time, speaks of 'the economy of a commonwealth' ('the Oeconomy of a Common-wealth' in the 1651 original). The young Petty was close to Hobbes (Aspromourgos 1996: 10, 54–7, 181).

Whatever significance one may attach to these uses, it seems clear that

Petty's passing references to *political economies* and *public economy* had no impact on subsequent English economic language. The emergence of a systematic notion of political economy in English economic literature belongs to the third quarter of the eighteenth century and evidently derives from French political economy. James Steuart's *Inquiry into the Principles of Political Oeconomy* (1767) is the only English work which could reasonably be described as a treatise on the subject, prior to *WN*, and the first to employ 'political economy' in its title, explicitly describing this as 'the science of domestic policy' in the subtitle. Economy and political economy are defined in the opening pages of the book. The former is conceived of in the traditional manner:[17] 'Oeconomy, in general, is the art of providing for all the wants of a family, with prudence and frugality'. The latter is defined by analogy with economy, but with 'essential differences' (Steuart 1767: 15–16; cf. 68). In particular, government is, and properly is, more constrained by historical circumstances:

> The great art ... of political oeconomy is, first to adapt the different operations of it to the spirit, manners, habits, and customs of the people; and afterwards to model these circumstances so, as to be able to introduce a set of new and more useful institutions.
>
> The principal object of this science is to secure a certain fund of subsistence for all the inhabitants, to obviate every circumstance which may render it precarious; to provide every thing necessary for supplying the wants of the society ....
>
> (Steuart 1767: 16–17; also 122, 124)

The 'statesman' properly guided by political economy is evidently to be a cautious reformer (cf. sec. 5.3.2 concerning Smith on theory and policy), and notice also the interchangeable use of 'art' and 'science'. But Steuart's appreciation of 'the variety which is found in different countries' is not a denial of 'universally true' principles of political economy. Indeed, it is from the vantage point of 'a citizen of the world', that 'the true principles are discovered', 'the principles of the science in general' (Steuart 1767: 16–17). It is also made clear that the qualification in the subtitle of the book, 'domestic policy *in free nations*', is not due to the scope of the science in general being limited in his view to such nations:

> I ... intend to confine myself to such parts of this extensive subject, as shall appear the most interesting in the general system of modern politics; of which I shall treat with that spirit of liberty, which reigns more and more every day, throughout all the polite and flourishing nations of Europe.
>
> (Steuart 1767: 18; also 216–17)[18]

In fact, Steuart's perception of the history of economic development leads him to the view that it has *promoted* the growth of liberty, and entering into that leads him well beyond the strict confines suggested by the subtitle's qualification (Steuart 1767: 216–17, 277–9). As with Smith and others of the French and

Scottish Enlightenments, history driven by economic forces is an important part of the inquiry. While Steuart's formal introductory statements on political economy do not explicitly make economic growth an element of it, growth (very much including population growth) and economic development are central. Employment and unemployment are also primary concerns, in striking contrast to Smith, who evidently relies upon a long-run mechanism of population adjusting to capital accumulation to put aside any such possible issue (e.g. *WN*: 98; and see pp. 98, 195–6). The definition of the object of political economy given above immediately continues with the addition of employment to the agenda (Steuart 1767: 17; also 28–9, 88). Steuart is emphatic that political economy is an art-science of general principles, but rather modest as to whether he has arrived at a fully-fledged system: 'I pretend to form no system, but, by tracing out a succession of principles, consistent with the nature of man and with one another, I shall endeavour to furnish some materials towards the forming of a good one' (Steuart 1767: 19). This stance also may be an expression of his sensitivity to the specificity of historical circumstances, even though he is explicit that such particulars do not deprive analysis of general principles.

In any case, all the conceptions of political economy from the century prior to Smith considered here, including that of Steuart, and as well, that of Smith himself, share one fundamental, common characteristic which stands in striking contrast to the conception of economics generated from the 1870s onward by the marginalist approach: they all focus upon the objective character of human socio-economic life, in terms of the production and reproduction of human subsistence and consumption, in a context of growth involving systematic qualitative change; that is to say, economic development.[19] (Cf. the thoughtful reflections of Larrère 2001b: 1070–1, on the significance of Quesnay's quantitative approach, for establishing the new science.) This is not a merely methodological difference, of no operational significance (see, in particular, the issue of demand and the theory of prices in Chapter 3). And in this, the pioneers of the science were more sensible – indeed, more scientific – than the marginalist theorists. To make human individual insatiability *essential* to the definition of the science is to ground it in a psychology that is at least dubious, certainly contestable, and in any case, likely to be highly historically contingent.

### *2.1.6 Cameralism and Linnaeus*

There are two further noteworthy strands of eighteenth-century intellectual development towards the concept of an economic science, though they are best regarded as conceptually distinct, in large part, from the French and British developments. The first is the rise in German economic literature of cameralism or cameral science, from the late-seventeenth century until its decline and replacement by *Nationalökonomie* from the end of the eighteenth century onward. It involved in some respects a somewhat more narrowly public administration (and public finance) conception, than the French and English notions of political economy, and had a definite mercantilist element; but in other respects, it is a broader, political, science than is political economy. Wilhelm von Schröder is a key early figure in this movement. The public administration temper of cameralism in a sense is an expression of its connection with the ancient Greek notion of estate management. The concept of *Haushalt* is commonly employed in that literature to conceive of political society as an extended family, for which the ruler (*Hausvater*) is responsible: 'For what is a good *Cammer*-President or Cameralist if not an experienced, good and prudent *Oeconomus* or householder' ('J.H.G.' from 1713, translated in Tribe 1988: 35). G.H. Zincke in 1744 also captures the spirit of the project:

> *The art of householding or the art of keeping house*, oeconomy, oeconomic science, is a practical science, wherein the wisdom, prudence and art of nearly all learned sciences are applied to the end of rightful concern for provisioning and economy ....
>
> (transl. in Tribe 1988: 51)

The meaning and significance of this literature have been very much elucidated and clarified by Keith Tribe (1988; 1995, chapter 2, a revised version of Tribe 1984; see also the survey by Magnusson 1994: 187–99). Later, traces of this cameralism are evident in the thought of J.W. von Goethe, connected with a notion of natural economy and 'organicism'. (He was also reading Smith.) James Steuart's rather more interventionist view of the role of government (the statesman) in economic life, relative to Smith, is probably at least partly due to the considerable time he spent in continental Europe, and consequent exposure to cameralist ideas. The second strand concerns developments in Sweden, particularly stimulated by the great botanist and naturalist, Carl von Linné (Carolus Linnaeus), towards an economic science understood as a kind of applied natural science. Since this concept is closely connected with the notion of 'the economy of nature', it is discussed in section 2.3.4.

A judgement can, however, be given here. Cameralism and the Swedish developments around Linnaeus are best regarded as conceptually quite distinct from the French, Italian and Scottish development of political economy, the latter three having a common root in the thought of the Physiocrats. The difference is thrown into sharp relief by noting that the German and Swedish lines of thought do not constitute a theory of economic society. The Swedish project is primarily focused on production and the technology of production, for human use and consumption. The developments around political economy 'proper', in France and Britain in particular, are more closely connected to the issue of State policy. To be sure, the Swedish programme, and cameralism, are policy sciences – no one was yet imagining economics as a purely theoretical endeavour – but the French and English projects are concerned with policy down to the deepest level: regime design or constitution building, so to speak, in the framework of an Enlightenment sensibility. Nevertheless, there are elements of commonality. The French and Scottish political economies also strongly focus on production; and all these lines of thought have roots in the Bacon-inspired project for 'the relief of man's estate':

> the greatest error of all ... is the mistaking or misplacing of the last or furthest end of knowledge.... [A] rich storehouse for the glory of the Creator and the relief of man's estate ... this is that which will indeed dignify and exalt knowledge .... [A]s both heaven and earth do conspire and contribute to the use and benefit of man; so the end ought to be ... to preserve and augment whatsoever is solid and fruitful: that knowledge may not be as a courtesan, for pleasure and vanity only, or as a bondwoman, to acquire and gain to her master's use; but as a spouse, for generation, fruit, and comfort.
>
> (Bacon 1605 [1951]: 41–3)

The role of nation-building as an impetus to the rise of a politico-economic science is also common to all of them. As to tensions between these various strands, it seems clear that cameralism had intrinsically a more conservative temper than the French project. Political economy proper, if not radical, certainly had an intrinsically radical potential; it constructed ideal systems in light of which actually existing societies could be judged. Part of Linnaeus's purposes in establishing professorial posts in something like 'economics' in Sweden was a reaction against cameralism (see sec. 2.3.4). The Milan professorial position commonly treated as one of the earliest academic Chairs of political economy was in fact designated in 'cameral science', under the auspices of Austrian rule, even if its holder gave to it a decidedly more 'French' – political economy proper – flavour (sec. 2.1.7).

### *2.1.7 Smith's achievement*

This survey of eighteenth-century developments in particular gives a clear enough sense of the historical context in which Smith embraced the designation 'political economy' for the science he was seeking to develop – from the elements of *LJ*, and with the benefit of the contributions of others, particularly Quesnay and the associated French writers, into its final form in *WN*. Our sketch of just some salient features of the formation of the idea of a political economy should be understood as just that, a sketch. There was a great deal more happening in relation to notions of economic management as an element of statecraft, and that programme as worthy of theoretical inquiry, than just this. A large number of, in particular, French, publications were appearing, which had recourse to 'economy' or variants in their titles, and Smith possessed a good number of them.[20] Much of these derived from Quesnay's lead. Steuart also was under the influence of the French literature, but probably most especially Cantillon (1755). The preponderance of French economic titles in Smith's own library is striking testimony to the mid-eighteenth-century primacy of French thought in the subject. Furthermore, in Glasgow in the 1750s and 1760s Smith attended a 'Political Economy Club' (Ross 1995: xxi, 107–8, 139–40; *Corr*: 104, n. 2; Rae

1895: 90–4). What is commonly regarded as the first European professorial position in political economy was established at the University of Naples from 1754, and held by Antonio Genovesi; what is often referred to as the second European Chair in political economy was established by Empress Maria Theresa at the Scuole Palatine in Milan from 1768–9, for Cesare Beccaria.[21] The further, partial qualification to these being the first two Chairs of 'political economy' is due to the Swedish developments, discussed in section 2.3.4. Thomas Malthus's position as Professor of Modern History and Political Economy at the College of the East India Company, from 1805, makes him the first holder of a Chair of political economy in Britain (Keynes 1933: 128–9). France had its first professor of political economy from 1830, in the person of J.-B. Say, at the Collège de France.[22]

The work which Pietro Verri saw as necessary to complete the task of turning political economy into a science (quoted in sec. 2.1.4) – linking separate theories harmoniously together, providing method and organization – may fairly be regarded as the singular achievement which raises Smith above all other eighteenth-century socio-economic thinkers. But that achievement should not be exaggerated; it was indeed, in large measure, a work of synthesis rather than original genius.[23] J.-B. Say was moved to write that until publication of *WN*, 'the science of political economy did not exist' (Say 1880 [1803]: xxxviii), a view that Smith himself would not have shared, given his comment that the Physiocratic system,

> with all its imperfections is, perhaps, the nearest approximation to the truth that has yet been published upon the subject of political oeconomy, and is upon that account well worth the consideration of every man who wishes to examine with attention the principles of that very important science.
>
> (*WN*: 678)[24]

In fact, Say is not wrong, if his proposition is read in terms of Smith's singular achievement. But Pierre-Samuel Dupont de Nemours, who republished Quesnay's writings (see n. 20) and conceived of the Physiocratic-inspired programme under the title of a 'new science' (*De l'Origine et du Progrès d'une Science Nouvelle*, 1767), was also not wrong, in responding: 'This idea that occurs to you to *reject* us … my dear Say, does not do away with the fact that you are through the branch of Adam Smith a grandson of *Quesnay*, a nephew of the great Turgot' (quoted in Skinner 1996: 178, from McLain 1977: 201). It appears that Smith would have dedicated *WN* to Quesnay, had he not died prior to its publication: Stewart (1811: 304) says that Smith 'told me himself'.

On the other hand, Smith certainly had no desire to publicly acknowledge James Steuart, famously commenting: 'I have the same opinion of Sir James Stewarts Book that you have. Without once mentioning it, I flatter myself, that every false principle in it, will meet with a clear and distinct confutation in mine' (*Corr*: 164). The absence of any reference to Steuart's *Principles* in *WN* is the result of a conscious policy. Edwin Cannan speculates that Smith may have chosen not to use 'political economy' in his title, because of its prior appropriation by Steuart. Commenting that Smith clearly regards his *WN* title as a 'synonym' for political economy, Cannan (1904: xviii) continues:

> it seems perhaps a little surprising that he did not call his book '*Political Œconomy*' or '*Principles of Political Œconomy*'. But we must remember that the term was still in 1776 a very new one, and that it had been used in the title of Sir James Steuart's great book .... Nowadays, of course, no author has any special claim to exclusive use of the title.... But in 1776 Adam Smith may well have refrained from using it simply because it had been used by Steuart nine years before, especially considering the fact that the *Wealth of Nations* was to be brought out by the publishers who had brought out Steuart's book.

In light of the above-quoted letter to William Pulteney, perhaps Smith was also motivated by a desire not to attract attention to Steuart's book.[25] In any case, Steuart's is not the only work in which Smith confronted the term and the concept (albeit in French and Italian), as we have seen.

## 2.2 Wealth as national product

### *2.2.1 Smith on 'wealth'*

Smith's prescriptive statement of the scope of political economy has four substantive terms: the *nature* and *causes* of the *wealth* of *nations*. What then is the meaning of 'wealth'? The overwhelmingly dominant notion of the nature of wealth is as the (flow of) national product:[26]

> Every increase or diminution of capital ... naturally tends to increase or diminish the real quantity of industry, the number of productive hands, and consequently the exchangeable value of the annual produce of the land and labour of the country, the real wealth and revenue of all its inhabitants.
>
> (*WN*: 337)

> A nation may import to a greater value than it exports for half a century, perhaps, together; the gold and silver which comes into it during all this time may be all immediately sent out of it; its circulating coin may gradually decay, different sorts of paper money being substituted in its place, and even the debts too which it contracts in the principal nations with whom it deals, may be gradually increasing; and yet its real wealth, the exchangeable value of the annual produce of its lands and labour, may, during the same period, have been increasing in a much greater proportion.
>
> (*WN*: 497–8)

> ... I shall endeavour to explain ... what are the reasons and causes which have induced almost all modern governments ... to contract debts, and what

> have been the effects of those debts upon the real wealth, the annual produce of the land and labour of the society.
>
> (*WN*: 688)

Subject to one qualification, this sense appears far more commonly than any other.[27] The qualification is that frequent passing reference is made in *WN* to wealthy persons, and nations (also towns and cities), in a manner which does not make clear whether the wealthy are understood as high-income and/or asset-rich entities.[28] In these contexts, Smith does not usually give an explicit asset versus income (stock versus flow) characterization; so that he could be referring to one or the other or both, when he speaks of wealth and the wealthy (and recall that it is the *real* wealth of nations which is explicitly identified with the *flow* of national product, immediately above). But where he is explicit, a stock concept is evidently intended.

Beyond the most frequent and definite sense of 'real' wealth as national product, and the frequent passing and rather indefinite references to wealth, some other distinct instances are noteworthy. In the *WN* chapter on wages, and a little elsewhere, Smith identifies wealth, not real wealth, with 'revenue and stock', or just stock, evidently intending to convey the sense of the aggregate expenditure devoted to employing labour (and by inference, devoted to labour consumption):

> The demand for those who live by wages … cannot increase but in proportion to the increase of the funds which are destined for the payment of wages. These funds are of two kinds; first, the revenue which is over and above what is necessary for the maintenance; and, secondly, the stock which is over and above what is necessary for the employment of their masters.
>
> . . .
>
> The demand for those who live by wages, therefore, necessarily increases with the increase of the revenue and stock of every country, and cannot possibly increase without it. The increase of revenue and stock is the increase of national wealth.
>
> (*WN*: 86–7; also 89, 91, 99, 105–6, 209, 266)

Perhaps this formulation is used (if one wishes to render it consistent with the concept of real wealth) because the associated aggregate labour employment generates the national product, or perhaps it is merely being used loosely here, as a variant of a stock concept.

The phrase 'real wealth and revenue', or variants thereof (in a small number of instances, not prefaced with 'real'), also occurs frequently, almost always explicitly identifying them with annual produce,[29] because for Smith 'revenue' can also serve as a synonym for national product (see sec. 4.2.1). Two instances of the phrase are less clear, but consistent with the identification of wealth and produce (*WN*: 515, 535); *WN* (105–6) equates 'wealth and revenue' with stock.

It may also be emphasized that 'wealth' is commonly articulated in explicitly dynamic contexts: 'the different stages of wealth and improvement', 'increase of wealth and improvement', 'the progress of wealth and improvement', 'the natural progress ... towards wealth and improvement', 'progressive wealth and increase' (*WN*: 206, 210, 235, 345, 378; also 207, 234, 242, 254, 497, 567, 596, 598, 625) – and as well, the wages and growth references cited directly above. There are many instances of wealth being coupled with power and social standing: 'wealth and distinction', 'wealth and greatness', 'wealth, and honours, and preferments', 'wealth and importance', 'wealth and power'.[30] Smith expresses a certain disdain for the individual pursuit of wealth, distinction and so on, at some of these instances (e.g. *TMS*: 50; see Chapter 5, n. 28).

Finally, there are extensive discussions of the mercantilist and Physiocratic concepts of wealth, the latter being also a notion of wealth as produce (but essentially, agricultural produce). Smith's treatment of the former is far more extensive, for the explicit reason of its far greater practical significance:

> That system which represents the produce of land as the sole source of the revenue and wealth of every country, has ... never been adopted by any nation, and ... exists only in the speculations of a few men of great learning and ingenuity in France. It would not ... be worth while to examine at great length the errors of a system which never has done, and probably never will do any harm in any part of the world.
>
> (*WN*: 663)

The contrast between what Smith regards as the mercantilist concept, and his own, is thrown into relief in the first reference to mercantilism and wealth in *WN*. Referring to those writers who have perceived a high value of money as evidence of poverty, he continues:

> This notion is connected with the system of political œconomy which represents national wealth as consisting in the abundance, and national poverty in the scarcity of gold and silver .... I shall only observe at present, that the high value of the precious metals can be no proof of the poverty or barbarism of any particular country at the time when it took place.... As the wealth of Europe ... has increased greatly since the discovery of the mines of America, so the value of gold and silver has gradually diminished. This diminution of their value, however, has not been owing to the increase of the real wealth of Europe, of the annual produce of its land and labour, but to the accidental discovery of more abundant mines than any that were known before. The increase of the quantity of gold and silver in Europe, and the increase of its manufactures and agriculture, are two events which, though they have happened nearly about the same time, yet have arisen from very different causes, and have scarce any natural connection with one another.
>
> (*WN*: 255)[31]

Most certainly, Smith is better disposed towards Physiocracy than mercantilism. His striking praise of the 'system' of 'The Oeconomists', quoted in relation to a comment of J.-B. Say above (sec. 2.1.7), continues:

> Though in representing the labour which is employed upon land as the only productive labour, the notions which it inculcates are perhaps too narrow and confined; yet in representing the wealth of nations as consisting, not in the unconsumable riches of money, but in the consumable goods annually reproduced by the labour of the society; and in representing perfect liberty as the only effectual expedient for rendering this annual reproduction the greatest possible, its doctrine seems to be in every respect as just as it is generous and liberal.
>
> (*WN*: 678)[32]

Before turning to the history of 'wealth' prior to Smith, two conceptual issues in relation to his notions of wealth may be raised: the distinction between *produce* and *the exchangeable value* of the produce; and the relation between wealth and consumption. With regard to the former, there appears to be some ambiguity as to whether real wealth is just the annual produce itself, or its exchange value. The most plausible resolution of this is that Smith's *ultimate* sense of wealth is as command over commodities (or resources for production of commodities). If one thinks of the physical annual produce as a single composite commodity, a fall in the exchange value of this produce with respect to another composite commodity (in which the possessors of the annual produce have some interest, for example, with a view to consumption) – even though the annual produce is unchanged – may in a sense be regarded as a fall in wealth. (For example, in modern terms, consider a decline in the terms of trade with no change in national product, though this illustration indicates that the distinction is only really significant at some disaggregate level or other.) In fact, such a notion of wealth as purchasing power is clearly expressed in his commentary on Hobbes quoted above (n. 30), which continues:

> The power which that possession [of wealth] immediately and directly conveys to him, is the power of purchasing; a certain command over all the labour, or over all the produce of labour which is then in the market. His fortune is greater or less, precisely in proportion to the extent of this power; or to the quantity either of other men's labour, or, what is the same thing, of the produce of other men's labour, which it enables him to purchase or command. The exchangeable value of every thing must always be precisely equal to the extent of this power which it conveys to its owner.
>
> (*WN*: 48)

The same view is differently expressed in a commentary upon the hypothetical possibility of a product for which there is no market:

> Unless a capital was employed in manufacturing that part of the rude produce which requires a good deal of preparation before it can be fit for use and consumption, it either would never be produced, because there could be no demand for it; or if it was produced spontaneously, it would be of no value in exchange, and could add nothing to the wealth of the society.
>
> (*WN*: 360–1)

But the identification of wealth as product, and of wealth as the exchange value of product, ends up also raising deep questions in relation to one particular aspect of Smith's economics: the coordination of capital accumulation (supply capacity over time) and demand (see secs 4.4.1, 5.2.3).

With regard to the relation between wealth and consumption, can one infer that the characterization of wealth as national product must be intended with a view to consumption, so that it would be as true to Smith's intention to articulate his notion of wealth-as-national-product as wealth-as-human-consumption? This may seem a small and innocuous step, but there is a substantive issue involved. It is an irrationality impossible to suppose Smith guilty of, that he would endorse a normative objective of growing national product, never to be realized in (above-necessary or surplus) consumption. It would be as if the economic system is to be an ever-expanding machine, aimed at maximum growth, in pursuit of (surplus) consumption realization which is *always* to remain in the future (cf. Chapter 4, n. 50). (Such irrationality is, after all, akin to his ultimate accusation against mercantilism.) His identification of wealth with the net revenue available for potential consumption may be understood in the light of this:

> gross rent ... comprehends whatever is paid by the farmer; ... neat rent, what remains free to the landlord, after deducting ... all ... necessary charges; or what, without hurting his estate, he can afford to place in his stock reserved for ... consumption .... His real wealth is in proportion, not to his gross, but to his neat rent.
>
> The gross revenue of all the inhabitants of a great country, comprehends the whole annual produce of their land and labour; the neat revenue, what remains free to them after deducting the expence of maintaining; first, their fixed; and, secondly, their circulating capital; or what, without encroaching upon their capital, they can place in their stock reserved for ... consumption .... Their real wealth too is in proportion, not to their gross, but to their neat revenue.
>
> (*WN*: 286–7; cf. 440; *LJA*: 83)[33]

Nevertheless, the time-paths of production and of desired (surplus) consumption remain distinct, depending on accumulation or saving through time. By focusing on output as such, rather than consumption, as wealth, Smith can leave open the question of the desirable path of consumption through time. This avoids a definite determination of the less clear-cut issue of trading off current (surplus) consumption in favour of future output (via current accumulation or investment) – or one may say, trading off current 'unproductive consumption' in favour of current 'productive consumption'.[34] A closer identification of wealth with consumption appears in the lectures on jurisprudence (*LJA*: 377–9, 384; *LJB*: 487, 503), though perhaps for a rhetorical purpose (ridiculing mercantilism); but there is in *LJ* no systematic use of a notion like 'real wealth' as it appears in *WN*.

### *2.2.2 Early meanings of wealth*

The English use of the term 'wealth' can be dated back to the thirteenth and fourteenth centuries, with parallel formations in the Middle Dutch *weelde*, *welde*, Middle Low German *welede*, and Old High German *welida*. From then right through to the seventeenth century in English it conveyed a wide sense of human well-being, not limited to material possessions: 'They sayd howe the noble men of the realme of Fraunce, knyghtes and squyers shamed the realme, and that it shulde be a great welth to dystroy them all' (1523); 'Christe ... liued ... and ... suffred ... for our sakes, and for our welthe' (1537); 'She ... procured both suche as was for the welthe of his soule, and prepared holsome meates for his body' (1541); 'In all tyme of our tribulacion, in all tyme of our wealth' (1548–9); 'The inuentyon of feates, helpynge annye thynge to the aduantage and wealthe of lyffe' (1551). The notion of wealth as material property is however also in use from the earliest times: 'For here es welth inogh to win, To make vs riche for euermore' (1352); 'all men shoulde haue and enioye equall portions of welthes and commodities' (1551; from Thomas More's *Utopia*); 'To [*sic*] late you shall repent the act When all my realme, and all your wealthes are sackt' (1574); '*Iulia*. What think'st thou of the rich Mercatio? *Lucetta*. Well of his wealth; but of himselfe, so, so' (1591; William Shakespeare); 'Wealth, howsoever got, in England makes Lords of Mechanicks, Gentlemen of Rakes' (1703; all from *OED*: 'wealth'). The *OED* provides just two prior instances of that phrase given perpetual currency by Smith's title: 'The winds were hush'd, the waves in ranks were cast, As awfully as when God's people past: Those, yet uncertain on whose sails to blow, These, where the wealth of Nations ought to flow' (Dryden 1667: prefatory 'Verses to ... the Dutchess'). 'To be poor, in the epick language, is only not to command the wealth of nations' (Johnson 1752: 238).[35]

From a modern standpoint, it is somewhat amusing to see that in its early life, from the thirteenth century to at least the sixteenth century, 'wealth' carries the generic sense of human well-being as such – of which, material well-being or material possessions are just one dimension.[36] The innovation of the eighteenth century, and perhaps a little earlier, is to make wealth to convey *only* a material or economic meaning (whether Smith's meaning, or another material notion). This may be read as an expression of the materialism of modernity and Enlightenment. Recall Bacon's influential dictum concerning 'the relief of man's estate' (quoted in sec. 2.1.6). Whatever Smith's personal views as to the significance of material acquisition for human well-being as such, his political economy makes the accumulation of consumable product synonymous with the acquisition of 'wealth', and this, to be the over-arching purpose of political economy, normative and explanatory. Of course, securing life itself, as well as liberty, is a more fundamental imperative, which material prosperity presupposes, and policy is required for the achievement of those conditions, as shall be seen most fully in Chapter 5. Conformity with the restraints of law is also required for the maintenance of life and liberty, the lives and liberty of all, and is further supported by a larger individual self-command than strict law entails. But beyond that, to the extent that well-being depends upon other things, it lies beyond the realm of policy. This is a manifestation of the liberal character of Smith's social thought: well-being in any wider sense is a private matter. (This implies no denial that Smith regards individual human well-being to depend upon things other than material consumption.) As a matter of fact, the pursuit of material accumulation is itself a private matter; but Smith is sure enough of his view of the character of human nature, to be confident that individuals *will* pursue material self-betterment. And whatever his view as to the limits of material accumulation as a means to individual well-being, he favours it as a *norm* for social theory. The pursuit of economic growth and development is a matter for public policy (including in this, regime design); the pursuit of, for example, God, is not.[37]

This point about the generic and wider original meaning of 'wealth' serves also to signal a warning as to how one perceives earlier texts in relation to this matter. In particular, with regard to ancient thought, since 'wealth' has no Greek (or Latin) root, what precisely are we considering when we inquire as to what, for example, Aristotle, regarded as 'wealth'?[38] The term commonly taken to convey the notion of the acquisition of 'wealth' in Aristotle (*chrematistic*), more properly and literally is to be understood as conveying the sense of acquisition of material things, and is most certainly not a synonym for human well-being in that frame of reference. Hence, in reading discussions of *chrematistic* as commentaries on 'wealth', one is a priori imposing upon those systems of thought, the sense of 'wealth' which has prevailed only with the rise of modernity and the advent of Enlightenment. The notion of human well-being in general is perhaps rather carried in Aristotle's Greek by the term *eudaimonia.* To be clear, however, this is not to say that consideration of Aristotle's view of *chrematistic*, contrasted with Smith's view of 'wealth' accumulation, is an utterly spurious or incoherent inquiry: it amounts to consideration of two contrasting, ancient and modern, views of the significance of material acquisitions to human well-being, not a pointless investigation. When Bonar (1893: 32–4), for example, as one among many others, indicates the Aristotelian view that there are finite limits to legitimate wealth acquisition, this is about precisely finite limits to legitimate material accumulation, which tells us something significant about a change from antiquity to modernity. But the difference between the Aristotelian notion of human well-being, and the modern view, is a wider subject, though material property is certainly a *requirement* for well-being or felicity, also for Aristotle (Barker 1946: l, 9, 118–19, 298–9).[39] What is in danger of being missed here is that important contrast: between ancient and modern notions of human well-being, where for our purposes here, it is the modern notion conveyed or implied by Smith's political economy, which is of particular interest. It may be added that to the extent there are causal connections between beliefs about the desirability or legitimacy of material acquisition, and *actual* material prosperity, one may conjecture that historically, they involved not merely a one-way causation from norms to actuality, but an interdependence. In pre-modern human history the technological infeasibility of general material abundance must have encouraged endorsement of austerity (and forms of collectivism); with the advent of modernity, the endorsement of material accumulation was surely stimulated by the experience of systematic material improvement.

The ancient philosophical strictures against the pursuit of material accumulation, buttressed by strands of Christian influence – or was the weight of relative influence the other way round? – ramify through the centuries of the Common Era up to the advent of modernity. The pursuit of material property becomes also a distraction from spirituality with a view to individual immortality in the world to come ('treasures in heaven': Matthew's Gospel, Ch. 6, verse 20). The demands of Christian charity towards the poor also tell against the legitimacy of unlimited individual accumulation. Rather than leading to any notion of the illegitimacy of material wealth and inequality, the latter became a stricture against unjust acquisition and use, and against dishonourable purposes and motivations (e.g. the sin of 'avarice', one of the seven 'deadly' sins dating from the sixth century). Not so much money or material possessions themselves, but 'the love of money', is repudiated (St. Paul's *New Testament* first letter to Timothy, Ch. 6, verse 10). 'Need' as a criterion for legitimate extent and use of material property serves as a highly elastic notion in this conception, as does the continuing recourse to a kind of Aristotelian mean between penury and excess. Against the pursuit of temporal material satisfactions, there is posited not merely the claims of well-being as felicity ('eudaimonia'), but those of salvation and eternal happiness, presumably an attractive prospect *vis-à-vis* damnation, since forever is a very long time. This also served the function of providing a certain solace to those who were at no risk of the alternative possibility of being overwhelmed by indulgence in material pleasures: it assisted in reconciling the poor to contentment with their lot. Resonating through much of this thought is a grappling with the significance of the calls to poverty by Jesus of Nazareth, as recorded in the Christian scriptures (e.g. Matthew's Gospel, Ch. 19, verse 21). The status of private individual property also was rendered tenuous in a framework of God's ownership of the world, and with the Church widening its temporal, material claims as its power grew. On the one hand, scientific developments which offered the prospect of sustained improvement in human physical and material well-being, and on the other, the rise (or revival) of a humanism which sought to 'redeem' humankind in *this* world, by way of human ingenuity and effort, eventually overcame the anti-materialist temper. But already, late-medieval (fifteenth-century) humanism was 'de-sanctifying' poverty; by the thirteenth century attitudes to material accumulation were shifting.[40] As shall be seen in Chapter 5, Smith will posit material well-being *for all*, in a certain sense, as the ultimate purpose of the social economy and of political economy.

If one were to take one's lead from Smith himself, then the most salient notion of 'wealth' prior to his own conception would be the alleged mercantilist identification of wealth and the precious metals (bullion and/or currency).[41] But how fair is Smith's characterization of the mercantile literature in this respect? There has been considerable discussion of that in the secondary literature. The very fact that the concept of 'mercantilism', more than two centuries on, persists as a common, if not now so dominant, mode of characterizing pre-Smithian economic thought is striking testimony to his success in shaping the latter-day perception of prior economic thought. To test Smith's view – and if need be, escape it – one must ask the most fundamental question. Is it sensible to suppose there was a more or less coherent or unified, and dominant, body of thought and/or practice in the two or more centuries prior to Smith, which can be characterized in terms of a single-minded policy objective of wealth understood as money? The best unequivocal answer is no. But the correct answer of course is contingent upon the exact definition of mercantilism, and with respect to that, one can choose from narrow and precise notions, across to broad and rather more elastic notions. In these terms, Smith's vulnerability on the issue is that his substantive critique of the mercantile system focuses on the narrow (regulation of economic activity, especially international trade and production for international trade), but at the same time he wishes to imply by this a repudiation of economic thought and practice much more widely.

There are three separate sets of economic beliefs involved here, which may be connected but are nevertheless distinct:

1 the desirability of state regulation of economic activity in general;
2 the desirability of state regulation of, in particular, international trade and production for international trade;
3 the desirability of a positive, or at least non-negative, national balance of foreign payments.

Smith is broadly against the first, and has arguments for his position independent of international trade and payments issues (that is to say, arguments which would apply in a closed system). There are also arguments *for* the first, which are independent of foreign exchange issues. (Somewhat further to this, see sec. 5.2.) The second is hardly intelligible without reliance on the third; but one can hold to the third and nevertheless reject the second – and one could subscribe to the second and third, while rejecting the first. Notice also that all three sets of beliefs are normative. The 'mercantilist' literature also generated descriptive theoretical statements, including statements which remain entirely valid today: for example, in a fixed exchange rate system, a balance of foreign payments surplus causes an increase in the domestic stock of money. The further common descriptive proposition – that an increase in the money stock is a necessary means, or an impetus, to increased domestic production – would be regarded more sceptically later (and now), but is not an entirely spurious idea.

Smith's concept of the mercantile system is unsatisfactory in at least two respects: if a narrow notion of mercantilism is adhered to (the second proposition above, supported by the third), then there is considerable non-mercantilist literature before Smith; if a broad notion of mercantilism is deployed (the first proposition), then the question becomes the degree of economic liberalism in pre-Smithian economic literature. This is not a meaningless question, but nevertheless, it is a question of degrees not principle. That earlier literature is by no means uniformly illiberal with regard to private economic activity. Furthermore, none of those above three normative propositions necessitate a belief that gold and silver constitute the only content of national 'wealth', nor that accumulation of the same should be the primary object of national economic policy. One may say, the 'mercantilists' could walk and chew gum at the same time, whether or not the concept is treated as a synonym for pre-Smithian economic writers in general. Mun (1664, but written decades earlier) became the archetypal English mercantilist text, a view already implied by Smith (*LJA*: 381), who owned a 1755 Glasgow edition of the work (Mizuta 2000: 177).

One may add that in truth, the accumulation of a national stock of gold and silver was not an utterly foolish objective: for example, for the purposes of a precautionary reserve of internationally acceptable purchasing power (with a view to national external security), or for the purposes of domestic production in economies in the process of monetizing exchange – both of these, and other aspects, being connected with nation-building. The very fact that these doctrines were so widespread gives reason to doubt that they were so entirely without merit, at least for their times. Economic doctrines are not like religious beliefs; they are somewhat more obliged to confront reality.[42] More generally, a less historically specific point may be made: to entirely dismiss external balance as a policy objective requires a supposition that balance of foreign payments problems (most notably, unsustainable deficits) are always either non-existent or trivial; or if they can be genuine problems, then their resolution is best left to private decisions, without the intervention of public policy. One or other variant of this position may or may not be sound, but it is not self-evidently foolish to dissent from such views. Keynes's (1936: 333–51) partial rehabilitation of mercantilism is in this spirit, even if not altogether historically well-informed.

### *2.2.3 Petty to Turgot*

It is certainly clear, once one arrives at the economics of Quesnay, that the concept of wealth as output, with the growth of wealth as the primary object of the science, has been fully embraced. Smith himself acknowledges that the Physiocrats share his correct conception of wealth (*WN*: 678; quoted in sec. 2.2.1). As a matter of fact, in the *Tableau* the calculation of national wealth includes the stocks of all assets (as well as the annual product); e.g. the capitalized value of land, housing, shipping, the money stock, and so on (Kuczynski and Meek 1972: v–xi, '3rd edn'). That is to say, wealth (*richesses*[43]) is taken to include the stocks resulting from previous flows of annual production; the parts of those earlier production flows not earlier consumed (though additionally, also the stock of land). As Quesnay says at another point, wealth is constituted by those things which have 'both use value and market value' (Kuczynski and Meek 1972: 9n; cf. viii, on the inclusion of land in wealth, both '3rd edn'). Notwithstanding the inclusion of money in the wealth calculation, there is a firmly anti-mercantilist commentary in a long note attached to the estimate for the money stock:

> The people believe that it is in money that the wealth of a state consists. But money, like all other products, constitutes wealth only in proportion to its market value; and it is no harder to acquire, by paying over other kinds of wealth for it, than any other commodity. Its quantity in a state is limited by the uses to which it can be put ....
>
> (Kuczynski and Meek 1972: ixn–xn, '3rd edn')

And further, and even more forcefully in the 'Maxims' accompanying the *Tableau*:

> money ... ought never to superabound in a country to the detriment of the use and consumption of the annual product, which ought through reproduction and mutual trade to perpetuate true wealth there.... Thus money is an active and really profitable form of wealth in a state only so far as it continually returns wealth for wealth, because money in itself is only sterile wealth.[44]... Although taxes are paid in money, it is not money which provides them: it is the wealth annually regenerated from the land. It is in this renascent wealth, and not as the vulgar believe in the nation's money stock, that the prosperity and power of a state consist.... Thus money should ... circulate for the purpose of reproducing the wealth which enables the nation to subsist and provides contributions for the sovereign.
>
> (Kuczynski and Meek 1972: 17n–18n; also 19n, both '3rd edn')

Also in the maxims one sees capital expenditure characterized as wealth (*richesses*), thereby emphasizing the circular character of production:

> men can obtain and perpetuate wealth only by means of wealth .... The more wealth a nation possesses for the purpose of enabling wealth to be annually regenerated, the fewer men does this annual reproduction employ, the more net product it yields, and the more men the Government has at its disposal for services and public works; and the more wages there are to enable them to subsist, the more useful are these men to the state by virtue of their occupations, and by virtue of their expenditure, which causes their pay to be brought back into circulation.
>
> (Kuczynski and Meek 1972: 20n; also 8, 13n, 14, all '3rd edn')[45]

Quesnay thus uses 'wealth' to include stocks as well as flows; but as has been shown above, this is true also of Smith. The key substantive point in relation to the conceptualization of political economy is that Quesnay, like Smith, centres the new economic science on the growth of 'wealth' in the sense of the flow of annual or national product. It is for Quesnay at one and the same time, the growth of *capital*, the growth of outputs that can serve as production inputs for further outputs, which is likewise true for Smith, as shall be seen in Chapter 4.

In so articulating the concept of wealth as the object of political economy, Quesnay no more than Smith fell out of the sky. There are many precursors for the idea of wealth as (consumable) output. One may focus here on some few of those, who possess also a notion of wealth so understood as the object of systematic theory – even fewer focused on the *growth* of wealth so understood. Richard Cantillon is Quesnay's most immediate predecessor as a genuine theorist of production and commerce. Most would agree that his remarkable *Essai* is the first genuine treatise in economic analysis of the modern era. Cantillon takes wealth (*la Richesse*) understood as produced outputs as his point of departure in the book. The very first, brief chapter, *De la Richesse*, opens: 'The Land is the Source or Matter from whence all Wealth is produced. The Labour of man is the Form which produces it: and Wealth in itself is nothing but the Maintenance, Conveniencies, and Superfluities of Life' (Cantillon 1755 [1931]: 3; cf. 31).[46] Notice, however, that the emphasis is on consumption as such (cf. Cantillon 1755 [1931]: 87–95). Cantillon certainly has a clear conception of production as a circular process in which produced outputs serve as inputs to further production. But growth of output via expansion of inputs and/or increase in the productivity of inputs – either as a mere possibility, or as an object of analysis and policy – is strangely absent from his text (see Aspromourgos 1996: 73–88). Cantillon evidently was significantly influenced by Pierre le Pesant Sieur de Boisguilbert, possibly including in relation to the notion of wealth, though there are certainly more definite traces of influence than that. In the context of a vigorous repudiation of gold and silver as wealth, he argues for 'true wealth' as 'complete enjoyment, not only of the necessities of life, but even of every superfluity and of anything which gives pleasure to the senses' (Boisguilbert 1707 [2000]: 17; also 1–3, 6, 8 and I.N.E.D. 1966: 497, 973, for the first edition; cf. Faccarello 1999: 66–7, 71, 83).

Cantillon also derived important elements of his system from Petty (Aspromourgos 1996: 107–12). The latter's conception of wealth is rather nuanced. Like Quesnay, Petty uses 'wealth' to denote both material stocks and flows; but he also deploys a hierarchical notion of the elements of wealth, ranking them from most durable down to least durable (see Aspromourgos 1996: 39–41). This enables him to preserve the good sense in mercantilism (e.g. the usefulness of a precautionary reserve of liquid purchasing power), without falling prey to any degree of excessive preoccupation with national accumulation of bullion or specie. Money is the most durable form of wealth – 'Universal Wealth' – yet it is also 'but the Fat of the Body-politick, whereof too much doth as often hinder its Agility, as too little makes it sick'.[47] The formula, 'Labour is the Father and active principle of Wealth, as Lands are the Mother', points squarely to produced output as the core meaning of wealth, as subsequently evident in Cantillon (Petty 1662: 68). Behind this formula probably stands the influence of Petty's mentor, Hobbes (1651: 160–1):

> The nutrition of a commonwealth consisteth, in the *plenty*, and *distribution* of *materials* conducing to life: in *concoction*, or *preparation* .... As for the plenty of matter, it is a thing limited by nature, to those commodities ... God usually either freely giveth, or for labour selleth to mankind.... [P]lenty dependeth, next to God's favour, merely on the labour and industry of men.

Near contemporary with Smith, Turgot's achievements with respect to theoretical substance and clarity place him on a par with the Scotsman as an economic analyst, in particular, in his most systematic work, the elegant and succinct *Réflexions* (1769–70).[48] Turgot, like Quesnay, identifies wealth with capital together with the capitalized value of land:

> if we add the revenue of all lands, that is, the net revenue ... and multiply them by the rate at which lands are sold, we would have the sum of all the wealth of a Nation in landed estates. To obtain the whole of a Nation's wealth, the moveable wealth ought to be added, which consist in the sum of capitals employed in enterprises of agriculture, industry and commerce, which ... must continually return to the entrepreneurs, to be reinvested in the enterprises, which could not continue without them. It would be a very gross error to confound the immense mass of moveable wealth with the mass of money that exists in a State; the latter is but a very small thing in comparison.
>
> (Turgot 1769–70 [1977]: 88–9)

Notice the emphasis on the circular character of production. He also goes on to include other durable assets which are potentially convertible into capital (Turgot 1769–70 [1977]: 90; recall the Petty–Cantillon inclusion of durables in wealth). Strikingly similar to Smith, Turgot identifies 'real' wealth with the annual produce as such:

> is it not evident that since the only real wealth of the State is the annual output of its land and of the industry of its inhabitants, its wealth will be at it greatest when the produce of each acre of land, and of the industry of each individual is carried to the highest possible level?
>
> (Groenewegen 1977c [1759]: 27)

Hence in the framework of circular production, Turgot speaks also of the annual output, especially in relation to agriculture, as 'renascent wealth' (Groenewegen 1977c [1767]: 123, 128). So had Quesnay.

One could say that in both Smith and earlier English literature, 'wealth' is constituting a kind of truism. It is being utilized to signify whatever particular and varying worthy thing, or things, that humans, or thinkers, or national policies choose to pursue, so that the proposition that analysis or policy should pursue 'wealth' is hardly more than a tautology. The issue of substance then is the change or difference in things aimed for. Hence, for example, Tribe (1984: 273) points out that in the German cameralist framework 'a primary form of wealth for a ruler consisted in the good order of his subject population'. And in the broadest historical terms, one can conclude, in a rough and ready way, that it is as if the content given to wealth-as-well-being narrows to a materialist conception. Put bluntly, the modern resolution of 'wealth' is that well-being *is* material. One might be tempted, from a twenty-first century vantage point (at least if the view is from within a developed social economy), to take the high moral ground with respect to this kind of materialism. Scepticism concerning material accumulation has latterly been increasingly encouraged: on the one hand, by a sense that in at least some respects individual consumption has reached the neighbourhood of what may be regarded as satiation; on the other, by a widening consensus that the depletion of non-renewable natural resources associated with that human material accumulation is unsustainable, if not a serious threat to human well-being into the future (on the latter, see Chapter 4, n. 31). (Who can say for sure that Smith, come back from the dead more than two centuries on, would not share these views, if it is at all sensible to pose such an unhistorical question?) However, any such moral scepticism with regard to contemporary material aspirations and their ecological or environmental consequences also should be tempered by historical sensitivity with regard to eighteenth-century aspirations. If we now question continuously increasing material consumption, it is from a level of comfort almost incommensurably higher than that of the eighteenth century. Any new-found appreciation, or rediscovery, of non-material well-being in recent decades, arising out of disenchantment with consumption and/or environmental concerns, should acknowledge that fact with respect to the Enlightenment materialist ambition. Perhaps, in a sense, Enlightenment has done its work in this respect. Is anyone today prepared to suggest that human beings should return to the material conditions of life of the average European in 1750, so long as there is a (sustainable) choice not to do so? Even so, pre-modern moderation with respect to individual consumption may not be now merely an anachronism.

## 2.3 Nature as a norm

### *2.3.1 Smith on 'nature'*

Notions of 'nature' and of the naturalness of a great variety of phenomena constitute the most pervasive generic concept in Smith's texts. A general consideration of them therefore usefully can be undertaken as a preliminary to the detailed consideration of his political economy in subsequent chapters. Three particularly common strands of use may be highlighted.

1 A thing, circumstance or situation is described as 'natural' or 'naturally' occurring if it is conceived of as predictable, to be expected, fitting or suitable, normal or ordinary.
2 Relatedly, 'nature' is objectified as the world or cosmos, and its structure – or similarly, as the character, structure, form, constitution or meaning of particular things in, or parts of, the world. As a subset of this, humans are one particular part of the world, whose nature is of special interest to Smith, of course, given his intellectual project: the constitution of human nature is the part of nature most extensively discussed by him.
3 Nature is also personified, as if it were an agent with definite intentions or purposes.

In addition to these three dominant, broad senses, other notable particular uses include: natural philosophy (*TMS*: 124–5, 313–14; *WN*: 766–71; *EPS*: 77, 119, 244–6, 249; *LRB*: 57, 144, 181); natural liberty (only in *WN*: 157, 324, 470, 530, 606, 687; cf. 608: 'natural and free' trade); natural jurisprudence (*TMS*: 218, 329, 340–1, 389; *LJB*: 397; *Corr*: 5); and, apparently identified, 'natural justice' and 'natural equity' (*TMS*: 340–1; *WN*: 898; *LJA*: 100, 105, 130). The terms 'natural law' or 'laws of nature' (*WN*: 382; *LJA*: 83, 93, 134, 154–5; *LJB*: 404, 443, 544, 554), 'natural rights' (*LJA*: 8, 13, 105; cf. 71; *LJB*: 399–401, 459, 471, 476) and 'natural reason' (*LJA*: 11, 82–3; *LJB*: 525, 538) also appear – though it is notable that save for one passing reference to inheritance rules in *WN*, these are all from *LJ*. Nature and the natural are also contrasted with 'art', 'habit, custom, and education', the 'acquired' and the 'Artificial' (*WN*: 458, 466–7; *EPS*: 178; *LRB*: 73; *LJA*: 16, 362; *LJB*: 459, 476; *edWN*: 572).

The sense of *natural* as expected, fitting or normal is everywhere in *TMS*, as well as *WN*, and indeed, across all Smith's writings.[49] In one way or another, many of those in *TMS* concern natural human feelings understood as proceeding from the actual constitution of human nature. And while at first glance these applications of the notion of the 'natural', in the *TMS* context of moral sentiments, might appear remote from *WN* economic applications, there is in fact a close kinship, and unity of intent. When Smith speaks of 'the natural and ordinary state of mankind', a 'natural and ordinary temper of mind', the 'ordinary standard of human nature', 'the natural and ordinary effects of … conduct', 'the natural and ordinary state of the mind', he conveys a sense of normality, which is constituted by his conception of human nature (*TMS*: 45, 57, 116, also 273n; *EPS*: 197; *edWN*: 571):

> Pain … is, in almost all cases, a more pungent sensation than the opposite and correspondent pleasure. The one, almost always, depresses us much more below the ordinary, or what may be called the natural state of our happiness, than the other ever raises us above it.
>
> (*TMS*: 121)

Likewise in *WN*, when he identifies natural prices and natural rates of remuneration to owners of production inputs, with 'ordinary' prices and rates of remuneration, he conveys a notion of the tendency for natural values to be realized in actual values as being the normal outcome of competition, which in turn is grounded in human nature. The explicit identification of the 'natural' and the 'ordinary' occurs also in other economic contexts: employments of labour and stock 'in their ordinary, or what may be called their natural state'; and 'natural risk' distinguished from 'extraordinary risk' (*WN*: 131, 132, 432). (All the instances of natural or ordinary economic magnitudes, most commonly related to prices and income distribution, are left for discussion in Chapter 3.) The same sense of economic effects as the predictable outcomes of the constitution of the human situation is expressed, for example, in relation to division of labour:

> in consequence of the division of labour, the whole of every man's attention comes naturally to be directed towards some one very simple object. It is naturally to be expected, therefore, that some one or other of those who are employed in each particular branch of labour should soon find out easier and readier methods of performing their own particular work .... A great part of the machines made use of in those manufactures in which labour is most subdivided, were originally the inventions of common workmen, who, being each of them employed in some very simple operation, naturally turned their thoughts towards finding out easier and readier methods of performing it.
>
> (*WN*: 20)

In this same sense, but rendered somewhat stronger, natural is sometimes equated with 'necessary'.[50]

The second sense, applied to the world or cosmos as a whole, is not so common, and in any case is not always easily distinguishable from the notion of nature personified (in *TMS*: 6, 36, 59, 92n, 140, 141n; in *WN*, for just Book I: 145, 183, 189, 206, 223, 235, 237, 246). This use, not surprisingly, is quite pervasive in *EPS* (e.g. 53, 185; but just twice in *LRB*: 74, 217n; and there are a small number of instances elsewhere – e.g. *LJA*: 334; *LJB*: 487; *edWN*: 570; *Corr*: 201). 'Nature' applied to the character or constitution of *particular* things is more commonly used, and more so in *WN*.[51] Nature as it appears in the title of *WN*, and the title of Book II, are instances of this. The larger phrase employed in the title of *WN*, 'nature and causes', appears only rarely (*WN*: 313, 679; *EPS*: 34; *edWN*: 562; cf. *LJB*: 535). Finally, the concept of a *human* nature appears regularly in *TMS*: there are 'original passions of human nature', 'unalterable principles of human nature'; 'the dread of death' is 'one of the most important principles in human nature' (*TMS*: 9, 13, 128; also in *TMS*, for just Parts I–II: 23, 25, 27–8, 31, 34, 43, 47–8, 51–2, 57, 58n–60n, 69, 77n, 79, 82, 85, 87, 93, 108). In short, there is an irreducible 'constitution of human nature' (*TMS*: 148), which serves thereby as a kind of anchor, so to speak, for science of human society such as political economy (cf. Campbell and Skinner 1976: 2–4). But it is a striking fact that there are only five explicit references to human nature in *WN*, and two of these refer to the thinking of others, quoting Mirabeau and describing pneumatology (*WN*: 679, 772). Nevertheless, one of the remaining three instances is fundamental to Smith's economic analysis (the other two are at *WN*: 93, 788):

> division of labour, from which so many advantages are derived, is not originally the effect of any human wisdom, which foresees and intends that general opulence to which it gives occasion. It is the necessary, though very slow and gradual consequence of a certain propensity in human nature which has in view no such extensive utility; the propensity to truck, barter, and exchange one thing for another.
>
> (*WN*: 25; cf. *LJA*: 347; *LJB*: 492–3; *edWN*: 570–71)

Furthermore, *WN* also includes considerable discussion of natural economic outcomes (evident as well in other texts), in particular, in terms of 'natural balance', the 'natural course' of events, and 'natural progress', further considered in Chapter 5. Beyond *TMS* and *WN* there occur only a few additional, rather slight references to human nature (*EPS*: 121; *LRB*: 85, 124, 131, 218; *LJA*: 36, 192; *LJB*: 543; *Corr*: 53, 56).

The final of the three dominant uses, nature personified, is also very extensively employed.[52] A striking instance which well captures also the notion of nature's economy is at *TMS* (87):

> In every part of the universe we observe means adjusted with the nicest artifice to the ends which they are intended to produce; and in the mechanism of a plant, or animal body, admire how every thing is contrived for advancing the two great purposes of nature, the support of the individual, and the propagation of the species. But in these, and in all such objects, we still distinguish the efficient from the final cause of their several motions and organizations.... The wheels of the watch are all admirably adjusted to the end for which it was made, the pointing of the hour. All their various motions conspire in the nicest manner to produce this effect. If they were endowed with a desire and intention to produce it, they could not do it better. Yet we never ascribe any such desire or intention to them, but to the watch-maker ....

References to the 'author' or 'director' of nature carry a similar sense:

> Though man ... be naturally endowed with a desire of the welfare and preservation of society, yet the Author of nature has not entrusted it to his reason to find out ... the proper means of attaining this end; but has endowed him with an immediate and instinctive approbation of that ... which is most proper to attain it. The oeconomy of nature is in this respect exactly of a piece with what it is upon many other occasions. With regard to all those ends which, upon account of their peculiar importance, may be regarded, if such an expression is allowable, as the favourite ends of nature,

> she has constantly … not only endowed mankind with an appetite for the end which she proposes, but likewise with an appetite for the means by which alone this end can be brought about, for their own sakes, and independent of their tendency to produce it. Thus self-preservation, and the propagation of the species, are the great ends which Nature seems to have proposed in the formation of all animals.… But though we are … endowed with a very strong desire of those ends, it has not been intrusted to the slow and uncertain determinations of our reason, to find out the proper means of bringing them about. Nature has directed us to the greater part of these by original and immediate instincts.
>
> (*TMS*: 77–8; part quoted in sec. 2.1.1)

These references point to the wider personification of nature as symptomatic of a natural theology; that is to say, a supposed rational theology not reliant upon revelatory scriptures. A god creates the universe, which then is governed by designed causation, humanly intelligible, which gives effect to the divine author's purposes, notably, preservation, and with no further divine intervention required. (Smith nowhere uses the term 'natural theology', but once refers to 'the natural principles of religion' – *TMS*: 170.) To that extent they may appear to be more philosophically significant than notions of naturalness merely as normality. On the other hand, these appeals to nature personified and nature's director could be read as mere stylistic embellishments, designed by the author of the texts to give a theological gloss to arguments that are logically independent of the existence of deity.[53] They then would be just metaphors for the humanly intelligible ordered causal structure of the observable world, and for Smith, the structure of human beings and human societies in particular. When Smith writes, for example, that 'Nature teaches us to hope' that a parricide will receive punishment after death (even if that punishment is of no social benefit), there is no sense other than metaphorical in which he can be understood (*TMS*: 91; cf. 132, 163–4, and the editorial comment at 400–1; also Lewis 1960: 41). It is just an elaborate way of saying that he perceives this hope as a typical or characteristic disposition, grounded in the human condition.

Doubt as to whether appeals to nature personified, and to an author/director of nature, are anything more than rhetorical devices employed for their usefulness to a moral treatise is strengthened by the virtually complete absence of such uses in *WN*. The author-director makes no appearance there; and only three passages can at all possibly be read as personifying nature, in the sense of suggesting nature is a purposive agent:

> If a nation could not prosper without the enjoyment of perfect liberty and perfect justice, there is not in the world a nation which could ever have prospered. In the political body, however, the wisdom of nature has fortunately made ample provision for remedying many of the bad effects of the folly and injustice of man ….
>
> (*WN*: 674)

> Though a husbandman should be employed in an expedition [i.e. a military undertaking], provided it begins after seed-time and ends before harvest, the interruption of his business will not always occasion any considerable diminution of his revenue. Without the intervention of his labour, nature does herself the greater part of the work which remains to be done.
>
> (*WN*: 694–5)

> [T]he hope of evading … taxes by smuggling gives frequent occasion to … penalties, which entirely ruin the smuggler; a person who, though no doubt highly blameable for violating the laws of his country, is frequently incapable of violating those of natural justice, and would have been, in every respect, an excellent citizen, had not the laws of his country made that a crime which nature never meant to be so.
>
> (*WN*: 898)

At least the second, if not the first, of these easily can read as nature objectified rather than personified; and the third is entirely intelligible as proceeding from a notion of human nature which requires no purposive 'Nature' or god. Furthermore, there are only two references to nature's author in the remaining four volumes of Smith's works (*EPS*: 156; *Corr*: 53; none in *LRB* or vol. 5), and only a very few passages which could at all conceivably be read as personifying nature (*EPS*: 136, 160, 163, 165, 168; *LJB*: 462; *Corr*: 55; none in *LRB*).

If natural theology were a vital foundation of his thought, one might expect to see more widespread visible evidence of it than this. Certainly, at minimum, one may ask how a person of traditional Christian beliefs could say the following of Hume, notorious during his life for alleged atheism: 'Poor David Hume is dying very fast, but with great chearfulness and good humour and with more real resignation to the necessary course of things, than any Whining Christian ever dyed with pretended resignation to the will of God' (*Corr*: 203). '… I have always considered him, both in his lifetime and since his death, as approaching as nearly to the idea of a perfectly wise and virtuous man, as perhaps the nature of human frailty will permit' (*Corr*: 221).[54] To be sure, these sentiments are consistent with Smith being a deist of some kind. But for the purposes of his separable science of political economy,[55] Smith's thought is reliant upon no natural–theological premises. His view that the structure of human nature and the world is such as to enable outcomes that support and advance human well-being, though this is by no means spontaneous in his understanding (see Chapter 5), may suggest to Smith a providential design, a teleological element in his thought (cf. Ross 1995: 340). But such providence plays no role in any of his causal explanations of economic processes and outcomes.[56]

### *2.3.2 Earlier concepts of 'natural'*

One instance in particular of Smith's language-concepts pertaining to nature is investigated in Chapter 3 below, natural price and its prehistory, and with various degrees of attention, Chapter 5 considers certain other naturalized concepts, also of direct pertinence to his political economy ('natural ...' progress, liberty, balance, course, distribution). Here we broadly consider the prehistory of the general notion of nature as a norm, in some sense, for human conduct, and thereby, for political, social and economic organization. Two aspects of this are worthy of particular attention: the notion of a 'science of man' in the Enlightenment, grounded in human nature; and the concept of 'the economy of nature'. The former implies a norm for social theory and for society, derived from the actual character of humankind. This may serve as a norm for social theory, both with respect to how humans actually behave and how they ought to behave; that is to say, with both descriptive and normative implications. This kind of human science is to take its bearings from how human beings *actually* are, both in its descriptive and prescriptive dimensions.

Hence there are two distinct senses in which nature can constitute a norm. The natural can be understood merely as the *normal* – in the sense of the common, typical, ordinary or usual, so that by corollary, the unnatural is the abnormal or aberrant, in the strictly descriptive sense that it designates phenomena which appear with relatively low frequency. Second, the natural can be supposed as also the good – e.g. because the natural is the effect of a benevolent supernatural author – with the natural thereby setting an ethical standard for human behaviour or for social organization, a genuinely normative notion. Smith in his social theory frequently employs the former sense of the natural as the normal, but certainly also has instances of the latter sense of nature as a norm. His moral philosophy is 'naturalistic' in a certain sense. It concerns human sociableness as normal behaviour, proceeding from the actual character of humanity, and from the structure of human life: behaviour at one and the same time, natural and worthy of moral approbation.[57] The naturalized concepts in the political economy – most notably, but not only, natural price – refer to phenomena that are both 'normal' in a certain sense, and also at the same time, are outcomes, conditions or processes worthy of approval. Natural price is the normal or 'ordinary' price, at least under certain institutional conditions which are themselves construed as natural (not least, under conditions of 'natural liberty'); it is also the most preferred price.

In a brute sense 'nature' can be understood as synonymous with the totality of elements making up the world or universe. But it acquires intellectual significance when it is employed to convey the notion of an intelligible structure of things. The essential nature is captured by principles or laws explaining the actual behaviour of things, or the *systematic* properties of things, which account for their systematic behaviours; fixed and universal laws which explain the constant change in nature understood as the totality of sense-perceptible things, change which includes the cycle of birth, maturation, decay and death. In this sense, to speak of the 'nature' of things is a purely descriptive intellectual project, albeit a more or less abstract one. Hepburn (2006: 517) observes that what nature means in a particular intellectual context is often most clearly seen by grasping what nature or the natural is being contrasted with. In relation to understanding human life, humanity can be contrasted with and distinguished from nature on the one hand, and can be conceived of as an element of nature on the other. (Smith has both; e.g. with regard to production on the one hand, and with regard to the principles of human nature on the other.) From the viewpoint of disjunction between nature and humankind, the relation between the two can further be conceived of as mediated by humanity's improving upon nature via ingenuity and labour; on the other hand, nature unaltered by human intervention can be idealized (Ruse 2005: 644). The same kind of idealization can be applied to humankind itself, unmodified by custom or society (Boas 1973: 347–8). Hence nature, human or otherwise, can be contradistinguished from convention or artifice; and of course, it can be contrasted with the supernatural.[58] If nature is understood as the humanly intelligible systematic structure of phenomena, then the history of the understanding of nature is virtually synonymous with the history of philosophy and science (as well as the humanities). Hence in early Western thought there are the Pythagorean geometrical forms of things, the transcendent Platonic forms, and the Aristotelian teleological realization of natures, in a kind of biological analogy. As against the analogy of nature as living organism, there is also nature as machine, an analogy which gained currency with the advent of modernity. And then beyond the purely descriptive, there is the question of nature and the good, or the relation of nature to value.[59]

Boas (1973: 346, 351) draws attention to 'at least sixty-six senses' of nature or natural – from antiquity, but influential through to modern times – detailed in Lovejoy and Boas (1935: 447–56; also Lovejoy 1927, with particular regard to aesthetic notions of nature). We can not do better on this matter than to quote their characterizations, with regard to a number of the most notable cases (with some instances of those to whom these notions are ascribed in parentheses):

> Genesis, birth. An infrequent sense of *physis*, though etymologically primary.
>
> [p. 447; Herodotus, Aristotle]

> The permanent and fundamental character (of a person), in contrast with transient manifestations or superficial appearances.
>
> [p. 448; Sophocles]

> the general cause of phenomena, the universal originating or moving power. (Cicero…) … The term in this sense tends to become a substitute for 'God as efficient cause'.
>
> [p. 448]

> the general philosophic antithesis of 'nature' and 'culture' or 'art'; here *physis* or nature is a generic or collective name for that which arises without human effort and contrivance, in contrast with that which man produces through his purposive action.
>
> [p. 449; Hippocrates, Democritus]

the 'nature' of a thing is its 'end' or the good towards which it tends, its final cause, that state in which its 'natural' development culminates ....

[p. 450; Aristotle]

'natural' in the Hippocratic writings and especially in modern languages, designates any phenomena or objects which are ordinary and usual, as opposed to the anomalous, the exceptional, or the monstrous.

[pp. 450–1]

As regular, 'nature' may mean that which happens from intelligible causes or in accordance with uniform law, in contrast with chance.

[p. 451; Democritus]

Good 'by nature' is any action to which men's impulses or instincts prompt them .... (Aristophanes, *Clouds*, 1078; the speech of Callicles in Plato's *Gorgias* ...)

[p. 452]

Since each species of living being has its distinctive 'nature' ... and since its good, according to Platonic and Aristotelian teaching, consists in the 'realization' of this nature, that is 'by nature' the good for man which most fully realizes the distinctive attribute of human nature ... – this attribute being diversely defined by Plato, Aristotle, the Stoics, and other ancient and modern writers.

[p. 453]

Since the objectively valid is that which is independent of private or local idiosyncrasies ... and since the 'light of nature' is supposed to be common to all men, 'nature' is the body of truths which are thus universally accessible, and the good or right or valid 'by nature' is identified with that which is actually practised, or at least known and approved, by mankind everywhere, in contrast with merely local or temporary customs .... [Aristotle, Cicero] ... The principle source of the uniformitarianism or standardizing tendency in 17th–18th century ethics ....

[p. 455][60]

With regard to human self-knowledge, and in relation to society in particular, to the extent that nature is understood as the essential character of humans as humans, it leads to the notion of a human nature. One empirical route to determining the content of this 'nature' is to search for characteristics, patterns, behaviours, standards or beliefs which can be read as common across the known variety of peoples and societies, thereby hoping to grasp that which is universal beneath the surface heterogeneity of human experience and practice. The premise that the universal is the essentially human, constitutes these supposed universals as knowledge of human nature, 'untangled' so to speak, from human particularities of time and place (the merely conventional). The additional premise, that the natural is the right and the good, then establishes this human nature as a benchmark, standard or norm for further thinking about society (cf. Boas 1973: 348).

The most significant element of the ancient pedigree of this line of thought, partly building on Platonism and Aristotelianism, is the Stoics, who exercised some considerable influence on Smith. Stoicism, originating around 300 BCE and an organized school or movement for some 500 years, brought a cosmopolitan doctrine of human equality to the Hellenistic (Greco-oriental) world. God is identified with reason and nature, a spark of which is in every man or every human being: 'all men equally should try to live by its common light; all men, if they do so, will be living according to the common law of nature' (Barker 1934: 408). From this derived a rather austere personal morality of self-control and tranquillity in the face of whatever life delivers, and a social philosophy of equality under natural law which should apply to all in common. (The latter had significant impact on the Roman Empire and Roman law.) The virtues to which the individual was to aspire were not merely self-directed; they included justice and a cosmopolitan notion of social duty. The natural law doctrines of the modern era, in particular, Grotius and Samuel Pufendorf in the seventeenth century, are ultimately derivative from this Stoic tradition, though a more or less radical transposition of it. Stoic social philosophy was not however purely an ethical or normative kind of theory:

> The world ... is a network of causal relationships capable in principle of being explained.... Human thoughts, actions, and decisions are a part of this causally deterministic system, but moral responsibility is not threatened ... since the decisive causal factor is the character and disposition of the agent as he or she reacts to the world.
>
> (Inwood 2006: 256–7)[61]

What did Smith take from all this? The *TMS* editors convincingly argue the impact of Stoicism as 'the primary influence' on Smith's moral philosophy, and also significant influence on his economics (Raphael and Macfie 1976b: 5–10, 18). In particular, Smith's conception of the virtues of prudence and self-command bear the strong imprint of Stoicism. These virtues are not only important elements of Smith's moral philosophy. They are also central to his conception of how individuals pursue their material interests in a sociable and self-restrained manner; in particular, they are characteristics which find an economic embodiment in the non-myopic pursuit of material betterment, via accumulation (see Chapter 3, n. 20; Chapter 4, n. 50). In the new Part VI of *TMS*, added to the sixth edition of 1790 (the last edition before Smith's death), the Stoic virtue of self-command takes on a foundational role in all virtue, 'making self-command a necessary condition for the exercise of other virtues':

> Great merit in the practice of any virtue presupposes that there has been temptation to the contrary and that the temptation has been overcome; that

> is to say, it presupposes self-command. 'Self-command is not only itself a great virtue, but from it all the other virtues seem to derive their principal lustre' (VI.III.11 [*TMS*: 241]). For Adam Smith, self-command has come to permeate the whole of virtue, an indication of the way in which Stoicism permeated his reflection over the whole range of ethics and social science.
>
> (Raphael and Macfie 1976b: 6)

Smith's admiration for Stoicism also extends to the higher virtues: at one point he comments that there can be no objection to most of the Stoic doctrines 'except that honourable one, that they teach us to aim at a perfection altogether beyond the reach of human nature' (*TMS*: 60). For the Stoics and for Smith, self-command is to live in accordance with nature. Nature as a harmonious system may even, perhaps, be said to inform Smith's notion of commercial society as a system of natural liberty (Raphael and Macfie 1976b: 7–8).[62] Smith was evidently more taken with Stoic ethics than with the substance of their natural science and humanity's place within it. From his contemporary and friend David Hume he accepted less with regard to ethics, but shared with him the eighteenth-century aspiration to a kind of unified human or social science.

### *2.3.3 A science of man*

The articulation of this modern intellectual programme, in terms of a 'science of man', is most notably due to Hume; and there is wide agreement about its broad contours. Introducing a collection of essays on aspects of the eighteenth-century Scottish conceptions of the science of man, Jones (1989: 1) characterizes the core notion as follows:

> French writers who spoke of 'the science of man', such as [Nicolas de] Malebranche, together with their English-speaking successors, such as Hume, never formally defined the notion. There is no difficulty, however, in identifying their concern to undertake a systematic investigation of man's nature, practices and social arrangements, parallel in rigour and comprehensiveness to the investigations of the natural world with which they were becoming familiar.

Of Hume in particular, whose name became most closely associated with the term, Wilson writes:

> Underlying all … [his] work was the ideal of creating a science of man rooted like natural science in the close observation of actual experience. Observation would reveal facts about human action that could then be subjected to a process of induction in order to identify the few principles that shape the whole system. Hume, of course, often tended to use this close observation to destroy the very ideal of building systems. But he backed

> away from embracing the total skepticism that his logical positions demanded.
>
> (Reill 1996: 208)[63]

In the same compendium, Wilson sketches the scope and content of the project and its subsequent transformation into the several social sciences that took definite shape in the nineteenth century:

> The use of the concept 'science of man' during the Enlightenment underscored the prevalent belief that the study of basic human nature could provide the material for creating a systematic body of reliable knowledge about human behaviour and character. The concept of a science of man also embodied the notion that the proper study of humankind should be separated from theology, religion, and metaphysics.
>
> Philosophes began to use the term with these new meanings around the middle of the eighteenth century, especially after David Hume incorporated it in his *Treatise of Human Nature*. In the flush of optimism about the power of human reason to uncover the lawful organization of the universe, some intellectuals, especially in Scotland and France, dreamed of bringing even human behaviour into the realm of mathematically expressed science. The concept lay under the whole program of the *Idéologues* during the French Revolution. It also informed enlightened searches for natural foundations of morality, political action, and economic behaviour.
>
> This general belief that human existence could be studied as a science modeled after the natural sciences helped to stimulate the development of specific new disciplines during the Enlightenment. Psychology, for example, began to emerge as a discipline separate from epistemology. Anthropology, as a cultural and physical study of humankind, also became a distinct subject. Elements of what would eventually become sociology appeared in the works of Montesquieu and some historians, but the distinct discipline was a nineteenth-century creation.
>
> (Reill 1996: 381)[64]

Another summary statement of the science-of-man programme goes a little deeper and points to one potentially problematic issue for that project, the relation between 'nature' and 'history' (especially human history):

> This science investigated the source of the cognitive skills that make man fit for life in human society and enable him to become civilized. It was an inquiry that questioned the importance of reason in shaping human behaviour and led to the development of an alternative, sentimental theory of human nature, which stressed the importance of speech and language in shaping the process of social interaction and the role of custom and habit in shaping the conventions out of which human culture is constructed. Hutcheson and Hume laid the intellectual foundations of this science of man. Both

> philosophers were influenced by Nicolas Malebranche and Jansenist metaphysics, by Pufendorf's natural law, and by [Bernard] Mandeville .... Both were interested in the origins of ideas of justice and property. Hutcheson attempted to create a Christian science of man. The roots of his thought are contained in his *Inquiry into Our Ideas of Beauty and Virtue* (1725), while his concern for natural theology is most evident in his posthumous *System of Moral Philosophy* (1756). Hume's non-Christian thought was influenced by Pierre Bayle's scepticism and by a desire to found the science of man on natural history rather than natural theology. Hume's philosophical perspective is set out in his *Treatise of Human Nature* (1739–40). The implications of that perspective for civil history are worked out in his *History of England* (1754–62), with the theological implications being developed in the posthumous *Dialogues concerning Natural Religion* (1779).
>
> (Phillipson 2001: 1197–8)

The question raised by this is the relation between the varieties and vagaries of human historical experience and change, and the unchanging nature of humankind which is evidently supposed, an issue taken up immediately below. It may also be added that to the extent that the science of man was an aspiration for social science – whether in a singular, unified and comprehensive form, or otherwise – to be of a kind with natural science, it was partly an ill-conceived project (an issue further considered in the Epilogue). That does not mean it was *entirely* ill-conceived.

Many commentaries rightly have emphasized the fundamental role in the science-of-man project of the idea of a human nature uniform across time and space. In truth, as a generic idea (apart from what substantive content was given to it), this is a notion already apparent in classical antiquity. The element of possible tension between the supposed uniformity of human nature and the variety of human historical experience – or if one prefers, a possible tension between uniformly operative nature on the one hand and contingency on the other – is evident in the account of Vyverberg (1989). There was a widespread Enlightenment belief in the uniformity of human nature through time, both physically and morally, and this was imbued with normative significance; for example, the 'attraction toward an abiding natural law', involving precepts of justice, and 'universal ingredients of human nature [such] as the quest for happiness, the persisting urges toward self-love and sociability, and the effective possibility of human choice and free will': 'no appearance of a new human breed would occur to upset that new science of man of which Hume and his contemporaries fondly dreamed'. But 'several types or degrees of universality in human nature' were acknowledged. Though human nature was understood to exhibit a fundamental uniformity with respect to 'senses, mental faculties, desires, passions and needs', universal motives and needs find different expression under various particular conditions. In short, there is enough uniformity of human nature 'to serve, it was hoped, as the basis for sound historical and sociological generalizations'. At the same time as nature was considered an objective and scientific concept, it was regarded also as a 'normative force' – 'fundamentally moral', with humanity possessed of 'instinctual ethical principles' (Vyverberg 1989: 34–5, 195–6, partly quoting Crocker 1959). Both the *Encyclopédie* and the French Enlightenment in general are supposed to have

> suffered from its age's inability to decide firmly in favour of either a scientific, descriptive view of nature, or a universalizing picture of nature as an ideal rather than as a complex of facts.... Nor was there significant dissent on the inclusion of both reason and passions in human nature, although their proper balance was the subject of much discussion.
>
> (Vyverberg 1989: 195)[65]

Hume's great hopes for the science of man, and his radical conception of its logical priority among the sciences, are sketched in the introduction to his *Treatise of Human Nature*. However unprecedented his conception may be, he is not the first thinker in human history to have lamented the lack of accord concerning the state and content of knowledge:

> Principles taken upon trust, consequences lamely deduced from them, want of coherence in the parts, and of evidence in the whole, these are every where to be met with in the systems of the most eminent philosophers, and seem to have drawn disgrace upon philosophy itself.
>
> (Hume 1739–40: xvii)

The state of 'the sciences' is such that

> even the rabble without doors may judge from the noise and clamour, which they hear, that all goes not well within.... Disputes are multiplied, as if every thing was uncertain; and these disputes are managed with the greatest warmth, as if every thing was certain.
>
> (Hume 1739–40: xvii–xviii)

The proffered way forward out of this mess is indeed the science of man. Since natural philosophy and even mathematics are *human* knowledge, then knowledge of the species, 'man', who discovers or makes this scientific and mathematical knowledge, is logically prior to the latter knowledge. They are 'in some measure dependent on the science of MAN; since they lie under the cognizance of men, and are judged of by their powers and faculties'. Understanding 'the human mind' is the necessary means to success in all 'philosophical researches':

> to march up directly to the capital or center of these [i.e. all] sciences, to human nature itself; which being once masters of, we may every where else hope for an easy victory. From this station we may extend our conquests over all those sciences, which more intimately concern human life .... There is no question of importance, whose decision is not compriz'd in the

> science of man; and there is none, which can be decided with any certainty, before we become acquainted with that science. In pretending therefore to explain the principles of human nature, we in effect propose a compleat system of the sciences, built on a foundation almost entirely new, and the only one upon which they can stand with any security.

This is a programme in which 'we ourselves are not only the beings, that reason, but also one of the objects, concerning which we reason' (Hume 1739–40: xix–xx).

In turn, the only solid foundation for *this* foundation is 'experience and observation'. (Notice also the subtitle of Hume's *Treatise*: 'an attempt to introduce the experimental method of reasoning into moral subjects'.) The lag between the application of the experimental method to human as against natural phenomena, 'above a whole century', is not surprising, he suggests: the original beginnings of these two parts of science (Socrates and Thales respectively) exhibit a similar time span to that between 'My Lord BACON and some late philosophers in *England*, who have begun to put the science of man on a new footing'. (An attached footnote explicitly names Locke, Anthony Ashley Cooper, the third Earl of Shaftesbury, Mandeville, 'Mr. *Hutchinson*' – i.e. Francis Hutcheson – and Joseph Butler.) The 'essence' of the human mind is as much unknowable as that of other bodies; its 'powers and qualities' can only be known by

> careful and exact experiments, and the observation of those particular effects, which result from its different circumstances and situations. And tho' we must endeavour to render all our principles as universal as possible, by tracing up our experiments to the utmost, and explaining all effects from the simplest and fewest causes, 'tis still certain we cannot go beyond experience; and any hypothesis, that pretends to discover the ultimate original qualities of human nature, ought at first to be rejected as presumptuous and chimerical.
>
> (Hume 1739–40: xx–xxi)

The 'impossibility of explaining ultimate principles' in fact is common to 'all the sciences' for Hume. He concludes his introduction with an admission suggestive of limitations to social science's capacity to become of a kind with natural science (though he resists this inference). Moral philosophy has the 'peculiar disadvantage, which is not to be found in natural' that the former cannot employ the experimental method in the same manner as the latter:

> We must therefore glean up our experiments in this science from a cautious observation of human life, and take them as they appear in the common course of the world, by men's behaviour in company, in affairs, and in their pleasures. Where experiments of this kind are judiciously collected and compared, we may hope to establish on them a science, which will not be

> inferior in certainty, and will be much superior in utility to any other of human comprehension.
>
> (Hume 1739–40: xxii–xxiii)[66]

To return to the issue raised above, how is the constancy of human nature to be reconciled with history, and even more importantly, reconciled with the role that a pioneering historiography commonly plays within the science-of-man project – including, not least, Smith's own historiography? (History and historiography are defined in the introduction to Chapter 5.) In fact, it does not require very much intellectual subtlety to appreciate the consistency which is possible, between an appreciation of the relativity of human practice on the one hand, and a belief in a singular and distinctive human nature on the other – with the latter also serving as a standard for normative propositions about behaviour and social organization. That is to say, a rather historicist temper towards human practices – behaviours and organization – is not in contradiction to the notion of an underlying uniformity of structure (e.g. the pervasiveness of 'reciprocity', however various its particular forms, as an operative principle in human relations). Indeed, the very diversity of human practices across time and space can be understood as pointing to the question of what is the *essentially* human, as against the merely customary or conventional and particular forms of human practice, in which the underlying nature of human life and society finds expression. The historical variety can become a means to uncovering that which is really general about humans. (The variety across space feeds into the historical consciousness as well, when the peoples discovered by European exploration in the 'New World' are read as evidence of the primitive form of all human society.)

The melding together of the descriptive and the normative does not so much involve a confusion of facts and values, a failure to see that normative propositions cannot logically be derived from descriptive statements (cf. Boudon 2004: 55–62, 89–90). In the case of Smith at least, it is rather a privileging with moral worth or ethical value, of those supposed intrinsic human traits which can be shown, at the purely descriptive level, to cause or bring about human and social outcomes which are posited as good – peace, order, prosperity and so on – though whether these posited aims themselves are given a plausible justification, as values, is another matter. (There may be a confusion of facts and values in particular instances, but an unconfused version of the idea can be articulated.) The further proposition, that humanity is *actually* so structured as to tend to produce these *good* outcomes, because designed by a benevolent god or nature, is the natural–theological or teleological element (with the 'invisible hand' idea then close at hand: see Chapter 5, n. 15). As shall be shown in section 5.3.3, Smith has a keen historical sensibility. This leads him to firmly believe that the appropriate socio-political organization and the best policies to implement, in particular times and places, are conditioned by the prevailing historical circumstances. This is not relativism. It is compatible with a universal standard of the good, but the implementation of it ought to be constrained by or adapted to circumstances. Nevertheless, if human history and the notion of an unchanging human nature are reconcilable in principle, this does not thereby mean that Smith's particular reconciliation of them is unproblematic. In particular, there is at least a tension between his history of human material development (the *very* 'slow progress of opulence') and the supposed naturalness of the system of 'perfect liberty' (liberal commercial society) – an issue taken up in Chapter 5 (esp. sec. 5.1.1 and n. 15).[67]

### *2.3.4 The economy of nature*

In relation to the formation of political economy in particular, the further notable expression of the idea of nature as constituting a norm for human life and society is the notion of *the economy of nature*. Broadly described, this notion shares in the conception of nature, generally including human nature and society, as providentially constructed by a god who is benevolent with respect to humankind (but not necessarily only with respect to humankind). It importantly incorporates further, the idea that this 'nature' is not only benevolent with regard to human ends, it is efficient in the achievement of those ends. It is an expression of the notion that, with regard to those ends, there is nothing superfluous in nature; the world has a providential, and an economical, organization. (The belief that this structure of the world is humanly intelligible, gained great impetus from, as well as giving impetus to, the revolutionary scientific developments of the seventeenth and eighteenth centuries, in a kind of virtuous circle, including of course, giving inspiration and impetus to the science of man.) The widespread uses of 'economy' to refer to management, organization or structure of a variety of particular things, noted in section 2.1.3 (n. 9: 'animal economy' and so on), are in fact just particular instances of this generic sense of the fittingness of these things (their structure and so on) to their purposes, for nature in general and for all its elements (hence, for example, the title of Russell 1755; there was a Latin edition the same year).

This idea of nature as an efficient machine for the achievement of definite and good ends, or as akin to a unified and efficient *organism*, would be generally the more appropriate metaphor, connects in an obvious manner with the latter-day secular idea of economic rationality as (choice of) the most efficient or economical means for achieving some definite objective(s). But the most immediately pertinent parallel with regard to the eighteenth-century development of political economy is good political management and organization of society's economic resources as an analogy from God or nature's management and organization of natural phenomena. The economy of nature notion seems to have roots in ancient Greek thought. At least its most fundamental aspect is much to be found in Aristotle (e.g. 'nature makes nothing purposeless or in vain': Barker 1946: 21). There is no Biblical equivalent of this idea; but with the subsequent addition of Judeo-Christian influence, the economy of nature appears as synonymous with divine economy, illustrated in early English instances in *OED* ('economy', 'economic'): 'God is the best economic; his house is exactly ordered for matter of good husbandry' (1656); 'the course and œconomy of nature' (1658); 'the method and Oeconomy of heaven' (1660); 'the civil Œconomy is formed in a chain as well as the natural' (1712).

The language of the 'economy of nature' seems to have become rather commonplace by the beginning of the eighteenth century. But it is via the agency of Linnaeus that the idea takes on its most intellectually substantial form. In a work under that name, he expresses an anthropocentrism (also evident in Bacon, quoted in sec. 2.1.6) symptomatic of the dependence of his conception on religious doctrine (a teleological element in the notion): 'when we follow the series of created things, and consider how providentially one is made for the sake of another, the matter comes to this, that all things are made for the sake of man … in order to pass his life conveniently and pleasantly' (quoted in Ghiselin 1974: 22, from a 1791 edition of a 1749 work). (The facts which Linnaeus saw as pointing to the world having been suited to humankind are of course also explicable by the inference that humankind has been suited to the world.) This is providential efficiency, so to speak. In this frame of thinking Linnaeus could regard economics as a kind of applied natural history; economics was united with natural science (see also Chapter 5, n. 40). It was a view common to the founders of the Swedish Royal Academy of Science in 1739. Economics meant the systematic description and application of technical innovation in agriculture and manufacture: Linnaeus's vision was of economics as 'the discipline of how to husband the natural world and, in doing so, order society on nature's model' (Rausing 2003: 185); 'in Linnaeus's eyes, oeconomia was about hardly anything more than natural history plus information on the uses made of its diverse objects in technology' (Müller-Wille 2003: 155).[68]

The idea of husbandry or stewardship of course connects also back to the ancient Greek conception of economy; and the idea of the efficiency of nature (whether or not the effect of a providential god) is clear as well in Aristotle. But also, in relation to the substantive content of French and British classical economics, it is well to remember in this context that the fundamental idea there, of the production of a social surplus, is about the viability of human socio-economic systems, their capacity to produce (or 'out put') at least as much as they use up or destroy in the form of inputs (see sec. 4.2.4). This is about production from nature by labour, and in relation to economic growth and development as the central focus of the explanatory theories of Quesnay and Smith, this also is an analogy from biology.[69] Smith read Linnaeus, and made some use of this in at least one of his essays (Ross 1995: 227–8). Later, the science of oecologie, which arose in the nineteenth century, supersedes or becomes the modern culmination of the economy of nature notion (Stauffer 1960: 235, n. 2; Worster 1994: 192). But prior to those developments, the term persists in Charles Lyell and Charles Darwin, though its meaning evidently had shifted.

Linnaeus's intellectual programme found expression in the establishment of academic Chairs in Sweden, in something resembling 'economics', or at least, something *perhaps* somewhat more closely resembling the intentions of French political economy proper, than were the cameralist academic developments (see sec. 2.1.6). During the early decades of the eighteenth century, in the context of working for educational reform, Linnaeus sought to have 'oeconomia', understood as a science of natural resources and their use for human life, included in university curricula, and Chairs of oeconomia established at Swedish universities. Chairs were established along these lines at Åbo (Turku, in Finland; 1747) and Lund (1760). Also, in 1759 the iron manufacturer Anders Borgström, with Linnaeus's encouragement, endowed a Chair in 'practical economics' at the University of Uppsala (the oldest university of northern Europe), partly with a view to counteracting the influence of the Uppsala professor in cameralism. (The first European Chairs in cameralism were at Halle, Frankfurt an der Oder and Rinteln, established in 1727, 1727 and 1730 respectively.) These Swedish Chairs combined teaching of mineralogy, zoology, botany and chemistry, as well as teaching pertaining to trade, mining, manufacturing, fishing and farming. The Åbo Chair, held by Pehr Kalm, a student of Linnaeus, was primarily devoted to applied natural science, but this was understood in terms of what in cameralism was called *Haushaltungskunst*: the arts of managing the national household. The first holder of the Lund Chair was Eric Gustaf Lidbeck. The Uppsala Chair appears to have been held by Pehr Niclas Christiernin.[70] Latter-day literature on these matters sometimes identifies the Uppsala Chair as the second European Chair of political economy or economics, after Naples. But as already intimated, this is a rather forced claim, turning on the matter of judgement as to whether the Swedish project, as with German cameralism, properly should be assimilated so closely with the French project of political economy proper. To resort, finally, to the cowardice of metaphor, the Swedish project and cameralist project are certainly 'relatives' of political economy, but more like cousins than siblings.

## 2.4 A 'new' science

The study of the history of economics most commonly concerns itself with the history of substantive economic ideas, and this is not a bad thing. But focus upon the range of substantive ideas in the history of economics – theories, doctrines, opinions, normative beliefs – should not allow an avoidance of, or even a failure to notice, what could be characterized as the most fundamental or elementary question for the history of economic science: how and why did the idea of political economy as a separable intellectual discipline emerge? Neglecting this question, one would run the risk of taking for granted the idea of an economic science as such, as a viable, separable intellectual project. That idea is not so self-evident that it is uncontestable. Its contestability is not so much due to any serious doubts that scientific methods can be applied, at least in some measure, to human socio-economic phenomena. It is rather due to doubts as to the legitimacy or desirability of a separable social science limited to 'economics', or to the domain of 'economic life'. In fact, much interest in Adam Smith's entire corpus, still, more than two centuries after his writing, springs from interest in a conception in Smith's thought (partly explicit, partly necessarily implicit), of a wider political economy than that entailed by modern marginalism (see n. 19 above and Chapter 1, n. 9), and as well, a more unified conception of social science, including its connections with philosophy (hence the title of Skinner 1996). The study of these matters and connections, e.g. the relations between *WN* and *TMS*, is important and valuable. But it surely cannot legitimately lead to the conclusion that Smith is against the idea of political economy as a separable science, albeit with scope, methods and theory that are variously different to those of modern economics. The very existence of *WN* is compelling prima facie evidence of Smith's position: if political economy in his view were inextricably interlinked with other forms of intellectual inquiry, then that book would not have been written.[71] Furthermore, as was pointed out in passing in section 2.1.2, Smith explicitly endorses the division of labour in scientific endeavour; for example:

> Philosophy or speculation, in the progress of society, naturally becomes, like every other employment, the sole occupation of a particular class of citizens. Like every other trade it is subdivided into many different branches, and we have mechanical, chymical, astronomical, physical, metaphysical, moral, political, commercial, and critical philosophers. In philosophy as in every other business this subdivision of employment improves dexterity and saves time. Each individual is more expert at his particular branch. More work is done upon the whole and the quantity of science is considerably increased by it.
>
> (*edWN*: 570; cf. the very similar statement at *WN*: 21–2)

As to the pervasive language of 'naturalness' in Smith's political economy and wider thought, this appears to have no essential explanatory role in the economic analysis, beyond just one element, but it is an absolutely fundamental element. The inessential role of appeals to naturalness will become clear at certain points in the ensuing chapters. It will be seen that in the domain of political economy at least, the naturalness of various phenomena has no informational content beyond a notion of normalcy under specified conditions: the outcomes that may reasonably be expected to result from, or to be ordinarily caused by, certain conditions. As to the absolutely fundamental element which is an exception to this conclusion, this is the role of human nature as constituting Smith's three fundamental 'drivers' of human economic behaviour: self-regard, the propensity to exchange, and the desire for material self-betterment. Their role and the relationship between them will also emerge in subsequent chapters. But it may be asked, why cannot these behavioural parameters also be posited merely as normal characteristics – simply as evident, observable (albeit only indirectly observable) facts, as to the typical pattern of actual human activity?

The answer is twofold. On the one hand, grounding those behavioural traits in a singular human nature is essential to the universal claims of the science: it is not offered as a science of eighteenth-century Englishmen, or of Europeans; it is (part of) a science of 'man', notwithstanding its being accompanied with a very strong historical sensibility. These drivers are understood to be uniformly operative in human beings across time and space, though it must be added, so is human sociability. Secondly, their naturalness and universality (though this does not require denying the existence of exceptional human beings) renders them essentially incapable of suppression or eradication; hence the political organization of socio-economic life must yield to their operation, at least up to a point. Happily for Smith, those natural drivers are benign or beneficial as to their socio-economic consequences, certainly (but not exclusively) under appropriate political arrangements. The happy outcomes do not require a perfection of political, social and economic organization. The irrepressibility of the drivers, and their beneficial effects, combine to support a normative conclusion, that the model for economic life is natural liberty. In relation to the happy socio-economic outcomes, Smith may 'decorate' his social theory with references to those outcomes as revealing the benevolence of nature or nature's author. But the actual *causal* processes offered to explain how, for example, self-regard combined with self-command, via the operation of competition, bring about a tendency of prices to gravitate towards desirable levels, in no way rely upon anything beyond those human-behavioural postulates and the conditions under which they operate.

Finally, one may ask how seriously ought one take Smith's notion of science as a means to mere *imagination* of unified explanation of the variety of phenomena, if applied to his own scientific activity?[72] Or, one may ask instead, how genuinely significant is this notion for Smith, as an epistemology of science in general? At least his science of political economy was not intended merely to be a speculative exercise to 'sooth' the mind with supposed understanding (*EPS*: 46). In Smith's own view, political economy is emphatically a *policy* science, 'policy' to be read in a deep sense – ultimately, a kind of constitution-building really. It is a tool for the betterment of human society; it is informed by a normative and practical purpose: 'The study of human nature in all its branches, more particularly of the political history of mankind ... gratified his ruling passion, of contributing to the happiness and the improvement of society' (Stewart 1811: 271). Can at least applied sciences, via their understanding of the world – in the case of political economy in particular, its understanding of human society – really be successful in their purpose of changing that world for the better, if their content is mere hypothetical imaginings, however soothing? (This is not to deny the central role of imagination in scientific endeavour, and in Smith's account of it.) Must they not have grasped, to some extent at least, the real inner workings of the phenomena? Could Smith deny this? Indeed, Vivenza (2001) convincingly contests taking Smith's views on astronomy in particular, as a justification for imputing to him a merely sceptical epistemology of scientific knowledge in general. Her argument is well summed up by McNamara (2004: 184–5):

> although Smith speaks sceptically in places about astronomical theories, this ... was an entirely orthodox position among non-sceptics because astronomy was believed to be a ... hypothetical endeavour, as opposed to physics .... Vivenza suggests that Griswold [1999] has both misunderstood

and illegitimately extended Smith's sceptical remarks in 'History of Astronomy' to Smith's corpus as a whole. The result is that Griswold overemphasizes Smith's scepticism to the neglect of his attachment to the 'empirical and experimental' ([Griswold 2001] p. 207) scientific method of his time ....

In Vivenza's own words:

> Smith poses questions of epistemology and method almost exclusively in his early works as a young scholar. He does not subsequently return to these themes, although he maintains his original position: anti-metaphysical, anti-dogmatic, empirical, perhaps even with an element of scepticism related to empiricism itself. I do not believe, however, that this element was a principle with which he defined himself as a man and as a philosopher, or an indirect means by which to embrace a doctrine without acknowledging it.
>
> (Vivenza 2001: 208, and 11–13, 27–8, 37–40, 206–9; also Vivenza 2005: 44–5, 49–54; Raphael and Skinner 1980: 19–21; Fleischacker 2004: 27)

The spirit of this conclusion is confirmed by a strong empiricist statement by Smith, in favour of empirical science, in a commentary on the history of science, in the context of the issue of funding education:

> In the antient philosophy, whatever was taught concerning the nature either of the human mind or of the Deity, made a part of the system of physicks.... Whatever human reason could either conclude, or conjecture, concerning them, made, as it were, two chapters, though no doubt two very important ones, of the science which pretended to give an account of the origin and revolutions of the great system of the universe. But in the universities of Europe, where philosophy was taught only as subservient to theology, it was natural to dwell longer upon these two chapters than upon any other of the science. They were gradually more and more extended ... till at last the doctrine of spirits, *of which so little can be known*, came to take up as much room in the system of philosophy as the doctrine of bodies, *of which so much can be known*. The doctrines concerning those two subjects were considered as making two distinct sciences. What are called Metaphysicks or Pneumaticks were set in opposition to Physicks, and were cultivated not only as the more sublime, but, for the purposes of a particular profession, as the more useful science of the two. The proper subject of experiment and observation, a subject in which a careful attention is capable of making so many useful *discoveries*, was almost entirely neglected. The subject in which, after a few very simple and almost obvious truths, the most careful attention can discover nothing but obscurity and uncertainty, and can consequently produce nothing but subtleties and sophisms, was greatly cultivated.
>
> (*WN*: 770–1; emphasis added)[73]

# 3 Competition, prices and distribution

*convergence of market prices towards natural prices*
*supply and demand*
*price as necessary cost*

> Mr. Malthus appears to understand, by his short phrase, '*the principle* of demand and supply' something different from what I should, as a reader of Smith only, have understood it to mean: I should have said, it meant that principle, which tends to bring the respective prices of things into such a state as will equalize, as nearly as is possible, the profits, &c., obtained in the production of each. But that principle does not then determine, what that state is.
>
> *Anonymous* (1821: 76–7)

Smith's political economy is commonly understood as first and foremost the economics of markets, of competition, and of prices. In a sense, this is not wrong, though its real object is the growth of wealth. It is a striking fact that in his elegant prefatory 'Introduction and Plan of the Work' Smith does not once mention prices or markets. Nevertheless, the concept of the competitive economy as a kind of self-regulating system, at least given an appropriate framework of law and property rights, is perhaps the most striking idea he contributed to the human sciences. It therefore is also commonplace for the lineage of more recent theories of competition to be traced back to Smith – most notably, the family of general equilibrium theories which rose to academic prominence after the Second World War. But how much kinship does Smith's political economy really have with those latter-day marginalist theories which originated about 1871? What follows takes up his conception of competition and prices. As a quite fundamental element of his overall system, this casts considerable light on that larger issue of the differences between Smithian political economy and modern marginalism.

*WN* actually begins with an analysis of production and technical change in terms of 'division of labour' (Book I, Chapters I–III); but insofar as the dynamics of production conditions are intimately connected with division of labour, they are necessarily associated also with exchange and hence markets. So the bulk of Book I concerns prices and income distribution. With regard to commodity prices, the centrepiece of Smith's approach is a dynamic process: the converging or 'gravitating' of market prices towards natural price via competition, the latter in turn arising out of self-interest. This is examined in the first section below. The 'anchor' for these price dynamics, the natural price, is a notion of the normal price under competitive conditions. Smith's conception of normal price is further examined in section 3.4, together with some consideration of his related theorizing of 'cost', and income distribution: his notions of competition and prices are applied also to distribution and costs, by way of analogy. This conceptualization of prices, so different from the later theories of 1871 and after, calls for a careful consideration of the precise meaning and role of 'supply' and 'demand', and related concepts, in *WN*, pursued in the second section. Section 3.3 then provides a systematic analysis of the role of demand in Smith's treatment of market prices. Because the language and concepts examined successively in these sections are so interrelated in earlier intellectual history, their histories prior to Smith are considered together, in the penultimate section. The final section provides a summing up and assessment of the strength of Smith's approach *vis-à-vis* modern theory.

## 3.1 Competition and prices

### *3.1.1 Concepts of price*

At the heart of Smith's conceptualization of commodity markets is a notion of natural prices as regulating the dynamics of market prices. The analytical centrepiece of the *WN* price theory is Book I, Chapter VII, 'Of the natural and market Price of Commodities'. Natural price is there defined in the following terms:

> When the price of any commodity is neither more nor less than what is sufficient to pay the rent of the land, the wages of the labour, and the profits of the stock employed in raising, preparing, and bringing it to market, according to their natural rates, the commodity is then sold for what may be called its natural price.
>
> The commodity is then sold precisely for what it is worth, or for what it really costs the person who brings it to market …
>
> Though the [natural] price … is not always the lowest at which a dealer may sometimes sell his goods, it is the lowest at which he is likely to sell them for any considerable time; at least where there is perfect liberty, or where he may change his trade as often as he pleases.
>
> (*WN*: 72–3)

Leaving aside fuller investigation of the notions of natural rates of wages, profit and rent until section 3.4.3, at core natural commodity price is a conception of a magnitude which just covers the necessary costs of supplying a commodity to purchasers (to the market) – in particular, just covering the sum of payments to owners of the inputs to its production (and marketing), at rates of remuneration which are 'necessary' in some sense (see also *WN*: 173, 219–20, 251).[1]

If the actual prices at which a commodity exchanges are below or above natural price, then input quantities and hence output quantities change:

> some of the component parts of its price must be paid below their natural rate. If it is rent, the interest of the landlords will immediately prompt them to withdraw a part of their land; and if it is wages or profit, the interest of the labourers in the one case, and of their employers in the other, will prompt them to withdraw a part of their labour or stock from this employment. The quantity brought to market will soon be no more than sufficient to supply the effectual demand. All the different parts of its price will rise to their natural rate, and the whole price to its natural price.
>
> ... [S]ome of the component parts of its price must rise above their natural rate. If it is rent, the interest of all other landlords will naturally prompt them to prepare more land for the raising of this commodity; if it is wages or profit, the interest of all other labourers and dealers will soon prompt them to employ more labour and stock in preparing and bringing it to market. The quantity brought thither will soon be sufficient to supply the effectual demand. All the different parts of its price will soon sink to their natural rate, and the whole price to its natural price.
>
> (*WN*: 74–5)

In latter-day terms, natural price is a notion of opportunity cost: it is the price which just enables payment to the owners of the employed inputs, the remuneration normally available in alternative uses. The concept and term also appear in *LJ*; but as the *WN* editors point out, it is there largely identified with labour cost, as if production is by means of unassisted labour alone.[2] Natural price includes elements of risk:

> A man ... has the natural price of his labour when it is sufficient to maintain him during the time of labour, to defray the expence of education, and to compensate the risk of not living long enough and of not succeeding in the business.
>
> (*LJB*: 495–6; also *LJA*: 355, 357; *WN*: 116–35)

However, some other risks are excluded (those from illegal transactions and exposure of commerce to crime are explicitly discussed), probably because regarded as more extraneous to production (*LJA*: 387; *LJB*: 509–10, 528). Smith also defines natural prices as net of commodity taxes and subsidies (*LJA*: 362–4; *LJB*: 533; also in *WN*: 216–17, 507, 895), though changing his view as to the effect of bounties on corn prices (*WN*: 506, n. 7).

If, on the one hand, natural price is the opportunity cost of supplying a commodity, then on the other hand, the notion that competition sets up a strong and general tendency for actual prices to converge upon opportunity cost, leads to the view that natural prices are the 'normal' prices in a competitive economy (our term; cf. Eatwell 1987: 598) – the prices that at least approximately, normally prevail. Hence Smith can speak of natural price as *ordinary price* (and identify ordinary and natural remuneration): the 'natural or ordinary rate' of the components of price (*WN*: 46). A clear and explicit identification of natural price with an 'ordinary price' arises in a discussion of the value of gold and silver:

> The lowest price at which the precious metals can be sold ... during any considerable time, is regulated by the same principles which fix the lowest ordinary price of all other goods. The stock which must commonly be employed, the food, cloaths and lodging which must commonly be consumed in bringing them from the mine to the market, determine it. It must at least be sufficient to replace that stock, with the ordinary profits.
>
> (*WN*: 189; also 72–3, 161–2, 172, 219, 652)

But notice that this refers to the 'lowest' ordinary price. At one point Smith discusses circumstances wherein 'ordinary price ... is at what may be called a monopoly price' (*WN*: 892–3). Ordinary price is also regularly equated with 'average' price.[3] These three notions of price – natural, ordinary, average – are reconciled by conceiving of ordinary price as the most common or typical or normal price, prevailing in a market over a significant stretch of time; and then this may be understood as synonymous with average price, either by definition or on the supposition that the highest frequency (most common) price within the set of actual transactions prices also approximates the mean of that set of prices; and finally, in markets subject to thoroughgoing competition, the ordinary price will tend to equality with the natural price.[4] In Book I, Chapter VII Smith defines monopoly price, rather emptily, as 'upon every occasion the highest which can be got', continuing:

> The natural price, or the price of free competition, on the contrary, is the lowest which can be taken, not upon every occasion, indeed, but for any considerable time together. The one is upon every occasion the highest which can be squeezed out of the buyers, or which, it is supposed, they will consent to give: The other is the lowest which the sellers can commonly afford to take, and at the same time continue their business.
>
> (*WN*: 78–9)

In markets subject to persistent monopoly conditions, ordinary price will exceed natural price. The natural price concept appears nowhere else in Smith's writings, beyond *WN* and *LJ*.

The concept of natural price is the most striking application in Smith's political economy, of an approach he more widely applies to analysis: a focus upon regular, typical or normal conditions or situations, including in this, the processes whereby normal outcomes occur. This is evidenced by his wider uses of 'average', 'ordinary', and also 'usual'. *Average* is most commonly employed by Smith in reference to commodity prices, 'average' and 'ordinary' frequently appearing as synonyms in this context, as shown above. The same identification of 'average' and 'ordinary' is applied to rates of wages, profit and rent, in turn identified with the 'natural rates' of these remunerations (*WN*: 46, 72, 105, 128, 219; cf. n. 4). With respect to wages, the average is distinguished from 'the most usual' rate, the latter being easier to ascertain; and due to the even greater difficulty in ascertaining average profit, Smith offers the 'usual market rate of interest' as a rough guide to profit rates (*WN*: 105). Averaging is applied also to a range of other economic variables.[5] Smith evidently intends 'average' in the standard sense of the mean of a series of quantities, though it is not to be taken so precisely and literally in all contexts.[6] The term nowhere appears in *EPS* or *LRB*, and just once in *TMS* (140), and in one letter in *Corr* (151). More strikingly, it is also not at all to be found in the documents collected in the fifth volume of the Glasgow Edition (but 'averaging' appears at p. 102). Average or ordinary or normal conditions are the object of analysis in *WN*, much more clearly than in the earlier lectures.

*Usual*, and by extension 'usually', is employed by Smith in the most generic sense to refer to that which is common, typical or normal. Hence it is used to describe a plausibly to be expected outcome, condition or course of events – 'the usual course of human affairs' (*TMS*: 244) – or that which is typical of a class of characters (*TMS*: 204), objects (*TMS*: 198), or behaviours: the 'usual pretences' of employees in entering into combinations; the 'usual idleness' of apprentices (*WN*: 84, 119). Similarly, usual is employed to characterize customary phenomena (*TMS*: 204; *EPS*: 41), with the phrase 'customary and usual' making them virtual synonyms in some contexts (*TMS*: 271). Likewise 'natural' and 'usual' can serve as synonyms (*TMS*: 149–51; *WN*: 172; *EPS*: 146), just as 'natural' and 'ordinary' can (see immediately below); e.g. combinations of employers (i.e. collusion) as 'the usual, and one may say, the natural state of things' (*WN*: 84). With regard to more substantial economic use, the 'usual' wage or 'price of labour' refers to the normal money wage understood as the most commonly paid rate for any particular class of labour (*WN*: 92, 94–5), thereby explicitly allowing for a dispersion of wage rates for the same work. As indicated in the previous paragraph, the most usual rate may not be equal to the 'average' wage (*WN*: 105), though elsewhere, usual price and average price appear to be identified (*WN*: 521–2). There is also reference to 'common and usual profit', but just once (*WN*: 114), whereas 'ordinary profit' appears very frequently. *Usual price* is also applied to commodities in general (*WN*: 231) and usual commodity prices are subject to change over time (*WN*: 447). The term 'common price' also appears occasionally (e.g. *WN*: 243, 359, 521).

The use of ordinary price and average price as synonyms has been indicated and, similarly, the identification of average and ordinary remuneration. Elsewhere the notion of 'ordinary' profit rates appears also on its own, clearly conveying a concept of normal or required rate of return.[7] Parallel to the possibility of a monopoly commodity price being the ordinary commodity price, monopoly can cause an ordinary rate of profit higher than the competitive rate (*WN*: 598–9, 612). In almost all instances however, ordinary profits refer to competitive remunerations. In fact, for the notion of a necessary rate of return on capital, Smith more frequently employs 'ordinary' than 'natural' – supporting the conclusion that his use of the language of 'naturalness' in economic contexts is not laden with any deeper philosophical significance. There are also references, very much fewer, to 'ordinary wages' (*WN*: 85, 95, 172, 720, 759, 864), 'the ordinary market rate of interest' and 'ordinary market price of land' (*WN*: 113, 357–9, 614, 840), and 'ordinary rent' (*WN*: 831, 843–4). 'Ordinary price' also appears on its own, without reference to average or natural price – again, less frequently than does ordinary profits.[8]

Other economic uses are: 'ordinary produce' (*WN*: 176, 838), 'the ordinary quantity of labour' input (*WN*: 182), an 'ordinary proportion' between prices (*WN*: 196, 229), the 'ordinary course' of international trade and payments (*WN*: 476–7, 488), 'ordinary [tax] revenue' (*WN*: e.g. 618), 'ordinary dividend' of the Bank of England (*WN*: 818), 'ordinary expence' of government (*WN*: e.g. 820), 'ordinary [agricultural] seasons' (*edWN*: 566) – and in correspondence, even 'the ordinary rate' for laundering (*Corr*: 41). It is again noteworthy that Smith's widespread articulation of his analysis in *WN*, in terms of ordinary and average magnitudes and conditions, is not at all so evident in the earlier lectures. Aside from more generic uses of 'ordinary', the economic uses are: 'ordinary' expenses (*LJA*: 103); the 'ordinary price' of slaves (*LJA*: 178); 'the ordinary and naturall progress of things', referring to the historical evolution of government (*LJA*: 228); the 'ordinary demands' of government (*LJA*: 263); 'ordinary [tax] revenue' (*LJA*: 270); 'ordinary price', more or less identified with natural price, and the 'price ordinary' of labour (*LJA*: 360); 'ordinary price', by itself, of corn (*LJA*: 365) – and in *edWN* (580), the 'ordinary high price' of tobacco. Beyond specifically economic uses, as with 'usual', 'ordinary' appears generically as a synonym for the *common*, *typical* or *normal* (e.g. *TMS*: 55, 72; *WN*: 55, 485–6, 691), and hence also as an antonym of *uncommon* (e.g. *TMS*: 25). So we are told of the typical situation in wage bargaining: the masters 'upon all ordinary occasions, have the advantage' over the workmen (*WN*: 83). As is the case for prices, wages, profits and rents, also in these wider uses 'ordinary' is often a synonym for natural.[9]

Smith's conception of market price is described in Book I, Chapter VII as follows:

> The market price of every particular commodity is regulated by the proportion between the quantity which is actually brought to market, and the demand of those who are willing to pay the natural price of the commodity .... Such people may be called the effectual demanders, and their demand the effectual demand ....
>
> (*WN*: 73)

It is also identified with '[t]he actual price at which any commodity is commonly sold' (*WN*: 73; also 46: 'market price, that is, the actual price of commodities'). It is 'competition' that causes market prices to deviate from natural price, when 'quantity' differs from effectual demand (as well as causing market or actual price deviations subsequently to be eliminated[10]):

> When the quantity of any commodity which is brought to market falls short of the effectual demand, all those who are willing to pay the whole value of the rent, wages, and profit, which must be paid in order to bring it thither, cannot be supplied with the quantity they want. Rather than want it altogether, some of them will be willing to give more. A competition will immediately begin among them, and the market price will rise more or less above the natural price ....
>
> When the quantity brought to market exceeds the effectual demand, it cannot be all sold to those who are willing to pay the whole value of the rent, wages and profit, which must be paid in order to bring it thither. Some part must be sold to those who are willing to pay less, and the low price which they give for it must reduce the price of the whole. The market price will sink more or less below the natural price, according as the greatness of the excess increases more or less the competition of the sellers ....
>
> (*WN*: 73–4)

So follows also, that when 'the quantity brought to market is just sufficient to supply the effectual demand and no more, the market price naturally comes to be either exactly, or as nearly as can be judged of, the same with the natural price'; and the metaphor from physics, of competition as like gravity: natural price is 'as it were, the central price, to which the prices of all commodities are continually gravitating'; the price towards which 'the market price of every particular commodity is ... continually gravitating, if one may say so' (notice the self-consciousness); market prices 'are constantly tending towards it' (*WN*: 74–5, 77; cf. 455, for another gravity metaphor, and similarly self-conscious).

Before proceeding further to consider Smith's uses of 'market price', what of his references to 'market' as such? The term appears only once in *TMS* (282), in relation to ancient slavery, and also only once in each of *EPS* (182) and *LRB* (188) – nor are any extensions of the term used in these works. The first uses in *WN* are under the list of 'Contents': the title of Book I, Chapter III ('That the Division of Labour is limited by the Extent of the Market'), followed by the reference to 'Market Price' in the title of Book I, Chapter VII (*WN*: 3). The notion of 'extent of the market' (sometimes conveyed also just by reference to 'the market') carries the sense of level of output, scale of activity in the production of a commodity, or sales volume – and closely related, 'market' as outlet or opportunity for sale (*WN*: 31–4).[11] But easily the most widely used sense is of 'market' as a place of trade or the places of trade in general, though not necessarily a *physical* place in space and time.[12] It might be thought – for instance, because of his regular references to 'bringing ... [commodities] to market' (e.g. *WN*: 161–2) – that Smith is thinking only of physical markets; but a reference to 'houses … brought to market' tells against this (*WN*: 862). At minimum, this indicates that he is not thinking only of markets in which the thing traded is taken to a physical market. References to, and distinctions between, 'general' and 'particular' markets convey also a sense of *degrees* of integration of transactions in specific commodities (*WN*: 219, 231, 455, 507, 533, 593, 638). Beyond these senses, the next most considerable use is market price. 'Home market', as distinct from foreign markets, also occurs frequently. There is significant discussion of 'the market rate of interest' (*WN*: 105–7, 109, 113–14, 319, 356–9, 611, 840, 845, 852, 915), and a few references to 'market towns' (*WN*: 31, 129, 137, 648; *LJA*: 10, 76; *LJB*: 470; *fA*: 582). The following are also noteworthy: 'an open and free market' (*WN*: 652); 'market place' (*LJA*: 139; *LJB*: 485); 'market time' (*LJA*: 193); 'marketing' (*WN*: 215); and 'the free competition of the market' (*WN*: 866). Smith nowhere finds it necessary to explicitly define 'market'.

Returning to market price in particular, when Smith identifies market price with the actual prices at which transactions occur (*WN*: 46, 73; two paragraphs above), how literally should this be taken? Notice that in one of these two instances, market price is defined as the actual price at which a commodity is *most commonly* sold. Whereas natural price is by definition a singular magnitude for each kind of commodity, the competitive processes whereby market prices deviate from natural price under conditions of 'market imbalance' (see n. 10 above) are consistent with, indeed likely to cause, transactions at non-uniform prices. That is to say, market price as literally the actual prices at which transactions occur when there is such market imbalance, is not in general a singular magnitude. This is confirmed by Smith's having recourse to the most common actual price, in order to be able to speak of a singular market price magnitude which can be compared with natural price, in terms of the direction of deviation between natural and market prices. Averages of market prices are also used elsewhere, for other purposes.[13] Essentially the same conceptualization of market prices, and of their relation to natural price, is expounded in *LJ*, if somewhat more primitively expressed:

> There are in every species of goods two separate prices to be considered, the natural and the market price. The 1$^{st}$ is that which is necessary <?to induce> one to apply to a particular business.… The market price often differs considerably from this, and is regulated by … 1$^{st}$, the demand or need for it …; 2$^{dly}$, the abundance of it in proportion to this demand; and 3$^{dly}$, the wea<l>th of the … demanders.… These two different prices, which appear at first sight to be noway connected nor to have the least dependance on each other, are very intimately related …. For if the market price be so high as to be more than sufficient to make up the naturall price … all will croud into it with expectations of making a fortune … and consequently it will … fall down to its naturall price.
>
> (*LJA*: 356–60)

Smith goes on to describe the symmetric process by which, if a 'trade by this or any other means becomes overstocked', the resulting deviation of market price below natural price will be corrected by supply adjustment (*LJA*: 360).[14] Explicit reference to 'market' prices occurs almost nowhere else in Smith's writings, beyond *WN* and *LJ* (*edWN*: 575; *Corr*: 151).

There are many other references to 'price' beyond these, most notably for our purposes, Smith's notion of 'real' versus 'nominal' price, considered in section 3.4.2 below. Passing or otherwise inconsequential references to prices in *WN* and *LJ* need not be detailed, but the following are worth noting: rent as 'the price paid for the use of land', and a 'monopoly price' (*WN*: 160–1, 840; cf. 185); interest as 'the price ... paid for the use of ... stock', or 'capital', or 'money' (*WN*: 352–4, 356–7; cf. *LJB*: 520); and most particularly, and far more pervasively, there are many references to labour remuneration as 'the price of labour'.[15] By thus articulating as 'prices', the payments for the three classes of inputs Smith categorizes as the collaborating means of production – though more especially for labour than capital and land – he seems to imply that their remuneration is analogous to commodity pricing (an issue further considered in sec. 3.4.3). There are no references of any kind to price, or any derivative of it, in *EPS*. There is only one in *LRB*, but a good few in the correspondence.[16] The term appears just once in *TMS* (53), as a metaphor, and is also once powerfully employed as a metaphor in *WN* (126). It is a curious fact that a person who did so much to found the political economy of modern commercial society, with prices and markets playing a vital role, should so little use 'price' as a metaphor. Metaphorically employed, it is precisely a notion of opportunity cost, the very deepest meaning of price: that which is foregone for the sake of having some other thing.

### *3.1.2 Smith on 'competition'*

As is already evident from *WN* (73–4), quoted above, the converging of market prices towards natural price – as well as deviation of market prices from natural price in the face of market imbalance – are understood to result from 'competition', either between potential buyers or potential sellers (and the term occurs there more frequently than just those quoted above). The concept of competition as a *regulative* force governing prices is at one point explicitly expressed using a variant of that term: 'Where there is an exclusive corporation [i.e. monopoly], it may perhaps be proper to regulate the price of the first necessary of life [referring to 'bread']. But where there is none, the competition will regulate it much better than any assize' (*WN*: 158). Natural price is the quantitative expression of that competitive force. As Smith puts it elsewhere, the actualization of 'the natural and proper[17] price' is the 'consequence of an open and free market' (*WN*: 652). Just as competition acts upon commodity prices, so also it appears similarly to act upon remuneration for inputs to production. With regard to labour:

> When in any country the demand for those who live by wages ... is continually increasing ... [t]he scarcity of hands occasions a competition among

> masters, who bid against one another, in order to get workmen, and thus voluntarily break through the natural combination of masters not to raise wages.
>
> (*WN*: 86)

> The funds destined for the payment of wages ... may be of the greatest extent, but if they have continued for several centuries of the same, or very nearly of the same extent ... [t]here could seldom be any scarcity of hands, nor could the masters be obliged to bid against one another in order to get them.... There would be a constant scarcity of employment, and the labourers would be obliged to bid against one another in order to get it. If in such a country the wages of labour had ever been more than sufficient to maintain the labourer, and to enable him to bring up a family, the competition of the labourers and the interest of the masters would soon reduce them to this lowest rate which is consistent with common humanity.
>
> (*WN*: 89; also 90, 111, 140, 145, 353)

Competition is also an influence upon wage relativities (*WN*: 121–2, 124, 146–50). With regard to capital:

> As the quantity of stock to be lent at interest increases, the interest ... necessarily diminishes, not only from those general causes which make the market price of things commonly diminish as their quantity increases, but from other causes which are peculiar to this particular case. As capitals increase in any country, the profits which can be made by employing them necessarily diminish. It becomes gradually more and more difficult to find within the country a profitable method of employing any new capital. There arises in consequence a competition between different capitals, the owner of one endeavouring to get possession of that employment which is occupied by another.... But when the profits which can be made by the use of a capital are in this manner diminished ... the price which can be paid for the use of it, that is, the rate of interest, must necessarily be diminished with them.
>
> (*WN*: 352–3; also 105–7, 110–11, 128, 140, 145)

This notion of competition acting upon rates of profit naturally gives rise to use of the phrase, ‘competition of capitals’, or similar terms (*WN*: 355–6, 361–2, 596, 598, 600, 604). The role of competition with regard to rents is not well specified: there is a suggestion that rents on corn land regulate other land-rents (*WN*: 165, 175, 245; see also *WN*: 841, 843–4), which is not very helpful for a theory of rents as such. In general, ‘free competition’ is Smith’s characteristic phrase for conditions of thoroughgoing competition, essentially understood as freedom of entry to and exit from markets, on the supply side in particular, to pursue gain or escape loss (for further uses, see sec. 5.2.1):

> Monopoly ... is a great enemy to good management, which can never be universally established but in consequence of that free and universal competition which forces every body to have recourse to it for the sake of self-defence.
>
> (*WN*: 163–4; cf. 755, where competition is likened to 'warfare')

There are many other references to 'competition' or variants thereof in *WN*, commonly deployed in the general sense of economic rivalry (cf. McNulty 1967).[18] Neither the term nor any variant of it appear at all in *LJ*; but there is, in the market-natural price analyses, a *concept* of competitive dynamics there. It does appear once in *edWN* (567). There are eight instances in *TMS* (26, 83, 138–9, 181, 214, 247, 258, 305), to convey various senses of rivalry or trade-off. It is nowhere in *EPS* and just one historical reference, in relation to ancient Greek competitions, in *LRB* (139). There are also two references to competition in the correspondence (*Corr*: 243, 245).

At core, 'competition' in Smith's economic uses, and indeed, more widely, is rivalry in the pursuit of (material) gain. It is therefore necessarily conflictual; even in situations characterizable as a positive-sum game, there is a trade-off over potential gain, an opposition of interests.[19] The force of competition is the force of self-interest or self-love. But Smith believes such self-regard can and must be both self-disciplined and otherwise limited by law in society. At one point in *WN* he argues for how competition makes for better product quality (in this particular instance, professional services), notably using the term *justle* (an archaic form of 'jostle', etymologically related to 'joust'):

> In every profession, the exertion of the greater part of those who exercise it, is always in proportion to the necessity they are under of making that exertion.... [W]here the competition is free, the rivalship of competitors, who are all endeavouring to justle one another out of employment, obliges every man to endeavour to execute his work with a certain degree of exactness.... Rivalship and emulation render excellency, even in mean professions, an object of ambition, and frequently occasion the very greatest exertions.
>
> (*WN*: 759–60)

And in another instance in *WN*, speaking of how increase of stock places downward pressure on profit rates and interest (the context was quoted two paragraphs above):

> There arises in consequence a competition between different capitals, the owner of one endeavouring to get possession of that employment which is occupied by another. But upon most occasions he can hope to justle that other out of this employment, by no other means but by dealing upon more reasonable terms.
>
> (*WN*: 353; also 599, 671)

Compare these with a striking passage in *TMS*, using the same term:

> Though it may be true … that every individual, in his own breast, naturally prefers himself to all mankind, yet he dares not look mankind in the face, and avow that he acts according to this principle.… When he views himself in the light in which he is conscious that others will view him, he sees that to them he is but one of the multitude in no respect better than any other in it.… [H]e must … humble the arrogance of his self-love, and bring it down to something which other men can go along with. They will indulge it so far as to allow him to be more anxious about, and to pursue with more earnest assiduity, his own happiness than that of any other person. Thus far, whenever they place themselves in his situation, they will readily go along with him. In the race for wealth, and honours, and preferments, he may run as hard as he can, and strain every nerve and every muscle, in order to outstrip all his competitors. But if he should justle, or throw down any of them, the indulgence of the spectators is entirely at an end. It is a violation of fair play, which they cannot admit of.
>
> (*TMS*: 83)

The jostling of self-interest has necessary limits.

The nature and significance of individual self-interest or self-regard – and its relationship to human sociability, moral sentiment, self-restraint and ethical behaviour – is a big and important subject for Smith.[20] But it is a subject separable from political economy as such – and so, it is not necessary to inquire further into it here. Indeed, one may even say that it is precisely in moral philosophy, more so than in economic inquiry, that systematic analysis of self-regard is most necessary. At first glance it might appear surprising that self-regard is much more discussed in *TMS* than *WN*. But for most of the purposes of Smith's political economy, self-interested individual pursuit of material gain – within a framework of generally law-abiding and otherwise self-disciplined behaviour, and in a well-ordered (and in particular, commercial) society – simply can be posited, leaving those more fundamental issues of ethics and law to 'jurisprudence' and moral philosophy (cf. Campbell and Skinner 1976: 18–19; Skinner 1996: 65–73). This is precisely an instance of the capacity for political economy to be pursued as a separate science. In the economics, self-regard can largely be taken for granted. It is the driving force which finds expression in competition (as well as other things, notably, capital accumulation). It is these – competition, accumulation and so on – which are systematically considered in the economics. It is in the moral philosophy that self-regard really has to be 'dealt with'.

Smith's vision of competition in relation to self-interest and justice is nicely summed up at the end of the penultimate Book IV of *WN*, the book which examines systems of political economy, following on from a repudiation of government regulation of economic activity:

> All systems either of preference or of restraint … being … completely taken away, the obvious and simple system of natural liberty establishes itself of

> its own accord. Every man, as long as he does not violate the laws of justice, is left perfectly free to pursue his own interest his own way, and to bring both his industry and capital into competition with those of any other man, or order of men.
>
> (*WN*: 687)

But if economic competition is an analogy from racing (see the *TMS* quotation two paragraphs above), then it is an imperfect one for Smith's conception. In the races of production, sale and consumption for gain, he is articulating a desired system in which there will be no (singular) winner; in particular, a system which tends to deliver the same 'prize' to all like contestants (uniform remunerations and prices). Some of the actual contestants – e.g. the proprietors who have carriage of commodity supply – might prefer to be sole winners (i.e. monopolists). Hence, it is not so surprising, if post-Smithian language may be allowed, that Smith is in favour of (competitive) capitalism, not capitalists. These are not the same thing. Indeed, rightly or wrongly, in his view capitalism *constrains* the power of capitalists.[21]

## 3.2 Supply and demand

### *3.2.1 Smith on 'supply' and 'demand'*

Adam Smith nowhere uses that phrase, 'supply and demand', or 'demand and supply', which in later times came to be regarded as so much signifying the pervasive subject matter of the science, as to be almost a synonym for it. That economics is 'all about' supply-and-demand (hereafter, SAD for short) appears to be something even widely 'known' to laypersons in more recent generations. While not using the phrase, Smith does extensively use 'supply' and 'demand'. The question is, what do they mean for him? The now very ordinariness, even triteness, of these terms can make them seem to represent mere common sense notions, so that Smith's understanding of them must be synonymous with our own. But whatever laypersons may take SAD to mean, the meaning he attaches to them is importantly different from that of latter-day economic theory, though to be sure, they are vitally important and pervasive elements in Smith's political economy.

*Supply* and variants of it in Smith's texts are considerably employed in verb rather than noun form, in part because Smith speaks of 'quantity brought to market' (or similar phrases), where we now would be inclined to speak of 'supply'. In relation particularly to 'supply' and 'demand' used together, 'supply the demand' and similar phrases are typical:

> The whole quantity of industry annually employed in order to bring any commodity to market, naturally suits itself … to the effectual demand. It naturally aims at bringing always that precise quantity thither which may be sufficient to supply, and no more than supply, that demand.
>
> . . .

> A monopoly granted either to an individual or to a trading company has the same effect as a secret in trade or manufactures. The monopolists, by keeping the market constantly under-stocked, by never fully supplying the effectual demand, sell their commodities much above the natural price, and raise their emoluments, whether they consist in wages or profit, greatly above their natural rate.[22]

While the application of this language is overwhelmingly to commodity markets, a small number of instances of application to labour also occur:

> Any rise in the average price of necessaries, unless it is compensated by a proportionable rise in the wages of labour, must necessarily diminish more or less the ability of the poor to bring up numerous families, and consequently to supply the demand for useful labour ....
>
> (*WN*: 872–3; also 98, 101)

*Supply the market* and similar phrases also are frequently used:

> When by an increase in the effectual demand, the market price of some particular commodity happens to rise a good deal above the natural price, those who employ their stocks in supplying that market are generally careful to conceal this change.
>
> (*WN*: 77)

> the corporation of butchers have the sole liberty of killing and selling all the flesh that is brought to market. Here the priviledge is not vested in the person of one man, but as the number is fixt they will readily enter into compacts to keep up the price of the commodity and at the same time supply the market but very indifferently with flesh.
>
> (*LJA*: 84; also *WN*: 53, 110–11, 199, 217, 224–5, 253, 329, 409, 521, 533–5, 537–9, 657, 856; *LJA*: 6; *Corr*: 243)

Variants of 'supply the ... wants' are also quite common, in one instance in relation to labour:

> The funds destined for the payment of wages ... may be of the greatest extent, but if they have continued for several centuries of the same, or very nearly of the same extent, the number of labourers employed every year could easily supply, and even more than supply, the number wanted the following year.
>
> (*WN*: 89; also 14, 27, 37, 73, 276–7, 351, 378, 447, 570; *LJA*: 335, 337, 340; *LJB*: 487; *edWN*: 566, 572)

Supply is also used to refer to national product, provisions, outputs, and the revenue of the monarch.[23] As well, the term and variants of it are employed in essentially non-economic senses across Smith's texts – notably, in the sense of 'provide', and sometimes 'substitute' (in the sense of to *supply the place of*).

Certainly in relation to commodities, the thing being supplied in these uses is generally a variant of the 'quantity brought to market', which together with demand (and more especially, $D^*$: see n. 10 above), plays such a central role in his conception of market prices and their relation to natural prices. Beyond all Smith's uses of 'demand' already detailed, and a further small number of particularly pertinent instances considered below, there are also considerable other instances of that term, which need not be considered or detailed. Suffice it to say that 'demand' finds pervasive use in wider contexts, not so strongly connected to price theory as to require our attention. Those wider references do provide some further indications of his views on the factors shaping demands. These include, for example, the wealth and wantonness of the demanders, the 'importance' of the commodity to them (*WN*: 74); 'fashion and fancy' versus 'use or necessity' (*WN*: 131); the requirements of subsistence (*WN*: 162); 'utility', in the sense of usefulness, versus 'beauty' (*WN*: 189–91); population and 'the progress of improvement' (*WN*: 247); the diffusion of 'taste' (*WN*: 407). All this is to make demands a creature of wealth and desire. Beyond that, it is perhaps most noteworthy that Smith conveys a general sense of demand as the autonomous element in output (as against price) determination, including in the dynamics of growth. To a certain extent this parallels the role of supply adjustment in the process of market prices converging towards natural price (examined in sec. 3.3.1): supply accommodates demand.

### *3.2.2 Smith on 'scarcity' and 'plenty'*

This clarification of the meaning of SAD in relation to prices in Smith's texts is further supported by finally considering his characteristic uses of 'scarcity' and 'plenty'. So far distant is his use of 'scarcity' from the modern marginalist notion of inexhaustible wants or uses confronting finite resources, that the two terms commonly serve as antonyms for Smith, with markets generally able to exhibit either situation:

> The high price of corn during these ten or twelve years past … seems evidently to have been the effect of the extraordinary unfavourableness of the seasons, and ought therefore to be regarded, not as a permanent, but as a transitory and occasional event. The seasons for these ten or twelve years past have been unfavourable through the greater part of Europe; and the disorders of Poland have very much increased the scarcity in all those countries, which, in dear years, used to be supplied from that market. So long a course of bad seasons, though not a very common event, is by no means a singular one; and whoever has enquired much into the history of the prices of corn in former times, will be at no loss to recollect several other examples of the same kind. Ten years of extraordinary scarcity, besides, are not more wonderful than ten years of extraordinary plenty.
>
> (*WN*: 217)

> If … ['a thing'] be usefull the price will be regulated according to the demand … and the plenty there is to supply it. A thing which is hardly of any use, yet if the quantity be not sufficient to supply the demand, will give a high price; hence the great price of diamonds. Precious metalls, which are certainly not so usefull as gold, bear a far greater price, partly on this account. Abundance on the other hand such as does more than supply all possible demands, renders water of no price at all and other things of a price the next thing to nothing. The scarcity on the other hand raises the price immoderately. — This also depends on … the riches or poverty of the demand[ers].
>
> (*LJA*: 358; cf. 333; *LJB*: 487, 496; *WN*: 44–5)

In such uses, scarcity is a synonym for a deficiency of supply – commonly, vis-à-vis normal demand – or just excess demand; and its antonym, plenty, a term for excess supply.[24] On the other hand, the later marginalist notion of scarcity is such that, unlike the case with Smith's notion, an opposite situation of 'plenty' is not possible for the human condition.[25]

When deployed in these senses to convey market (or just supply–demand) imbalance (see n. 10), scarcity and plenty are naturally identified by Smith with dearness and cheapness respectively, in the sense of high and low market prices (as well as sometimes high and low *natural* prices – see below). In some of these instances, evidently *abnormally* high or low prices are intended: 'sudden and extraordinary plenty' associated with 'a cheap year' and 'sudden and extraordinary scarcity' associated with 'a dear year' (*WN*: 103–4); 'high rent of enclosed land … owing to the scarcity of enclosure' (*WN*: 167); 'scarcity must necessarily raise … price' and 'plenty … obliges … to sell cheaper' (*WN*: 243); 'high price' in a 'season of scarcity', compared to 'ordinary … price' in 'times of moderate plenty' (*WN*: 259).[26] This identification is most explicitly stated in *LJ*: 'dearness and scarcity, abundance and cheapness, are we may say synonimous terms' (*LJA*: 362; also *LJB*: 487, 497). Scarcity-as-excess-demand is also applied to labour, in the very first reference to 'scarcity' in *WN*:

> When in any country the demand for those who live by wages … is continually increasing; when every year furnishes employment for a greater number than had been employed the year before … [t]he scarcity of hands occasions a competition among masters, who bid against one another, in order to get workmen … .
>
> (*WN*: 86)

> The funds destined for the payment of wages … may be of the greatest extent, but if they have continued for several centuries of the same, or very nearly of the same extent … [t]here could seldom be any scarcity of hands, nor could the masters be obliged to bid against one another in order to get them. The hands, on the contrary, would, in this case, naturally multiply beyond their employment. There would be a constant scarcity of employ-

> ment, and the labourers would be obliged to bid against one another in order to get it.
>
> (*WN*: 89; also 88, 132, 156; *LJA*: 192)

While scarcity is commonly contrasted with plenty, 'abundance' is also often employed as an antonym (*WN*: 156, 171, 178, 192, 212–13, 236, 255, 431; *LJA*: 362; *LJB*: 487, 496–7; *edWN*: 575). Sometimes scarcity conveys just a general sense of supply as such, or limited supply, or small quantity, rather than excess demand in a strict sense (e.g. *WN*: 172, 431, 943; *LJA*: 370). In one striking instance Smith notes that demand may be influenced by scarcity; that is to say, demand is not independent of supply conditions, or is positively influenced by cost:

> With the greater part of rich people, the chief enjoyment of riches consists in the parade of riches, which in their eyes is never so compleat as when they appear to possess those decisive marks of opulence which nobody can possess but themselves. In their eyes the merit of an object which is in any degree either useful or beautiful, is greatly enhanced by its scarcity ....
>
> (*WN*: 190–1)

The same point is made in *EPS* (182–3), and the editor draws attention to the kinship with Thorstein Veblen's snob effect (Wightman 1980: 174).

While thus commonly used to convey the sense of abnormal supply deficiency or excess demand, in some other instances 'scarcity' refers to conditions causing high or rising cost and natural price:

> That the silver mines of Spanish America, like all other mines, become gradually more expensive in the working, on account of the greater depths at which it is necessary to carry on the works, and of the greater expence of drawing out the water and of supplying them with fresh air at those depths, is acknowledged by every body who has enquired into the state of those mines.
>
> These causes ... are equivalent to a growing scarcity of silver (for a commodity may be said to grow scarcer when it becomes more difficult and expensive to collect a certain quantity of it) ....
>
> (*WN*: 232)

> Those things which are scarcest bear the highest price, as they become the purchase of the richest persons who can afford to bid highest. They alone purchase diamonds, rubies, and all manufactures which by the work required are scarce, tho of no great additionall reall worth, and in generall all productions whether of art or of nature which are scarce and ill to be come at.
>
> (*LJA*: 361–2)[27]

In this sense, Smith speaks also of 'natural rise' in prices (*WN*: 259, more fully quoted in n. 26). In a rather symmetric manner, apart from 'plenty' as excess supply, the term is also used for conditions of low or falling natural cost and price. The two distinct notions – of, one might say, temporary versus persistent plenty – are nicely brought together at one point, where he writes of the introduction of cultivation of various animal foods. Smith continues:

> After it [the cultivation] has become general, new methods of feeding are commonly fallen upon, which enable the farmer to raise upon the same quantity of ground a much greater quantity of that particular sort of animal food. The plenty not only obliges him to sell cheaper, but in consequence of these improvements he can afford to sell cheaper; for if he could not afford it, the plenty would not be of long continuance.
>
> (*WN*: 243)

Extended to commodities in general, plenty as low prices is synonymous with 'opulence' (see sec. 5.1.1):

> It is the great multiplication of the productions of all the different arts, in consequence of the division of labour, which occasions, in a well-governed society, that universal opulence which extends itself to the lowest ranks of the people … and a general plenty diffuses itself through all the different ranks of the society.
>
> (*WN*: 22; cf. *LJA*: 362)

> The third thing which is the object of police is the proper means of introducing plenty and abundance into the country, that is, the cheapness of goods of all sorts. For these terms plenty and cheapness are in a manner synonimous, as cheapness is a nec<e>ssary consequence of plenty.
>
> (*LJA*: 333; also 378)

Hence Smith deploys dual senses of scarcity and plenty: scarcity and plenty may be associated with market prices above and below normal prices, more or less temporarily; or they may be associated with high and low natural costs and prices.[28] 'Dearness' and 'cheapness', or variants thereof (including 'dearth'), are also frequently juxtaposed by Smith – separate from reference to scarcity and plenty – in one instance explicitly articulating the same dual sense: dear/cheap as market price above/below normal price, or as high/low normal price (*WN*: 231). It may be added that the notion of scarcity as high or rising natural cost is no more the marginalist concept of scarcity than is Smith's other, excess-demand notion: it entails no supposition of insatiable wants; rather, only a notion that quantity demanded causes an extent or extension of supply such as to require implementation of inferior production methods (or more vaguely, a notion of cost so high as to render a commodity purchasable by only a minority of persons).[29] We may conclude by drawing attention to one remaining instance of (a variant of) 'plenty', not already noted, which occurs in one of Smith's two key definitions of political economy, fully quoted at the opening of section 2.1.1: the aims of political economy are 'to provide a plentiful revenue ... for the people' and 'to supply the state ... with a revenue sufficient for the publick services' (*WN*: 428). Notice the contrast: plenty for the people, sufficiency for the State.

## 3.3 Market prices, supply dynamics and the role of demand

### *3.3.1 Role of supply versus demand*

While Smith nowhere uses the phrase 'supply and demand' or 'demand and supply' when he articulates the determination of market prices, he uses language which easily, but dangerously, can be translated into those terms.[30] That phrase, later to become so commonplace, is indeed somewhat suggestive of *symmetric* forces, which is precisely how later marginalist theory sought to conceptualize supply and demand, in terms of a kind of equilibrium balancing of opposing forces. Smith's characteristic expression – 'supply the demand' and similar phrases – rather is suggestive of a certain *a*symmetry: of supply adjusting to demand. This in turn flows from his notion of $D^*$ the fixed point, $(D^*, p^n)$, the centre of gravity, with $Q$ adjustment doing the work of balancing the market. That the given quantity $D^*$ presupposes $p^n$, serves to confirm that Smith treats $p^n$ as independent of $Q$, at least in relation to *just* the quantity variations associated with correction of 'market imbalances'. If that were not so, $D^*$ could not be given independent of quantity supplied. Smith's characteristic treatment of $p^m{}_i$ behaviour under competitive conditions is a description of the dynamic motion of actual prices in situations of market imbalance: the dynamics of deviation and convergence of $p^m{}_i$ with respect to $p^n$. This conception does not entail SAD in the latter-day sense of supply and demand functions. Consider first the role of demand, in order to see how the convergence dynamics do not rest upon demand functions in any essential way.

Smith nowhere makes reference to demand functions in which individual and/or market demands for commodities bear a well-defined negative relation to the uniform own-prices of commodities.[31] Nevertheless, are latter-day demand functions needed in order to make sense of what Smith actually does say about market price behaviour? That is to say, is such a notion necessary to his explicit argument linking market imbalances, $p^m{}_i$ and $p^n$? If demand functions were necessary to Smith's argument, one might be inclined to infer that he tacitly supposes them. Suppose for the sake of argument that $p^m{}_i$ dynamics may be thought of as occurring in a sequence of time periods (call them 'market periods') so short as to not allow the quantity of each commodity supplied to markets to vary within the period – or at least, not to vary upwards (withdrawal of supply from the market, discussed further below, remains possible). Then the role of demand can be approached by decomposing the issue into three questions:

1 How can market imbalance ($Q/D^* \neq 1$) lead to deviation between $p^m{}_i$ and $p^n$?[32] Can such deviation lead to some degree of convergence between $Q$ and demand
2 within the market period and/or
3 across a sequence of market periods?

In relation to all three, the issue is whether demand functions are necessary to these processes. It is useful to consider the two possibilities – a) $Q > D^*$ and b) $Q < D^*$ – separately and successively, generating six questions.

Suppose initially $Q/D^* > 1$.

a.1 By supposition, not all of $Q$ can be sold for at least $p^n$ in this situation – if one ignores the possibility that market sales ($Q^s$) can exceed $D^*$ at $p^m{}_i \geq p^n$, with this satisfied as a strong inequality for at least one market price.[33] Why might this situation induce at least some suppliers who perceive the imbalance, to offer at least some parts of $Q$ at $p^m{}_i < p^n$? Such an inducement could be provided by the conviction that some additional demands will be forthcoming at prices below $p^n$ – and that if this is so, the resulting losses from selling at such prices are preferable to no sale at all. But neither a belief on the part of suppliers that $Q^s$ exceeds $D^*$ at market prices below $p^n$, nor that supposition being actually correct, is necessary to induce suppliers to make offers at below-normal prices: even if, as at least some $p^m{}_i$ deviate below $p^n$, $Q^s$ were invariant (and equal to $D^*$), there would still be inducement for suppliers to make offers at below-normal prices, in an attempt to bid demanders away from each other (i.e. from other suppliers). Furthermore, if some or all the effectual demanders also perceive the overall situation of market imbalance, they may be induced to resist paying $p^n$ – which would further encourage suppliers to contemplate a loss-minimizing offer of outputs at below-normal prices, rather than risk no sale at all.

a.2 Within the market period, below-normal prices can only lead to convergence, a narrowing of the initial imbalance, either by at least some supply offers at below-normal prices inducing a market demand greater than $D^*$, or market conditions inducing suppliers to withdraw a part of $Q$. In the latter case, quantity actually offered diverges from $Q$.

a.3 The possibility of a withdrawal of part of $Q$ as market prices deviate below $p^n$ means that convergence between quantity and demand in the market period can occur without any tendency of market demand to be greater than $D^*$ at below-normal prices. In any case, such market-period convergence is not necessary to Smith's convergence dynamics: so long as the average (or most common) of $p^m{}_i$ deviates from $p^n$ in the appropriate direction, a quantity response comes into play beyond the market period, as a result of the repulsion of below-normal profits (but see n. 35), and with $p^m{}_i$ converging back towards normal price.

Suppose now the opposite case of initially $Q/D^* < 1$.

b.1 In this situation, all of $Q$ *could* be sold for $p^n$, with unmet demand ($D^* - Q$): by supposition, not all demands can be met when all elements of $p^m{}_i = p^n$. Why might this situation induce at least some suppliers who perceive the imbalance, to offer at least some parts of $Q$ at $p^m{}_i > p^n$? Such an inducement could be provided by the conviction that at least some part of the demand $D^*$ will be forthcoming at prices above $p^n$, so that above-normal profits can be reaped if quantities can be sold at such prices. Furthermore, if at least some of the effectual demanders *are* willing to transact at least some quantities at above-normal prices, and they perceive the overall situation of market imbalance, they may be induced to offer above-normal prices – in an attempt to bid suppliers away from each other (i.e. from other demanders). And actual transactions at above-normal prices will only occur at all, if in fact there *are* some demands at those prices: in the absence of that, supply offers at above-normal prices would be pointless. But this requirement to ensure a plausible basis for appropriate price deviations is not a requirement for a latter-day demand function: if market demand were invariant (say equal to $D^*$) as at least some market prices deviate above $p^n$, there is *greater* inducement for suppliers to make offers at above-normal price.

b.2 Within the market period, above-normal prices can only lead to convergence by inducing a market demand less than $D^*$.[34]

b.3 Convergence between quantity and demand in the market period can only occur if there is a tendency for market demand to be less than $D^*$ at above-normal prices. But again, as in a.3, such market-period convergence is unnecessary to Smith's convergence dynamics of $p^m{}_i$ with respect to $p^n$: so long as the average (or most common) of $p^m{}_i$ deviates from $p^n$ in the appropriate direction, a quantity response comes into play beyond the market period, as a result of the attraction of above-normal profits (but see n. 35), and with $p^m{}_i$ converging back towards normal price.

Three further points may be emphasized. Even if market demand varies negatively in response to $p^m{}_i$ deviations from $p^n$ when $Q \neq D^*$, this would be understood by Smith to involve transactions at a variety of market prices, rather than at a uniform non-normal price. Second, in situations of market imbalance, an element of bargaining power is in play, analogous to Smith's characterization of the labour contract (see sec. 3.4.3). It follows that it therefore would not be a robust supposition, that hypothetical price/demand combinations for individual (potential) transactors – showing prices they are willing to pay for various particular quantities – could be posited independent of (knowledge of) the overall market situation. Such combinations (even if they were otherwise sensible constructs), to the extent that they depend upon the balance of bargaining power, would not in general be independent of the degree of market imbalance. Third and most importantly, convergence between quantity offered in the market and market demand, in the initial market period, is not at all necessary to Smith's subsequent dynamic process driving $p^m_i$ towards $p^n$. By excluding variations (or at least expansions) in outputs supplied, *by construction*, the very essence of the Smithian dynamics is removed. Even if aggregate quantities demanded are strictly invariant to $p^m_i$ deviations with respect to $p^n$, supply adjustments across market periods suffice to effect Smith's convergence process.

Furthermore, these dynamics serve to determine not the magnitudes of $p^m_i$, but mere deviation between the average (or most common) of $p^m_i$, and $p^n$. While Smith gives $p^n$ quantitative expression, $p^m_i$ are expressed only in terms of direction of deviation – and, sooner or later, direction of movement – with respect to $p^n$. The process for a particular commodity, thought of in terms of a sequence of discrete market periods, can be summarized by a three-step causal chain.

1 At least some $p^m_i$, and hence also the average or most common market price (in period '*t*'), will be below (above) $p^n$ if $Q_t > D^*$ ($Q_t < D^*$), where $Q_t$ is supply in period t.
2 $Q_{t+1}$, the quantity brought to market in the subsequent period, will be above (below) $Q_t$ if the difference between average market price and $p^n$ in period *t* is positive (negative), on the supposition that the latter difference corresponds to an average profitability of commodity supply above (below) the required profitability, the opportunity cost of capital or natural rate of profit.[35]
3 The difference between average market price and $p^n$ will sooner or later diminish in response to the diminishing difference between $Q_t$ and $D^*$ – sooner or later, because this process is consistent with 'overshooting', in the sense of $p^m_i/p^n$ divergence continuing temporarily to widen in the face of $Q_t/D^*$ imbalance narrowing. The difference between average and required profitability thereby also diminishes (the same correspondence utilized under the second step).

As $Q_t$ converges upon $D^*$, prices and profitability converge upon their natural rates. Prices stabilize when all elements of $p^m_i$ equal $p^n$ and $Q_t/D^*$ equals unity, but with the resulting $p^n$ unexplained by SAD. No demand functions are needed for this competitive process of convergence.

However, while Smith's dynamics of $p^m_i$ convergence do not require demand functions, at one point he supposes that deviation of market prices below $p^n$ (due to initial $Q > D^*$) is associated with total market demand above $D^*$: 'When the quantity brought to market exceeds the effectual demand … [s]ome part must be sold to those who are willing to pay less' (*WN*: 74; quoted more fully in sec. 3.1.1). This points to an auxiliary function of demand responsiveness to price deviations from $p^n$ – not about price convergence, but rather, ensuring limits to price deviation. That is to say, this pertains to the behaviour of $p^m_i$ in response to the initial imbalance or shock, *before* $p^m_i$ come under the 'pull' of capital adjustments in response to that $p^m_i/p^n$ divergence – two distinct stages in the process, one may say. In the absence of price stickiness, such demand responsiveness (in both directions) ensures that $p^m_i$ do not exhibit explosive behaviour. (Such variations of demand around $D^*$ may come from final users or from dealers – wholesale or retail merchants, who have a considerable presence in *WN* – absorbing excess supplies before $p^m_i$ reach zero, or reducing demands below normal before $p^m_i$ go to infinity.) In the absence of price stickiness, or rapid $Q$ adjustment, or dealers absorbing imbalances, responsiveness of final users' demand is the only safety valve limiting price volatility. Smith's far more extensive and systematic consideration of supply-side adjustment – in *WN*, Book I, Chapter VII, and throughout *WN* – is due to the fact that in the convergence dynamics it is the supply side which is doing all the work.[36] Higher (lower) demand at below-normal (above-normal) prices provides temporary alleviation of pressure on $p^m_i$, in time-horizons shorter than required for supply adjustment. But Smith's interest is in convergence upon $p^n$, $D^*$, and for this, a demand/$p^m_i$ relation can have at most only a contingent and auxiliary significance.

The convergence dynamics certainly require at least some $p^m_i$ to deviate from $p^n$ in the face of market imbalance. The possibility of above-$D^*$ demand at below-normal prices may assist those dynamics, by providing additional impetus for suppliers to offer output at below-normal prices, as well as impetus for demand-side offers at below-normal prices. (With regard to the latter, persons other than the effectual demanders, perceiving the market imbalance, could be induced into the market with below-$p^n$ offers, as well as the effectual demanders, also perceiving the imbalance, being induced to resist paying $p^n$.) But belief in such a possibility on the part of suppliers, sound or otherwise, is not necessary to induce such offers. Even in the face of a belief (and reality) that below-normal prices will not induce a total market demand above $D^*$, suppliers still have grounds to make offers at below-normal prices, in order to avoid ending up as the suppliers with no or insufficient sales (given the overall market imbalance), by bidding demanders away from other potential suppliers. If competition of this kind makes sales at $p^n$ generally doubtful or unlikely, whatever beliefs motivate that behaviour, the only alternative open to any particular supplier is to withdraw from the market, if this appears less unprofitable than selling at the feasible below-normal prices.[37] (Of course, to the extent that withdrawal occurs, the pressure towards sales at below-normal prices is relieved.) In short, the possibility of demand above $D^*$ at below-normal prices can play a supporting though inessential role in the price convergence dynamics, in the $Q > D^*$ case; but even this potential auxiliary role of a demand/price relation is not symmetric: in the $Q < D^*$ case, the less the responsiveness of total demand to higher prices, the greater the encouragement to $p^m_i$ deviations above $p^n$.[38] It is in *limiting* price volatility in the face of market imbalances, in both directions, that a demand responsiveness to prices has a function.

### *3.3.2 Indeterminacy of demand-prices*

In view of all these considerations concerning the role of demand behaviour versus supply-side adjustment, it becomes manifest how inadequate is a partial-equilibrium, two-dimensional representation in price-quantity space (e.g. Larsen 1977: 227–8), for expressing Smith's treatment of market prices. Market price in general is not a singular magnitude in situations of $Q/D^* \neq 1$. $D^*$ is represented by a point in that space. Demand at non-normal prices cannot be represented by a given latter-day demand curve (nor in terms of a uniform market price at each demand level). More will be said about supply behaviour below. But it may be noted already that, within any market period, Smith's $Q$ cannot be represented by a vertical supply curve, since this asserts that all individual suppliers are willing to dump their component of $Q$ at *any* prices below $p^n$ (and all receive the same price), which Smith does not suppose. (What might occur from Smith's point of view, with respect to supply within a market period when $Q/D^* < 1$ and at least some of $p^m{}_i > p^n$, also cannot be represented by a vertical supply curve, which similarly supposes all suppliers receiving the same price.) Even if one could translate $Q$ into a strictly inelastic supply curve, this still would not determine an equilibrium market price in situations of market imbalance: a vertical curve confronts a point not on that curve.[39]

What follows from all this is that Smith's formulation of market price 'determination' is not a theory of the magnitude or level of market prices at all. To the extent that it is a (very minimal) theory, it is a theory of differences of $p^m{}_i$ with respect to a norm, under conditions of market imbalance. The proportion $Q/D^*$, which is Smith's characteristic 'explanation' of $p^m{}_i$ (or of their average or most common value), cannot be about the level of market price: that ratio can tell us nothing quantitatively definite about total market expenditure on a commodity, relative to quantity transacted (cf. Garegnani 1987: 565–6; Ciccone 1999: 70–1). Furthermore, the dynamics he enunciates in his treatment of $p^m{}_i$ convergence only require that the extent of the deviation of the average or most common $p^m{}_i$ from $p^n$, will sooner or later diminish in response to a narrowing $Q/D^*$ imbalance. No absolute magnitudes of market prices are required. This interpretation gains additional confirmation, and deeper clarification, by consideration of Smith's conclusions about price behaviour under (unusual) conditions in which supply constraints due to particular finite natural resources mean that $Q$ can *never* accommodate $D^*$ (a possibility tacitly put aside in all our commentary so far).

The most significant instance of this is worth quoting at length. Smith employs a threefold classification of raw materials, in order to discuss the course of their prices in growing economies, and continues:

> The first comprehends those which it is scarce in the power of human industry to multiply at all.... In the progress of wealth and improvement, the real price of the first may rise to any degree of extravagance, and *seems not to be limited by any certain boundary*.... It consists in those things which nature produces only in certain quantities, and which being of a very perishable nature, it is impossible to accumulate together the produce of many different seasons.... When wealth and the luxury which accompanies it increase, the demand for these is likely to increase with them, and no effort of human industry may be able to increase the supply much beyond what it was before

> this increase of the demand. The quantity of such commodities, therefore, remaining the same, or nearly the same, while the competition to purchase them is continually increasing, their price may rise to any degree of extravagance, and *seems not to be limited by any certain boundary.*
>
> (*WN*: 234–5; emphasis added)

Similar sentiments are expressed elsewhere in the same chapter (Book I, Chapter XI – 'Of the Rent of Land'):

> It sometimes happens ... that the quantity of land which can be fitted for some particular produce, is too small to supply the effectual demand. The whole produce can be disposed of to those who are willing to give somewhat more than [$p^n$] .... The surplus part of the price ... may commonly, in this case, and in this case only, *bear no regular proportion* to the like surplus in corn or pasture, but may exceed it *in almost any degree* .... The whole quantity of ... [certain] wines that is brought to market falls short of the effectual demand .... The whole quantity, therefore, can be disposed of to those who are willing to pay more .... The difference is greater or less, according as the fashionableness and scarcity of the wine render the competition of the buyers more or less eager. *Whatever it be*, the greater part of it goes to the rent of the landlord.
>
> (*WN*: 172; emphasis added; also 173–5)

Already, the possibility of prices prevailing, persistently, which are indeterminate from a theoretical standpoint – due to such situations of what may be called 'absolute' supply inelasticity (maximum feasible $Q < D^*$) – is raised in the *WN* price theory chapter: 'enhancements of the market price ... the effect of natural causes which may hinder the effectual demand from ever being fully supplied, and which may continue, therefore, to operate for ever'. This is raised there precisely in the context of possible causes of market prices persistently in excess of $p^n$, the other two notable sources being '[s]ecrets' and monopoly (*WN*: 77–8, esp. para. 20). The parallel between price under conditions of absolute supply inelasticity and under monopoly (of course, not mutually exclusive situations) is confirmed by the common language used to discuss them. Considering possible taxation of those wines for which $Q$ persistently 'falls so much short of the effectual demand', Smith comments that price is 'already *the highest that could be got* for the quantity commonly sent to market' (*WN*: 893; emphasis added). In *WN*, Book I, Chapter VII, monopoly price is described as 'upon every occasion *the highest which can be got*'.[40]

What is common to Smith's treatment of $p^m{}_i$ dynamics in the face of temporary market imbalance, and his treatment of instances of supply incapacity to accommodate $D^*$, is that limitations on $Q$ responsiveness – temporary on the one hand, persistent on the other – makes the prices outcome a creature of demand conditions. Smith quite rightly recognizes that theory cannot give determinate, quantitative expression to prices under those two circumstances.

Monopoly is then a further instance where constraint upon supply responsiveness deprives $p^n$ of the capacity to regulate $p^m{}_i$. These three sets of situations are distinct and particular embodiments of a single principle: *the indeterminacy of price magnitudes when competition acting through supply adjustment is impeded from causing convergence towards* $p^n$, or equivalently, the indeterminacy of demand-prices. For Smith's political economy there is no such thing as a theory of demand-price. Recall his characteristic phrase, supply-the-demand and the like, illustrated in section 3.2.1. The three sets of situations compared here are circumstances wherein supply-the-'demand' ($D^*$) does not occur, either temporarily or persistently, and therefore $p^n$ does not prevail. In the latter two cases, the result is a market price[41] persistently regulated by demand-prices which are essentially untheorizable, save to say that market price will exceed $p^n$, and vary in a definite direction with respect to the factors which shape demand.[42] These are not determinate prices because, implicitly but clearly enough, Smith's view is that demand-price cannot be theorized as can normal price (or 'supply-price', if one prefers). When he writes as he does at *WN* (234–5), this can only be made sense of in terms of Smith's believing that normal prices of (sufficiently) reproducible commodities can be determinately theorized, in a manner which the prevailing prices of insufficiently reproducible commodities, which hence reflect demand-prices, cannot. Supply- or normal price can be given determinate, quantitative theoretical expression; demand-prices, which prevail for commodities in inelastic supply with respect to $D^*$, cannot.

## 3.4 Competitive price and concepts of cost

Smith's theory of prices and income distribution is systematically presented in *WN*, Book I. But the very title of *WN*, Book I[43] points to the fact that the importance of prices is derivative from their significance for the production and distribution of wealth – the growth of product per worker and its division between wages, profits and rents – the fundamental object of Smith's science of political economy. The importance of price behaviour, including remuneration for production inputs, derives from the role of prices in production and distribution in decentralized market societies. It is also evident from the preceding sections that the magnitude of normal price, the anchor for market price behaviour, is determined by the natural rates of remuneration to owners of inputs, together with 'the' production method in use for each commodity.[44] To complete consideration of Smith's conceptualization of prices, we now inquire into the concept of 'cost' associated with the notion of normal price, as well as other notions of cost. The focus is upon Smith's conceptual framework. However, to clarify two aspects of the conceptualization in particular – the absence of latter-day supply functions, and the analogy (or otherwise) between natural pricing of commodities and natural remuneration for inputs – it is necessary also to enter into discussion of Smith's substantive theories of normal prices and of income distribution. We turn first to the question of commodity supply functions. It is clear from the argument of previous sections that Smith's treatment of $p^m{}_i$ convergence towards

$p^n$ has no recourse to latter-day demand functions: demand/price relations serve only to limit $p^m{}_i$ volatility in the face of market imbalances. What about relations between quantity supplied and prices? For the sake of completing an account of SAD in relation to his price theory, some consideration of (in particular, normal) prices in relation to quantities produced is in order. As a first approximation, this issue may be approached by considering how a supposition of what may be called 'quasi-constant costs' can be applied to the analysis.

### *3.4.1 Normal price and scale of production*

Smith's treatment of market price dynamics in terms of a $p^n$ anchor associated with a given level of production ($D^*$) might convey the impression that his normal price theory is a rather 'static' construction (cf. Campbell and Skinner 1976: 25–30; Skinner 1996: 140, 150, 164). But Smith evidently regards the normal prices of *WN*, Book I and the growth dynamics of Book II as elements of a single, unified theory. As a first approximation, any perception of tension or contradiction between the two may be corrected by interpreting normal price, in modern terms, as the average or unit cost of production, at natural rates of remuneration, associated with use of the 'dominant' method of production (Eatwell 1987: 599): the most widely employed method at any point in time, operated at the normal or desired level of capacity utilization of the associated configuration of plant, machinery, and so on; i.e. the fixed capital, or 'plant' for short (cf. Chapter 4, n. 61).[45] This is to define normal price as the unit opportunity cost associated with that particular or 'given' quantity of output, the normal capacity output. To be sure, this given quantity is not $D^*$. In general it will be some fraction of $D^*$, so long as normal capacity output is less than $D^*$. But what is true for this normal capacity output also will be precisely true for any magnitude, $D^*$, which is a whole-number multiple of this quantity, that number then determining the cost-minimizing number of plants, associated with the dominant production method, required in the industry. It will be roughly true, when $D^*$ is a non-integer multiple of that normal capacity output; and it will be more nearly approximately true, as the non-integer multiple becomes larger.[46] But it is not necessary for Smithian competition to prevail, that this multiple be a *very* large number, implying a very large number of plants: his concept of competition has far more kinship with the notion of 'contestable markets' than the notion of perfect competition.[47] Freedom of entry and exit, not a very large number of firms, is the key – freedom and *ease* of (i.e. low barriers to, or low costs of) entry and exit, one may more fully say.

Normal price so understood is entirely capable of playing a regulative role with respect to $p^m{}_i$ in situations of capital accumulation, growth and output variations in general, at least so long as production methods for each commodity or process are not subject to too rapid change.[48] The independence of $p^n$ from output changes under such quasi-constant-cost conditions, makes the supposition of given $p^n$ consistent with the output changes associated with converging of $p^m{}_i$ towards $p^n$, *and* consistent with output changes associated with the dynamics of accumulation and growth. Care must be taken here to distinguish between two different kinds of potential variations in costs as $Q$ varies:

1 variations in unit cost, hence diverging from $p^n$, as $Q$ deviates and converges with respect to $D^*$;
2 changes in normal cost and hence $p^n$, associated with changes in $D^*$ and normal industry output.

The former are of no relevance to the quantity/price outcome at $Q = D^*$ and $p^m{}_i = p^n$ – and we may put aside the possibility of any such cost variations fully or more than fully counteracting the non-normal profit signals which drive supply adjustment and the convergence dynamics when $p^m{}_i \neq p^n$. (Many such $Q$ adjustments will involve only variations in capacity utilization.) On the other hand, growth dynamics – involving as they do for Smith, changing effectual demands which typically are accompanied by technical change, as well as change in normal rates of remuneration – almost inevitably involve change in normal prices.[49] Hence, quasi-constant normal costs will not do as an account of his view of normal prices in relation to quantity produced, in general. For Smith, there are two particularly important manifestations of technical change associated with a path of accumulation and growth (with the rate of growth itself a highly contingent phenomenon): most especially, labour productivity growth associated with division of labour and extent of the market, but also, increasing scarcity of some natural resources. The course of normal distribution in the context of growth, also a determinant of the course of normal prices, will also be highly contingent.

To be sure, some of these forces shaping $p^n$ through time appear internal to particular industries, as the role of 'extent of the market' suggests. Two striking examples may be quoted:

> increase of demand … though in the beginning it may sometimes raise the price of goods, never fails to lower it in the long run. It encourages production, and thereby increases the competition of the producers, who, in order to undersell one another, have recourse to new divisions of labour and new improvements of art, which might never otherwise have been thought of.
> (*WN*: 748)

> In multiplying … the quantity of fish that is brought to market … ['the efficacy of human industry'] is … both limited and uncertain. It is limited by the local situation of the country, by the proximity or distance of its different provinces from the sea, by the number of its lakes and rivers, and by what may be called the fertility or barrenness of those seas, lakes and rivers, as to this sort of rude produce. As population increases, as the annual produce of the land and labour of the country grows greater and greater, there come to be more buyers of fish …. But it will generally be impossible to supply the great and extended market without employing a quantity of

> labour greater than in proportion to what had been requisite for supplying the narrow and confined one.... The fish must generally be sought for at a greater distance, larger vessels must be employed, and more expensive machinery of every kind made use of.
>
> (*WN*: 252–3)

The first of these clearly concerns economies internal to the industry; but they are not a result of quantity variation really, rather, a result of *the influx of competitors* stimulated by increasing demand. The second more directly pertains to variation of quantity, and the associated need to employ more costly production methods. Both are essentially dynamic processes, but more especially the former: distinct values of $p^n$ associated with different production methods at different points in time. Accounting for these two classes of phenomena will not lead to a priori supply functions, and certainly not to the notion of normal price in general as an increasing function of quantity produced. As to production methods, the course of normal costs and prices depends upon the contingent and competing influence of human ingenuity and natural scarcity.[50] Furthermore, these factors cannot be conceived of as entirely internal to particular industries: technical change interacts complexly and contingently with capital accumulation and distribution in the context of growth at the system-wide level, matters further considered in Chapter 4. But for the purposes of the quantity variations associated with eliminating $Q \neq D^*$, the supposition of constant normal costs and normal prices best fits Smith's accounts. Accounting for change in normal costs and their relation to scale of activity belongs to another level of analysis.

There is another vantage-point from which one can grasp that Smith's treatment of supply in relation to $p^n$ cannot resemble the latter-day notion of rising supply-price as quantity produced increases. This in turn helps further to explain why commodity demand functions would be uninteresting to Smith, even if he had ever conceived of them as a possibility. The concept of rising normal (or 'long-period') supply-price rests necessarily upon the SAD or marginal productivity approach to distribution. Demand functions for 'factors of production' – derived from supposed factor substitution in response to relative 'factor prices' – together with factor supplies, are deployed to determine market-clearing factor prices. But marginalist theory commonly assumes constant physical returns to scale in the technology available for commodity production. Why then does long-period supply-price rise as the quantity produced of any particular commodity increases? Supposedly, the equilibrium prices of the factors of production used relatively intensively in the production of that commodity rise as the demand for them rises, thereby inducing changes in factor proportions, and possibly factor supplies, so as to keep total factor demands and supplies equal (see Garegnani 1983). Smith has no such idea of factor prices. To take just the case of wages, in essence he has a bargaining-power approach, wherein the rate of capital accumulation relative to the rate of population growth proxies for the balance of power (see section 3.4.3). This is 'supply' (population growth) and 'demand' (capital accumulation) in a certain sense; but it is not the post-1871 sense, as is evident from the absence of any reference by Smith to a role for variable factor proportions in this context. In the absence of commodity supply functions of this kind, for the theory of normal prices latter-day commodity demand functions are otiose: the only demand that matters is $D^*$. And for his account of the competitive process linking $p^m{}_i$ and $p^n$, Smith requires only that, in the face of market imbalance, $Q$-net-of-$D^*$, and the difference between the average or most common value of $p^m{}_i$ and the level of $p^n$, vary appropriately in relation to each other.[51]

### *3.4.2 Four concepts of cost*

Smith's normal price is a concept of unit cost, a cost-price, in turn determined by production methods in use and normal rates of remuneration for inputs used up in production processes.[52] He does not explicitly consider the possibility of multiple production methods simultaneously in use in the production of particular commodities (see n. 44), a situation which would impose the question, *which* production method is associated with normal cost. It is as if he tacitly supposes an identical production method for all producers, or a single method extensively used; though Smith certainly attaches great importance to consideration of technical change over time. With production methods at any point in time treated as data, the determination of normal cost at that point in time reduces, for Smith, to the question of the determination of normal remuneration rates for inputs. Prior to a consideration of that issue, we examine his uses of 'cost'.

The *WN* price theory chapter takes as its point of departure the proposition that insofar as natural price is equivalent to opportunity cost, when a commodity is sold at normal price it 'is then sold precisely … for what it *really costs* the person who brings it to market' (*WN*: 72; emphasis added; also 505). Notice that this concerns the real cost *to the supplier*: it is the measure of cost relevant to the supply behaviour which drives $p^m{}_i$ convergence towards $p_n$, the process which is the central subject of that chapter. Elsewhere Smith deploys a different notion of real cost, along the lines of the inputs used up in the production of commodities, focusing particularly on labour input:

> It does not cost less labour to bring silver to Amsterdam than to Dantzick; but it costs a great deal more to bring corn. The real cost of silver must be nearly the same in both places; but that of corn must be very different.
>
> (*WN*: 209)

> The acquisition of … talents, by the maintenance of the acquirer during his education, study, or apprenticeship, always costs a real expence, which is a capital fixed and realized, as it were, in his person.
>
> (*WN*: 282)

> The debtors of such a bank, as … I have been giving some account of, were likely … to be chimerical projectors … who would employ the money in

> extravagant undertakings ... which, if they should be compleated, would never repay the expence which they had *really cost*, would never afford a fund capable of maintaining a quantity of labour equal to that which had been employed about them.
>
> (*WN*: 316; emphasis added; also 65–7; *LJA*: 333)

His tendency to identify inputs used up with labour is probably an expression of his conviction that the costs of production of commodities are reducible to wages, profits and rents (*WN*: 65–9), so that insofar as capital itself consists of produced commodities, this implies that all inputs are reducible to labour and natural resources. Natural resources are not a cost to society but are freely appropriated from nature (even if private property in land entails payment of rent), apart from any labour required for their appropriation: nature's 'labour costs no expence' (*WN*: 363; also 67, 265, 364). While the two notions of cost are different – opportunity cost to suppliers in Book I, Chapter VII, versus cost as inputs used up in production – they nevertheless are each particular expressions of a fundamental generic sense of cost: that which is foregone, given up or destroyed, in the gaining or acquiring of a thing.[53]

It is not necessary also to exhaustively detail the hundreds of references to 'expense' – or the more common spelling, 'expence'. That term frequently serves as a synonym for cost (e.g. *WN*: 178, 245, 460, 666–7 – as well as in other writings); but more often it is used to refer more generally to expenditures. The term is employed also in non-economic or figurative senses; for example: the labourer's 'dexterity at his own particular trade seems ... to be acquired at the expence of his intellectual, social, and martial virtues' (*WN*: 782). More important for Smith's various senses of 'cost' is that the second notion of cost noted immediately above, as inputs used up in production, is connected with a third notion of cost or price. Smith makes a distinction between real and nominal price, where the former refers to the exchange-value of a thing in terms of labour or commodities (but more particularly, labour), as distinct from its exchange-value in money (i.e. silver or gold).[54] The connection is explicit:

> [The] rise ... in the nominal or money-price of ... rude produce has been the effect, not of any degradation in the value of silver, but of a rise in their real price. They have become worth ... a greater quantity of labour and subsistence than before. As it costs a greater quantity of labour and subsistence to bring them to market, so when they are brought thither, they represent or are equivalent to a greater quantity.
>
> (*WN*: 245–6)

> the real price both of the coarse and of the fine manufacture, was ... much higher in ... antient, than it is in the present times. It cost a greater quantity of labour to bring the goods to market. When they were brought thither, therefore, they must have purchased or exchanged for the price of a greater quantity.
>
> (*WN*: 263; also 49–50)

*WN*, Book I, Chapter v is devoted to this concept of real price. The justification for it is worth quoting at length:

> Every man is rich or poor according to the degree in which he can afford to enjoy the necessaries, conveniencies, and amusements of human life.... The value of any commodity, *therefore*, to the person who possesses it ... is equal to the quantity of labour which it enables him to purchase or command ....
>
> The real price of every thing, what every thing *really costs* to the man who wants to acquire it, is the toil and trouble of acquiring it. What every thing is really worth to the man who has acquired it, and who wants to dispose of it or exchange it for something else, is the toil and trouble which it can save to himself .... What is bought with money or with goods is purchased by labour as much as what we acquire by the toil of our own body. That money or those goods indeed save us this toil. They *contain* the value of a certain quantity of labour which we exchange for what is supposed at the time to contain the value of an equal quantity. Labour was the first price, the original purchase-money that was paid for all things. It was not by gold or by silver, but by labour, that all the wealth of the world was originally purchased; and its value, to those who possess it and who want to exchange it for some new productions, is precisely equal to the quantity of labour which it can enable them to purchase or command.
>
> (*WN*: 47–8; emphasis added)

In this conception Smith conflates two distinct notions. On the one hand, he proposes an empirical, observable measure of value: the money price of a commodity divided by the money wage of some category of labour. On the other hand, in justifying this measure he appeals also to a psychological category, the pains of labour understood as the ultimate human cost of a commodity: not a measure at all.[55] Smith also speaks of the 'real price' of labour as the commodity real wage – 'the real command of the necessaries and conveniencies of life' – which is to make it the reciprocal of the real price of commodities (*WN*: 87; also 95–6, 104, 219, 224). He cannot define the real price of labour in the same manner as commodity real prices: the 'labour-commanded' value of a unit of labour is a unit of labour. His uneasiness with the concept of the real price of labour, due to its inconsistency with the idea of labour as the ultimate standard, is evident at *WN* (51), where it is called a (merely) 'popular' notion.

Even putting aside the ultimate-human-cost notion with its empirically empty psychologizing, the justification for the labour-commanded measure is that it reflects the command that possession of a commodity gives a person, over consumption goods in general ('necessaries, conveniencies ... amusements ... therefore'). This is strictly true only if the labour theory of value applies – only if commodities exchange in proportion to the labour time directly and indirectly required in their production.[56] Nevertheless, Smith also has an entirely sound motivation for the labour-commanded measure: the desire to provide a means of distinguishing changes in money values of commodities due to change in the production conditions or cost of the monetary instrument (gold and silver), from changes due to change in the production conditions or cost of the commodities themselves (*WN*: 49–50). However, labour-commanded value does not satisfactorily meet that objective. Since real price of a commodity so understood is just the reciprocal of the real wage expressed in that commodity, change in a commodity real price is synonymous with change in the commodity real wage. This may be associated with a change in production conditions and labour productivity with respect to consumed commodities or the commodity currency, but may also occur without any such change in production methods.

What then is the significance of real price as labour commanded? Putting aside the psychological notion, which is really a fourth notion of cost, logically separable from labour commanded, the whole drift of, for example, the *WN* (260–5) discussion of real price, as well as elsewhere (see n. 57), points to the answer. What Smith is seeking to capture, however inadvisable his chosen means, is a singular measure of true cost, conceived of as reducible to required labour input, and he also incorrectly believes this will serve as an adequate measure of command over other commodities.[57] Generally, certainly for manufacture, though not for all agriculture, Smith sees real prices falling in the course of material development; i.e. wages expressed in terms of those commodities rising. In any case, the important and operational scientific concept of cost-price – normal price as opportunity cost – in no way depends upon either the fruitless idea of grounding cost in 'ultimate' psychological phenomena, or the validity of labour commanded as a measure of something or other. Smith is more right than he realizes, when he comments:

> As it is the nominal or money price of goods … which finally determines the prudence or imprudence of all purchases and sales, and thereby regulates almost the whole business of common life in which price is concerned, we cannot wonder that it should have been so much more attended to than the real price.
>
> (*WN*: 55)[58]

### *3.4.3 Income distribution as pricing*

This leads naturally to a final issue, the theory of distribution which lies behind normal commodity prices. This is pertinent, in part, because of the apparent analogy between normal commodity prices and normal remuneration for inputs; and so, perhaps a parallel between the convergence of $p^{m}{}_{i}$ towards $p^{n}$, and the convergence of actual remunerations towards normal remunerations under competitive conditions. Already in sections 3.1 and 3.2 it has been shown how much Smith articulates remuneration for inputs (labour, capital, land), as 'prices', though far more commonly with regard to labour than capital and land, and as prices upon which competition acts. This suggests that commodity pricing and remuneration for production inputs are analogous processes. His theory of commodity price behaviour treats the natural rates of remuneration to labour, capital and land as given opportunity costs. That is to say, potential commodity suppliers or providers of inputs respond to the remuneration implied or offered in commodity prices, relative to merely assumed, alternative normal rates, available elsewhere. This involves no logical incoherence, but it leaves normal remunerations unexplained.

Does Smith provide accounts of normal rates of wages, profits and rents which are analogous to the theory of natural prices, and parallel conceptions of convergence of actual rates of remuneration towards natural rates? There are analogous aspects, but the parallels are far from complete, and less complete than Smith seems to suppose. The case of normal real wages offers the closest analogy. Here, the money value of the customary subsistence real wage is conceived of as the analogue for labour of the cost of production for commodities. It is the cost of (re)production of labourers, but including in this, the cost of altering population size in accord with the dictates of labour demand:

> the demand for men, like that for any other commodity, necessarily regulates the production of men; quickens it when it goes on too slowly, and stops it when it advances too fast. It is this demand which regulates and determines the state of propagation in all the different countries of the world .... The wages paid to journeymen and servants of every kind must be such as may enable them, one with another, to continue the race of journeymen and servants, according as the increasing, diminishing, or stationary demand of the society may happen to require.
>
> (*WN*: 98; also 162, 180, 568)

> The wages of the inferior classes of workmen ... are every where necessarily regulated by two different circumstances; the demand for labour, and the ordinary or average price of provisions. The demand for labour, according as it happens to be either increasing, stationary, or declining; or to require an increasing, stationary, or declining population, regulates the subsistence of the labourer, and determines in what degree it shall be, either liberal, moderate, or scanty. The ordinary or average price of provisions determines the quantity of money which must be paid to the workman in order to enable him, one year with another, to purchase this liberal, moderate, or scanty subsistence.
>
> (*WN*: 864 and *passim* to p. 876; cf. 103)

To this account of inferior wages, Smith adds a theory of competitive wage relativities under five principal heads, to determine normal wage rates in general (*WN*, Book I, Chapter VIII, esp. 85–6, with Chapter X, esp. 116–35). Bargaining power, expressed especially, though not exclusively, in the (im)balance of labour demand and supply, explains deviations of wages away from normal rates. But also, importantly, bargaining power enters as well into the explanation of the magnitude of the subsistence wage, as it differs between expanding, stationary and contracting economies:

> When in any country the demand for those who live by wages; labourers, journeymen, servants of every kind, is continually increasing; when every year furnishes employment for a greater number than had been employed the year before, the workmen have no occasion to combine in order to raise their wages. The scarcity of hands occasions a competition among masters, who bid against one another, in order to get workmen, and thus voluntarily break through the natural combination of masters not to raise wages.
>
> (*WN*: 86)

> In a year of sudden and extraordinary plenty, there are funds in the hands of many of the employers of industry, sufficient to maintain and employ a greater number of industrious people than had been employed the year before; and this extraordinary number cannot always be had. Those masters, therefore, who want more workmen, bid against one another, in order to get them, which sometimes raises both the real and the money price of their labour.
>
> The contrary of this happens in a year of sudden and extraordinary scarcity. The funds destined for employing industry are less than they had been the year before. A considerable number of people are thrown out of employment, who bid against one another, in order to get it, which sometimes lowers both the real and money price of labour.
>
> (*WN*: 103–4; also 83–91, 97–9, 101)

This is to make the subsistence real and money wage too elastic or flexible a concept to be a plausible anchor for actual wages, analogous to $p^n$ an anchor for $p^m{}_i$ (see also *WN*: 91–7). In particular, insofar as it varies with the three alternative growth possibilities, this purported anchor is not independent of SAD imbalances.[59] The tenuousness of the determination of wages by reference to any definite notion of subsistence is confirmed by Smith's treatment of tax incidence (see sec. 4.4.2). In addition, for the purposes of a general theory of normal commodity prices, there is a circularity: the normal money prices of commodities depend upon the normal rates of money wages, which in turn depend upon the normal money prices of all the commodities entering into the subsistence consumption. Nevertheless, the unsatisfactory conception of the wage anchor does not necessarily compromise the analogy between $p^m{}_i$ convergence and deviation with respect to $p^n$, and market wage convergence and deviation with respect to normal wages. That is to say, supposing that a normal real wage rate (and wage relativities) can be taken as plausibly determined in *some* manner, or treated as given (independent of SAD imbalances), then there is a genuine analogy between market commodity price dynamics and market wage dynamics, and as with commodities, it is the labour supply side which does the work of adjusting imbalances. This requires also that the circularity involved in the interdependence of normal money wages and the normal money prices of commodities entering into subsistence consumption can be resolved, so that the normal money wage rates are determinate magnitudes (see n. 94 below).

However, even this limited analogy does not extend to the cases of profit rates and rents. Nothing at all resembling an anchor is offered for the determination of profit rates (*WN*: Book I, Chapter IX), though the maximum and the minimum 'ordinary' profit rates are defined (*WN*: 113) and profit relativities are treated in Book I, Chapter X. The highly unsatisfactory attempt at a theory of rents in the following chapter of *WN* – the longest of the book (more than 12 per cent of the entire text) – is even more problematic (see Hollander 1973: 163–79; Brewer 1995). Hence while there is some important analogy between commodity pricing and labour pricing in Smith's approach to income distribution, this is far less so for profits and rents. There is therefore also no genuine symmetry between determination of normal values for the three sets of distributive variables. Nevertheless, here also, as with wage determination, if normal rates of profits (and rents on substitutable or homogeneous land) can be treated as given or otherwise satisfactorily determined, then under competitive conditions there is a genuine analogy between convergence and deviation of actual prices with respect to normal prices and convergence and deviation of actual remuneration rates with respect to normal rates.[60] Of course there is also something more than analogy in the relation between prices and remunerations: by the definition of normal price, equality of, or difference between, market and normal price entails equality of, or difference between, actual and normal remunerations.

The genuine analogy with respect to convergence is importantly revealing in one respect in particular. The mistaken idea that his treatment of commodity prices is akin to the SAD functions of latter-day marginalism, taken together with the evident parallels between commodity and labour pricing, could lead to the conclusion that SAD functions also are applied to labour. In fact, it was shown above that the behaviour of market prices under conditions of market imbalance proceeds from the impact of bargaining power, together with competition. Hence the true parallel for Smith is that in *both* the case of commodities and the case of labour, it is the balance of bargaining power which regulates the market outcomes for actual prices or actual wages, notwithstanding the absence of a satisfactory account of the anchor for the labour case. (Stated more positively, the absence of an anchor in the latter case is an expression of the fact that bargaining with respect to labour pricing determines also the *natural* wage.) The consistency between Smith's notion of market prices as signifying the particular concrete prices at which particular actual transactions occur, and his minimalist theoretical statements about average or most common market price, is to be understood in terms of the *overall* market imbalance influencing at least some if not all *actual* transactions prices. Overall market imbalance influences bargaining power in commodity transactions, in a manner analogous to Smith's conception of bargaining power informing the labour contract, both being embodiments of 'the higgling and bargaining of the market' associated with the human 'propensity to truck, barter, and exchange' (*WN*: 25,

49). (In any singular actual transaction, the proportion between 'supply' and 'demand' of course is necessarily unity.) Just as SAD in Smith's treatment of commodity markets is not SAD functions, so SAD in his treatment of wages is not SAD functions. In both domains, supply/demand balance[61] informs the behaviour of prices or wages by its impact upon the balance of bargaining power between the two sides involved in the exchanges or contracts. This is an important unifying conception behind his view of commodity pricing on the one hand and distribution on the other.

## 3.5 Prices and costs prior to Smith

### *3.5.1 Etymology*

We turn now to examine the history of concepts of price, supply, demand and cost, prior to Smith. But first, the etymology of these terms may briefly be considered. The term 'price' originates in thirteenth-century Middle English, from Old French, *pris* and late Latin, *precium* – conveying 'price, value, wages, reward', and in Old French, also 'honour, praise, prize'. The Middle English *pris* (and various other spellings) had all the Old French senses of 'price, value, honour, prize, praise'; but from the seventeenth century its literal meaning narrowed to just the modern sense: 'Money, or the like, paid for something': 'To haue vytaylles at reasonable prys' (1481); 'This making of Christians will raise the price of Hogs' (1596; Shakespeare); 'the Marchant thinketh that he cannot sell his goods at the prise currant' (1599); 'Purchased ... at the prise of much blood' (1656); 'The common price of the Bagnio [bathhouse], is two Aspres [a Turkish coin] to the Master' (1687). From almost the earliest times in English use, 'price' also has been figuratively employed to convey a generic notion of cost: '[w]hat it costs to obtain some advantage; that which is given, surrendered, or undergone, for the sake of something else' (*OED*: 'price'). 'Cost' itself entered fourteenth-century English from Old French, *cost* and *coust*, in turn from Roman. Variants of it appear in a wide range of European languages. Its primary meaning was always the one which it still conveys: 'That which must be given or surrendered in order to acquire, produce, accomplish, or maintain something; the price paid for a thing'. Interestingly, the term 'prime cost' – to refer to cost-price net of charges for distribution, wholesaling and retailing (i.e. cost of production) – evidently was in use before Smith (*WN*: 72–3): 'Some small quantity which was sold below the prime cost' (*c.* 1724; Jonathan Swift). From the earliest times, cost has been used also to convey the related sense of outlay or expenses (*OED*: 'cost').

'Supply' originates from Old French, *so(u)pleer* – earlier, *soup(p)leier,-oier*, later *supplier* – in turn from Latin, *supplēre* (*plēre*, to fill). In English from the fourteenth and fifteenth centuries, the verb carried the senses of to assist, succour, support, maintain; 'to make up a deficiency'; to 'fulfil, satisfy (a need or want) by furnishing what is wanted' (and also, to act as a substitute for): 'That he knowe not but that I haue supplyed All that I can his matter for to spede' (*c.* 1520); 'These ... virtues ... supplyeth y^e^ defautes that be lefte in y^e^ powers of the soul by synne' (1526); 'He supplyed vp the number of Senatours that were greatly decayed' (1579–80); 'Nature is supplide in him by Art' (1615); 'All living creatures he doth feed, And with full hand supplies their need' (1623). The noun came into use somewhat later, to convey the results of the actions denoted by the verb – assistance, succour, support, relief; 'The act of making up a deficiency, or of fulfilling a want or demand' – or to convey that which is supplied: 'Thow art ... My hope, support, and haill supplie' (1567); 'Heere will I lie in a bush to make a supply, if you shall faile in anything' (1598); 'To expend your time with vs a-while, For the supply and profit of our Hope' (1602); 'Why are usefull things good? because they minister to the supply of our wants and desires' (1768) (*OED*: 'supply').

'Demand' originates from the French, *demander* (and noun, *demande*) – in turn, derived from the Latin, *dēmandāre*. The *OED* comments:

> The transition from the Latin sense 'give in charge, entrust, commit, commend' to the Romanic sense 'request, ask', was probably made through the notion of *entrusting* or *committing* to any one a duty to be performed, of *charging* a servant, or officer, with the performance of something, whence of *requiring* its performance of him, or *authoritatively requesting* him to do it. Hence the notion of *asking* in a way that commands obedience or compliance, which the word retains in English, and of simple asking, as in French.... The verb probably passed into the vernacular from its legal use in Anglo-French.

Hence, from the fourteenth and fifteenth centuries, follows the senses of the English verb and noun: 'To ask for (a thing) with legal right or authority'; 'To ask for (a thing) ... in such a way as to command attention'; 'To call for or require as necessary; to have need of': 'Hys heyre myght haue an actyon for to demande the hole payement of hys wages' (1489); 'The Portugals demaunded [to know] the state of the realme' (1600); 'Those girles of Italy, take heed of them, They say our French lacke language to deny If they demand' (1601; Shakespeare). Derivative from this, the noun conveys then the act or action of so demanding. This notion of demand as authoritative request, which of course is still current, has a certain natural kinship with the subsequent economic sense of demand as material want backed by ability and willingness to pay. It is notable that in detailing and defining this sense, the *OED* cites no instances earlier than the eighteenth century: 'The calling for a thing in order to purchase it'; 'a call for a commodity on the part of consumers'; 'The manifestation of a desire on the part of consumers to purchase some commodity or service, combined with the power to purchase' (*OED*: 'demand'). In this economic context, demand as 'request' gains 'authority' precisely from being backed by ability to pay. To that extent, it is understandable that 'demand' came to serve as shorthand for the buy side of the market, during the eighteenth century.

### *3.5.2 The century prior to Smith*

It has been seen that for Smith (*WN*: 46, 73), market prices are actual prices, the particular prices at which actual transactions occur. This is not an equilibrium concept, in the sense of a uniform market price resulting from some form of competitive or arbitrage process, whereby differences in prices at which exchanges occur are eliminated. Nevertheless, it was also seen how Smith, by recourse to the most 'common' market price, can use a concept of market price – not merely to refer to a set of disparate prices at which actual transactions occur, but as a single magnitude – for the purposes of comparison with natural price and inferring price dynamics (sec. 3.1.1). Cantillon's influential *Essai* has much of the core Smithian conception of normal prices (in a certain sense), and of market prices, and of the relation between the two. He, more than Smith, comes close to the notion of a theoretically conceived, uniform market price. This arises in the context of a discussion of the role of towns which hold weekly markets, in effecting the circulation of commodities. Cantillon details advantages from villagers in a region all bringing their products to one central market in town, including the following:

> It would be almost impossible to fix the price of the produce and the merchandise in the Villages, between the Merchants and the Villagers. In one Village the Merchant would refuse the price asked for produce, hoping to find it cheaper in another Village, and the Villager would refuse the price offered for his merchandise in the hope that another Merchant would come along and take it on better terms.
>
> All these difficulties are avoided when the Villagers come to Town on Market-Days to sell their produce and to buy the things they need. Prices are fixed by the proportion between the produce exposed for sale and the money offered for it; this takes place in the same spot, under the eyes of all the Villagers of different Villages and of the Merchants or Undertakers [*Entrepreneurs*] of the Town. When the price has been settled between a few the others follow without difficulty and so the Market-price of the day is determined.
>
> (Cantillon 1755 [1931]: 11–13; also 27, 277–9)

Notice Cantillon's recourse to 'proportion' (*la proportion*) in articulating market price, which at first glance is suggestive of Smith's proportion between quantity brought to market and effectual demand. But in fact, at least the denominator of Cantillon's ratio is different from that of Smith. Even supposing Cantillon's notion of quantity supplied is equivalent to Smith's notion of quantity supplied, the latter has for the denominator a quantity of the commodity – the quantity which would be demanded if supplies are offered at the normal price – whereas the former has a quantity of monetary expenditure (or at least a quantity of expenditure 'offered'). Hence Cantillon's explanation of market price comes dangerously close to being a tautology: the market price on any market day, supposed as a uniform magnitude, is identically equal to the monetary expenditure on the commodity divided by the quantity supplied. The only thing that would enable avoidance of this inference is the recourse to expenditure 'offered', which might not mean *actual* expenditure; that is to say, which might be interpretable as a magnitude distinct from actual expenditure. Elsewhere, he offers a somewhat different formulation, less vulnerable to the charge of tautology, but also rather loosely expressed: 'the quantity of Produce or of Merchandise offered for sale, in proportion to the demand or number of Buyers, is the basis on which is fixed or always supposed to be fixed the actual Market Prices'. Cantillon admits at the same page, that the determination of market prices, so understood, 'has no exact or geometrical foundation, since it often depends upon the eagerness or easy temperament of a few Buyers or Sellers' (Cantillon 1755 [1931]: 119; cf. 47–53, 199, 277–9). This is reminiscent of Smith's position on demand-prices, and of Petty's disavowal of giving any precise determination to market prices, due to their contingent character (the latter, quoted below).

In any case, whether or not one gives it a generous interpretation, Cantillon's formulation concerning market prices appears to bear the imprint of Locke's economic writings, with which Cantillon certainly was familiar. Like Cantillon, Locke comes close to a tautological treatment of market prices:

> The *change* of … Marketable value of any Commodity in respect of an other Commodity or in respect of a standing common Measure, is … the alteration of some proportion, which that Commodity bears to something else.… This proportion in all Commodities, whereof money is one, is the proportion of their quantity to the vent. The Vent is nothing else, but the passing of Commodities from one owner to another in Exchange; and is then call'd quicker, when a greater quantity of any species of Commodity, is taken off from the Owners of it, in an equal space of time.… This Vent is regulated, *i.e.* made quicker or slower, as greater or less quantities of any Saleable Commodity are remov'd out of the way, and course of Trade; separated from publick Commerce; and no longer lie within the reach of Exchange.
>
> (Locke 1696: 67; emphasis added)

Again, as with Cantillon, even supposing Locke's supply side is equivalent to Smith's quantity supplied, the articulation of the demand side can be read in terms of just the actual expenditure. But it can be rescued from characterization as tautology by, perhaps charitably, supposing 'vent', in the sense of outlet for sale, to represent some notion of the strength of demand. (Law 1705: 5 criticizes Locke's language, replacing 'Vent' with 'Demand'.) In any case, Cantillon definitely parts company from Locke, and advances beyond him with regard to price theory, in having a conception beyond market price: a conception of an underlying cost-price towards which market prices will be drawn.

Instances of some variant or other of SAD being offered as an explanation of market price behaviour in the century or so prior to Smith could be multiplied many times over; but it is evident enough from the examples of Locke and Cantillon, that it would be a mistake to read these as SAD functions in the manner of latter-day marginalist theory.[62] They are also not identical to Smith's treatment of market prices, in terms of the relation between quantity supplied and effectual demand. They are rather, a kind of common sense notion of SAD imbalances, commonly more about explaining mere market price *fluctuations*, rather than *levels* of market prices. For all Locke's elaborate and sustained recourse to quantity and vent (or variants) in his economic writings, in the end he is offering little more than that, with respect to the behaviour or structure of prices:

> The *value* or *price* of any thing, being only the respective estimate it bears to some other, which it comes in Competition with, can only be known by the quantity of the one, which will exchange for a certain quantity of the other. There being no two things in Nature, whose proportion, and use does not vary, 'tis impossible to set a standing regular price between them. The growing plenty or scarcity of either in the Market; (whereby I mean the ordinary places, where they are to be had in Traffick) or the real Use, or changing fashion of the place bringing either of them more into demand than formerly, presently varies the respective value of any two Things. You will as fruitlessly endeavour to keep two different Things steadily at the same price one with another, as to keep two Things in an *Æquilibrium*, where their varying weights, depend on different Causes.
>
> (Locke 1696: 169–70)

That the common sense notion is not Smith's conception, certainly on the demand side, is evident from the fact that his demand-side conception presupposes the notion of normal price – and most of these authors in the century or so prior to Smith have no such conception. All they are generally offering is a common sense law of markets whereby the interplay of SAD causes price fluctuations.

In fact, one need not overstate this point. Even if some or other of the rather imprecisely articulated appeals to variants of SAD in early modern economic literature are attempts to account for levels of market prices, rather than merely changes, this is of no moment for interpreting the significance of those key developments during the century prior to Smith, which point beyond this notion, towards the Smithian conception of market prices versus normal price. North (1691: 518), for example, like Locke, refers price changes to something like SAD: 'plenty makes cheapness… as Corn, Wool, &c. when they come to Market in greater Quantities than there are Buyers to deal for, the Price will fall'. But Fortrey (1673: 239), on the other hand, articulates something like SAD in a manner which appears intended to be more about price level: 'Where the commodity is scarce, and the vent great, the purchase is alwaies dear'. Smith's approach, and its putting aside any pretence of giving determinate, quantitative theoretical expression to market prices in general and demand-prices in particular (sec. 3.3.2), was and remains sound, and exposes the frailty or emptiness of any such apparent SAD 'explanations' of market price levels. Prior to Smith, notions of interacting supplies and demands influencing prices led to no definite price magnitude, as an outcome of such processes, unless accompanied by some notion or other of cost of production. In particular, it is the introduction of a role for the discipline of competition, in enforcing a tendency towards a definite cost-price, which is the crucial breakthrough, culminating, to a certain extent, in Smith's price theory. From this perspective, earlier SAD accounts of prices which may be read as being about market price levels, if they have no recourse to a notion of cost-price, are incapable of giving any definite and less vague explanation of price magnitudes, precisely because the absence of competitive markets means that market prices are not 'unified' and disciplined by supply-side normal cost.[63] In the absence of any notion of a normal price magnitude regulating SAD, all that can be in play in any such SAD interpretations of the level of market prices is just the balance of bargaining power between potential suppliers and demanders, with no definite quantitative outcome determinable (cf. Roncaglia 2005: 142–3). Smith's theory of normal prices, and those of the writers before him who advanced similar notions, introduce a discipline upon bargaining power and pricing, enabling a determinate theory of price, given sufficient time for competition to assert itself.

In the century or so prior to Smith one indeed does see an emerging tradition of a theory of normal prices, explained by reference to objective determinants – that it to say, factors observable in principle – and with those prices understood as the values towards which market prices will tend. Supplies and demands thereby come to be understood as subject to the discipline of this anchor, by some form or other of competitive market activity. This is entirely compatible with the common-sense law of markets, but is itself a vital new and additional theoretical advance in the making of modern political economy. As is seen clearly in Smith, as a culmination of these pioneering developments, while the balance of supplies and demands may be the proximate cause of price behaviour, in a system of integrated markets regulated, in some measure, by competitive activity, those supplies and demands themselves will be regulated by deeper forces: normal price (and thereby its determinants), or more precisely, differences between normal price and market prices.[64] It is this kind of conception of an anchor for market prices, some notion or other of normal price, which is very much less to be found prior to Smith, as against common sense SAD approaches to market price behaviour. From that standpoint, whether or not the conceptualizations of market prices along the lines of Locke or Cantillon may properly be regarded as tautological is of no great moment. Even if these are treated as at least roughly equivalent to Smith's conception of the temporary, or day-to-day, determination of market prices, the important issue is whether or not earlier writers have a conception of an objective anchor explaining a more persistent dynamic tendency of market prices; that is to say, a notion of natural or normal price, along something like the lines Smith articulated. Cantillon does; Locke does not. Cantillon himself has a clear understanding of this difference between his theory and Locke's contribution (even if tacitly unfair to at least Petty, in asserting that this judgement applies to 'all' English writers):

> the real [or 'intrinsic'] value of everything used by man is proportionable to the quantity of Land used for its production and for the upkeep of those who have fashioned it.... Mr Locke who, like all the English writers on this subject, *has looked only to Market Prices*, lays down that the value of all things is proportionable to their abundance or scarcity, and the abundance or scarcity of the silver for which they are exchanged.... I consider that Mr Locke's idea is correct in the sense of the following Chapter ['Of Market Prices'], and not otherwise.
>
> (Cantillon 1755 [1931]: 115–17; emphasis added)[65]

Before Smith, there emerges in a line of intellectual development running from Petty through Cantillon to the Physiocrats, Turgot and Steuart, a clear and definite conceptualization of normal prices, towards which market activity would draw actual or market prices, with the normal price of any particular commodity explained by reference to objective factors of one kind or another. However those objective factors might differ as between these various writers, what is common to them all is that they involve a notion of cost of production, in turn explained by reference to production methods and the remunerations for use of inputs used up in production. The earliest clear formulation of a general *explanatory* or descriptive notion of normal price, so understood as a kind of centre towards which actual or market prices in fact will be drawn, is to be found in Petty (1662: 90).[66] He defines 'natural dearness and cheapness' in terms of production conditions, in particular, labour input: 'the few or more hands requisite' to production of a commodity. It is symptomatic of the pre-capitalist character of the social economy Petty theorizes, that he distinguishes this natural cost from 'Political Cheapness [which] depends upon the paucity of Supernumerary Interlopers into any Trade over and above all that are necessary'. This 'true Political Price computed upon naturall grounds', expressed in terms of 'the common artificiall Standard Silver', then gives 'the true Price Currant'.

In Petty's world, competition cannot be relied upon to ensure technically efficient production methods are in use, so that political price in general is the benchmark expressing the objective determinants of price. He immediately indicates that a variety of 'contingent Causes' can 'adde or take away from the price of things' – 'in the judicious foresight and computation whereof lies the excellency of a Merchant' (Petty 1662: 90). This comment indicates clearly enough that the distinction between natural and political price on the one hand, and contingent influences upon prices on the other, is intended to capture a distinction between the objective and persistent determinants of prices ('the permanent Causes', he calls them at the same page), and factors causing market price fluctuations or deviations around the objective benchmark. This is confirmed elsewhere, where Petty proposes a form of labour theory of value to explain the price of corn and of gold, in terms of silver. This, he says, is 'the way of pitching the true proportion' between their values, 'which many times is set but by popular errour, sometimes more, sometimes less, diffused in the world', and continues: 'This, I say, to be the foundation of equallizing and ballancing of values; yet in the superstructures and practices hereupon, I confess there is much variety, and intricacy' (Petty 1662: 43–4; cf. 50–1; Aspromourgos 2000: 67–8).

If it is unclear what forms of exchange and market processes are implied by Petty's price theory, Cantillon's formulation some seventy years later certainly is articulated in terms of a social economy in which markets operate so as to draw prices into the neighbourhood of normal price, which he most commonly conveys by the term 'intrinsic value' (*valeur intrinseque*). This is a notion of cost of production in terms of land and labour input; hence the title of the key chapter dealing with it: '*The Price and Intrinsic Value of a Thing in general is the measure of the Land and Labour which enters into its Production*'. The cost of production is constituted by the quantity and cost of land (i.e. the rental price) and the quantities and costs of the various kinds of labour required for production. Market prices can diverge from intrinsic value, due to SAD imbalances: for example, the influence of 'the Humours and Fancies of men' on the demand side; or on the supply side, if 'the Farmers in a State sow more corn than usual, much more than is needed for the year's consumption' (Cantillon 1755 [1931]: 27–9). Hence follows Cantillon's general perspective on the subject, close to Smith's conception in a formal sense:

> the impossibility of proportioning the production of merchandise and produce in a State to their consumption causes a daily variation, and perpetual ebb and flow in Market Prices. However, in well organised Societies the Market Prices of articles whose consumption is tolerably constant and uniform do not vary much from the intrinsic value ....
>
> (Cantillon 1755 [1931]: 31; also 97, 117–21)

As to the determination of intrinsic value, production methods for commodities are simply taken as given. The wage-rates used in the calculation of these Cantillonian normal prices are understood as those associated with customary subsistence real wages, different for different kinds of labour, together with a range of other factors entering into wage relativities (e.g. skill, risk, trust), strikingly similar to the factors suggested also by Smith. Furthermore, land-rent is included as an element of the cost of production entering into the determination of intrinsic value. The latter two aspects, taken together, lead to a remarkable result, of which Cantillon is well aware: intrinsic values will be proportional to the quantity of land directly and indirectly required to produce the various commodities, including in this, the land required to produce the consumption of required labour. That is the ultimate objective content of his intrinsic values.[67]

The objective approach to theorizing the structure and behaviour of prices developed by Petty and Cantillon gains greater maturity in the hands of others in the eighteenth century, most notably, Quesnay, Turgot and Steuart. In Quesnay, this is articulated in terms of 'fundamental price' (*prix fondamental*), and in Steuart, in terms of 'real value' – though both their theories are compromised by a degree of indeterminacy with regard profits in relation to prices.[68] One may say that the key divide between Smith and all the earlier writers with an objective approach to the determinants of a normal price, with one exception, is the absence of any clear notion of profits or rate of return on capital as such, incorporated as an element of normal price (cf. Chapter 4, n. 87). That it to say, normal price is a cost-price not inclusive of normal profit per unit of output, in the manner of Smith. To that extent, these theories from the century before Smith are concerned with a pre-capitalist social economy, though there is certainly a form of competition at work, already even in Cantillon's conception, and Quesnay pioneers capital theory (see sec. 4.3.7). The one exception is Turgot. His remarkable *Réflexions* enunciate clearly the dynamic, competitive tendency to equalization of returns, and its significance for the behaviour and structure of prices. Various forms of income-earning wealth are distinguished: land, interest-bearing loans, and capital advances in manufacture, agriculture and merchandising (Turgot 1769–70 [1977]: 64–77). The functional distinction, not to be found in Cantillon, between pure profits as a return for capital advanced, versus entrepreneurial returns as quasi-wages for superintendence and risk-bearing, is also clearly drawn. Turgot illustrates this at one point with the example of an owner of capital in leather manufacture,

> who will wait for the sale of the leather to return him not only all his advances, but also a profit sufficient to compensate him for what his money would have been worth to him, had he turned it to the acquisition of an estate [i.e. a landed estate], and moreover, the wages due to his labour and care, to his risk, and even to his skill; for surely, if the profits were the same, he would have preferred living without any exertion on the revenue of the land which he could have purchased with the same capital.
>
> (Turgot 1769–70 [1977]: 70; also 71, 74, 86)

That competition tends to establish a systematic relation between the alternative yields in the five employments of income-earning wealth is also entirely explicit: 'the annual product which can be drawn from capitals invested in these different employments, are influenced by each other, and are all related to the current rate of the interest of money'. The rate of return on land ownership is generally the lowest yield, because it entails little superintendence and the least risk. Interest rates on loans will be somewhat higher than returns on land because, though the superintendence is even less than that associated with land ownership, the lender faces the possibility that 'the insolvency of his debtor may cause him to lose his capital'. (That is to say, the difference is that a landowner faces no risk of losing the asset itself.) In turn, investments in agricultural, manufacturing and merchandising enterprises will require yet higher returns: 'for since these employments require, in addition to the capital advanced, much care and labour, if they were not more lucrative, it would be more advantageous to secure an equal revenue which might be enjoyed without having to do anything'. Here, 'besides the interest of the capital', the yield must compensate the entrepreneur's

> care, his labour, his talents and his risks, and to furnish him in addition that with which he may replace the annual wear and tear of his advances, which he is obliged from the very first to convert into effects which are liable to deterioration and which are, moreover, exposed to all kinds of accidents.

The difference in these yields therefore 'does not prevent them from having a reciprocal influence on each other, nor from establishing a kind of equilibrium amongst themselves' (Turgot 1769–70 [1977]: 85–7; also 75).

In this account, one sees a clear conceptualization of a competitive tendency towards equalization of the net returns from holding wealth in the variety of major forms Turgot perceives as available in the mid-eighteenth-century French social economy. However, no definite direction of causation between the various yields is suggested. That is to say, one can infer from the logic of Turgot's argument that, given the general level of any one of the five categories of yields, the premia required to compensate for differences in entrepreneurial superintendence and risk in the other categories, will determine the other four sets of yields, under the pressure of competition. There is just one degree of freedom here for the levels of yields across the board. But Turgot does not specify any one among these yields as the independent variable determining the others. All he specifies is that the yields will tend to a definite relation with each other – '*are limited by each other*'. The interest rate on loans is suggested as 'a kind of thermometer' or 'index' of yields in general; but this is not about causation from interest to other yields. It is just to indicate, as does Smith (*WN*: 105–6), that interest rates are the most visible evidence of the general level of yields. The systematic implications of the equalization of net returns for the structure of prices, in terms of the determination of *normal* prices, are not laid out with the clarity and fullness provided by Smith, but the link is made. Contemplating a situation in which the required net rate of return on capital in a nation is 2 per cent rather than 5 per cent, Turgot comments: 'as its manufacturers and merchants can content themselves with a lower profit, they will place their goods on all markets at a much lower price' (Turgot 1769–70 [1977]: 87–8). Furthermore, the entire discussion of net yield equalization makes clear that the prices associated with this process are understood to cover production costs, including depreciation of capital, as well as profit rates gross of entrepreneurial required returns. There is also a variant of SAD offered, evidently intended to explain market prices in general, in terms of prices 'determined by the chaffering of seller and buyer; by the balance between the offer and the demand' (Turgot 1769–70 [1977]: 77; also 81). These inferences are confirmed by other writings.[69]

### *3.5.3 Market prices and the 'just' price*

Thus in the century prior to *WN* one observes the development of objective theories of price built around some concept or other of cost-price; and it was a cumulative scientific development, in the sense that Smith and the others built upon predecessors. More widely, the early modern economic literature at the same time is replete with SAD interpretations of prices or price changes. From the standpoint of the early modern theorists of an objective notion of price, from Petty forward, SAD and the market prices or price changes associated with SAD naturally appeared as transitory ebb and flow – a conception which finds a beautiful clarity and culmination in Smith's treatment of natural and market prices, but also in Turgot. To be more precise, SAD appear not as the ultimate causes of prices; they appear as the merely proximate causes, causes which themselves ultimately will be regulated by any divergences between market prices and cost-price, via the agency of competition in some sense or other. From this viewpoint, shifting balances of bargaining power in the market, associated with the ebb and flow of SAD imbalances are now anchored by the discipline of cost-price. Hence Cantillon's comment (quoted above), that Locke *et al.* had considered 'only' market prices. In short, in early modern economic literature prices, their changes or levels, are understood by reference either to variants of SAD, or to SAD together with a deeper notion of cost-price. Only in the latter framework could the significance of differences between market prices and normal price come into play. Only the notion of a cost-price anchor could give definite content to the determination of a *level* of price. What of the understandings of prices prior to the modern era, in medieval and ancient thought?[70] To the extent that the intellectual developments around concepts of normal price sketched above are a reflection of reality, one has reason to infer that the systematic role of competitive forces in market processes in general is a phenomenon that emerges only in the eighteenth century. This by itself gives reason, a priori, to doubt that there would be descriptive theories of prices in earlier times, for anything resembling a decentralized, competitive market economy. That is to say, it gives reason to doubt that ancient and medieval thought would offer anything commensurate to price theory in the modern sense. These doubts are confirmed by a consideration of the character and significance of such earlier writings on exchange and prices.

With regard to Scholastic economic thought, the concept of the 'just price' is of primary interest (hereafter, $p^j$). Though at first glance it might seem that notions of $p^j$ are quite distinct from the question of the determination and behaviour of actual prices, in practice the former kind of inquiry is inseparable from the latter: to form a judgement concerning the divergence between, or coincidence of, $p^j$ and actual prices, one must almost inevitably posit an understanding of the factors determining actual prices as well as $p^j$. Two distinct currents appear to run through the medieval rendering of $p^j$. Or at least, there are two distinct currents of latter-day interpretation of its meaning: on the one hand, a mere notion of the prevailing market price; on the other, a sense of a cost-price (more on the latter below). We say 'mere' market price because the notion of the prevailing market price simultaneously could incorporate a notion of cost-price, if conditions are supposed in which prevailing market price is at one and the same time, cost-price – or market prices are understood as strongly tending towards cost-price. (This is precisely what the subsequent objective approach of Smith and others certainly involves, under competitive conditions.) The idea of the prevailing market price as the $p^j$, itself has three distinct strands of possible meaning:

1 it could be that price at which *any* particular, individual, voluntary exchange occurs;
2 it could be a *common* market price, associated with the generality of exchanges in the market at a point in time, so that any particular exchanges at prices different from that ordinary price may be deemed unjust;
3 or it could be an even stronger sense of the latter, a notion of a common or ordinary market price *of some persistence through time.*

The second is significantly different from the third, because the latter allows the possibility of a price which even 'everybody' has to pay, at some particular point in time, being nevertheless unjust. The obvious example is an extraordinary, adverse supply shock to the market for an agricultural staple of consumption (typically, a crop failure). The unusually high market price, or average market price, which is then likely to prevail temporarily – though by the standard of the second strand, common and hence just – could be deemed unjust by the standard of the third strand (cf. Hamouda and Price 1997: 196, 199, 204–6, on the medieval economy as 'an economy of shortages'). Both the second and the third are expressions of a kind of normative 'law of one price' (see p. 118).

Cajetan (Tomas de Vio) in the sixteenth century provides an example of the notion of any particular price resulting from voluntary exchange being just, in terms of the price paid 'in a certain place and in a certain way of selling'; so that if a house valued at 4,000 sells for a quarter of that, '[w]e say that the just price is one thousand as today no buyer was prepared to pay more' (quoted in Chafuen 2003: 81). Variants of one or other of the second and third strands of identification between market price and $p^j$ – common market price, in some sense, as $p^j$ – are expressed in Scholastic thought, in terms of the $p^j$ as the common estimate of the market. Hence Francisco de Vitoria in the sixteenth century proposes that, in a market of many buyers and sellers, 'common estimation' sets the $p^j$; an exchange at any other price, due, for example, to 'frauds and deceits', is unjust. Since Vitoria explicitly says that neither the labour required to produce a commodity, nor any price previously paid for it, is relevant to the $p^j$, it is avowedly made independent of cost (quoted in Chafuen 2003: 82–3). Monopoly, especially with respect to consumption staples, constitutes another source of price deviating from the common market version of $p^j$, much condemned in ancient and medieval literature (Wood 2002: 138–43). Approaches to common market price along the lines of the third strand are evident in Kaye's (1998: 89) characterization of regulatory practice in the fourteenth century and beyond:

> princes and city councils maintained the right to regulate market prices in the name of the common good. Maximum price edicts remained a traditional government response to economic crises. As a rule, however, such interference was never more than temporary. In the all-important area of grain, wine, and other agricultural products, prices were expected to fluctuate and were allowed to do so. [Footnotes are attached to some of these sentences.]

Kaye (1998: 126–7) also contrasts the position of Aquinas, who regarded a very high grain price during times of abnormally limited supply as unjust, with that of Peter John Olivi (both thirteenth century), who regarded it as acceptable and beneficial. Olivi also defended the legitimacy of buying cheap and selling dear, because 'otherwise the whole *communitas* would be sinning since everyone desired it', but interestingly, qualified this by reference to whether exchange-value expressed the 'common estimate of the common good' (Kaye 1998: 154; also 126, n. 41). That the broad thrust of the medieval Scholastic literature was against the first strand of interpreting $p^j$ is confirmed by Langholm's (1992: 93) conclusion that the maxim of the Roman law commentators (to which they themselves did not, in any case, strictly adhere) – that a thing is worth as much as it can be sold for – contradicts the Scholastic doctrine of justice in exchange, which 'presumes the existence of a just price which may be different from the highest price obtainable in any given situation'. Wood (2002: 135–6), in opposition to de Roover's (1958) view that $p^j$ was simply the current market price, takes a more nuanced view, that such a normal price could have legal and moral significance, without necessarily being just as such, noting Aquinas's ambivalence. She also emphasizes medieval economic literature's deriving from two distinct traditions: the Christian scriptures and Aristotle on the one hand, as well as Roman law on the other (Wood 2002: 132–3, 147–9).

The notion of mere-market-price, in one or other sense, as the benchmark for $p^j$ appears as a kind of conventionalism: the $p^j$ is whatever exchange-ratio voluntary market exchange gives rise to, the only question being whether this is true for any particular exchange, or for only some notion of the common market exchange rate. Furthermore, the market price so understood, independent of cost, would appear to be explained as a price resulting from the interplay of SAD in some sense. This SAD conventionalism is evident in San Bernadino's fifteenth-century distinction between an objective and natural use-value ('*virtuositas*'), and desirability ('*complacibilitas*'), where the latter, with scarcity ('*raritas*'), determines legitimate exchange-values (Chafuen 2003: 81). It is evident also in the willingness of some among the Scholastics to declare that it was legitimate to charge a high price for bread in times of famine. But this apparently radical conventionalism commonly was underpinned by a belief that provisioning of the poor and so on, was a responsibility of the community as a whole, rather than a responsibility of merchants in exchange (Chafuen 2003: 88–90). Indeed, while at first glance the common-estimate-of-the-market notion of $p^j$ might appear as a mere variant of SAD, in some cases at least, it appears intended rather as a kind of communal standard, imbued with social norms or custom, not the price outcome of a market of interacting, anonymous and asocial individuals – hardly surprising in the circumstances of pre-modern societies (cf. Wood 2002: 136, 138). Baldwin (1959: 20) describes the $p^j$ conception in ancient Roman law as

> a normal and customary price, which can be determined in commerce of free exchange which is regular and orderly. It is contrasted with an overcharged or a trifling price or a price based on the prejudiced affections of one of the parties. In all cases the just price seldom appears as a general transcendental standard of value but rather as an individual estimation for each case [i.e. for individual *commodities*, not persons] based on the market conditions of the time and place.

Kaye (1998: 91–2) comments on this:

> The identification of just price with market price is conveyed in two nearly identical texts from the *Digest* (a sixth-century compendium of Roman law) that state: 'The prices of things are determined not by their value and utility to individuals, but by their value determined commonly.'

Quoting Langholm (1987: 125) – *communis aestimatio* 'came to mean specifically the kind of estimate which the total community makes unintentionally through the impersonal working of the economy' – Kaye (1998: 93) further comments: 'the just price achieved through a supra-personal process, as the product of a common estimation that shifted according to common need and scarcity … was understood within both canon and civil law as a shifting, relativistic determination'. Why this should be understood as unintentional and impersonal is not so clear. In any case, distinguishing a mere SAD notion of common estimate from a customary-norm notion of common estimate is inherently difficult, since customary notions of normal price could not be independent of (temporally persistent) conditions of production, natural scarcity – and demand, indirectly, via the possible influence of quantity produced upon cost. (Natural scarcities certainly imposed themselves with greater force in the pre-modern world.) Hence, from the standpoint of modern political economy, the second and third strands of the notion of $p^j$ as prevailing market price, but not the first, can be read as norms for regulating or judging bargaining power in relation to individual exchanges – whether with respect to a conventional, common market price from day-to-day, or a more temporally persistent common market price (or indeed, a cost-price: cost can change over time as well).[71]

To that extent, the $p^j$ appears as an institution aimed at playing the role in the pre-modern social economy, which free competition plays in the economy theorized by Smith and others. Or to put the point the other way around, Smith's natural price concept can be conceived of as a kind of transposition of a Scholastic ethical notion of just price. This is so insofar as the latter is, in some sense or other, market price under normal conditions, with unjust prices resulting from abnormal or extraordinary bargaining power in circumstances of abnormal market imbalance (on one side or the other, though more typically, on the supply side). In fact, Smith's normal prices have normative significance as well (see n. 17 above). His willingness to endorse a legal maximum interest rate, though at a level in line with market-determined rates (*WN*: 356–7), and to at least entertain the possibility of government price regulation in circumstances where a staple commodity is subject to monopoly supply (*WN*: 158), have some kinship with medieval $p^j$ notions. (The context of *WN*: 158 makes clear enough that Smith regards competition as a substitute for traditional price regulation.) This willingness to contemplate legal regulation, because competition enforcing natural price cannot be guaranteed, confirms that Smith regards natural prices as just exchange rates in some sense; though for him, in the case of produced commodities, these are definitely exchange rates in accordance with cost under competitive conditions (but cf. n. 78 below). For Smith, competition is a substitute for legal enforcement of $p^j$. But the debt market is an exception, and where competition does not prevail, traditional legal interventions might be desirable.

### *3.5.4 Aristotle's formula*

The ancient roots of European medieval thought, especially in Aristotle, is as much evident with regard to prices and exchange as other social topics. But as Kaye (1998: 64–5) points out, no definite theory of a 'just price' is to be found in Aristotle. Here are the key Aristotle passages on the matter, in an account of justice in exchange which runs to a mere three pages or so in modern print:

> let *A* be an architect, *B* a shoemaker, *C* a house, and *D* a shoe. Then the architect must receive from the shoemaker the latter's work and must himself[72] ... give him in return his own work. First, then, if the proportion is an equality and reciprocity takes place, what will be done is what we have called 'just'.... [N]othing prevents the product of one artist from being better than that of another, and these should be equalized.... For an association for exchange is not formed by two doctors but by a doctor and a farmer, and, in general, by artists who are different and unequal and who require equal exchanges.
>
> ... Accordingly, as an architect is to a shoemaker, so should the number of shoes be to one house; for if this were not so, there would be neither exchange nor association. But this proportion would be impossible if the goods exchanged were not somehow equal. All goods to be exchanged, then, should be measurable by some standard .... In reality, *this measure is*

the *need* which holds all things together; for if man had no needs at all or no needs of a similar nature, there would be no exchange or not this kind of exchange.... That need holds these together as a single thing is clear from the fact that if the two parties, whether both or only one, do not need each other, they do not make the exchange .... A coin, ... like a measure, by making goods measurable by the same unit, makes their equalization possible; for neither would an association of men be possible without exchange, nor exchange without equalization, nor equalization without measurement by the same unit. It is true that goods whose difference is great *cannot be measured by the same unit*, but when *referred to* the *needs* of men *they become sufficiently measurable.*

(Apostle 1975: 87–8; emphasis added)[73]

What definite content does this give to the determination of exchange ratios, actual or just? Langholm (1992: 186) rightly interprets Aristotle's 'square of exchange' between the architect (characterized as a 'builder' in some translations) and the shoemaker merely to mean that 'need or demand is the *cause of exchange*', rather than 'need or demand, quantitatively expressed [by means of money, determining] ... the just exchange ratio'. Hollander (1965: 621–2) takes a somewhat similar view, with respect to both Aristotle and Aquinas, that the role of demand is of a kind with the classical economists' view that use-value is merely prerequisite to exchange-value. The latter is also emphatic that for both, $p^j$ is explained by reference to relative costs including remunerations at least partly determined by a social hierarchy of occupations (Hollander 1965: 618–22). But it is drawing too long a bow to infer from Aristotle's rather slight discussion of exchange, with its oblique implications of something like labour and/or cost, that there is a notion of cost-prices there. Baldwin's judgement is to be preferred in this respect:

> By declaring that human want was the true and universal standard of value of [*sic* – 'in' intended?] exchange, Albert the Great and Thomas Aquinas were completely Aristotelian in their analysis. The two medieval commentators, however, did not stop at that point. Beginning with Albert, the two theologians added a second basis which was foreign to the text of Aristotle. Value was also based upon the factors of labor and expenses (*labores et expensae*).
>
> (Baldwin 1959: 74; cf. Vivenza 2001: 146–50)

In any case, one must ask: what could the notion of equality in exchange, based upon a supposed standard of human need (or want, or demand) possibly mean? Neither Aristotle, nor indeed, any who subsequently followed his lead, give any definite content to this idea, unless the conventionalist identification of $p^j$ with some variant of market price is regarded as imputing definite content to it. This notion of equal exchange, so much discussed in the secondary literature on Aristotle and in the subsequent Aristotle-inspired medieval literature, seems quite empty.

The point may be made as follows. Use-value for Aristotle is far from having a 'subjective' meaning, in the manner of the later marginalist approaches to price theory, in terms of reduction to some kind of homogeneous substance ('utility', pleasure or satisfaction), in turn grounded in individually idiosyncratic preferences. Nor does it have any kinship with the weaker notion of subjectivity, in terms of a supposed arbitrariness of human desires, individual or collective. He rather has an objective conception of use: the use-value of a chair is sitting, the use-value of a hat is covering the head, and so on. Use-values are heterogeneous, each specific to qualitatively distinct human purposes that things are fitted to serve. (This is likewise true for Smith: see p. 124.) Such a notion of distinct use-values, given order or hierarchy by reference to need and ultimate human purposes, is evident in Aristotle's discussion of household management in the *Politics* (Barker 1946: 1–38, being Book I). This is the key statement of the distinction between use-value and exchange-value:

> All articles of property have two possible uses.... The one use is proper and peculiar to the article concerned; the other is not. We may take a shoe as an example. It can be used both for wearing and for exchange.... Even the man who exchanges a shoe, in return for money or food, with a person who needs the article, is using the shoe as a shoe; but since the shoe has not been made for the purpose of being exchanged, the use which he is making of it is not its proper and peculiar use. The same is true of all other articles of property.... Exchange is possible in regard to them all: it arises from the natural facts of the case, and is due to some men having more, and others less, than suffices for their needs.
>
> (Barker 1946: 23; cf. Chapter 2, n. 39)[74]

For the purposes of exchange, 'need' as such, can then be understood as giving ethically informed hierarchy to the various distinct use-values, reducing them to a kind of commensurability. That is to say, a hierarchy of legitimate or 'natural' human needs provides a kind of standard for determining legitimate exchanges.[75] But though it might provide some guidance as to how an individual ought to decide, or actually decides, whether or not to engage in a particular exchange, it supplies no means of arriving at definite exchange-values between commodities held by different individuals. Nor can it determine any 'equality', in terms of a need (or want, or demand) standard, between the things exchanged in transactions. Suppose a person *A* produces a quantity of bread in excess of own-needs, and stands in need also of wine; and a person *B* produces a quantity of wine in excess of own-needs, and stands in need also of bread. A quite sensible and ethically defensible standard of 'need' makes an exchange between the two similarly sensible (not to say likely). But this cannot by itself tell us at what ratio they will or should exchange; and it would be impossible or meaningless, on this basis alone, to derive one particular ratio which would involve 'equality' in the exchange. Given the circumstances specified, both will benefit from exchange. What could it mean to ask whether they have benefited 'equally'? Of course, if one takes a further step in this thought experiment and imposes a situation of competitive markets in the manner of Adam Smith's theoretical world, then an equality of exchange founded upon cost-price becomes plausible, as at least the centre of gravity of exchange ratios (whether or not 'just'). The latter standard is objective and genuinely quantitative, in a way in which 'need' never could be. But this world of competition is not Aristotle's world and is hardly to be found in medieval thought either.[76]

In short, differences across history in the conceptualization of 'economic' subjects, such as exchange, of course may be due to differences in the character of actual economic organization and behaviour. There is then the question of the extent to which medieval and ancient socio-economic life do or do not resemble modern economic society. This is a matter of controversy. Vivenza (2001: 158, n. 106; cf. 149, n. 66) observes that the unimportance, in ancient political theory, of commerce and market exchange in the modern sense, may not be due to the insignificance of such market exchange in the ancient world, but rather, to the fact that ancient thought was uninterested in such phenomena – the disdained form of 'chrematistics' (see Chapter 2, n. 39). She also there draws attention to Karl Polanyi's distinction between 'commerce' and 'market' in ancient civilizations, insofar as the existence of the latter does not entail the former. Meikle (1995: 147–79) provides an excellent appraisal of contending views, 'primitivist' versus 'modernist', concerning the pertinence of modern economic categories to the actual character of ancient socio-economic organization. He largely favours, in a nuanced way, the former position, which is exemplified by the writings of Finley (e.g. 1970, 1992; see his combative opening argument at pp. 17–27 of the latter). Even an idea now so elementary to us, the 'law of one price' (LOOP), presupposes the existence of what may be called 'regular markets',[77] and competition in the sense of Smith requires much more (notably, free mobility of capital and labour between economic activities). Theorizing competition between capitals had to await the eighteenth century. Schefold (1999: 126) observes that Plato at one point writes, that traders should not charge different prices for the same commodity in the same market. But notice that this is a prescription, not a description of markets – a kind of normative LOOP. Schefold also there takes the view that Aristotle's treatment of exchange-value is not in the context of regular markets, in our sense. Lowry (2003: 20) takes the same view, though his interpretation is generally much compromised by marginalist preconceptions. He makes the further observation that the very substantial contract law of the Romans, culminating in the Emperor Justinian's sixth-century codifications, was in part a substitute for the absence of 'stable' markets (Lowry 2003: 21). De-Juan and Monsalve (2006: 103–6) emphasize the absence in the medieval world of free competition in the sense of Smith, or the presence of market power, as the motivation for Scholastic $p^j$ doctrines.[78] De Roover (1958: 427, 429–31) suggests that at least by the late-medieval era, regular markets existed for staple commodities, though not for luxuries, but at the same time, acknowledges that adverse supply shocks ('crop failures') caused recurrent havoc.

### *3.5.5 Some latter-day interpretations*

Our account of Smith's approach to the theory of prices leads to the conclusion that Maurice Dobb's (1973: 112–18) 'two-streams' interpretation of Smith – the notion that Smith is a substantive source for both the classical and marginalist traditions – should as much be rejected as the interpretations of Smith as a primitive Marshallian or marginalist. A detailed criticism of Dobb's interpretation is provided by O'Donnell (1990). His book is a very thorough study of Smith's overall theory of distribution and prices; but it is more concerned with the former than the latter, the opposite of our emphasis here. Perhaps its even greater strength is in providing a critical history of key interpretations of Smith, in four distinct chapters. O'Donnell puts to shame, and to the sword, much of the prior secondary literature. Indeed, his book is really geared to the purpose of exposing the frailty of the Maurice Dobb interpretation, together with that of Samuel Hollander (1973).[79] The critique of the latter project of imputing to Smith a primitive version of general equilibrium marginalism is thorough and compelling (O'Donnell 1990: 171–96). In presenting this refutation of Hollander, O'Donnell also details the secondary literature which has sought to impute variants of the marginalist or 'subjective' approach to value, to economic writings all the way back to medieval and ancient thought. This points to the fact that those with a clearer eye for the absence of anything resembling a subjective or primitive-marginalist approach to price theory in *WN*, can yet make another interpretive error: that Smith's approach involves a departure from a long earlier tradition of subjective approaches to explaining prices, anticipatory of marginalism.

Those who take this erroneous view can also (but need not) add the judgement, that Smith thereby committed a great folly: whether or not this would have been a folly on Smith's part, supposing such an earlier tradition really did exist, is a logically separate issue. No one has taken this line of interpretation to more absurd extremes than Kauder (1953). The opening sentences reveal the mistake which compromises his entire story:

> Several times the history of the marginal utility theory had to be rewritten. The triumvirate Jevons, Menger, Walras knew only Gossen as their forerunner. To-day we recognise that the analysis of subjective elements in economic valuation starts with Aristotle. He begins a trend of thought whose traces abound in the writings of the Middle Ages, the Renaissance and the enlightenment.
>
> (Kauder 1953: 638)

This is to write as if a role for demand in the behaviour of prices were synonymous with marginal utility theory, or at least, synonymous with a more or less primitive anticipation of it. Smith's treatment of prices alone is enough evidence to rebut that tacit presupposition, since demand certainly plays a role in market price dynamics (and the pricing of supply-inelastic commodities). But it has no role in the natural prices of reproducible commodities, except indirectly, insofar as quantity produced influences normal cost of production.

A few examples suffice to illustrate the unhistorical misreadings which result. For Aristotle, we are told, '[e]conomic goods ... derive their value from individual utility, scarcity and costs. If the amount of goods is increasing the value decreases and can even become negative' (Kauder 1953: 638–9). The quotation from Aristotle offered in support of this is:

> External goods, like all other instruments, have a necessary limit of size. Indeed all things of utility [including the goods of the body as well as external goods] are of this character; and any excessive amount of such things must either cause its possessor some injury, or, at any rate, bring him no benefit.
>
> (Kauder 1953: 639, n. 1, quoting Barker 1946: 280–1; the square-bracketed intervention is Barker.)

This says nothing of the sort Kauder claims, and is straightforwardly and sensibly interpreted, as indicated earlier, in terms of use-values as the definite, qualitatively distinct human purposes of things, *not* reducible to a supposedly homogeneous, latter-day 'utility' substance. Hence those things have properly a finite, limited usefulness in relation to legitimate needs.[80] In supposing further that Grotius and Pufendorf in the seventeenth century, along with a raft of earlier thinkers, regard commodity value to be determined by 'utility and scarcity', Kauder (1953: 640) misses the simpler and more plausible meaning: these writers, having no notion of competitive markets in which bargaining among sellers and buyers is subject to the discipline of normal cost of production, are left with nothing more to say than that market prices are subject to the ebb and flow of SAD, sometimes combined with a rather vague notion of cost (more on cost below). Put summarily, this essentially amounts to Smithian market prices without Smithian natural prices. Even Pufendorf's treatment of cost is much closer to the medieval approach than to that of Smith (Theocarakis 2006: 29–32).[81]

A vital analytical fact must be reiterated here (see sec. 3.4.1): a SAD theory of normal commodity prices (or long-period equilibrium prices, to use a latter-day phrase) becomes possible only if normal unit and marginal costs of commodities, in general, are a systematic and well-defined positive function of market supply. The marginal productivity theory of distribution is the only foundation for such well-defined commodity supply functions, under conditions in which producers are free to vary input use and input proportions. Where, in Aristotle, the medieval writers, or the early modern theorists of the seventeenth and eighteenth centuries, is this to be found? Appeals in these literatures to wants, desires, uses, use-values, however subjectively understood – and indeed, references to scarcity – do not the marginalist theory of value make.

In short, in staking a claim for a long prehistory of marginalism in Western thought, Kauder sets himself too easy and inadequate a task, by merely appealing to such 'evidence'. In fact, immediately following the comment on Grotius, Pufendorf and medieval literature, he rather gives the game away by conceding: 'Their value theories are a mixture of costs and subjective values, of objective prices and valuations. Utility is more often than not the general welfare of a community and not the specific pleasure of an individual' (Kauder 1953: 641). When he further writes of the sixteenth-century Italian, Gian Francesco Lottini, that he 'almost discovers the infinity of wants and ... knows about the underestimation of future wants', Kauder again straight away retreats to the concession that 'Lottini apparently was not aware of the fact that he was dealing with economic subjects', just as with the sixteenth- to eighteenth-century Italian writers (Bernardo Davanzati *et al.*), he finally admits: 'No doubt the Italian economists were often near the correct solution, but they did not reach it. They cannot grasp it, because they lack the marginal method' (Kauder 1953: 643, 647). For one final example, Kauder (1953: 645) proposes that Ferdinando Galiani, a contemporary of Smith, has a theory of interest with 'a strong resemblance to the explanation presented by the Austrian economist [Eugen von Böhm-Bawerk]. Interest, so the young abbé claims, is the difference between present and future money'. This is not a theory at all, but merely a *definition* of interest, as embodied in contracts for the receipt of money at (typically) one date, in exchange for delivery of money at a stream of future dates. Kauder (1953: 650) concludes his essay with a tone of high drama, though it is properly to be viewed as melodrama:

> it was the tragedy of these writers that they wrote in vain, they were soon forgotten. No scholar appeared to make out of these thoughts the new science of political economy. Instead, the father of our economic science wrote that water has a great utility and a small value. With these few words Adam Smith had made waste and rubbish out of the thinking of 2,000 years. The chance to start in 1776 instead of 1870 with a more correct knowledge of value principles had been missed.[82]

Douglas (1928: 80, 95) is another who expresses perhaps even more remarkable outrage at Smith's objectivism, albeit without the attempted vast pre-Smithian historical sweep of Kauder:

> By failing to follow up the hints which ... [Locke and Joseph Harris] had developed, Smith helped to divert the writers of the English Classical school into a cul-de-sac from which they did not emerge, in so far as their value theory was concerned, for nearly a century, while he also helped ... to give rise to the economic doctrines of nineteenth-century socialism.
>
> ...
>
> There are, it seems to me, few more unfair instances in economic thought than the almost complete unanimity with which the English-speaking economists of the chair have heaped condemnation upon the over-worked and poverty-stricken Marx, who worked under such great difficulties, and, save

> for the comments of Jevons and a few others, have heaped praises upon Smith and Ricardo. The failure was the failure not of one man but of a philosophy of value, and the roots of the ultimate contradiction made manifest to the world in the third volume of *Das Kapital* lie imbedded in the first volume of the *Wealth of Nations*.

One may say, *contra* Kauder and Douglas, that if there had been such a primitive-marginalist tradition, Smith would have been entirely sensible, and much to be applauded, for breaking with it. But there was no such tradition. (We pass over Douglas's other historical and analytical judgements, without comment.) Robertson and Taylor (1957) to some extent take Kauder to task, though in the end, they fall short of giving Smith his proper due, because they share the unsympathetic belief that 'scarcity and utility are basically essential for any satisfactory treatment of value theory' (p. 186; also 188 – at 188n they describe Douglas's above-quoted statement as 'eloquent'). When one considers, to take a notable example, Hutcheson's (1755, vol. 2: 53–64) commentary on price determination – in light of the clarity of Smith's distinction between market prices and natural prices, and his distinct explanations of the factors determining them – it is evident that Hutcheson's appeals to demand and cost, in effect, are a conflation of market and natural prices.

Hutcheson does treat cost in a rather sophisticated way, though hardly more so than is to be found in medieval literature (more on this below): 'difficulty of acquiring' is influenced not only by the labour required, but also 'the rarity or scarcity of the materials in nature' (including in this 'such *accidents* as prevent plentiful crops'), 'the great ingenuity ... requisite in the artists', 'the dignity of station in which, according to the custom of a country, the men must live who provide us with certain goods' (Hutcheson 1755, vol. 2: 54–5; emphasis added). As well, in accounting for something resembling necessary supply-price or cost-price, he includes an element of profit as a kind of quasi-wages and compensation for risk, reminiscent of entrepreneurial remuneration in Cantillon's *Essai* published the same year (see n. 67 above). The profit element is captured in Hutcheson's concluding summary statement on price, which also bears the imprint of Scholastic influence:

> In matters of commerce, to fix the price we should not only compute the first cost, freights, duties, and all expences made, along with the interest of money employed in trade, but the labours too, the care, attention, accounts, and correspondence about them; and in some cases take in also the condition of the person so employed, according to the custom of our country. The expence of his station of life must be defrayed by the price of such labours; and they deserve compensation as much as any other.[83] This additional price of their labours is the just foundation of the ordinary profit of merchants, on which account they justly demand an higher price in selling, than what answers all that was expended upon the goods. Their value *here* is augmented by those labours, as justly as by those of farmers or artisans.

> As there are many contingent losses by the perishing of some goods, or their receiving damage, these losses may be justly compensated by a further augmentation of the price of such as are safe. As merchants lose sometimes by the falling of the rates of goods on hand, they may justly take the contingent advantage too of goods on hand, when the rates of such goods rise by any accident which makes them scarce. Men who are fortunate in these accidents may be much enriched, without any fraud, or extortion. The constant profit [i.e. the average over a series of price fluctuations and losses from other causes] is the just reward of their labours.
>
> (Hutcheson 1755, vol. 2: 63–4)[84]

It is true also that at one point Hutcheson (1755, vol. 2: 54) seeks to suggest a kind of symmetry between demand and cost in relation to price determination:

> When there is no *demand*, there is no price, were the *difficulty* of acquiring never so great [i.e. use-value is a necessary condition for exchange-value]: and were there no *difficulty* or labour requisite to acquire, the most universal *demand* will not cause a price … [i.e. cost is also a necessary condition for exchange-value]. Where the demand for two sorts of goods is equal, the prices are as the difficulty. Where the difficulty is equal, the prices are as the demand.

But the last two sentences here are meaningless.

The proposition that usefulness of *some* kind is 'prerequisite' to exchange-value is a much weaker notion than a subjective theory of value: it says only that it is a necessary condition for a thing to be produced and enter into exchange, that it be 'in demand', so to speak, insofar as being 'in demand' is treated as synonymous with a thing having use-value in some sense. This is what Hutcheson (1755, vol. 2: 53) means when he writes: 'The natural ground of all value or price is some sort of use which goods afford in life; this is prerequisite to all estimation' – and in his statement at the following page, quoted immediately above.[85] (Indeed, in between these two statements he sketches a version of the paradox of value.) The notion of use-value as a prerequisite for exchange-value on the one hand, and the conflation of accidental SAD influences on prices with the role of cost-price on the other, come together in the following statement:

> when some aptitude to human use is presupposed, we shall find that the prices of goods depend on these two jointly, the *demand* on account of some use or other which many desire, and the *difficulty* of acquiring, or cultivating for human use.
>
> (Hutcheson 1755, vol. 2: 54)

Is this about market prices or natural prices? In a sense, it is about neither and it is about both at the same time; but it is certainly in no way marginalism, whose distinctive interplay of SAD in the determination of equilibrium commodity prices, essentially requires the SAD or marginal productivity theory of factor pricing.

It is true that Smith himself can be read as denying that use-value is even a precondition for exchange-value (*WN*: 44–5; and similarly, *LJA*: 358; *LJB*: 487), so that Douglas (1928: 78), for example, can conclude that for Smith, 'utility' is 'not even a necessary prerequisite' for exchange-value. He *does* speak of things having exchange-value and 'little or *no* value in use' (*WN*: 44). But this should be read as rhetorical flourish, designed to throw into sharper relief the independence of exchange-values from use-value. In fact, Smith immediately follows this, with reference to the example of diamonds, by saying that they have '*scarce* any value in use' (*WN*: 45), and the initial comment, in any case, says '*little*' or no use-value. Hence also, at *LJA* (358), diamonds are described as '*hardly* of any use', and at *LJB* (487), it is said of diamonds that 'their *real* use seems not yet to be discovered' (emphasis added in all these quotations).[86] This statement in fact points to the objective sense Smith intends by 'value in use'. The implied conception appears little different from Aristotle: every kind of thing has its particular, qualitatively distinct use-value for humans. Combined with a kind of ethically constituted hierarchy of human needs, this enables him to deem, for example, the use-value of diamonds as trivial.[87] To the extent of the hierarchy of uses, Robertson and Taylor (1957: 184) are right to say that in *WN* use-value is an 'ethically tinged' notion. If there is a 'paradox of value' in pre-marginalist thought, this is it. A thing of trivial or morally dubious use (e.g. gold or diamonds for self-adornment, or in pre-modern thought, as instruments of acquisitiveness) can have a very high exchange-value due to natural scarcity or cost; a thing of primary human need, like water, can be free (cf. Vivenza 2001: 141–2, 154). This contrast is also the point of the ancient Midas fable: King Midas, granted his wish for the power to turn anything he touched into gold, faces starvation surrounded by gold, and repents his wish.

Robertson and Taylor (1957: 189) set themselves the task of addressing the 'unsolved problem' thrown up by Kauder's interpretation, of why, in *WN* at least, Smith turned away from the allegedly long tradition of subjective approaches to value. In fact, there is no problem to solve: for the kind of social economy which is emerging in his time, Adam Smith takes the great and correct step forward of imposing the discipline of competition upon the interplay of supplies and demands. Smith undoubtedly stands in a tradition of thought in which Grotius, Pufendorf and Hutcheson are key early modern elements. But Smith found his own way, and a better way, with regard to price theory for a competitive social economy, drawing on the development of cost-price theories from Petty forward, and with *LJ* a kind of way station on the route to *WN*. As has been shown in previous sections, this particularly pertains to the dynamics of the supply side. The high drama created by Kauder and Douglas, around Smith's lack of a systematic role for demand in his theory of normal prices is fictional. Part of the reason for such false dramatizing is their failure to grasp correctly the role of demand in the marginalist theory they wish to uphold. In the absence of any systematic basis for commodity supply functions (rising normal or long-period unit and marginal costs), there is no systematic role for commodity demand functions in normal price determination, even if it is otherwise reasonable to posit such demand functions. Actually, it is not otherwise reasonable to suppose such functions anyway (see sec. 3.6).

### *3.5.6 Cost and pre-modern thought*

It was observed above, in introducing Scholastic views on prices, that there are two distinct currents in the retrospective interpretation of $p^j$: mere-market-price, whether one or other of three possible interpretations of that, versus cost-price in some sense. How can the answer to such an apparently straightforward question – whether or to what extent a cost-price concept is incorporated in pre-modern notions of $p^j$ – be so much disputed? Partly it is because the articulations in the literature, possibly interpretable as concepts of cost, or as SAD, are often rather vague or oblique. This is certainly true, with regard to the role of cost, suggested by some commentators, in Aristotle's account of exchange in the famous *Nicomachean Ethics* argument, discussed above. Nevertheless, it is beyond doubt that cost enters into at least many versions of the medieval $p^j$ and accounts of actual prices. Hamouda and Price (1997: 191–2, and the attached, extensive notes on twentieth-century, secondary literature; also Friedman 1980: 235, notes 6, 7), in an excellent analysis, examine divergent retrospective interpretations of the medieval $p^j$, which they rightly argue, with copious references to primary sources, reflect divergent views in the medieval literature itself. That literature refers,

> on the one hand to price as determined by the cost of production, whose components are raw materials, labour and adequate resources to support the needs of oneself and one's family, and on the other hand to price determined by supply and demand with the emphasis on scarcity on the supply side and need and utility on the demand side.... [R]eferences to both these methods of price determination are readily available and frequently in the same medieval works.
>
> (Hamouda and Price 1997: 193)

For the former view, they instance Robert de Courçon, Albertus Magnus and Aquinas; for the latter, John Buridan and Henry of Langenstein (also known as Henry of Hesse). They are also careful not to identify 'need' with 'utility' (Hamouda and Price 1997: 193–5). In fact, Hamouda and Price, in a sense, resolve the interpretive tensions by arguing that it was maldistribution of incomes and wealth, highlighted by the contrast been cost-prices and need, which led to the development of at least some of the $p^j$ doctrines:

> It was not due to the medievals' failure to analyse price formation astutely but rather due to their wary perception of the inherent injustices in the pure

economic forces of price formation which led them to draw ethics into the economic picture.

(Hamouda and Price 1997: 195–6; also 200–2)[88]

Hollander (1965: 624–8) provides another plausible attempt at resolving the cost versus demand (or versus SAD) dualism, not necessarily incompatible with the Hamouda and Price resolution: 'the assumption of a single criterion of justice is false. A different rule was adopted in different circumstances.' Hollander's resolution is that relative costs, informed by a hierarchy of remunerations based upon social status, applies to customary exchange in the 'traditional' social economy, whereas common market price, though qualified by some ethical prescriptions, pertains to non-traditional market situations. Notice the recourse to including under cost an adequate standard of living for the producers (in the quotation from Hamouda and Price 1997: 193 above; also 203–4; Sewall 1901: 8), which included considerations of the social status of the producers, as Hollander's account also attests. This points to a notion of just remunerations, parallel with $p^j$, such remunerations necessarily then becoming an element entering into $p^j$. Wood (2002: 144–57) provides a summary account of notions of the just wage in medieval thought. Once a thinker had embraced such a notion (e.g. Aquinas, and Antoninus of Florence in the fifteenth century), whether based upon a market criterion analogous to the common market commodity price, or some other standard, it is logically inescapable that just commodity price must be understood to cover the costs associated with just remunerations. Social status could mean different just remunerations for different classes of labourers and other labour-like socio-economic functions (e.g. merchants), or different payments for professional services (e.g. lawyers, teachers), depending upon the social status of the *purchaser* of the service. Just as with commodities, particularly staple consumption goods, monopoly was an issue with respect to wages and other labour-like remunerations, notably, in relation to the craft and merchant guilds (Wood 2002: 140–3, 146–7).[89] Transformed into the notion of normal subsistence, the notion of customary remunerations plays a role in modern descriptive theories of cost of production; e.g. Smith's natural wage as a component of normal cost of production, though perhaps combined with more considerable confidence than in Scholastic thought, that a market economy will deliver such an outcome.

Kaye (1998: 90; cf. Sewall 1901: 7) traces the conventionalist doctrine of $p^j$ as a mere SAD-determined price to Roman law: 'a thing is worth what it can be sold for', thereby *defining* worth as whatever will voluntarily be paid for a commodity; hence follows also the more general principle of Roman law, that 'a willing party is not injured'. But this was not completely unqualified: fraud was an exception. As Kaye (1998: 91) goes on to point out, the minus-50–plus-50 per cent rule (see n. 71 above), derived from Roman law but extended and generalized in the medieval era, entailed that voluntary exchanges beyond this band are at unjust prices. The conventionalism of that rule is within limits. Furthermore, in the context of the earlier Roman law, it seems that '[a] legally sufficient equality between cost and value was *assumed* to exist in all sale agreements entered into freely' (Kaye 1998: 90; emphasis added), whatever precisely that means. Is it a tautology, or a description of what was expected to be the normal situation with respect to most transactions? Kaye (1998: 106–7) also draws attention to the firm opposition to a conventionalist interpretation of $p^j$ by Henry of Ghent (thirteenth century), for whom 'a thing is worth not what it *can* be sold for ... but rather what it *ought* to be sold for'. What determines the latter for Henry is unclear: probably a customary normal price is intended, though elements of cost (including mercantile costs) are clearly taken into account (Kaye 1998: 139–40). In any case, he was definitely reacting against the moral emptiness of a conventionalist notion that the mere voluntary character of an exchange makes it just. Aquinas, Kaye (1998: 97–8) also acknowledges, repudiated the identification of just price with common market estimate, Kaye interpreting this as due to theological and ethical beliefs which prevented Aquinas from embracing such conventionalism. He does allow for some latitude in the justness of prices, around a particular value, but not to the extent of the minus-50–plus-50 per cent rule (Kaye 1998: 185).

All this points to consideration of the implications of the level of actual market prices for the standard of living of those on the demand side of commodity markets, as well as the supply side. Hence the diagnosis of Hamouda and Price (1997), indicated above, and the notion of the $p^j$ as an attempted response to the economics of more or less chronic shortage. To the extent that $p^j$ theories were motivated by demand-side considerations, they ultimately were about market prices relative to the money incomes of the poor and less well off; that is to say, they were about the level of real incomes or real wages, at least as measured in terms of staple consumption items. To illustrate, if one specifies that the money price of grain cannot justly exceed one dinarius per unit of grain, on the basis (tacit or explicit) that the wage of a poor labourer is twenty dinarii, one is really proposing that the money price of grain cannot justly exceed one-twentieth of the money wage of that labour. This relative upper bound ultimately is being rationalized on the objective – or if one prefers, customary – basis of the consumption needs of a poor labourer (a minimum of twenty units of grain). Hence Herlihy (1958: 37) comments in relation to the claim that $p^j$ represents mere market price, that '*justus* frequently bears the sense of "true", "real", "established or utilized without deceit or fraud"' – that is to say, without any deeper ethical significance – but adds: 'in regard to the necessities of life, especially in regard to grain, the [northern Italian] city governments for the most part recognized that here justice demanded that the price be kept ever within the reach even of the poorest citizens'.

Raymond de Roover (1958) made a key contribution to repudiating the interpretation, widely influential earlier (see pp. 418–20), that the $p^j$ was understood as a kind of ideal price, posited independently of actual market outcomes. But de Roover's argument, even if sound, does not foreclose the question as to whether common market price was understood to reflect production cost in some sense. He himself, on the one hand says 'the just price did not correspond to cost of production as determined by the producer's social status' (de Roover 1958: 420–1). On the other hand, with particular respect to Albertus Magnus and Aquinas, he resolves any perceived contradiction between market price and cost-price elements of their treatment of $p^j$ as follows:

> In their comments on Aristotle both Albertus and Aquinas insist that arts and crafts would be doomed to destruction if the producer did not recover his outlays in the sale of the product.... In other words, the market price could not fall permanently below cost. If so, there is no contradiction, since the market price would then tend to coincide with cost or to oscillate around this point like the swing of a pendulum.... This ... agrees with classical and neoclassical economic analysis.
>
> (de Roover 1958: 422)

In short, de Roover is rather indifferent to whether or not the just common market price was understood also as cost-price, but does not reject the proposition. His purpose is to dispose of the ideal-price interpretation. But while de Roover (1958: 421–2) drips sarcasm in critiquing earlier interpretations which would make of Aquinas a Marxist, one may ask whether it is any less silly to turn him into a Marshallian. Hollander (1965: 629–30) rightly observes: 'we cannot ascribe to ... [Aquinas] a full-fledged Marshallian theory of price determination'; there is no 'classical or neo-classical mechanism' to be found there. This follows from Hollander's plausible interpretation (with regard to Aquinas, but not Aristotle), that the significance of cost-price in the Aristotle and Aquinas accounts of just exchange was as an expression of customary norms governing remunerations or distribution in a tradition-based social economy:

> neither Aristotle nor Aquinas ... explain how the exchange ratios will come to reflect costs of production. The topic under discussion was exchange between individual craftsmen, who were not to engage in any form of bargaining; the just rate was well defined *prior* to the act of exchange.... In short, there is no mechanism whereby current prices are related to production costs.... It is evident that social opprobrium, or the 'self-interest' and above all the 'conscience' of the craftsmen must have been relied upon. There is no economic mechanism to explain the cost 'determination' of price.
>
> (Hollander 1965: 630; also Wilson: 1975: 62–9, for a similar view)

The various currents in medieval treatments of prices and justice – mere-market-price versus cost-price, and various notions as to the relevant market price – all come together in a commentary by Langholm (1992: 303–6) on the views of Giles of Lessines in the thirteenth century:

> How Aristotle actually conceived of just value in exchange is unclear, but the scholastics, following Albert the Great, picked up some hints... related

them to the patristic and legal traditions and formulated two main sets of criteria. One was based on labour and other costs of production, transportation and storage, including risk. The other was based on supply and demand, the latter being an expression of general need (*indigentia*) .... Though never explicitly stated by Giles of Lessines, these sets of criteria are both implied on numerous occasions .... Giles extends the rule of justice in exchange by analogy from a commodity exchange to the hire of labour, and elsewhere suggests that a reasonable reward for labour and other cost factors may serve to estimate the just price. Risk attached to a thing reduces its value; a merchant may hope to make a profit simply in order to balance the risk of losing. On other occasions Giles suggests that the just value may vary from time to time and from place to place owing to the scarcity or abundance of goods and other conditions, thus clearly implying some sort of market estimate.[90]

. . .

While cost and market conditions are often brought to bear on the estimation of a just price ... Giles occasionally invokes the right and ability of free agents to reach their own agreements about justice in exchange. In a compilation of quotes ...one easily recognizes the three pithy maxims of legal origins... viz. the ownership maxim of the Justinian *Code* stating that anyone is arbiter of his own thing, the maxim of the *Digest* echoing Aristotle to the effect that a willing party is not injured, and (supported by these two) the *commune dictum* of the Gloss on the *Digest* defining value as obtainable price:

> The true owner of a thing ... can give or sell the ownership of the thing or the use or fruits of any possession .... Every exchange made by the free will of the owners is made justly. From this it follows that whoever by buying or selling should receive more than they give, receive it justly and as being made their own, by the free will of the owners.... A thing is justly estimated according to the utility which it brings to its possessor, and it is justly worth as much as it can be sold for without fraud.[91]

Our purpose in this section, of course, has not been to resolve all of the controversies around the interpretation of the character and significance of medieval and earlier literature concerning prices and related matters. Rather, it has been to convey a sense of the currents of thought concerning prices, SAD and costs, running through this vast literature, across a span of many centuries. The difficulties due to the scale of the literature and the span of time involved are compounded by the fact that the further one goes back in time, the harder it becomes to grasp the conceptual world(s) in which 'economic' propositions are being articulated. One has a strong sense that the secondary literature on these writings often has too unselfconscious recourse to the apparently everyday language of 'price', 'supply' and 'demand', 'cost', but deploying it with degrees of preconception derivative from the marginalist theories of 1871 and after.[92] Once these terms are understood from that particular, latter-day framework, they cease to be mere everyday or common-sense terms of reference; they become particular theoretical constructs, alien to the territory they are being used to survey, and of questionable plausibility in their own right. One can easily sympathize with the sentiment of Wilson (1975: 58), which would be just as accurate if it referred to yet other examples of latter-day thought intruding into interpretation: 'some economists see Aristotle and Aquinas as forerunners of the Austrian school of economics of the 1870's [*sic*], and others see them as predecessors of the cost-of-production theorists. A few see them as predecessors of both!'

These considerations amount to a warning against misperceiving the extent of continuity in intellectual history. But of course, there *is* continuity, as well as change, and getting the balance right as between the two, on any particular issue, is often a delicate matter of judgement. This is especially true, in our context here, with respect to 'cost'. A figure like Hutcheson, and also, for another example, Verri on ordinary price (n. 68 above), evidence continuity with Scholasticism, as does the role of customary living standards in both medieval and classical-economics notions of cost. As to change, there are three key innovations in the transition to early classical economics in the eighteenth century. The natural or normal price, emphatically a cost-price, is strongly identified with the tendency of actual prices under conditions of competition in regular markets. At least by the time one arrives at Turgot and Smith, this involves a *system* of markets, integrated via the mobility of capital and labour. Second, the determination of normal costs is theorized, rather than merely assumed, again, particularly with respect to competitive conditions. (On both, recall Hollander's sound criticism of de Roover, quoted above.) But the extent of this latter innovation should not be exaggerated. On the one hand, there is that continuity with respect to custom entering into determination of wage levels. On the other, whatever sense of competition and regular markets might be involved in elements of the medieval literature, there is no notion of normal profit rates on capital (equalization of net returns) in the pre-modern literature. It could even be argued that normal cost of production was not 'really' theorized until the nineteenth and twentieth centuries, when the classical objective approach to prices was released from the restrictive confines of the labour theory of value. Finally, there is the deeper sense of cost which emerges in the formation of modern political economy: the inputs used up in production of the gross social product, a concept of cost which in general can only be understood at the level of society, or of an economic system as a whole. This is not at all to be found in the pre-modern literature, prior to Petty; but that is a subject for Chapter 4.

The cost which anchors prices in the emerging objective tradition of the century or so to 1776 ultimately is grounded in technology (production methods) and remunerations for inputs. Smith, and others in that period, certainly seek to theorize the development of production methods. Nevertheless, taking the methods of production of commodities as given for the purposes of price theory (as Smith does), the theorizing of normal costs in the eighteenth century essentially reduces to the question of what determines the distributive variables which enter into costs. This, most obviously, points to the theorizing of wages, together with profit rates on capital once one arrives at the Turgot and Smith formulations of normal prices, and also land-rents in some formulations. Functional distribution, to be sure, is not very deeply theorized prior to the nineteenth century, but certainly there is a notion of normal distribution with respect to wages, at least partly governed by social conventions as to customary subsistence, independent of the ebb and flow of SAD.[93] With regard to determination of the general level of profit rates, Smith achieves little. In Turgot one even sees propositions which might suggest that the rate of interest, understood as a kind of underlying benchmark for the levels of profit rates, is to be explained by reference to something like SAD in the market for loans (following what was by then a reasonably long tradition of thought). But if there is any definite causation supposed by him – and in our view, this is not at all evident – the rate of interest appears to be derivative from the profitability of capital (see Groenewegen 1971: 299–304). In any case, here, one must look forward to a crucial analytical development after the eighteenth century, in particular, associated with Ricardo. With given production methods and given normal real wage rates, the general rate of profit is fully determined: it is not possible, under these conditions, to put forward also a separate theory of the general level of interest rates and/or profit rates, whether via recourse to SAD in the market for loans or anything else. In short, the successive attempts to theorize the elements of functional income distribution in the development of the objective theory of competitive cost-price in the eighteenth century is a process of intellectual development still far from completed by the achievements of Smith. Indeed, if the forces determining functional distribution are themselves changing over time, such intellectual development might *never* be completed, except at a most fundamental level of understanding. Such historical change surely applies to the distribution of the social net product in the long-term evolution of human societies. The 'rules of the game' shift and social theory must also move – with a view to keeping up with them, or *catching up* with them. Furthermore, from a retrospective standpoint also, one must be honest enough to admit that the rules are less clear the further we look back in time, and therefore our understanding of them, almost inevitably more conjectural.

## 3.6 Competition theory without supply-and-demand functions

The conclusions of the preceding sections with regard to Smith's treatment of prices may be summarized under four heads.

1 There are three essential elements forming the causal chain which constitutes his dynamic conception of market price adjustment in relation to normal price: market imbalance ($Q \neq D^*$) causes at least some $p^m{}_i$ to deviate from $p^n$; deviation from $p^n$ of the average of $p^m{}_i$ causes $Q$ adjustment over time; convergence of $Q$ upon $D^*$ causes $p^m{}_i$ to converge upon $p^n$.
2 Latter-day demand functions are not necessary to this conception, and

Smith in any case does not posit them, though responsiveness of total market demand to price provides some additional motivation for $p^m{}_i$ deviating from $p^n$ in the presence of market imbalance, and at the same time, limits price volatility in those circumstances.

3 Latter-day supply functions are not necessary to Smith's conception either, and are not posited: the possible relations between quantity produced and normal price are conceived of in dynamic terms and are highly contingent (and commonly irreversible). They depend upon the contending factors, division of labour and natural resource scarcity, and normal cost is also dependent upon wider forces (e.g. the influence of capital accumulation upon distribution).

4 Smith's analyses of situations in which production is inelastic in relation to $D^*$ confirms a tacit supposition of his treatment of market prices: demand-prices are incapable of determinate quantitative, theoretical expression. When Robertson and Taylor (1957: 191) pose the ill-conceived question, why Smith did not follow through in *WN*, with his market price analysis of *LJ*, part of their answer nevertheless rings truer than they realize: 'Smith felt that … subjective analysis was leading nowhere. It had not … proved capable of being employed in any actual quantitative measurement'.

It was shown also that Smith has recourse to four distinct notions of cost. First, there is the concept of normal price as opportunity cost, which provides the anchor for market price behaviour under competitive conditions. Second, there is the concept of cost as the inputs used up in commodity production, commonly reduced to, or equated with, labour. This then provides part of the justification for a third concept – real price as labour commanded – which is taken to capture cost in the second sense, as well as measuring purchasing power in terms of commodities, both incorrect in general. Real price has a further sensible motivation, to ascertain sources of variation in production methods and costs, but is unsatisfactory for that purpose. Finally, in support of the third, Smith also appeals to pains, toil and trouble in the human acquisition of commodities as the *ultimate* cost of them to humankind. However, this subjective notion is not necessary to the third concept, or indeed, the first two. It is the first and the second which have scientific substance. (The significance of the second is considered in Chapter 4.) There is also an attempted analogy between commodity pricing and remuneration for inputs. This is far less complete than Smith's language and arguments suppose or imply. For wages there is a kind of anchor analogous to normal commodity price, but not for profits and rents. Even allowing for a normal customary real wage, somehow plausibly determined, there is circularity involved in the derivation of the associated normal money wage rates, though this difficulty can be overcome.[94] With regard to profit rates and rents, only with Ricardo forty years later, will their determination in association with a given real wage be placed on a coherent and plausible basis. The result is that once real wages, production methods and the quantities of outputs (in particular, the outputs which require scarce natural resources for their production) are given, profitability and rents are fully determined. No theories of profits and of rents, separate from and independent of the determination of real wages, are necessary, or even possible, under these conditions. But Ricardo left much undone with regard to satisfactorily representing this resolution of income distribution and competitive prices. After more than another century of contributions from a number of sources, Piero Sraffa from the 1920s began to construct a system of equations which would culminate in a genuinely satisfying formulation of the classical approach.[95]

Why might these findings with regard to Smith be significant? In relation to the role of demand, it is important that his competitive process does *not* depend upon such onerous assumptions as are entailed by demand functions. The postulates upon which demand functions are founded – e.g. the autonomy of individual preferences with respect to the economic processes in which individuals engage (production, consumption, prices and others' preferences) – are not so innocuous that one would be indifferent as to whether or not a certain chain of economic reasoning requires such functions. Occam's razor alone tells us that all else given, the attractiveness of Smith's treatment of competition and market prices is enhanced by its *not* requiring the existence of latter-day demand functions.[96] Market price convergence towards normal prices is a central element of Smith's political economy, and of the supposed self-regulating character of competitive systems. If this key process does not depend upon positing demand functions, *ceteris paribus* Smith's analysis is rendered more plausible – and more attractive than modern marginalist treatments. This conclusion does not entail a denial of substitutability in consumption (see, e.g. *WN*: 104, 182–4, 843, 884, 892–3, 897). Rather, it is an affirmation that supply-side adjustment is sufficient for a coherent account of competitive price dynamics, with demand responsiveness to prices serving only as a mechanism for placing bounds upon price volatility in the face of market imbalances. With regard to prices and supply, Smith's approach to market prices show that only very weak postulates about supply response in relation to non-normal prices are required, in order to capture the competitive process of convergence. His approach to normal prices and supply, by respecting the complexities and contingencies in the evolution of production methods and normal rates of remuneration in the framework of growth dynamics, eschews simple a priori presumptions about functional relations, as well as keeping the focus on dynamics.[97]

Smith's dynamic treatment of $p^m{}_i$, when thus clearly understood, is and remains attractive because it is so much more plausible than modern marginalist treatments of market price in terms of demand functions and supply functions at particular points in time. In these latter-day exercises, the demand functions have no quantitative basis in observable phenomena. To be clear, those latter-day functions are not objectionable so much for their imposing restrictions on preferences, such as consistency and completeness over some relevant domain of choice, though those restrictions are not completely unproblematic. What is more unsatisfactory is the suppositions of autonomous and independent preferences governing choices, together with the inescapable incapacity to give genuine quantitative expression to the inferred demand functions, so that they will *always* be nothing more than drawings from imagination. Their basis in intrinsically unobservable 'phenomena' means that these supposed functions will always lack any authentic quantitative, empirical basis: $E = mc^2$ is an equation; $D_x = f(p_x)$ is a cartoon. To be sure, the human sciences may commonly have to proceed on conjectures of a psychological nature; but where these can be avoided they should be. With regard to price theory, Smith has shown a way to proceed which requires minimal suppositions about the behaviour of demand and its psychological underpinnings.

The absence of a theory of demand-prices, together with the more minimal and contingent (rather than a priori) treatment of prices and supply, point to the character of Smith's theory of competition and prices as rather 'minimalist' in comparison with marginalism (or Marshallianism). But because it is more modest in its reach, its theoretical aims and claims, it is also more robust. This points more generally to an approach to economic analysis which gives a more limited domain to theory, more limited scope for generality and determinateness. His approach to prices (as well as income distribution) is not a primitive anticipation of marginalism; it is qualitatively different and at least on this subject, superior, even with a view to contemporary economic conditions. This is not to say that 'supply-and-demand' is unimportant to Smith; it is very important, but understood differently to the theories of 1871 and after. Nor is this to say that the particulars of his approach are in no need of modern reconstruction, including in some very important respects. Our three-step characterization of Smith's dynamic feedback mechanism in section 3.3.1, describing the essential character of his market price dynamics (summarized also at the opening of this section), relies upon the suppositions that deviation of market prices from normal price will cause actual profit rates to deviate in the same direction from normal or required profitability, and that changes in supply reduce market imbalance. Some modern formalizations have shown that these causal links may not be so unproblematic as might appear at first glance – the two sources of the potential difficulty being the interdependence of costs and prices in general, and the influence of output changes on demands.[98] Happily, it seems that post-Smith there are still some useful tasks for modern economic theory to pursue.

# 4 Production and capital accumulation

*division of labour and labour productivity*
*gross revenue and net revenue*
*capital and productive labour*

> Consumption ... is the sole end and object of all economic activity.... Aggregate demand can be derived only from present consumption or from present provision for future consumption. The consumption for which we can profitably provide in advance cannot be pushed indefinitely into the future.... The obstacle to a clear understanding is ... an inadequate appreciation of the fact that capital is not a self-subsistent entity existing apart from consumption.
>
> *John Maynard Keynes* (1936: 104, 106)

The ultimate object of Smith's political economy as a system of descriptive theory is the growth of wealth understood as annual national product; and connected with this, its ultimate normative purpose is high or rising consumption per capita, widely distributed (on the latter, see sec. 5.1.1). Production therefore could not but be a primary concern of *WN*. The three opening chapters of Book I indeed focus on production methods, in terms of the dynamics of 'division of labour' in relation to the growth of markets and labour productivity. The title of Book I, it may be noted, makes no reference to prices. It describes the contents in terms of production and distribution: 'Of the causes of Improvement in the productive Powers of Labour, and of the Order according to which its Produce is naturally distributed among the different Ranks of the People' (*WN*: 13). The concept of division of labour and its significance, in particular, as the source of labour productivity growth, is taken up in the first section below. But it is in *WN*, Book II – 'Of the Nature, Accumulation, and Employment of Stock' – that Smith systematically exposits his theory of growth. Beyond division of labour, the two key elements of the conceptual framework he employs there are the distinction between gross and net revenue and that between productive and unproductive labour. These are examined in sections 4.2 and 4.3 respectively. The accumulation of capital is closely connected with all three of these fundamental elements of growth processes, but Smith's concept of capital particularly comes into play in relation to net revenue and even more so, productive labour. The propensity to save is the driver of the rate of accumulation, and hence, with productivity growth, the cause of the growth of production capacity. The propensity to save in turn derives from one of three fundamental psychological parameters upon which Smith's political economy relies: the desire for material self-betterment, grounded in human nature. The proportion between a society's productive and unproductive labour is an expression of that propensity. The final section is particularly concerned with the absence of an account of the coordination of saving and investment, and of commodity supplies and demands, in the context of Smith's growth dynamics. It also clarifies his conception of the social surplus: that part of national product available for free disposal.

## 4.1 Division of labour and labour productivity

### *4.1.1 Smith and division of labour*

The phrase 'division of labour' first appears in the very first sentence of *WN*, Chapter I,[1] where its causal significance for labour productivity growth is announced: 'The greatest improvement in the productive powers of labour, and the greater part of the skill, dexterity, and judgment with which it is any where directed or applied, seem to have been the effects of the division of labour' (*WN*: 13). It is then systematically discussed over the first three chapters.[2] In a nutshell, division of labour is specialization of labour in production processes, motivated by the consequent productivity gains: 'The separation of different trades and employments from one another, seems to have taken place, in consequence of this advantage', 'a proportionable increase of the productive powers of labour' (*WN*: 15). As Richardson (1975) well argues (also Sylos-Labini 1976: 200, 225–6), the dynamics of division of labour and the associated technical change constitute a second dimension of competition, additional to convergence of market prices towards natural price, both deriving from the same driving force: the desire for material betterment (discussed in sec. 4.3.2). The scope for these productivity gains is much more to be found in manufacture than agriculture, and they arise from three sources: improved labour dexterity, time-saving from no longer shifting between tasks, and introduction of, or innovations in, machinery.[3] Division of labour also is fruitfully applied to philosophy or science (*WN*: 21–2; *LJA*: 347; *LJB*: 492; *edWN*: 570, 574). In Chapter II it is presented as the 'very slow and gradual' consequence of a uniquely human, natural 'propensity to truck, barter, and exchange one thing for another', 'not originally the effect of any human wisdom, which foresees and intends that general opulence to which it gives occasion' (*WN*: 25; cf. 29–30; also *LJA*: 347, 348–9, 351; *LJB*: 492–3; *edWN*: 570–1).[4]

It is noteworthy that Smith here goes on to wonder aloud, whether this propensity is an irreducible datum of human nature – 'one of those original principles in human nature, of which no further account can be given' – or whether it proceeds from the faculties of reason and speech, adding: 'it belongs not to our present subject to enquire' (*WN*: 25).[5] Just as self-regard can be taken as a given for the purposes of price theory under competitive conditions (see p. 76), so here the propensity to exchange with a view to individual gain also can be taken as a datum for the purposes of political economy, even though that propensity is not irreducible.[6] Indeed, the self-regard which lies behind competition is naturally brought into play in the persuading which is characteristic of exchange processes, as Smith makes explicit:

> man has almost constant occasion for the help of his brethren, and it is in vain for him to expect it from their benevolence only. He will be more likely to prevail if he can interest their self-love in his favour, and shew them that it is for their own advantage to do for him what he requires of them. Whoever offers to another a bargain of any kind, proposed to do this. Give me that which I want, and you shall have this which you want, is the meaning of every such offer .... It is not from the benevolence of the butcher, the brewer, or the baker, that we expect our dinner, but from their regard to their own interest. We address ourselves, not to their humanity but to their self-love ....
>
> (*WN*: 26–7; also *LJA*: 347–8; *LJB*: 493; *edWN*: 571–2)

In Smith's conception of the dynamics of this technical change, division of labour is causally connected with two phenomena: labour productivity growth ('improvement in the productive powers of labour') on the one hand and 'extent of the market' (Book I, Chapter III) on the other. He is also emphatic that specialization is not primarily a result of natural differences in individual human capacities:

> The difference of natural talents in different men is, in reality, much less than we are aware of; and the very different genius which appears to distinguish men of different professions ... is not upon many occasions so much the cause, as the effect of the division of labour.
>
> (*WN*: 28; also *LJA*: 348; *LJB*: 493; *edWN*: 572–4)

It is 'the power of exchanging' that 'gives occasion' to division of labour; so that 'the extent of this division must always be limited by the extent of that power, or, in other words, by the extent of the market' (*WN*: 31; also *LJA*: 355–6; *LJB*: 494; *fA*).[7] The division of labour is most evident, and most highly realized for goods or services of limited transportability, in cities (*WN*: 31–2). But there is wider division and more extensive markets as well, including international division of labour: 'such ... are the advantages of water-carriage, it is natural that the first improvements of art and industry should be made where this conveniency opens the whole world for a market to the produce of every sort of labour' (*WN*: 34; also *fB*). International free trade favours opulence, by enabling the dynamic benefits from greater extension of markets and hence also greater division of labour (*WN*: 446–8, 680–1; *LJA*: 390–2; *LJB*: 512–13, 529; *edWN*: 562, 577; cf. Stewart 1811: 343). Hence improvements in the ease and cost of transportation, by extending potential markets, enable extension of division of labour and its benefits (*WN*: 32–4; *LJA*: 356; *LJB*: 494; *fA*: 583; *fB*). Smith does not think it an accident that civilization began in the countries bordering the Mediterranean, and that the most materially developed parts of Asia exhibit similar advantages of water transportation (*WN*: 34–6; *fB*).

The causality between specialization, productivity and scale in the division of labour dynamics is not straightforward. Productivity growth certainly is the effect of which specialization is the cause; but does growth of the market cause specialization or does specialization cause the growth of exchange and of markets? In Book I, Chapters I–III (esp. Chapter III) the former direction of causation might seem intended; but this is not so unambiguously stated. The process could be thought of as a kind of interplay between the two phenomena, a mutual rather than one-way causation. The scope for labour specialization is limited by the scale of production; but this proposition is possibly consistent with, for example, productivity growth arising from increased specialization, in some manner simultaneously extending the market, via the resulting growth of incomes sustaining demand growth in line with the associated growth of potential output (cf. sec. 4.4.1).[8] Hence in the homely examples of specialization and extension of exchange at *WN* (27–8; also in *edWN*: 572), the latter appears to proceed from the former. On the other hand, a very similar illustration in *LJA* (348; cf. 351–2; also *LJB*: 493) concludes that 'the certainty of being able to exchange the surplus produce of their labours in one trade induces them [savages] to seperate themselves into different trades'. This implies that marketability induces or enables specialization, though this example actually begins from a kind of accidental specialization. (Very similar formulations concerning the role of 'certainty of being able to exchange' appear at *WN*: 28 and *edWN*: 572.) Likewise, further on in the same text we are told that '[t]he being of a market first occasioned the division ... of labour, and the greatness of it is what puts it in ones power to divide it much' (*LJA*: 355; also 356). Similarly, in *fA* (582) we read:

> Every species of industry ... will be more or less accurately subdivided into the different branches according to which it is capable of being split, in proportion to the extent of the market .... When the market is very small it is altogether impossible that there can be that separation of one employment from another which naturally takes place when it is more extensive.

The same logic is evident in the opening pages of *WN*, Book II:

> the number of workmen in every branch of business generally increases with the division of labour in that branch, *or rather it is the increase of their number which enables* them to class and subdivide themselves in this manner.
>
> (*WN*: 277; emphasis added)

These formulations suggest that Smith rather favours a one-way causation from market opportunities to specialization, so that the process appears as *demand-led*: it is the growth of market demand which drives extension of specialization and hence productivity growth. This is a dynamic not at all akin to the supply-led vision of later marginalist economics, in which commodity and input demands ultimately accommodate supplies of 'factors of production'. Recall also that Smith's dynamics of market price convergence towards normal price posited given, normal effectual demands (sec. 3.1.1).

Beyond the first three chapters, the most systematic consideration of division of labour in *WN* occurs in Book V, Chapter I (781–8). In the context of discussing public provision for education, Smith paints a dismal picture of the impact of division of labour on the labourer:

> In the progress of the division of labour, the employment of the far greater part of those who live by labour, that is, the great body of the people, comes to be confined to a few very simple operations .... But the understandings of the greater part of men are necessarily formed by their ordinary employments. The man whose whole life is spent in performing a few simple operations ... has no occasion to exert his understanding, or to exercise his invention in finding out expedients for removing difficulties which never occur. He ... generally becomes as stupid and ignorant as it is possible for a human creature to become. The torpor of his mind renders him, not only incapable of relishing or bearing a part in any rational conversation, but of conceiving any generous, noble, or tender sentiment .... Of the great and extensive interests of his county, he is altogether incapable of judging; and unless very particular pains have been taken to render him otherwise, he is equally incapable of defending his country in war.... His dexterity at his own particular trade seems, in this manner, to be acquired at the expence of his intellectual, social, and martial virtues. But in every improved and civilized society this is the state into which the labouring poor, that is, the great body of the people, must necessarily fall, unless government takes some pains to prevent it.
>
> (*WN*: 781–2; also 697–8; *LJB*: 539–41)

One may say, bluntly, that the growth of labour productivity from division of labour is due to its making labourers like machines, with associated ill consequences for their intellectual and physical constitution, and their sensibilities (cf. *WN*: 684, on slaves as machines). It is this, really, which makes this specialization partly *cause* the invention of new machines: the resulting increase in the simplicity and repetitiveness – indeed, in the mechanical nature – of labour activity provides increasing scope for labour to be replaced with machines, including in this process the workers themselves perceiving potential innovations in machinery.[9] The point is cast in sharp relief by Ferguson (1767: 280): 'Manufactures ... prosper most, where the mind is least consulted, and where the workshop may, without any great effort of imagination, be considered as an engine, the parts of which are men'.

By expressing so strongly his belief that the reduction of labour to increasingly mechanical activities is destructive of labourers' human qualities, Smith strikingly evidences that he is not an ideologue for commercial society or liberal capitalism. An ideologue or mere apologist would suppress or downplay such uncomfortable consequences. Recall also in this context our earlier comment, that Smith is in favour of capitalism not capitalists (see p. 77). Nevertheless, the necessary role of labour specialization in the growth of output per capita, and hence its essential role in pursuing the normative objective of political economy, the growth of consumption per capita, means that such specialization is an inescapable element of material progress. It also means that everything which flows from specialization is a necessary concomitant of such progress as well: decentralized market exchange, with all its institutional and behavioural (including ethical) requirements (e.g. the emergence of a monetary economy: *WN*: 37–8, 47, 221; *LJA*: 374; *LJB*: 500). The productivity and consumption gains which can proceed only from labour specialization makes decentralized exchange the inevitable historical outcome for humankind. To state the point more conditionally, decentralized exchange economies are as inevitable as the unwillingness of humankind to forgo the gains from specialization in production. Commercial society is necessary for material progress:

> It is the great multiplication of the productions of all the different arts, in consequence of the division of labour, which occasions, in a well-governed society, that universal opulence which extends itself to the lowest ranks of the people. Every workman has a great quantity of his own work to dispose of beyond what he himself has occasion for; and every other workman being exactly in the same situation, he is enabled to exchange a great quantity of his own goods for a great quantity … of theirs … and a general plenty diffuses itself through all the different ranks of the society.
>
> (*WN*: 22)[10]

Hence follows the very considerable attention devoted to commodity pricing and distribution in *WN*, Book I (i.e. exchange of one kind or another) before Smith turns to his ultimate object, the growth of wealth, in Book II.[11]

### *4.1.2 Earlier conceptions of division of labour*

William Petty probably deserves the credit for first clearly articulating the potential for labour specialization to increase productivity per worker, in two distinct passages of text. One occurs in the context of his extolling the economic and other benefits of populous cities, the emphasis being on population density:

> *Manufactures* will beget one another, and each *Manufacture* will be divided into as many parts as possible, whereby the Work of each *Artisan* will be simple and easie; As for Example. In the making of a *Watch*, If one Man shall make the *Wheels*, another the *Spring*, another shall Engrave the *Dial-*

> *plate*, and another shall make the *Cases*, then the *Watch* will be better and cheaper, than if the whole Work be put upon any one Man. And we also see that in *Towns*, and in the *Streets* of a great *Town*, where all the *Inhabitants* are almost of one Trade, the Commodity peculiar to those places is made better and cheaper than elsewhere.
>
> (Petty 1683a: 473)

In linking the division-of-labour/productivity nexus to populousness, Petty here also connects the phenomenon with scale of the market, albeit in a somewhat oblique way: in the absence of cheap commodity transportation, population density proxies the size of the market. He makes the same connection to market size in the second instance. Again, it is not quite as explicit as Smith is later to make it, and certainly not as systematically treated:

> Those who have the command of the Sea Trade, may Work at easier Freight with more profit, than other at greater: for as Cloth must be cheaper made, when one Cards, another Spins, another Weaves, another Draws, another Dresses, another Presses and Packs; than when all the Operations above-mentioned, were clumsily performed by the same hand; so those who command the Trade of Shipping, can build long slight Ships for carrying Masts, Fir-Timber, Boards, Balks, *&c.* And short ones for Lead, Iron, Stones *&c.* One sort of Vessels to Trade at Ports where they need never lie a ground, others where they must jump upon the Sand twice every twelve hours; One sort of Vessels, and way of manning in time of Peace, and cheap gross Goods, another for War and precious Commodities; One sort of Vessels for the turbulent Sea, another for Inland Water and Rivers; One sort of Vessels, and Rigging, where haste is requisite for the Maidenhead of a Market, another where 1/5 or 1/4 part of the time makes no matter. One sort of Masting and Rigging for long Voyages, another for Coasting. One sort of Vessels for Fishing, another for Trade. One sort for War for this or that Country, another for Burthen only. Some for Oars, some for Poles, some for Sails, and some for draught by Men or Horses, some for the Northern Navigations amongst Ice, and some for the South against Worms, *&c.*
>
> (Petty 1690: 260–1; editorial footnotes are attached to a couple of these sentences)

Petty (1683a) was in Smith's library; it is likely he was familiar also with the latter work (Mizuta 2000: 27; *WN*: 534–5; *Corr*: 288). Petty's insights into technical division of labour were undoubtedly stimulated by his involvement in the Bacon-inspired 'history of trades' project (see Aspromourgos 2005: 7–12).

Between Petty and Smith, a number of writers draw the connection from specialization to labour productivity, though it is not at all clear that they have ongoing productivity growth in mind, in the manner of Smith. Henry Martyn's (1701: 65–73) strikingly detailed account of productivity gains and cost reductions from specialization is evidently derivative from Petty: Martyn uses the same three examples of cloth, watches and ships. He is, perhaps, somewhat more explicit concerning the role of market size: 'if the Demand of Watches shou'd become so very great as to find constant imployment for as many Persons as there are Parts in a Watch' (p. 69). Mandeville (1733: 335–6; also 149) argues that in a polity with laws securing property and life, '[n]o Number of Men ... will be long without learning to divide and subdivide their Labour'. Contemplating a fivefold division of labour, he comments that each employment then will 'receive much greater Improvements, than if all had been promiscuously follow'd by every one of the Five'. Like Petty, he also instances watchmaking. Hutcheson's (1755, vol. 1: 287–90) account has something of a dynamic feel, but only via the role of market size in terms of a hypothetical progression from an isolated individual, to a family, to a few families, to society. He seems to have been considerably influenced by Gershom Carmichael's commentaries on Pufendorf (1682), though the latter's passing reference to something akin to division of labour is of very slight substance (Skinner 1996: 113–14; Moore 1927: 89). Joseph Harris (1757: 16–22) sketches the benefits of 'mankind ... betaking themselves severally to different occupations': 'each becoming expert and skilful in his own particular art ... performed in a much better manner, and with much less toil, than any one of them could do of himself'. Turgot (1769–70 [1977]: 43–50, 64, 69–71) outlines the significance of the technical division of labour, in terms of higher productivity from specialization, as well as the historical development of the social division of labour (see n. 15 below on this distinction). He also connects division of labour with the need for capital advances. But one does not get from Turgot's text either, a sense of ongoing technical progress.[12]

Reflections on the social and economic divisions of labour as such, are not an innovation of modern thought; they are to be found in literature all the way back to antiquity. But in contradistinction to Smith, in pre-modern thought the socio-economic division of labour is rather statically understood, and not unrelated to this, it is naturalized. As Vivenza (2001: 128) puts it, in the context of a valuable discussion of earlier secondary literature on the ancient versus the Smithian conception of division of labour, 'in the one, social and economic stratification and a lack of choice as to work; in the other, social mobility and a free labour market'. Absent from pre-modern thought is the Smithian view that individuals' socio-economic and other differences are a result of the division of labour, rather than the division of labour being a consequence of individuals' differences, the latter understood as natural in some sense. Likewise absent is the link from labour specialization to increasing labour productivity, understood dynamically, as *an ongoing process*. The prospect of such ongoing technical progress is one crucial aspect of the larger idea of human progress, which has its genesis only in the seventeenth and eighteenth centuries (Bury 1955: 1–97) – though in the case of Smith at least, optimism concerning human progress in general is moderate and qualified (see sec. 5.3.2).[13] On the foundation laid by Petty and other subsequent writers, Smith could plausibly posit for political economy a normative goal of high or rising consumption per capita. The technical progress made possible by division of labour and associated mechanization is the empirical basis for the normative principle. Of course, that prescriptive principle cannot be deduced from the descriptive theory. Something more must be added, some notion of a right of all to share in the social bounty provided by technical progress.[14] This does not need to be a supposition of *equal* individual rights to a share in the bounty, but a sense of natural human equality certainly provides support for Smith's normative principle (cf. Vivenza 2001: 133). Both the descriptive theory and the norm involve a break with pre-modernity: the prospect of productivity growth from division of labour *enables* the norm of generalized high or rising consumption.

Here is the text from Plato's *Republic* most commonly cited in comparisons of Plato and Smith on division of labour:

> 'Well then,' I said, 'a city, as I believe, comes into being because each of us isn't self-sufficient but is in need of much. Do you believe there's another beginning to the founding of a city?'
>
> 'None at all,' he said.
>
> 'So, then, when one man takes on another for one need and another for another need, and, since many things are needed, many men gather in one settlement as partners and helpers, to this common settlement we give the name city, don't we?'
>
> 'Most certainly.'
>
> . . .
>
> 'Now wait,' I said. 'How will the city be sufficient to provide for ... [food, housing, clothing and so on]? Won't one man be a farmer, another the housebuilder, and still another, a weaver? Or shall we add to it a shoemaker or some other man who cares for what has to do with the body?
>
> 'Certainly.'
>
> . . .
>
> 'Now, what about this? Must each one of them put his work at the disposition of all in common – for example, must the farmer, one man, provide food for four and spend four times as much time and labor in the provision of food and then give it in common to the others; or must he neglect them and produce a fourth part of the food in a fourth part of the time and use the other three parts for the provision of a house, clothing, and shoes, not taking the trouble to share in common with others, but minding his own business for himself?'
>
> And Adeimantus said, 'Perhaps, Socrates, the former is easier than the latter.'
>
> 'It wouldn't be strange, by Zeus,' I said. 'I myself also had the thought when you spoke that, in the first place, each of us is naturally not quite like anyone else, but rather differs in his nature; different men are apt for the accomplishment of different jobs. Isn't that your opinion?'
>
> 'It is.'

> 'And, what about this? Who would do a finer job, one man practicing many arts, or one man one art?'
>
> 'One man, one art,' he said.
>
> ...
>
> 'So, on this basis each thing becomes more plentiful, finer, and easier, when one man, exempt from other tasks, does one thing according to nature ....'
>
> (Bloom 1968: 45–7; 369b–370c; an editorial note is attached to one of these sentences)

In a sense, in his famous commentary on how the differences between a 'common street porter' and a 'philosopher' are not 'so much the cause, as the effect of the division of labour', Smith turns Plato on his head, as well as pre-modern thought generally (*WN*: 28–30; *LJA*: 348–9; *LJB*: 493; *edWN*: 572–4). Rather than the division of socio-economic functions and activities among individuals or groups being the result of natural differences among human beings, division of labour determines at least much of the differences between individuals or groups undertaking different socio-economic activities, differences which hence cease to be conceived of as natural. This doctrine has an evidently and inherently subversive implication for the social division of labour, whatever Smith's intentions in this regard.[15] For example, if an actual aristocracy is not a natural aristocracy, acquiescence in the associated socio-economic order is that much less compelling (cf. *WN*: 622, 707, 944, concerning 'natural aristocracy'). Smith's idea is attractive in its egalitarian recourse to a certain kind of natural equality of individuals. The arbitrariness of individuals' socio-economic positions (including at birth, but even before), and the associated differences in modes of consumption, in education, in the work or 'work-like' functions that individuals are applied to, and in the whole constellation of life activities, make a substantial part of the differences in what individuals are and what they become. But that idea requires at least qualification, subsequent to the development of genetics. Nevertheless, the fact of genetic differences does not contradict the truth that social and technical division of labour also makes individuals different. The political exploitation of genetic pseudo-science in the twentieth century is not irrelevant to this point.[16]

The above quotation from the *Republic* certainly lacks Smith's link between extent of the market and division of labour (and the role of capital); but at first glance it might seem suggestive of his link from specialization to labour productivity growth. In a judicious assessment of the similarities and differences between Plato and Smith on this subject, and a consideration of pertinent ancient literature more widely, Vivenza (2001: 129–40) disposes of this inference. She also systematically considers the three factors Smith offers to explain how specialization increases labour productivity (see sec. 4.1.1), comparing them with Plato's treatment. With regard to labour productivity growth, Vivenza (2001: 131–2; cf. 139, n. 33 and Schefold 1999: 126) – with explicit and particular reference to the last sentence of our quotation from the *Republic* ('more plentiful') – comments:

> Plato's point is that the man who dedicates himself to one work only rather than to many will perform it better because he will do so with ever greater experience, an understanding of the way it works, and professional competence ['a finer job', in our quotation from the *Republic* above]. The result, in short, is a better product, even if to put it like this is to misrepresent somewhat the thought of a philosopher whose principal concern is not so much for the product ... as for the man making it.... His comment should therefore be understood in the obvious sense that by sticking to a single form of work one will get more of it done than if one were to carry out two or three together.

Plato's account, it may be emphasized, also lacks the notion of productivity growth as an ongoing process. Vivenza's interpretation involves a qualified endorsement of Foley (1974), but certainly not of his subsequently expressed view, that there are ancient (albeit not Platonic) origins even for Smith's notion of individual differences being the consequence rather than the cause of the division of labour (Vivenza 2001: 126–9, 137–9; Foley 1975). McNulty (1975) had drawn just this contrast between Plato (together with pre-modern thought in general) and Smith, as we have above. Vivenza (2001: 127, n. 5, 129, n. 8) notes that the same point was earlier made by Bonar (1922: 15–17, 155; and the same pages in the 1st edition).[17]

Schumpeter (1954: 56) made the somewhat pejorative observation that division of labour is the 'eternal commonplace of economics'. But what are from one vantage point elementary and obvious notions, are from another, fundamental ideas. In any case, the connection between division of labour and technical progress is not at all a widespread belief before Smith. Furthermore, specialization of economic and social functions is synonymous with interdependence among humans, and thereby, a fundamental social fact which could hardly be ignored by anyone, at any time, seriously thinking about the nature of economic society. Levy (1999: 243–5) rightly emphasizes the *intrinsically* social character of individuals in Smith's economic theory and we have shown how even insatiability of individuals' wants is conceived of in intrinsically social terms by Smith (Chapter 3, n. 25). The 'Robinson Crusoe' model of economic behaviour (see White 1987), more congenial to latter-day economics due to its methodological individualism, cannot be imputed to Smith's conception of individuals. The propensity at the foundation of Smith's interpretation of division of labour is a sociable propensity, grounded in the human capacity for language, at the same time as it is self-regarding (*WN*: 25). It is also notable that the division of labour is given priority as the first topic addressed in *WN*, even though this sequencing was by no means logically necessary. To truck, barter and exchange is an activity not possible for an isolated individual. Modern economics pays little explicit attention to division of labour; but this is perhaps more due to its being taking for granted, than a rejection of the significance of division of labour for labour productivity (cf. Groenewegen 1977a: 391, 398–9). Some developments in modern economics may be read as attempts to engage with the consequences of division of labour for economic and social organization; e.g. the theory of the firm (Seabright 2004: 152). The absence of any treatment of the firm in Smith means that it is unclear, in his account, to what extent the process of 'vertical disintegration' entailed by division of labour – the separation or reduction of the production of final goods into more and simpler, activities – involves the emergence of more (and more specialist) firms and markets, or occurs internal to firms. (To the extent that greater specialization occurs within firms, it does not entail greater market exchange.) This issue is taken up in later economics (see Vassilakis 1987; Vincent-Lancrin 2003; cf. n. 15 above). The dynamic interaction of productivity growth and demand growth, though in a form involving more mutual causation than in Smith's account of division of labour, was much emphasized by Nicholas Kaldor (n. 8 above).

Seabright (2004) provides a thoughtful reflection on the nature and significance of division of labour in contemporary society, including the institutional, social and ethical conditions for a system of exchange among strangers – and its dangers. He never addresses Smith's concerns about the consequences of specialization for workers' well-being. Were those concerns unfounded – or is it that modern labour specialization does not generate so much debilitating mechanical activity? As a matter of fact, Smith's reflections on the role of education in offsetting the ill consequences of division of labour provide reasons, from his viewpoint, for concluding that such consequences are no longer pertinent (*WN*: 784–8; cf. Winch 1978: 113–20). In arguing that people 'of rank and fortune' do not suffer the consequences of division of labour that workers do, Smith provides grounds which would imply that twenty-first century workers, at least in the most developed economies, would not generally be subject to those consequences either. Those people of rank and fortune,

> are generally eighteen or nineteen years of age before they enter upon that particular business, profession, or trade, by which they propose to distinguish themselves in the world. They have before that full time to acquire, or at least to fit themselves for afterwards acquiring, every accomplishment which can recommend them to the publick esteem, or render them worthy of it.
>
> (*WN*: 784)[18]

In addition, the employments in which they 'spend the greater part of their lives' are not 'simple and uniform'; they are 'extremely complicated', exercising 'the head more than the hands', and these people 'generally have a good deal of leisure' (*WN*: 784; cf. *EPS*: 187). The circumstances of the average twenty-first century worker in a developed economy are more like this than like that of an eighteenth-century labourer.[19]

## 4.2 Gross revenue and net revenue

### *4.2.1 Smith and social 'net revenue'*

The term 'revenue' is employed very extensively in *WN*, by itself, as a synonym for various species of income; e.g. of countries, the State, society, the people, labour, stock, land and individuals.[20] This wide-ranging use of the term does not occur in *LJ*, where it is used exclusively to refer to revenues of government or of governing classes, in one sense or another.[21] This is likewise true of the one reference in *edWN* (567) and the few references in *Corr* (245–6, 250, 262, 271, 273–4, 289–90). Hence also, the *WN* distinction between gross and net revenue is not to be found in the pre-*WN* writings. The transition from a purely public finance use of the term, to a notion of the revenue of nations or societies, is evident from a comparison of Smith's definitions of jurisprudence and of political economy. The 'author' or amanuensis of *LJB* gave them the title, 'Juris Prudence or Notes from the Lectures on Justice, Police, Revenue, and Arms …' (396). This accurately reflects Smith's own conception there of the elements of jurisprudence, understood as 'the theory of the general principles of law and government', with its 'four great objects … Justice, Police, Revenue, and Arms' (*LJB*: 398; similarly, *LJA*: 5–7). The key *WN* definition of political economy 'proposes two distinct objects; first, to provide a plentiful revenue or subsistence for the people … and secondly, to supply the state or commonwealth with a revenue sufficient for the publick services' (*WN*: 428; quoted more fully in sec. 2.1.1). Here in *WN*, the people's 'revenue' has priority of place; but in truth, this notion of political economy was already implied in *LJ*.

It was concluded in section 2.1.1 that for Smith the science of political economy is a branch of jurisprudence. The opening paragraphs of *LJA* confirm this. After introducing the first of the four elements of jurisprudence ('justice'), Smith continues:

> When … internall peace … is secured, the government will next be desirous of promoting the opulence of the state. This produces what we call police. Whatever regulations are made with respect to the trade, commerce, agriculture, manufactures of the country are considered as belonging to police.… The 3$^{d}$ part of police[22] is bon marché or the cheapness of provisions, and the having the market well supplied with all sorts of commodities.… This is the most important branch of police ….
>
> (*LJA*: 5–6)

Smith goes on to comment also on government revenue and external defence, as well as international relations. Hence in this language of *LJ*, political economy is concerned with the second and third objects of jurisprudence: the non-trivial part of 'police' (but part of the justice dimension of police has been put aside), together with government revenue. However, external defence also has a place. In a prefatory note to the 1790 sixth edition of *TMS*, Smith comments on an undertaking he had made in the concluding paragraph of the previous five editions, to publish an account of jurisprudence: 'In the *Enquiry concerning the Nature and Causes of the Wealth of Nations*, I have partly executed this promise; at least so far as concerns police, revenue, *and arms*' (*TMS*: 3; emphasis added; cf. 342).

Our concern here is with Smith's conception of the gross and net revenue of societies or nations. But before turning to that directly, two additional aspects of these terms may be outlined: his identification of revenue with production or output ('produce') and his uses in general of 'gross' and 'net' (actually, almost always, 'neat'). The former identification is stated very explicitly in the following terms: 'the annual revenue of every society is always precisely equal to the exchangeable value of the whole annual produce of its industry, or rather is precisely the same thing with that exchangeable value' (*WN*: 455–6). This equality is repeated very frequently, albeit more casually, throughout the book, commonly expressed with recourse to the phrase 'real wealth and revenue' or 'real revenue and wealth'.[23] Hence we have an identification of revenue, income and the value of annual produce. This in turn is connected with the Smithian doctrine of the reducibility of the value of the annual national produce to what are regarded by him as the three ultimate forms of income from production: wages, profits and rents (*WN*, Book I, Chapter VI):

> As the price or exchangeable value of every particular commodity, taken separately, resolves itself into some one or other or all of … [wages, profits and rent]; so that of all the commodities which compose the whole annual produce of the labour of every country, taken complexly, must resolve itself into the same three parts, and be parcelled out among different inhabitants of the country, either as the wages of their labour, the profits of their stock, or the rent of their land. The whole of what is annually either collected or produced by the labour of every society, or what comes to the same thing, the whole price of it, is in the [*sic* – 'this' intended?] manner originally distributed among some of its different members. Wages, profit, and rent, are the three original sources of all revenue as well as of all exchangeable value. All other revenue is ultimately derived from some one or other of these.
>
> (*WN*: 69; also 265, 286)

Hence interest payments are merely a transfer, 'a derivative revenue' – from profits, if the borrowings are used for investment, or from any of the three ultimate revenues in the case of consumption loans. Similarly, '[a]ll taxes, and all the revenue which is founded upon them, all salaries, pensions, and annuities of every kind, are ultimately derived from some one or other of those three original sources of revenue' (*WN*: 69–70; also 825).

A theoretical issue arises here, in relation to the significance of the parallel between the reducibility of the price of any individual commodity to wages, profits and rents (elaborated at *WN*: 65–9), and the reducibility of the annual product to the same three incomes. This is the chapter prior to Smith's key price theory chapter (Book I, Chapter VII). The identification of the value of the annual product with the revenue proceeds from its sale is sensible, indeed, can be *constructed* to be true, by appropriate accounting definitions. For 'circular' production systems,[24] this will be true in both gross and net terms: net of the value of material inputs used up in the annual cycle of gross production, the value of the remaining product (i.e. the net product) accrues as net incomes to the three classes of owners of inputs; in gross terms, the value of the material inputs used up will also accrue as the additional income making up, together with net income, total gross income. Smith is also correct that this accounting identity can be applied as well to the value or sale price of any particular commodity: deducting the value of material inputs used up in the production of a commodity, what remains of its sale price[25] will resolve into incomes to the three classes of input owners collaborating in its production; and in gross terms, the cost of the material inputs used up will also accrue as additional income, making up the total price of the commodity. But when Smith moves to the *theory* of normal prices in the subsequent *WN* chapter, he supposes that this allows him to proceed as if the rates of wages and profits entering into those prices are separably determined. This is an additional step beyond the above accounting identities, and is taken up further in section 4.3.5.

Finally, before turning specifically to gross and net revenue of society, Smith's overall use of 'gross', 'net' and variants thereof may be sketched. In *TMS* 'gross', and extensions of the term, are considerably used in moral senses: excessive, coarse or indecent (e.g. *TMS*: 32, 81, 175, 209, 257, 328). This moral sense is also employed in *WN* (e.g. 40, 350, 518, 764, 788, 794, 802–3, 945). *Engrossed* appears in the sense of absorbed, or taken control of, in *TMS* (57), and this term and variants thereof are extensively used to describe monopolistic situations in *WN* (112, 143, 382, 385, 396, 525, 528, 538, 532–4, 572–3, 596, 628, 630, 744). This sense also appears in *LJ* (*LJA*: 197–8; *LJB*: 516, 524–5, 579, 581). The first use of the economic sense of 'gross' in distinction from *neat* (the latter, also first employed here) is in relation to profit rates net of compensation for 'extraordinary' or 'occasional losses to which every employment of stock is exposed' (*WN*: 113; also 753, 818 – the latter netting out 'expence of management'). Net profit is also called 'clear profit' (*WN*: 113) and 'neat revenue' is employed in a couple of instances as a synonym for net profit (*WN*: 488, 852). By way of analogy to gross rent versus net rent of a private estate, a distinction is drawn between the 'gross revenue' and the 'neat revenue' of a society, the latter being 'what remains free … after deducting' the cost of maintaining the capital stock, 'or what, without encroaching upon their capital, they can place in their stock reserved for immediate consumption' (*WN*: 286–7). This is precisely the concept of particular interest to us here, thoroughly investigated directly below. 'Gross produce' also occurs (*WN*: 184, 186, 219, 562, 665, 882, 888, 896), and 'neat produce', particularly in relation to Smith's appraisal of Physiocracy (*WN*: 665–75, 847–8, 896). But notwithstanding his identification of national product and revenue, these uses of gross and net produce never refer to a system-wide concept (national output), but rather to agricultural outputs or the gross proceeds from taxes. Hence gross and net tax revenues are distinguished as well (*WN*: 727n, 882, 885, 888, 896–7). At one point, 'gross estimation' is employed in the sense of a rough or approximate measure (*WN*: 756). Smith uses 'nett' or 'net' rather than the more usual 'neat' on only four occasions (*WN*: 750, 753, 753n; *Corr*: 289–90). All Smith's economic uses are particular instances of the generic notion of net quantity as that 'remaining after all necessary deductions' from gross quantity (*OED*: 'net'). This is very clear, indeed explicit, in the quotation from *WN* (286) above, as well as in the following: a 'neat salary' as salary '[a]fter all deductions are made'; 'nett revenue' as gross revenue 'clear of all deductions and … charges' (*WN*: 720, 750; also 882, 896).[26]

It is in the second chapter of *WN*, Book II, subtitled 'of the Expence of maintaining the National Capital', that Smith enunciates his concepts of the gross and net revenue of society.

> The gross revenue of all the inhabitants of a great country, comprehends the whole annual produce of their land and labour; the neat revenue, what remains free to them after deducting the expence of maintaining; first, their fixed; and, secondly, their circulating capital; or what, without encroaching upon their capital, they can place in their stock reserved for immediate consumption, or spend upon their subsistence, conveniencies, and amusements. Their real wealth too is in proportion not to their gross, but to their neat revenue.
>
> (*WN*: 286–7)

This is to make net national revenue equal to the value of annual output net of the replacement of capital used up in the annual production cycle.[27] The meaning of 'capital' is explored further in the next section. Here it suffices to say that putting aside fixed capital for now, circulating capital embraces four elements: 'money, provisions, materials, and finished work' (*WN*: 288). The content of circulating capital will be further considered below. The latter three embrace material inputs which will be used up in production processes, embodied in commodities subsequently to be used for consumption or maintenance of fixed capital (generally via sale to others, but possibly also by direct use), together with stocks in the latter-day sense of inventories (see *WN*: 279–80, 282–4).

But in determining net revenue, Smith does not wish to deduct the value of the latter three from annual produce or gross revenue, unless and until they subsequently contribute to the maintenance of fixed capital. His reason is that otherwise, they will finally be realized in 'stock reserved for immediate consumption', when sold to 'users and consumers' (*WN*: 282, n. *a*, 283, n. *c*), or transformed into commodities which are then so sold:

> The maintenance of those three parts of the circulating capital, therefore, withdraws no portion of the annual produce from the neat revenue of the society, besides what is necessary for maintaining the fixed capital.

> The circulating capital of a society is in this respect different from that of an individual. That of an individual is totally excluded from making any part of his neat revenue, which must consist altogether in his profits. But though the circulating capital of every individual makes a part of that of the society to which he belongs, it is not upon that account totally excluded from making a part likewise of their neat revenue. Though the whole goods in a merchant's shop must by no means be placed in his own stock reserved for immediate consumption, they may be in that of other people, who, from a revenue derived from other funds, may regularly replace their value to him, together with its profits, without occasioning any diminution either of his capital or of theirs.
>
> (*WN*: 288)[28]

As to the first of Smith's four elements of circulating capital, he is including in capital the quantity of money available for use in exchange on the basis of its role in the circulation of commodities, in particular, the circulation of the other three circulating capital elements (*WN*: 282, 288–92; also 438). It is certainly sensible to exclude this money element from net revenue, as Smith does (*WN*: 289); but it would also be more sensible to exclude it from capital altogether. It is not part of the annual produce and it is not an input to production in any meaningful sense; but if it is to be treated as capital at all, it is really more akin to fixed capital, as Smith somewhat acknowledges (*WN*: 288–9, 291). Here he draws poorly the conceptual line between production processes and other, connected but distinct, economic processes which are part of the overall system, notably, exchange and circulation. Smith would have done better to more distinctly separate conceptually money's role in circulation from the concept of capital in production. This would be analogous to his separation of unproductive labour from productive labour, while nevertheless allowing that the former may be useful or even necessary in some larger sense than production as such (see sec. 4.3.2). The statement that money is neither a part of output nor of net revenue also requires one qualification: once money is treated as part of required capital in production, then the costs of maintaining, or if required, augmenting, the quantity of money will constitute a deduction from net revenue (*WN*: 289, 291–5). In the case of augmentation, the newly produced money should then also form a part of annual produce.

The importance of the concept of net revenue to Smith's political economy is that it provides one of the three fundamental building blocks of his treatment of capital accumulation and economic growth: division of labour as the driver of productivity growth; net revenue as setting the upper bound of potential net accumulation of capital; and the proportion of gross (or net) revenue allocated to employment of productive labour as determining the actual extent of gross (or net) capital accumulation, as against unproductive consumption. Whatever difficulties may attach to his substantive definition of society's net revenue in relation to capital, its conceptual significance is to constitute a notion of (say, annual) national income available for expenditures, after allowance for the preservation or restoration, intact, of the capital stock inherited at the beginning of the annual cycle of production. (The difficulties are further discussed in secs. 4.2.4, 4.3.1 and 4.4.2.) The allocation of this net revenue between, in latter-day language, investment and (surplus) consumption – or in Smith's language, between productive labour and unproductive labour – is a crucial determinant of growth. The potential growth paths include for Smith the possibility of negative accumulation and negative growth (a 'declining' state), if unproductive consumption exceeds net revenue. Such an outcome can occur, in a closed system, by way of 'consumption' of the existing capital stock (e.g. *WN*: 342). Again, these issues will be taken up more fully in the examination of Smith's treatment of capital and productive labour in section 4.3. This all points toward the issue of whether Smith has a conception of the social surplus: that part of national product or income which is available for free disposal, after deducting that which is necessary for restoring the capital stock to its initial situation, as it was at the beginning of the annual production cycle.[29] If there is such a conception in Smith, then the key question is what is to be netted out from gross national or social product, to arrive at the surplus.

### *4.2.2 The concept of a social surplus*

This question will be resolved in sections 4.3 and 4.4. With a view to providing a benchmark for that analysis, a statement of the concept of surplus may be presented here. While Chapter 3 was particularly concerned to recover Smith's scientifically valuable conception of normal price as the opportunity cost regulating the dynamics of market prices, it was indicated in section 3.4.2 that a second Smithian notion of cost also has important scientific content: cost as the inputs used up or destroyed in the process of producing a particular product; that is to say, the real, physical loss that is the consequence of obtaining an output, and under conditions of technically efficient production, the *necessary* consequence.[30] Considered at the level of a closed socio-economic system as a whole, this leads directly to the concept of 'surplus'. The real cost of production of the gross outputs of such a system, say produced in an annual cycle, is the set of aggregate quantities of required inputs used up; the surplus, roughly speaking, is the difference between those gross outputs and the aggregate necessary inputs.[31] This is just the concept of 'price', in its deepest or most elementary sense: that which is sacrificed; that which is given up, in 'exchange'; that which is foregone. For the science of wealth there are two important expressions of this idea, one clear in Smith, one not so clear, as we shall see. Normal price as suppliers' opportunity cost, regulating market prices under competitive conditions, represents what is foregone *at the level of individual producers*. Second, the inputs used up in production of the gross national product represent what is foregone *by the (closed system) society or socio-economic system as a whole*, the difference between these two sets of quantities being the social surplus.

There will be a set of activities (or processes, or industries) in any economic or social system, in which a variety of material inputs and a variety of types of human labour inputs are combined in certain quantities, for the production of certain quantities of material outputs. The concept of surplus captures the capacity of such a production system to be self-replacing or self-reproducing, its capacity for outputting quantities in excess of those inputted. Labour cannot merely be input in such systems: humans require consumption to subsist through time; in a viable system they must be 'reproduced' as well. By supposing a definite set of kinds and quantities of commodities defining necessary consumption per unit of labour, per time period, for each type of labour, the required labour inputs to the production system can be reduced to quantities of commodities. Then the production system may be characterized entirely in terms of commodity flows, and the 'viability' of the system can be defined in terms of the aggregate input of each and every commodity not exceeding its aggregate output (but see n. 31 above).

As a simple formal illustration of this, suppose a production system in which there are just two economic activities undertaken in a uniform, discrete time period, producing three material outputs by means of three material inputs plus homogeneous labour. $C_C$, $M_C$, $T_C$ and $C_M$, $M_M$, $T_M$ are the quantities of material inputs in the two activities (C, M), respectively; $L_C$, $L_M$ are the respective labour inputs; $C^C$, $M^C$, $T^C$ and $C^M$, $M^M$, $T^M$, the quantities of joint outputs from each activity respectively. Necessary consumption per unit of labour may be represented by a given quantity of just commodity C ($c$); that is to say, M and T do not directly form a part of subsistence. This generates the input–output configuration:

$$C_C, M_C, T_C, cL_C \rightarrow C^C, M^C, T^C$$

$$C_M, M_M, T_M, cL_M \rightarrow C^M, M^M, T^M$$

The viability condition for this system may be stated as:

$$S^C = (C^C + C^M) - [(C_C + C_M) + c(L_C + L_M)] \geq 0$$

$$S^M = (M^C + M^M) - (M_C + M_M) \geq 0$$

$$S^T = (T^C + T^M) - (T_C + T_M) \geq 0$$

where $S^C$, $S^M$, $S^T$ are the surplus quantities of the three material commodities, and the production of a surplus further requires that at least one of these is satisfied as a strict inequality.

A particular construction may now be placed upon commodity T. Suppose it in fact is homogeneous land which comes out of each of the two activities, as output, in exactly the same quality and quantity as it enters each process as input: land is assumed to come through each production process completely unchanged. In this special case, $T_C$ and $T^C$ ($T_M$ and $T^M$) are identical in economically relevant character and quantity, so that $S^T$ is zero. To that extent, with regard to formulating the concept of surplus, one may suppress the role of land, taking for granted its entry to and exit (unchanged) from the production system.[32] Then, putting aside $T_C$ (and $T^C$), $T_M$ (and $T^M$) and adding also the simplifying supposition of no other joint production ($M^C$, $C^M$ take zero values), the superscripts on outputs identifying the process from which they come can be dropped. The resulting system, akin to single production (i.e. an absence of joint production), can be represented by:

$$(C_C + cL_C), M_C \rightarrow C$$

$$(C_M + cL_M), M_M \rightarrow M$$

$$C \geq [(C_C + C_M) + c(L_C + L_M)]$$

$$M \geq (M_C + M_M)$$

with the production of a surplus requiring at least one of these two inequalities to be satisfied as a strict inequality. The circular character of production and associated concept of surplus formed the framework for analysing and binding the structure of distribution and prices, as well as capital accumulation and consumption, in classical economics and beyond. The approach can also be formulated in terms of labour (and was). To see in a simple manner how one may translate between necessary commodity input and surplus product on the one hand, and necessary and surplus labour on the other, add these further two suppositions: neither commodity employs input of commodity M ($M_C$, $M_M = 0$) and no surplus of commodity C is produced ($C$ equals $C_C + C_M + cL_C + cL_M$). Then, $C$ and $M$ become the system's necessary input and surplus output respectively, and $L_C$ and $L_M$, necessary and surplus labour respectively. Indeed, one may conceive of necessary labour as producing surplus commodities, or of necessary commodity inputs producing surplus labour, just as much as one may conceive of labour producing surplus labour or commodities producing surplus commodities.[33]

The concept of 'surplus' so understood is a particular species of which the genus is the idea of system (or 'national') net product or net income. It has the peculiarity, from a modern standpoint, that necessary or subsistence consumption of the labour required to produce the gross product is also netted out. Does this difference matter; and is not the classical notion obsolete for modern economies, in which instances of labour consumption or wages in the neighbourhood of subsistence are apparently rare? It can matter, and subsistence consumption may remain pertinent even in economies in which the consumption of relatively few persons approximates subsistence in any plausible sense. (The latter issue is considered in the Epilogue.) In his modern reconstruction of the classical approach to distribution and prices, Sraffa (1960: 9–10) puts aside necessary labour consumption, at least for his immediate purposes in that book, but with some reluctance. The reluctance is understandable: it is evident that labour and its necessary consumption are essential to the viability of circular production systems, in a way in which above-necessary consumption is not. Necessary labour consumption is akin to other necessary commodity inputs to production. But while in the first instance the concept of surplus is best regarded as an elementary notion of system net product or net income, at a deeper level it conveys the notion of a system-level residual, available for free disposal after replacement or reproduction of the inputs used up (but see n. 31 above). A net product could be identified also in marginalist models incorporating circular production systems, but it is not generally available for free disposal with respect to its income distribution dimension. That is to say, putting aside the issue of whether or not to net necessary labour consumption out of gross output, the net product *becomes* a surplus in this deeper sense, when it can be conceived of as free to be distributed in a variety of ways. Certainly in Smith's approach, a variety of distributional outcomes is regarded as consistent with a given set of property relations, rather than functional distribution being uniquely determined by the requirements of competitive system equilibrium, as in latter-day marginalist theory. Or at least, that theory has sought such a result.

### *4.2.3 Etymology*

The term 'revenue' emerges in fifteenth-century English, from the Old French *revenu*, the past participle of *revinir*, to return – from the Latin *revinire* (return), *re-* (back) and *venire* (come). It early had some use in the literal sense of return: 'now uppon the Kyngs revenue into his owne realme' (1532). But from the beginning, it had the primary sense of 'return, yield, or profit' from lands or other property; that 'which comes in ... as a return from property or possessions, esp. of an extensive kind; income from any source (but esp. when large and not directly earned)': 'Other profitz or revenuz that longeth to the seid cominaltee' (1433); 'He ... caused the partyes to be contented with such reuenuse & profytes as they had resayued' (1494); 'Whervpon is the reuenew of my fermes spente or wasted?' (1565); 'I haue a Widdow Aunt, a dowager, Of great reuennew' (1599; Shakespeare); 'One gave all of his goods to the poore at once, the other kept all the inheritance and gave the revenue' (1649). As Gilibert (1987) observes, it thereby is essentially a synonym for 'income' in later English, though 'revenue' is more particularly applied to income from assets rather than from labour before Smith. (In fact, 'income' was somewhat used in the sense of revenue, as early as the seventeenth century.) Revenue was also employed figuratively: 'the reuenues of your vertues wilbe inualuable' (1576); 'The grace of God is the best revennewe of this towne, and his blessings our greatest rentes' (1626). From early, it was also deployed in the particular sense of the income of monarchs, governments or States: 'His majesteis yeirlie revenew and patrimony of his croun' (1580); 'The Revenue now in time of Peace, will yield above all charges 1500000 *l.* per An.' (1690; all quotations from *OED*: 'revenue').

'Gross' originates in Middle English, from Old French *gros*, *grosse* (big, thick, coarse), from late Latin, *grossus* (thick). It conveyed these senses in English from the fifteenth and sixteenth centuries, and the related senses of 'corpulant', 'unwholesomely … fat', 'palpable', 'easy to apprehend', 'flagrant', 'monstrous', the largest part of something, general as opposed to particular, density, 'material or perceptible to the senses' (as contrasted with the impalpable), as well as common, inferior, dull, stupid, rough, clumsy, indelicate and unrefined. The technical sense of the term, which is of primary interest in relation to Smith, is a kind of precise crystallization of the gross as the large: the '[e]ntire, total, whole', in particular, 'before necessary deductions have been made': 'Cast togyther in one grosse sum' (1539); 'I cannot instantly raise vp the grosse Of full three thousand ducats' (1596; Shakespeare); 'Comets … haue … Power and Effect ouer the Grosse and Masse of things' (1625). This precise sense also generally gives 'gross' a definite quantitative meaning. The concepts of gross and net at this level are inextricably interconnected. The gross concept at least implies a net magnitude; the technical or quantitative sense of net certainly entails a gross concept: the net magnitude as that remaining after all pertinent, necessary deductions have been made from the gross quantity. 'Neat' also arises in Middle English from French. The senses of the term relating to elegance, smartness and so on may be put aside, though it may be noted that they have an underlying connection with the technical sense of the term. The latter is in English use by the seventeenth century, as one dimension of the senses of 'neat' relating to purity: 'free from dirt or impurities', 'unadulturated', '[f]ree from any reductions': 'neate and cleane from the faultes which S. Paule condemneth' (1579); '600000 ducates of golde, neat and free of all charges' (1599); 'She saw me mix water with my wine … she and her women drank it neat' (1686); 'The Commander has … Two-Eighths of the neat Produce of every Prize' (1747).[34]

### *4.2.4 Earlier concepts of net revenue*

It is the net concept which is of primary interest in relation to 'revenue'; and it is the deployment of that concept *at the level of society as a whole* which is the important scientific development for economic theory in the eighteenth century. Prior to Smith, the most decisive theoretical advance with regard to that system-level conception of net revenue is due to Quesnay, though one may suggest that his advance is only to make more explicit, more systematic and more formal, a notion of social surplus already clear in Petty and Cantillon. Here, Petty – as ever, intellectually inventive – deserves to be regarded as the originator. As with his insights concerning the connection from technical division of labour to labour productivity (sec. 4.1.1), it is the environment and intellectual atmosphere provided by the Bacon-inspired intellectual programme of the circle of Samuel Hartlib, and of the Royal Society, centred on applied science, technology and production methods, which evidently was the stimulus (see Aspromourgos 2005). Petty's basic theoretical conceptualization is developed in three arithmetical models in the *Treatise of Taxes* (Petty 1662: 30–1, 42–3, 89–90), and it is widely applied by him to policy and statecraft. On the foundations of Petty's surplus concept, Cantillon develops a systematic analysis of the production and circulation of commodities in general. The socio-economic system is demarcated into classes, primarily in terms of landowners, entrepreneurs (of which farmers are a subset) and labourers. It is also demarcated spatially, in particular, in terms of town and country, though this is not quite equivalent to manufacture and agriculture. The net revenue of the system is identified with land-rents and taxation revenue, as is the case also for Petty:

> The overplus of the Land [of a society] is at the disposition of the Owner: he pays part of it to the Prince or the Government, or else the Farmer does so directly at the Owner's expense.
>
> As for the use to which the Land should be put, the first necessity is to employ part of it for the Maintenance and Food of those who work upon it and make it productive: the rest depends principally upon the Humour and Fashion of Living of the Prince, the Lords, and the Owner ....
>
> (Cantillon 1755 [1931]: 7; cf. 63, 75–95)[35]

From the point of departure provided by Cantillon's text, Quesnay developed a remarkable piece of theoretical machinery for the conceptualization and analysis of economic society, most notably embodied in the *tableau économique*, in which the net revenue of society is identified with a surplus produced by agriculture alone. That theoretical system has received much analysis and appraisal, and a repetition is not necessary here.[36] Turgot made important advances upon that system. Nevertheless, Turgot remains within the Physiocratic framework, to the extent that he regards land-rents (gross of taxation) as the net 'revenue' of society, implying that the associated net product of agriculture is the social net product as a whole. He entertains the idea of 'pure profits' (our term) being part of the surplus, equivocates, but then rejects it. In this regard Smith is in advance of Turgot, insofar as Smith recognizes that pure profits are, in principle at least, a taxable surplus. Associated with this, in Smith not only agriculture is productive of surplus. Other industries or activities – manufacture, as well as, for example, transportation and distribution services – in general contribute to production of the social surplus, as well as their outputs, in part, forming part of the surplus (see secs 4.3.2–4.3.3, with 4.4.2). Turgot's apparent Physiocratic position on net revenue implies a rejection of that sound Smithian view; but, inconsistently, other Turgot arguments appear to step beyond the limits of that view and closer to Smith. In terms of the illustrative model employed in section 4.2.2 to clarify the concept of surplus, the Physiocratic view, consistently expressed, is akin to the limiting case discussed there, where it is assumed that commodity M is not required as input for the production of commodity C, with all production activities other than agriculture being like the production of commodity M (or like 'silk' in the model employed in section 4.3.3 to clarify the meaning of productive labour in Smith). That is to say, the Physiocratic doctrine strictly requires that agriculture be a self-subsistent production sector: the proposition that agriculture alone produces a surplus is inconsistent with the proposition that agriculture requires as inputs, commodities produced by other industries (cf. Vaggi 1987b: 25–6).[37]

Turgot's Physiocratic position is enunciated in an extended passage of argument at the end of the *Réflexions* (Turgot 1769–70 [1977]: 90–5). He raises the question of how to locate owners of capital within his tripartite division of society, in terms of the productive cultivators, the industrial class, and landowners ('the disposable class'). Interest on capital – which for Turgot represents the rate of return on capital net of that part of the return compensating for entrepreneurial activity – 'seems … a disposable portion'. That is to say, it is not a necessary cost of production. But he immediately indicates that this conflicts with the Quesnay doctrine, which Turgot embraces, 'that only the class of [land] proprietors … [have] a revenue properly so called, a disposable revenue'. We need not go through all the detail of his strained argument for excluding those pure profits from the surplus revenue available for free disposal (and for that reason, the revenue susceptible to taxation without compromising the reproduction of the economic system). His conclusion is quite emphatic:

> they are … the price and the condition of … [capital] advances, without which the enterprise could not be carried on. If this return is diminished, the capitalist will withdraw his money, and the enterprise will come to an end.… In short, the capitalist lender of money ought to be considered as a dealer in a commodity absolutely necessary for the production of wealth ….

The element of equivocation or ambivalence in Turgot's position is evident in the following comment in these last few pages of the *Réflexions*: 'the person who lends money belongs properly to the disposable class as to his person, *because he has nothing to do* [in the production process]; but not as to the nature of his wealth' (emphasis added). He also there explicitly acknowledges that saving and capital accumulation occur, not just out of the disposable revenue of the landowners, associated with 'the net product of land', but also out of profit income (as well as wage income, to some extent), because the recipients 'have … a surplus beyond their subsistence' (cf. Turgot 1769–70 [1977]: 65 and n. 29, 69). On any sensible reckoning, this means that the latter incomes really share in the social net revenue.[38]

Two questions are raised by the existence of this emerging tradition of analysis, from Petty to Turgot, built around a concept of society's net revenue or income, understood as the value of the surplus output of the production system as a whole. Given Smith's familiarity with that tradition, why did he utilize a different conception of social net revenue, which is less coherent from the point of view of conceptualizing both the freely disposable net product and capital accumulation (issues taken up further below)? Second, how and why did such a net revenue concept come to be deployed at the level of society as a whole, an application both wider and deeper than the mere accounting notion of net income in one form or another, applied to particular entities below the level of nations or societies (e.g. individuals, corporations, the State)? Gilibert (1987) offers an answer to the former question, in terms of Smith's 'trying to take into account workers' consumption … in assessing the prosperity of a nation'. Hollander (1973: 199–204) takes a similar view. This has some plausibility; and the fact that wages share in the social surplus in Smith's system – as shown below – provides some further justification for his conceptualization of net revenue. In any case, the effect of that conceptualization is to leave the social surplus submerged, in Smith's analysis of capital accumulation and growth. Or should one rather conclude that the concept of a social surplus is simply not there? As shall be seen, that concept is certainly entailed by his economics: it is most evidently operational in the theory of tax incidence, where the distinction between necessary inputs and surplus revenue cannot be avoided. And if it is there, and required, in one dimension of the analysis of commercial society, it cannot be absent in another dimension of the analysis of the same object; it can only be submerged. Whatever the plausibility of Gilibert's judgement, the effect of Smith's definition is to muddy the distinction between gross and net capital accumulation. All these matters are resolved in sections 4.3 and 4.4.

As to the question of how and why the social net revenue concept came to be deployed, the 'how' is considerably explained by the developments from Petty to Turgot sketched above, with its genesis in Petty connected with the seventeenth-century Bacon-inspired technology programme. Perhaps there is more to the story as well. One wonders whether the formation of the concept was supported or assisted by way of analogies drawn from concepts of net income which arose in the development of accounting practices and theory, around double-entry bookkeeping in particular, of which there are written records showing its Italian genesis from as early as the thirteenth century (cf. Chapter 3, n. 60, on the role of analogy in the development of science). Double-entry bookkeeping virtually *obliges* attention to a net receipts notion, of one kind or another, via the imposed identification of the change in the net value of the assets of an entity between two points in time, and the balance of profit or loss over the intervening time period (Yamey 1987: 919). If the accounting literature did play a role, then the national income accounting of Gregory King might have been something of a bridge between the earlier accounting literature and eighteenth-century economic theory (cf. Larrère 2001b: 1070–1). King was the great founder of such social accounting methods, following on Petty's seminal efforts in what he called 'political arithmetic'. But against this conjecture, the 'net' element focused upon in both the national accounting of Petty and of King is a form of saving or accumulation. This is indeed very much in the spirit of the private accounting identity between change in net assets and profit/loss. It is not the surplus of the eighteenth-century economists; it is equivalent to that part of the surplus not consumed. The social surplus proper, and the associated net income concept, *are* elements in a kind of social accounting; but in any case, the possible role of the earlier accounting literature is a speculation which cannot be resolved here.[39]

As to why the social net revenue concept was developed, just as the emergence of political economy itself is in part an expression of the imperatives of early modern nation-state building (see sec. 2.1.3), so also the emergence of the concept of the social surplus and associated net revenue of society or the nation is the development of one, important intellectual tool of political economy, for statecraft and policy. Not the least aspect of policy relevance is taxation: the surplus is equivalent to that part of national income which is available for free disposal, and hence susceptible to taxation without damaging the reproduction of the economic system (see sec. 4.4.2). Petty's deployment of the concept is closely connected with policy, including taxation policy. This tax issue is also highly pertinent to the Physiocratic programme, in terms of what kinds of taxation will avoid inhibiting the reproduction of economic activity levels, capital accumulation and growth. This dimension of the theory is rendered possible because, when deployed at the level of society as a whole – or more precisely, at the level of the economic system as a whole – the net revenue can acquire the deeper significance of being the income equivalent of the surplus output of the production system as a whole. This grounding of the net revenue in production – the production of a physical surplus of outputs – in general cannot be applied at the level of sub-national entities. Particular industries which are part of a wider production system are not viable on their own: they require inputs produced by other industries; they cannot replace their inputs in physical terms, only in value terms. Hence in the (effectively, two-commodity) model of surplus utilized in section 4.2.2, a commodity surplus in general cannot be defined for one industry independent of the other. It is a system-level concept.[40]

## 4.3 Capital and productive labour

Division of labour, the first of our three key elements of Smith's growth process, is necessarily associated with decentralized exchange (sec. 4.1.1). So also, labour specialization and the consequent lack of individual self-sufficiency entails that the consumption requirements of workers during production must be accumulated as a prior stock. Hence division of labour is also necessarily associated with the accumulation of 'stock' or 'capital'. So the summary 'Introduction' to *WN*, Book II links capital accumulation back to the division of labour, the subject matter which opens Book I:

> In that rude state of society in which there is no division of labour, in which exchanges are seldom made, and in which every man provides every thing for himself, it is not necessary that any stock should be accumulated or stored up beforehand in order to carry on the business of the society. Every man endeavours to supply by his own industry his own occasional wants as they occur.... But when the division of labour has once been thoroughly introduced, the produce of a man's own labour can supply but a very small part of his occasional wants.... A stock of goods of different kinds, therefore, must be stored up somewhere sufficient to maintain him, and to supply him with the materials and tools of his work .... As the accumulation of stock must, in the nature of things, be previous to the division of labour, so labour can be more and more subdivided in proportion only as stock is previously more and more accumulated.
>
> (*WN*: 276–7; also *LJB*: 521–2, 527)

Here again, as with the relation between labour specialization and productivity growth on the one hand, and extent of the market on the other, there is the possibility of reverse causation, from specialization to the growth of stock, or mutual causation (see sec. 4.1.1). Hence Smith concludes the above-cited *LJ* discussion with the comment, intended historically: 'till some stock be produced there can be no division of labour, and before a division of labour take place there can be very little accumulation of stock' (*LJB*: 522). Notice also how the title of Book II, Chapter I of *WN* ('Of the Division of Stock') mirrors the title of Book I, Chapter I ('Of the Division of Labour'; cf. the parallel between specialization of stock and of labour at *WN*: 530).

However, it is quite clear that Smith understands the causation to run from accumulation of stock or capital to extent of specialization (even if, we may add, the prospect of productivity gains from specialization perhaps may historically have provided stimulus for accumulation). This is evident from *WN* (276–7, partly quoted directly above), and for a further instance, neatly summarizing Smith's conception of the growth process:

> The annual produce of the land and labour of any nation can be increased in its value by no other means, but by increasing either the number of its productive labourers, or the productive powers of those labourers who had before been employed. The number of its productive labourers, it is evident, can never be much increased, but in consequence of an increase of capital, or of the funds destined for maintaining them. The productive powers of the same number of labourers cannot be increased, but in consequence either of some addition and improvement to those machines and instruments which facilitate and abridge labour; or of a more proper division and distribution of employment. In either case an additional capital is almost always required. It is by means of an additional capital only that the undertaker of any work can either provide his workmen with better machinery, or make a more proper distribution of employment among them.
>
> (*WN*: 343; also 676)

It is in the first three chapters of Book II (*WN*: 279–349) that Smith presents his capital theory and the closely related concept of 'productive' labour.

### *4.3.1 Smith on 'capital'*

Smith's concept of capital does not make it a synonym for 'stock'. Capital is that part of stock which generates a revenue or profit to the owner. In this distinction, individuals are characterized as being in possession of stocks of commodities or other physical assets (say, at the beginning of an annual production cycle), with this stock then being divided between the person's own consumption and investment in capital.[41] In other words, the stocks include consumption goods, including consumer durables, as well as capital goods. The latter part of total stock can in turn be conceptually divided into fixed and circulating capital. The former embraces 'things as yield a revenue or profit without changing masters, or circulating any further': 'improvement of land, … machines and instruments of trade', 'profitable buildings', 'the acquired and useful abilities of all the inhabitants or members of the society' (*WN*: 279–82). Capital in the most generic sense then appears to be constituted by that part of the existing stock of commodities and physical assets which at any point in time is to be invested in production, with a view to sale and profit. Hence, for example, a house may be stock but not capital:

> The stock that is laid out in a house, if it is to be the dwelling-house of the proprietor, ceases from that moment to serve in the function of a capital, or to afford any revenue to its owner. A dwelling-house, as such, contributes nothing to the revenue of its inhabitant ….
>
> (*WN*: 281)

Even a house that is rented out, for use as a residential house, is not capital from the standpoint of society as a whole:

> as the house itself can produce nothing, the tenant must always pay the rent out of some other revenue which he derives either from labour, or stock, or land. Though a house, therefore, may yield a revenue to its proprietor, and thereby serve in the function of a capital to him, it cannot yield any to the publick, nor serve in the function of a capital to it, and the revenue of the whole body of the people can never be in the smallest degree increased by it.
>
> (*WN*: 281)

This latter illustration points to what Smith seems really to intend in his core definition of capital as revenue-producing stock: capital is stock which produces value added, as will become clearer in the consideration of productive labour below.[42] The method of dividing the 'capital stock'[43] into its fixed and circulating components is a little odd by latter-day standards: 'the characteristick' of fixed capital is 'that it affords a revenue or profit without circulating or changing masters'; 'the characteristick' of circulating capital is 'that it affords a revenue only by circulating or changing masters' (*WN*: 282). The four elements making up the circulating capital have been indicated in section 4.2.1 (*WN*: 282–3). The striking instance of the potential for this mode of demarcation to generate odd results is the resulting characterization of agricultural seed input:

> The whole value of the seed … is properly a fixed capital. Though it goes backwards and forwards between the ground and the granary, it never changes masters, and therefore does not properly circulate. The farmer makes his profit, not by its sale, but by its increase.
>
> (*WN*: 281)

On the other hand, Smith's observation that fixed capital is ultimately the product of circulating capital used up is a better conceived idea:

> Every fixed capital is both originally derived from, and requires to be continually supported by a circulating capital. All useful machines and instrument of trade are originally derived from a circulating capital, which furnishes the materials of which they are made, *and the maintenance of the workmen who make them*. They require too a capital of the same kind to keep them in constant repair.
>
> (*WN*: 283; emphasis added)

A final diagnosis of Smith's fixed versus circulating capital distinction is provided below (esp. n. 55).

The list of circulating capital elements at *WN* (282–3) at first glance appears not to include wages or consumption of labour, but it is clear in many places that Smith does indeed include wages in circulating capital, though the wages of *productive* labour only (see below). Indeed, the quotation directly above, two paragraphs further on from this list, makes that explicit, and the point is reiterated in the paragraph which follows it as well. There are many other references to wages as part of capital; for example: 'The quantity of industry which any capital can employ, must, evidently, be equal to the number of workmen whom it can supply with materials, tools, and a maintenance suitable to the nature of the work' (*WN*: 295).

> That part of the annual produce … of any country which replaces a capital, never is immediately employed to maintain any but productive hands. It pays the wages of productive labour only. That which is immediately destined for constituting a revenue either as profit or rent, may maintain indifferently either productive or unproductive hands.
>
> Whatever part of his stock a man employs as a capital, he always expects … to be replaced to him with a profit. He employs it, therefore, in maintaining productive hands only; and after having served in the function of a capital to him, it constitutes a revenue to them.
>
> (*WN*: 332)[44]

The inclusion of some wages as part of capital indicates also that Smith's net revenue is not a measure of net income in the sense of a surplus available for free disposal. To the extent that labour input requires necessary consumption, net revenue is a wider concept than just the surplus, since it evidently includes also subsistence: 'the neat revenue of the society … the stock reserved for immediate consumption, the subsistence, conveniences, and amusements of individuals' (*WN*: 289; also 287). Insofar as net revenue therefore includes replacement or reproduction of wages associated with the current level of employment, it is not really all potentially available for net employment growth, but only a part of it.

Putting aside the considerable references to capital crimes and punishment (together with a slight number other non-economic uses), there are in *LJ* only a small number of minor references to 'capital', all of them referring to financial capital and all in *LJB* (484, 513, 517, 536). However, there are many references there to 'stock' – with the implication of stock, in at least some of these instances, as commodities used as inputs in production – and as well, the notion of saving as the source of accumulation is indicated clearly enough. In one of these commentaries on stock, the argument concerning saving and stock is allied with illustrative references to financial capital, suggesting that Smith was still well short of his mature view of capital and stock (*LJB*: 513; also 508, 514). A parallel argument, without reference to capital, appears as the final extant pages of *LJA* (393–4; also *LJA*: 377–80; *edWN*: 578). It is also explicitly argued that 'stock', notably for the consumption of labourers employed, is a prerequisite to production (e.g. *LJA*: 365–6, 382; *LJB*: 498, 519–22). The absence of capital theory – the absence of a developed analysis of the functional and socio-economic distinction between capital and profits on the one hand, and labour and wages on the other – is the great 'gap' in *LJ* relative to *WN*. One can hardly observe this disjunction, together with the fact of Smith's time spent in Paris between the lectures and publication of *WN*, and not be drawn to the conclusion that the French economists played a crucial role in advancing his thinking in this dimension (more on this in sec. 4.3.7). Nevertheless, the treatment of stock in *LJ* indicates that he at least had then a grasp of the significance of capital in the sense of produced means of production.

### *4.3.2 Smith on 'productive labour'*

The chapter of *WN* in which the notion of productive labour is systematically exposited (Book II, Chapter III) announces an intimate connection between capital and productive labour in its title: 'Of the Accumulation of Capital, or of productive and unproductive Labour'. The opening sentence appeals to value added for the defining distinction between productive and unproductive labour:

> There is one sort of labour which adds to the value of the subject upon which it is bestowed: There is another which has no such effect. The former, as it produces a value, may be called productive; the latter, unproductive[45] labour.

The illustration Smith offers contrasts manufacturing labour and 'menial servants'. The former produces a 'vendible commodity' which covers the worker's wages as well as generating profit; the menial servant 'adds to the value of nothing', his services 'generally perish in the very instant of their performance' (*WN*: 330). The proportion in which total employment, and hence also that part of the annual product devoted to labour consumption, is divided between productive and unproductive uses then constitutes a key determinant of economic growth:

as a smaller or greater proportion of it [i.e. 'the annual produce'] is in any one year employed in maintaining unproductive hands, the more in the one case and the less in the other will remain for the productive, and the next year's produce will be greater or smaller accordingly; the whole annual produce, if we except the spontaneous productions of the earth, being the effect of productive labour.[46]

Though the whole annual produce of the land and labour of every country, is, no doubt, ultimately destined for supplying the consumption of its inhabitants, and for procuring a revenue to them; yet when it first comes either from the ground, or from the hands of the productive labourers, it naturally divides itself into two parts. One of them ... is ... destined for replacing a capital, or for renewing the provisions, materials, and finished work, which had been withdrawn from a capital; the other for constituting a revenue either to the owner of this capital, as the profit of his stock; or to some other person, as the rent of his land....

That part of the annual produce of the land and labour of any country which replaces a capital, never is immediately employed to maintain any but productive hands. It pays the wages of productive labour only. That which is immediately destined for constituting a revenue either as profit or as rent, may maintain indifferently either productive or unproductive hands.

(*WN*: 332; also 350, 353, 355–6, 360, 862, 887, 927)

The wages of $L^u$ on the other hand, as well as the incomes of 'those who do not labour at all', are not part of capital. While employment of $L^u$ by wage-earners is possible, '[t]he rent of land and the profits of stock are every where ... the principal sources from which unproductive hands derive their subsistence' (*WN*: 333). Smith sums up the argument:

The proportion, therefore, between the productive and unproductive hands, depends very much in every country upon the proportion between that part of the annual produce, which ... is destined for replacing a capital, and that which is destined for constituting a revenue, either as rent, or as profit.

(*WN*: 333–4)[47]

The dichotomy between $L^p$ and $L^u$ is also expressed in terms of 'industry' versus 'idleness' (*WN*: 335–7):

The proportion between capital and revenue ... seems every where to regulate the proportion between industry and idleness. Where-ever capital predominates, industry prevails: wherever revenue, idleness. Every increase or diminution of capital, therefore, naturally tends to increase or diminish the real quantity of industry, the number of productive hands ....

(*WN*: 337; also 71)

The growth and contraction of the capital stock in turn depends upon 'parsimony, and … prodigality';[48] by what a person 'saves from his revenue he adds to his capital' and 'employs it … in maintaining an additional number of productive hands, or enables some other person to do so, by lending it to him for an interest':

> As the capital of an individual can be increased only by what he saves from his annual revenue or his annual gains, so the capital of a society, which is the same with that of all the individuals who compose it, can be increased only in the same manner.
>
> Parsimony, and not industry, is the immediate cause of the increase of capital. Industry, indeed, provides the subject which parsimony accumulates. But whatever industry might acquire, if parsimony did not save and store up, the capital would never be the greater.
>
> Parsimony, by increasing the fund which is destined for the maintenance of productive hands, tends to increase the number of those hands whose labour adds to the value of the subject upon which it is bestowed. It tends therefore to increase the exchangeable value of the annual produce of the land and labour of the country.
>
> (*WN*: 337)[49]

Finally, the inclination to save or accumulate in turn is grounded in a fundamental principle or desire in human nature, already encountered, or at least implied, in relation to competition, and in relation to division of labour:

> the principle, which prompts to expence, is the passion for present enjoyment; which … is in general only momentary and occasional. But the principle which prompts to save, is the desire of bettering our condition, a desire which … comes with us from the womb, and never leaves us till we go into the grave. In the whole interval which separates those two moments, there is scarce perhaps a single instant in which any man is so perfectly and completely satisfied with his situation, as to be without any wish of alteration or improvement, of any kind. An augmentation of fortune is the means by which the greater part of men propose and wish to better their condition … and the most likely way of augmenting their fortune, is to save and accumulate some part of what they acquire …. Though the principle of expence, therefore, prevails in almost all men upon some occasions, and in some men upon almost all occasions, yet in the greater part of men, taking the whole course of their life at an average, the principle of frugality seems not only to predominate, but to predominate very greatly.
>
> (*WN*: 341–2)[50]

The relation between capital and $L^p$ serves to cast light on Smith's understanding of both. All labour employed by capital is $L^p$; and $L^p$ is defined by reference, on the one hand, to its producing value added, on the other, to its product being vendible commodities (more on the latter immediately below). Hence one *perhaps* may say that for Smith capital is constituted by inputs to production, other than unimproved natural resources, in activities which generate value added. Since all $L^u$ is employed in activities other than production and accumulation of capital, it must be devoted, in one way or another, to production of luxury consumption or otherwise 'non-necessary' activities, using the term non-necessary advisedly (see three paragraphs below). The division or proportion between $L^p$ and $L^u$ thereby is an expression of the rate of capital accumulation, though the productivity of productive labour – 'productivity' here in the ordinary sense of net output per worker – also enters into determination of the accumulation rate. The accumulation rate is then attributed by Smith to the extent of saving, with the natural tendency to save – which he regards, on average, as dominating 'the passion for present enjoyment' (*WN*: 341) – proceeding from individuals' desire for self-betterment.

Competition in Smith's price theory, and the propensity to trade in his account of division of labour, proceed from self-regard – properly, restrained by law, self-command, sociableness and so on – self-regard which can be taken as a datum for the purposes of political economy. So likewise, the saving behaviour which is supposed to drive capital accumulation derives from the self-regarding desire for material improvement, which also is treated as a given of human nature. These three fundamental dynamics of Smith's political economy all are ultimately grounded in this same human characteristic, the self-regarding desire for material betterment: competition, acting in particular upon market prices and input allocation; division of labour, arising from the exchange propensity, but aimed also at material self-betterment, and given impetus by competition; and accumulation here. The exchange propensity in particular is a manifestation of a sociable self-regard; the sociable persuading associated with it appeals to the self-regard of the other, because one knows from self-knowledge that this is the kind of appeal which *will be* persuasive. Of these three fundamental psychological parameters – self-regard, the exchange propensity, the desire for material betterment – the last is the most fundamental. It is the thing to which self-interest is directed, and the purpose of labour specialization and exchange.

Along with the non-value-adding characteristic of $L^u$, the second defining characteristic of $L^p$ versus $L^u$, in terms of vendible versus non-vendible outputs, is connected in Smith's thinking with a distinction between physical commodities and services. Certainly, for private production the vendibility condition is a necessary feature of the output of $L^p$, since this is the means via which the value added is realized, by way of sales revenue. Is it also his view that only physical commodities are capable of embodying realizable value added, so that service-producing labour is neither productive nor a vehicle for capital investment or accumulation? Smith comes very close to this position but ultimately, and somewhat contradictorily, doesn't quite fully embrace it. Transportation, wholesaling and retailing are emphatically productive activities for Smith (*WN*: 360–3) and on any sensible rendering, they are services. Consider further the range of particular activities that he nominates for unproductiveness. 'Menial servants' constitute his archetypal example (e.g. *WN*: 330, 669, 675, 887). Beyond this, the most detailed listing of $L^u$ is at the beginning of the key chapter on $L^p$ and $L^u$:

> The sovereign ... with all the officers both of justice and war ... the whole army and navy .... Their service, how honourable, how useful, or how necessary soever, produces nothing for which an equal quantity of service can afterwards be procured. *The protection, security, and defence of the commonwealth, the effect of their labour this year, will not purchase its protection, security, and defence, for the year to come.* In the same class must be ranked, some both of the gravest and most important, and some of the most frivolous professions: churchmen, lawyers, physicians, men of letters of all kinds; players, buffoons, musicians, opera-singers, opera-dancers, &c.... Like the declamation of the actor, the harangue of the orator, or the tune of the musician, the work of all of them perishes in the very instant of its production.
>
> (*WN*: 330–1; emphasis added; also 333, 676)

Government employment is quite prominent here, and in his taxation analysis Smith puts a rather general proposition, that 'the revenue of the sovereign ... seldom maintains any but unproductive labourers' (*WN*: 862; also 898, 924–5; *LJB*: 514–15 has an intimation of this, and cf. *LJA*: 393–4). But this is not an unequivocal statement of principle ('seldom'). A similarly qualified statement appears earlier: 'The whole, or almost the whole publick revenue, is in most countries employed in maintaining unproductive hands' (*WN*: 342). The possibility of public employment devoted to production of capital, whether or not a desirable situation, cannot be ruled out. Skinner (1996: 165) therefore somewhat overstates the case in suggesting that for Smith all government services are unproductive 'by definition'.[51]

The distinction between $L^p$ and $L^u$ is first and foremost a descriptive rather than an ethical concept for Smith, though it acquires normative significance once the growth of wealth is accepted as an objective of policy. On his terms, maximizing growth of produce in any time period is synonymous with minimizing the quantity of $L^u$. Nevertheless, Smith is entirely conscious that at least some elements of $L^u$ are not just useful but absolutely indispensable to the functioning of society in general ('necessary', in the quotation from *WN*: 330–1 above), and therefore also necessary to the 'productive' part of the economy. To mention the most obvious, those parts of the apparatus of State requisite for guaranteeing property rights are thereby necessary to the conduct of all economic activity.[52] This necessity or usefulness of at least some $L^u$ is not a failing with regard to how Smith draws the line between $L^p$ and $L^u$. It is an analytical distinction for a particular intellectual purpose, the analysis of reproduction and growth, not a judgement of the intrinsic worth of activities. It expresses another instance of political economy, as a particular branch of science, treating certain aspects of reality as data. Just as the science proceeds on the basis of certain given characteristics of humans (self-regard and so on), so also, in analysing production and growth, the socio-political infrastructure of economic activity can be taken as given, for these limited purposes. Smith is not thereby required to deny the necessity or usefulness of $L^u$, and does not; indeed, he affirms it for at least some $L^u$.[53] On the other hand, his attempt to exclude services as such from productive activity, on the basis of their non-vendibility and/or their immateriality, leads to contradiction. His inclusion of transportation, wholesaling and retailing under $L^p$ exposes that (as does the role of education in capital accumulation: n. 51). They are as much services which 'perish ... in the ... instant of their performance', as any of the unproductive activities which Smith lists, but they are also emphatically 'vendible' (*WN*: 675). Furthermore, those transportation and distribution services are of course value-adding activities, as Smith explicitly acknowledges, by virtue of their being productive (e.g. *WN*: 362). Why not some other services as well?

The 'menial servants' example, which so much dominates Smith's mind when he thinks of $L^u$, is a 'good' example for him, in the sense that it fortifies his conviction about services. Such direct personal services are non-value-adding activity, a form of luxury consumption, as well as involving no physical commodity output; they are suggestive of, for example, the retainers of wealthy landowners. For sure, such activity belongs in the $L^u$ category, on any coherent rendering of it. But consider instead one of his examples of a 'frivolous' unproductive service, opera singers. Opera singing is entirely capable of being a vendible service *and* of generating value added in Smith's sense, as part of an opera company in which production inputs are (successfully) invested for profit. This points to the truth that the characterization of $L^p$ as workers who 'reproduce ... together with a profit, the full value of their consumption' (*WN*: 339) does not really quite capture the coherent distinction between productive and unproductive labour or inputs that Smith's analysis of capital and growth is in need of. An opera singer in a profitable opera company can cover the cost of her consumption and generate a profit as well. When Smith says the following concerning his favourite example of $L^u$, menial servants, he conflates two separate characteristics of labour activity:

> Their maintenance and employment is altogether at the expence of their masters, and the work which they perform is not of a nature to repay that expence. That work consists in services which perish generally in the very instant of their performance, and does not fix or realize itself in any vendible commodity which can replace the value of their wages and maintenance.
>
> (*WN*: 675)

Producing a service which is consumed in the moment of its performance is compatible with selling that service at a price which recovers its production cost together with profits, which therefore also means that it embodies value added. The opera singer's singing may perish in the moment of its performance but that service can still be sold at a profit.[54]

### *4.3.3 Productive labour: a rational reconstruction*

What then *is* the distinction which would give coherence to Smith's productive versus unproductive demarcation? While an opera singer's services can be sold at a price which covers her cost and returns a profit, what an opera singer in a profitable company cannot do, by way of that singing activity, is actually contribute to the production of the necessary inputs required for the company's work, including in this her and the other opera workers' necessary consumption or subsistence (the costumes, the musical instruments and so on, as well as the food and other commodities consumed by the members of the company). At least this is true, so long as attending opera performances is not itself part of necessary consumption or other inputs. In fact, this aspect of the situation is implied in a sentence in Smith's detailed list of $L^u$ at *WN* (330–1), quoted (and emphasized) three paragraphs above: the provision of government services of justice and defence this year, 'will not purchase [them] ... for the year to come'. The output generated by the State personnel involved in provision of these services does not form part of their own consumption, nor does it produce other inputs necessary to the production of their services; someone else must produce that. In short, $L^p$ is labour employed with capital goods (labour consumption goods and other inputs), to produce further capital goods. To see the essential character of the issue here more clearly, consider an illustrative model, along similar lines to that employed in section 4.2.2 to clarify the concept of social surplus.

Suppose a social economy producing just three distinct kinds of commodities, 'corn' (C, representing agriculture), a 'machine' (M, representing manufacture), and a commodity we may, for the moment, just refer to as 'silk' (S). Assume all three commodities are infinitely divisible and that there is no public sector and therefore also no taxes. There is an annual cycle of production in which the three commodities are produced, in terms of the following given, constant-returns-to-scale production methods:

$$a_{MC}, l_C \rightarrow \textit{1 unit of corn}$$

$$a_{MM}, l_M \rightarrow \textit{1 unit of machines}$$

$$a_{MS}, l_S \rightarrow \textit{1 unit of silk}$$

where $a_{MJ}$ and $l_J$ (J = C, M, S) are the annual machine and labour inputs, respectively, per unit of each output, with all these six parameters taking positive values.[55] By taking production methods as given here, and further below, the Smithian dynamics of technical change and productivity growth associated with division of labour and expansion of markets are put aside. Suppose further that normal conditions prevail, so that labour receives an annualized wage equal to the value of its subsistence consumption ($c$), assumed to consist only of a quantity of corn. (The analysis is essentially unchanged if we suppose, in line with

Smith's thinking, that in growing systems this given real wage can be at a level higher than minimum subsistence.) Then, the input requirements per unit of outputs may be restated as:

$a_{MC}, cl_C \rightarrow$ *1 unit of corn*

$a_{MM}, cl_M \rightarrow$ *1 unit of machines*

$a_{MS}, cl_S \rightarrow$ *1 unit of silk*

Assuming away rents for simplicity, one can then specify price equations which capture the Smithian notion of normal prices, but with the circular nature of the production system explicitly accounted for (see n. 24 above):

$$(p_M a_{MC} + wl_C)(1 + r) = p_C$$

$$(p_M a_{MM} + wl_M)(1 + r) = p_M$$

$$(p_M a_{MS} + wl_S)(1 + r) = p_S$$

$$w = p_C c$$

$$p_S = 1$$

where $w$ is the wage, $p_J$ (J = C, M, S) are the normal prices of the three commodities, all measured in a conventional unit of account (say, shillings and pence), and $r$ is the uniform annualized rate of profit.[56] (The supposition of a uniform rate of profit across all activities puts aside the differential characteristics of capitals that are associated with differential competitive or normal returns, which Smith systematically considers in *WN*, Book I, Chapter X.) A unique and economically meaningful solution exists for the rate of profit and the commodity prices, so long as the production methods and real wages are suitably restricted.[57]

Now notice that in fact the price equation for silk can be removed from this system and the remaining four equations will suffice to generate an economically meaningful solution for the profit rate and the prices of corn and machines (though the use of silk as numeraire, to express relative commodity prices, the fifth equation, will have to be amended, making corn or machines the numeraire instead). These variables are determinable independently of silk, with the price of silk then determinable posterior to them, by inserting the solutions for the corn and machine prices and the profit rate into the silk price equation. This asymmetry is also manifest in the fact that the restriction required to ensure an economically meaningful solution for this system is independent of silk and its production conditions (see n. 57 above). 'Silk' in this illustrative model can cover its costs in value terms, and generate the normal rate of profit on capital, but it cannot participate in the reproduction of itself in physical terms,[58] in the manner of a system of 'basic' commodities (the latter, here represented by agriculture plus manufacture). Silk, it may be added, could just as well be read as a representation of the opera singer and her associated instruments for providing her services, or even the menial servant (if hired out for profit). In that sense, opera singing, as well as other examples of $L^u$ Smith offers, are instances of 'silk', or properly understood, 'non-basics' (see n. 24). The basic/non-basic distinction, which Smith does not fully grasp, is the coherent form of his $L^p/L^u$ distinction (cf. Eltis 1975: 434–5, or 1984: 77–8). The coherent distinction is between commodities (and the associated labour) which are inputs to production in general, and commodities which contribute only to final (above-necessary or luxury) consumption. The labour of opera singers, and of Smith's menial servants, State personnel and so on, does not contribute to production of the former.

A brief digression may be useful here. At a point such as this in our interpretation of Smith, and in relation to the use of algebraic formulations more widely in this chapter, some might be tempted to the view that we are ourselves illegitimately reading latter-day modes of thought back into Smith's text. Such interpretive methods are sometimes accused of being 'teleological' (Winch 1978: 180–1; 1996: 20; 1997: 385–6, 399, 402) or 'rational reconstruction' (Blaug 1999). The inappropriateness of interpreting Smith via the frame of latter-day theory alien to his thought has been emphasized in Chapter 3 in particular. But recourse to latter-day theoretical developments which share Smith's approach, and thereby assist in clarifying the meaning of his economics, is another matter. 'Teleology' applied to intellectual history, perhaps also (wrongly) associated with 'Whig history', surely is a misuse of the term. Teleology entails some notion that the final purpose of a thing in some sense 'explains' it. Such teleological explanation is entirely alien to all our notions, now, of causation, which is no doubt why it is used pejoratively in relation to historiography. No one who engages in anything that could be characterized as Whig history is really arguing that earlier ideas, which can be perceived as imperfect articulations of later ideas, are in any sense *explained* by the later ideas. To suppose that Sraffa's concept of non-basics is a kind of perfection of Smith's notion of unproductive labour is in no sense a teleological explanation. Is it Whig intellectual history, a portrayal of earlier ideas as elements in the progress towards later, superior ideas? In a limited sense, perhaps it is; but there *is* scientific progress, at least with respect to particular and well-defined questions, especially questions of a transparent analytical kind. To the question – what kind of employments are capable of enabling the growth of national produce? – the answer, 'labour producing basics in the sense of Sraffa', is conceptually and analytically superior to the answer, 'productive labour in the sense of Smith'. It is superior from the standpoint of Smith's own frame of reference.

Such conceptual-cum-analytical progress is part of the history of ideas as well. To reject the legitimacy of such comparisons as that between Smith's unproductive labour and Sraffa's non-basics, is therefore to suppress part of intellectual history; to grasp the parallel is to better understand both the limits and the enduring strength of Smith's thought. To contend, even further, that Smith's intellectual framework and Sraffa's intellectual framework are entirely incommensurable universes or 'paradigms' is just obscurantism. Garegnani (2002: 242n) has provided an acute response to Blaug's (1999: 213) poorly thought out notion of rational reconstruction ('the tendency to view history as a relentless march of progress from past errors to present truths'), as supposedly opposed to historical reconstruction. Rational reconstruction, better conceived of as reconstructing the logical structure of a past theory, is really just analogous to 'a contemporary grammar of classical Latin, in which a Latin writer of the period should recognize the rules he consciously or unconsciously followed in expressing himself; so Blaug would [surely] agree, the grammar would constitute a *historical* reconstruction of that Latin'. (See also the compelling response by Kurz and Salvadori 2002, a concise version of Kurz and Salvadori 2003, and the very careful diagnosis of the relations between mathematical modeling, rational reconstruction and intellectual history in Waterman 2003: 555–60, 564.) In truth, if rational reconstruction as Blaug literally understands it were to be purged from historiography, then the very notion of, for example, 'classical economics' – and every other term or concept not actually used by earlier writers – would have to be excluded from the interpretation of those authors. Whether or not 'classical economics' is a useful concept for some purposes, such a general exclusion is neither possible nor desirable (cf. Jardine 2007 on 'anachrophobia', reviewing Park and Daston 2006). We cannot write the history of 1776 as if we were living in 1776; and if we could, it would not then be 'history'. Historiography is of its very nature backwards-looking. While we cannot see and feel precisely as Smith did, with some effort, we can understand his texts (cf. the epigraph to Chapter 1).

### *4.3.4 Growth dynamics*

The kind of illustrative modelling employed above to clarify the meaning of Smith's $L^p/L^u$ distinction may also be used to give transparency to his characterization of growth dynamics. The masters who control production can be conceived of as having possession of the entire gross product produced in period t, at the end of period t. Collectively, their decisions about how to use this product in period t+1 may be thought of as determining its allocation as follows. Assume for simplicity that corn is not at all consumed by the masters, that it is the consumption good of labour only, so that the gross output of corn ($Q_{c(t)}$) is entirely devoted to employment of labour in period t+1:

$$Q_{c(t)} = c(l_c Q_{c(t+1)} + l_M Q_{M(t+1)} + l_s Q_{s(t+1)})$$

where the t, t+1 subscripts denote the time period in which these gross outputs of corn, machines and silk are produced. The machine gross output is not directly consumed at all and is analogously allocated between the production of the three commodities in the following period:

$$Q_{M(t)} = a_{MC}Q_{C(t+1)} + a_{MM}Q_{M(t+1)} + a_{MS}Q_{S(t+1)}$$

The silk gross output from period t is entirely consumed, in period t+1, by the masters. Finally, the masters' decisions as to what proportion of the value of period t output (net of the silk output in period t) to devote to accumulation or saving may be represented by a given aggregate parameter, $\sigma$:

$$(1-\sigma)(p_C Q_{C(t)} + p_M Q_{M(t)}) = (p_C cl_S + p_M a_{MS})Q_{S(t+1)} \qquad 1 \geq \sigma > 0$$

Hence $(1-\sigma)$ is the proportion of the value of period t output[59] which is devoted to production of masters' consumption goods in period t+1, $(p_C cl_S + p_M a_{MS})$ being the capital (or cost) per unit of silk output, and with the resulting silk consumed in period t+2. It may also be assumed that there is no labour supply constraint upon growth, in line with Smith's view of the long run (see pp. 195–6).

Given the stocks of commodities produced in period t and available for use in period t+1, and with normal prices determined as earlier, the third equation contains only one variable, $Q_{S(t+1)}$, which is thereby fully determined by that equation alone. The first two equations then *might* determine a solution for $Q_{C(t+1)}$, $Q_{M(t+1)}$. The resolution of this system in fact is not quite so simple. Given the determination of $Q_{S(t+1)}$ via the third equation, a unique and economically meaningful solution for $Q_{C(t+1)}$, $Q_{M(t+1)}$ requires further restrictions, which need not be considered in mathematical detail here. It suffices to offer the following intuition. The ratio between the total corn input and total machine input employed in production of silk, corn and machines in period t+1 will be a function of the corn/machine ratios associated with the three production methods ($cl_C/a_{MC}$, $cl_M/a_{MM}$, $cl_S/a_{MS}$), together with the relative levels of the three outputs. If the initial stocks of corn and machines are treated as parameters of arbitrary magnitude, there may exist no combination of period t+1 outputs which will enable the initial stocks of both inputs simultaneously to be fully employed in production of the period t+1 outputs. So long as $Q_{S(t+1)}$ is limited to levels such that neither all of $Q_{C(t)}$ nor all of $Q_{M(t)}$ is devoted to production of $Q_{S(t+1)}$, a set of positive feasible values for $Q_{C(t+1)}$, $Q_{M(t+1)}$ exists. Depending upon the corn/machine ratios in corn and machine production, there will exist a certain range of values of the initial corn and machine stocks, which generates a unique and economically meaningful combination of $Q_{C(t+1)}$, $Q_{M(t+1)}$, for any such value of $Q_{S(t+1)}$. (To be more precise, the proportion between the stock of corn net of that used in silk production, and the stock of machines net of those used in silk production, must lie between $cl_C/a_{MC}$ and $cl_M/a_{MM}$.) If such a unique solution exists, it is just that $Q_{C(t+1)}$, $Q_{M(t+1)}$ combination which ensures full employment of the corn and machine stocks inherited from period t.

This diagnosis points to the conclusion that the notion of given stocks should be treated advisedly in interpreting Smith's growth dynamics. It is more true to his conception of capital and growth to regard the initial stocks of commodities in our formal exercise above, available for use as capital or for masters' consumption, as not merely arbitrarily given – which would be rather like conceiving of them in the manner of the initial endowments of latter-day marginalist theory – but as the result of a history of masters' attempts to adjust capital stocks to commodity demand conditions. At any point in time, those collective attempts may turn out to have been less than perfectly successful, so that there is underutilized stock.[60] From this standpoint, imposing restrictions on the first two equations so as to guarantee a unique solution is, at minimum, not necessarily less sensible than treating the stocks inherited from period t production as arbitrary magnitudes.

There arises here also a further and distinct issue. While on the one hand there is the question of whether the stocks carried over from one period to the next can be sufficiently utilized by feasible levels of production, on the other, there is the issue of whether the associated new supplies of output will find a sufficient demand. Even if a unique set of outputs such as to satisfactorily employ the stocks carried over exists, there may be a mismatch with demand, either excess supplies or excess demands. If the unique set of outputs happens to coincide with aggregate demands for outputs at normal prices – demands in the *next* period, in the manner of our modelling above – this would be a happy situation of supplies balancing demands, together with initial aggregate stocks being at appropriate levels to meet those demands.[61] (If output levels are not correctly adjusted to demand conditions, then of course market prices will tend to deviate from natural price.)

Putting this demand issue aside until section 4.4.1, suppose there is a unique solution for outputs (whether or not matching demands), due to stocks being sufficiently adapted to production methods and the outputs the masters desire to produce. Then three key features of Smith's conception of accumulation may be highlighted. First, the asymmetric roles in growth dynamics of the 'productive commodities' (corn and machines) on the one hand, and unproductive silk-making on the other, are expressed in the first two equations directly above, in the incapacity of $Q_S$ to contribute to production and growth of $Q_C$, $Q_M$. Second, the role of accumulation-cum-saving can be seen in a two-step causation: higher values of $\sigma$ entail lower $Q_{S(t+1)}$, which in turn increases the net stocks of corn and machines available for production of further corn and machines. But due to the heterogeneity of the capital goods, it is quite possible that a reduction in $Q_{S(t+1)}$ will lead to an ambiguous change in $Q_{C(t+1)}$, $Q_{M(t+1)}$: in a system of multiple distinct commodities, a rise in the outputs of all commodities, save one for which there is a fall in output, is an ambiguous change. Suppose therefore an even simpler production system, with machines assumed away and corn production treated as a vertically integrated activity: corn and silk are produced by means of corn and labour alone ($a_{CC}$, $l_C$ per unit of corn output; $a_{CS}$, $l_S$ per unit of silk output). The following two equations then represent the distribution of the corn stock between production of corn and of silk, and the masters' choice concerning consumption versus accumulation:

$$Q_{c(t)} = (a_{cc} + cl_c)Q_{c(t+1)} + (a_{cs} + cl_s)Q_{s(t+1)}$$

$$(1 - \sigma)Q_{c(t)} = (a_{cs} + cl_s)Q_{s(t+1)}$$

The second equation determines $Q_{s(t+1)}$, which, inserted into the first equation, then determines the growth of capital:

$$Q_{c(t+1)} = (1 + r)\sigma Q_{c(t)}$$

This throws into sharp relief the second key feature of Smith's conception: the growth of corn output, or capital, is a positive function of $\sigma$.[62] There is a maximum growth rate when $\sigma$ is unity – finite, due to the circular character of production – the net growth rate then being equal to $r$ (see n. 61). Net growth becomes negative when $\sigma$ takes values less than $1/(1 + r)$. For the intuition behind this result notice that $1/(1 + r)$ is equivalent to corn capital input per unit of gross corn output (see n. 62). Hence, when the fraction of $Q_{c(t)}$ carried forward for production of corn in the next period ($\sigma$) is equal to this proportion ($a_{cc} + cl_c < 1$), the corn capital allocated to production of $Q_{c(t+1)}$ is identical to the corn capital devoted to production of $Q_{c(t)}$, and so the levels of those two successive outputs are also the same. The maximum growth rate is associated with zero consumption by the non-labourers or masters. While one may notionally imagine a situation of such zero luxury consumption, it should be recalled that $L^u$ includes activities which are certainly necessary to economic life in a wider socio-political sense. Smith in any case is not adamantly opposed to all luxury (see, e.g. *WN*: 796–7, quoted in Chapter 2, n. 37; n. 50 above and sec. 4.3.8; cf. Winch 1978: 132–5; 1996: 59–80). The third and final key feature is Smith's use of the ratio of a society's productive labour to its unproductive (or total) labour, as a proxy for accumulation-cum-saving behaviour. With $L^p$ and $L^u$ in period t+1 given by $l_cQ_{c(t+1)}$ and $l_sQ_{s(t+1)}$ respectively, the ratio of productive to unproductive labour is indeed a positive function of $\sigma$:

$$L^p/L^u = (l_c/l_s)(p_s/p_c)[\sigma/(1 - \sigma)]$$

But notice the role also of production methods, as expressed here in terms of labour productivities and relative prices (and the latter are not independent of the former). A rise of $L^p/L^u$ could occur independently of $\sigma$, though also, $\sigma$ may not be independent of relative prices.[63]

Further with regard to the maximum growth rate, Smith makes some emphatic statements that the social economy is for human consumption, particularly in his critical commentaries on the mercantile system and the associated notion of wealth-as-money. Indeed, his most emphatic statement of what later comes to be called 'consumer sovereignty' fittingly occurs at the end of the eight-chapter critique of mercantilism in Book IV:

> Consumption is the sole end and purpose of all production; and the interest of the producer ought to be attended to, only so far as it may be necessary

> for promoting that of the consumer.... But in the mercantile system, the interest of the consumer is almost constantly sacrificed to that of the producer; and it seems to consider production, and not consumption, as the ultimate end and object of all industry and commerce.... It cannot be very difficult to determine who have been the contrivers of this whole mercantile system; not the consumers, we may believe, whose interest has been entirely neglected; but the producers whose interest has been so carefully attended to ....
>
> (*WN*: 660–61)

In one sense this expresses a real and fundamental truth of modern humanism and Enlightenment: the economic system exists for 'the relief of man's estate', to use the phrase of that seminal modern, Francis Bacon (quoted more fully in sec. 2.1.6). But as prefigured in section 2.2.1 in relation to wealth-as-product versus wealth-as-consumption, the issue is not so simple in relation to the growth path of consumption. The time-paths of production versus consumption, and hence the time-path of investment, have implications for the intertemporal distribution of consumption; e.g. higher unproductive consumption in period t+1, and lower accumulation, reduces potential unproductive consumption in period t+2. To say that ultimately the only defensible purpose of economic activity is human consumption does not resolve this issue.

There is one further and final point concerning the productive versus unproductive distinction. That distinction is really about the *uses* to which commodities are put, not the qualitative characteristics which define any particular kind of commodity. Each unit of corn produced, for example, is not productive as such. Hence, in the treatment of growth directly above, in any time period part of the previous period's output of corn or of machines is being used productively, to produce further corn and machines, and part of it is being used unproductively, to produce silk. (However, silk, by construction in our model above, is capable only of unproductive use.) Similarly, to take one of Smith's instances of a productive service, a retailer can be selling a necessary subsistence good to a productive worker at 3.00pm, and be selling a luxury consumption good to the menial servant of a landlord at 3.01pm. In this situation, the same retail labourer, in (virtually) the same kind of activity, is contributing to productive activity in one moment and to non-productive activity in the next. Smith is certainly aware of this, most notably, in relation to the alternative uses of stock, either as capital or for unproductive consumption, and well aware that 'productiveness' may and should be applied to any and all of the inputs which are necessary to reproduction of inputs. Productiveness is not a peculiar characteristic of labour alone. In the context of his analysis of tax incidence, Smith comments:

> The rent of houses, though it in some respects resembles the rent of land, is in one respect essentially different from it. The rent of land is paid *for the use of a productive subject.* The land which pays it produces it. The rent of

houses is paid for the use of an unproductive subject. Neither the house nor the ground which it stands upon produce any thing. The person who pays the rent, therefore, must draw it from some other source of revenue ....

(*WN*: 842; emphasis added)

As the *WN* editors indicate, this connects with a passage of argument in the last chapter of Book II:

> Not only ... [the farmer's] labouring servants, but his labouring cattle, are productive labourers. In agriculture too nature labours along with man; and though her labour costs no expence, its produce has its value, as well as that of the most expensive workmen .... The labourers and labouring cattle, therefore, employed in agriculture, not only occasion, like workmen in manufactures, the reproduction of a value equal to their own consumption, or to the capital which employs them, together with its owners [*sic*] profits; but of a much greater value. Over and above the capital of the farmer and all its profits, they regularly occasion the reproduction of the rent of the landlord.
>
> (*WN*: 363–4; see also 346–9 on durable consumption and productive labourers)

Insofar as employment of some of a society's land is necessary to the production of value added – or more coherently stated, necessary to the production of inputs to the production of further capital – that land is as much productive as the labour likewise employed. Furthermore, when Smith speaks of 'productive stock' (e.g. n. 42 above, and the productive cattle in the quotation directly above) he is correctly attributing the same productiveness to produced means of production employed in generating further capital. The productive stock is not only the consumption of the productive workers; it includes also their instruments of production.[64]

#### *4.3.5 Reducibility of normal prices*

There is one further issue worthy of comment here. We hinted in section 4.2.1 that Smith's notion of the reducibility of normal prices to remunerations for the three collaborating forms of inputs, labour, capital and land, is somewhat problematic (see pp. 148–9). The model employed above to clarify the $L^p$ concept (sec. 4.3.3) may be used also to clarify this issue. Consider, in the terms of that model, the determinants of Smith's 'real prices', the labour-commanded prices, focusing upon the two capital goods, corn and machines. Their Smithian real prices ($p_{CW}$, $p_{MW}$) are expressed by dividing their money prices by the money wage:

$$p_C/w = p_C/p_C c = 1/c$$

$$p_M/w = p_M/p_C c = (p_{MC})(1/c)$$

where $p_{MC}$ is the price of machines expressed in terms of corn. The equality of $p_{CW}$ and $1/c$ is merely a consequence of the supposition of a given real wage, since Smithian real price is just the reciprocal of the real wage expressed in terms of the commodity under consideration. A 'solution' for the real price of machines may then be derived, by recourse to the earlier machine price equation:

$$p_{MW} = l_M(1 + r)/[1 - a_{MM}(1 + r)]$$

It is evident that for this to be an economically meaningful solution the denominator must be positive, which is guaranteed by the restriction that $r$ is less than $(1 - a_{MM})/a_{MM}$. This has a straightforward and satisfying economic interpretation: the profit rate, in particular, in machine production, cannot be so high as to exhaust or more than exhaust the revenue from sale of output, net of the value of the machine input used up in the machine production cycle. The machine input per unit of machine gross output ($a_{MM}$) must also be less than unity, otherwise machine production is incapable of generating any value added at all. These restrictions also mean that $a_{MM}(1 + r)$ is less than unity. The solution for $p_{MW}$ therefore can be expressed by the following approximation:

$$p_{MW} \approx l_M(1 + r)\{1 + [a_{MM}(1 + r)] + [a_{MM}(1 + r)]^2 + \ldots + [a_{MM}(1 + r)]^k\} \quad k \to \infty$$

This expression reveals the element of soundness in Smith's intuitive reduction (at least once one has put aside his unsatisfactory treatment of rents). It shows the labour-commanded price as a function of the labour directly and indirectly required to produce a machine, compounded by the profits earned at each conceptual 'stage' of the production process – conceptual or logical time rather than real time (see n. 65). The first term, $l_M(1 + r)$, is the labour directly required to produce a machine, marked up by the profit factor. Now consider the expansion of $1/[1 - a_{MM}(1 + r)]$, which is the multiplicand of $l_M(1 + r)$. The first element (unity) accounts for the direct labour input, when multiplied by $l_M(1 + r)$. The second term – $[a_{MM}(1 + r)]$, likewise multiplied by $l_M(1 + r)$ – accounts for the *indirect* labour input in the production of the direct machine input required to produce a machine ($a_{MM}$, also marked up by the profit factor). But this machine input itself previously required machine input in its production, which is represented by the third term – $[a_{MM}(1 + r)]^2$, again multiplied by $l_M(1 + r)$ – and so on, back and back, to successive, conceptually or logically 'prior' production cycles. Hence the real price can be approximated by a reduction to a series of dated labour inputs – derived from the given, current production method – compounded by the given rate of profit.[65] Furthermore, if the normal price of machines were expressed in the conventional unit of account or any other numeraire, rather than being expressed in labour commanded, an analogous approximation could be derived, showing the machine price reduced to dated wage cost compounded by the rate of profit. This is something of a vindication of Smith's intuition concerning the reducibility of normal prices, but not entirely. This real price equation was only advisedly called a 'solution' above, because the determination of $r$ is unclear from this equation alone. (In fact, an explicit solution for $r$ is not necessary in order to see the character of this reduction.) The assumption of a given real corn wage means that the real price of corn is fixed, as the reciprocal of that real wage. But just as for the real price of machines, the real price of corn also, at one and the same time, will be equal to the labour directly and indirectly required to produce a unit of corn, compounded by the profit factor. By recourse to the earlier corn price equation, together with the solution for $p_{MW}$, the real price of corn can be expressed as:

$$p_{CW} = 1/c = l_C(1 + r) + \{l_M a_{MC}(1 + r)^2/[1 - a_{MM}(1 + r)]\}$$

$$1/c \approx l_C(1 + r) + [l_M a_{MC}(1 + r)^2]\{1 + [a_{MM}(1 + r)] + [a_{MM}(1 + r)]^2 + \ldots + [a_{MM}(1 + r)]^k\} \quad k \to \infty$$

With a given real wage, the only variable in this equation or in the approximation is $r$, which hence must be fully determined by that equation.[66] Notice therefore also, that the production methods of *both* corn and iron enter into that determination of the general profit rate: not only the labour-output and machine-output ratios in corn production ($l_C$, $a_{MC}$) are involved, but also those in machine production ($l_M$, $a_{MM}$), together with the real wage ($c$). This result is an expression of the simultaneity of prices and costs in circular production systems, an issue discussed also at a number of points in Chapter 3. As our set of five equations in section 4.3.3 shows, with a given real wage, $r$ is determined simultaneously with $p_C$ and $p_M$, and so, normal costs are determined simultaneously with normal prices. In circular production systems, costs in general cannot be known independently of prices. All these parameters – the production methods for all basic commodities in the system (corn and machines in our illustration) and the real wage – therefore also enter into determination of $p_{MW}$, via their role in determining $r$.

Perhaps Smith's intuition extended to *some* sense of this result: he does see the need to refer back to indirect labour to justify his reducibility notion, and so, at least by implication, perceives the need to refer to the production methods of produced inputs employed in the production of any particular commodity, for which the reduction is being contemplated.[67] But as to the rate of profit being so determined as to ensure that the reciprocal of the real wage just equals the profit-compounded direct and indirect labour input required, Smith is unaware of this kind of functional connection between real wages and the rate of profit. The notion of arriving at the magnitude of normal price by adding up natural or normal wages and natural or normal profits per unit of output, with the associated rates of wages and of profits evidently regarded as separably determined, is to that extent misguided.[68,69] On the other hand, the non-basic commodity reveals an unsurprising asymmetry. Its real price, like the real prices of the basic commodities, is expressible in terms of labour directly and indirectly required, compounded by profit. But since it does not enter into production as an input, there is a one-way causation running from $r$, $p_M$ and $p_C$, together with the production method for silk, to the normal price of silk. In that sense, a cost-of-production theory of normal price is adequate for explaining the pricing of such commodities, but only such non-basic commodities, and only once the prices of basics are determined.

### *4.3.6 Prehistory: capital, cattle, chattels*

The term 'capital' comes into substantial use in English in the fifteenth-century, from the French *capital*, in turn from the Latin *capitāle*, *capitālis* – referring to 'head-, principal', and to capital in the sense of 'principal sum of money, capital, wealth, property' (*OED*: 'capital'; 'cattle'). For the purposes here, non-economic senses of capital, which pertain, in one way or another to 'the head', may be put aside. In English, it is only from the seventeenth century that 'capital' gains currency in its general economic senses of 'the original funds of a trader, company, or corporation; principal'; '[t]he stock of a company, corporation, or individual with which they enter into business and on which profits or dividends are calculated' (*OED*: 'capital'). Prior to that, from at least the fourteenth century, variants of *cattle* and *chattel* conveyed these kinds of economic senses of capital in English, though some seminal sixteenth-century instances of 'capital' have been unearthed in the accounting literature, evidently arising by way of translation of Luca Pacioli (Cannan 1921; Richards 1926; Hatfield 1926, 1934). As the *OED* ('capital') indicates, the actual French descendant of the Latin is *cheptel*, pronounced *chetel*; and further:

> Under the feudal system the application [of *cattle*, *chattel* and variants] was confined to movable property or wealth, as being the only 'personal' property, and in English it was more and more identified with 'beast held in possession, live stock', which was almost the only use after 1500, exc. in the technical phrase 'goods and catells (cattals)' which survived till the 17th c. In legal Anglo-French, the Norman *catel* was superseded at an early period by the Parisian *chatel*; this continued to be used in the earlier and wider sense (subject however to legal definition), and has in modern times passed into a certain current use as CHATTEL, so that the phrase just cited is now also since 16th c. 'goods and chattels'.
>
> (*OED*: 'cattle')

Hence senses of 'capital' in early English use are conveyed by economic applications of all three of these terms, and least so by the term 'capital': 'By loue of worldly catall' (1495); 'I giue and bequeth all my chattelles and houses' (1549); 'The custodie, not of the landes onely … but of the goods and chattels also' (1570–6); '*Capital*, wealth, worth; a stocke, a man's principall, or chiefe, substance' (1630–9 [1611]); 'Catals comprehend in it selfe all goods mooveable & immooveable, except such as are in nature of freehold … Catals are either reall or personall' (1641); 'Such anticipations upon all kinds of receipts for monies borrowed and already spent, that they had no capital for future security' (1647); 'An Act for Enlarging the Capital Stock of the Bank of England' (1709; all quotations from *OED*: 'capital'; 'cattle'; 'chattel').

Traces of this etymology live on in Smith's texts and in his thought. Opening his critique of mercantilism, he mentions in passing that for the Tartars, '[w]ealth … consisted in cattle' (*WN*: 430). To be sure, this is there connected by him with the use of cattle as a monetary instrument, both as means of exchange and unit of account (cf. *WN*: 38). Nevertheless, this identification proceeds from the notion of cattle as durable stock, whether for production or as a potential means of payment.[70] In the latter sense it involves, for Smith, the traditional misidentification of wealth and money. So, in the mercantilist literature, monetary reserves or balances are commonly referred to as 'stocks'; but this nevertheless captures an idea of wealth as stocks available for use. In any case, to the extent that the etymological connection between 'cattle' and 'capital' is attributable to the function of cattle as primary (non-human) means of production in traditional pastoral societies, it is interesting that in discussing the resolution of commodity prices into wages, profits and rents, Smith equates the maintenance of labour with the maintenance of cattle employed in production: 'In the price of corn, for example, one part pays the rent of the landlord, another pays the wages or maintenance of the labourers and labouring cattle employed in producing it, and the third pays the profit of the farmer' (*WN*: 68). In a similar manner, in the context of illustrating his distinction between fixed and circulating capital, Smith writes that the 'maintenance' of a farmer's 'labouring cattle' is 'a circulating capital in the same manner' as 'the wages and maintenance of his labouring servants' (*WN*: 280). Insofar as the consumption goods of labour are included as an element of the stocks of capital goods required as temporally prior advances in the production processes of Smithian commercial society, then labour is indeed like livestock. Labour, or rather, $L^p$, is a part of the capital. The capital of a society, in the sense of means of production, is reducible to labour, together with the unimproved natural resources also used in production.

It was shown in section 2.2.1, that for Smith wealth is output not capital; but in relation to his notion of $L^p$, capital as produced means of production can be characterized as output or wealth well used, in the production of more wealth. The *OED* ('capital') itself conveys an idea very close to this, in defining 'capital stock or fund' as '[t]he accumulated wealth of an individual, company, or community, used as a fund for carrying on fresh production; wealth in any form used to help in producing more wealth'. This circular or circulation conception of capital and production is also central to Quesnay's economics, as has already been seen (see pp. 21, 40). In an unpublished manuscript, Sraffa notes the *WN* (68) text quoted immediately above – or more precisely, notes the effectively identical Smith analogy between labour consumption and 'maintenance' of 'a labouring horse', also at the same page – precisely because of its reduction of labour input to the commodities required to maintain labour (Sraffa Papers, Trinity College, Cambridge, folder D3/11/37: folio 6). There is, of course, at least a tension between thus treating wages as capital in the form of the consumption by labour, and at the same time, as part of society's net revenue. Also relevant here is the element of analogy Smith notes between slaves and livestock (albeit involving a very different system of property rights to that pertinent to the labourer in commercial society): 'In order that they [slaves] may work well, it is the interest of their master that they should be fed well and kept in good heart, in the same manner as it is his interest that his working cattle should be so' (*WN*: 939; also *LJA*: 181, 187; *LJB*: 451; *WN*: 586–7). In fact, the *OED* ('cattle') observes that the term 'cattle' actually was '[a]pplied by slaveholders to their slaves', but strangely, gives only one instance, rather late in the history of Western slavery, from *Uncle Tom's Cabin*, published in 1852: 'What have any of you cussed cattle to do with thinking what's right?'

### *4.3.7 Quesnay: the invention of capital theory*

To the question of the origins of the concept of capital, Marx for one, suggests a clear-cut answer: 'the system of the physiocrats [i.e. "Quesnay ... and his ... disciples"] is the first systematic conception of capitalist production' (Marx 1967, vol. 2: 360; also vol. 3: 784; Marx 1963: 44). Since the actual term, conveying various notions of wealth, property or assets, was extant before Quesnay (both in French and English), Marx cannot have intended that Quesnay's writings gave birth to the concept of capital as such. It is rather that Quesnay begins the *theory* of capital. Hence in relation to earlier senses of 'capital' conveyed under the terms 'capital', 'cattle' and 'chattels', as indicated above in considering the etymology, the sense of capital that Quesnay can be regarded as having originated is a deeper and more precise notion, constructed for the purposes of an economic theory. In the context of theorizing a mid-eighteenth-century social economy in which capitalism is coming into being – but has not yet fully arrived (certainly has not yet fully arrived in economic theory) – there are two key aspects to that conception. First, capital is produced means of production (including labour consumption, in eighteenth-century economics), necessary as inputs to production processes, so that those inputs must be 'advanced' for production to take place. In this aspect, it is important that the concept of capital is couched at the level of the physical inputs used and used up in production, deeper than the mere financial notion of capital. Second, capital is a property right attached to those means of production, which generates a claim to a share of the revenue from production and sale – that it to say, which *ex ante* requires a return of profits – and a return realized *ex post*, to the extent that prices more than cover the production costs of outputs, including the cost of the capital goods used up. Cannan (1894: 217–18) more or less accords with this two-part definition: 'originally the term seems to have been confined to loans of money.... [I]n the natural course of historical development the term ... received a wider meaning.... [C]apital is considered primarily as a source of profit.' And, he goes on to say, the concept develops into a notion of '*that part of wealth set aside for future production*' (original emphasis), which captures the first element of our definition (at least if one excludes unimproved natural resources from 'wealth').

The property-right sense obviously presupposes the produced-means-of-production aspect; but one can have a social economy in which produced means of production are in use, while the property-right aspect is absent. (Hence the presence of the produced-means-of-production notion in a text cannot be taken as evidence, by itself, of the presence of the property-right notion; cf. Sewall 1901: 30–1, 45–8, on pre-modern thought.) Marx is right: nowhere earlier than Quesnay can there be found a conception of capital combining these two dimensions, a combination which points towards Turgot's theory of fundamental prices and Smith's theory of natural prices. In both Turgot and Smith, the equalization of the net returns or advantages of investing in the various alternative assets or activities available to property owners is a central organizing principle of the treatment of income distribution and prices. What has not yet 'arrived' in Quesnay's theory, and is likewise absent from all other economic writers before Turgot and Smith, is this notion of a tendency towards a uniform net rate of return on income-earning property in all its forms. When Marx speaks of Physiocracy as the founding of capital theory he has Turgot in mind as well.[71]

Quesnay's *Tableau* characterizes a position of the economic system in which the '*advances* … employed in cultivation [i.e. agriculture]', and the '*advances* … employed for the capital [*les fonds*] and costs of trade, for the purchase of raw materials for manufactured goods, and for the subsistence and other needs of the artisan until he has completed and sold his work', are restored for the next annual cycle of production via gross revenue from sales covering those capital costs (Kuczynski and Meek 1972: i–iii, '3rd edn'). That is to say, the *Tableau* contemplates a situation of the economy in which reproduction is successfully realized in exchange. The *Tableau* is hardly at all explicit about net profits being returned from sale, along with capital costs. The rather tentative and uncertain place of profits in Quesnay's economics is partly a consequence of the doctrine that only land-rents constitute the genuine social net revenue. On the other hand, Quesnay does perceive the role of a return of profits – notably, in agriculture – resulting from a 'good' price (*bon prix*), in enabling and facilitating net capital accumulation. Meek (1951: 320) goes so far as to suggest that 'French Physiocracy was, in the broadest sense, a theory of capital accumulation'. He is not wrong to thereby imply that this was the primary purpose of Quesnay's economics, both with regard to descriptive theory and normative application. The animating policy objective is economic growth, which in turn requires capital accumulation. The *Tableau*, the concept of the surplus, the price theory, the taxation doctrines, notwithstanding their limitations in relation to theorizing a capitalist economy, are all ultimately about the determinants of that capital accumulation, and the conditions for facilitating it. Vaggi (1987c: esp. 58–93, 121–64, 190–2) has done much to clarify the systematic significance of prices and profits for Quesnay's economics.[72] To put the conclusion briefly, capital is present in Quesnay's economics, as a claim to a share of the revenue from production, for advancing produced inputs – a share over and above those capital costs. But as a claim to profits, its presence is rather tenuous.

It has already been suggested above that the absence of capital theory from

*LJ*, together with Smith's time spent in Paris between the lectures and publication of *WN*, points to Quesnay's crucial contribution – directly, and/or via Turgot – in relation to this central aspect of Smith's economics.[73] In this regard, the argument of Lundberg (1964), though unconvincing as to its central thesis, is of some interest. Her primary purpose is to argue for the possibility that Smith was responsible for the 1793 English translation of Turgot's *Réflexions*, an edition which is actually in Smith's library (Mizuta 2000: 258; though obviously, only in 'his' library after his death!). Viner (1965: 135–8) convincingly rebuts this proposition. What is intriguing is that Lundberg (1964: 65–73) partly rests her argument on Smith's use in English of the French forms, '*a* capital' and 'capital*s*' – indeed rather odd, or at least awkward, expressions in English – and Turgot's use of the equivalent French terms. In response, Viner points to instances of these terms in English texts before Smith and in French texts other than Turgot. Nevertheless, while the case for Smith as Turgot translator is not made, Viner (1965: 134) acknowledges:

> It is true that Smith in *The Wealth of Nations* repeatedly used expressions like 'a capital,' 'an equal capital,' 'two capitals,' 'their capitals,' and so forth, and I suppose it is also true that English-speaking persons before and after Smith would in similar contexts normally write 'capital,' 'capital equal in amount,' and so forth, if they used the word 'capital' at all. I also concede the probability that Smith was here influenced by French usage and especially by Turgot's usage in the *Réflexions*. Miss Lundberg's demonstration of the verbal correspondences between *The Wealth of Nations* and the *Réflexions* I accept, therefore, as a significant addition to the case against Cannan's skepticism with respect to Smith's even having seen the *Réflexions* before writing *The Wealth of Nations* . . . .[74]

Lundberg's more extreme and less plausible claims rest upon negative propositions which in principle can be disproved by the evidence of a single exception; e.g. 'Smith ... uses the term "capital" as only the French have ever used it', referring to the use of both *a capital* and *capitals* (Lundberg 1964: 65). This is precisely how Viner responds. But while this linguistic aspect of *WN* does not carry the weight of Lundberg's conjecture concerning the translation of Turgot, it does support the conclusion that Smith's capital theory has a French origin. In relation to the term 'capital' in French, Marx (1963: 44) also notes that the Physiocrats gave fixed and circulating capital 'other names' (i.e. original and annual advances), and that Turgot 'uses the term capital for *avances* more frequently than Quesnay' (Marx 1967, vol. 2: 360, n. 37). Such negative propositions, in any case, can never strictly be proven, even in the absence of any known counter-instances, unless one can confidently claim to have scrutinized all conceivably relevant texts prior to those for which one is making the claim – effectively, an impossibility. Hence, strictly speaking, this applies also to propositions such as ours, that there is not to be found before Quesnay any deployment of the notion of capital in the two-part sense we have enunciated above.[75]

### *4.3.8 Luxury, unproductiveness and surplus before Smith*

The main currents of the historical background to Smith's concept of $L^p$ come clearly into view if one focuses on his concept in terms of the coherent representation it can be given, via Sraffa's distinction between basics and non-basics (see secs 4.3.2, 4.3.3). It will be recalled from there that the lack of consistency in Smith's multiple definitions of the term can be overcome by identifying services with luxuries and setting aside the proposition that $L^u$ cannot produce value added.[76] To be clear, both of these steps involve departing from Smith's texts; they give more coherence to the concept than he provides it with himself. In any case, the effect of this representation is to make the $L^p/L^u$ dichotomy to parallel a distinction between production of capital goods and production of luxuries. However, for this identification of $L^p$ versus $L^u$ with capital versus luxuries to be completely satisfying as a coherent reconstruction, the categories 'capital' and 'luxuries' must be both mutually exclusive and collectively exhaustive. We will not want there to be commodities which are both capital and luxuries, or neither capital nor luxuries. For then there will be labour which is both productive and unproductive, or neither productive nor unproductive.

In two important respects, capital and luxuries may not be mutually exclusive and collectively exhaustive for Smith. In speaking of consumption he commonly makes a threefold distinction between 'necessaries', 'conveniencies' or 'conveniences', and 'luxuries' or some analogous term (e.g. *TMS*: 50; *WN*: 47, 87, 95, 181, 287, 289–90, 299, 405; *LJA*: 338; *edWN*; 563; cf. Raphael and Macfie 1976b: 50). To the extent that labourers consume conveniences, the tripartite characterization of consumption may be regarded as imparting a lack of mutual exclusiveness to the capital/luxuries distinction, if the conveniences consumed by labour are regarded as part of the wages (of $L^p$) advanced as capital in the production process – and at the same time, those conveniences are assimilated to the concept of luxury. Or it may be regarded as imparting a lack of collective exhaustiveness, if labour conveniences are treated as neither capital advances nor luxuries. Secondly, the possibility of activities which are neither capital-producing nor luxury-producing pertains also to the status of government. It was shown in section 4.3.2 that Smith clearly understands at least some substantial elements of governmental activity to be essential to the operation of economic society – not least, to the operation of a fully-fledged commercial society – even while he explicitly characterizes them as unproductive. The professor of philosophy whose lectures on jurisprudence run to hundreds of pages in print, much of them about property rights, could hardly have failed to see the necessity of some infrastructure of government and law for the conduct of economic activity. So in a sense, essential government infrastructure is neither capital nor luxury. But as argued in sections 4.3.2 and 4.3.3, this is not a conceptual failure on Smith's part: government, largely, does not produce capital goods in his world, and that is what merits its exclusion from the category of productive activity, with no need then to deny that at another level, it is nevertheless necessary.

For the purpose of considering the relation between Smith's $L^p$ concept and earlier thought, especially pre-modern thought, we may put aside any notion of elements of consumption which are neither necessities nor luxuries – either by putting conveniences aside, or by regarding any such above-*strictly*-necessary consumption as productive and hence, part of the capital advanced in production. (The other possibility broached immediately above – that conveniences consumed by labour, or at least by $L^p$, are simultaneously capital and luxury – is too alien to the Smithian frame of reference.) In fact, treating conveniences consumed by $L^p$ as productive consumption is consistent with Smith's 'elastic' notion of subsistence (sec. 3.4.3; cf. n. 91 below). We may also put aside the resources allocated to the non-economic essentials for economic society to function, notably, the necessary infrastructure of government which protects life, at least some liberties, and property rights. (In a real sense, this includes the resources necessary for external defence.) On these two suppositions, unproductive activity strictly reduces to production of luxuries. The $L^p/L^u$ dichotomy then resonates down the ages, all the way back to ancient thought, as well as in the forms ancient thought took when intertwined in the West with Christian thought in the Common Era. It resonates in various forms of a dichotomy between natural needs and artificial wants (Perrotta 2004: 24–7).

In pre-modern thought the dichotomy serves first and foremost as the basis for a moral judgement against luxury, with the consumption dichotomy closely aligned with a virtue versus vice or corruption dichotomy (Wahnbaeck 2004: 13–15). It is only really in the early modern era that luxury is considered, and reconsidered, in a framework of arguments which are both economic and descriptive or empirical. In order to gain a concise view of the whole picture of luxury in Western thought, and especially of the transition from pre-modernity to modernity, the range of positions with regard to luxury can be represented in two dimensions: in one dimension, there are arguments for and against luxury; in the other, there are moral versus economic arguments for or against. So represented, in principle, there can be four kinds of views. The pre-modern views are overwhelmingly of a moral character, as against the economic arguments and views which come into play with modernity. In the for-and-against dimension, pre-modernity overwhelmingly takes a position against luxury. To take notable examples, this is true of those two ancient thinkers foundational to Western thought, Plato and Aristotle, though the latter, at least, is hardly a puritan; in the Common Era, the thought of St Augustine of Hippo is foundational for the Christian antipathy to luxury. Favouring luxury, for moral reasons, is certainly the least commonly to be found of the four views; but even in pre-modernity one perhaps can find instances of something like this view (Perrotta 2004: 25–6, on Isocrates). The economic arguments concerning luxury which arise in the seventeenth and eighteenth centuries are less overwhelmingly on one side or the other, for or against, though the secondary literature of recent times has tended to emphasize the modern trend towards views in favour of luxury. Mandeville is widely and rightly regarded as the most striking representative of this view.[77]

This two-by-two representation of views on the issue goes to the heart of the matter; but it should not at all be taken to imply that each particular thinker or writer necessarily can be uniquely placed in one or other camp, in each of these dimensions. For example, one could be against luxury for the labouring classes but not against luxury for others (Sekora 1977: 97, on some eighteenth-century English literature). In Roman thought there is a moral distinction between private and public luxury, the latter having a desirable political function (Wahnbaeck 2004: 14; cf. sec. 5.1.2). More importantly for our purposes here, Smith himself occupies a nuanced and complex position, straddling at least two or three of the elements of the two-by-two characterization. While the rise of modern views in favour of luxury has been emphasized in recent scholarship, the emerging political economy of the seventeenth and eighteenth centuries also expresses a definite opposition to luxury, for non-mercantilist reasons. Smith has this view. By virtue of his favouring capital accumulation and the productive use of labour, Smith is in the category of being against luxury for economic reasons. But in taking this view he is, as in many other things, a moderate (see sec. 5.3.2). He is not at all obdurately opposed to all luxury, as noted in section 4.3.4 (also n. 50 above). Most significant in this context is his endorsement of real wages above strict subsistence, and even more, his favouring high or rising real wages (sec. 5.1.1). If this is not exactly an endorsement of luxury for the labouring classes, it is an endorsement of material comfort (those aforementioned 'conveniences'). But this view of labour consumption is essentially a *moral* stance; it is not based on any descriptive understanding of an economic function of high or rising labour consumption. There are also in Smith other contending strands of belief concerning the moral significance of the development of commercial society, and its attendant material progress and opulence. For example, commercial society, by reducing the dependency of labourers, reduces criminality; and commercial life itself leads to greater honesty (see Chapter 5, n. 21). On the other hand, there is the adverse impact of division of labour on the intellectual and moral qualities of labourers (sec. 4.1.1).

It is a striking fact that of the four elements of our two-by-two characterization of views on luxury, the one which is most evidently absent in Smith is any *economic* argument for luxury (The closest thing to such an argument is at *WN*: 346–9; though in the end, it is not really that.) Those moderns who favour luxury for economic reasons, rather than favouring it as intrinsically desirable in itself, in one way or another are doing so because they perceive luxury as providing a source of demand to support the potential production capacity of the social economy – luxury as a demand outlet for aggregate output which otherwise would lack a sufficient demand. Most particularly, this is about favouring luxury consumption as a means to higher levels of labour employment than otherwise would occur. This is evident, for example, in Mandeville and Jean-François Melon (Wahnbaeck 2004: 24–9). A further, common idea in the early modern literature, which might appear as an additional economic argument, is not really such: notions along the lines of the human desire for luxury, or material comfort more widely, providing the necessary spur to material progress. This kind of idea, when expressed at this general level, is hardly 'economic', and hardly an 'argument' at all. It amounts to little more than saying that the desire for material progress or opulence leads to material progress or opulence.[78] Material progress, opulence or luxury are being favoured for themselves. The absence in Smith of anything like the (genuinely) economic argument for luxury is ultimately due to his identification of saving and investment. His thereby subscribing to a saving-is-spending doctrine means that for Smith, luxury is not needed as a solution to a kind of primitively stated, quasi-Keynesian problem of insufficient aggregate demand at the level of the economic system as a whole (cf. Winch 1996: 79, 89, 365–6). Capital accumulation, which is at one and the same time saving, can fulfill the role of supporting the production capacity of the system, without need of assistance from luxury consumption. At least, this is so if the saving-is-spending doctrine is plausible, an issue examined in section 4.4.1.

The moral versus economic distinction in the foregoing sketch of views on luxury should not be misidentified with a normative/descriptive distinction. All of these views are views for or against luxury and therefore all have normative content, as well as descriptive content. If, like Smith, one has a theory in which capital accumulation is the condition for economic growth – and capital accumulation is self-validating with regard to sufficiency of aggregate demand to support production capacity – then production of luxuries is at the expense of growth. To get from this descriptive theory to a normative judgement about production of luxuries, one must add a normative principle, along the lines of 'growth is good' – or at least, better than luxury, up to some point. Neither are the pre-modern views against luxury merely the positing of a priori moral judgements, bereft of descriptive content. They commonly involved empirical content, for example, about causation between luxury and loss of martial spirit (Berry 1994: 56–60). Here also, of course, to arrive at a normative judgement against luxury, a normative principle has to be added, along the lines of 'martial spirit is good'. The modern pro-luxury economic argument is based on a normative principle that high or higher employment is good; but embedded within it is also a descriptive theory of some kind, however inchoate, concerning labour employment and aggregate demand for commodities. If, as against Smith's view, saving is *non*-spending, then those who took that view may be said to have had a point. Most satisfactorily stated, Smith's descriptive distinction between $L^p$ and $L^u$ is a distinction between capital-producing and other-producing activities. (In his less satisfactory formulations, it is about physical-commodity-producing versus service-producing activities, and value-adding versus non-value-adding activities.) To the extent that capital accumulation and growth are to be favoured over luxury consumption, then $L^p$ is to be preferred to $L^u$. But what is to guarantee 'the extent of the market' for the output of $L^p$?

Another early modern dichotomy which can be associated with the prehistory of the $L^p/L^u$ distinction is that between 'industry' and 'idleness' (e.g. Child 1668: 14; and Smith himself: *WN*: 337; quoted in sec. 4.3.2). A further dichotomy, with close analogy to that one, and getting very close to the substance of Smith's conception, is the distinction between productiveness and 'sterility'. Here one may note an intriguing apparent clash of metaphors in the history of the characterizations of productiveness and of luxury. The generic concept of the 'productive' in modern European languages derives from the classical Latin *prōdūcere*, 'to extend … to prolong … to bring forth … to advance … to bring into existence, to give birth to'. Derivative from this, 'productive' from the seventeenth century in English conveys, among other senses, 'creative, generative', and 'fertile' (*OED*: 'produce'; 'productive'). Hence follows the identification of unproductiveness with sterility or barrenness.[79] On the other hand, Seabright (2004: 76) suggests that up until the seventeenth century, 'luxury' was identified with 'lechery', and somewhat analogously, until the late nineteenth century, 'expense' was a synonym for orgasm. These language practices, he further suggests, are perhaps symptomatic of human unease about sex intertwining with unease about material wealth. The *OED* ('lecher'; 'luxury') does not completely confirm Seabright's account; but it does show that to 'spend' conveyed the meaning, '[t]o ejaculate; to have an orgasm', and in fact, continued in such use in the twentieth century. The *OED* ('spend') provides a striking instance from Samuel Pepys's *Diary*, indeed tinged with a moral tone favouring abstinence:

> I went up to her and played and talked with her and, God forgive me, did feel her; which I am much ashamed of, but I did no more, though I had so much a mind to it that I spent in my breeches.

So we have, at one and the same time, the unproductive as barren, and the associated superfluous excess as an expression of wantonness. One could perhaps reconcile these two perceptions by construing lechery (luxury) as 'wasted' ejaculation or orgasm (expenditure) – in different dimensions, trade-offs between spending and abstinence or saving (the latter now not being construed as a kind of spending, in the manner of Smith)!

By happy coincidence, the Pepys diary entry dates from the very year of Petty's *Treatise of Taxes* (1662), a work seminal to the development of the descriptive $L^p$ concept, in the political economy of Quesnay, Turgot and Smith. The language of productiveness and sterility is much employed by Quesnay and the Physiocrats. By virtue of his being the first theorist of 'capital' (in the substantial sense defined in section 4.3.7), it is not so surprising that Quesnay also provides the first, explicit concept of productive versus unproductive activity. But to the extent that in Quesnay, $L^p$ is more directly conceived of in terms of surplus-producing labour (in agriculture) than capital-producing labour, there are clear antecedents for the concept in the writings of Petty and Cantillon in particular. The development of the notion of the social surplus (outlined in sec. 4.2.4), and the development of the notion of $L^p$ as surplus-producing labour, are two sides of the same coin. The key point to make with regard to Petty and Cantillon is that capital accumulation in the sense of Quesnay and those who followed his lead is not to be found in their writings.

With regard to the treatment of $L^p$ from Quesnay to Smith, one may conclude with a key analytical point. The two notions of $L^p$ – as capital-producing labour and as surplus-producing labour – coincide, if 'capital' is understood to include all the produced means of production necessary for production. This is the case when the wages, or the consumption, of (capital-producing) labour are treated as necessary cost or necessary input, and included as part of capital, as they are in Quesnay, and somewhat more equivocally, in Smith. The productive sector of the economy is then that set of activities wherein capital is devoted to the production of more capital, a self-subsistent subsystem of the economy as a whole (cf. p. 157 and notes 37, 62 above). The sector's productiveness is manifest in its producing a surplus: the output of capital goods exceeds the input of capital goods used up. The social surplus hence can be construed either as the net product of the subsystem – or as the gross product of the economic system as a whole, net of the gross product of the capital-goods subsystem. (The latter will exceed the former, by the amount of the value added in the part of the economic system producing other than capital goods.) To the extent that capital goods are devoted to production of more capital goods, rather than to production of 'luxury' consumption or other non-capital-producing uses, the surplus is realized in positive capital accumulation. The supposition that wages no more than cover the 'necessary' consumption of labour would mean also that the social surplus is entirely realized in non-wage income (land-rents and profits, gross of taxation). But the proposition that wages do not at all share in the surplus is too simple to adequately represent Smith's views (sec. 4.4.2).[80]

## 4.4 Two problems

Smith's political economy as descriptive or explanatory science arrives at its core *raison d'être* in the analysis of accumulation and growth. Its prescriptive and ultimate purpose is 'general opulence', universal high or rising consumption, examined in Chapter 5. In the end, the growth of capital and production can only be for the purpose of consumption, sooner or later, as Smith so frequently and emphatically argues in his repudiations of mercantilism. The pace of growth is attributed to three key factors: division of labour as the driver of technical progress and hence, growth of output per worker; net revenue as setting a finite upper bound to accumulation of capital; and the rate of accumulation-cum-saving itself, as determining the actual share of net income or revenue devoted to increasing the capital stock. The growth of capital, or at least stock – driven by saving behaviour and expressed in the proportion between a society's productive labour and its unproductive labour – is the prerequisite for expanding division of labour and increasing productive consumption and production. 'Unproductive production' is not really a contradiction in terms for Smith (but cf. n. 46 above); 'unproductive capital' is, at least putting aside the money-as-capital issue (n. 42 above) and a further qualification due to 'misconduct' (n. 48 above). The latter is not a mere quibble. It points to the fact that Smith largely takes for granted that capital advances will be realized in profitable sales. That is to say, he is supposing a tendency towards normal conditions in which supplies balance effectual demands and normal prices prevail (see further to this, sec. 4.4.1). As was argued in section 3.4.1, the natural prices of *WN*, Book I are understood, entirely reasonably, to apply to the growth dynamics of Book II.

Campbell and Skinner (1976: 43, 48–9; also Groenewegen 1977a: 395–7; Rashid 1998: 21–3, 27) suggest that placing so much emphasis upon the division of labour dynamics led Smith to underrate the importance of machinery ('mechanization') for productivity growth. Perhaps there is some truth in this, but these two phenomena are intimately intertwined in Smith's accounts (see pp. 136, 139, including notes 3 and 9). It is not, in any case, a meaningful question to ask – what has been the contribution to productivity growth of changing or increased labour skills, versus the contribution of new machinery? – unless those contributions are separable and additive, which they are not. The same kind of error concerning the contribution to growth of capital versus division of labour lies behind the thesis that 'the role of capital came to dominate ... [*WN*] and ... to replace the division of labour as the major influence on growth' (Bowley 1975: 361; also 367–8, 372–4). Both capital accumulation and division of labour are *necessary* to rising output per worker. Furthermore, new divisions of labour and introduction of new machinery are generally two sides of the same coin, technical progress being simultaneously embodied in both. They are not independent factors in productivity growth. (The non-separability of division of labour and capital accumulation embodied in new machinery is very explicit at *WN*: 343, quoted at p. 161) The only sense in which capital may be given a priority is that growth without division of labour dynamics is conceivable; growth without capital accumulation is not. Put bluntly, the division of labour as Smith understands it is about making workers more machine-like, out of which, of itself, naturally grows increasing possibilities of replacing human labour with machines (Groenewegen 1987b: 902). The problematic concept of net revenue points to the absence in the growth theory of an explicit and systematic recourse to a notion of surplus, similar to that employed by the Physiocrats, which would set the genuine finite upper bound to net accumulation.[81] The great gap in his treatment of capital accumulation is the absence of an account of the coordination of saving and investment; and related to this, the coordination of demands and supplies, in the *dynamic* context of accumulation and growth.

### *4.4.1 Growth dynamics and demand/supply coordination*

In relation to that omission, one may raise this question. The three building blocks of Smith's growth theory – labour productivity growth, the level of net revenue and the rate of saving – jointly determine the growth of production capacity. What is there in this theory to guarantee that this capacity growth will be matched by a sufficient growth of demand to validate it? This is, one may say, the Keynesian question, in the framework of a long-run or growth analysis (see the epigraph to this chapter). Recall also, in this context, the apparent relatively autonomous role of demand, both in the market price dynamics and in the division of labour dynamics. (The productivity growth associated with the latter is also capacity growth.) Neither is suggestive of any notion of demand adapting to an autonomous growth in the supply of capital.[82] Probably part of the reason that this question escapes Smith is due to his commonly proceeding on the basis of an identification of saving decisions and investment decisions, a fact highlighted in modern commentary by Garegnani (1978–9: 338–41). To that extent, the question of the coordination of saving and investment flows, *flows arising in general from the saving and spending decisions of different sets of individuals*, is sidestepped, by treating a decision to save and a decision to invest as one and the same decision.

The following is the fullest and most striking statement of this identification:

> What is annually saved is as regularly consumed as what is annually spent, and nearly in the same time too; but it is consumed by a different set of people. That portion of his revenue which a rich man annually spends, is in most cases consumed by idle guests, and menial servants, who leave nothing behind them in return for their consumption. That portion which he annually saves, as for the sake of the profit it is immediately employed as a capital, is consumed in the same manner, and nearly in the same time too, but by a different set of people, by labourers, manufacturers, and artificers, who re-produce with a profit the value of their annual consumption. His revenue, we shall suppose, is paid him in money. Had he spent the whole, the food, cloathing, and lodging which the whole could have purchased, would have been distributed among the former set of people. By saving a part of it, as that part is for the sake of the profit immediately employed as a capital *either by himself or by some other person*, the food, cloathing, and lodging, *which may be purchased with it*, are necessarily reserved for the latter. The consumption is the same, but the consumers are different.
>
> (*WN*: 337–8; emphasis added)

The first emphasized phrase indicates that Smith thinks it makes no difference to his analysis whether or not the identification holds, without any explicit justification.[83]

It is important to understand that in resolving the problem of ensuring a growth of demand to validate the capacity growth associated with capital accumulation, the saving/investment identification entails abandoning consideration of a genuinely decentralized economy. To ensure that validation, the identification must be accompanied by a supposition, either that capital is homogeneous, or that the masters who make accumulation decisions are identical in all economically relevant respects except the scale of their activities (i.e. the accumulators are homogeneous). In relation to the first supposition, consider the equation for $Q_{c(t+1)}$, employed in section 4.3.4 to capture two key features of Smith's growth theory. Suppose, in this context, that there are a large finite number of individual masters who have ownership of output and engage in accumulation, each with a distinct saving rate, $\sigma_i$. The homogeneity of capital in this formulation ensures that no obstacle to supply validation results from this heterogeneity of the masters: each one 'saves' a distinct proportion of his or her output, and at one and the same time 'demands' that portion by devoting it to expansion of productive capacity (accumulation) – with the resulting aggregate $\sigma$ just the average of the $\sigma_i$s, weighted by the proportions of $Q_{c(t)}$ controlled by each respective master.

If, on the other hand, capital is heterogeneous, so that in general masters cannot satisfy their accumulation plans merely by saving/demanding a part of their own output from the previous period, then achieving those plans requires decentralized exchange and genuine saving/investment coordination (see the second emphasized phrase in the *WN*: 337–8 quotation immediately above). In such a world of heterogeneous commodities, the homogeneous-capital solution can be replicated by supposing steady-state growth dynamics (see n. 61 above); but even in a steady-state framework it must be supposed that each individual master's activity is a microcosm of the system as a whole, otherwise the problem of decentralized coordination of saving and investment returns. Hence there is effectively only one accumulator in this framework, and indeed, only one (albeit composite) commodity. In either case, the coordination of demand and supply in the context of growth is resolved, as if for a single saver/investor. These are precisely conditions in which no markets are needed and no decentralized coordination required. The growth process is intelligible only as a kind of expanding self-reproducing machine, akin to the growth model of von Neumann (1937). While a self-sustaining steady-state growth path exists for such an economy, the question in need of an answer is how non-steady growth occurs in a decentralized economy subject to random disturbances as well as systematic structural change. When the issue at hand is coordination in a decentralized economy, it is no comfort to know that a centralized economy has no such coordination problems. Keynes (1936) is right; there is a problem (see Garegnani 1978–9, 1988; cf. Tobin 1992: 126–8, though he is rather too kind to Smith).

At least since 1936, economists of all persuasions have been obliged to approach the question of the relation between saving and investment broadly in the following terms. There are agents (typically conceived of as 'households') who undertake saving and an in general different set of agents (typically conceived of as 'firms') who undertake investment expenditures; how are these two sets of decisions coordinated so as to generate a balance between aggregate planned saving and aggregate planned investment? (There of course must also be a balance of demands and supplies at the level of individual commodities, in any such equilibrium.) In broad terms, to this question two distinct answers have been given. Saving adapts to investment, and so aggregate supply adapts to aggregate demand, the latter determined by 'autonomous' elements of demand plus 'multipliers' linking autonomous and induced demands, via variations in activity levels. This is the Keynesian answer. Alternatively, investment may be conceived of as adapting to (the full employment level of) saving, ultimately via reliance on mechanisms which ensure that the demand for 'factors of production' adapts to the supply of factors, most notably, labour demand adapting to labour supply. This is the answer offered by marginalist theory – unsatisfactory, and in any case, not to be found in Smith.

What is his answer to the question? In truth, he does not really address it (but see directly below, further to labour demand and supply in particular). This exposes the absence of any substantial theory of the determination of aggregate activity levels in Smith's political economy: his growth theory is really a theory of how production *capacity* can grow, or one may say, a theory of *potential* growth. By proceeding as if an act of saving is identical with an act of investment (saving is spending), it is as if saving decisions were all akin to a corn farmer who 'saves' by putting aside a part of the crop, for use as seed input and labour consumption in the next production cycle, so that the farmer's abstaining from consumption is synonymous with investment or accumulation (with no wider exchange relations required). If something like this were so, saving and investment automatically would balance for each individual, and so also at the aggregate level. No such assumption is made by Smith; it is rather that he thinks the absence of such a comprehensive identification will not affect his analysis. Such an assumption in fact is inconsistent with the social economy Smith is theorizing. There is plenty of external financing in *WN*, equity as well as debt, and there is much about banks (see, in particular, *WN*, Book II, Chapter IV).[84]

There are two further issues to which the problem of demand/supply coordination in the context of growth dynamics is also relevant. It is pertinent to Smith's account of division of labour, to the extent that there is a chicken-and-egg problem with regard to the causation between growth of market demand on the one hand, and increasing division of labour on the supply side on the other. Recall the complex interaction of processes one can draw from his account: growth of the market influences, or at least provides the scope for, division of labour; division of labour, as a form of capacity growth, may influence growth; and distribution is influenced by the rate of output and hence employment growth, relative to growth of population and hence of the workforce. But in Smith's account, demand growth appears as the relatively autonomous factor. In any case, as emphasized in section 3.4, this set of dynamic system-wide forces is certainly a long way from latter-day industry supply functions, and obviously involves irreversibilities (e.g. technical innovation).

Second, there is the issue of labour demand/supply balance. Smith suggests a kind of full employment mechanism, but this notion of a process whereby population and labour supply growth adapt to growth of labour demand has no resemblance to the latter-day marginalist full employment mechanism. In a rough sense, it exhibits an *opposite* causation to the marginalist mechanism. The latter has labour demand adjusting to labour supply, principally via the influence of relative factor prices upon demand for factors of production. The radical difference between the two notions of labour demand/supply balancing is thrown into sharp relief by noticing that Smith's conception entails the conclusion that there is no long-run labour supply constraint on the level of activity or its growth rate. Recall the blunt statement quoted more fully in section 3.4.3: 'the demand for men, like that for any other commodity, necessarily regulates the production of men' (*WN*: 98). It would be absurdly ahistorical to describe Smith as a 'Keynesian'; it would impute more coherence to his demand-supply growth dynamics than they possess. But with regard to the relative autonomy of extent of the market and of labour demand, he is closer to Keynes than to marginalism (cf. Garegnani and Palumbo 1998: 16–17).[85]

### *4.4.2 The content of the social surplus*

There remains one final issue: the status and content of the concept of social surplus in Smith's political economy. The importance of 'net revenue' is that it defines the finite maximum increase in the capital stock, understood to include the consumption of $L^p$, between any two time periods. Hence, given the initial capital stock, it determines the maximum growth rate of capital. (Even putting aside productivity growth, this is not quite the same thing as the growth rate of output, to the extent that capital-output ratios are variable, though Smith never considers the issue of capital utilization rates). The maximum *net* growth rate, however, is constrained by the magnitude of the social surplus, properly defined (sec. 4.2.2), not by Smith's net revenue. The latter includes necessary consumption of productive labourers previously employed (though not all $L^p$), as well as new additions to $L^p$. His distinction between gross and net revenue confounds gross and net accumulation. Net revenue being exclusive of fixed capital maintenance makes saving out of net revenue to that extent net accumulation; net revenue being inclusive of circulating capital components means that saving out of net revenue is to that extent gross accumulation. The net revenue specification would cease to be unsatisfactory if one made the assumption that necessary labour consumption could be ignored: then the net revenue measure of society's net income would coincide with the surplus, and more or less correctly constitute the upper bound to net accumulation. But Smith is very explicit at many places in his texts, that substantial parts of labour consumption are necessary input. They are therefore not part of the social net product properly understood. The treatment of wages as capital advances, detailed in section 4.3.1, ultimately rests upon the imperative to keep labourers alive and functioning during the production cycle. The oft-stated causal relation from money prices of subsistence (notably, corn) to money wages is pertinent here as well, since it implies a concept of subsistence labour consumption as a necessary cost of production in real terms (e.g. *WN*: 509–10; *LJA*: 101; *LJB*: 502). Though on the other hand, *any* given levels of real wage rates, at subsistence or above, generates such causation (*WN*: 103–4). Depending upon the strength of capital accumulation and growth, real wages can be persistently above minimum subsistence, or 'subsistence' can be above minimum (*WN*: 91–9).

When Smith says that the replacement or maintenance cost of fixed capital is not part of net revenue (*WN*: 287), he means to convey that the material inputs and $L^p$ devoted to maintenance of the stock of fixed capital are not available for consumption or direct production of consumption. But this should apply equally to the elements of circulating capital used up, or to be used up, in production, or otherwise not available for consumption (e.g. inventories). To be sure, putting aside money, the elements of Smith's circulating capital which are not to devoted to maintenance of fixed capital *will* indirectly or directly end up being available for subsequent surplus consumption (though they alternatively may be saved and thereby devoted to accumulation). Nevertheless, it remains true for any definite time period under consideration – say, the annual production cycle – that the commodities used by producers as circulating capital during that period are not available for such use. Those commodities may end up in a subsequent time period in such use; but this is to abandon the discipline of defining flows by reference to definite time periods. Smith of course recognizes the need for circulating capital to be replaced:

> circulating capital being continually withdrawn from it [i.e. from the total stock of circulating capital], in order to be placed in the other two branches of the general stock of the society [i.e. in fixed capital and net revenue]; it must in its turn require continual supplies, without which it would soon cease to exist.
>
> (*WN*: 284)

> the whole annual produce … naturally divides itself into two parts. One of them … is … destined for replacing a capital, or for renewing the provisions, materials, and finished work, which had been withdrawn from a capital ….
>
> (*WN*: 332)[86]

If one contemplates a sufficiently long time period, such that all of the items of fixed capital inherited at the beginning of that time period will be entirely used up in that period, then 'fixed' capital becomes of a kind with circulating capital. The distinction between fixed and circulating evaporates, which is not problematic. More importantly, Smith's distinction between gross and net revenue also evaporates. On his definitions, the whole of the annual produce (the gross revenue) would then be identical with net revenue, since no deduction for maintenance of fixed capital would be necessary. (There is no fixed capital.) The only purpose of this thought experiment is to highlight the inappropriateness of his net revenue definition. For under these circumstances, there are still used up inputs to be replaced, in order to restore productive capacity, before the genuinely 'net' income available is determined.

There is in fact another dimension of Smith's political economy which bears quite directly on the issue of the social surplus. More precisely, it bears upon the question of what is necessary cost, and therefore, what has to be replaced or maintained, in order to reproduce or maintain the system's activity levels (leaving the stock of productive inputs intact), versus what is over and above this, available for free disposal. That dimension is the treatment of tax incidence. Smith's tax incidence theory can reveal the real surplus notion in his economics, by showing precisely what he regards as necessary costs, insofar as they are regarded as incapable of carrying the burden of tax incidence. For this purpose, the concept of surplus should be viewed in terms of gross income net of necessary costs of production, the *genuine* (not Smith's) social net revenue or net income. This is the value equivalent of the gross outputs of the economic system net of necessary inputs used up.

Consider first taxes on profits. Smith distinguishes conceptually between 'interest' on capital employed and the remainder of the profit earned over and above this, the latter compensating for the 'risk and trouble' of production:

> This latter part of profit is evidently a subject not taxable directly. It is the compensation … for the risk and trouble of employing the stock. The employer must have this compensation, otherwise he cannot, consistently with his own interest, continue the employment. If he was taxed directly, therefore, in proportion to the whole profit, he would be obliged either to raise the rate of his profit, or to charge the tax upon the interest of money; that is, to pay less interest. If he raised the rate of his profit in proportion to the tax, the whole tax, though it might be advanced by him, would be finally paid by one or other of two different sets of people, according to the different ways in which he might employ the stock of which he had the management. If he employed it as a farming stock in the cultivation of land, he could raise the rate of his profit only by retaining a greater portion, or, what comes to the same thing, the price of a greater portion of the produce of the land; and as this could be done only by a reduction of rent, the final payment of the tax would fall upon the landlord. If he employed it as a mercantile or manufacturing stock, he could raise the rate of his profit only by raising the price of his goods; in which case the final payment of the tax would fall altogether upon the consumers of those goods. If he did not raise the rate of his profit, he would be obliged to charge the whole tax upon that part of it which was allotted for the interest of money. He could afford less interest for whatever stock he borrowed, and the whole weight of the tax would in this case fall ultimately upon the interest of money. So far as he could not relieve himself from the tax in the one way, he would be obliged to relieve himself in the other.
>
> (*WN*: 847; cf. 113)

In short, insofar as profitability net of interest[87] is regarded as a kind of necessary cost, reflecting a necessary entrepreneurial contribution to production, the actual incidence of any taxes imposed upon it will be shifted to rents, non-necessary consumption or pure profits (interest, in the case of borrowed capital). Undoubtedly land-rents are a taxable surplus in Smith's understanding (e.g. *WN*: 812, 830, 843–4, 847–8); but he recognizes also that pure profits are strictly analogous to land-rents, and so likewise a taxable surplus:

> Like the rent of land, it [i.e. interest] is a neat produce which remains after compleatly compensating the whole risk and trouble of employing the

> stock.... The ordinary rate of profit ... is every where regulated by the quantity of stock to be employed in proportion to the quantity of the employment, or of the business which must be done by it. But the quantity of the employment, or of the business to be done by the stock, could neither be increased nor diminished by any tax upon the interest of money.... [T]he portion of this profit necessary for compensating the risk and trouble of the employer, would likewise remain the same .... The residue, therefore, that portion which belongs to the owner of the stock, and which pays the interest of money, would necessarily remain the same too. At first sight, therefore, the interest of money seems to be a subject as fit to be taxed directly as the rent of land.
>
> (*WN*: 847–8; also 857–8)

But asymmetric with the case of rents, Smith seeks to avoid the conclusion that profits are an appropriable surplus, equally susceptible of tax incidence, marshalling two arguments. Taxation of pure profits, for various reasons, is impracticable. Second, proprietors will tend to shift their stock to another country, in response to attempted taxation of profits (*WN*: 848–9; cf. 906, 927–8; *LJB*: 531–3). Neither objection goes to the issue of principle. How could Smith respond, with regard to his second objection, to this thought experiment: suppose all countries simultaneously tax pure profits at the same rate and by the same method? This question is just a way of indicating that truly general economic theory must reconcile itself with closed systems. Smith does not reject the proposition that pure profits are an appropriable surplus; he rather rejects just the auxiliary proposition, that they are capable of being taxed in practice.

The relation between wage income and the social surplus has already been touched upon a number of times, at least indirectly, via the question of the relation between wages and subsistence. It has been suggested in section 3.4.3 that wages are connected to subsistence, but that subsistence is a rather flexible notion in Smith, too loose for subsistence to serve as an anchor for a determinate real-wages outcome, even in the long run. The capacity of real wages to be unmoored from minimum subsistence requirements manifests itself also in his treatment of wages and tax incidence. Smith reiterates his earlier argument, that money wages of 'the inferior classes of workmen' are determined by the growth rate of labour demand, which determines whether subsistence will be 'liberal, moderate, or scanty', together with the 'ordinary' money prices of the relevant subsistence commodities. He infers: 'While the demand for labour and the price of provisions, therefore, remain the same, a direct tax upon the wages of labour can have no other effect than to raise them somewhat higher than the tax'.[88] Since wages are advanced as part of capital, the increase in prices, as a result of the tax-induced higher wage costs, will be even greater than the increase in wage cost, since there must be also additional profits paid in relation to the higher wage capital. Smith expects the incidence of such taxation to fall upon commodity prices and/or rents, unless the tax feeds back negatively on growth and thereby reduces real wages (*WN*: 864–5; also *WN*: 466, 508; *LJA*: 359–63; *LJB*: 496–7).

Furthermore, to the extent that wage differentials relative to the wages of the lowest classes of labour are a compensation for costs of acquiring labour skills (as well as disagreeableness and risk, among other factors), the notion of these higher wage rates as also necessary costs, from Smith's standpoint, is entirely plausible, particularly in light of the fact that entrepreneurial incomes, at least under competitive conditions, are regarded as necessary costs of production. Hence Smith adds:

> The recompence of ingenious artists and of men of liberal professions … necessarily keeps a certain proportion to the emoluments of inferior trades. A tax upon this recompence, therefore, could have no other effect than to raise it somewhat higher than in proportion to the tax. If it did not rise in this manner, the ingenious arts and the liberal professions, being no longer upon a level with other trades, would be so much deserted that they would soon return to that level.
>
> (*WN*: 866)[89]

Putting aside the possibility of these taxes finally falling upon rents, the influence of taxes on money wages, in order to maintain a definite purchasing power of the after-tax wage (and with given wage relativities), therefore feeds through to higher commodity prices, via the impact upon wage costs and hence also capital and profits per unit of outputs.[90]

When Smith turns subsequently to consider direct taxes on consumption goods, he distinguishes their incidence, depending upon whether they are imposed on necessities or luxuries. A tax on necessaries 'operates exactly in the same manner as a direct tax upon the wages of labour' (*WN*: 871).

> It is otherwise with taxes upon … luxuries; *even upon those of the poor*. The rise in the price of the taxed commodities, will not necessarily occasion any rise in the wages of labour.… The high price of such commodities does not necessarily diminish the ability of the inferior ranks of people to bring up families. Upon the sober and industrious poor, taxes upon such commodities act as sumptuary laws, and dispose them to either moderate, or to refrain altogether from the use of superfluities which they can no longer easily afford.… Any rise in the average price of necessaries, unless it is compensated by a proportionable rise in the wages of labour, must necessarily diminish more or less the ability of the poor to bring up numerous families, and consequently to supply the demand for useful labour …. Taxes upon luxuries have no tendency to raise the price of any other commodities except that of the commodities taxed. Taxes upon necessaries, by raising the wages of labour, necessarily tend to raise the price of all manufactures …. Taxes upon necessaries, so far as they affect the labouring poor, are finally paid, partly by landlords in the diminished rent of their lands, and partly by rich consumers … in the advanced price of manufactured goods ….
>
> (*WN*: 871–3; emphasis added; also 874–6, 885–6, 888, 905–6, 936, 938)[91]

This seems a strangely flawed argument. Once it is allowed that the real wage includes an above-subsistence component, the idea that a rise in the money price of subsistence commodities – whether due to taxation or any other persistent cause – will necessarily lead to a compensating rise in money wages loses force. For once there is non-necessary consumption included in the real wage, a rise in subsistence prices can be as much accommodated by a reduction in luxury consumption, as can a rise in luxury prices. What would make the argument work is to suppose, in a situation of heterogeneous labour, that the lowest class of workers earns a wage just equal to the value of subsistence, and therefore has a level of consumption with no luxury component. Other kinds of labour earn wages which include above-subsistence consumption, with the wage relativities determined by one or more of the five factors Smith offers to explain wage differences (e.g. the degree of 'trust' required – *WN*: 122). A rise in the prices of subsistence commodities would raise the money wages of the lowest class of workers, in order to preserve their capacity to purchase subsistence, and this would flow on to all wages, in order to preserve competitive relativities. But against this suggested resolution, Smith seems in the above quotation to be conceiving of non-necessaries as consumed even by the lowest-income workers (see also *WN*: 888).

What then can be construed as the social net income which is residual or surplus with respect to replacement of necessary inputs or recovery of necessary costs? There is a concept of a finite net social product (net revenue). There is also a clear conception of subsistence consumption requirements and an explicit notion of minimum wages. Smith would undoubtedly affirm these propositions: if the workforce is to be reproduced or maintained from one production cycle to the next, the aggregate quantities of commodities required for their consumption must be deducted from the net product (in value terms, from the 'net revenue'); satisfying such reproduction means that this part of net revenue is not available for free disposal in other uses. But his conception of the residual revenue, income or product available for free disposal in a society – that part of payments which does not in any sense reflect necessary costs or inputs – is less than the gross social product net of necessary labour consumption, and more than the gross product net of wages. Entrepreneurial activity is also understood to be necessary, and some part of labour incomes is not strictly necessary. Hence, in its income dimension Smith's surplus is land-rents plus pure profits, together with some elements of wages, certainly for higher classes of workers; but perhaps even the wages of the lowest classes of workers include a surplus component.[92] The very fact that the saving decisions which are supposed to generate accumulation are indeterminate, as Skinner (1996: 165) indicates, points to a realm of freedom rather than necessity, with regard to the division of the associated incomes between surplus consumption and investment. Recall in this context that in Smith's view accumulation can be undertaken by even lowly wage workers, in least in principle (notes 41, 44 above).

The production of a social surplus formed the framework for analyzing both distribution and growth, in classical economics and beyond (e.g. John von

Neumann, Wassily Leontief and Sraffa). It is not merely an esoteric theoretical concept of no practical relevance.[93] The viability of economic systems over time, their capacity to continue to reproduce themselves, is a very real practical problem – especially with respect to non-renewable resource depletion, a pressing issue for human development and survival (cf. notes 31, 32 above). The existence of a social dividend available for free disposal is also of considerable socio-economic significance, to the extent that it implies a spectrum of feasible income distributions (cf. sec. 4.2.2). That which is appropriable by taxation is also privately appropriable, via shifts in the bargaining power which governs the distribution of private income, as Smith makes clear himself.

# 5 Opulence and policy

*the progress of opulence*
*the system of natural liberty*
*policy and theory*

> You have formed into a regular and consistent system one of the most intricate and important parts of political science, and if the English be capable of extending their ideas beyond the narrow and illiberal arrangements introduced by the mercantile supporters of Revolution principles, and countenanced by Locke and some of their favourite writers, I should think your Book will occasion a total change in several important articles both in police and finance.
>
> *William Robertson*, 1776 (*Corr*: 192)

In the introduction to his collected *Papers Relating to Adam Smith*, Andrew Skinner has elegantly summarized the relation between the various major parts of Smith's intellectual project as a whole, taking his bearings from an important 1790 statement of Smith himself – in a prefatory note to the sixth edition of *TMS*, which appeared shortly before his death. Smith writes:

> In the last paragraph of the first Edition of the present work, I said, that I should in another discourse endeavour to give an account of the general principles of law and government, and of the different revolutions which they had undergone in the different ages and periods of society; not only in what concerns justice, but in what concerns police, revenue, and arms, and whatever else is the object of law. In the *Enquiry concerning the Nature and Causes of the Wealth of Nations*, I have partly executed this promise; at least so far as concerns police, revenue, and arms. What remains, the theory of jurisprudence, which I have long projected, I have hitherto been hindered from executing, by the same occupations which had till now prevented me from revising the present work.[1] Though my very advanced age leaves me, I acknowledge, very little expectation of ever being able to execute this great work to my own satisfaction; yet, as I have not altogether abandoned the design, and as I wish still to continue under the obligation of doing what I can, I have allowed the paragraph to remain as it was published more than

> thirty years ago, when I entertained no doubt of being able to execute every thing which it announced.
>
> (*TMS*: 3)

Skinner (1996: 2–3) comments:

> the ethics, jurisprudence, and economics were … seen by Smith as the parts, separate but interconnected, of an even wider system of social science.… In fact, the theory of jurisprudence was never completed, although generous traces of the historical perspective to which Smith referred appear in books III and V of the *Wealth of Nations*, and in the two sets of lectures on jurisprudence which have so far been discovered.
>
> The links between the parts of this great plan are many and various. The *TMS*, for example, may be regarded as an exercise in social philosophy, which was designed in part to show the way in which so self-regarding a creature as man erects (by natural as distinct from artificial means) barriers against his own passions, thus explaining the observed fact that he is always found in 'troops and companies'. The argument places a good deal of emphasis on the importance of general rules of behaviour which are related to experience and which may thus vary in respect of content.
>
> The historical analysis, with its four socio-economic stages, complements this argument by formally considering the origin of government and by explaining to some extent the forces that cause variations in accepted standards of behaviour over time. Both are related in turn to Smith's treatment of political economy. The historical argument explains the origins and nature of the particular type of socio-economic structure with which the economic analysis of the *Wealth of Nations* is concerned, while *The Theory of Moral Sentiments* provides an account of the psychological assumptions upon which both analyses depend.

Skinner is importantly right to speak of '*separate* but interconnected', though the latter term's suggestiveness of mutual dependence is perhaps not so felicitous. As we have sought to stress at a number of points in the preceding chapters, Smith does not so much propose a unified and comprehensive social science made up of inseparable parts. At least with regard to political economy, the dependence is largely unidirectional, as Skinner's last sentence quoted above indeed indicates (but see n. 21 below). When Smith speaks of political economy as '*a branch* of the science of a statesman', one should take the word 'branch' seriously; though one should also take seriously that at the same time, he speaks of '*the*' science (*WN*: 428; emphasis added; quoted more fully, sec. 2.1.1; cf. 678–9, also quoted there). To that extent, there is implied both a separable science of political economy (but not thereby autonomous), and a wider, singular or unified policy science. This raises two intriguing questions. What are the other branches of this policy science? What is the relation of history and of historiography to political economy in Smith's understanding? (By 'history' we mean the set of actual, concrete and particular, past events; by 'historiography', the study, writing and interpretation or theorizing of history.) Perhaps the most important and substantial connection between history and economic analysis in *WN* is in relation to 'opulence', which is considered in historical terms in Book III, though there are as well many other historical commentaries and illustrations in the book. Opulence also provides the normative purpose of political economy: '[i]t proposes to enrich ... the people' (*WN*: 428). As the ultimate purpose of this policy science, opulence is examined in section 5.1. Smith's conception of 'policy' and 'police' is then taken up in section 5.2. The benchmark or ideal type for evaluating policy, policy regimes, and the economic significance of political arrangements in general, is his notion of the 'system of liberty', which is also considered there. Section 5.3 contemplates the relation between the ideal and policy further, and thereby also the question of the relation between theory and policy – and connected with this, the question of the significance of history and historiography for Smith's political economy. The concluding section contemplates the self-conscious limits of Smith's political economy as a theoretical science, and the limitations of his political economy in its normative aspect.

## 5.1 The progress of opulence

### *5.1.1 Smith on 'opulence'*

In fact, no formal definition of 'opulence' is really provided in *WN*, notwithstanding that the term appears in the titles of Book III and Book III, Chapter I (*WN*: 5, 376). Rather, various aspects or dimensions of it are described. The closest to a statement of a defining characteristic occurs at *WN* (209–10), where 'real opulence' is illustrated by the 'very rich' societies of Holland and Genoa, 'opulence and prosperity' being coupled together, and contrasted with 'poverty and distress'. It is division of labour which brings about the rising output per worker which, at least in 'well-governed' societies, effects a '*universal* opulence which extends itself to the lowest ranks of the people', so that 'a general plenty diffuses itself through all the different ranks of the society' (*WN*: 22; emphasis added; also 25, which speaks of 'general opulence', 35). The causal connection between opulence and division of labour is also explicit in *edWN* (564–6, 570, 572, 577), and extensively treated in *LJ* (*LJA*: 342–3, 349–50, 355–6, 390–2; *LJB*: 489–92, 494). In short, opulence is high consumption – and universal or general opulence is the extension of high consumption to all of society in general. Hence, consumption per worker is 'more liberal in a society advancing to opulence than in one that is standing still' (*WN*: 53; cf. 88). The title of Chapter 2 in *edWN* strikingly parallels the title of *WN*: 'Of the nature and causes of *public* opulence' (562; emphasis added); wealth understood as consumable output, and opulence, are (almost) one and the same thing. It is in *edWN* that perhaps the most vigorous enunciation of general opulence as the standard for judging economic development is to be found:

> in an opulent and commercial society labour becomes dear and work [i.e. output] cheap .... The high price of labour is to be considered not meerly as a proof of the general opulence of society which can afford to pay well all those whom it employs; it is to be regarded as what constitutes *the very essence* of public opulence, or as *the very thing in which public opulence properly consists*. That state is properly opulent in which opulence is easily come at, or in which a little labour, properly and judiciously employed, is capable of procuring any man a great abundance of all the necessaries and conveniencies of life.... National opulence is the opulence of the whole people, which nothing but the great reward of labour, and consequently the great facility of acquiring, can give occasion to.
>
> (*edWN*: 567; emphasis added; also 575)[2]

While productivity growth from division of labour *enables* general opulence, it is all the conditions for high output and labour productivity growth – and for its realization in generalized high consumption – which are necessary to ensure it. The 'uniform, constant, and uninterrupted effort of every man to better his condition' is 'the principle from which publick and national, as well as private opulence is originally derived', because from that principle comes the accumulation of capital (*WN*: 343). The 'natural progress ... towards wealth and improvement' results from

> capital ... accumulated by the private frugality and good conduct of individuals, by their universal, continual, and uninterrupted effort to better their own condition. It is this effort ... which has maintained the progress ... towards opulence ....
>
> (*WN*: 345; also 334, 346, 349)[3]

Recalling the causal connection between division of labour and extent of the market (sec. 4.1.1), it is not surprising that Smith also comments: 'In opulent countries the market is generally so extensive, that any one trade is sufficient to employ the whole labour and stock of those who occupy it' (*WN*: 134). And just as the scope for productivity gains from division of labour are greater in manufacture than agriculture (again, sec. 4.1.1), so also '[t]he most opulent nations ... generally excel all their neighbours in agriculture as well as in manufactures; but they are commonly more distinguished by their superiority in the latter than in the former' (*WN*: 16; also 17; *LJA*: 342–3; *LJB*: 490–1; *edWN*: 566).

There are also two notable political aspects of opulence commented upon in *WN*. Smith observes that there is less direct subordination of people to the rich in 'opulent and civilized' societies, compared with earlier stages of society (excepting the very earliest), though 'authority of fortune' remains 'very great': '[t]hat it is much greater than that, either of age, or of personal qualities, has been the constant complaint of every period of society which admitted of any considerable inequality of fortune' (*WN*: 712). Second, in any conflict between the requirements of national defence and the pursuit of opulence, the former should prevail: legislation protecting the naval capacity of Great Britain is 'the wisest of all the commercial regulations of England', even though 'not favourable to … the growth of … opulence' (*WN*: 464–5; cf. 518, 522–3). The scope Smith perceives for such conflict should not however be exaggerated: elsewhere he argues for the superior military capacity of opulent nations over poor and barbarous ones (*WN*: 706–8; cf. *LJA*: 238–40; *LJB*: 412–15).

The requirements for high output and productivity growth, realized in high consumption, which is synonymous with opulence, are not only the direct economic factors, examined in Chapter 4 (esp. secs. 4.3.1–4.3.2). They include also, in particular, secure property rights – security in the broadest sense, from within and without the polity. In the context of linking opulence to capital accumulation, Smith emphasizes that even under less than good government, net capital accumulation goes on, 'in all tolerably quiet and peaceable times' (*WN*: 343). The quotation from *WN* (345), two paragraphs above, pursues the same line of argument; more fully: '[i]t is this effort, *protected by law and allowed by liberty*, … which has maintained … progress' (emphasis added). While secure property rights are largely taken for granted in *WN* – another aspect of the given (but not necessarily irreducible) parameters within which Smith's separable political economy proceeds – the largest part of *LJ* is devoted to analysis of those rights, and the history of those rights in particular. The first of the four purposes of government contemplated under jurisprudence is:

> to maintain justice; to prevent the members of a society from incroaching on one anothers property, or siezing [*sic*] what is not their own. The design here is to give each one the secure and peacable [*sic*] possession of his own property.
>
> (*LJA*: 5)

Second to this priority of 'internall peace', is 'promoting the opulence of the state' – and third and fourth, government revenue-raising and external security: even if internal security is in place, 'if there be no security from injuries from without the property of individualls can not be secure' (*LJA*: 5–6; also *LJB*: 398) In the only reference to opulence in *EPS* (51), Smith connects the emergence of philosophy in ancient Greece to the presence of '[l]aw and order', 'security and leisure', external security and opulence. In the only references to the term in *LRB* (137–8), he makes opulence a prerequisite to the historical development of the fine arts, explicitly associating the concept with 'ease and Security'. Stewart (1811: 322) quotes from a 1755 manuscript by Smith, then in Stewart's possession:

> Little else is requisite to carry a state to the highest degree of opulence from the lowest barbarism, but peace, easy taxes, and a tolerable administration of justice; all the rest being brought about by the natural course of things.[4]

Smith regards the history of human economic or material development as susceptible of systematic theoretical interpretation, in terms of the 'progress' of opulence (*WN*, Book III).[5] In fact, what is emphasized is the *slow* progress of opulence in human history. Since opulence is one and the same thing as growth of output and of labour productivity, realized in high consumption, the impediments to opulence are as one with the impediments to such growth and its consumption realization. Putting aside the problem of original accumulation, first and foremost this is about the historic insecurity or inappropriate structure of property rights, which, along with other political factors, undermines accumulation (*LJB*: 522–5, 528). With regard to other political impediments, in *WN* it is about national policies which have inverted the natural order of material progress, with the economic advancement of cities and towns leading the development process – rather than agricultural development leading, which would be the natural course.[6] Indeed, Smith regards the two systems of political economy he systematically criticizes in *WN*, Book IV – understood here especially as policy regimes – as expressions of particular historical experiences of economic development ('[t]he different progress of opulence in different ages and nations' – *WN*: 428). But even if natural and political conditions favour accumulation and division of labour, what is to guarantee that high growth and high or rising output per worker are realized in generalized high or higher consumption?

No policy is offered to ensure that result; it is rather conceived of as the natural outcome of a competitive economy exhibiting rapid accumulation and growth, and hence also exhibiting strong growth of labour demand and therefore liberal wages (see secs 3.4.3 and 4.3.2). Or, one may perhaps better say that commercial society – with the rule of law enforcing property rights, free competition and so on – *is* the policy for bringing about general opulence, though nothing in this formula guarantees high accumulation, other than human nature (see sec. 4.3.2, esp. n. 50, concerning saving behaviour and the desire for material betterment). To the extent that high accumulation does occur, then, under competitive conditions, on the basis of Smith's understanding, greater division of labour, high real wages and low profit rates also occur. Hence general opulence is a kind of unintended consequence of the propensity to accumulate and producer innovation, arising out of individuals' desire for material self-betterment – an 'invisible-hand'-like mechanism (see n. 15 below). Hence 'bad police' is policy which impedes free competition – in particular, by restricting market prices from convergence towards natural prices (whether by taxes, bounties, monopolies or other regulation) – militating against opulence and contributing to its slow development (*LJA*: 362–6; *LJB*: 497–9, 521–30; *edWN*: 575–81). Smith's major critical target on this account is of course mercantilism and the erroneous identification of opulence with accumulation of a national stock of money (*LJA*: 378, 381, 384–5, 388, 390–2; *LJB*: 430, 503–13, 515, 519; *edWN*: 576–8).[7] From this standpoint, good economic policy – in particular, with regard to forms and levels of taxation and public expenditure – concerns the least detrimental ways of financing essential or otherwise desirable activities, which are beyond the capability of private production. With regard to the pursuit of general opulence, economic policy is about providing the best framework within which human nature – acting through accumulation, division of labour and competition – can procure generalized high consumption for all.

By way of his notion of general or universal opulence, Smith makes the purpose of political economy, and the material purpose of government and of the social economy, the advancing of the material welfare of the labouring classes, because they are the most numerous in society. Hence follows this striking passage in the *WN* chapter on wages, which, though it does not refer to general or public opulence, connects closely with that normative standard:

> The common complaint that luxury extends itself even to the lowest ranks of the people, and that the labouring poor will not now be contented with the same food, cloathing and lodging which satisfied them in former times, may convince us that it is not the money price of labour only, but its real recompence, which has augumented [*sic*].
>
> Is this improvement in the circumstances of the lower ranks of the people to be regarded as an advantage or as an inconveniency to the society? The answer seems at first sight abundantly plain. Servants, labourers and workmen of different kinds, make up the far greater part of every great political society. But what improves the circumstances of the greater part can never be regarded as an inconveniency to the whole. No society can surely be flourishing and happy, of which the far greater part of the members are poor and miserable. It is but equity, besides, that they who feed, cloath and lodge the whole body of the people, should have such a share of the produce of their own labour as to be themselves tolerably well fed, cloathed and lodged.
>
> (*WN*: 96)

By this standard, if the richest person in a society were made better off, with no improvement in the position of anyone else, this would not be a social or 'welfare' improvement. It is the material welfare of the great majority which is the concern of Smith's political economy; and since the labouring classes make up the bulk of the population, the general opulence at which it aims, requires high or higher consumption for at least the bulk of those. Recall our proposition at the end of section 3.1.2, that Smith is in favour of capitalism not capitalists. Does this make Smith's politics in some sense 'left-of-centre'? Perhaps it does. But on the other hand, Eltis (2004: 154, and more expansively, 151–7) has strongly made the case that the proffered means to this general prosperity is really a variant of 'trickle-down'. One resists applying such a vulgar conception to Smith, except that, actually, the application seems valid.

For Smith, it is competitive commercial society with strong capital accumulation which delivers the best possible outcome for labourers. His following contention, surely inspired (and surely, consciously) by John Locke's similar suggestion a century earlier, is an evocation of trickle-down:

> the accommodation of an European prince does not always so much exceed that of an industrious and frugal peasant, as the accommodation of the latter exceeds that of many an African king, the absolute master of the lives and liberties of ten thousand naked savages.
>
> (*WN*: 24)[8]

The point is made even more explicitly in *LJA*. Notwithstanding the deductions from the product of the labourer in civilized states, which do not occur in savage states, the labourer is better off:

> mankind are far better provided in all the necessaries and conveniences of life in a civilized than in a savage state; ... plenty and opulence is far greater. The unassisted industry of a savage can not any way procure him those things which are now become necessary to the meanest artist. We may see this ... in comparing the way of life of an ordinary day-labourer in England or Holland to that of a savage prince, who has the lives and liberties of a thousand or 10000 naked savages at his disposall. It appears evident that this man, whom we falsly account to live in a simple and plain manner, is far better supplied than the monarch himself.... [P]erhaps the affluence and luxury of the richest ['European grandee'] does not so far exceed the plenty and abundance of an industrious farmer as this latter does the unprovided and unnesisted [*sic*] manner of life of the most respected savage.... The labour and time of the poor is in civilized countries sacrificed to the maintaining the rich in ease and luxury. The landlord is maintained in idleness and luxury by the labour of his tenents, who cultivate the land for him as well as for themselves. The moneyd man is supported by his exactions from the industrious merchant and the needy who are obliged to support him in ease by a return for the use of his money. But every savage has the full enjoyment of the fruits of his own labours; there are there no landlords, no usurers, no tax gatherers. We should expect therefore that the savage should be much better provided than the dependent poor man who labours both for himself and for others. But the case is far otherwise.... The division of labour amongst different hands can alone account for this.
>
> (*LJA*: 340–1; also 338–9)

A similar passage of argument is in *LJB* (489–90).[9] Yet again, the same line of argument appears in the opening pages of *edWN* (562–4, 566), but with a decidedly more negative moral tone concerning 'so much oppressive inequality':

> In a civilized society the poor provide both for themselves and for the enormous luxury of their superiors.... [W]ith regard to the produce of the labour of a great society there is never any such thing as a fair and equal division.... On the contrary those who labour most get least.... [T]he poor labourer ... bears, as it were, upon his shoulders the whole fabric of human

society, seems himself to be pressed down below ground by the weight, and to be buried out of sight in the lowest foundations of the building.

(*edWN*: 563–4)

To be clear, 'trickle-down' does not and cannot merely convey the proposition that the employers as a whole provide the wage-paying employment of the workers as a whole. This is just to describe an evident fact of capitalism, or of Smithian commercial society. (Nevertheless, the question of what *causes* or determines the level of employment is a different and more difficult matter, than the question of the provision of the employment: see sec. 4.4.1.) Trickle-down must be about workers, in some ascertainable sense, being better off as wage workers in commercial society, than they otherwise would be – and further, that this provides ethical justification for their lower-class position and the associated inequality. To the extent that Smith is subscribing to a position close to this (though I think, with more than a hint of ethical ambivalence), when the texts illustrative of trickle-down acknowledge that (unequal) distribution is expropriation or deduction from the product of the workers, this should be read as a frank admission of what is simply *an evident fact*, rather than as some kind of leftism (cf. the apologetic tone at *edWN*: 566). In this regard, one must accept that Smith at least comes close to a position which will appear strangely unreasonable to many modern readers: the distribution of material resources is, in significant measure, arbitrary – but nevertheless ethically defensible. The element of arbitrariness pertains not only to *personal* distribution (e.g. whether a person is a worker or a proprietor), but also to *functional* distribution, insofar as the latter is an expression of bargaining power, in Smith's understanding (sec. 3.4.3). As was seen in section 4.4.2, Smith's theory of tax incidence also exposes the element of arbitrariness in functional distribution.[10]

The normative aspect of the trickle-down doctrine – the implication that trickle-down in some measure justifies liberal capitalism and its attendant inequality – acquires further significance in relation to Smith's narrow conception of justice (see n. 56 below). The narrowness of his theory of justice makes trickle-down vital to ensuring the coherence of Smith's social theory. If there is no obligation in justice to provide resources to the poor, and in the extreme, trickle-down does not so operate as to guarantee the subsistence of the poor, then the dynamics of capitalism might threaten their very survival. This would be an impossible conclusion for Smith's social theory to allow, because it would contradict a principle at the very foundation of all modern liberal theory: the fundamental natural equality of all individuals, an equality which must extend at least so far as to allow that all have an equal right to life itself. In other words, that conclusion would expose a deep contradiction in the system of thought. If its operation can be relied upon, trickle-down in liberal capitalism disposes of that possible incoherence. Whether, even then, it can justify the economic inequality associated with liberal capitalism is another matter. Smith does not offer any standard by which that inequality could be judged, and possibly condemned (and thereby perhaps even justifying the intervention of policy). In this regard, the issue is not so much whether the inequality *should* be condemned. It is whether there is any standard in Smith's social theory, by which the inequality could *ever* conceivably be condemned as unjust. Short of the distribution of material resources in commercial society threatening the very lives of people, the answer appears to be no. But on the other hand, Smith's willingness to entertain progressive taxation (see sec. 5.2.3) implies a willingness to make normative judgements about material distribution, and implement those judgements via policy.

### *5.1.2 Extending opulence*

'Opulence' entered English in the sixteenth century from the French *opulence*, conveying 'great richness', in turn derived from the classical Latin *opulentia*, 'wealth, riches, affluence, sumptuousness, splendour'; and similarly, 'opulent' from the French *opulent*, 'rich, wealthy … abundant', and the classical Latin *opulentus*, 'rich, wealthy, grand, sumptuous, rich in literary or intellectual resources'. It conveyed these same senses in English: 'He … was troubled with strange imaginations, first with the felicitie of the llande, next of the opulencie of the inhabitants' (1584); 'The Hanses should growe opulent, and possesse the whole trade of the realme' (1601); 'The potentest Monarchies, the prowdest Republiques, the opulentest Cities have their declinings and periods' (1647); 'The Hollander and Fleming may infuse this secret into us from that wonderous degree of opulence, and pompe, which both by Trade have ascended unto' (1648); 'The British language claims [honour] … for its Opulence' (1667); 'Rome and its tumultuous Joys, Its Crouds, and Smoke, and Opulence, and Noise' (1749; all quotations from *OED*: 'opulence'; 'opulency'; 'opulent'). Notwithstanding the ancient antipathy to luxury (see sec. 4.3.8), a certain qualified endorsement of opulence seems to have originated in the Roman world, by way of a distinction between the vice of private luxury and the public opulence (*magnificentia*: splendour) of the State and of the elite:

> The *princeps* [emperor] himself became the bearer of public luxury: the grandiosity of public works reflected the *maiestas* of the Roman Empire.… Excess in private luxury … was condemned in the case of the bad *principes* such as Caligula, Nero and Vitellius; the good *principes* such as Augustus, Vespasian and Trajan, however, combined public *magnificentia* and private *frugalitas*.
>
> (Corbier 2005: 907; see also Veyne 1990)

Corbier cites also the maxim of Caligula: 'A man must be either frugal … or Caesar.' Hence, notice the political dimension of the definition of *ŏpŭlentĭa* in Simpson (1968: 415): '*wealth, riches, opulence*' (citing Sallust); and '*the power, greatness of a state*' (citing Sallust, Virgil, Tacitus). This State opulence included public works in which the mass of people shared enjoyment, up to a point – perhaps the most notable example being the Colosseum, initiated by Vespasian.

This is, in any case, not the opulence of Adam Smith; or at least it is not his opulence when he qualifies the term with 'general' or 'universal'. His use of the term with the qualifiers, 'national' and 'public', might be read as conveying something more like the traditional notion of State magnificence; but his use of those phrases does not support that inference (see sec. 5.1.1). (Nevertheless, the advocate of the productive use of labour is not thereby unswervingly opposed to all government luxury, or private luxury, as indicated in section 4.3.) The high consumption intended by Smithian opulence cannot possibly be identified with the material trappings of the polity and its ruling and elite classes. One may suggest that he tacitly – and surely, consciously – indicates the contrast with traditional opulence, precisely by using those qualifiers, to project a new notion of opulence for all. But is Smith the first to project this possibility? Coats (1958) details the emergence of English views favouring high or rising real wages in roughly the quarter century from 1750, contesting the earlier account of eighteenth-century views on wages by Furniss (1920); Vanderlint (1734) is the earliest instance Coats uncovers. (He does not address *why* this change of view started to appear in that period, though there is an implication that it is at least partly attributable to the possibility of high wages having been opened up by technical progress.) Perrotta (2004: 223–43) provides a more detailed overview of pertinent European economic literature in the late-seventeenth and eighteenth centuries, tracing high-wage views somewhat earlier than Coats (e.g. Martyn 1701). In supporting high or rising real wages, Smith therefore is not unique in the eighteenth century. But he is the most striking instance, for two reasons. It seems that no one before Smith so clearly and emphatically posited that high or rising labour consumption should be the prime economic aim of State policy, certainly in comparison with the instances considered by Coats and Perrotta. Secondly, in Smith, this normative principle is accompanied by the most plausible and satisfying descriptive theory in that century, of how the politico-economic system could deliver output growth per capita, and rather more contingently, widely diffused consumption growth per capita.

In respect of the first of these two aspects, it is worth comparing Smith with the stance of Quesnay, as the major figure in the advent of modern political economy before Smith, apart from Turgot. In Quesnay's *Tableau* the reader is offered the maxim – '*Abundance plus dearness equals opulence*' – followed immediately by the proposition that low agricultural prices reduce the 'well-being' of 'the lower classes'. An accompanying note rationalizes this by supposing that the money wage is set as a fixed multiple of the price of corn, but the actual consumption of corn by the labourer is a *smaller* quantity than this multiple. It follows that a higher corn price leaves the labourer with higher money income net of expenditure on corn, to spend on 'other needs', though in fact, even under these suppositions, real wages only increase with a higher corn price if the prices of the other things consumed rise in a lesser proportion. Quesnay suggests that 'all other classes' also gain a real benefit – 'the cultivators', 'the proprietors' and the State (Kuczynski and Meek 1972: 9–10; '3rd edn'). This idea that everybody's real incomes could rise in this process of moving to a higher price must have as a necessary condition that output per agricultural worker rises as a result – that there is an accompanying technological improvement. In any case, the seemingly rather strained argument with respect to real wages does not amount to Smithian opulence in terms of high or rising real wages, nor does the scenario as a whole amount to ongoing technical progress in the manner of Smithian division of labour. In contrast to ongoing change, note that Quesnay prefaces the thought experiment with the statement: 'A high price of corn ... *provided that it is constant*, is more advantageous to the lower classes' (Kuczynski and Meek 1972: 10n; '3rd edn'; emphasis added).[11]

This contrast between a kind of one-off improvement in Quesnay, and the ongoing dynamics of Smith, points to one final issue in relation to the general opulence notion of the latter. As against Quesnay's hopes for what high prices will achieve, Smith's opulence maxims look towards low prices (sec. 5.1.1, esp. n. 2). There may appear in our discussion in this chapter, and the previous one, some ambiguity as to whether general opulence in Smith means high real wages, or rising real wages, or high *and* rising real wages. Both can be inferred from his treatment of growth and economic development in commercial society. High accumulation and growth in such a society *ceteris paribus* makes for high real wages, via the impact on the balance of bargaining power with regard to the labour contract (e.g. *WN*: 87; and sec. 3.4.3). Furthermore, if such a commercial society is at the same time competitive and hence innovative, it will exhibit ongoing labour productivity growth from continuous progress in the division of labour (Chapter 3, n. 19; sec. 4.1.1). Combined with the spread of new forms and higher levels of customary consumption by labourers, perhaps partly via emulation, this strongly implies rising labour consumption as well. With regard to diffusion of new and higher consumption, recall the following, quoted more fully in section 5.1.1: 'luxury extends itself even to the lowest ranks of the people, and ... the labouring poor will not now be contented with the same food, cloathing and lodging which satisfied them in former times' (*WN*: 96).[12]

## 5.2 Policy and the system of liberty

### *5.2.1 Smith on 'liberty'*

It is by way of variations on the phrase *system of liberty* that Smith enunciates the ideal or standard by way of which the variety of socio-political arrangements are to be judged, though that phrase as a whole does not appear frequently. The fullest statement of the notion occurs at the end of Book IV, in the context of rebutting Physiocratic-inspired policy which gives preference to agricultural industry over manufacture and foreign trade, and as a bridge to the systematic and detailed consideration of policy in Book V:[13]

> every system which endeavours, either, by extraordinary encouragements, to draw towards a particular species of industry a greater share of the capital of the society than what would naturally go to it; or, by extraordinary

> restraints, to force from a particular species of industry some share of the capital which would otherwise be employed in it; is in reality subversive of the great purpose which it means to promote. It retards, instead of accelerating, the progress of the society towards real wealth and greatness; and diminishes, instead of increasing, the real value of the annual produce of its land and labour.
>
> All systems either of preference or of restraint … being … completely taken away, the obvious and simple system of natural liberty establishes itself of its own accord. Every man, as long as he does not violate the laws of justice, is left perfectly free to pursue his own interest his own way, and to bring both his industry and capital into competition with those of any other man, or order of men. The sovereign is completely discharged from a duty, in the attempting to perform which he must always be exposed to innumerable delusions, and for the proper performance of which no human wisdom or knowledge could ever be sufficient; the duty of superintending the industry of private people, and of directing it towards the employments most suitable to the interest of the society. According to the system of natural liberty, the sovereign has only three duties to attend to; three duties of great importance, indeed, but plain and intelligible to common understandings: first, the duty of protecting the society from the violence and invasion of other independent societies; secondly, the duty of protecting, as far as possible, every member of the society from the injustice or oppression of every other member of it, or the duty of establishing an exact administration of justice; and, thirdly, the duty of erecting and maintaining certain publick works and certain publick institutions, which it can never be for the interest of any individual, or small number of individuals, to erect and maintain; because the profit could never repay the expence to any individual or small number of individuals, though it may frequently do much more than repay it to a great society.
>
> (*WN*: 687–8)

This, and *WN*: 606 (see n. 13), are the only instances where Smith speaks explicitly of the system of liberty as 'natural'. Elsewhere, he writes of 'the liberal system', with particular reference to unrestricted international trade (*WN*: 538–9). The 'mercantile system [i.e. mercantilism], in its nature and essence a system of restraint and regulation' is contrasted with 'allowing every man to pursue his own interest his own way, upon the liberal plan of equality, liberty and justice' (*WN*: 663–4). The Physiocratic system on the other hand, whatever other faults it may have, is a 'liberal and generous system': it recognizes that 'the most perfect freedom of trade' raises output and hence the potential stock of capital; that 'a state of the most perfect liberty' generates 'the highest prosperity' (*WN*: 671–3).[14] Smith endorses this Physiocratic view; though he goes on here to chide at least Quesnay, for supposing that only implementation of the ideal system, only such a perfection of political arrangements, will enable economic prosperity (*WN*: 673–4) – an argument discussed in section 5.3.2. As to Smith's endorsement, he goes on to make this more explicit in relation to maximization of national product via unrestricted commerce:

> in representing the wealth of nations as consisting, not in the unconsumable riches of money, but in the consumable goods annually reproduced by the labour of the society; and in representing perfect liberty as the only effectual expedient for rendering this annual reproduction the greatest possible, its doctrine seems to be in every respect as just as it is generous and liberal.
>
> (*WN*: 678; cf. 11)

Earlier in his critique of mercantilism, Smith acknowledges that import restrictions can increase the quantity of stock and labour employed in the thus protected domestic industries, but makes his crucial criticism by raising the question of whether such policies will 'either ... increase the *general* industry of the society, or ... give it the most advantageous direction' (emphasis added):

> The general industry of the society never can exceed what the capital of the society can employ.... [T]he number of workmen ... that can be continually employed by all the members of a great society, must bear a certain proportion to the whole capital of that society, and never can exceed that proportion. No regulation of commerce can increase the quantity of industry in any society beyond what its capital can maintain. It can only divert a part of it into a direction into which it might not otherwise have gone; and it is by no means certain that this artificial direction is likely to be more advantageous to the society than that into which it would have gone of its own accord.
>
> (*WN*: 453)[15]

To be sure, Smith here may sound somewhat tentative in denying that the direction of capital allocation under discriminatory policy will be more socially advantageous (and he is similarly tentative prior to this, same page). But Smith very commonly expresses tentatively, views that he holds emphatically (see Henderson 2004). The tentativeness of expression raises no doubt as to his stance. Neither does the infrequent use of the system-of-liberty phrase tell against the importance of the notion, for Smith. Further expressions of the same conception as the system of natural liberty are provided by his frequent reference to 'natural balance' (or more dynamically expressed, 'natural course', and as well 'natural distribution'), which in particular, convey a sense of the normal outcome of free competition – commonly, to refer to the quantities of outputs and/or production inputs associated with situations in which normal prices prevail.[16] The same sense is conveyed also by reference to just 'perfect liberty': normal price as the lowest at which a commodity will be sold 'where there is perfect liberty, or where ... [the supplier] may change his trade as often as he pleases' (*WN*: 73, and similarly at 79); equalization of the net remunerations for inputs of labour or stock, 'where things were left to follow their natural course, where there was perfect liberty' (*WN*: 116; and similarly, 135; also 669, 673–4,

678, where the phrase is frequently deployed in relation to Physiocracy). 'Natural liberty', without explicit reference to 'system' also appears: 'artificial' legal restriction of labour mobility as 'an evident violation of natural liberty and justice' (*WN*: 157; also 470). Similarly, legal restrictions on the deployment of stock, as well as labour, are described in near identical terms (*WN*: 530–1). Nevertheless, Smith explicitly overrules this 'natural' liberty in one instance (or two, if one includes also the party-walls themselves). Legal restriction on the forms of paper money or credit,

> may, no doubt, be considered as in some respect a violation of natural liberty. But those exertions of the natural liberty of a few individuals, which might endanger the security of the whole society, are, and ought to be, restrained by the laws of all governments; of the most free, as well as of the most despotical. The obligation of building party walls, in order to prevent the communication of fire, is a violation of natural liberty, exactly of the same kind with the regulations of the banking trade which are here proposed.
>
> (*WN*: 324)

More widely, liberty is frequently coupled by Smith with 'security': 'upon the impartial administration of justice depends the liberty of every individual, the sense which he has of his own security' (*WN*: 722–3; also *TMS*: 81; *WN*: 395, 405, 412, 541, 944; *LJA*: 313, 315, 338; *LJB*: 421–2, 480). It is also commonly coupled with 'justice': Jean-Baptiste Colbert, 'instead of allowing every man to pursue his own interest his own way, upon the liberal plan of equality, liberty and justice', gave 'extraordinary privileges' to some industry and placed 'extraordinary restraints' upon others (*WN*: 664; also *TMS*: 81, 238; *WN*: 138, 674). This coupling also occurs in connection with what is perhaps his most well-known 'anti-capitalist' comment – '[p]eople of the same trade seldom meet together … but the conversation ends in a conspiracy …' – Smith continuing (interestingly): 'It is impossible … to prevent such meetings, by any law which either could be executed, or would be consistent with liberty and justice. But … the law … ought to do nothing to facilitate such assemblies' (*WN*: 145). Liberty is also connected with 'independency' (*TMS*: 230, 290; *WN*: 399; cf. 567, 572 and *LJA*: 188, 313); and it often appears together with 'property': the separation of judicial and executive powers 'is the great advantage which modern times have over antient, and the foundation of that greater Security which we now enjoy both with regard to Liberty, property and Life' (*LRB*: 176; also *TMS*: 297; *WN*: 857, 944; *LJA*: 179, 313, 325; *LJB*: 422, 425, 434, 451). Other notable instances of his use of liberty are: liberty as an antonym of 'confinement' (*TMS*: 151); 'liberty of trade' (*LJA*: 255, 257); 'liberty of exchange' (*LJB*: 514, 529; *edWN*: 577); 'the common liberty' versus 'oppressive monopolies' (*WN*: 140); monopoly or corporations as a kind of 'sole liberty' (*LJA*: 84); liberty as being 'free to chuse' (*WN*: 763; also 116). Nowhere is there anything resembling a formal definition of liberty in general (cf. Forbes 1975: 193).[17]

What of 'freedom', including variants? In *WN* the term is generally narrowly employed in economic senses. 'Freedom of trade', 'free trade' and variants (e.g. 'free commerce') are very frequently used. Other notable uses in *WN* are: 'free competition' (*WN*: 78, 140, 142, 164, 329, 516, 530, 545, 576, 759, 853, 866); 'perfect freedom' (*WN*: 131, 329, 534, 580, 637, 670–1, 687, 885–6, 900); 'free circulation of labour and stock' (*WN*: 135, 151–2, 155); and a couple of other renderings of free economic activity (*WN*: 138, 171). The core element of Smithian free competition, freedom of entry on the supply side (see sec. 3.1.2 and p. 91), is captured also in the coupling of 'free' and 'open': the policy of Europe treats 'country labourers' as 'common labour', therefore not requiring apprenticeship, and so 'free and open to every body' (*WN*: 119; also 631, 652). The term is very little used, with any substantial socio-political or economic intent, in *TMS*, *EPS* or *LRB*. Just as with liberty, so freedom is coupled with independence (*TMS*: 57, 201, 290; *EPS*: 252, but translating Rousseau; also *LJA*: 246, 271, 333). The 'free' is also identified with the voluntary (*TMS*: 78–9). And again, as with liberty, freedom is coupled with security, referring here, essentially to property rights (*WN*: 540–1). The phrase 'free government', and similar expressions for notions of political freedom in some sense (e.g. 'a free people'), are used frequently (*WN*: 324, 326, 585–7, 589, 622, 683–4, 696, 774–6, 788, 804, 813, 853; *LJA*: 374; *LJB*: 417, 502, 530–1; and in a slight manner, *LRB*: 112, 158, 195); but little substantive content is given to the idea in *WN*. Somewhat greater substance is provided in *LJ*. Individual freedoms (e.g. in 'commerce' and marriage) are grounded in natural rights, together with a theory of justice: 'the right one has to the free use of his person . . . when it does not prove detrimentall to any other person' (*LJA*: 8; cf. *LJB*: 401). Freedom of speech is defended (*LJA*: 125–6, 298; *LJB*: 421, 481; cf. *LRB*: 41, 56, on freedom of thought), and the power of the British House of Commons *vis-à-vis* the monarch, as a support for the security of liberty and property (*LJA*: 262, 270–1, 274; *LJB*: 421–2). An independent judiciary, together with the jury system, is a further foundation of this 'happy [political] mixture' (*LJB*: 421–2; *LJA*: 213, 271, 274, 286–7; *Corr*: 144); but the power of the judiciary must be constrained as well (*LJB*: 480). The role of 'good temper and moderation' in the behaviour of 'contending factions' (in effect, political parties) is also commended as 'the most essential circumstance in the publick morals of a free people' (*WN*: 775; cf. 788). 'Opulence and freedom' are 'the two greatest blessings men can possess' (*LJA*: 185).[18]

### *5.2.2 Smith on 'police' and 'policy'*

Smith's uses of 'policy' – and 'police', a term he also uses (up to a point, a synonym for the former) – are also worthy of systematic consideration. Nowhere in *WN* does he provide definitions of these terms; but both *LJA* and *LJB* open with an outline of the elements of 'jurisprudence', within which police is located (discussed also in the opening paragraph of sec. 4.2.1). Jurisprudence is 'the theory of the rules by which civil governments *ought* to be directed' (emphasis added). It is therefore a normative science; but Smith immediately adds: 'It attempts to shew the foundation of the different systems of government in different countries and to shew how far they are founded in reason'. The normative theory is used to scrutinize actual governments – hence the strongly historical character of *LJ*. The direction or aims of government – 'the design of *every* government' (emphasis added) – divides into four elements.[19] The first is 'justice' or 'internall peace', in particular, 'to give each ... the secure and peacable possession of his own property'. The second is 'opulence': 'This produces what we call police'; '[w]hatever regulations are made with respect to the trade, commerce, agriculture, manufactures of the country are considered as belonging to the police' (*LJA*: 5). Police in turn divides into three components, the first two of which are too trivial to require the intellectual inquiry of jurisprudence (except for a sub-component concerned with the prevention or punishment of personal injuries, which properly belongs in the treatment of justice rather than police). Hence the analysis of police focuses on the third part:

> bon marché or the cheapness of provisions, and the having the market well supplied with all sorts of commodities. This must include not only the promoting a free communication betwixt the town and the country, the internall commerce as we may call it, but also on the plenty or opulence of the neighbouring country.
>
> (*LJA*: 6)[20]

Just as for jurisprudence in general, so for police in particular, the theory is applied to historical scrutiny of actual systems of commercial regulation: 'we shall consider the different regulations that have subsisted in different countries and how far they have answered the intentions of the governments that constituted them; and this we shall <?> to ancient as well as modern times' (*LJA*: 6). After justice and police, the remaining two elements are public finance ('revenue') and external defence and international relations (*LJA*: 6–7).[21]

This is to make police and political economy, as Smith would later define the latter, effectively *almost* synonymous, confirming political economy's *raison d'être* as a policy science devoted to the theory of, and policy for, opulence (cf. sec. 2.1.1) – except that revenue obviously, and defence and external relations at least partially, have a place in political economy as well (see pp. 147–8). Even the rather incomplete and vague implied definition of opulence here, in terms of 'cheapness' and 'well supplied' markets, resonates in the mature treatment of the subject, in a passing definition of the purpose of political economy at *WN* (748; quoted in Chapter 4, n. 22). The question was raised in the introduction to the present chapter, what are the remaining elements or 'branch[es]', over and above political economy, making up the legislative or policy science? The outlines of the contents of jurisprudence at the beginnings of *LJ* provide a quite clear answer. The legislative science as a whole is synonymous with 'jurisprudence', which can be regarded as the all-encompassing *political science*, in Smith's conception. He does not himself use that term; but it perhaps better conveys to the modern mind the intent behind this comprehensive policy science, than does jurisprudence or legislative science.[22] It embraces 'legislation' in the deepest and widest sense – to the extent of the constituting, along ideal or otherwise desirable lines, of the polity itself. (The desirability or otherwise of implementing 'the' ideal constitution goes to the question of the relation between theory and practice, discussed in sec. 5.3.2.) However, in conceiving of Smith's jurisprudence as an all-encompassing political science, care must be taken in one respect: jurisprudence concerns also relations between individuals at what may advisedly be called a 'sub-political' level (see, for example, *LJA*: 7–8, 13, 141; family relations are an instance). But these relations as much are, or become, creatures of legislation and of government as do the rights of citizens qua citizens, the powers of government, and the economic relations involving property and contract. (That which is 'private' – beyond the intrusion of the State – is defined by the State as well.) This comprehensive science is the political science insofar as its architectonic purpose is the policy of States, actual as well as ideal or desirable – their constitutions, laws and regulations – with a view to the betterment of the human condition.

Consider, a little further, how Smith's classification of the elements of social inquiry compares with the modern demarcation of the social sciences. His jurisprudence, as a kind of comprehensive science of State policy, encompasses jurisprudence in the modern sense, political philosophy and political science, as well as political economy. But in modern terms, Smith's economic science contains some sociology, as do the parts of his jurisprudence concerned with justice and political constitutions: the sociability of the self-regarding human animal is decisive for the feasibility and desirability of political and economic arrangements, insofar as those arrangements depend upon what are feasible and ethically defensible social relations. But more properly, for Smith the theory and analysis of the sociability and social relations which inform the politics and economics belong in the moral philosophy or moral science embodied in *TMS*: '[t]he two useful parts of moral philosophy … are Ethics and Jurisprudence'; but with regard to the latter, 'it belongs not to our present subject to enter into any detail' (*TMS*: 340, 218; also 389, quoted and discussed in n. 43 below). (Recall from sec. 2.1.2, Smith's treating 'science' and 'philosophy' as synonyms, including a definite characterization of moral philosophy as a science.) This is even more true of psychology: both the psychology and the sociology of the self-regarding but sociable human animal are essentially separable from and logically prior to Smith's jurisprudence. The elements of the latter depend upon the moral science, but the moral science does not depend upon them. In particular, it has been seen at a number of points in Chapters 3 and 4, how Smith's political economy proceeds on the basis of certain psychological parameters, but parameters which are not thereby irreducible, and indeed, are capable of further investigation by other branches of the human sciences. His economic science also includes some of what would now be called political science or political philosophy. As well as containing descriptive analysis of the economic consequences of various political arrangements, it seeks to determine some appropriate rights and powers, of particular economic relevance; it does not merely treat political and legal rights and powers as given.[23]

The location of descriptive sciences like psychology and sociology in moral philosophy might seem at first glance strange; but in this regard, the essential character of Smith's particular form of 'moral philosophy' must be kept in mind. It is not so much inquiry into rationally derivable principles or rules of right conduct or of good behaviour. It is rather, inquiry into how and why most humans *actually do* most of the time act more or less sociably and decently – though it certainly also has normative purpose and content (Haakonssen 1981: 135–6). In this sense, Smith's moral philosophy is a kind of naturalistic ethics: it seeks to explain why, on the basis of their natural and actual constitution, humans actually do behave in certain socially desirable ways. To that extent, in the way we now use these terms, it is at least as much social science as it is philosophy. In this context, it is pertinent to recall the opening sentence of *TMS* (quoted also in Chapter 3, n. 20):

> How selfish soever man may be supposed, there are evidently some principles in his nature, which interest him in the fortune of others, and render their happiness necessary to him, though he derives nothing from it except the pleasure of seeing it.
>
> (*TMS*: 9)

That this is the very first sentence of the book renders it additionally surprising that '*das Adam Smith problem*' has had such longevity in the evaluation of Smith's thought – the notion that there is some tension between Adam Smith, philosopher of ethics in *TMS*, and Adam Smith, supposed philosopher of selfishness in *WN* (see Raphael and Macfie 1976b: 20–5; Montes 2003a). At very least, this opening sentence shows that the problem of reconciling individual self-regard and human sociability was at the centre of his thinking, at least as early as the writing of that book, some two decades prior to publication of *WN*. The fact that Smith was revising and reissuing *TMS*, from 1759 all the way forward to his death in 1790, is a further piece of prima facie but compelling evidence against inconsistency between the two books. In truth, Smith's simultaneous authorship of the moral philosophy and the political economy is just a testimony to the near-common-sense proposition that self-interest is not a self-subsisting and sufficient basis for society; that self-regard needs containment within a sensibility of moral conduct and restraint (certainly for it to be socially efficacious).

In contemplating the differences between Smith's branches of inquiry into human society and the modern demarcations of the social sciences one should not lose sight of a fundamental fact. Whatever progress has occurred in the social sciences undoubtedly has been due in substantial measure to intellectual division of labour. And we cannot understand the world without breaking it up into parts; the prescription that we cannot understand the parts of the world without understanding the whole may easily become a recipe for intellectual paralysis. But in one respect the idea of, or aspiration to (or perhaps dream of?), a unified social science rings true: in the end, the demarcations within the social sciences are ad hoc, driven by the several agendas, questions, and methods of the inquirers; the phenomena *are* ultimately indivisible. (Attraction to the idea of a unified social science, as a motive for interest in Smith in recent decades, was discussed in the opening paragraphs of Chapter 1 and in section 2.4.) The divisions of intellectual effort are, one may say, divorces of convenience; but they may have unsatisfactory wider consequences. Some aspects of this with respect to modern economics are taken up in the Epilogue.

To return to Smith on policy, beyond the *LJ* definitions of the scope of police, 'policy' and 'police' are commonly employed to convey the sense of a comprehensive policy regime, or an overall system of regulation, of a State or States – both economic and wider regulation. The 'policy of Europe' is a common catchphrase for Smith's critical target in this respect – a system which includes 'laws and customs', a system 'not leaving things at perfect liberty' (*WN*: 119, 135; also, e.g. 146, 151–2, 374, 396, 431, 441, 528–9, 681, 683). Policy and police, in this sense of regime or overall system, when applied to economic matters, become synonyms for 'political oeconomy' employed, albeit less frequently, in the same sense (*WN*: 679), as noted in section 2.1.1. The sense of policy and police as an overall regime of government regulation is also to be found in *LJ* (e.g. *LJA*: 300; *LJB*: 525; also *edWN*: 581). While policy and police can be synonyms, police is also employed in narrower, more particular senses: to refer to the actual enforcement or execution of laws or of order (*WN*: 512, 541, 698), which is essentially how the term continues to be used in English to the present; or the actual laws and regulations themselves (e.g. *TMS*: 90, 102; *LJA*: 332; *LJB*: 486); or the actual services of policing, where this includes public safety in relation also to hygiene and fire (*WN*: 815; *LJA*: 5, 331; *LJB*: 398, 486). The more than singular meaning of the term is strikingly evidenced at *LJB* (541–2), where 'Police' and 'Arms' are first distinguished, Smith then turning to consider the police of 'defence' (i.e. arms). In two places he speaks of 'publick police', referring to public provision of transport infrastructure as a 'branch' or 'department' (*WN*: 729–30), and in *edWN* (575), asserting the tendency of market prices towards normal price, 'unless there is some great error in the public police' (also, *TMS*: 90, 187 refer to 'civil police' and 'civil policy'). Of course also in *WN*, government 'regulations of police' impede the realization of natural or normal prices (*WN*: 77; also 79); and the variety of 'laws and policy' may influence wage and profit differentials, 'rules of police … as foolish as can well be imagined' (*WN*: 80, 137; also 116). The 'best police' is to leave 'every thing' to its 'naturall course' (*LJA*: 366; *LJB*: 499). Rather in the same spirit, the fundamental source of opulence, division of labour, 'is not … the effect of any human policy' (*LJA*: 347). In one instance, policy in the sense of national expediency is contrasted with 'humanity' (*LJB*: 549, 551); and in another, police in the sense of artifice or convention is distinguished from 'nature' (*LJB*: 447). Policies are ascribed also to individuals (*WN*: 856; *LJA*: 265).[24]

### *5.2.3 Economic liberty: justification and limits*

What then are the ultimate grounds of Smith's stance towards economic liberty and discriminatory regulation? At the level of substantive economic analysis, his position proceeds from the supposition that discriminatory policy – either favourable or adverse to particular economic activities – cannot increase the stock of capital or the pace of capital accumulation in a society. Such discrimination at best can only redirect capital in ways which diminish its efficacy as a whole in producing consumable-or-investible output, and/or diminish the rate of growth of output – aggregate output and its growth in turn constituting the stocks available for potential future use as capital.[25] Hence the very clear, substantive statement at *WN* (453; quoted more fully above, sec. 5.2.1; emphasis added): 'The general industry of ... society never can exceed what the capital of the society can employ.... No regulation of commerce can increase the quantity of industry in any society *beyond what its capital can maintain*.' Regulation will only redirect capital to less socially advantageous avenues than those to which natural liberty would have allocated it.

Is this position robust? There are two distinct postulates lying behind this view, the first of which is rather less overt: a denial that the total quantity of capital can be increased by discriminatory policy; and a denial that such policy can lead to a better allocation of the capital stock. Smith is on quite firm ground with regard to the second of these: a *general* presumption in favour of non-discriminatory policy as between particular commodities or industries (though it is not thereby necessarily a universally applicable principle). Hence he observes that no prudent family attempts to make for themselves a commodity for consumption, which they can more easily and cheaply acquire by purchase. The tailor buys his shoes; the shoemaker buys his clothes (*WN*: 456–7).

> What is prudence in the conduct of every private family, can scarce be folly in that of a great kingdom. If a foreign country can supply us with a commodity cheaper than we ourselves can make it, better buy it of them with some part of the produce of our own industry, employed in a way in which we have some advantage.
>
> (*WN*: 457)

This is to reaffirm the productivity benefits of specialization and division of labour – and to deny the State has any capacity to improve upon the outcomes, by discriminating between particular commodities.

With regard to the first and rather more unobtrusive postulate, that policy cannot favourably influence the actual *scale* of the capital stock, Smith's position is weaker. However unobtrusive it may be, he states it explicitly enough – indeed, for one instance, immediately following the quotation directly above. The very next sentence states: 'The general industry of the country, being always in proportion to the capital which employs it, *will not thereby be diminished* ... but only left to find out the way in which it can be employed with the greatest advantage' (emphasis added). And a few lines further on – in the context of a somewhat oblique commentary, but clearly enough directed against infant industry arguments for protection – Smith is even clearer.[26] Though such regulations may develop the production of a particular manufacture more quickly in a society,

> it will by no means follow that the sum total, either of its industry, or of its revenue, can ever be augmented by any such regulation. The industry of the society can augment only in proportion as its capital augments, and its capital can augment only in proportion to what can be gradually saved out of its revenue. But the immediate effect of every such regulation is to diminish its revenue, and what diminishes its revenue, is certainly not very likely to augment its capital faster than it would have augmented of its own accord, had both capital and industry been left to find out their natural employments.
>
> (*WN*: 458)

This is to assert that such policy cannot increase the overall stock of capital (in some sense), this stock in turn depending upon the national revenue and the rate of saving out of this revenue. Such discriminatory policy just reallocates the stock (for the worse). Supposing rates of saving to be unaffected by such policies, this amounts to saying that those policies cannot increase national revenue, only reduce it, relative to the non-discriminatory situation. But in one passage of argument, contemplating the consequences of an end to the British monopoly of the American colony trade, Smith virtually concedes that at least a *dramatic* policy change in favour of international trade liberalization can destroy both labour employment and capital: 'To open the colony trade all at once to all nations, might not only occasion some transitory inconveniency, but *a great permanent loss* to the greater part of those whose industry or capital is at present engaged in it' (*WN*: 606; emphasis added). To be clear, he downplays this risk, and in any case, remains committed to the pursuit of 'perfect liberty'.[27]

Here Smith opens a door, just a little. If liberalization can diminish the capital stock – due to a sudden and dramatic loss of previous demand – is it inconceivable or a priori dismissible, that regulation or policy of some kind can augment the capital stock? This point connects with the issue raised in section 4.4.1, concerning the problem of causation between aggregate demands and productive capacity in the context of Smith's growth dynamics. If, at least in principle, there are government policies that can conceivably influence the growth of aggregate demand, and changes in the growth of demand can induce changes in accumulation, then it becomes possible for policy to favourably influence growth and accumulation. In Smith's language directly above, policy thereby is capable of influencing 'revenue' and overall 'capital', even if it has no influence on *rates* of saving. (Apart from the possibility of government policy being capable of inducing demand growth and capital accumulation, there is the further aspect, that the public sector in principle can itself directly produce capital in the sense of production inputs: see n. 54 below.) An a priori blanket prohibition on economic policy intervention is then not so compelling.

Smith's position here rests on a tacit denial that government expenditures can generate and favourably alter demands for private sector outputs. It therefore also tacitly denies the further links: from demands for private sector outputs to private incomes, and from private incomes to the size of the capital stock – whether the latter link is via saving from private incomes or, more plausibly, via induced demands for capital. In this respect, for Smith, government taxes and expenditures are just a drain from private revenue, with the latter only capable of being *unfavourably* influenced by the former. A blanket opposition to policy intervention is not so compelling, if policy plausibly can favourably influence aggregate demand and overall accumulation. Opposition to discriminatory policies merely designed to favour particular commodities or trades would remain entirely compelling – particularly if merely for the benefit of particular private producer interests (e.g. commodities or trades associated with friends of a governing political party).[28] Of course the possibility, in principle, of policies that can favourably influence activity levels and accumulation gives rise to further issues: how likely *in practice* are such policies to do more good than ill; how plausible is it to trust politicians not to misuse possible good theoretical reasons for policy intervention, to justify ill-motivated and bad policy interventions? A policy that increases aggregate activity and capital might at the same time deteriorate the allocation of capital. But this is precisely part of the point being made here: the issue is more complicated than to warrant a response of mere a priori prohibition.

In fact, blanket opposition even just to discriminatory interventions with respect to particular commodities or activities is not Smith's position, once it comes to the detail of policy. What appears, perhaps for rhetorical effect, as frequent statement of unwavering opposition, turns out to be really just a statement of general presumption. Consider the range of particular policy interventions he endorses. He is not averse to a little discrimination along the lines of 'vice taxes' (our term) – hence his support for sumptuary laws with respect to 'strong beer' and other luxuries of 'the poor', as indicated in section 4.4.2 (*WN*: 871–2; also 891). (There is some tension between this and the policy objective of general opulence; or at least, the advocate of perfect liberty here implies that the State to some extent may direct the content of the labourers' high consumption.) In commenting on the crucial role of coal costs in wage determination, and hence both indirectly and directly in manufacturing production costs in general, Smith at least halfheartedly favours a transport subsidy: 'If a bounty could in any case be reasonable, it might perhaps be so upon the transportation of coals from those parts of the country in which they abound, to those in which they are wanted' (*WN*: 874). His support in 1780 correspondence for a form of import protection on something akin to infant industry grounds has already been noted (n. 26 above), and his strong endorsement of government regulation of paper money or credit (sec. 5.2.1).[29] Further exceptions to perfect liberty are detailed by Skinner (1996: 183–208), in a valuable, comprehensive treatment of Smith on the role of the State in general – though not every instance Skinner offers is entirely convincing as exceptions to 'non-intervention' (his term) or non-discrimination. Beyond those noted already (and one further, immediately below), these include: product quality validation; control of currency; 'temporary monopoly', but very emphatically temporary (*WN*: 754–5), for new and risky foreign trade ventures, and for new inventions and books; discriminatory taxation to alter individual economic behaviours (in relation to production – *WN*: 831) that are *not* socially beneficial; and legal regulation of interest rates, though in a certain conformity with market-determined rates (Skinner 1996: 186–7).

But Viner (1928; also published earlier: Viner 1927) provides the most comprehensive treatment of all the exceptions to natural liberty endorsed by Smith, noting also the following: laws obliging payment of wages in money rather than in kind are 'quite just and equitable'; laws obliging landowners to cultivate their land, at pain of forfeiture, are useful; road maintenance cannot be entrusted to private control; and government, at least in principle, can successfully run commercial enterprises, postal services being the best example (*WN*: 158, 572, 726–7, 817–19; Viner 1928: 135, 145, 148, 151).[30] With regard to product quality validation (*WN*: 138–9), Viner (1928: 145) rightly draws the inference that '[u]nqualified adherence to the principle of *caveat emptor* was apparently not a necessary implication of Smith's laissez faire doctrines'; but this applies with equal force, albeit in a somewhat different manner, to some of his views on regulating labour contracts and land-rent contracts. (With regard to rents, this is evident in some of the discriminatory taxes Smith endorses: see n. 31 below.) Notwithstanding all these exceptions to natural liberty, a government role with respect to public health is strikingly absent. But Viner (1928: 150) notices a passing comment by Smith, that government should give 'serious attention' to prevention of the spead of 'loathsome and offensive' diseases, even if not 'mortal' or 'dangerous' (*WN*: 787–8). From this Viner draws the reasonable inference that Smith would 'support public action taken to prevent the spread of dangerous diseases, and thus would include public hygiene among the proper functions of government', a conclusion partly confirmed by the inclusion of 'public ... cleanliness' in the definitions of police in *LJ* (*LJA*: 5; *LJB*: 398).

There is one further, notable instance of discriminatory policy, and perhaps the most surprising: Smith's endorsement of progressive taxation. As one of four general maxims concerning taxation, he posits:

> The subjects of every state ought to contribute towards the support of the government, as nearly as possible, in proportion to their respective abilities; that is, in proportion to the revenue which they respectively enjoy under the protection of the state.... In the observation or neglect of this maxim consists, what is called the equality or inequality of taxation.
>
> (*WN*: 825)

But further on in the same Part II of Book V, Chapter II on taxation, he somewhat tentatively endorses a measure disproportionately taxing the rich:

> A tax upon house-rents ... would in general fall heaviest upon the rich; and in this sort of inequality there would not, perhaps, be any thing very unreasonable. It is not very unreasonable that the rich should contribute to the publick expence, not only in proportion to their revenue, but something more than in that proportion.
>
> (*WN*: 842)

Furthermore, at *WN* (827) Smith cites Lord Kames's *Sketches of the History of Man* with regard to taxation, the *WN* editors quoting in an attached note the latter's six rules for taxation, including: 'To remedy the "inequality of riches" as much as possible, by relieving the poor and burdening the rich'.[31]

Beyond all the particular exceptions, there is as well, provision of the legitimate services of government – in enforcement of justice, external defence and public works, the latter involving in particular, transport infrastructure and education (Skinner 1996: 188–200; note that compulsory education is endorsed – *WN*: 786). Indeed, the first and second of these especially, point to the truth that, first and foremost, the limits to perfect liberty are that *the system of liberty itself, however 'natural', is not spontaneously self-creating*. It requires a political infrastructure of government and law – in particular, the establishment and enforcement of property rights and contracts – in turn necessitating taxation to shift the necessary resources to public use. The systems of expenditure and taxation, however, should conform with notions of equity – including some directing of taxes to users of the publicly provided services (hence really user charges, where these users are an identifiable subgroup in society) – and with a design to encourage producer efficiency in provision of those services (see Skinner 1996: 189–92).

One could contemplate the several roles of government that Smith enunciates, together with the further array of exceptions he allows to the complete implementation of perfect liberty, and conclude that he is deeply inconsistent or even hypocritical. His willingness to take employment as a Commissioner of Customs (1778–90) also could be read as a contradiction between his theory and his personal 'practice' (see Ross 1995: 305–33). But these aspects of the thought and the life can also rather be treated as evidence against the perception of Smith as strict and uncompromising economic libertarian, and in favour of viewing him as moderate and pragmatic concerning the relation between theory (or the ideal) and practice (cf. Winch 1996: 46–7). This is the central theme of the following section. Indeed, one may allow that his political or practical purpose, to advance reform in the face of the actual policy regimes he confronted, itself justified a vigorous and commonly unqualified policy rhetoric of liberty, freedom and emancipation – a rhetoric which overstates his actual case. That manner of articulation is then quite consistent with taking seriously the considerable policy qualifications to liberty and Smith's conception of the positive role of government, as well as his strong aversion to idealistic zealotry in politics. (The latter is considered in sec. 5.3.2.) When contemplating his many apparently unequivocal endorsements of the system of liberty, it is well to remember what kind of world Smith was confronting by way of State regulation of 'economic life' and economic behaviour (as well, of course, as other dimensions of life). This was emphatically regulation of *lives*, of persons, not merely regulation of some abstract category, 'markets'. It was such as could reasonably justify an unequivocal rhetoric. Smith's underlying theory with regard to whether or to what extent capital is preserved or destroyed in the face of shifts in demand is vulnerable, not to say frail. But there is nevertheless genuine moral feeling behind his attacks on regulation of labour:

> To remove a man who has committed no misdemeanour from the parish where he chuses to reside, is an evident violation of natural liberty and justice. The common people of England ... have now for more than a century together suffered themselves to be exposed to this oppression without a remedy.... There is scarce a poor man in England of forty years of age ... who has not in some part of his life felt himself most cruelly oppressed by this ill-contrived law of settlements.
>
> (*WN*: 157; also 470)[32]

### *5.2.4 Early meanings of liberty and freedom*

The term 'liberty' arises in English use in the fourteenth and fifteenth centuries, from the French *liberté*, in turn from the Latin *lībertāt-em*, from *līber* (free). It has always been generally a synonym for freedom. It seems that use of the term, and to that extent also the concept, is originally connected with the practice of slavery, notably in relation to the history of captivity in the Jewish scriptures, where the concept had both political and spiritual dimensions. Then, by way of analogy, in the Christian scriptures the term attaches to the notion of Christian religious redemption. Hence, liberty understood as '[e]xemption or release from captivity, bondage, or slavery'; '[f]reedom from the bondage of sin, or of the [Old Testament] law': 'where is the spirit of God, there is liberte' (1382); 'He [God] brought me forth ... in to lyberte' (1535); 'This libertie, which Christians haue, is a spirituall libertie, a heauenly liberty, a liberty of the soule' (1604) (*OED*: 'liberty'). The same meanings contemporaneously attach to 'freedom' (*OED*: 'free'; 'freedom'). Notice that in the Christian religious conception, this liberation partly concerns emancipation from strictures of Old Testament religious law, which has obvious resonance with later meanings of political liberty (not least, including economic freedoms): limits upon the reach of political law in restricting or directing individuals' behaviour (cf. Bouwsma 1995: 222–3). The terms 'free' and 'freedom' emerge in English during the same period as 'liberty'. Here also there is an intimate connection with the practice of slavery. The *OED* ('free') observes:

> The primary sense of the adj. is 'dear'; the Germanic and Celtic sense comes of its having been applied as the distinctive epithet of those members of the household who were connected by ties of kindred with the head, as

> opposed to the slaves. The converse process of sense-development appears in Lat. *līberī* 'children', literally the 'free' members of the household.

The term derives from Germanic languages. The Old English *fréo* corresponds to Old Frisian, Old Saxon and Old High German *frî*, Old Norse *frí-r*, Gothic *frei-s* and Old Teutonic *frijo-*. These in turn derive from Old Aryan *priyo-*, represented by Sanskrit *priyá* (dear) from the root *pri* (to love: Sanskrit *prî*, to delight, endear; Old Church Slavonic *prijatelĭ*, friend; Gothic *frijôn*, Old English *fréon*, to love; from which derives also 'friend') (*OED*: 'free').[33]

Somewhat later, liberty and freedom are being used to convey notions of people's security from 'arbitrary, despotic, or autocratic rule or control', or 'civil liberty', or 'existing under a government which … does not encroach upon individual rights' (*OED*: 'free'; 'liberty'), though the *OED* examples are not greatly informative as to what rights are being supposed: 'Till the iniurious Romans did extort This Tribute from vs, we were free' (1611; Shakespeare); 'They … vindicate that liberty left them as an inheritance by their Ancestours, from the incroachments … of the Court of Rome' (1654); 'The Liberty of Man, in Society, is to be under no other Legislative Power, but that established by Consent in the Commonwealth' (1690; Locke); 'Freedom consists in a people's being governed by laws made with their own consent' (1725; Swift); 'Those who would give up essential liberty, to purchase a little temporary safety, deserve neither liberty nor safety' (1759; Benjamin Franklin; variously from *OED*: 'free'; 'freedom'; 'liberty'). The *OED* ('liberty') further distinguishes: natural liberty as 'the state in which every one is free to act as he thinks fit, subject only to the laws of nature' (citing Hobbes, 1651); civil liberty as 'natural liberty so far restricted by established law as is expedient or necessary for the good of the community' (citing John Milton, 1644); liberty of conscience as 'a member of a state … [being] permitted to follow without interference the dictates of his conscience in the profession of any religious creed or the exercise of any mode of worship' (from the sixteenth century forward); liberty of the press as 'recognition by the state of the right of any one to print and publish whatever he pleases without previous governmental permission' (citing William Blackstone, 1769).[34] Among other senses of liberty in use before 1776, less significant for our purposes here, the *OED* details: '[t]he condition of being able to act in any desired way without hindrance or restraint'; 'being free from the control of fate or necessity'; 'freedom … beyond what is granted or recognized as proper' (i.e. in the sense of licence); '[p]rivileges, immunities, or rights enjoyed by prescription or by grant' (*OED*: 'liberty'). Identical or near identical definitions to these appear under 'freedom'.

The *OED* defines 'free trade' to particularly pertain to international trade: 'open and unrestricted trade', and more fully (citing Smith):

> Trade or commerce left to follow its natural course, i.e. without the interference of customs duties designed to restrict imports or of bounties intended to foster home production. Also, the legislative establishment or maintenance

> of this state of things, and the principles of those who advocate it; opposed to *protection*.

Smith does indeed overwhelmingly (though not quite entirely) use the phrase 'free trade' and variants in *WN* to refer to international trade (but including in this the colony trade), and therefore, quite naturally, it is mainly used in Book IV (see the citations in n. 18 above). The earliest instances the *OED* offers of that long resonant phrase are from the seventeenth century, though the very earliest is a metaphor: 'Wit's become a free trade for all sorts to live by' (1606); 'A Remedie ... vnder good and Politike Gouernment ... will bee Free Trade' (from Malynes 1622: 105); 'they desired not only the free Trade, but even the Monopoly of plundering to themselves' (1642–3); 'Our Plantations ... would have been much increased and inriched by a Free Trade, more than by this restraint' (1670; all from *OED*: 'free trade, free-trade'); 'They permit Free Traders on their Island Bombaim [probably referring to São Tomé Island, off the west African coast]' (1698; *OED*: 'free-trader'). The following also have some kinship with free trade: 'Their Free-martes, or Markets' (1631); 'Nothing is so advantageous to it [trade] as a free-port' (1711); 'The Privileges of Cities, Towns, Persons, Free-fairs, and other Exemptions' (1714); 'Free ships render the merchandize on board free' (1753; all from *OED*: 'free').

While the earliest instances of liberty and freedom offered in the *OED* might seem to point to a Judaic origin, Raaflaub (2003: 609–10) observes that '[d]espite their charter myth of liberation from Egyptian slavery ... the Hebrews ... began to use freedom politically only under Hellenistic influence'. He traces the very earliest articulations of liberty to commentary around slavery, as well as 'individual or collective freedom from dues, taxes, and other obligations as old as communities with centralized government':

> These concepts are attested in Egyptian and Mesopotamian documents and the Hebrew Bible. Nevertheless to these civilizations – as to ancient China – the concepts of free citizens or of political freedom were unknown. Typically, near-eastern societies were ... ruled by autocratic and divinely sanctioned monarchs or an absolute divine law.... Such conditions were not conducive to recognizing freedom as a political value.
>
> (Raaflaub 2003: 609)

As to etymology, Raaflaub (2003: 610) conjectures that *eleutheros* and *liber* 'probably both derive from I[ndo-]E[uropean] *leudh-* (perhaps initially "grow"), designating the legitimate member of a descent group or community'. (This accords with the *OED* account of *līberī* and *priyá*, documented above.) The available evidence suggests that 'freedom was first given *political* value by the Greeks, in a world of small *poleis* ... which were not subject to imperial control, where power was not centralized, autocratic, or divinely sanctioned but broadly distributed'. (For a thorough account of the genesis of political liberty in Greek thought and language, see Ostwald 1995.) The dangers of enslavement and especially,

> the confrontation with the autocratic Persian state made the Greeks aware of the free character of their societies. Earliest allusions to political freedom and the emergence of an abstract noun (*eleutheria* [*ελευθερια*]) date to the Persian Wars of 480/79 and their aftermath (e.g. Aeschylus, *Persae* 403).
>
> (Raaflaub 2003: 610)

The causes of the politicization of *libertas* in Roman civilization are unclear; but it is noteworthy that Roman *libertas populi*, rather than being egalitarian and participatory, was concerned with 'equality before the law and the protection of individual citizens from abuse of power by magistrates'; during the empire 'liberty was increasingly reduced to ... security and protection under the law' (Raaflaub 2003: 610). The individualism embodied in the cosmopolitan natural law doctrine of Roman Stoicism supported the development of Roman law (Laslett and Cummings 2006: 658).

Concepts of freedom in ancient philosophy of course extend beyond mere political liberty, which is appropriately our focus here, for the purposes of placing liberty in Smith's political economy in historical context. Raaflaub (2003), for example, comments on moral-political aspects, such as the Sophists' views on rights to emancipation from mere conventional socio-political constraints and the Socratic opposition to individual freedom understood as licence or libertinism. The question of free will and determinism, or free will versus necessity, is also an important ancient theme (e.g. in Stoicism). In the medieval synthesis of revealed religion and ancient philosophy this takes also the form of reconciling human free will and divine omniscience or providence (Marenbon 1998: 19–23; Davies 1998: 253–6). As to political liberty in medieval thought, Augustine's influential theology, with its 'severe view' of human corruption resulting from 'the Fall', led to a negative conception of earthly states as largely coercive institutions made necessary by that human condition. The rise of Aristotelianism in the West from the twelfth century, particularly after Aristotelian texts reached the West from the Islamic world, led to 'a more optimistic view of human nature, society, and the civil state'. For example, in Aquinas, 'divine grace was seen as completing and fulfilling human nature, rather than dramatically abrogating it in the Augustinian manner'; the State was not merely a remedy for sin. There is not much akin to modern political liberty to be found in medieval Aristotelianism, but Thomistic and other Scholastic natural law provided grounds for a theory of legitimate political power, and hence for limits to that power, and so also justification for resistance to tyranny as a kind of lawlessness (Henry 2006: 99–100, 104; cf. Laslett and Cummings 2006: 658–60, who observe that right of resistance in Aquinas is not by virtue of any claim to rights of the individual). The situation of the independent Northern Italian city-states from the twelfth century created an intellectual climate not dissimilar to that of the ancient Greek city-states, which first gave birth to concepts of political liberty. This, along with ancient sources, including the example of the Roman republic, provided inspiration for the Renaissance development of civic humanist and republican ideas (Laslett and Cummings 2006: 660–1; Bouwsma 1995: 206–19; Mundy 1995: 103–12, 123, 127–9, 133–4).[35]

### *5.2.5 Modern political liberty*

How precisely may one isolate political liberty from the wider issues of human freedom in ancient and medieval, as well as modern thought? Political liberty may be understood as an attribute of systems of government and law which limit the intrusion of others – including (perhaps especially) intrusion by the organs of government itself – upon the life, thought, speech, action and material possessions of the individual. (Political liberty so understood is first and foremost a property of *political constitutions*, rather than individuals.) At core, this is a notion of individual privacy: the political construction of a domain within which government and law are silent. Such a definition of course does not in any manner solve the problems, both theoretical and practical, which have long plagued consideration of liberty. There are degrees of such privacy. The liberty of each, which is consistent with the liberty of all, is inevitably a matter of controversy, partly pointing to the norm of an equality of liberties, also much contested as to its content. The rights of government to overrule individual freedoms by due process of law, notably, with regard to crime and taxation, are disputable. So are the rights of the individual versus the majority in democratic polities which embody political liberty in some measure or other. A considerable amount of the contention, past and present, flows from the issue of possible trade-offs between equality and liberty.

From the point of view of this conception of political liberty, which is very much in the spirit of Smith's approach to the idea, Berlin (2005: 517) emphasizes how thoroughly modern the notion is, compared with the ancient Greek conception of political liberty as mere participation in law-making:

> In the modern world, a new idea … makes itself felt, namely that there is a province of life – private life – with which it is thought undesirable, save in exceptional circumstances, for public authority to interfere. The central question posed by the ancient world is 'Who shall govern me?' Some said a monarch, some said the best, or the richest, or the bravest, or the majority, or the law courts, or the unanimous vote of all. In the modern world, an equally important question is 'How much government should there be?' The ancient world assumed that life was one, and that laws and the government covered the whole of it – there was no reason to protect any corner of it from such supervision. In the modern world, whether historically because of struggles of the Churches against intervention by the secular State, or of the State against the Church, or as a result of the growth of private enterprise, industry, commerce, and its desire for protection against State interference, or for whatever reason, we proceed on the assumption that there is a frontier between public and private life; and that, however small the private sphere may be, within it I can do as I please … provided this does

> not interfere with the similar rights of others, or undermine the order which makes this kind of arrangement possible.

A variety of lines of criticism of the limitations of this negative conception of liberty develop after Smith, by way of appeal to freedom, not merely *from* restriction or coercion of the individual, but *for* something or other in the nature of self-realization (e.g. social and political participation, rationality). In the economic dimension, this criticism turns on the question of what significance one can attach to abstract freedoms in the absence of material means to exercise or realize human *capacities*, within that space provided by negative liberty. An equality of formal 'negative' freedoms can subsist with great inequality of means or opportunity to exercise that freedom, the latter pointing to an absence of 'substantive freedom' (see Reeve 2003a; Norman 2005; n. 33 above). The issue of material inequality is taken up further in section 5.4.

The sources of the distinctly modern liberalism built around negative liberty are first and foremost to be found in English political theory of the seventeenth century, notably, Hobbes and Locke. While Hobbes's political theory may appear illiberal from a latter-day standpoint, it forges the modern approach by making the protection of the individual the foundation of theorizing. His striking formula in Chapter 21 of *Leviathan*, that beyond the inalienable right of individuals to protect their own lives (which in Hobbes's view can never legitimately be overruled by government), 'liberties ... depend on the silence of the law', formulates the issue in precisely the modern liberal manner (Hobbes 1651: 143). Though Smith, following Hume, eschews the contract approach of Hobbes and Locke to the theory of legitimate government, Smith is at one with Locke in making the protection of the life, liberty and possessions of the individual the standard for assessing the worthiness or legitimacy of governments and political constitutions. Where precisely Smith stands in relation to all the currents of modern intellectual developments concerning political liberty prior to 1776 has been a source of some controversy, no doubt partly due to the absence of a fully explicit and thoroughly detailed political theory in Smith's extant writings. It is pertinent here that Smith himself regarded his writings as part of a larger intellectual project that, in the end, he was unable to complete (see p. 251), perhaps because it was incapable of coherent completion (Winch 1978: 9–12; Griswold 2006; Ross 2006).[36]

Forbes (1975) provides the finest and most historically sensitive treatment of the issue of Smith's politics, in particular relation to liberty, and his lead is followed in this respect in the larger and more systematic study of Winch (1978; also Haakonssen 1981: 93–8, 127–33). The key point is that the sense of political liberty which is the governing norm of Smith's political theorizing and analysis (and likewise for Hume) is:

> liberty in the sense of the Civilians and Grotius, Pufendorf, and the authoritative exponents of natural law: the personal liberty and security of

> individuals guaranteed by law, equivalent to justice, peace, order, the protection of property, the sanctity of contracts.
>
> (Forbes 1975: 184)

The evaluation of the forms of political constitution in the separate dimension of the distribution of political power – democracy, aristocracy, monarchy and so on, including mixed forms – takes its bearings from this standard (Forbes 1975: 184–6, 191–3, 198). Giving a priority to 'personal liberty' so understood, over the dimension of political liberty in terms of the degree of democracy, does indeed fit with Smith's uses of liberty and freedom detailed in sec. 5.2.1. The associated interpretation of Smith as standing within the modern natural law tradition of Grotius, Pufendorf and Hutcheson – though rather transformed by the influence of Hume – is also supported by the important study of Haakonssen (1981: 2, 12, 147–51). One further important issue canvassed by Forbes (1975: 194–201) in relation to liberty is whether in Smith's thought 'there is a natural and necessary connection between the progress of improvement [economic development] and liberty', the latter understood in the sense of a liberal, secular and democratic polity, an interpretation suggested by Cropsey (1957: 64–70, 93–8). The persuasive conclusion is that there is in Smith 'no "law" of commerce giving rise to liberty' (Forbes 1975: 200). This is pertinent also to our earlier point, that for Smith orderly commercial society is not a spontaneous product of human nature (n. 15 above).[37]

The causal connections between commerce and negative economic liberty are certainly a fundamental issue in Smith and other eighteenth-century thought. Aside from causation, necessary or contingent, from economic development to negative or personal liberty, there is also of course the more straightforward possible causation in the opposite direction: liberty, at least in the economic dimension, as the condition for opulence. But in the case of Smith, economic liberty in any strong sense is not the precondition for opulence as such, since he clearly believes that (human) nature will be working away producing material progress, even in the absence of ideal conditions (see sec. 5.3.2). In Smith, liberty can be said to be the condition for *general* opulence: the fullest realization of opulence in a diffusion to the population in general. Forbes (1975: 201) has a valid point when he concludes that for Smith '[o]ne cannot have freedom without commerce and manufactures, but opulence without freedom is the norm rather than the exception'. But this is only valid if opulence is understood as less than Smith's general opulence (cf. Fleischacker 2004: 55–7, who too much downplays the significance of general opulence in Smith). The connection between commerce and opulence is also somewhat contingent (see *LRB*: 137, cited by Forbes).

For Smith, the rise of commerce in Europe acted to promote personal liberty, by replacing feudal relations of *direct* dependence of the poor upon the rich, with market relations (*WN*: 411–27; Lieberman 2006: 232–3, 239–43). But this was not a necessary or an inevitable outcome:

> For Smith, there is, in a sense, nothing natural about the 'system of natural liberty'. If mankind had, by degrees, unevenly and uncertainly, emerged

> from tutelage, it was less a testament to the power of interest than to unanticipated consequences of actions or to fortuitous combinations of interests.... Establishing the 'system of natural liberty' under which every-man is 'left perfectly free to pursue his own interest his own way' [*WN*: 687] is ... a *task*, rather than something that comes naturally ....
>
> (Mehta 2006: 255–7).

The relations between commerce and opulence on the one hand, and liberty (even just personal liberty) on the other, are more nuanced, complex and contingent than the simple formulas, 'commerce inevitably leads to liberty' or 'liberty (in some strict sense) is the necessary precondition for commerce or opulence'. Their mutual dependence and interaction are well captured by Rothschild and Sen (2006: 334–7): 'The progress of opulence ... can be seen as a virtuous circle, in which legal and political improvement leads to economic improvement, and economic improvement in turn leads to further improvement in political and legal institutions'.[38]

Economic liberty – individuals' freedom to make use of the material assets and labour capacities they possess, as they see fit – is but a subset of political liberty as privacy, as absence of government intrusion (adverse or favourable). But whatever the forms of constitution and government, democratic or otherwise, the liberty of the individual – negative liberty in Berlin's sense, personal liberty in Forbes's sense – is a creature of political society and its law. It is an expression of this, that as a matter of sheer fact, property, as against mere *possession*, has no existence independent of polity (cf. Hume 1739–40: 501). This is so notwithstanding those forms of political libertarianism which seek to make radical claims for the political inviolability of individuals' material possessions. Libertarians cannot properly speak of 'property' as if it has an existence independent of political constitution, law and society. 'Private' property exists always and only by virtue of a self-denying ordinance of political societies and their systems of law (cf. Forbes 1975: 130–2, 148, on Hobbes versus Smith). In relation to the Hobbes maxim quoted above, concerning liberty as the silence of the law, material property is an element of that silence too. It is that political self-denial by the State with respect to individuals' material possessions (including incomes) which libertarians must justify, not some impossible notion of private property as existing by virtue of natural rights, independent of polity. Robert Nozick (1974) provides the most significant latter-day attempt to justify such a libertarian view. This is pertinent to the legitimacy of government regulating individuals' economic activities in production and exchange, but more importantly, also to the question of legitimate taxation. Rather than libertarian, Smith is a decidedly moderate liberal, especially on the taxation issue (sec. 5.2.3; notes 54, 55 below; cf. Fleischacker 2004: 174–202).

### *5.2.6 The idea of police*

'Police' comes into English use in the fifteenth and sixteenth centuries from the French *police*, conveying 'public order, administration, government' – and more specifically, from the thirteenth to the seventeenth century, in French, variously: 'regulation of trades, etc., in a town'; 'good order, good administration' (note the normative dimension); 'public order assured by the state'; 'collection of legislative or administrative measures governing and facilitating social life'; 'organization or body for public order'; 'order and regulations established in a society, assembly, or other body' (*OED*: 'police'). The French term in turn derives from the post-classical Latin *politia*, which carried the senses of 'citizenship', 'political organization, government', from the ancient Greek *πολιτεία*, 'citizenship, government, administration, constitution, polity, form of government' (*OED*: 'police'; 'policy'). (Hence we return to where we started, in sec. 2.1.3, with the origins of 'political' economy in ancient Greek thought.) In English, 'police' conveyed the same senses as the French: before 1776, '[s]ocial or communal organization'; '[t]he regulation and control of a community; the maintenance of law and order, provision of public amenities, etc.'; '[p]ublic regulation or control of trade in a particular product'; 'a controlling body, within a community' (*OED*: 'police'). It was also partly a synonym for 'policy', which – also from the fifteenth century, or a little earlier – before 1776 carries the senses of '[t]he art, study, or practice of government or administration; the conduct of public affairs'; '[p]olity, civil order; an organized … system or form of government or administration'; '[a] principle or course of action adopted or proposed as desirable, advantageous, or expedient, *esp.* one formally advocated by a government'; 'method of acting on matters of principle, settled practice'; 'skill or shrewdness in public affairs; statecraft' (*OED*: 'policy'). The following illustrate early uses of the terms: 'He exercisyd his knyghtly labowris … in grete police' (*c.*1450); 'To the subvercion of the policy and gode rule of this lond' (1488–9); 'knowlege … expedyent to be lerned for the conservacion of their good pollices' (1536); 'Suche peoples as do lyue to gethere in a cyuyle pollycye and good ordre' (1551); 'Neuer did bare and rotten pollicy Colour her working with such deadly wounds' (1598; Shakespeare); 'There is no art that hath bin more canker'd in her principles, more soyl'd, and slubber'd with aphorisming pedantry then the art of policie' (1641; Milton); 'a police upon grain, as might keep the price of it within determined limits' (1767; Steuart; all from *OED*: 'police'; 'policy').[39]

Farge's (2001) account of 'police' in seventeenth- and eighteenth-century France portrays something of a contrast between the theory and the reality. Policing is defined in terms of 'governing human beings and making them happy in light of the general interest'; 'assuring the repose of the public and of individuals … purging … disorder, … procuring abundance, and … allowing each person to live in accordance with his status and his duty'. In the practice, the objective of order appears as dominating happiness: policing aimed 'to prevent and repress'; it 'came to resemble the operation of a gigantic eye'; it involved an attitude of 'insinuating oneself into every location' and 'extravagant powers … to establish rules and regulations where none had previously existed' (Farge 2001: 1063–7). Notwithstanding this emphasis on a 'police state' (in the latter-day sense) interpretation of French police or policy, there are also economic and public health dimensions to the French theory and practice (as Smith himself indicated: *LJA*: 331; *LJB*: 486). The police power was responsible for 'public safety, food supplies, and sanitation'; its duties included 'the procurement of supplies', 'street cleaning', 'supervision of Jews, foreigners, booksellers, and gaming', administering 'fees paid by members of crafts and professions', 'regulation of cabs, gutters and lanterns, fairs, markets, weights and measures, soldiers and recruits, innkeepers, domestic servants, wet nurses and schools, transportation', and responsibilities with respect to 'roads and transportation, and trade' (Farge 2001: 1066, 1068–9).[40]

The general French idea of police as aimed at the happiness of the citizenry might at first glance make it seem very close to Smith's conception, as to the (at least ostensible) purpose of the former, even allowing that the latter is perhaps more economically focused. But it is not at all evident that in the French conception, rising consumption of the lower classes is included in 'happiness', as it certainly is included in Smith's conception of the aims of police or policy (see secs. 4.3.8, 5.1.1–5.1.2, 5.2.2). Farge's preoccupation with the crime-and-punishment dimension of French theory and practice, as against the economic aspects (which she touches upon relatively lightly), may unduly downplay the role of the material consumption of the population within it, though she has some support from Smith himself on this. He comments critically on the extensiveness of French police (in the sense of the quantity of regulations and laws with respect to crime), linking this to an excess of 'retainers' and 'menial servants'; i.e. unproductive labour (*LJA*: 331–3; *LJB*: 486–7; see n. 21 above; Smith also there comments on the origins of the term and concept). From the point of view of the oppressiveness of French police practice portrayed by Farge (even if, one may suspect, this is rather overstated; cf. Emsley 1983: 6–7), Smith's theory of police and policy appears as substituting for the French system a relatively light regime of State regulation – as sufficient for both public order (certainly, orderly economic life) and general prosperity. Human nature, even if not *spontaneously* producing these outcomes, will do most of the work, given a sound framework of law. However similar or dissimilar the objective of French police and the objective of Smith's political economy (and his police, and his politics), in his understanding of prosperous commercial society – with general opulence resulting from strong capital accumulation and growth, in turn associated with a high proportion of productive labour relative to unproductive labour – less *actual* policy is needed than has commonly been thought and practised. This is the Smithian potential virtuous circle, where liberty might enable prosperity and prosperity enhance liberty. The capacity of the French police power to make and simultaneously enforce laws, on the run so to speak (Farge 2001: 1067), is also an element of legislative and executive arbitrariness inconsistent with Smith's conception of well-constituted polities.[41]

Smith wants less police, in the sense of government regulation, than the existing policy regimes of Europe have implemented. To reprise an earlier quotation (sec. 5.2.2), 'the best police [is] to leave things to their natural course' (*LJB*: 499; *LJA*: 366). But in terms of objective, he enlarges police by aiming to extend opulence to the population in general. Winch (1983b: 506) asserts that 'secure provision of "cheapness and plenty" *in matters of subsistence* was the central problem of "police" in the eighteenth century' (emphasis added). Internal peace and public order were evidently at least as central. In any case, even focusing upon just the more economic dimension of police, Smith's objective is certainly larger than the mere (current) subsistence or survival of the people. In the *TMS* invisible hand parable, Smith might seem to speak as if the *merest* subsistence is all that really matters for human welfare in relation to consumption:

> It is to no purpose, that the proud and unfeeling landlord views his extensive fields, and without a thought for the wants of his brethren, in imagination consumes himself the whole harvest that grows upon them.... The capacity of his stomach bears no proportion to the immensity of his desires, and will receive no more than that of the meanest peasant.... The rich ... consume little more than the poor, and in spite of their natural selfishness and rapacity, though they mean only their own conveniency, though the sole end which they propose from the labours of all the thousands whom they employ, be the gratification of their own vain and insatiable desires, they divide with the poor the produce of all their improvements. They are led by an invisible hand to make nearly the same distribution of the necessaries of life, which would have been made, had the earth been divided into equal portions among all its inhabitants, and thus without intending it, without knowing it, advance the interest of the society ....
>
> (*TMS*: 184–5; cf. notes 9, 15, 28 above)

The implication that the difference between the consumption of the rich and the poor is unimportant cannot be taken as a judgement that above-necessary consumption is unimportant. The significance of 'general opulence' for Smith's political economy and police too much contradicts it (see secs 5.1.1–5.1.2; cf. sec. 4.3.8 concerning 'conveniences'; Young 1997a: 165–8).

## 5.3 Theory, policy, history

### *5.3.1 Smith on 'theory'*

Smith does not extensively use the term 'theory' or variants – except, of course, that it appears in the very title of *TMS*. As argued in section 5.2.2, because of the approach to ethics taken in that work, it at least as much belongs to the domain of social science as to that of moral philosophy, as we would now use those terms. To that extent the title is testament to Smith's conviction of the possibility of theory, the centrality of theorizing, for understanding human society – in this case, human sociableness being precisely the subject. From the fourth edition of 1774, the title – *The Theory of Moral Sentiments* – was expanded by the addition, '*or, an essay towards an analysis of the principles by which men naturally judge concerning the conduct and character, first of their neighbours, and afterwards of themselves ...*'

(Raphael and Macfie 1976b: 39–42). Theory is about principles. The title proper, though not in any degree the content of Smith's theory, was almost certainly inspired by Louis-Jean Lévesque de Pouilly's *Théorie des Sentimens Agréables* ... (1747), translated as *The Theory of Agreeable Sensations* ... (1749). Smith's title also expresses his conception of the proper subject matter of moral philosophy as a whole, rather than describing his particular contribution to it, and captures his conviction, in contrast to Hutcheson and Hume, that human moral sentiment is multiple rather than singular.[42] In the prefatory 'Advertisement', added in the sixth edition of 1790, Smith identifies 'the general principles of law and government' with 'the theory of jurisprudence' (*TMS*: 3). Since political economy is for Smith the remainder of jurisprudence, beyond the theory of justice (implied clearly enough here but confirmed elsewhere: see sec. 5.2.2), this implies there is a theory of political economy as well. Likewise, the last paragraph of *TMS* (341–2), to which the advertisement actually addresses itself, makes the same identification even more tightly: 'a system of ... natural jurisprudence, or a theory of the general principles which ought to run through and be the foundation of the laws of all nations'; a 'general system', a 'philosophy of law ... treated of by itself, and without regard to the particular institutions of any one nation'; 'a system of ... principles'. Part VII, entitled 'Of Systems...' of moral philosophy, opens by referring to 'the different theories' that have been offered, concerning the nature and origin of moral sentiments – again identifying system, theory and 'principles' (*TMS*: 265). These three instances beyond the title itself are all those to be found in *TMS*.

The *TMS* (341–2) definition of natural jurisprudence, quoted immediately above, placed side by side with the opening sentence of *LJB* (397) – 'Jurisprudence is that science which inquires into the general principles which ought to be the foundation of the laws of all nations' – shows an identification of theory and science.[43] All this takes us back to where we began this study, in Chapter 2 (especially sec. 2.1.2), with the concept of science and the identification of philosophy, science and systems – and now as well, more explicitly, those three also identified with theory and general principles. On the following page of *LJB*, Smith switches back to use of 'theory' (and in parallel text in *LJA*): 'Jurisprudence is the theory of the general principles of law and government' (*LJB*: 398); 'Jurisprudence is the theory of the rules by which civil governments ought to be directed' (*LJA*: 5). The implication from the *TMS* advertisement, that political economy is amenable to theorizing, is confirmed in *WN*. In the 'Introduction and Plan of the Work', Smith sketches how different nations have followed different 'plans' with regard to economic development, dichotomizing these plans into those that have favoured 'the country' and those that have favoured 'towns', and pointing to the contents of Book III. (Intimating the contrary view that he will end up putting in the book, Smith adds: 'Scarce any nation has dealt equally and impartially with every sort of industry.') This then leads into a statement of the purposes of the Book IV critique of mercantilism and Physiocracy:

> Though those different plans were, perhaps, first introduced by the private interests and prejudices of particular orders of men, without any regard to,

> or foresight of, their consequences upon the general welfare of the society; yet they have given occasion to very different theories of political œconomy; of which some magnify the importance of that industry which is carried on in towns, others of that which is carried on in the country. Those theories have had a considerable influence, not only upon the opinions of men of learning, but upon the public conduct of princes and sovereign states. I have endeavoured, in the Fourth Book, to explain, as fully and distinctly as I can, those different theories, and the principal effects which they have produced in different ages and nations.
>
> (*WN*: 11)

Notice how this describes theories as arising out of practice, and then feeding back upon practice or policy. At another point, Smith refers to the 'very ingenious theory' of the Physiocrats (though not thereby correct), with particular regard to taxation of rents (*WN*: 830). These are the only two explicit references to theory in *WN*.

The (eventual) emergence of a theory or theories of political economy also receives passing mention in *LJA* (235). Discussing the Roman republic's increase of power and opulence, Smith observes how 'peace and tranquillity at home' provides the basis for 'cultivation of the arts', and adds: 'Commerce too will naturally introduce itself, tho' not, as now, particularly studied and a theory laid down'. Another lecture opens with the comment that he had begun in the previous lecture 'to give some account of those bad practicall effects which proceeded from that system or theory which placed the opulence of a nation on its coin and money' (*LJA*: 388). Later in the same lecture he introduces a further ill consequence of mercantilism – 'not … so prejudiciall … as it has affected the theory more than the practise' – connected with Mandeville's 'theory that private vices were publick benefits' (*LJA*: 393). Apart from the two *LJ* references to jurisprudence as theory, quoted directly above, these are the only three further instances of theory in those manuscripts. Beyond these references to theory, specific to political economy, the 'History of Astronomy' in *EPS*, as an exercise in the history of science, naturally refers to theory. In the context of outlining his notion of scientific systems of explanation as soothing the human imagination (discussed in Chapter 2), Smith refers to the 'theory and history' of philosophy (*EPS*: 46). There are also references to 'the theory of the heavens' (*EPS*: 54, 87, 89), Newton's theory (*EPS*: 99) and 'the theory of gravity' (*EPS*: 100–1, 103) – uses all closely connected with systems of explanation. Hence in the one further instance in the 'Astronomy', he speaks of 'system or theory', just as he had at *LJA* (388; quoted immediately above):

> Philosophers, long before the days of Hipparchus, seem to have abandoned the study of nature, to employ themselves chiefly in ethical, rhetorical, and dialectical questions. Each party of them too, had by this time completed their peculiar system or theory of the universe ….
>
> (*EPS*: 65)[44]

### *5.3.2 Theory and practice*

Theory is science and/or an intellectual system or systems, systems of general principles, for understanding and explanation, in various domains. With regard to social theory in particular, Smith certainly believed that he had fashioned a political economy, self-consciously building on the earlier work of others, which captures the true causes of the wealth of nations, a theory which correctly grasps the fundamental factors determining the distribution and growth of output. It might seem a small step from this conviction, to the conclusion that a more or less wholesale implementation of the ideal system in practice, is desirable in any time or place. But Smith does not, tacitly or explicitly, embrace that conclusion: policy is not, or ought not be, such a straightforward application of right theory; correct policy is not necessarily a simple embodiment of the ideal. He pursues this line of thought consciously, and in more than one place; so much so, that one may say Smith has the rudiments of a kind of meta-theory of the relation between theory and practice. The moderateness, the aversion to intellectual and political zealotry, is not merely an instinct of temperament on Smith's part; it is a thought out, reasoned conclusion. Though there is not a vast number of instances of 'theory' in his texts, given the synonyms for the term, the issue could just as well be characterized as the relation between (social) science or principles and practice/policy. To be clear, the science of political economy is certainly for the service of legislation or policy. This was made evident already in section 2.1.1 – a branch of the science of a legislator – and confirmed in the previous sections of this chapter. Nevertheless, Smith takes the view that the authentic legislator will exercise prudence, particularly by way of taking into account the history and situation of the particular nation under policy consideration. This is discussed at some length in an important passage of argument in *TMS* (231–4; cf. 216 on the 'superior prudence' of 'the great statesman … the great legislator').

Considering the leader of a political faction or party who gains power, Smith contemplates the possibility that 'from the very doubtful and ambiguous character of the leader of a party, he may assume the greatest and noblest of all characters, that of the reformer and legislator of a great state'. On the other hand there is 'a certain spirit of system' which leads to 'fanaticism', to proposals to 'new-model the constitution', and to intoxication with 'the imaginary beauty of this ideal system':

> The violence of the party, refusing all palliatives, all temperaments, all reasonable accommodations, by requiring too much frequently obtains nothing; and those inconveniencies and distresses which, with a little moderation, might in a great measure have been removed and relieved, are left altogether without the hope of a remedy.

The reformer-legislator on the other hand,

> will accommodate, as well as he can, his public arrangements to the confirmed habits and prejudices of the people; and will remedy as well as he

> can, the inconveniencies which may flow from the want of those regulations which the people are averse to submit to. When he cannot establish the right, he will not disdain to ameliorate the wrong ... when he cannot establish the best system of laws, he will endeavour to establish the best that the people can bear.

The man of system, 'wise in his own conceit', is

> often so enamoured with the supposed beauty of his own ideal plan of government, that he cannot suffer the smallest deviation from any part of it. He goes on to establish it completely and in all its parts, without any regard either to the great interest, or to the strong prejudices which may oppose it. He seems to imagine that he can arrange the different members of a great society with as much ease as the hand arranges the different pieces upon a chess-board. He does not consider that the pieces upon the chess-board have no other principle of motion besides that which the hand impresses upon them; but that, in the great chess-board of human society, every single piece has a principle of motion of its own, altogether different from that which the legislature might chuse to impress upon it ....
>
> Some general, and even systematical, idea of the perfection of policy and law, may no doubt be necessary for directing the views of the statesman. But to insist upon establishing, and upon establishing all at once, and in spite of all opposition, every thing which that idea may seem to require, must often be the highest degree of arrogance.
>
> (*TMS*: 232–4)

This is a vigorous statement for moderation in the implementation of principles in politics, and by inference (confirmed below), concerning the proper relation between theory and policy. Smith firmly repudiates engineering society on the mere basis of theoretical reasoning or principles, without attention to the concrete situation – and by implication, attention to the history from which that situation has arisen. A similar sentiment – which resonates with the chessboard metaphor at *TMS* (234; quoted above) – is expressed in a quotation by Stewart (1811: 322), from a 1755 Smith manuscript:

> Man is generally considered by statesmen and projectors as the materials of a sort of political mechanics. Projectors disturb nature in the course of her operations in human affairs; and it requires no more than to let her alone, and give her fair play in the pursuit of her ends, that she may establish her own designs.

At least partly, Smith's position concerning men of system and political projectors is evidently driven by an aversion to actually existing politicians. The sense conveyed above, of the noble legislator as the exception among politicians, is confirmed by his disparagement of the latter:

> When the judicial is united to the executive power, it is scarce possible that justice should not frequently be sacrificed to, what is vulgarly called, politics. The persons entrusted with the great interests of the state may, even without any corrupt views, sometimes imagine it necessary to sacrifice to those interests the rights of a private man.
>
> (*WN*: 722)

> They whom we call politicians are not the most remarkable men in the world for probity ....
>
> (*LJB*: 539)

Further to this, in a discussion of the American colonies and the attractions (i.e. temptations) to their 'leading men' of colonial representation in the British parliament being allowed, Smith comments:

> Instead of piddling for the little prizes which are to be found in what may be called the paltry raffle of colony faction; they might then hope, from the presumption which men naturally have in their own ability and good fortune, to draw some of the great prizes which sometimes come from the wheel of the great state lottery of British politicks.
>
> (*WN*: 622–3)[45]

But more than merely from a cynical – or clear-eyed (the reader may judge) – view of politicians, Smith's own ideal of natural liberty itself is also, and more fundamental, ground for antagonism towards much political experimentation. (Hence there are two levels to the issue: the correct theory tells against political interventions generally; but even implementation of the correct theory should take account of practice.) It follows also from this, that it would be wrong to see his position on this matter as just straightforward political conservatism – in the sense of an a priori presumption against political change and experimentation as such, and in favour of the status quo for its own sake. After all, the noble legislator of *TMS* (231–4) is characterized as a 'reformer'. Apart from any other evidence, the dominant policy drift of *WN*, and its opposition to the prevailing policy of Europe, compellingly tells against this view (sec. 5.2.2). Furthermore, Smith elsewhere – and it is also in *TMS* (at 185–7) – speaks in very positive terms of how 'love of system' encourages individuals to 'promote the public welfare':

> The perfection of police, the extension of trade and manufactures, are noble and magnificent objects. The contemplation of them pleases us, and we are interested in whatever can tend to advance them. They make part of the great system of government, and the wheels of the political machine seem to move with more harmony and ease by means of them. We take pleasure in beholding the perfection of so beautiful and grand a system, and we are uneasy till we remove any obstruction that can in the least disturb or encumber the regularity of its motions.

But before continuing along this line, he immediately adds a caution which reminds of the man of system. The 'sole use and end' of political constitutions is 'to promote the happiness of those who live under them':

> From a certain spirit of system, however, from a certain love of art and contrivance, we sometimes seem to value the means more than the end, and to be eager to promote the happiness of our fellow-creatures, rather from a view to perfect and improve a certain beautiful and orderly system, than from any immediate sense or feeling of what they either suffer or enjoy.
>
> (*TMS*: 185; cf. 316)[46]

A statement in favour of the role of precedent in legal adjudication shares the same attitude, in this instance, explicitly referring to the limitations of theory alone:

> The Sentences of former Cases are greatly regarded and form what is called the common law, which is found to be much more equitable than that which is founded on Statute only, for the same reason as what is founded on practise and experience must be better adapted to particular cases than that which is derived from theory only.
>
> (*LRB*: 175)

This rather non-doctrinaire approach to the implementation of principles and theory in policy and practice no doubt was supported in Smith's thinking by his conviction that humankind, and more particularly, nations, could prosper even under imperfect and adverse political arrangements; the outcomes available are not merely, either perfection or disaster. The point is made in the context of a discussion of the Physiocrats' advocacy of 'perfect liberty':

> Some speculative physicians seem to have imagined that the health of the human body could be preserved only by a certain precise regimen of diet and exercise, of which every, the smallest, violation necessarily occasioned some degree of disease or disorder proportioned to the degree of the violation. Experience, however, would seem to show that the human body frequently preserves, to all appearance at least, the most perfect state of health under a vast variety of different regimens; even under some which are generally believed to be very far from being perfectly wholesome. But the healthful state of the human body, it would seem, contains in itself some unknown principle of preservation, capable either of preventing or of correcting, in many respects, the bad effects even of a very faulty regimen. Mr. Quesnai, who was himself a physician, and a very speculative physician, seems to have entertained a notion of the same kind concerning the political body, and to have imagined that it would thrive and prosper only under a certain precise regimen, the exact regimen of perfect liberty and perfect justice. He seems not to have considered that in the political body, the natural effort which every man is continually making to better his own con-

> dition, is a principle of preservation capable of preventing and correcting, in many respects, the bad effects of a political œconomy, in some degree, both partial and oppressive. Such a political œconomy, though it no doubt retards more or less, is not always capable of stopping altogether the natural progress of a nation towards wealth and prosperity, and still less of making it go backwards. If a nation could not prosper without the enjoyment of perfect liberty and perfect justice, there is not in the world a nation which could ever have prospered. In the political body, however, the wisdom of nature has fortunately made ample provision for remedying many of the bad effects of the folly and injustice of man ....
>
> (*WN*: 673–4)

Smith expresses here a conviction that even under second-best (or worse) constitutions, regimes and policies, 'nature' is still in play, working away for the good.[47]

The refusal to treat (desirable) practice as simply a straightforward implementation of correct theory is evident at the level of political constitutions, but is also expressed with regard to economic policy. It was pointed out in section 5.2.3, how Smith entertains the possibility that a sudden and dramatic loss of foreign markets could diminish the national capital stock, the context being the possible loss of the British monopoly of the American colony trade. He conceives of this monopoly as having dangerously distorted the British economy into an excessive reliance on one market:

> A small stop in that great blood-vessel, which has been artificially swelled beyond its natural dimensions, and through which an unnatural proportion of the industry and commerce of the country has been forced to circulate, is very likely to bring on the most dangerous disorders upon the whole body politick.
>
> (*WN*: 604–5)

This unfortunate predicament does not persuade Smith to abandon the goal of unrestricted trade; rather, he advocates gradualism and deference to practical judgement:

> moderate and gradual relaxation of the laws ... seems to be the only expedient ...; and which, by gradually diminishing one branch of her industry and gradually increasing all the rest, can by degrees restore all the different branches of it to that natural, healthful, and proper proportion which perfect liberty necessarily establishes, and which perfect liberty can alone preserve.
>
> (*WN*: 606)

Even the precise form of that gradual policy implementation cannot be decided a priori, by reference to principle alone:

> In what manner ... the colony trade ought gradually to be opened; what are the restraints which ought first, and what are those which ought last to be taken away; or in what manner the natural system of perfect liberty and justice ought gradually to be restored, we must leave to the wisdom of future statesmen and legislators to determine.
>
> (*WN*: 606)

It is an issue for practice not theory.

Another substantial expression of the same kind of stance occurs in a consideration of the desirability of maintaining or restoring free importation. The first is raised in the context of whether or not a nation should 'retaliate' against restrictions on its exports by other nations. Smith thinks retaliation 'may be good policy', if it leads to repeal of the foreign nations' protection; otherwise, not. As to whether retaliation will induce repeal:

> To judge ... does not, perhaps, belong so much to the science of a legislator, whose deliberations ought to be governed by general principles which are always the same, as to the skill of that insidious and crafty animal, vulgarly called a statesman or politician, whose councils are directed by the momentary fluctuations of affairs.
>
> (*WN*: 467–8)

The science of political economy, constituted by universal general principles, cannot judge the contingencies of the particular situation. The second – the desirability of restoring free importation – goes to the same issue as *WN* (604–7). If substantial domestic industries have grown up under import protection,

> [h]umanity may in this case require that the freedom of trade should be restored only by slow gradations, and with a good deal of reserve and circumspection. Were those high duties and prohibitions taken away all at once, cheaper foreign goods of the same kind might be poured so fast into the home market, as to deprive all at once many thousands of our people of their ordinary employment and means of subsistence.
>
> (*WN*: 469)

Smith provides reasons why this problem may not be so considerable, touched on above (*WN*: 469–71; n. 27 above); but he nevertheless reiterates that substantial abolition of protection 'should never be introduced suddenly, but slowly, gradually, and after a very long warning' (*WN*: 471).

In the context of these considerations, Smith offers a comment on the chances of implementing policy perfection, which resonates with his comments on Physiocracy at *WN* (673–4), discussed above, and provides a fitting conclusion to this issue of the relation between theory and practice:

> To expect ... that the freedom of trade should ever be entirely restored in Great Britain, is as absurd as to expect that an Oceana or Utopia should ever be established in it. Not only the prejudices of the publick, but what is much more unconquerable, the private interests of many individuals, irresistibly oppose it.[48] Were the officers of the army to oppose with the same zeal and unanimity any reduction in the number of forces, with which master manufacturers set themselves against every law that is likely to increase the number of their rivals in the home market; were the former to animate their soldiers, in the same manner as the latter enflame their workmen, to attack with violence and outrage the proposers of any such regulation; to attempt to reduce the army would be as dangerous as it has now become to attempt to diminish in any respect the monopoly which our manufacturers have obtained against us. This monopoly has so much increased the number of some particular tribes of them, that, like an overgrown standing army, they have become formidable to the government, and upon many occasions intimidate the legislature. The member of parliament who supports every proposal for strengthening this monopoly, is sure to acquire not only the reputation of understanding trade, but great popularity and influence with an order of men whose numbers and wealth render them of great importance. If he opposes them, on the contrary, and still more if he has authority enough to be able to thwart them, neither the most acknowledged probity, nor the highest rank, nor the greatest publick services can protect him from the most infamous abuse and detraction, from personal insults, nor sometimes from real danger, arising from the insolent outrage of furious and disappointed monopolists.
>
> (*WN*: 471)

### *5.3.3 History and political economy*

It is a short step from the issue of theory and practice to the importance of history and historiography for Smith's approach to social theory: the importance of the particular points to the importance of history for understanding. Indeed, the historical treatment of all subjects is a pervasive feature of his *oeuvre*. *TMS* extensively considers previous systems of moral philosophy (especially Part VII: *TMS*: 265; cf. Raphael and Macfie 1976b: 4–6). *EPS* and *LRB* are largely exercises in the history of science, literature and human sensibility. *LJA* and *LJB* are in largest part studies of the historical development of law. As to *WN*, along with the history of human economic development in Book III, there are many other, often lengthy, historical commentaries on a variety of issues: a detailed treatment of the historical evolution of production methods for a wide range of commodities (Book I, Chapter XI); a lengthy examination of banking systems (Book II, Chapter II); considerable historical commentary on colonies (Book IV, Chapter VII); extensive discussions of the history of public finances in a number of places (esp. Book V, Chapter I, Parts I–II); and more. In short, in Smith's texts in general, and in his political economy in particular, one sees far more history than in any modern economic treatise along marginalist lines. In section 5.2.2 some consideration was given to Smith's understanding of the place of political economy within the social sciences, compared with the modern demarcation of the social sciences. But the relation between historiography (as defined in the introductory paragraphs of this chapter) and political economy – a question raised in those opening paragraphs – was not considered there. How integral is history to Smith's political economy project? Does historiography form a *part* of political economy; or is it merely a very salient supplement to the political economy proper? What seems the correct answer requires a fine balance and delicate judgement. Skinner (1996: 250–2) takes the view that for Smith history is not integral to political economy, in the way it is for Hume (as well as for Steuart, Galiani and other eighteenth-century economic writers):

> In Smith's hands, the history of civil society is essential for our understanding of the exchange economy and of the social and political environment it may produce. But here, history is the *preface* to political economy rather than integral to the treatment. In the event, Smith did not use the historical method in dealing with economic questions ....

There is truth in this; and, one may add, notwithstanding all the mass of historical narrative with economic pertinence in *LJ*, Smith *chose* to exclude most of it from *WN*. One might say, historiography may be essential for understanding how commercial society arose, but once that system arrives, political economy can proceed to understand it without necessary recourse to history (cf. Campbell and Skinner 1976: 4, 17). Nevertheless, Skinner (1996: 252) goes a little too far in suggesting that the perspective generated by the historical approach of Steuart *et al.* – 'a perspective ... that *policy* recommendations must always be related to the circumstances that prevail' – is not shared by Smith.[49] Perhaps he has a more universalistic approach than these other writers, but Smith is nevertheless firmly of the view that the legislator must take into account prevailing circumstances. There is truth in Skinner's resolution of the relation between history and political economy, to the extent that – given the emergence or existence of a fully fledged commercial society with due process of law and so on – it is possible in Smith's terms of reference to apply the general principles of political economy to understanding the operation of the socio-economic machine. But there is in Smith's political economy another layer of meaning, one may say a deeper layer of meaning, to the role of history in economic processes (and so a role for historiography). The scope of theoretical determinateness in the economics is more limited than is the case in latter-day marginalist economics, and so a considerable domain for contingency, and hence history, is opened up *within* the economic analysis itself. (This issue is taken up further in the Epilogue, in relation to modern economics.)

The dependence of the level of real wages upon the contingencies of bargaining power is the notable example, at the very heart of Smith's theory of distribution and prices. The customary content of subsistence also makes subsistence, whatever the plausibility of its status as an anchor for wages, necessarily a creature of history. This is a kind of theory which, via that domain of indeterminateness, provides 'space' for contingency and thereby for history; e.g. a role for particular norms concerning minimum socially acceptable consumption, and particular institutions such as labour law and (later) unions, to shape the bargaining outcome. Nevertheless, one does well to avoid merely semantic distinctions. What matters is not so much whether or not historiography has a place within the defined scope of Smithian political economy, whether historiography intersects with political economy. Rather, what matters is the importance or otherwise of historical understanding for the proper conduct of an economic science. Whether, in definitional terms, historiography is auxiliary or integral, then does not matter. In any case, notwithstanding the very wide, or one may say 'soft', use he makes of the term 'science' (see sec. 2.1.2), Smith never calls history or historiography a science – with the exception of the particular case of 'natural history' (*EPS*: 248).

From the standpoint of economic subjects, the most striking historical dimension of Smith's thought is a four-stages conception of the history of human material development, in terms of hunting, herding, agriculture and commerce.[50] Whether or not there is such a thing as an historical science for Smith, this historiography certainly has a 'theoretical' character, though it is Dugald Stewart (1811: 292–6), not Smith himself, who aptly names this form of inquiry '*Theoretical* or *Conjectural History*'. It is history, up to a point, with a certain determinate logic, because it is the working out of nature, especially human nature, in history. (Recall also the sense in which Smith perceives nature working away, for the good, in economic outcomes, even under imperfect or worse political constitutions and policy regimes, in his comments on Physiocracy discussed in sec. 5.3.2.) One may say, therefore, that a central element of Smith's historical writing is to account for the effects of the operation of the fundamental human psychological characteristics (the desire for material self-betterment and so on) – under various institutional conditions in the widest sense – though with resulting human behaviour effecting alteration in those conditions, both intentionally and unintentionally. But that working out in history of human nature and of its universal principles of action is by no means deterministic. Indeed the central point of the *WN*, Book III treatment of economic development is to show how little the *actual* development has followed 'the natural course'. (The sceptic at this point, and at others, might inquire: if the liberal system is so 'natural', why has it taken so much human history for it to emerge, even in imperfect forms?) And the materialism evident in the four-stages theory – materialism in the sense of economic forces shaping wider human and socio-political development – is also soft, rather than deterministic. The historiography is 'conjectural' in the sense that it is partly (but by no means exclusively) based upon speculation as what *must have* been the course of history, based upon knowledge of human nature, together with knowledge or conjecture about the circumstances in which humans found themselves at earlier times. There is plenty of actual history in Smith's text as well, or at least what purports to be accurate accounts of actual history.

The recourse to conjecture does not at all reflect an indifference towards 'well authenticated history' (*WN*: 702). In truth, notwithstanding a degree of latter-day fascination with Smith's theoretical history, in both *LJ* and *WN* the balance between the conjectural and the actual favours the latter.

Certainly for Smith, consciously, theory informs the study of history, and whether or not it is science, the study of history is properly about cause and effect. *LRB* (104–16) includes two lectures on '*the History of Historians*', ancient and modern – second-order historiography so to speak (in terms of our definition of historiography): study of the history of history-writing. Machiavelli is singled out for particular praise, and the reason is interesting: 'Machiavel is of all Modern Historians the only one who has contented himself with that which is the chief purpose of History, to relate Events and connect them with their causes without becoming a party on either side' (*LRB*: 115; cf. *TMS*: 217). In *WN* (790), Hume is described as 'the most illustrious philosopher and historian of the present age'. John Millar wrote of Smith himself:

> I am happy to acknowledge the obligations I feel myself under to this illustrious philosopher, by having, at an early period of life, had the benefit of hearing his lectures on the History of Civil Society, and of enjoying his unreserved conversation on the same subject. The great Montesquieu pointed out the road. He was the Lord Bacon in this branch of philosophy. Dr. Smith is the Newton.
>
> (quoted in *EPS*: 275, ed. note 4; cf. *Corr*: 99, n. 1)

*LJ* are certainly very much in the same spirit (pun intended) as Montesquieu (1748): with regard to historical method and an associated measure of relativism, in terms of a kind of functional explanation of particular principles and practices of law, with respect to particular kinds of societies (but on their differences, see Forbes 1954: 646). On the other hand, Montesquieu's chapters on commerce and money are of not much substance, relative to the genuine political economy which appears in the subsequent three decades (Montesquieu (1748 [1989], Books 20–22: 337–426).

Whether or not historiography is an element of political economy as Smith understood the science, it is a compelling fact that he was imbued with a deep and wide-ranging historical sensibility:

> By instinct ... he is a historian in the sense that he sees narrative as the very type of human thought-procedure; but his interest in it is also that suggested by Hume's description of history's records as 'so many collections of experiments by which the moral philosopher fixes the principles of his science'.
>
> (Bryce 1983: 19)

The considerable historical commentaries in *WN*, noted above (the actual rather than theoretical history) should also be seen as partly embodying an empirical concern, albeit of a commonly long-run kind – rather than solely expressing a role for history in economic inquiry. Be that as it may, overall in Smith's thought, one has a sense of his aiming for a delicate combination: on the one hand, enunciation of universal principles (of explanation, and of justice as he comprehended it), and on the other, strong appreciation of the historical specificity of the conventional expression of those universals, in particular times and places. Smith died with a long expressed ambition of completing a wide-ranging historico-theoretical project, or set of projects, unfulfilled. In 1785 he writes: 'I have … two other great works upon the anvil; the one is a sort of Philosophical History of all the different branches of Literature, of Philosophy, Poetry and Eloquence; the other is a sort of theory and History of Law and Government' (*Corr*: 286–7; cf. 168). As the editors of the correspondence point out (p. 287, n. 5), elements of all this are preserved in *EPS*, *LRB* and *LJ*. In the same letter Smith admits the unlikelihood of his plans being brought to completion (cf. *Corr*: 310–11).[51]

## 5.4 Limits of theory and limits of Smith's policy

Stepping back from the substantive content of both the theory and the policy Smith enunciates, one may see how he draws stricter limits to the proper domain of theory in political economy, than has become customary since the twentieth century. The legitimate claims of economic theory are rendered more modest (an issue pursued further in the Epilogue). Smith's political economy in no essential way relies upon the project of theoretical history, however valuable or insightful or intriguing the latter may be. But history, actual and speculative, nevertheless plays a much bigger role in his economics than it does in modern economics. There may be substantial and good reasons for this. To come at the issue from another vantage point, Smith's political economy is appealing because in one sense it is bigger than modern economics, and consciously connected with social science more widely. In another sense it is smaller than modern economics, insofar as the domain of determinate theoretical results is smaller. Is this just because he was working at an early stage in the theoretical development of the science, and so produced a lesser number of determinate results than we are now capable of? There is truth in that; but there is more to the matter as well.[52] The domain of theory (and determinacy) and the domain of history (and contingency) are differently drawn by him. Smith's refusal to make practice and policy a straightforward application of his essentially universalistic politico-economic theory is another and a different expression of the limits of theory. His manner of constituting the scope of political economy is also of considerable interest. This is not so much because a literal return to his conception is to be recommended; rather, because it assists us to see more clearly the particularity and frailties of our own taken-for-granted conceptions of the science and its relations (or lack thereof) with other sciences, in particular, other social sciences. It surely cannot be said that the current academic demarcations of the social sciences are satisfactory or unproblematic.

As to the substantive content of Smith's theory and policy, almost enough has been said by way of appraisal in the previous chapters, as well as earlier in this chapter. Its relation to subsequent developments will be discussed in the Epilogue as well. The only remaining and fundamental issue deserving of consideration here concerns Smith's treatment of distribution and its significance for the limitations of his first-best, most preferred economic policy in pursuit of his normative purpose for political economy.[53] As was clarified in section 5.1.1, general opulence is the ultimate normative purpose of his political economy. As a policy science, it shares the same prescriptive economic purpose as good government. The descriptive theoretical content of the science is naturally governed by that over-arching purpose: to grasp the means to prosperity; to understand and explain the causes of the distribution and growth of output and of consumption. Much has been written criticizing Smith's characterizations of what he called the mercantile system (see sec. 2.2.2). He certainly oversimplified – one may even say, misrepresented – the corpus of mercantile literature in his portrayal and critique of it. But even if that is true, one should not lose sight of the rightness of his position *vis-à-vis* mercantilism, 'in the large', so to speak, whether or not his account of it is true to all the detail of that literature. In making general opulence the normative purpose of political economy, Smith forcefully enunciates that the (legitimate) purpose of the social economy is to advance the per capita consumption of the labouring classes, the bulk of the population.

> 'Tis true indeed that … gold lasts for a long time and … claret is very soon consumed, but this makes no odds. For to what purpose do all those things which a nation possesses serve? To no other but the maintaining the people? And how is <it> that this end is answered? By being consumed. It is the *consumptibility* of a thing which makes it usefull. To what purpose does industry serve but to produce the greatest quantity of these necessaries.… The business of commerce and indust<r>y is to produce the greatest quantity of the necessaries of life for the consumption of the nation …. The production of the necessaries of life is the sole benefit of industry.… The whole benefit of wea<l>th and industry is that you either employ a greater number or give those already employed a more comfortable subsistence ….
> (*LJA*: 390–1; cf. *LJB*: 511–12; also *WN*: 660–2, part quoted in sec. 4.3.4)

How many of the mercantilist writers can be read as enunciating such a view of the economic purpose of society? In truth, that literature largely treats the labouring classes as little more than fuel for the economic machine, that machine being geared to other grand politico-economic purposes of State.

That is all to the good, as to the legitimate *end* of economic society. But offering the system of natural liberty as the *means* to that end, amounts to offering trickle-down as the (largely) sufficient policy for that purpose: the workers are better off, as wage workers in liberal commercial society, than they otherwise would be. To put it mildly, this is not in any straightforward sense a testable empirical proposition (what are the 'otherwise' possibilities?). Let us accept that Smith is right concerning the more limited proposition, that as between the 'savage' socio-economy and the commercial socio-economy, the median or average person in the latter is better off than the equivalent person – or even the materially *best-off* person – in the former. Still, two further contestable steps are required in order to get to an ethical justification of the trickle-down conclusion, along the lines implied by the Smith texts considered in section 5.1.1, together with his general presumption concerning policy outlined in section 5.2. First, the superior situation of the median individual in commercial society is a result of higher labour productivity; but does this require inequality (as Smith evidently believes) – and if it does, what precise extent and forms of inequality does it require? Could not the median individual be even better off by way of redistribution of resources, in some further alternative socio-political framework or other – e.g. social democracy or some variant of socialism (going beyond the redistribution sanctioned by Smith himself) – at least if the higher labour productivity can be preserved under such alternative social arrangements? (Of course, many have offered various pro and *contra* answers to this kind of question, since 1790.)

In allowing that progressive taxation is legitimate (sec. 5.2.3), Smith takes a step in the direction of opening up this possibility. Is he not then subject to the following, telling charge that Keynes directs at Friedrich von Hayek, concerning liberalism and planning, in a letter of 28 June 1944, written in response to Keynes's reading Hayek's *Road to Serfdom* (1944)?

> You admit here and there that it is a question of knowing where to draw the line. You agree that the line has to be drawn somewhere, and that the logical extreme is not possible. But you give us no guidance whatever as to where to draw it. In a sense this is shirking the practical issue. It is true that you and I would probably draw it in different places. I should guess that according to my ideas you greatly under-estimate the practicability of the middle course. But as soon as you admit that the extreme is not possible, and that a line has to be drawn, you are, on your own argument, done for, since you are trying to persuade us that so soon as one moves an inch in the planned direction you are necessarily launched on the slippery path which will lead you in due course over the precipice.
>
> (Moggridge 1980: 386–7)

Smith's trust in 'nature' makes him not so worried about economic society going over a precipice. As for deciding where the line is to be drawn, Smith could offer only the prudence of the legislator (*TMS*: 216) – though this is not to deny that his use of the phrases, 'not very unreasonable' that the rich pay 'something more' than proportional taxation (*WN*: 842), certainly suggests that *his* practical judgement would be to favour very moderate progressivity. In any case, this does not provide a definite and defensible principle or rule for where to draw the line on redistribution.[54]

The second necessary but contestable step in arriving at an ethical justification for a general policy of trickle-down in a liberal commercial society goes to this issue: even if great or extreme inequality were a necessary element of commercial society and its high labour productivity, this would not justify the resulting particular socio-economic outcomes for each of the particular individuals or families making up that society. (The inheritance of wealth and the associated intergenerational transmission of inequality alone point to that.) However necessary the functional distribution – and as a matter of fact, as has been seen, for Smith functional distribution itself is arbitrary up to a point (see p. 211) – the ethically arbitrary character of personal distribution is a compellingly obvious fact. Beyond justice (as he understands it), defence and some quite limited public works, Smith has a general presumption in favour of a non-interventionist State – notwithstanding a good number of particular exceptions that he allows. One may say that he gives himself too easy a target, in advancing the case for perfect liberty, by attacking discriminatory policies as between particular commodities and activities – especially when the sole purpose (or at least the sole benefit) is to favour particular private interests.[55] Such policies are only part of the potential picture.

What of possible policy intervention to address unemployment? At least for the very long run, this is not plausible as a policy problem in Smith's system: labour supply adapts to accumulation and the associated growth of labour demand. What of possible policy to address income or wealth maldistribution, or poverty? This is not (or hardly) entertained either; but there is nothing in Smith's system to guarantee a morally defensible personal distribution of material resources, or functional distribution of income, in liberal commercial society.[56] The only hope of any rational argument in defence of such elements of arbitrariness in material inequality must be along the lines of dangers from political intervention in the distribution of property (wealth or incomes), such as to outweigh any possible benefit.[57] This is not the place to consider socio-economic arrangements alternative to a more or less strict form of liberal capitalism along Smithian lines.[58] But the least one may say is that it is a long bow of an argument which would draw a trajectory from, say, progressive income tax, or inheritance taxation – or even social democracy – inexorably to the Gulag. To Smith's suggestion that the rich and the poor are more substantially on an equal footing than might at first appear (see n. 9 above), there is a rather obvious response: if this is so, the rich should have no reason to be troubled by any prospect of exchanging places with the poor.

# Epilogue

> It has sometimes been said of political economy, that it approaches to the strict science of mathematics. But I fear it must be acknowledged, particularly since the great deviations which have lately taken place from the definitions and doctrines of Adam Smith, that it approaches more nearly to the sciences of morals and politics.
>
> *Thomas Malthus* (1827: 2)

## 1

Economics has travelled a great distance since 1776; whether entirely in a desirable direction is another matter. It might seem a preposterous possibility that there are respects in which Adam Smith's outlook and approach to economic analysis are superior to those which have resulted from more than two centuries of subsequent development in the discipline. But there are reasons why progress *in all respects* is not guaranteed in this field. In the social sciences, the marketplace of ideas cannot be relied upon to ensure that only fruitless ideas are cast aside. One cannot confidently assume that the state of economic science – say, as embodied in the consensus of the academic literature of the most recent twenty years – captures all that is worthy of preservation in prior economic thought. In considering the prehistory of Smith's conception of political economy in its relation to 'nature', in section 2.3.3, we suggested that the eighteenth-century science-of-man project, to the extent that it aspired to a social science of a kind with natural science, was partly ill-conceived. There are *qualitative* differences between the social sciences and (much of) the natural sciences which no amount of intellectual progress will ever eliminate.

Economics by its very nature is always and everywhere vulnerable to ideological corruption or capture. As a scientific endeavour, it is almost uniquely subject to a kind of pincer movement which is a continual threat to its integrity. On the one hand, it deals with the distribution of material resources among humans, a subject close to the hearts of those with material interests, and power; on the other, its doctrines are generally not subject, in any straightforward manner, to the discipline of compellingly evident facts. This combination makes the discipline extremely attractive for, and very vulnerable to, such corruption and capture. If we observe two chemists, one with Left political views and one with Right views, we do not really think this information is pertinent to the scientific status of their respective intellectual work as chemists (though it may influence the problems to which each chooses to devote his or her efforts). But if we observe two economists with similarly divergent political views, we are far more likely to think this relevant to the status of their intellectual work, even if that is not inevitably so. The point to be emphasized is that in the main the socio-political beliefs of natural scientists don't matter to the scientific status of their work; they do to the work of economists. This is not merely, or even primarily, a matter of economists consciously pursuing ideological purposes in their work. It is due also to socio-political values influencing the work of social scientists, in ways which are irrelevant to most of natural science.

In social science, there is not a strict independence between the beliefs of the scientific observer and the behaviour of the phenomena constituting the domain of inquiry. The theories can influence the phenomena.[1] The capacity of theories about the social world to influence behaviour in part hinges on human values being shaped by human beliefs about the objective structure of the relevant world – the structure of society, economy, polity, and so on. Our beliefs as to what is desirable can hardly be independent of our beliefs as to what are feasible or possible states of the world. To take a substantial example, and one pertinent to the contrast between Adam Smith and modern economics, what is possible and desirable *vis-à-vis* the distribution of income between wages and non-wage income can hardly be independent of our beliefs about what are the feasible distributional outcomes, in the kind of mixed capitalist economy in which we live. One could, on the one hand, believe that there is a unique competitive equilibrium distributional outcome under those conditions (the conventional view, associated with marginalist theory); or on the other hand, that a considerable spectrum of distributions is feasible (as does Smith). One's values concerning what distributional outcomes are desirable, and perhaps worth pursuing, in such a socio-economic framework – whether via public policy or the policies of other organizations – could hardly be independent of those beliefs.

The phenomena can also influence the social scientist. Consider again a substantial example pertinent to the difference between Smith's view and contemporary economics. Acquiescence in the particular kind of methodological individualism which is commonplace in economics – treating each individual's preferences as autonomous with respect to the preferences of others, and autonomous with respect to the socio-economic processes in which individuals engage – is surely partly symptomatic of acquiescence in a rather shallow kind of contemporary liberalism. It is no doubt also partly explained by what may be called 'methodological opportunism': convenient assumptions for generating neat results. As is evident from the preceding chapters, neither that methodological individualism, nor that kind of liberalism, is to be found in Smith. Social science is persistently prone to failures as a result of these intrinsic difficulties arising from lack of independence between the observer and the phenomena, and these failures are not necessarily systematically eliminated through time. Social science therefore is not subject to systematic intellectual progress in the same manner as the natural sciences broadly speaking. The study of the intellectual history of the social sciences teaches this cautionary lesson. We see, more easily in retrospect, the roles that prejudice, ideology and so on play in these intellectual endeavours, as well as the capacity of theories to influence behaviour. This is one reason why social science has need of an understanding of its history, in a way in which natural science does not. This is not to say that there is *no* progress. In particular, on a strictly analytical level, there most certainly is progress; for example, in the formal development of competitive price theory, from Turgot and Smith, through Ricardo and Marx, to von Neumann and Sraffa. Indeed, this kind of progress is what enabled us, in Chapters 3 and 4, to grasp certain limitations of Smith's treatment of normal prices and distribution, and of his notion of productive labour.

In relation to this issue, a recent repudiation of the postmodern attack on science is instructive: it is a defence of natural science alone.[2] It thereby throws into sharp relief the qualitative difference between natural science and social science. For in the end, the authors have a simple but compelling argument: (natural) *science works* (e.g. Gross and Levitt 1998: 112). That is compellingly true of natural science, from the technological evidence of its success, in a way that is not true of social science. In relation to that limitation of their defence to natural science, Gross and Levitt (1998: 12) report what they regard as a general university opinion:

> For decades certain assumptions about the epistemological ranking of various fields have prevailed, though rarely explicitly, among academic intellectuals. The rule of thumb has been that the hard scientists produce reliable knowledge, assembled into coherent theories. Historians, it is conceded, generate reliable factual knowledge (as long as they keep their methodological noses clean); but this is often contaminated by unprovable and bootless speculation. Economics has rigor of method; but its assumptions are serious, often fatal, oversimplifications of the real world. In the other social sciences impressionistic description and subjective hermeneutics rule, though they may come dressed in elaborate statistical costumes. The more theoretical the social scientists are, the less respect they get. Literary criticism, finally, has been looked upon as a species of highly elaborated connoisseurship, interesting and valuable, perhaps, but subjective beyond hope of redemption, and thus out of the running in the epistemological sweepstakes.

Notice the ambivalence about economics. But the very fact economics is being ranked, epistemologically, between the natural sciences and the other social sciences, suggests that economics is nevertheless being rather too generously rated. There are parts of economics not so different from literary criticism.[3]

**2**

Let us proceed however, in a spirit of optimism, in the knowledge that authentic scientific work in economics *is* possible. There is then also the issue of the demarcation of the science *vis-à-vis* human knowledge in general. Smith's understanding of the scope of political economy may be seen as symptomatic of the porous borders between the several latter-day social sciences. Scope is properly defined by reference to purpose. At first glance, from a latter-day standpoint, Smith's project – aimed at understanding production, distribution and growth, with a view to generalized high or rising consumption – might appear narrow. But ultimately, the factors relevant to that purpose embrace everything which shapes the narrowly 'economic' factors that are the proximate causes: labour productivity growth and capital accumulation. This includes, for example, political governance and the forms of legal regulation (especially property rights); the particular histories of nations for which policy is being formulated; and the 'moral sentiments' which form the social framework of norms and conventions within which production and exchange take place. (The moral sensibilities of peoples have a history too: *TMS*: 194–211, 341.) There is a legitimate and fruitful intellectual division of labour which enables a 'narrow' political economy to proceed, by taking various factors as given; but there is also a larger frame of reference pointing to the possibility of a unified science of society.

In relation to the post-Smithian demarcations between the social science 'disciplines', one may ask, is a discipline a subject matter or an intellectual method? It may be either. The modern social sciences have been divided, primarily by reference to subject matters, but also to some extent by intellectual methods, though perhaps increasingly less so in the latter respect. (Of course, ultimately, we are all obliged to have recourse to the same tools, deduction and induction – and only those.) Supposed generic analytical methods – notably, rational choice theory in general and game theory in particular – have spread across the social sciences. To that extent, in terms of discipline-as-intellectual-method, one may say that a singular 'discipline' is being practised across a range of subject-disciplines. This rational choice method could be regarded as fulfilling that hope for a unified 'science of man', to which the eighteenth century gave birth. But its methodological individualism stands in contrast to Smith's social theory. Furthermore, the political economy branch of Smith's overall social theory is constituted by subject matter not method. It is emphatically about the 'bread-and-butter', material dimension of life (cf. n. 4 below). It is not in any way a pretence to a generic theory of human behaviour as such, an idea which arose in the late-nineteenth century, with marginalism (see Chapter 1, n. 9; Chapter 2, n. 19). Put crudely, Smith might say in response to the practice of economics as a generic science of human choices as such, that economists should be busy about the proper business of economics: 'business'.

It was concluded in Chapter 5 that Smith's political economy is narrower than modern economics also in another sense: it has a more limited domain of determinate theory, is less expansive in its claims for theoretical knowledge, versus the role given to history and contingency. There is a passage of argument pertinent to the latter in a review of Kenneth Carpenter's (2002) study of the French dissemination of *WN*. The reviewer notes that there are a number of ways in which the study provides an understanding of how Smith's work was appropriated in France over time:

> One concerns the sheer nomenclature surrounding the work itself. How did French readers conceive of the WN in generic terms? What kind of a work was it? How did they perceive its purpose and scope? In fact, the answer to this question is not as easy as it may seem, and it is a mistake to assume, as is often done, that the work has always been viewed straightforwardly as a work in political economy.
>
> The earlier responses, continuing through the revolutionary period, tend to be quite flexible and unspecific in their descriptions of the field or 'science' to which Smith's work belongs. Several saw him as a general theorist of social relations.... [The] notion of Smith as a general theorist of human development and of civilized society is a recurring one in the sources Carpenter has assembled .... Sometimes, the science to which he is contributing is called that of 'political economy', sometimes it is 'social economy', and sometimes it is something else again, such as 'public economy' ....
>
> (H.C. Clark 2004: 177–8)

Smith's political economy in some respects *was* indeed all these things. In terms of modern meanings, it was an economics, a (little) sociology, some political science, and with a substantial recourse to history, but taking a psychology of human nature as more or less a datum. Clark perhaps suggests more significance for the differences of nomenclature assigned – political economy, public economy, social economy – than is warranted. But the characterization of Smith as theorist of human development captures something important about his approach to social theory: its essentially macro-historical and dynamic character. Compared to modern economics, his intellectual ambitions in this regard certainly do not appear as excessively modest. The 'expansiveness' of modern economics, especially in recent decades, is of a rather different kind: *reducing* such wider human phenomena to 'economics', in the particular narrow form of rational choice theorizing, projecting a unified social science built upon methodological individualism, in terms of autonomously constituted individuals, optimizing subject to constraints.[4]

One may say that in a substantial and significant sense political economy as understood by Smith is a different intellectual discipline to 'economics', as the latter was developed in the twentieth century, within the framework of marginalism. But there is a need for balanced judgement here, to recognize both change and continuity. There is not likely to be an 'end of history' with regard to intellectual disciplines. In the last 2,500 years, intellectual disciplines have come into being and have ceased to exist, and no doubt will continue to do so, though inertia in linguistic practices may give the impression of more continuity than there has been in fact. But there *is* also continuity, the most important element of which, making Smith's economic thought still relevant for us, is the persistence of liberal capitalism – in at least fundamental respects, the same today as it was (or was coming to be) in the late eighteenth century. One supposes that economics will always be forced, sooner or later, to return to the material substance of its traditional and primary subject matter: production, distribution, accumulation, activity levels, and so on – most particularly, in the context of mixed capitalist economies. As to the demarcations between the social sciences, one should not get too caught up in mere semantics. Does it really matter, in the end, whether something is said to be part of psychology, or sociology, or political science, rather than economics – or vice versa? But demarcations and the manner of constituting subject matters are not merely of semantic significance. Where the boundaries are drawn between the human sciences, together with the humanities – including the institutional boundaries, in terms of academic departments, schools and faculties – influences the substance and totality of the intellectual work carried out within them as a whole.

Furthermore, in the human sciences at least, intellectual methods and constructs do not simply derive from the phenomena, in a one-way process. The methods and constructs can determine the subject matter – for example, technique determining the problems and questions considered, rather than vice versa:

> Sometimes, our sciences create kinds of people that in a certain sense did not exist before. I call this 'making up people'.
>
> What sciences? The ones I shall call the human sciences, which, thus understood, include many social sciences, psychology, psychiatry and, speaking loosely, a good deal of clinical medicine. I am only pointing, for not only is my definition vague, but specific sciences should never be defined except for administrative and educational purposes. Living sciences are always crossing borders and borrowing from each other.
>
> The engines used in these sciences are engines of discovery but also engines for making up people.
>
> (Hacking 2006: 23)

This points also to the fact that in an important sense the various modern social sciences do not really demarcate mutually exclusive domains of inquiry (whether or not in some sense also collectively exhaustive). This is hardly surprising, since the dimensions of human society and human life ultimately are not so separated either. Rather, their subject matters inevitably intersect; they can even turn out to be, in many instances if not altogether, different approaches to the same phenomena. In Hacking's analogy, close to Smith's own notion of modes of understanding as 'machines' (*EPS*: 66), they are different engines for pulling the same load; they are different discoveries, or claims of discovery, in relation to the same phenomena. As already implied above, this fact is nowhere more strikingly evident within the social sciences, than from the vantage point of twentieth-century economics. More than any of the other social sciences, economics has made claims for having in its possession an 'engine' – the notion of constrained, optimizing, individual rational choice – which can pull all loads, a universal social-scientific method. From this perspective, as well as there being a difference of scope or object between Smith's political economy and modern economics, there is also a difference of theoretical approach to the same subject matter. The engines are different but not thereby incommensurable. There are also commonalities of method; for example, the central role of profit maximization in the dynamics of markets and prices.

Andrew Skinner (1996: 178–9) approvingly quotes Hutchison's (1988: 355, 370) comments that 'Smith was unwittingly led by an invisible hand to promote an end that was no part of his intention, that "of establishing political economy as a separate autonomous discipline"'; 'from an analytical point of view "the losses and exclusions which ensued after 1776 ... were [...] immense"'. It has been a key strand of argument in the preceding chapters that Smith most certainly projected political economy as a *separable* science. But an 'autonomous' economic science is inconceivable (see sec. 2.4). In the case of Smith, it is a sheer inescapable matter of fact that political economy is not autonomous; and he makes no such claim for it. On the contrary, Smithian political economy consciously and explicitly rests upon suppositions of psychology, and in its normative dimension, principles of political theory. Nor is modern economics free of logically prior suppositions. But there are profound differences between Smith and modern economics as to the manner of the separability of economic analysis. There *is* a kind of pretended 'autonomy' inherent in the marginalist approach: it is the autonomy of the individual agents of the theory, stripped of their identities as anything other than pursuers of their independently given preferences; people without characteristics as social or political actors; people without any history. If political economy had not taken this course in the latter half of the nineteenth century, it is unlikely that the other social sciences would have developed as they did either. One wonders whether sociology, for example, in at least some respects filled a vacuum resulting from the impoverishment of economic analysis. In any case, it is quite clear, in broad terms, what Smith would have thought of the results. The historian of science and historian of histories (*LRB*: 104) might even take the view that social scientists with a better sense of their own history, of the intellectual history of their disciplines, would have been less prone to some wrong turns which have occurred.[5]

## 3

The most significant substantive wrong turn was and remains the marginal productivity theory of distribution, and connected with this, the supply-side determination of economic activity levels and growth. For Smith, normal ('natural') real wage rates are an outcome of the balance of bargaining power around the labour contract, in part reflecting the balance (including persistent imbalance) between workforce growth and employment growth. (Bargaining power is central also to the behaviour of commodity *market* prices, but – given sufficient time for competition to exert its influence – they are anchored to natural or normal prices, which are independent of supply-and-demand imbalances.) If Smith had grasped the inverse functional relation between real wage rates and the profitability of capital (under given production methods for commodities[6]) – a relation certainly understood from Ricardo forward – this bargaining approach to wages would suffice to determine functional distribution as a whole; i.e. rates of profits and rents, as well as wages. But Smith imagines that at least real wages and profitability can vary independently of each other, and so, attempts unsuccessfully a separate theory of the profitability of capital. To be sure, Smith has some notion of a binding constraint on distribution.[7] But the technological constraint binding together real wage and profit rates is not perceived by him, partly because of the vexed Smithian treatment of rents.

One could respond, that as against Smith's bargaining power approach, the marginal productivity theory presupposes a spectrum of production methods for each of the several commodities produced in the economic system, at any singular point in time (in the limit, the supposition of an infinite number of production methods). Hence, one could say, it is the *absence* of this from Smith's scheme which explains his different – and by implication, special and limited – theory of distribution. In fact, it is the marginal productivity theory which turns out to be 'special': profit-maximizing choice of technique with regard to normal or competitive equilibrium prices will not generate the conventional marginalist factor demand functions, except under the condition of there being just one 'basic' commodity produced in the economic system (see n. 6 above, and for the concept of 'basics', Chapter 4, n. 24). Smith is right: competition is compatible with a range of values of the real wage, the particular outcome which emerges being a function of a range of socio-economic circumstances and forces, including institutions and history (see Aspromourgos 2009; Pivetti 1991).

For the purpose of the theory of normal prices, or competitive equilibrium prices if one prefers, once the real wage is taken as given – determined by reference to the balance of those socio-economic circumstances and forces – the normal prices are indeed magnitudes essentially independent of supply and demand fluctuations, as Smith supposes. (Over time, again as Smith supposes, normal prices will depend upon the dynamics of activity levels, via the dependence of production methods upon increasing returns and natural scarcities.) The formal price equations utilized in Chapter 4 are a simple illustration of this, with the assumption of constant physical returns to scale serving as a simplifying device, to abstract from any influence of scale upon production methods. The normal prices so defined act as the anchor for market price dynamics in response to such fluctuations, prices being drawn towards normal levels under competitive conditions. There is no need in this competitive process for the absurdity of individual preferences which are autonomous with respect to the individuals' environment – both other individuals and the processes the individuals engage in. That was correct in 1776, and remains so: the notion of the associated individuals' commodity demand functions as similarly autonomous with respect to the processes individuals engage in is an incredibly strong supposition. It is obvious that consumption changes people, just as it is obvious that individuals are socially formed, and similarly obvious that participation in markets alters character. When one contemplates the individual agents who inhabit marginalist theory, one wonders what sort of beings they are, and one is tempted to conclude that they must be gods. Abandoning commodity demand functions might be a matter for regret, if they offered any prospect of adding genuine knowledge. But as constructs grounded in psychological (alleged) data, they are bereft of any definite quantitative content, a mere pretence of exact knowledge.[8]

## 4

Accept, for the sake of argument, that distribution is determined by these kinds of socio-economic circumstances and forces. It might nevertheless seem that the concept of labour subsistence consumption is irrelevant in contemporary, developed economies, where rates of real wages, overwhelmingly, are evidently well above subsistence, in any sense of the term – and therefore also, that the concept of surplus derived from it is irrelevant. One might then further conclude that just the modern notion of net national product or income, which ignores any notion of necessary labour consumption, suffices for consideration of income distribution. It should be noted immediately that this proposition that real wages are above subsistence presupposes the empirical meaningfulness of the concept of subsistence consumption, still, and to that extent, somewhat negates the supposed inference. More substantively, a notion of conventionally determined subsistence remains operational in modern societies, broadly defined by reference to the standard of living associated with welfare systems or social security 'safety nets'. That is to say, the level and kind of consumption enabled by transfers from government to those unable to work (and lacking other private sources of income), or willing to work but unable to find work, defines the socially acceptable minimum consumption. That minimum is by no means irrelevant to the distribution of the rest of the social net product. Quite apart from the distributional implications of the means of financing such government expenditures on the poor, that socially defined minimum sets the lower bound of the wages outcomes of the employed. If, with Smith, we conceive of the outcomes of the labour contract as resulting from the balance of bargaining power between the participants, then the conventional subsistence income sets a limit to the operation of those forces, on one side. The surplus genuinely available to be distributed remains less than the net national product or income. At another level, the shifting balance of social forces within which functional income distribution is worked out can effect alteration in the socially acceptable minimum itself. In short, we cannot really now generally proceed in economic analysis as if the net national income were entirely available for 'free' disposal, like the Smithian surplus.

As to the more general question of what actually may properly be regarded, for a contemporary society, as constituting necessary inputs or necessary costs, to be deducted from gross products or income in arriving at the system's surplus product or net income, Smith's answer seems still to be largely sound. The most important qualification one must make with respect to his conception is to abandon the supposition that government production or expenditures are (almost) entirely surplus to requirements. This is so even if one puts aside the government-provided infrastructure of property rights and their enforcement, as Smith does, which are obviously essential to the very existence of the 'private' economy, which Smith of course does not deny. Even the most ardent opponent of government's role in economy and society can hardly deny that, in fact, some part of what it provides much more directly enters into the production of commodities in an essential way, or contributes to the subsistence of the population. This is true, for example, of large parts of education and health services, transport infrastructure and welfare payments.[9] Wages and labour consumption are certainly in part still necessary costs or inputs, as well as part surplus, as indeed they were for Smith; and land-rents and pure profits remain, again as they were for Smith, strictly surplus, putting aside the subsistence consumption of the recipients (on 'pure' profits, see chapter 4, n. 87). The one remaining significant point with regard to the content of necessary cost versus surplus is the matter of entrepreneurial incomes, under competitive conditions, which, as was seen above (sec. 4.4.2), were treated as necessary costs in Smith's analysis of tax incidence. It is vital to keep in mind that the entrepreneurial activities Smith thereby treats as necessary inputs to production are those associated with entrepreneurial incomes which persist under conditions of free competition. It would include, for example, the risk-bearing of the self-employed. There are certainly extensive elements of incomes along these lines, which should be treated as necessary costs: for example, the margins between paid wage work and incomes of the self-employed as necessary to enabling or at least inducing certain kinds of economic activities, necessarily undertaken by entrepreneurs in the generic sense (cf. Kurz and Salvadori 2005: 429–31).

The significance of the social surplus for economic growth is that it constitutes the finite upper bound upon net investment: if the entire surplus product took the form of new investment or additions to the capital stock, rather than above-necessary consumption, net accumulation would be maximized for any given gross product. Equivalently, this would entail all surplus income being devoted to net saving – all income over and above that required to satisfy necessary consumption and induce necessary entrepreneurial activity (as well as that required to replace inputs used up in the annual production cycle). (In Smith's framework, functional distribution could influence net saving if rates of saving out of income differ across different functional categories, but see also Chapter 4, n. 62.) Beyond these propositions, there is also the question of the direction of causation in growth dynamics, as between the growth of aggregate demand on the one hand and the growth of supply and production capacity on the other; or equivalently, causation between aggregate investment and aggregate saving.

Here, one must depart from Smith in one particular, but fundamental, respect. He sees the growth process as being driven by those three fundamental psychological parameters which he understands as generating output and consumption growth per capita – in terms of their role with respect to saving (identified with capital accumulation), productivity growth (division of labour) and of course, competition itself (see pp. 166–7) – the most fundamental of these three for Smith being the desire for material self-betterment. The element of this vision which most definitely needs to be put aside is the notion of saving as determining – indeed, synonymous with – accumulation. His intuitions of a relatively autonomous role for demand (revisited immediately below) are to be preferred. Keynes's approach to the coordination of aggregate demand and supply, or of investment and saving, with the former determining the latter, is superior to that of Smith; and a synthesis of Smith's approach to distribution and prices, and Keynes's demand-led approach to long-run activity levels is entirely viable (see Garegnani 1978–9; Eatwell and Milgate 1983; Kurz 1990).

In relation to this conclusion, recall from section 5.2.3 that Smith's endorsement of limited state intervention in economic activity is based on two postulates, at least with regard to the narrowly economic aspects of the issue: policies discriminatory as between particular commodities or activities, in general, do not lead to a better allocation of society's capital; and the more unobtrusive postulate, policy interventions can only decrease the overall capital stock, or leave it unchanged, they cannot increase the capital stock. Something akin to the same result is derived in latter-day marginalist theory, but there, from an explicit supply-side theory of full resource utilization under competitive conditions, with the growth rate regulated by the exogenous growth of the supply of primary factors of production (notably, labour). This supply-side theory of activity levels is just another aspect of the marginal productivity theory of distribution, since the latter involves the adaptation of factor demands to relatively autonomous factor supplies, in association with equilibrium 'factor prices'. Government regulation, expenditures and taxes thus can only redirect resources, not expand activity levels. Even though marginalism thus arrives at a somewhat similar result, this is not Smith's theory. His position is more a mere assertion, and one which he himself undermines in other parts of his analysis (sec. 4.4.1). The compatibility of Smith's approach to distribution and prices and Keynes's approach to activity levels, in enabling a synthesis of the two, thereby also can repair the absence in Smith of a determinate account of the coordination of demands and supplies in the context of growth dynamics. This is a route to reconciling that which is enduringly worthwhile in Smith's system, with Keynes's sound repudiation of the supply-side doctrine of marginalism and his positive alternative approach to activity levels, built around the principle of effective demand. Of course, the possibility thereby opened up, that policy can favourably influence activity levels and growth, does not in and of itself prove that scepticism as to the competence and good intentions of government in so proceeding is spurious.

These considerations with respect to growth and the question of the relative autonomy of (input) supply factors versus (output) demand factors in growth and accumulation dynamics, remind that – however much his theory may differ from marginalism – Smith has his own psychological postulates, taken as given for the purposes of economic analysis in general, and accumulation and growth in particular. While autonomous individual preferences, in the manner of marginalist theory, are in no respects data for Smith's political economy, one may ask: how do the data he actually has recourse to, including, but not only, his psychological parameters, compare with the data of marginalist theory? The three fundamental data of the latter are technology (the set of methods available for producing the various commodities), the resource 'endowments' of the individuals in the economy, and the individuals' preferences – the individuals then being supposed as choosing efficient means for the maximum satisfaction of those preferences (see Chapter 1, n. 9). With regard to the first of the two non-psychological data, technology, Smith certainly does not treat production methods as exogenous to economic phenomena in general. The dynamic increasing returns associated with division of labour are sufficient evidence of that, innovation being endogenous to competition. Nevertheless, Smith is prepared to take production methods as given for certain definite purposes or particular parts of theory: natural prices are posited on given production methods.

With regard to endowments, in the analysis of growth Smith certainly treats of situations in which stocks of resources are given at a point in time, with the allocation of those resources between alternative uses entering into the determination of the path of the economy into the future, and hence its 'reproduction' (whether expanding, stationary or contracting). But this is just to defer to an evident fact, that at any point in time, *everything* can be taken as given. There is no notion in Smith's political economy of taking the stocks of available production inputs as data, for the purposes of the theory of normal prices and income distribution. In that part of his theory, the quantities employed of capital goods (including at least a considerable part of consumption by wage-earners), workers and lands are treated as endogenous to production methods and effectual demands. While Smith provides no genuine account of how commodity demands and supplies as a whole are coordinated, or equivalently, of the coordination of aggregate saving and investment, in both the analysis of market price dynamics and in the analysis of division of labour, commodity or market demands appear as the autonomous element, with commodity supplies adapting to demands. (See also the issue of capital destruction in sec. 5.2.3.) Such a conception implies that, if prices achieved their normal levels, with market supplies balancing effectual demands, then the quantities of inputs in use for the purposes of production and supply of commodities would ultimately be caused or induced by commodity demands. The Cantillonian element in Smith's thought, concerning labour supply (Chapter 4, n. 85), is just the most striking expression of this: 'the demand for men, like that for any other commodity, necessarily regulates the production of men' (*WN*: 98). One can suggest that Smith should be just as happy with the proposition that the demand for capital, like the demand for any commodity, regulates the production of capital – not least, since wages are part of capital.

How do Smith's psychological data compare with the latter-day marginalist psychological data of given individual preferences which are efficiently pursued, in terms of individuals' choosing their most preferred outcome subject to any given constraints? With regard to demand for consumption goods, no such notions are entailed or implied by Smith's treatment of effectual demands, though he certainly recognizes the existence of substitutability in consumption. On the other hand, the tendency of prices and remunerations to owners of inputs to converge towards uniformity for homogeneous commodities or inputs, strongly implies a fundamental rationality at a more elementary and *objective* level, across (if not all then many) participants in market exchange. These kinds of processes do not in any way depend upon the peculiar form of methodological individualism which is embodied in marginalism, in terms of autonomous individual preferences. They proceed simply from an unwillingness of individuals to pay more as purchasers, or to be paid less as sellers, than is on offer elsewhere in the market; minimizing cost or maximizing revenue, with respect to observable magnitudes.

With regard to the optimizing behaviour supposed in marginalist theory, this might appear to bear a similarity to the Smithian pursuit of self-interest, but in fact, caution is in order on this front too. On the one hand, the marginalist conception of the efficient pursuit of preference satisfaction may be conceived of in abstract terms, as involving desires which are not necessarily connected with one's own pleasures at all: desires that one's neighbours be happy, or that the material condition of poor people far away be bettered. In this conception, the treatment of the pursuit of individual preferences, in one sense, certainly acquires great generality; but in another sense it is thereby emptied of content: it can say nothing more about human behaviour than the rather empty formal hypothesis, that people pursue their purposes, whatever these purposes may be, efficiently. Such a proposition, to put it mildly, is not easily susceptible to empirical test (cf. Sippel 1997). Apart from the supposition of efficient choice of means, it is little more than a statement that people do what they do. On the other hand, the marginalist conception may be conceived of in terms of preferences directed to individual pleasures or satisfactions which are independent of others' outcomes. (Certainly, to deliver any definite results, the marginalist theory needs to head in this direction: allowing individual preferences which depend upon the outcomes achieved by others will wreak havoc with the theory.) This comes closer, in a sense, to the psychology underpinning Smith's economics. The notion of bettering one's material condition, as the bedrock purpose to which self-regard is directed in economic behaviour, is a notion of material self-regard. But even here, Smith's individuals in commercial society are most certainly not selfish automatons: they take care of themselves, in a framework of sociable and socially constructed conduct, and law; they pursue gain, as owners of labour, stock and land. Their psychology is more substantively construed than the abstract preferences of marginalist 'rational economic man'.

**5**

Hugh Blair wrote to Smith shortly after publication of *WN*, predicting that the book 'in some degree' would become 'the Commercial Code of Nations' (*Corr*: 188). The phrase 'in some degree' was well chosen. In fact, even after the neo-liberal successes of the late-twentieth century, the socio-economic role of the State – and in particular, the shares of government revenues and outlays in GDP – surely remain way beyond what Smith would have countenanced in 1776. They show little sign of being rolled back even by governments of supposed economic-liberal persuasion. Even for those developed economies with among the lowest government revenues and outlays as shares of GDP, like the UK and USA, around one third of the national 'revenue' and 'produce' is at the disposal of government. Though the market as an institution for decentralized allocation has certainly been vindicated, the public sector and transfer payments continue to function as very significant redistributive mechanisms in all economies, together with collective provision of a considerable range of outputs, especially tertiary goods and infrastructure. One should be clear also that 'market' and 'State' can be a false dichotomy: considerable government outlays are channeled through private decisions and markets. If anything, the tendency for at least salient elements of tertiary goods to naturally absorb a larger proportion of incomes and expenditures as income per capita rises, favours further growth of public provision of such services (notably, education and health), if not by direct provision then at least by public funding support.

The public sector and the share of government revenue in GDP have been able to grow to such an extent, partly due to the increase over the long term in the social surplus per capita – the truly *net* national income which is available for free disposal, and hence, susceptible of a range of distributions and allocations, and therefore capable also of redistribution. (We say 'partly', because of the earlier-mentioned fact that part of public sector outlays is funding necessary production inputs or necessary consumption.) One can say that the capacity of the public sector to expand is in part due to Smith's technology optimism being vindicated (see Chapter 3, n. 50). The openness of distribution of the surplus to 'contest' is pertinent to both the balance between the relative sizes of the private and public sectors, and the distribution of income within the private sector. The soundness of Smith's approach to wage levels, as not uniquely determined by reference to competitive conditions, means that (within bounds) the determination of income distribution lies in the realm of freedom not necessity. That is to say, a *spectrum* of distributive outcomes is possible in a competitive capitalist economy; there is no unique, and therefore necessary, distributive outcome associated with the working out of competition. Distribution can therefore be a subject of choice, of policies, potentially conflicting policies, of workers and employers, as well as governments; and it can be shaped by the contingencies of particular histories.

In a mixed capitalist economy the distribution which has to be resolved by the whole range of pertinent economic, social, political and institutional forces and circumstances is not only that between wages, pure property income and entrepreneurial incomes. It concerns also the distribution between the sum of private incomes in all these functional categories and the tax share of GDP. Hence one sees in Smith's treatment of taxation, how the burden of taxes might be shifted, but must ultimately fall (only) on some or other of the surplus components of private incomes (sec. 4.4.2). This illustration in relation to taxation and distribution points to the fact that a surplus which is appropriable in the form of taxation is also, in principle, appropriable in the form of a redistribution between private income categories. A shift in bargaining power or in wider forces regulating the distribution between real wages and pure profits could lead to a redistribution from pure profits to higher surplus real wages. And since real wages are above customary subsistence and thereby include a share of the social surplus, just as wages can incur tax incidence, so a shift in bargaining power can enable the owners of capital and/or entrepreneurs to increase their share of the surplus via lower real wages (or lower growth of real wages if per capita productivity is growing). In short, a taxable surplus is a contestable surplus.

In relation to policy, there is another aspect of the production and distribution of the social surplus which should be recalled here. It was merely touched upon in Chapter 4 (because Smith does not really engage with it, at this level): the depletion of non-renewable natural resources are properly to be regarded as contributing *negative* elements to the set of commodity flows making up the surplus in any time period (Chapter 4, n. 31). This truth acquires more pressing practical significance now, since the sustainability of the modes of human use and depletion of natural resources has become an issue of pressing concern. Taking this problem together with the levels of per capita private consumption which have been achieved in the most developed economies, one should contemplate amending Smith's formula for the normative purpose of political economy to: advancing the per capita consumption *or leisure* of the bulk of the population. That is to say, taking into account the sustainability or otherwise of rising material consumption per capita, for all human beings, one might conclude that the purpose of economic society should be enunciated in terms of higher labour productivity being realized in either higher material consumption, or lower average time worked, or a combination of the two. In the limit, beyond some level of consumption per capita, any continuing labour productivity growth could be realized in average per capita hours worked falling roughly at the same rate. The question of the sustainability of the natural environment connects with the question of the distribution of command over resources. Could every human being on the planet today live as average Americans or Europeans do, in terms of the resulting natural resource depletion? The course of economic development and rising per capita consumption in populous poorer nations like China and India may give a tangible answer to that question. The contest for primary resources which could result would certainly give concrete expression to prevailing inequalities.

## 6

The classical political economy which Smith first fashioned into a satisfying general system of inquiry or science remains in broad terms a sound approach to the analysis of mixed capitalist economies, centred on the dynamics of economic development. Of course the substantive content Smith gave to it is imperfect and incomplete; it was so then, and is more so now. The treatment of prices and distribution requires the benefit of a better account of functional distribution, an account pioneered by Ricardo and others, and brought to a certain degree of completion by Sraffa and von Neumann. The treatment of demand/supply coordination in the context of growth dynamics is rendered coherent by incorporating Keynes's approach to outputs, activity levels and growth, whereby a relatively autonomous role is able to be given to elements of aggregate demands. The modesty of theoretical claims, and associated role for history and institutions, is also a Smithian methodological temper worthy of emulation. Likewise, at least in principle, the strong sense of economics as a policy science aimed at human material betterment – in Smith, combined with moderation concerning the application of theory to particular historical circumstances – is a desirable temper for an economic science today, or any day. One hesitates a little on this last point because one sees the capacity for normative economics since 1776 to end up serving the material interests and values of particular groups, consciously or otherwise. But of course, this was true in 1776 and earlier as well, and Smith was very aware of it. That awareness made him thoroughly realistic, but it did not make him a pessimist. In the end, the only *intellectual* counterbalances to such dangers are a thorough-going commitment to empiricism and objectively based theory, combined with open public conversation and contest around the issue of socio-economic values.

Up to a point, the modern project of an economic science, viewed from its origins – notably its connection with statecraft and Enlightenment – can be seen to be *functional* for modern society. In this regard it is not like literature and literary criticism. We may be very glad to have had the benefit of Shakespeare; but it is not the case that if he had not existed, we would have to invent him. Shakespeare is a kind of 'luxury', inessential to the functioning of our societies. But *what* of economics is functional? Not the whole edifice and activity of contemporary academic economics. The 'lower' levels are functional; for example, the conceptual frameworks and methods for the analysis of large volumes of economic data, essential to the running of complex decentralized societies, essential to both public and private governance in contemporary societies. So also are the fundamental theoretical constructions which enable realistic understanding of the system behaviour of modern economies (e.g. Keynes, Leontief, Sraffa), and are capable of application to policy. Many parts of the 'higher' reaches of (especially theoretical) economics are little different from literature and literary criticism in their functional significance. These activities are 'luxuries' (or unproductive labour), living off the essential role of academic economics in providing the 'lower-level' economics for professional education.

There is also a dark side. In section 2.1.3, the role of state building in the genesis of political economy as a distinct science was noted. But this kind of functionalism of economics with respect to political society is a two-edged sword. Its 'usefulness' includes, or may easily become, not just an organon for practical organization and socio-economic management at a technical level, but also, provision of ideological support for dominant interests.

One could conclude that economics is so difficult to do properly, and so vulnerable to corruption, that one should abandon it. But while this option is of course open to individuals, it is not really available to humankind, and to societies and polities. Apart from the functionalism mentioned immediately above, 'grand' socio-economic theory – in the manner of Smith, Marx, Walras and Keynes – is an almost inevitable aspiration of the species. We seek a unified explanation of the structure of human society, commonly with a view to changing it in the pursuit of definite and worthy ends, 'policy' in the largest sense. The economic dimension will always be a vital, indeed primary, element of that. These truths, Smith well understood. His efforts and success at such grand theory are what make him of enduring interest to us.

# Notes

## 1 Introduction

1 This is from a manuscript in the Sraffa Papers, Trinity College, Cambridge (folder D3/12/4: folio 14), quoted in Pasinetti (2001: 153).

2 In the quotation from Thomas Pownall which serves as the epigraph to Chapter 2, he speaks of *WN* as containing the principles of the laws of motion 'by which the system of the human community is framed'; but our choice of term was not inspired from that source. Nor should our use of the term 'framing' evoke in the reader any connection with a more recent sense: 'framing effect' as '[a]n effect of the description, labelling, or presentation of a problem on responses to it'; in particular, the same individual making different choices in two situations, 'although the two frames [i.e. situations] are merely different ways of describing the same problem' (Colman 2006: 295).

3 It is of no moment, precisely how many concepts, twelve or more, these key terms and fundamental elements make up. The notions of supply and of demand are conceptually separable; but their interest here is in relation to their joint role in the explanation of price behaviour. The notion of gross revenue virtually entails the notion of net revenue, and vice versa; so that they are quite inextricably connected in a singular meaning. The notions of capital and of productive labour are closely bound together in Smith's thought, but they are not so inseparably linked in general.

4 An exercise such as this, comprehensively accounting for every use Smith makes of various terms, is enabled by the technology of machine-searchable text. That technology is not strictly necessary for undertaking such a task; but the endeavour would be impracticable without it. The most salient example in Smith's case is his very prolific use of 'nature' (and variants thereof). Machine-searchable text enables one to examine every one of the thousands of instances of Smith's use of this term, with sufficient speed, that by the time one examines the last use, one is able still to retain in one's head the meaning of the first use. The reader should be in no doubt, however, that even with this machine assistance, these processes of inquiry are very considerable tasks (and many more than the ones reported here have been undertaken in the course of this study).

5 Merton (1993) and Merton and Barber (2004) are interesting and intensive studies, tracing the history of just one phrase and one term respectively. (They also bear a close connection to each other: see Robert Merton's 'Afterword' in the latter work, the main text of which dates from 1958.) The former concerns an idea most commonly associated with Isaac Newton – 'If I have seen farther, it is by standing on the shoulders of giants' (Merton 1993: xx) – but in fact dating from at least as early as the twelfth century. (The 1993 edition contains the text of the first edition, evidently verbatim, plus Umberto Eco's foreword for the 1991 Italian edition, Merton's preface and Denis Donoghue's afterword to the 1985 edition, and a 1993 'Postface' by Merton.) As it happens, the concept of 'serendipity', insofar as it concerns unintended outcomes, has some kinship with an aspect of Smith's thought (see Chapter 5, n. 15).

6 As against the notion that language is the primary 'reality' of intellectual history, Thompson (2004: 127) sensibly concludes:

> The contrary presumption, that language is purely a reflection of material reality, is also severely flawed, if not so drastically. Rather, there is ... a dialectic between them – they work to constitute each other, and that is how historical change and development occurs, but non-linguistic reality is the primary term of the relationship.

Smith himself had more than a passing interest in language, and a review of Samuel Johnson's *Dictionary* (1755) was almost his first published work (Smith 1755; cf. *EPS*: 257–60, for one slight earlier publication). There is also Smith's 'Considerations Concerning the First Formation of Languages' (1761). In introducing this work, Bryce (1983: 25) sums up 'Smith's vision of the organic connection between thinking and speaking' in the following terms: 'Language and thought are generated together .... He ... had learned ... to see "parts of speech", not as dead terms in school grammar, but as operations of the human intellect, and "grammar" itself as the image of logic.' Furthermore, Smith's no longer extant 1751 dissertation for the Chair of Logic and Rhetoric at the University of Glasgow was entitled *De Origine Idearum* (Bryce 1983: 23).

7 The corpus of writings is substantial but not huge. Smith made a considered decision to have most of his private papers destroyed (wise perhaps, from the standpoint of his own interest, but unhelpful to intellectual historians). Stewart (1811: 327–8) gives a detailed account of the events leading up the manuscript writings being 'committed to the flames' at about the time of Smith's death, and offers suggestions as to motive. He also points out that Smith had formed this intention many years earlier, reproducing a 1773 letter to Hume expressing that desire. (The corrected text of the latter is at *Corr*: 168.) Ross (1995: 404–6) conjectures on the contents of the destroyed manuscripts, their relation to the extant writings, and also Smith's possible motives.

8 *The Glasgow Edition of the Works and Correspondence of Adam Smith, with Supplementary Texts*, Charlottesville, VA: Intelex Corporation, 2002 (Past Masters: Humanities Databases, Full Text Scholarly Editions), ISBN 1–50785–339–8. The supplementary texts included are Ross (1995), Skinner (1996) and Mizuta (2000). While the CD-ROM has been employed as a research tool, all quotations are taken from the physical text of the Glasgow Edition (and likewise for the supplementary texts).

9 The marginalist theory arose in the latter part of the nineteenth century and continues to dominate the mainstream of academic economic thinking today. 1871 is a symbolic date for representing its advent, since two of the three figures commonly regarded as the founders published key works that year (William Stanley Jevons 1871; Carl Menger 1871; the third is Léon Walras 1874, the second volume of which appeared in 1877). Alfred Marshall (1890) was also important, for giving the theory an apparently more operational character, thereby greatly contributing to its gaining acceptance in that 'Marshallian' form. In the early twentieth century, that theory crystallized into a core conception of 'scarcity', understood as unlimited individual human wants confronting finite resources for the satisfaction of those desires.

Marginalism took most clear and striking theoretical form in the shape of general equilibrium theories, in which the three fundamental data of the theory are: *technology*, constituting the methods available for producing commodities with inputs of produced commodities and other resources ('factors of production'); the *preferences* of the individuals in the economy (individuals' preferences being assumed autonomous with respect to those of others, and autonomous with respect to the processes and endogenous variables of the theory); and the quantities of resources available for use and their distribution among the individuals ('*endowments*'). Under competitive conditions, these data might then generate well-defined supply and demand functions for commodities and factors of production – on the further supposition that individuals choose efficient means for the maximum satisfaction of their preferences. This, it was at least hoped, would enable determination of a meaningful set of 'equilibrium' prices, outputs and quantities of factors employed – by reference to conditions of generalized market-clearing (balance or equilibrium between aggregate supplies and demands, for all commodities and factors). The term 'marginalism' reflects the optimization conditions associated with the equilibria of the theory, embodied in marginal equalities or inequalities.

## 2 The science of wealth

1 In all variants of 'economy', Smith's (Glasgow Edition) texts employ the digraph, *oe*; but not consistently the ligature, *œ*. Generally, in *WN* the ligature is employed, unless the term (including variants) appears capitalized. *WN* (678; quoted below in relation to J.-B. Say) and *WN* (679, 755), are the only counter-examples of *oeconomy*; *WN* (663) has an instance where the ligature is employed in the capitalized form, *Œconomy*. In *TMS* the ligature does not appear at all, and this is likewise true of the few references in *EPS*, *LJB*, *edWN* and *Corr*. Here, we quote all the terms precisely as they appear in the Glasgow Edition text. Note also, in relation to the *WN* (428) definition of political economy, that when Smith speaks of the 'sovereign' this need not denote merely the monarch. He comments with respect to England: 'the king is not here the sovereign. The sovereign power … is lodged in the king and Parliament together' (*LJA*: 311; also *LJB*: 433).

2 In the fourth edition of his *Essay on the History of Civil Society*, Adam Ferguson (1773: 242) defers to Smith's forthcoming work as 'a theory of national œconomy, equal to what has ever appeared on any subject of science whatsoever'. The sense of political economy as a policy regime can be seen at *WN* (372): 'the great object of the political œconomy of every country, is to encrease the riches and power of that country' (also *WN*: 674, 679 – and 755, where the sense could be theory, policy regime, or both). And on the mercantilist policy regime in particular as a political economy: it 'being established … that wealth consisted in gold and silver … it … became the great object of political œconomy to diminish … importation … and to increase … exportation' (*WN*: 450; also 255, 430, 434–5). Mercantilism and Physiocracy (not his terms) are the two systems of political economy Smith evaluates in *WN*, Book IV, the latter much more briefly (*WN*: 663). The mercantilist literature is distinguished, at least in Smith's view, by a preoccupation with policy aimed at balance of foreign trade surpluses, and thereby, accumulation of gold and silver (see sec. 2.2.2). Physiocracy is a vitally important mid-eighteenth-century school of economic thought, with which Smith has a much more positive relation.

3 This English text is provided by the editor (p. 312n), from Stewart's *Collected Works*, and is supposed to be a translation of Bacon, from *De Augmentis Scientiarum*, Book VIII, Chapter iii. (Stewart's actual 1811 text provides just the Latin.) But the precise passage from Bacon's text that Stewart intends is unclear.

4 This comment presumes that Millar would identify the content of the fourth part of the lectures, as he describes it, with political economy as a whole. Perhaps he would not.

5 The quotation from *EPS* (51) in the previous paragraph is a continuation of this quotation ('the study of Philosophy, of that science which pretends'). Smith's text continues: 'they [mankind] pursue this study for its own sake, as … good in itself, without regarding its tendency to procure them the means of many other pleasures'.

6 Further references to science occur at *TMS* (19–20, 125, 268, 272); *WN* (143, 149–50, 761, 763–4, 773, 780–1, 796, 812); *EPS* (71, 77, 80, 85, 97, 107, 121–4, 185–6, 205, 212, 245–9); *LRB* (113); *LJA* (216, 349); *fA* (582); *Corr* (70, 176–7).

7 Further to Smith's conception of science, see Becker (1961) and Lindgren (1969) who emphasize the significance of Smith's theory of language for his conception of science, interpreted as 'conventionalistic'. Skinner (1996: 21–3, 25–47, incorporating work first published in the 1970s) reads the same Smith writings more moderately, as

just allowing for a subjective element in scientific theorizing. See also Vivenza (2001: 9–40), and on Smith's identification of philosophy and science, Raphael (1985: 91–3). Redman (1997: 207–58) provides a nuanced view of the extent to which Smith's social science can be regarded as 'Newtonianism'. Montes (2003b; reproduced in Montes 2004: 130–64) as well argues against the notion of Smith's following a Newtonian model of scientific inquiry. Both Redman and Montes raise the further question of how 'Newtonian' Newton was.

8 The editor comments:

> though he is speaking of the household only in the beginning of the sentence, Aristotle also includes the polis at the end. 'Economy' ... though it literally means only household management, is treated by him in its political as well as its domestic aspect ....
>
> (p. 21n; see also 22, n. E)

And further: *oikonomia*

> dealt partly with household management ... and partly with public economy or state finance.... It is a theory of the ways in which households and cities can properly use the means at their disposal for the better living of a good life.
>
> (p. lvi; cf. Theocarakis 2006: 10, n. 2)

See also Pomeroy (1994: 41, and *passim*): 'The polis was a community of oikoi rather than of individual citizens'. Screpanti and Zamagni (2005: 30) assert, without citing any specific authority or original sources, that 'as early as in the first century BC, the term *politikè oikonomìa* was already used by some Epicurean philosophers'.

9 See also the discussion of 'policy' in section 5.2. With regard to *economy* in Latin coming to represent a generic notion of management or organization, as indicated in *OED* and mentioned by Groenewegen (1987c), the former gives examples of the economy of a poem or building, animal economy and vegetable economy. For our purposes here, the most interesting and significant instance of such wider notions of economy as management or organization is the concept of *the economy of nature* (taken up further in sec. 2.3.4) – not least, due to Smith's own use of it (see sec. 2.1.1).

10 For a particularly positive assessment of the significance of Montchrétien's achievement, see Magnusson (1994: 178–80, 183–5). Schumpeter (1954: 167–8) dismisses him with the judgement that using the term political economy in his book title was 'his only merit'. For another view see also Bridel (1987).

11 It has been suggested that 'Enlightenment' is not a term of the eighteenth century, in any European language, and apparent synonyms from that century (*le siècle des lumières*, *die aufklärung*) do not necessarily coincide in meaning with the latter-day concept, a product of the late nineteenth century (J. Clark 2004). (But 'Light' as a metaphor for knowledge or truth has ancient roots.) Be that as it may, *enlightenment* is a pertinent and useful term to describe a set of early modern intellectual developments across various parts of Europe. Commonly the term is employed to refer to eighteenth-century rationalism and the associated rise of scientific social and historical theory (e.g. Thompson 2004: 115–16, 130). There is no reason to get overly excited about naming conventions; but it is reasonable also, at another level, to view the scientific revolution of the previous century or so (most notably associated with the names of Galileo Galilei, René Descartes and Newton) as forming a singular intellectual development with the eighteenth-century Enlightenment, in relation to the deployment of human reason to advance human well-being. Certainly the programme of Bacon and of the Royal Society is about human enlightenment in the generic sense, aimed at the improvement of human *material* life in particular, via technology and science. Robertson (2005) rightly emphasizes the place of material betterment in the Enlightenment view of social progress, providing a rich account of the intellectual

background to the formation of political economy in Scotland and Naples. See also the excellent and balanced overview of Kramnick (1995), who dates the Enlightenment era from the 1680s to the 1790s, thereby including the publications of John Locke and Newton, a part expression of his emphasis on the place of natural science and technology in the Enlightenment (pp. x–xiii). (Kramnick also includes in his anthology a selection from Bacon.) Furthermore, those intellectual developments across the two centuries can be regarded as constituting the advent of modernity, at the level of self-conscious thought (cf. Thompson 2004: 115–17, 132; Aspromourgos 2001: 64). Roncaglia (2005: 18–23) provides a thoughtful general account of the intellectual background to the formation of political economy as a distinct science, suggesting also the significance of Niccolò Machiavelli. Winch (1971: 5–26) remains a good, balanced account of issues in interpretation of the rise of political economy in the mid-eighteenth century, as is Groenewegen (2002b).

12 To be clear, the conclusion embraced here is that the 'birth' of 'political economy' is to be located in the seminal modern efforts towards the self-conscious construction of a distinct and separable science and/or art of politico-economic understanding and policy. (It is in this sense that Hume should be understood when he writes: 'Trade was never esteemed an affair of state till the last century' (Miller 1985: 88). Miller follows the 1777 edition of Hume's *Essays*, first published in late 1741, with some additions.) This of course is not without its own prehistory and antecedents, as briefly indicated above. It is also unsurprising that wherever human written records are to be found, there will be found accounts of 'economic' matters, a subject in which a material being such as humankind, is likely always to take a close interest. But this does not justify making economic science coeval with human written records concerning material or economic matters. Not going this far, Lowry (1987: 11, 23–4) is nevertheless an example of the view that the ancient Greeks, in some definite and substantial sense, invented economic analysis. Roll (1961: 31), in a more general history of economics, is another example, suggesting Aristotle is in some sense the founder of economics ('the first analytical economist'). It is better to regard the character and significance of economic ideas in ancient thought as constituting a *different* intellectual project. (A view along these lines has been put most vigorously by M.I. Finley. See Chapter 3, n. 76.) At the same time, mere semantic differences in articulation of the significance of ancient thought should not be mistaken for differences of substance, as to the economic content of the ancient writings.

13 The fuller title is given in n. 20 below. Quotations are from the translation by Meek (1962), principally from the 1764 edition. He indicates also that this work by Mirabeau involved close collaboration with Quesnay, who probably provided many of the leading ideas (Meek 1962: 37n). Quesnay undoubtedly was the key figure in the eighteenth-century French formation of political economy, as Smith himself implies (*WN*: 678–9), at least prior to Turgot.

14 These quotations are from Meek's translation of 'General Maxims for the Economic Government of an Agricultural Kingdom', in *Physiocratie* ... (Quesnay 1767–8; see n. 20 below). The fuller title is given in n. 20 below. See also, from the same 'Maxims', the comments on agricultural 'reproduction' and 'good administration in political economy' (Meek 1962: 243–4). Elsewhere in the primary Physiocratic documents translated in the same work, there are also forms of appeal, direct or indirect, to 'economic science' (Meek 1962: 154, 183n, 204, 211, 213), in one instance, acknowledging the difficulty of resolving confusion 'in a science which is still little known and obscured by private interests and dominant prejudices' (Meek 1962: 230). The 1767–8 statement quoted in the text (from Meek 1962: 232) is itself a variant of a statement at the end of the 'Maxims' accompanying the 1764 version of the *Tableau*, in the context of a concluding comment on 'the true principles of the science of economic administration' (*les vrais principes de la science du Gouvernement économique*):

> This science is not confused here with the trivial and specious science of financial operations whose subject-matter is only the money stock of the nation and the monetary movements resulting from traffic in money, in which credit, the lure of interest, etc., as in the case of gambling, bring about nothing but a sterile circulation which only in exceptional circumstances can be of any benefit. It is in a knowledge of the true sources of wealth, and of the means of increasing and perpetuating them, that the science of the economic administration of a kingdom consists.
>
> Economic administration opens up the sources of wealth; wealth attracts men; men and wealth make agriculture prosper, expand trade, give new life to industry, and increase and perpetuate wealth.
>
> (Kuczynski and Meek 1972: 21–2, '3rd edn')

On the significance of the circular or reproduction conception of production, see section 4.2.2.

15 The spelling of *economy* here is an error of the Hull edition; the 1683 text has '*Oeconomy*'. Also in his *Treatise of Taxes* Petty (1662: 60) comments:

> We must consider in general, that as wiser Physicians tamper not excessively with their Patients, rather observing and complying with the motions of nature, then [i.e. than] contradicting it with vehement Administrations of their own; so in Politicks and Oconomicks the same must be used ....

It is interesting to compare this with Smith's chiding of the Physiocrats in general and Quesnay in particular, also using a medical metaphor, at *WN* (673–4; quoted in sec. 5.3.2). Both Petty and Quesnay were medical doctors. Petty's statement of course is interesting also for expressing a certain economic liberalism (see the context). The strange spelling of *economics* in this quote, absent the digraph and no 'e', is verbatim the 1662 edition, so probably a printer's error, misreading a longhand digraph. In relation to Petty's use of *politics and economics*, a 1622 instance recorded in the *OED* ('politic', sec. 3 – 'politics') is worth noting: 'Morall Philosophie ... hath three parts: Ecclesiastickes, Oeconomickes, and Politickes'. See also the young Petty's (1647: 8–9, 19) coupling of the terms economy and policy.

16 See HROnline (2002), which provides machine-searchable transcriptions of the manuscripts. Much of the use of the term concerns specification of natural resources and produced commodities, their uses, and the methods of producing them, especially best and innovative methods. (See Aspromourgos 2005, esp. pp. 6–7, for discussion of one particularly important instance; cf. Aspromourgos 2001: 50, 83–5.) The connection with a broad sense of 'husbandry' is therefore close (and sometimes very explicit in the documents), giving these uses an element of traditional meaning. There are also frequent listings of sciences or species of knowledge in which, in particular, ethics and/or theology, economics and politics are commonly grouped together. These formulations (another instance of which is given in n. 15 above, from the *OED*), rather than suggesting a combining of economics and politics, are probably best viewed as persistence of a form of Aristotelian division of knowledge, so pointing to separation of the two. Still, demarcations of knowledge which regularly placed economics and politics side-by-side may have stimulated Petty. A more thorough investigation of the significance of *economy* in Hartlib's archive, undertaken by someone proficient in Latin, might prove enlightening.

17 Though Steuart proceeds to rather artificially impose upon the household a political conceptualization that only makes real sense at the level of States.

18 The 1966 Skinner edition quoted here throughout, follows the 1805 edition, which incorporates corrections made to the 1767 text by Steuart prior to his death in 1780; but significant changes from the 1767 edition are editorially noted by Skinner.

19 The marginalist conception is crystallized in Lionel Robbins's (1935: 15–16)

definition, replicated in one form or another in the opening chapters of virtually all introductory textbooks in more recent decades:

> Here ... is the unity of subject of Economic Science, the forms assumed by human behaviour in disposing of scarce means.... The economist studies the disposal of scarce means. He is interested in the way different degrees of scarcity of different goods give rise to different ratios of valuation between them, and he is interested in the way in which changes in conditions of scarcity, whether coming from changes in ends or changes in means – from the demand side or the supply side – affect these ratios. Economics is the science which studies human behaviour as a relationship between ends and scarce means which have alternative uses.

This seminal formulation is actually not well articulated: the 'means' are not 'scarce' in themselves; it is the finiteness of means *relative to the extent of potential human uses* which constitutes the scarcity (though the idea is better stated further on, pp. 22–3). Subjectivism is essential to the definition, in terms of the role of supposed unlimited wants in constituting the central and organizing conception of scarcity. Probably P.H. Wicksteed was the decisive influence in the formation of Robbins's notion (ironically, coming at the tail-end of the worst of the Great Depression). He explicitly, if rather incoherently, aims the definition against the classical economists' 'materialist' (Robbins's inverted commas) approach; the Physiocrats and Smith are explicitly mentioned (pp. 7–9). It is also more than ironic that Robbins (1935: xiv) supposes, 'as a result of the theoretical developments of the last sixty years, there is no longer any ground for serious differences of opinion on these matters' – just prior to John Maynard Keynes's (1936) fundamental assault upon the new orthodoxy (of course, not unrelated to the first irony).

20 For example: J.-J. Rousseau (1758) *Discours sur l'Oeconomie*; F. Quesnay (1759) *Tableau Œconomique*; C.F. Tiphaigne de la Roche (1760) *Essai sur l'Histoire Œconomique des Mers Occidentales de France* (ASL); Victor Riquetti (Marquis de Mirabeau) (1763) *Philosophie Rurale, ou économie générale et politique de l'agriculture...* (ASL); J.F. de Villeneuve (1763), *L'Économie Politique. Projet pour Enrichir et pour Perfectionner l'Espèce Humaine* (enlarged edn 1767); J.C. Valmont de Bomare (1764) *Dictionnare Raisonné Universel d'Histoire Naturelle ... et le détail de leurs usages dans ... l'économie domestique & champêtre ...* (ASL); P.J. Macquer (1766) *Dictionnaire de Chymie, contenant la théorie & la pratique de cette science, son application ... & à l'économie animale ...* (ASL); F.V. de Forbonnais (1767) *Principes et Observations Oeconomiques* (ASL) and (1767) *Observations Oeconomiques sur Divers Points du Sistême de l'Auteur du Tableau Oeconomique* (ASL); J. Steuart (1767) *An Inquiry into the Principles of Political Œconomy ...* (ASL); R. Dossie (1768) *Memoirs of Agriculture, and Other Oeconomical Arts* (ASL); F. Quesnay (1767–8) *Physiocratie, ou constitution naturelle du gouvernement ...* (ASL) and (1767–8) *Discussions et Développemens sur quelques-unes des Notions de l'Économie Politique ...* (ASL; the two vols, ed. P.-S. Dupont de Nemours); G.F. Le Trosne (1768) *Recueil de Plusieurs Morceaux Économiques ...* (ASL); P. Verri (1771) *Meditazioni sulla Economia Politica* (ASL; 2nd edn 1772 – both in Smith's library); A. Young (1771) *The Farmer's Letters to the People of England .... To which are added ... occasional tracts on husbandry and rural œconomics* (3rd edn; ASL); G. Ortes (1774) *Della Economia Nazionale*; A. Young (1774) *Political Arithmetic .... Addressed to the œconomical societies established in Europe ...* (ASL); P.-S. Dupont de Nemours (1775) *Tableau raisonné des principes de l'économie politique*; A. Genovesi (1775) *Lezioni di Economia Civile*. Those followed by 'ASL' in parentheses were in Smith's library (see Mizuta 2000). A number of these works were published anonymously. Jean-Jacques Rousseau's *Discours* (commonly referred to as the 'Third Discourse') first appeared in 1755, as 'De l'Économie Politique', in volume 5 of the celebrated *Encyclopédie ou Dictionnaire*

*Raissoné des Sciences, des Arts et des Métiers* ... (eds D. Diderot and J. le Rond d'Alembert).

21 In fact, the Naples Chair was designated in 'Meccanica e Commercio', but Genovesi discarded mechanics after reading articles by François Véron Duverger de Forbonnais, a mercantilist opponent of the Physiocrats, in the *Encyclopédie* (Wahnbaeck 2004: 60). The Milan Chair was designated in 'Scienze Camerali', but this was changed to 'Istituzioni Economico Politiche' when Alfonso Longo succeeded to the Chair in the early 1770s (Bruni and Porta 2003: 372). It was also subsequently abolished, in the 1780s. Along with Verri, Beccaria is the most significant of the eighteenth-century Italian economic writers, though also evidently much derivative of French economics – including in this, the Irishman Richard Cantillon's French treatise published in 1755 (Groenewegen 1987a). The growth of wealth understood as national product is also at the centre of Beccaria's conception of the science (public economy). See also Groenewegen (1983). Groenewegen (1987d) and Porta and Scazzieri (2002) provide accounts of Verri's conception of political economy, and Bruni and Porta (2003), an interpretation of 'civil economy' in eighteenth-century Italian economic thought (also Bruni and Zamagni 2004; Wahnbaeck 2004 – and the interesting exercise by Guidi 1994). Robertson (2005: 28–31, 371–6) presents the development of political economy in Scotland and Naples as the creation of a science of economic development, as an agent of the Enlightenment project of material betterment. Institutionalization of economic analysis in Spain was partly inspired by Neapolitan influence, with a kind of 'Chair' as early as 1784 – not within a university, but involving teaching – sponsored by an economic society. Spanish university Chairs in political economy were established in the 1840s (Almenar and Llombart 2001: 110–13).

22 Keynes (1933: 129n) notes that the title originally proposed for the Malthus Chair had been 'Professor of General History, Politics, Commerce, and Finance'. Notice therefore the ambivalence as to designation, in relation to all the early Chairs of 'political economy'. From 1819, Say was Professor of Industrial Economics at the Conservatoire des Arts et Métiers. On university developments around German, cameralist economic ideas, with kinds of 'economics' Chairs as early as 1727, see Tribe (1988, Chapters 3–5).

23 This was quite strongly suggested by Stewart (1811: 322–3; quoted sec. 2.1.2) himself, and more recently, has been turned into something of an indictment of Smith (Rashid 1998). See also Chapter 5, n. 22, concerning contemporaries of Smith appealing to the notion of a 'political science', in categorizing his political economy project. This is in the context of a consideration of the place of political economy within the social sciences, section 5.2.2.

24 Ross (1995: 410) evidently overlooks Say, in supposing that Henry Cockburn (1856: 45–6) is the first to make Smith 'the founder of the science'.

25 Peter Groenewegen privately suggested to me the further possibility that the publisher of the two works, Thomas Cadell, may himself have wanted a title differentiated from that of Steuart.

26 Smith's framework for understanding the *causes* of wealth is considered below, especially Chapter 4. As to why 'nations' appear in the definition of political economy – implying that polity is in some sense the most fundamentally pertinent human collectivity, for the purposes of economic analysis – two reasons may be suggested. The compelling pertinence of polities follows from this 'branch of the science of ... [the] legislator' being a *policy* science (*WN*: 428). But also, while Smith certainly has a cosmopolitan moral and intellectual temper, his cosmopolitanism is qualified: 'while accepting the idea of world citizenship, he rejects the Stoic view that this should obliterate stronger ties of feeling for smaller groups.... Smith argues, it is nature that teaches us to put family, friends, and nation first' (Raphael and Macfie 1976b: 10, with 7). Nevertheless, his title is cosmopolitan, not parochial: not an inquiry into the

wealth of Britain, or of *the* nation, but of *nations*. For an expression of Smith's cosmopolitanism, see *TMS* (229).

27 *WN* (6, 12, 207–8, 254–5, 258, 337, 339–40, 344–5, 364, 366–7, 447–9, 451, 513, 517, 663–4, 668, 673, 844, 929). At one point, agricultural produce is described as 'the principal source of the wealth of every great country' (*WN*: 857; cf. 364, 427 – and n. 28 below concerning land as wealth). *LJA* (362) refers to 'naturall wea<l>th of the state', implying that it is equivalent to the flow of national product for consumption (cf. 391, 394). *LJA* (359) employs 'real wealth' to refer to the exchange value in terms of other commodities, rather than money, of a diamond.

28 For just Books I–III of *WN* (the first 427 of 950 pages), at (48, 74, 112–13, 129, 152, 174, 178–9, 192, 200, 206–10, 220, 234–5, 242, 253–4, 256, 347, 373, 376, 379, 402, 405, 411, 422–3, 426–7); also *TMS* (51); *LRB* (112, 138, 149–52, 156, 204). There are also some such passing references in *LJ*, which need not be noted here. *WN* (113, 152) provides fairly clear instances of a stock concept of (personal) wealth – also *LJA* (187, 208, 215–6); *LJB* (520). At *WN* (258 – just two sentences on from an instance of Smith's defining real wealth as annual produce – he writes of land as 'by far the greatest, the most important, and the most durable part of the wealth of every extensive country', though linking this to its productiveness. Indeed, elsewhere the 'real wealth' of the landlord is characterized as his 'real rent ... his power of purchasing the labour, or the produce of the labour of other people' (*WN*: 264; also 265; cf. *LJA*: 245). The term 'wealth' (or extensions of it) appear nowhere in *EPS*; there are only a few general references in the context of historical narrative in *LRB*; and apart from a few references to *WN* itself, almost none in *Corr*.

29 One is quoted, and the other twenty or so instances included in the citations of this sense, above.

30 *WN* (617, 366); *TMS* (83); *WN* (619, 496); also *TMS* (50, 61–2, 64, 72, 166–7, 181–3, 253, 272); *WN* (367, 564, 566, 687, 713, 728, 946); *LRB* (155). Smith quotes with qualified approval the dictum (inspired by Hobbes), wealth is power, adding that the wealthy person does not thereby necessarily acquire political power, 'civil or military': 'His fortune may, perhaps, afford him the means of acquiring both, but the mere possession of that fortune does not necessarily convey to him either' (*WN*: 48). The term 'commonwealth' is used extensively by Smith, never with any definition, but clearly identifying it with polity or the executive political power.

31 See also *WN* (340, 429–30, 438–40, 497–8, 517, 555, 561, 651); *LJA* (300, 345, 381, 384–5, 387–91); *LJB* (535). At *WN* (430–1 and 449–50), Smith concedes that some of these writers have *not* limited wealth to money, and have included 'consumable goods'. Only Locke is explicitly named.

32 See also *WN* (6, 663–4, 668, 673–4, 676, 679). While systematic criticism of mercantilism occurs in both *LJ* and *WN*, there is no discussion at all of Physiocratic ideas in *LJ*. Between the lectures and the completion of *WN* Smith spent considerable time in France during the mid-1760s, meeting important intellectual figures including Quesnay and Turgot (see Ross 1995: 195–219).

33 The following comment in the context of Smith's analysis of capital is noteworthy as well:

> To maintain and augment the stock which may be reserved for immediate consumption, is the sole end and purpose both of ... fixed and circulating capitals. It is this stock which feeds, cloaths, and lodges the people. Their riches or poverty depends upon the abundant or sparing supplies which those two capitals can afford to the stock reserved for immediate consumption.
>
> (*WN*: 283)

See also *WN* (678) on the Physiocratic concept of 'the wealth of nations as consisting ... in the consumable goods annually reproduced by ... labour', quoted two paragraphs above, and the reference to wealth as consumable goods in relation to mercantilism, in n. 31 above. The concepts of gross and net revenue are examined in section 4.2.1.

34 Smith does not use *precisely* these terms, but they accurately capture a part of his intention. (See secs. 4.3.2–4.3.4, concerning 'productive' inputs, and sec. 4.4.2.). To the extent that Smith treats the wages or consumption of productive labour as part of the capital advances required for production, then consumption and capital accumulation are not mutually exclusive. Therefore, the analogue of the modern distinction between consumption and investment, in Smith's framework, is a distinction between unproductive consumption and investment. The trade-off between consumption and growth is addressed also in section 4.3.4. For the concept of 'surplus', see section 4.2.2.

35 It is a curious fact that one of these two instances is from the creator of the first great English dictionary. Smith became in 1775 a member of the famous and highly select 'Club', of which Samuel Johnson was a founder in 1764. Smith apparently did not like him and probably the feeling was mutual (Bate 1978: 35, 180, 366, 399, 504–5; *LRB*: 228). Ross (1995: 191–2) comments on their relationship, including the anecdote (of perhaps doubtful veracity) that Smith in a face-to-face altercation called Johnson a 'son of a bitch', and apparently not in a friendly way, possibly in response to his speaking ill of Hume. (The source for this is alleged to be John Millar, via the recollection of Walter Scott: Ross 1995: 427, n. 3.) Recall also that Smith reviewed the dictionary (Smith 1755; see Chapter 1, n. 6). Smith owned an edition of *The Rambler* (Johnson 1771) and a *Works* of John Dryden containing the relevant poem (Mizuta 2000: 81, 133; Dryden 1760, vol. 1: 48). (There is as well a further edition of Dryden's poetry in Smith's library: Dryden 1701.) Dryden is discussed at *TMS* (198); *EPS* (33, 221, 234–6, 239); *LRB* (229–30). But if there was any particular source of inspiration for Smith's choice of phrase, perhaps it more likely was the Physiocrats (Scott 1937: 322–3, n. 2; cf. Ross 1995: 76, on George Berkeley).

36 A couple of instances of the non-economic senses of wealth were included also in the epigraph quotations for this study as a whole (see p. xi), as a – perhaps there overly subtle – little joke: the *OED* indicates that the wider senses of wealth as well-being in general, including 'spiritual' well-being, are obsolete ('*Obs.*')!

37 On individual self-restraint and liberty, see pp. 75–7, and section 5.2.1 concerning the system of natural liberty. On human nature and material self-betterment, see sections 2.3.1 and 2.4, and the discussion of saving in section 4.3.2. With regard to the non-establishment of religion, see the argument at *WN* (792–814), concerning the benefits of competition among religious groups, though Smith nowhere there actually uses the term 'competition' to describe this. The following comments are particularly notable:

> if politicks had … dealt equally and impartially with all the different sects, and … allowed every man to chuse his own priest and his own religion as he thought proper … zeal must be altogether innocent where the society is divided into two or three hundred, or perhaps into as many thousand small sects, of which no one could be considerable enough to disturb the public tranqillity.
>
> (*WN*: 792–3)

> Science is the great antidote to the poison of enthusiasm and superstition; and where all the superior ranks of people were secured from it, the inferior ranks could not be much exposed to it.
>
> (*WN*: 796)

> frequency and gaiety of publick diversions … painting, poetry, musick, dancing … all sorts of dramatic representations and exhibitions, would easily dissipate, in the greater part of … [the people], that melancholy and gloomy humour which is almost always the nurse of popular superstition and enthusiasm. Publick

> diversions have always been the objects of dread and hatred, to all the fanatical promoters of those popular frenzies. The gaiety and good humour which those diversions inspire were altogether inconsistent with that temper of mind, which was fittest for their purpose, or which they could best work upon.
>
> (*WN*: 796–7)

> In a country where the law favoured the teachers of no one religion more than those of any other ... the ... executive power ... would have no occasion to give himself any concern about them, further than to keep the peace among them, in the same manner as among the rest of his subjects ....
>
> (*WN*: 797; cf. 538–9, quoted in Chapter 5, n. 48)

Unlike economic competition, which is designed to enhance economic outcomes, the purpose of religious competition is to assist in neutralizing religiosity; but in both instances, individuals are restrained by the competition. (The 'melancholy ... humour' Smith mentions here may be compared with the characterization of 'melancholy moralists' at *TMS*: 139; also 283.) Hont and Ignatieff (1983a: 8–12, 43–4) suggest how Smith may be understood to conceive of a reconciliation between the pursuit of material wealth and a certain, limited sense of 'virtue'. See further to this, Chapter 5, n. 56.

38 Aristotle is more than merely an arbitrary example from ancient thought: however slight his 'economic' commentaries, they are more considerable than those of any other ancient writer, and were easily the dominant ancient philosophical influence in the Common Era (Meikle 1995: 1–4; also Langholm 1983).

39 In Aristotle, the art of material acquisition is legitimated by properly serving household management: 'True wealth has a limit of size, determined by the purpose of the association it serves' – notably, the household or polis (Barker 1946: 21; also 19, 27–8). This is 'natural', as opposed to unlimited and unnatural, acquisition of material things; and usury is the most unnatural of all (Barker 1946: 21–7, 29). ('True wealth' translates *ho alêthinos ploutos*: Meikle 1995: 48.) The conclusion of Aristotle's diagnosis is well summed up in accompanying editorial commentary: 'true wealth' is determined by 'the ... needs of the household, and is limited by those needs'; unnatural accumulation arises from 'a misconception of the purpose of life and of the nature of well-being' (Barker 1946: 26, n. 1, n. 2; also Meikle 1995: 48–51, 68–81; Pomeroy 1994: 218–19). From his very different standpoint, Aristotle therefore arrives at a similar conclusion to Smith, in one negative respect: it is false to identify true wealth with money (Barker 1946: 25, citing also the Midas fable). Beyond Aristotle's more fundamental negative proposition concerning unlimited acquisition, no very definite content is given to the finite and legitimate material acquisition (see, for example, Barker 1946: 66–8). On the nuances of *chrematistic* as the art of material acquisition, see Barker (1946: 22, n. E, 27, n. F) and Meikle (1995: 43–67); and on *eudaimonia*, best conveyed by the English, 'felicity', but more a state of *activity* than merely a state of mind, see Barker (1946: lxxv–lxxvi, 118, n. 1).

40 Wood (2002: 42–68, 84, 207). On all these matters, see Langholm (1992: e.g. 74–8, 99–100, 206–10, 251–5, 383–6, 566–9; also Langholm 1983: 46–66); and most especially, Perrotta (2004), which provides a detailed account of the perceptions of consumption and wealth from the ancients, through patristic, medieval and mercantilist thought, up to the eighteenth century.

41 Smith nowhere speaks of 'mercantilism'. It seems to have entered English in the late-nineteenth century, by a doubling back into English from the German transliteration (*merkantilismus*) of Smith's actual phrase, 'the mercantile system' (e.g. *WN*: 429, 642). This is the view of Winch (2002: 5), supported by Viner (1955: 3), the latter also suggesting that Smith's characterization of mercantilism as the 'commercial' or 'mercantile' system derives from Physiocracy. The *OED* ('mercantilism') on the other hand, tentatively suggests the term may have derived from the French *mercan-*

*tilisme*, which arose earlier in the nineteenth century. Though 'mercantile system' is not used in *LJ*, the critique of mercantilism is there (n. 31 above). Smith also acknowledges the Physiocratic conception of wealth, very close to his own, but took the view that it had had little impact on practice, certainly little influence relative to the mercantile system (*WN*: 663, 678; and see the discussion of Quesnay below).

42 Heckscher (1955) is an influential and monumental interpretation of mercantilism, more or less in accord with Smith's view. Viner (1955) is likewise in the tradition of Smith on mercantilism, but not uncritical of his position (e.g. in relation to the supposed money/wealth identification). For valuable and generally more positive interpretations, see Coleman (1969), Appleby (1978), Grice-Hutchinson (1978), Hutchison (1988: 87–96, 149–55), Magnusson (1993; 1994), Perrotta (2004: 112–78, 204–22) and Roncaglia (2005: 41–52). On British mercantilist practice, distinct in significant respects from Continental policy, see Morgan (2002). As to defining mercantilism, only a fairly narrow construction can enable the term to serve any useful purpose in historical interpretation. Earlier, I had recourse to a definition combining the descriptive and the normative: 'the doctrine that changes in the quantity of circulating currency, due to the balance of foreign payments, significantly influence the level of domestic activity; and that government regulation can systematically and successfully influence that balance' (Aspromourgos 1996: 205, n. 6). This definition in terms of economic doctrine does however leave aside the important, perhaps even primary, political element: protecting and advancing the position of the State in international relations; in a blunt phrase, money as the sinews of war (Malynes 1623: Ep. Dedi.):

> *but forasmuch that neither wisdome nor valour can well subsist without treasure, since Moneys have obtained the title of the sinowes of war, and the life of Commerce: I hope that the accumulating thereof may properly be called* The Præheminent study of Princes, *when the same is procured by Trade: which is the sole peaceable instrument to inrich Kingdomes and Common-weales.*

On political power versus economic prosperity as goals of mercantilism, see Viner (1948). On economic liberalism in pre-Smithian economic thought, see in particular Grampp (1952; or, a slightly revised version, 1965). John Locke and Dudley North are probably the two most striking examples of English 'liberal' economic writers before Smith. Smith concedes himself, that the former does not limit wealth to money (n. 31 above).

43 This is the French term, commonly translated into English as 'wealth'. An exhaustive examination of Smith's use of the term *riches* makes evident that it is a synonym for 'wealth', and similarly to wealth, may be a stock or flow (asset or income) concept in his use (cf. sec. 2.2.1). But 'real riches' is certainly a synonym for 'real wealth' precisely understood as the flow of produce or revenue, or their purchasing power (e.g. *WN*: 290, 298, 560; *LJA*: 472; *LJB*: 503–4, 508). Of the two terms, 'riches' is much less used by Smith than 'wealth'; but perhaps 'riches' is the more common of the two terms for material possessions, in earlier, general English use. Of only two works in Smith's library with 'wealth' in their titles, one is *Reflections on the Formation and Distribution of Wealth. By M. Turgot … Translated from the French* (London, 1793), a translation of Turgot (1769–70), but notice, published after Smith's death. Lundberg (1964) argues the possibility that Smith was the translator, but this is unconvincing (see Viner 1965: 131–8; this is a long essay by Viner introducing a facsimile reprint of Rae 1895; also sec. 4.3.7). In any case, this translation of Turgot's title identifies *richesses* and *wealth*.

44 There is some kinship between this conceptually somewhat awkward notion of sterile wealth and Smith's notion of money as an element of circulating capital (see sec. 4.2.1). Also, Petty had much earlier argued the possibility and undesirability of an excess money stock, and in the spirit of his 'political arithmetic', calculated the national stock required for transactions purposes (Aspromourgos 1996: 34–6).

45 Two similar characterizations of wealth producing wealth were quoted in the discussion of Physiocracy in section 2.1.4, from Meek (1962: 232) and in the accompanying n. 14, from Kuczynski and Meek (1972: 22, '3rd edn').

46 The assertion on the original title page of the *Essai* (Cantillon 1755 [1931]: 1), that it was published in London, is a fiction. The book was published with no author attribution, which contributed to delaying recognition of Cantillon's significance for the history of political economy – as well, by obscuring the fact that it was written at least two decades prior to its date of publication. Smith owned a copy (Mizuta 2000: 45). The tangled history of this book, and indeed, of its author, is much clarified by Murphy (1986: 299–321, with regard to the book). The Higgs edition provides both the French text and an English translation, on facing pages.

47 Petty (1691a: 147; 1691b: 113; also 1690: 259–60, 269). *Verbum Sapienti* (Petty 1691b) was only ever published as an appendix to *The Political Anatomy of Ireland*, prior to the 1899 Hull edition, but is a free-standing, separately written work. The durability doctrine is also to be found in Cantillon (1755 [1931]: 89–91).

48 It is therefore all the more surprising that this work apparently had such an accidental genesis (Groenewegen 1977b: XVII–XIX). It was composed in 1766 and first published in serial form. Since it is little more than fifty pages in modern print, in terms of substance per page it compares more than favourably with Smith's 950-page magnum opus. Other Turgot writings quoted and cited here are from the translations in Groenewegen (1977c), with date of original publication or composition in parentheses.

49 So much so that it would be tedious to cite them all. All instances of this sense, for just Parts I–II of *TMS* (the first 108 of 342 pages), are at (5, 10, 13–14, 17–22, 24, 27–9, 31–7, 41–5, 47–9, 51, 53–4, 58, 61–2, 68–71, 73, 75–6, 79–90, 91n–92n, 94, 99, 101–4, 107–8); and similarly, for just Book I of *WN* (275 of 950 pages) at (3, 11, 13, 19–20, 26, 28, 32, 34, 38, 44, 49–50, 65, 69, 84, 86–7, 89, 91, 94, 97–8, 100–1, 104–5, 108, 116, 118, 123, 125, 131–2, 135, 139, 142, 146, 160–2, 167, 169, 199–200, 202, 207–9, 224, 230, 234–5, 238–9, 242, 244, 246–8, 252, 255, 258–60, 265).

50 *WN* (19, 454, 627, 767, n. *i* and n. *j*, 802, 814); *LJA* (275, n. *b*, 338); *edWN* (568, 580); *Corr* (383). See also editorial n. 13 at *WN* (19), on other juxtapositions of 'naturally' and 'necessarily'.

51 In *TMS*, for just Parts I–II (6, 8, 17–18, 34, 37, 40, 49, 59, 65–6, 72, 85, 92); in *WN*, for just Book I (1, 3, 4, 11, 14, 16, 20, 28–30, 40, 46, 63, 72, 80, 89, 100, 111–12, 116, 119, 122, 128, 131–4, 143, 146, 157, 176, 181, 235, 243, 246, 250).

52 Again, it is unnecessary to cite them all. For Parts I–II of *TMS* all instances are at (7, 11, 22, 25, 28, 37, 47, 52–3, 58–9, 71, 77–8, 82, 86–7, 91, 93, 105–8). Instances in other of Smith's writings of his general uses under the first two of the three broad senses indicated at the beginning of this section will not be documented, unless pertinent to his political economy.

53 Note his self-conscious apology in the previous quotation, when speaking of nature's 'favourite' ends ('if such an expression is allowable'). Other references to the author of nature or similar phrases occur at *TMS* (93, 105–6, 128, 128n, 166, 169, 235–6, 273, 289, 298). The *TMS* editors note changing practice across the six editions with respect to the use of an upper-case initial letter in printing the word 'nature', especially for instances of personification or near-personification, and indicate that Smith's letters in his own hand employ an initial capital (Raphael and Macfie 1976b: 44, 49).

54 Smith's timidity concerning involvement in public controversy over religion is strikingly illustrated by his unwillingness to accede to his friend's deathbed wish, that Smith oversee posthumous publication of Hume's *Dialogues Concerning Natural Religion*. Smith's biographer speculates also on a deeper explanation for this behaviour (Ross 1995: 302–4, 338–41, 416; elaborated upon in Campbell and Ross 1982;

and for related correspondence, see the '*Dialogues*...' entry in the *Corr* index). See also further to this issue, the two different versions, public and private, of Smith's letter on the death of Hume (*Corr*: 203–4, esp. 204, n. 4, and 217–21), and Raphael and Macfie (1976a, App. II, esp. 398–401) concerning Smith's removal for the *TMS* sixth edition of a passage in relation to Christian belief which was in the earlier editions. (Also, the 'Whining Christian' of *Corr*: 203 may be compared with the 'whining ... moralists' of *TMS*: 139; also 283.) His views on the non-establishment of religion quoted above (n. 37), are views which could only be held by a person indifferent to all the varieties of Christian belief. Rothschild (in Hanley *et al.* 2004: 160–1) offers some thoughtful conjectures on Smith's religious beliefs, or lack thereof (cf. Raphael and Macfie 1976b: 19–20, 39; Ross 1995: 118; Winch 1996: 35–40). As to Hume's *actual* beliefs, as opposed to the contemporaneous perceptions of his beliefs, this is a murky issue. His scepticism and religious unbelief, more positively expressed, are probably most correctly construed as a belief in the unknowableness of deity, or 'First Cause', or of the extra-natural in general. Incidentally, Hume also in print speaks of 'that beneficent Being, who means the good of all his creatures' (Miller 1985: 467).

55 That it is separable does not mean that it is 'autonomous'. See section 2.4.

56 Puro (1992) provides a rather muddled or contrived classification of Smith's uses of nature (and variants) in *WN*, concluding that there are eight distinct notions of nature to be found there. This is not a useful multiplication, relative to the threefold classification we have suggested; and his interpretation suffers also, of course, for being limited to *WN*. Griswold's (1999: 311–17) interpretation, in terms of seven senses of nature in Smith, is more considered – and in any case, entirely consistent with our threefold characterization. The issue also arises in Hanley *et al.* (2004: 139, 156): Werhane argues that 'an unquestioned natural rights theory and some vague notions of natural order' underpin Smith's moral philosophy; Rothschild concurs with Griswold as to the 'dizzying variety' of senses in which Smith uses nature and variants. (Rothschild's assertion at the same page, that Smith never speaks of 'natural right', is incorrect, at least with regard to *LJ*: see p. 44.) A further comment on this issue probably gets the balance right:

> Smith certainly refers to the universal dispositions or original principles of human nature .... He says very little, all the same, about the foundation or grounding of his own system in an account (an abstract science, or an anthropology, or what would later have been called a psychology) of human nature.
>
> (Rothschild in Hanley *et al.* 2004: 152; see also Cremaschi 1989, discussed in n. 67 below)

Montes (2003a: 77; reproduced in Montes 2004: 15–56) asserts that, unlike *TMS* (which is 'full of them'), in *WN* 'there is no reliance on Nature (except *WN*, V.ii.k, p. 870), or any other metaphor (except the elusive invisible hand) with a theological or deistic connotation'. (At the same place, Montes also suggests that the *TMS* appeals to nature and the deity can all be removed, without doing any violence to the structure and content of that work.) This is an overstatement – particularly with regard to the role of *human* nature in the political economy (see sec. 2.4) – but nevertheless, correct 'in spirit', so to speak. (For a rather different view, see Schabas 2005: 79–101, also published as Schabas 2003.) However, the nomination of *WN* (870) as the one instance of Smith's relying on 'Nature' in that work is actually rather odd: that instance implies much less a personification of nature than the three passages from *WN* provided above (preceding paragraph). Generally on this issue, see also Pack (1995), mentioned at n. 57 below.

57 See, for example, *TMS* (63, 77, 85–6, 113–14, 158–9, 200, 265); cf. Haakonssen and Winch (2006: 386–7, 392). To be sure, there *are* human behaviours that Smith regards as both natural and worthy of moral disapprobation; for example: 'The love

of domination and authority over others ... is naturall to mankind' (*LJA*: 192). Nevertheless there are also naturalistically expressed ethical and prescriptive dimensions to his thought: prescriptive norms that are intended to be 'realistic', in the sense of not being ethically too demanding of actually existing human beings, of being in accordance with the actual character of the average human being. Pack (1995) documents considerable examples of Smith's disapproving of behaviours or practices which he characterizes as natural. Pack's point is somewhat overstated however: many of these refer to instances where Smith means only to convey that a phenomenon is the normal or to-be-expected outcome of some particular set of circumstances or conditions, or they involve 'nature' conveying just the character or constitution of a phenomenon.

58 The supernatural could be understood as inherently of superior value to the natural, but not necessarily: e.g. Christian 'demons'. Also, under the influence of the Christian tradition, humanity could be seen as a being participating both in nature and in a transcendent sphere, a being with an animal and a spiritual dimension (Boas 1973: 346–7).

59 On all this, see Hepburn (2006), Boas (1973) and Ruse (2005), upon which the account here is based.

60 As to the etymology, the English use of nature and natural dates back to the fourteenth century, and a little earlier, from Old French *nature*, *naturel* (the latter French form was also used in Middle English), and from Latin *nātūra*, *nātūrālis*. The French noun conveyed the senses of the 'active force that establishes and maintains the order of the universe ... properties or characteristics that define objects ... constitution'; the classical Latin, 'birth, constitution, character, the genitals, the creative power governing the world, the physical world, the natural course of things' (*OED*: 'natural', 'nature'). The ancient Greek equivalents are *physis* (nature) and *ta physika* (natural things). A valuable essay by Lewis (1960: 24–74), on the history of *natura*, *physis* and *kind*, serves to confirm that those who complain about the variety of senses of *nature* in Smith (n. 56 above) are in a sense 'shooting the messenger': he is simply reflecting the multi-faceted meaning of the term in the history of Western thought. As part of a larger and deeply thoughtful discussion of the fate of 'nature' in the Enlightenment, Larrère (2001a) surveys the ambiguous and contradictory meanings attributed to it in Enlightenment thought as a whole.

61 Hence Stoicism was also not at all merely a human and social philosophy. It included a pantheistic physics of a providential nature – as Hallie (1967: 21) puts it, 'all change is immanent in God and unchanging in its laws' – and pioneering systematization of logic (as well as epistemology and philosophy of language). The Stoics, 'more than any other ancient school, emphasized the interdependence among the parts of philosophy' (Inwood 2006: 254, referring to logic, physics, ethics). Neither should the austerity of the Stoic personal moral code be exaggerated. As Inwood (2006: 257) illustrates: 'Stoic rejection of passions' means that since, for example, 'wealth is not a strict good, we should not be elated at achieving it (though there is nothing wrong with enjoying it)'. On all these matters, see Barker (1934), Hallie (1967) and Inwood (2006), upon which the account here is based.

62 For Smith's further discussion of Stoicism in *TMS* (see 272–93, 306–7, his key criticism being at 292–3; also *Corr*: 56). Stoic science is discussed in *EPS* (62–3, 65, 85, 108, 116–17, 121n–23n, 127–8, 253); also *LRB* (193). The system of natural liberty is examined in section 5.2.1. Heise (1995) also argues for the importance of the Stoic influence upon Smith (cf. Vivenza 2001: 202–6, for a substantial critique), and it is central in Brown's (1994) interpretation of Smith's overall thought. Fleischacker (2004: 112–13, 120, 291, n. 29) downplays it, but his argument is not compelling. For her deeply thoughtful and considered view on the Stoic influence, see Vivenza (2001: 209–12). Smith's *TMS* (60) statement is somewhat reminiscent of Montesquieu's (1748 [1989]: 466) comment on Stoicism: 'It exaggerated only those things in which there is greatness: scorn for pleasures and pains'.

63 Schabas (2005: 163, n. 1) also repudiates the view of Hume as a radical sceptic: 'Although Hume was traditionally portrayed as a skeptic, since the 1970s most scholars agree that a careful reading shows that he was not (see, e.g., Stroud 1977; and Baier 1991)'.

64 Redman (1997: 104) observes that while first use of the term *social science* has been commonly ascribed to John Stuart Mill, it was already in French and English use prior to him. She offers French instances from 1808 (François Marie Charles Fourier) and 1827 (Jean Charles Leonard Simonde de Sismondi).

65 With regard to nature's uniformity versus the particularity of the conventional in human practices, Schreyer (1989: 151) goes so far as to say:

> The study of nature and the study of man, natural and moral philosophy, were considered two parts of the same discipline. It was the overruling scientific endeavour of the time to establish a science of man that was to be as certain and methodologically sound as the natural philosophy of a Boyle or Newton.... The underlying assumption was that there was no basic difference in the subject matter of natural and moral philosophy, that the science of man like the science of nature ultimately rested on observation and experience, that it was the task of the philosopher to establish a causal relationship between the principles of nature and observable phenomena. For moral philosophy, this meant that a causal relationship was assumed between the principles of human nature and man's cultural achievements, a relationship that – given identical circumstances – would result in a uniform pattern of human development.

A striking example of the contingency of particular conditions in shaping particular histories, in Smith's economic analysis, is the role he perceives the geography of the Mediterranean to have played in the growth of human civilization in that part of the world (*WN*: 34–6). For a more detailed interpretation of the historiographical dimension of the Scottish Enlightenment, see Redman (1997: 114–28). Wood (1996) also examines the role of 'natural history', derived from Bacon, in the science-of-man literature. Bacon, Newton and Locke were the three figures who commonly served as the intellectual inspiration for the project.

66 The diversity of meanings which can be imputed to 'nature', even by one and the same author (and a very able one), is also evident in Hume. Hence, defending his denial that justice is a 'natural virtue', he comments:

> I make use of the word, *natural* [here], only as oppos'd to *artificial*. In another sense of the word; as no principle of the human mind is more natural than a sense of virtue; so no virtue is more natural than justice. Mankind is an inventive species; and where an invention is obvious and absolutely necessary, it may as properly be said to be natural as any thing that proceeds immediately from original principles, without the intervention of thought or reflexion. Tho' the rules of justice be *artificial*, they are not *arbitrary*. Nor is the expression improper to call them *Laws of Nature*; if by natural we understand what is common to any species, or even if we confine it to mean what is inseparable from the species.
>
> (Hume 1739–40: 484; cf. 473–6).

Further to Hume, nature and the science of man, see Schabas (2005: 58–78). Skinner (1996: 250–2) comments on the influence of Hume's conception upon Smith.

67 For a more negative assessment of Smith's attempt to reconcile an empirical and a normative account of human nature, see Cremaschi (1989: 92–5, 100–2, 106): Smith belongs to the natural law tradition, in a certain sense; but to the extent that for him, the rule of nature takes its bearings from sentiments rather than reason, it may be regarded as a precarious basis for normative theory (in particular, a theory of justice). Edmund Burke is another striking contemporaneous instance of a thinker who seeks to reconcile nature and history. Notwithstanding his historical sensibility, he could

write to Smith with regard to *TMS*: 'A theory like yours founded on the Nature of man, which is always the same, will last, when those that are founded on his opinions, which are always changing, will and must be forgotten' (*Corr*: 46). It may be added that the nature versus history issue has much more force with respect to humanity than any other elements of the world which science seeks to explain. From a human standpoint, as between ancient Greece and contemporary Greece, the way fire burns, or even the way sheep or birds behave, appear much more constant than the way humans behave and organize themselves.

68 Interestingly, according to Koerner (1999: 106) the Swedish Academy founders initially designated it the 'Economic Society of Science'; but '[i]n their first protocoled meeting, chaired by Linnaeus, they changed the name to the grander-sounding "Academy"'. Along with Koerner (1999) and Rausing (2003), on all these matters in relation to the economy of nature, see also Worster (1994), Redman (1997: 141), Müller-Wille (2003) and Schabas (2005: 4–5, 29–35, 40–1) – the last of these, in the context of a larger inquiry into the place of nature in the formation of modern economic science in the eighteenth and nineteenth centuries. (Koerner and Rausing are one and the same person.)

69 The very name of the Physiocratic school expresses an appeal to nature, deriving from the title of the 1767 collection of Quesnay's writings edited by Dupont de Nemours (see n. 20 above): 'The term … indicates the importance ascribed by these authors to natural forces, and derives from the Greek: *phýsis*, nature, and *kràtos*, power' (Vaggi 1987a: 869). The Physiocrats understood their doctrine to involve bringing the politico-economic order into conformity with nature or natural law (Fox-Genovese 1976: 9–11); 'government by nature', as Larrère (2001a: 897) succinctly puts it. She also draws attention to the parallels between Quesnay's viewpoint and Linnaeus's unified 'natural economics' (Larrère 2001a: 898). This, and more specific evidence, raises the possibility of an influence of Linnaeus upon Quesnay (Charles 2005: 145). Müller-Wille (2003: 166–7; cf. Rausing 2003: 177) is probably more right to conclude that any parallels rather reflect a 'common background in belonging to a scientific community that shared certain methodological vantage points'. Banzhaf (2000), partly following the work of others (see 546), makes a case for the significance of Quesnay's medical inquiries for his political economy, connected also with his broader conception of natural law; but Linnaeus plays no role in this account. This raises the question of the role of 'nature' in the Physiocratic doctrine of agriculture's unique productiveness, in terms of being able to generate a surplus.

70 On all these matters, see Tribe (1988: 42–4), Lempiäinen (1994: 586–8), Koerner (1996: 125–7), Koerner (1999: 106–8) and Rausing (2003: 180–2). In Koerner (1999: 108), Borgström is named as Eric Ericsson Borgström; in Rausing (2003: 180), as Anders Borgström. On the Uppsala Chair, compare Koerner (1999: 108) and Bernholz (2001: 207). Rausing (2003: 182) sums up the fate of Linnaeus's economics project: 'this newfound discipline left no lasting heritage'.

71 Here, one may draw a distinction between 'free-standing' or 'autonomous', and 'separable': the former may be taken as having a stronger sense, of independence from any logically prior suppositions. Smith's political economy is self-consciously not free-standing in that sense, while nevertheless separable. See the discussions of competition and self-regard in section 3.1.2, division of labour and the propensity to exchange in section 4.1.1, and saving and bettering one's condition in section 4.3.2. The notion that political economy at some point becomes an 'autonomous' discipline is not a useful idea: neither in 1776, nor 1817, nor 1871, was economic science an 'autonomous' discipline *in fact*, whatever later such claims there may have been. Nor is contemporary economics: most obviously, even in its purely deductive forms, it is dependent upon psychological and mathematical axioms. This is discussed further in the Epilogue. For a different view of the character and methods of Smith's political economy, but mostly not particularly in conflict with the account given here, see

Redman (1997). Force (2003: 276; also 200–7, 237, 251–5, 262–3) appears to give some prominence to a notion of the 'autonomy' of 'economic science', at least from the beginning of the nineteenth century; but in fact, what rather concerns him is the question of the autonomy of economic life or behaviour, with respect to ethics and politics (cf. Larrère 2001b). In any case, our interpretation of Smith's political economy as a separable science is not inconsistent with Force's interpretation of Smith. Viner (1928: 119–20) goes too far in endorsing the existence of an 'Adam Smith problem' (see pp. 220–2) and in implying an autonomy for political economy; but nevertheless, his argument provides something of a useful antidote to the opposite view:

> It is a commonplace among the authorities on Adam Smith that it is impossible fully to understand the *Wealth of Nations* without recourse to the *Theory of Moral Sentiments*. The vast bulk of economists, however, who have read the *Wealth of Nations* without reading the *Theory of Moral Sentiments*, have not regarded Smith's masterpiece as an obscure book, as one especially hard to understand. On the other hand, the very authorities who are most emphatic in asserting the need of reference to the *Theory of Moral Sentiments* to understand the *Wealth of Nations*, once they embark upon their self-imposed task of interpreting the latter in the light of the former, become immersed in difficult problems of interpretation for which scarcely any two writers offer the same solution.

72 This view, noted in section 2.1.2, is expressed in 'The History of Astronomy'. Here are the key statements, quoted more fully:

> when law has established order and security, and subsistence ceases to be precarious, the curiosity of mankind is increased .... The leisure which they then enjoy renders them more attentive to the appearances of nature ... and more desirous to know what is the chain which links them all together.... Those of liberal fortunes, whose attention is not much occupied either with business or with pleasure, can fill up the void of their imagination, which is thus disengaged from the ordinary affairs of life, no other way than by attending to that train of events which passes around them.... Their imagination, which accompanies with ease and delight the regular progress of nature, is stopped and embarrassed by ... seeming incoherences; they excite their wonder, and seem to require some chain of intermediate events, which, by connecting them with something that has gone before, may thus render the whole course of the universe consistent and of a piece. Wonder, therefore, and not any expectation of advantage from its discoveries, is the first principle which prompts mankind to the study of Philosophy, of that science which pretends to lay open the concealed connections that unite the various appearance of nature; and they pursue this study for its own sake, as an original pleasure or good in itself, without regarding its tendency to procure them the means of many other pleasures.
>
> (*EPS*: 50–1)

> even we, while we have been endeavouring to represent all philosophical systems as mere inventions of the imagination, to connect together the otherwise disjointed and discordant phaenomena of nature, have insensibly been drawn in, to make use of language expressing the connecting principles of this one [i.e. astronomy], as if they were the real chains which Nature makes use of to bind together her several operations.
>
> (*EPS*: 105; cf. 45–7)

73 We emphasize 'discoveries' in this statement, by way of contrast with the notion of scientific theories as *inventions* (see *EPS*: 105, quoted in n. 72 above). Vivenza's conclusion is confirmed also by Smith's position, expressed more than once, that it is the pursuit of human material subsistence and betterment (rather than mere 'wonder' – again, see n. 72) which is the stimulus for the development of the arts and sciences:

> to supply the wants of *meat*, *drink*, cloathing, and lodging allmost the whole of the arts and sciences have been invented and improved.... Geometry, arithmetick, and writing have all been invented originally to facilitate the operation of the severall arts.... [I]n a certain view of things all the arts, the science<s>, law and government, wisdom, and even virtue itself tend all to this one thing, the providing meat, drink, rayment, and lodging for men .... [T]he far greater parts of the arts and sciences have been invented and improved to supply three great wants of mankind ... food, cloaths, and lodging ....
>
> (*LJA*: 337–40; also *LJB*: 488–90; *TMS*: 183)

### 3 Competition, prices and distribution

1 All other references to natural prices beyond Book I, Chapter VII are at *WN* (3, 46, 165–6, 216–17, 326, 507, 630, 651–3, 893).

2 *LJA* (84, 356–7, 360–4, 370, 387, 389); *LJB* (494–8, 510, 528, 533); Campbell and Skinner (1976: 20); Meek *et al.* (1978b: 34–5). See also n. 85 below. With regard to natural price involving only labour cost, there is however at one point a suggestion of the need to recover interest and profit understood as the opportunity cost of capital invested in labour education (*LJA*: 357).

3 *WN* (53–4; 'the temporary and occasional price' versus 'the average or ordinary price' of corn) and similar articulations at *WN* (63, 76, 194–8, 215, 236, 259, 527). All these instances point to a notion of normal prices associated with normal market conditions. Further uses of ordinary price occur at *WN* (132, 164–5, 168, 186, 202–3, 229, 249, 358–9, with regard to land prices, and the ordinary rate of interest, also 614, 482–3, 527, 652, 864). Only a few slight and passing uses of it occur in *LJA* (178, 360, 365), and one in *edWN* (580).

4 Recall in the definition of natural price from *WN* (73), quoted directly above, and also in the quote directly following here, the phrase 'for any considerable time' (also at 220). It may also be noted that an equality of natural price and average price under competitive conditions is not a *definition* of natural price: this would make natural price merely an artefact of actual prices, depriving it of the independent definition essential for its causal role as regulator of market prices. Rather, equality of natural price and average/ordinary price is an expression of the conviction that competition will indeed prevail upon actual prices, tending to bring them into line with opportunity cost, so that actual prices at least on average approximate natural price. Vianello (1989: 102–5) cogently argues that such approximation of the average of actual market prices to natural price is only really plausible on the supposition of unchanging natural prices. Smith indicates also that competition can extend to international price equalization, for some commodities, with explicit allowance for the role of transport costs (*WN*: 185, 208; cf. 426). International mobility of capital is also considered a little (*WN*: 848–9, 906, 927–8; cf. Book II, Chapter V).

5 The following is the most pertinent to price theory:

> in some employments the same quantity of industry will in different years produce very different quantities of commodities; while in others it will produce always the same, or very nearly the same.... It is only the average produce of the one species of industry [i.e. the former] which can be suited in any respect to the effectual demand; and as its actual produce is frequently much greater and frequently much less than its average produce, the quantity of the commodities brought to market will sometimes exceed a good deal, and sometimes fall short a good deal of the effectual demand. Even though that demand therefore should continue always the same, their market price will be liable to great fluctuations ....
>
> (*WN*: 75–6)

The point is reiterated at *WN* (132). Other economic averages appear at *WN* (63, 125, 206, 213, 226–7, 342, 461, 508, 519, 534, 555, 661, 888).

6 There are some explicit calculations of averages in the precise sense (*WN*: 204, 211–18, 267–75, 889–90).

7 All such references to ordinary (without reference to 'average' or 'natural') profits in Smith's *Works* are in only *WN* (70, 111–14, 118, 122, 127–8, 160–1, 163, 175, 182, 184, 187, 189, 245, 264, 310, 377, 438, 454, 505–6, 518, 529–30, 545, 562, 596, 598–9, 612, 665–6, 670–2, 744, 755, 837, 840, 848, 865).

8 See the citations in n. 3 above, as well as those cross-referenced with the quotation from *WN* (189) above. This use occurs particularly in Book I, Chapter XI, *Of the Rent of Land* (pp. 160–275).

9 This was indicated in section 2.3.1. Some further instances of this identification may be given here: 'the natural and ordinary state of mankind' as the condition of 'the greater part of men', 'natural and ordinary temper of mind' (*TMS*: 45); the 'ordinary standard of human nature' as average behaviour (*TMS*: 57; also, for example, 80–1, 119, 260, 309); 'the natural and ordinary effects of … conduct' (*TMS*: 116); 'a natural event … according to the ordinary course of things' (*TMS*: 141); 'the natural and ordinary state of … mind' (*TMS*: 273, n. *e*); the 'ordinary and natural state of animals' (*edWN*: 571).

10 See above this section, the quotation from *WN* (74–5). Hereafter, in the consideration of Smith's market price dynamics, effectual demand is represented by $D^*$ and 'market imbalance' is employed as a shorthand for inequality between 'quantity … brought to market' and $D^*$.

11 On 'extent' of the market, and related notions like 'extended' and 'extensive', see also *WN* (130, 134, 246–7, 249, 253, 447, 496, 507–9, 535, 537, 575, 577, 580, 591–2, 595, 637, 680–2, 730, 833, 838, 900–1, 935, 1070); *LJA* (355–6); *fA* (582); *fB* (585). Occasionally, Smith speaks also of 'narrowness' of the market (*WN*: 129–30, 246, 267, 447–8, 680, 727–8; cf. *LJA*: 366). On market as outlet for sale, see also *WN* (32, 34, 163, 171, 180, 185, 192, 194, 220–2, 246–7, 249, 376, 411, 443, 448, 489, 494, 503, 531, 534, 536, 545, 547, 578, 580–1, 592, 632, 635, 671, 684); *LJA* (83, 256); *LJB* (525); *fA* (583); *Corr* (241).

12 For just Book I of *WN* (275 of 950 pages) at (16, 41–2, 48–50, 52–5, 57–9, 60, 67n, 69–79, 93–4, 98, 101, 110–11, 113, 125, 129, 132, 134, 140–41, 149, 158, 161–5, 167–8, 172–5, 178–9, 182, 184, 189, 194–5, 198, 207–9, 211–14, 216–20, 224–5, 228–37, 243–5, 249–53, 257–9, 263, 272); *LJA* (6, 33, 84, 163, 257, 357–8, 364, 368–71, 375, 377–8, 382, 389); *LJB* (496–500, 502–3, 507, 510, 512, 516, 525, 527–9, 537); *edWN* (567, 574–5); *fA* (582–4); *fB* (585); *Corr* (243, 245–6).

13 *WN* (200–1, 215, 235). All other references to market prices beyond Book I, Chapter VII are at *WN* (3, 59–60, 62–3, 132, 213, 482–6, 839); and *WN* (352, 356–8) speak of interest as a market price, and of the market price of land.

14 An analysis in very similar terms occurs at *LJB* (494–8). All other references to market prices in the lectures are at *LJA* (361–2, 364, 377); *LJB* (503).

15 For just Book I of *WN* (51, 53–4, 56 ('the current prices of labour'), 77, 84 ('the price of work'), 87, 92 (the 'common' and 'the usual price of … labour'), 93–6, 98, 101, 103–4, 122, 127, 133–4 (the 'common price of common labour'), 143, 148, 150 (the 'usual price of teaching'), 156, 164, 207, 209, 218–19, 224); *LJA* (192, 317, 341, 343–4, 350, 355 ('the naturall price of labour'; also 361 and *LJB*: 495), 359–62, 387); *LJB* (491); *edWN* (567, 575). *LJA* (361) is the only instance where Smith *explicitly* refers to a 'market price' of labour; but the notion of there being labour markets is more widely implied, in particular by his treatment of labour remuneration as analogous to commodity pricing.

16 *LRB* (157); *Corr* (48, 60, 139–41, 151–4, 177–8, 245–6, 248, 251, 263, 270, 277, 294). They are all inconsequential from a conceptual and theoretical point of view, with one exception (*Corr*: 251; see n. 57 below).

17 The explicit imputation of normative significance by calling it 'proper' – natural price as the desirable outcome – is repeated at *WN* (652, also at 630, in relation to profits and prices) and *LJA* (84). On competition and its effects as a natural norm for human society, see also the discussion of 'the system of natural liberty', and 'natural balance' and related terms, in section 5.2.1.

18 *WN* (17, 79, 93, 132, 135–6, 145–6, 158, 172, 174, 185, 209, 224, 235, 249, 267, 357, 460, 465–7, 469, 471, 494, 496, 500, 526, 547, 557, 597, 607–8, 632, 637, 644, 656, 660, 669, 684, 687, 734, 736–7, 741–2, 744, 746, 748–9, 780, 881, 902).

19 In this deepest or most generic sense, 'competition' also informs the meaning of the 'anchor' (not a Smithian metaphor) of market price behaviour itself: natural price as opportunity cost is natural price as the (best) competing alternative foregone. Notice also the coercive force of competition with regard to individual behaviour, in the quotation from *WN* (163–4) given in the text immediately above ('self-defence'). Kurz (2008) has drawn out the significance of this aspect of the classical conception of competition, for the endogeneity of technical innovation with respect to competition. That is to say, at another level of analysis there is a second and important dimension of competition in Smith, whereby competition acts upon production methods (sec. 4.1.1). This in fact is somewhat implied in the quotation from *WN* (759–60), immediately below; and for a clearer instance, see the quotation from *WN* (748), in section 3.4.1 below. For an intriguing parallel with economic competition, consider also Smith's views on non-establishment of religion, discussed in Chapter 2, n. 37.

20 Smith uses both terms, 'self-interest' and 'self-love', but it is far, far more discussed in *TMS* than in *WN*. The other typical articulation is in terms of people's desire of 'bettering' their 'condition'. (On this, see the discussion of Smith on saving in sec. 4.3.2, especially n. 50, also for the role of self-command and prudence.) 'Self-regard' is not used by him; but this softer term perhaps better captures Smith's sense of a combination of self-interest and sociable 'self-command' (his term) or self-restraint, than do self-interest and self-love, which, one may suggest, have a rather harder tone to them, for the twenty-first-century ear (cf. Faccarello 2005: 702). The very opening sentence of *TMS* (9) acknowledges human selfishness while at the same time affirming a natural human sociableness (albeit connected with individual pleasure, though this does not make it selfish: cf. *TMS*: 317):

> How selfish soever man may be supposed, there are evidently some principles in his nature, which interest him in the fortune of others, and render their happiness necessary to him, though he derives nothing from it except the pleasure of seeing it.

On the naturalness of self-regard see, for example, *TMS* (212, 219); *edWN* (579); *Corr* (56). The key *WN*, Book I, Chapter vii (74–5, 79) on price theory explicitly appeals to individuals' 'interest' as motivating the behaviour generating competition. It should be added that the relationship between morals or manners and commerce, in Smith's understanding, is not entirely one-way, not just a relationship of orderly commercial society presupposing a certain standard of moral behaviour (see Chapter 5, n. 21). In *LJ*, Smith also observes that the human infant's lengthy dependence on its parents naturally socializes humans, by enforcing a habitual and accommodating restraint of the individual will (*LJA*: 142–3; *LJB*: 438) – a useful reminder that social theories which take fully formed adults as their starting point are overlooking an important elementary fact. Valuable discussions of self-regard in Smith's thought are provided by Raphael and Macfie (1976b: 20–2), Fitzgibbons (1995: 137–52), Griswold (1999: 76–96), Roncaglia (2005: 122–6) and, perhaps especially, Force (2003). Hirschman (1977) is a contribution of enduring significance, tracing the relations between human 'passions' and 'interests' in seventeenth- and eighteenth-century thought.

21 Hence the disdain Smith sometimes expresses for masters, owners of capital and so

on, while it has been a source of some latter-day amusement and bemusement, is not at all genuinely paradoxical:

> Our merchants and master-manufacturers complain much of the bad effects of high wages .... They say nothing concerning the bad effects of high profits. They are silent with regard to the pernicious effects of their own gains. They complain only of those of other people.
>
> (*WN*: 115, and in near identical terms at 599)

> People of the same trade seldom meet together, even for merriment and diversion, but the conservation ends in a conspiracy against the public ....
>
> (*WN*: 145)

> Whenever the legislature attempts to regulate the differences between masters and their workmen, its counsellors are always the masters.
>
> (*WN*: 157; cf. 584)

> To widen the market and to narrow the competition, is always the interest of the dealers ... an order of men ... who have generally an interest to deceive and even to oppress the publick ....
>
> (*WN*: 267)

> To found a great empire for the sole purpose of raising up a people of customers, may at first sight appear a project fit only for a nation of shopkeepers. It is, however, a project altogether unfit for a nation of shopkeepers; but extremely fit for a nation whose government is influenced by shopkeepers.
>
> (*WN*: 613)

See also *WN* (84–5, 266, 471, quoted in sec. 5.3.2, 570); *TMS* (50–66). Consider as well, Smith's concerns about the impact of specialization on workers (sec. 4.1), and the primary place he gives to workers' consumption in the normative objective of political economy ('opulence': sec. 5.1.1). In the *WN* (613) quotation, the first edition of the book has, instead of the phrase 'whose government is influenced', the words 'that is governed' (cf. *WN*: 570). On the use of the post-Smithian term 'capitalism', see Chapter 5, n. 58.

22 *WN* (75, 78; also 74–9, 165, 172, 174–5, 228, 242–3, 370, 529, 579, 638); *LJA* (358, 361, 381); *LJB* (496). Other instances of 'supply' and 'demand' explicitly juxtaposed occur at *WN* (193–4, 199, 206, 211, 221, 235, 539, 601, 607, 755, 757).

23 *WN* (10–11, 283–4, 548, 912); *LJA* (260, 267–9, 326, 384, 387, 421). Other and incidental references to 'supply' and variants of it, of an economic nature, occur at *WN* (22, 47, 66, 93, 130, 137 (applied to labour), 147, 169, 176, 178, 192, 207–9, 212, 254, 256–7, 264 (for just Book I)); *LJA* (196, 325, 335, 339, 343, 351, 355, 356, 363, 377, 379, 383, 385–8, 390–2); *LJB* (488–9, 503, 510); *edWN* (562, 566, 572). There are in *TMS*, *EPS* and *LRB*, no instances of a genuinely economic kind, though there are some of a non-economic nature.

24 All other instances of scarcity and plenty explicitly juxtaposed in relation to commodity prices are at *WN* (100–4, 183, 189, 204, 215–18, 243, 259, 424, 461, 507, 514–15, 526, 538–9, 875); *LJA* (359, 361–2, 383); *LJB* (487).

25 That there is a qualitative difference between Smithian and marginalist concepts of scarcity is not undercut by his regarding human desires as unlimited. Smith expresses such a view, for example, at *WN* (181):

> the desire of the conveniencies and ornaments of building, dress, equipage, and houshold furniture, seems to have no limit or certain boundary.... What is over and above satisfying the limited desire [for food], is given for the amusement of those desires which cannot be satisfied, but seem to be altogether endless.

See also *WN* (190–1); *TMS* (50–1). The desires described there, however insatiable, are *social* in character, unlike the autonomous individual preferences of latter-day marginalist theory. In any case, the key question is whether such desires play a role in his explanation of prices. They do not; only $D^* > 0$ as a necessary condition for anything to *have* a market and a price, of any persistence (cf. Smith's distinction between $D^*$ and 'absolute demand' at *WN*: 73). Such notions about human desire are not equivalent to subscribing to the marginalist theory of relative commodity prices. A hint of human insatiability can even be found in the Bible: 'The lover of money will not be satisfied with money; nor the lover of wealth with gain' (Ecclesiastes Ch. 5, verse 10); 'Human eyes are never satisfied' (Proverbs Ch. 27, verse 30). But the marginalist theory, of course, is not to be found there. None of this is to deny that the extent of human desire plays a wider role in Smith's economics, for example, as a general spur to industriousness. See in particular, the discussion of bettering one's condition in section 4.3.2; also Rosenberg (1968), on Smith's conception of the historical course of economic development.

26 See also *WN* (178, 212–13, 303); *LJB* (496). The phrase 'moderate plenty' is employed by Smith a number of times, to convey a sense of normal market conditions:

> in many places the money price of labour remains uniformly the same sometimes for half a century together. If in these places, therefore, the labouring poor can maintain their families in dear years, they must be at their ease in times of moderate plenty, and in affluence in those of extraordinary cheapness.
>
> (*WN*: 92)

> In the present season of scarcity the high price of corn no doubt distresses the poor. But in times of moderate plenty, when corn is at its ordinary or average price, the natural rise in the price of any other sort of rude produce cannot much affect them.
>
> (*WN*: 259; also 215, 424, 452, 459, 515, 682, 875 – and especially 526)

27 See also *WN* (190–1, 242–3, 466, 521, 563); *LJA* (380). All other (and rather more incidental) references to scarcity or variants thereof, employed in economic senses, are at *WN* (323, 437–8, 442, 524–8, 531, 533, 536, 540, 636, 940); *LJA* (364, 383); *LJB* (509, 511, 524). (This listing does not include Smith's frequent use of 'scarce' as an archaic form of 'scarcely', in the non-economic sense of 'barely' or 'hardly'.) There are no economic uses of scarcity or variants of it at all in *TMS*, *EPS*, *LRB* or *Corr*. Note that the key *WN* Chapter on price theory proceeds without any reference to scarcity (the first is at p. 86), circumstantial confirmation of the argument below, that the substance of that theory does not belong to the same family as the later marginalist theories. Nevertheless, the assertion by Robertson and Taylor (1957: 184) – that 'Smith makes only passing reference to … "scarcity" and makes no reference to it at any critical point in his discussion of value' – is at best an exaggeration.

28 For other instances of plenty as excess supply see *WN* (174–5, 537–9, 841 (with regard to ground-rent)); *LJB* (525). For plenty as opulence, see also *LJA* (6, 340–41, 355–6, 363–6, 381–2); *LJA* (487) – and for plenty as cheapness, also *WN* (565–6, 570, 573; all with respect to land); *LJA* (331, 360); *LJB* (472, 486–7, 526). All other incidental references to plenty or variants of it, not cited elsewhere here, are at *TMS* (56, 168); *WN* (99, 165, 223, 241, 323, 421, 429, 480, 483, 534, 567–8, 572, 614, 748, 841, 876); *EPS* (49); *LJA* (159, 196, 400); *LJB* (499, 507); *Corr* (66–7). Some of these are not 'economic', in any significant sense, or only slightly so (e.g. *WN*: 876 – 'the most plentiful … diet'). As implied by this listing, the term or variants appear hardly at all in *TMS* (twice), *EPS* (once), *LRB* (nowhere) and *Corr* (twice, but both non-economic senses).

29 To more clearly see this, consider the following hypothetical world. Labour is the only primary (i.e. non-produced) input in the production of commodities (though for

Smith, in a certain sense labour is a reproducible input: see *WN* (98, quoted in sec. 3.4.3). The labour, or number of workers, available for production is finite. Commodities are produced by means of inputs of labour and produced commodities, via constant-returns-to-scale production methods. Scarcity in Smith's second sense described in the text is not present in this world, since outputs can be expanded without any rise in input requirements per unit of outputs. (But of course, the existence of commodities exhibiting high prices relative to most individual incomes cannot be excluded.) Nevertheless, the additional supposition of insatiable human wants would make this situation exhibit marginalist – or what may be called 'subjective' – scarcity, since the maximum feasible output quantities are finite, due to the finite labour availability.

30 For discussion of the origin of that phrase, see Groenewegen (1973, 1987e) and Thweatt (1983). The latter, at minimum, creates a potentially misleading impression when he says that in 'Smith's *Wealth of Nations* ... we find the *couplet* "supply and demand" on 14 occasions' (Thweatt 1983: 288; emphasis added). To repeat, and notwithstanding Thweatt's unfortunate use of inverted commas here, that phrase is nowhere used by Smith (and in any case, there are more than fourteen such couplings: see n. 22 above). Hereafter, $p'''_i$ $(i = 1, 2, \ldots, k)$ is commonly used to denote the set of market prices at which transactions in a commodity actually occur (and sometimes just to denote market prices in general); $p''$, to denote normal price (our preferred term for Smith's 'natural price'); and $Q$, to denote Smith's notion of 'quantity ... brought to market'. That is to say, the set of market prices in general involves multiple values whereas normal price is necessarily singular.

31 However, there is one point in the argument of *WN*, Book I, Chapter VII where Smith has recourse to a relation between total market demand and market prices, to which we return immediately below.

32 The 'deviations' may be interpreted in either of two ways. Supposing initially that $Q/D^* = 1$ and all elements of $p'''_i = p''$, how does the imbalance cause a *change* in at least some $p'''_i$, away from $p''$? Making no supposition of initial prices uniformly equal to normal price, how does $Q/D^* \neq 1$ cause a *difference* between at least some $p'''_i$ and $p''$? (Smith once uses the term 'deviations' in this manner himself – *WN*: 80; cf. 197.) The special case of identical $p'''_i$ occurs when $p''$ prevails throughout the market (and $Q/D^* = 1$). Such a uniform $p'''$ is also possible under conditions of market imbalance, but it is obviously far less compelling in that situation.

33 In other words, the possibility that total demand and sales might exceed effectual demand as at least some $p'''_i$ deviate *above* $p''$ is excluded from consideration. $Q^s$ is the sum total of quantities actually transacted between suppliers and demanders, in general at a variety of market prices, in the market period.

34 A withdrawal of some part of $Q$ from the market is not impossible, e.g. for storable commodities, as a result of expectations of future price rises, but this possibility may be put aside here.

35 Actually, Smith does not employ such a simple correspondence between market/normal price differences and actual/required profitability differences. Rather, he supposes merely that in general such price differences will cause payments to some or other of the owners of collaborating inputs – capital, labour, land – to deviate from required returns. That is to say, it is supposed that the burden of non-normal prices may fall on any of the three parties, and their responses in principle can suffice to push commodity supply in the appropriate direction. This is more satisfactory for supply contractions than supply expansions: putting aside the role of rents, if prices are below $p''$, suppliers (here equated with the owners of capital) who are continuing to receive required profitability – while the wages of their labourers are below required remuneration – will tend to be deserted by labour. But if prices are above $p''$, and suppliers (who we may identify with the owners of capital) are continuing to receive just the required profitability – while wages are above required remuneration

– attempted labour influx to the industry might induce no supply expansion (cf. Ciccone 1999: 85, n. 3).

36 Ciccone (1999: 71–2) rightly distinguishes two sources of $Q/D^*$ imbalance discussed in *WN*: imbalance between capital or productive capacity and normal effectual demand (thereby requiring, ultimately, an adjustment of industry capacity); and transitory imbalances or shocks, from either the demand or supply sides, which require no such changes in capacity. Transitory demand shocks may lead to no $Q$ variations, just a temporary imbalance between $Q$ and (abnormal) demand. See also the careful analysis by Vianello (1989: 93–7) of sources of variation in demands and quantities supplied.

37 The possibility of suppliers withdrawing from the market rather than accepting below-normal prices when $Q > D^*$ is explicitly considered by Smith, and he indicates the significance of perishability for this possibility (*WN*: 74). It may be added however, that even supposing the commodity can be held by suppliers at zero storage cost and is strictly imperishable, still it may not be held back from the market until it can be sold for $p^n$. On Smith's own reasoning concerning capital and profits, the normal price for a commodity stored over a sequence of $k$ periods will be $p^n(1 + r)^k$, where $p^n$ is here to be read as the normal price at the completion of production and marketing (before storage) and $r$ is the normal rate of profit: the capital tied up in the stored commodity must return normal profits over the periods of storage. Hence, if a holder of the commodity for potential supply has no expectation that normal (or otherwise expected actual) prices will rise in something like this manner over subsequent periods, there is incentive to sell at some range of prices below $p^n$.

38 As above (n. 35), for simplicity the suppliers may be identified with the owners of capital.

39 Ciccone (1999: 75–6) points out that, whatever superficial similarities it may have to Smith's approach to market prices, Marshall's notion of 'temporary equilibrium price' differs qualitatively, 'in the very conception of the latter as an equilibrium price, i.e. as a price which makes the amount buyers are willing to purchase just equal to the amount which sellers are willing to sell'. Larsen (1977) acquiesces in just this identification of the Smithian and Marshallian concepts. Ciccone might have added that the conformity of Marshall's temporary equilibrium prices to the 'law of one price' (LOOP; temporary price as a singular magnitude) also makes it an equilibrium concept in a sense in which Smith's $p^m{}_i$ are not. The fact that Cantillon employs something akin to the LOOP (see sec. 3.5.2), and that Smith was very familiar with that work (Mizuta 2000: 45), suggests that he chose consciously to not treat market price as a uniform magnitude. Ciccone (1999: 88, n. 18) reminds us also of Marshall's tendency to colonize classical economics with his own ideas. See further to this, Groenewegen (1993). Hollander (1973) is the most substantial latter-day example of the persistence of this Marshallian tendency in the literature.

40 *WN* (78; emphasis added). The notion of indeterminate price under conditions of absolute supply inelasticity is not explicitly stated in *LJ*, but it is implied by the characterization of 'demand-prices' (not a Smithian term) under those conditions as arbitrary (*LJA*: 358–9; also 361–2; *LJB*: 496):

> *When there is not enough produced to serve every body*, the fortune of the bidders is the only regulation of price.
>
> The story which is told of the merchant and the carrier in the desarts of Arabia is an evidence of this. The merchant gave 10,000 ducats for a certain quantity of water. His fortune here regulated the price, for if he had not had them, he could not have given them, and if his fortune had been less, the water would have been cheaper.
>
> (*LJB*: 496; emphasis added, and the same parable at *LJA*: 358)

Notice also the use, in relation to desire, of the phrase 'no limit or certain boundary', at *WN* (181; quoted in n. 25 above), so similar to the *WN* (234–5) language in relation to demand-prices.

41 Market prices in these situations are more likely to tend to uniformity.

42 For Smith, the determinants of demand essentially reduce to wealth and desire (sec. 3.2.1), where 'wealth' may convey assets or income, but most probably real income is primarily intended (e.g. *WN*: 290; and more fully, sec. 2.2.1).

43 'Of the Causes of Improvement in the productive Powers of Labour, and of the Order according to which its Produce is naturally distributed among the different Ranks of the People'.

44 At least for the purposes of his treatment of market price convergence, Smith seems tacitly to suppose that for each commodity, industry or activity, all producers at any point in time employ the same production method, or that there is a single method employed by the great bulk of producers. (Nevertheless, as taken up in sec. 4.1.1, for the purposes of his analysis of growth dynamics new production methods are more or less continuously being introduced; and since they are not introduced by all producers simultaneously, this entails multiple production methods at any point in time, even if there is a singular dominant method.) Insofar as multiple methods of production at any particular point in time are not contemplated, the associated uniform input–output relations may be read as embodying the production method which is both input-minimizing and cost-minimizing, at least when production methods are subject to competition, so that normal price just covers both necessary cost, as well as necessary remunerations. These are distinct insofar as the payment of necessary remunerations, but with use of production methods which are not cost-minimizing (at given rates of remuneration), would generate above-necessary costs (cf. Petty's distinction between political and natural prices, discussed in sec. 3.5.2).

45 For the purposes of this discussion, the cost of bringing output 'to market' is put aside.

46 An illustration may assist. Suppose the normal capacity output of the dominant plant in some particular industry is 100 units. If $D^*$ is 200, 300 or 800 units, there can be precisely two, three or eight such plants, each producing at normal capacity and normal cost. If $D^*$ is 864, there can be eight plants each producing 108 units or nine plants each producing 96 units – in either case, reasonably close to normal capacity. However, if $D^*$ is 252, and supposing again that each plant has the same share of normal output, two plants would each be producing 126 units (which might even be an unfeasible over-utilization) or three plants, 84 units each (a considerable under-utilization).

47 See Willig (1987); cf. McNulty (1967), Richardson (1975: 353–8) and Sylos-Labini (1976: 200–2). Putting aside the issue of single plants controlled by more than one firm, the desirable plant size, or normal capacity, associated with the dominant production method is equivalent to the minimum, economically viable firm size (e.g. for potential entrants); and thereby, together with $D^*$, determines the maximum number of viable firms. For Smithian competition to be consistent with Smithian dynamic increasing returns from division of labour, at each point in time the ratio of normal plant capacity to $D^*$ must be such as to allow sufficient firms for free competition or contestability of markets.

48 If technical change is very rapid, there may be no well-defined dominant method of production (cf. *WN*: 131–2). Consider computer technology in the last two decades of the twentieth century: change was so rapid that there perhaps were no well-defined normal prices for some of the associated products. On this issue, see also Kurz (2008) on competition, technical innovation and normal prices in relation to Smith, classical economics and Joseph Schumpeter.

49 The possibility of the convergence dynamics inducing technical change (e.g. by *temporary* alterations in the size of the market) may be put aside. The possibility of their inducing change in normal remunerations is even less plausible.

50 See, for example, *WN* (260). Recall, from the argument of section 3.2.2, that this variant of Smith's notions of 'scarcity' is in contradistinction to the 'subjective scarcity' of marginalist theory. In relation to ingenuity versus scarcity, Smith is most definitely a technology optimist: overall, productivity growth is the dominant force, not natural scarcity. (See also Sylos-Labini 1976: 205–6 on the irreversibility of Smith's dynamic increasing returns.) The arrival of a stationary state (zero growth) economy in commercial society, due to natural resource constraints, is evidently a remote possibility for Smith (*WN*: 111–12). Heilbroner (1973), in particular, imputes excessive significance to this possibility (cf. Winch 1978: 142–4).

51 Given $p''$, this implies increasing $Q$ as market prices rise above $p''$; but that relation of course does not correspond to, and is not by Smith grounded upon, a short-period marginal cost function.

52 As with commodity prices, we shall prefer the term 'normal', where Smith speaks of natural, ordinary or usual rates of remuneration.

53 The difference is evident in the fact that for an economic system as a whole, the normal value of its gross outputs is equal to cost in the first sense, but generally will be in excess of cost in the second sense, that excess being an expression of the social surplus or net product (see secs 4.2.2 and 4.4.2). All other instances of 'cost', for just Books I–II of *WN*, are at: (38, 66, 77, 95, 110, 129–30, 163–4, 167, 178, 196, 224, 242, 249–50, 262, 265, 292, 310, 330, 347, 363) – and in *LJ*, at: *LJA* (79–80, 120, 185, 195, 219, 300, 341, 343, 363, 369–70, 385); *LJB* (409, 475, 509, 531). Neither the term nor variants of it appear anywhere in *TMS* or *LRB*; there is one in *EPS* (184) and four in *Corr* (49, 178, 206, 216), though three of the latter are figurative.

54 Smith is clear that he means by money or nominal value the quantity of gold or silver embodied in the currency, not its conventional denomination: '[b]y the money-price of goods ... I understand always the quantity of pure gold or silver for which they are sold, without any regard to the denomination of the coin' (*WN*: 63; also 213, 254).

55 At *WN* (47–8), quoted immediately above, he uses the phrase 'toil and trouble'; elsewhere, 'pains' (*LJA*: 17, 25). Neither represents a homogeneous substance which could provide a unit or standard for measurement. When Smith continues further in relation to reducing heterogeneous labour to a common substance, commenting that it is 'not easy to find any accurate measure either of hardship or ingenuity' (*WN*: 48), one cannot but agree: it is impossible. The misguided attempt to justify 'labour' as 'the ultimate and real standard' (*WN*: 51) of value continues to p. 54. Pownall (1776: 344–5) is also critical of this subjectivism: 'the same person will, in different habits, relations and circumstances of life, estimate ... labour ... as of very different value'. Blaug (1962: 49), on the other hand, judges it a virtue of Smith's analysis: 'Adam Smith tried to go deeper .... The "real value" of a commodity is ... not a certain number of man-hours but units of disutility.' (The statement is repeated in subsequent editions.) Young (1997a: 79–103) also seeks to draw a subjective theory of costs out of Smith's texts.

Smith is much concerned about the impact of work on the state of mind of the labourer (see sec. 4.1). It is by him nowhere reduced to a supposed homogeneous substance, 'disutility' (a term not to be found in Smith's texts) – let alone any suggestions that 'utility' also is reducible to a homogeneous and measurable substance, and that both utility and disutility are reducible to a singular substance. The appeal to labour pains is little more than philosophico-anthropological background noise to the science proper. When it comes to actually measuring, it is, of course, observable phenomena which are deployed: labour-time, corn and so on. (Naldi 2003: 552 interprets the labour pains notion in a more objective manner.) Pownall (1776: 342; also 343–5) as well rejects the notion that labour commanded is an adequate measure of cost in the sense of input used up:

> it is not simply the labour, *but the labour mixed with ... objects*, that is

> exchanged; it is *the composite article, the laboured article*: Some part of the exchangeable value is derived from the object itself; and in this composite value, which is the thing actually exchanged, the labour bears very different proportions of value, according to the different nature of the object on which it is employed.

This, in effect, is an intuition that the labour theory of value is not an acceptable assumption (see n. 56 below).

56 So Smith continues a little further on: The wealth of a person conveys

> the power of purchasing; a certain command over ... labour, *or over all the produce of labour* .... His fortune is greater or less, precisely in proportion to the extent of this power; or to the quantity either of other men's labour, or, *what is the same thing*, of the produce of other men's labour, which it enables him to purchase or command.
>
> (*WN*: 48; emphasis added)

But it is only 'the same thing' if the labour theory of value holds. (It is as if Smith is continuing to think of the relation between labour embodied in producing commodities and labour commanded, as if commodity exchange continues as in the 'rude state': see *WN*: 65.) Suppose $p_x$, $p_y$ and $w$ are the money prices of a commodity $x$, a commodity $y$, and homogeneous labour, respectively. The labour theory of value is the proposition that the relative price of $x$ with respect to $y$ ($p_x/p_y$, the $y$-commanded value of $x$) is equal to the labour-time directly and indirectly required to produce a unit of $x$, relative to that required to produce a unit of $y$; hence the latter is, at the same time, equal to the ratio of the labour-commanded price of $x$ ($p_x/w$) and of $y$ ($p_y/w$). Furthermore, for the labour-commanded price of a commodity to strictly equal the labour-time directly and indirectly required to produce it requires a special case of the labour theory of value so understood – in effect, the case which Smith characterizes for the 'rude state', the human condition before rents and profits enter as elements of price. Naldi (2003) conjectures that some of the difficulties of making sense of Smith's labour-commanded notion indeed may be due to the residual presence of a labour theory of value in the text of *WN*, from earlier thinking which Smith subsequently discarded. But Naldi acknowledges that such an interpretation is impossible to demonstrate.

Sylos-Labini (1976: 207–8) notes that in relation to the primary practical purpose for which Smith utilizes the labour-commanded measure – to estimate technical and productivity changes over time – constancy over time of the wage share (of direct *plus indirect* labour employed), for any particular commodity, makes changes in the labour-commanded price of the commodity an accurate reflection of changes in the direct plus indirect labour employed per unit of output in production of the commodity. (Indirect labour refers to the labour required to produce the material inputs required for production of a commodity, alongside the direct labour input.) Smith makes no such assumption about wage shares. But in any case, this result is due to nothing more than the fact that the wage share of direct *plus indirect* labour, in the gross value of output, is equal to the real wage per worker (measured in the commodity under consideration) times the labour-time directly and indirectly required to produce a unit of the commodity. Constancy of that wage share over time therefore entails that any percentage change in direct plus indirect labour-time required (the reciprocal of total labour productivity) is matched by an equal percentage change, but of opposite sign, in the real wage (the reciprocal of the labour-commanded price). Furthermore, the constancy of Sylos-Labini's measure of the wage share in general will only be associated with constancy of the wage share in the ordinary sense of the term – the wage share of *direct* labour in *net* value added – if the labour theory of value holds. In short, his constant-wage-share conjecture is not really an alternative way of making sense of Smith's labour-commanded measure, such as to require weaker restrictions than the labour theory of value.

57 Sometimes real price is expressed in terms of 'corn' or 'subsistence', as well as labour (*WN*: 194, 236, 250, 254, 262, 515 – and 245–6, quoted above); but these are evidently serving as proxies for labour. Smith makes explicit elsewhere that the relative stability of the corn wage, combined with the greater difficulty of ascertaining money-wage rates across time and space (versus corn prices), provide pragmatic grounds for using corn as a standard of real value (*WN*: 53–4, 56; cf. 206; see also Sylos-Labini 1976: 209–16). In the first edition of *WN* Smith had rather overstated the significance of corn as a standard, and amended his text in response to James Anderson, though one may say, still leaving it overstated (see *WN*: 515–16, with ed. n. 28; *Corr*: 251). All other references to real and/or nominal price are at *WN* (3, 4, 46, 51, 53–5, 81, 210, 224, 234–5, 249–50, 253–4, 259, 509, 514–15, 555). These terms are not employed in *LJ*, but the real versus nominal price distinction is intimated there, with particular regard to money and to labour (*LJA*: 100–2, 343–4, 350, 359–62, 375; *LJB*: 491, 502–3; also *edWN*: 567). Smith also sometimes uses 'real value' to denote real price (see n. 58). In a detailed exegesis, O'Donnell (1990: 62–81) seeks to impute more coherence to Smith's real measure(s) of value, and in the process, provides a guide to the large and far from unanimous secondary literature on this matter.

58 Smith also makes very extensive use of 'value', and variants. In *WN* and *LJ* it is generally employed as a synonym for the exchange-value of things, including aggregates, especially in terms of money, but also in terms of commodities or labour – or simply, price. The phrase 'real value' is sometimes employed as a synonym for real price (e.g. *WN*: 53, 206–7, 355, 535), as well as being used in other senses, and there is a concept of value added (e.g. *WN*: 66, 83, 330, 667). 'Real value' also appears a little in *LJA*, but never in the sense of labour commanded; it is not at all to be found in *LJB*, but at p. 503 Smith asserts that 'labour, not money, is the true measure of value'. He once, rather tentatively, refers to 'naturall value' (*LJA*: 370; but see also the index reference at *WN*: 1033). *WN* (44–6) distinguishes exchange-value and use-value. There are also non-economic uses of the term, in the senses of importance or esteem or worth, and as well in his other writings. When money is characterized as 'the measure of value', this is really meant in the sense of a measure of esteem or worth (e.g. *WN*: 429; *LJA*: 367; *LJB*: 499–500).

59 Stirati (1994: 57, 83–4) does not read Smith as having a notion of different subsistence wage rates for expanding, contracting and stationary economies, though Smith's use of the language of multiple subsistence levels is acknowledged. Rather, there are multiple natural wage rates with a single subsistence wage, the latter identified with the minimum natural wage consistent with the prevailing social conventions of a given time and place. (On Smith's understanding of the role of social conventions in constraining the terms of individual labour contracts, see the important argument at Stirati 1994: 58–65.) This is more a semantic than a substantive difference of interpretation with respect to our view here. At the level of general theory, nothing very definite can be said about the magnitude of Smith's natural real wage anchor, whether or not it is regarded as expressing multiple subsistence wage rates. But he does also clearly enunciate the idea of a minimum customary real wage (*WN*: 85, 89–91, 113). Stirati also draws attention to the fact that the dependence of the real wage on bargaining makes it possible that customary subsistence itself may be altered by real wage changes of sufficient persistence, a phenomenon explicitly considered by James Steuart (Stirati 1994: 66–8, 83–4; also Garegnani 1984: 320, n. 49). Indeed, for the customary natural or subsistence real wage to change over time, in logic there must be deviations of market wage-rates from the (previous) natural wage, of sufficient persistence as to enable a different real wage to become habitual – a kind of hysteresis of the real wage (cf. sec. 5.1.2). See further, Chapter 4, n. 85, on the related issue of wages and unemployment.

60 Cremaschi (2002: 90, 107, 109–10) argues for the importance of metaphor and analogy in the development of science and the process of concept construction: explanation proceeding by way of likening a phenomenon to something else – 'as if' explanation. The latter is certainly the more significant intellectual step: metaphor merely suggests that a phenomenon is 'like' something else; it can amount to little more than rhetorical decoration. Analogy moves to explanation, proposing that a phenomenon behaves in a manner parallel to some other, already understood thing. But the distinction between metaphor and analogy can be very fine in particular instances: *gravitation* with regard to market and natural prices is little more than metaphor; *circulation* in relation to commodities and money is more genuinely analogy. (The latter metaphor-cum-analogy is very much in use earlier than Smith; e.g. Misselden 1623.) Skinner (1996: 11, 43) draws attention to Smith's own recognition of the importance of reasoning by analogy in the history of science, including false analogy. The parallel between commodity pricing and functional income distribution is one such, partly false, analogy. It may be added here also that Smith's competition-of-capitals approach to determining normal profit rates has significant kinship with Hume's views on interest and profits (Miller 1985: 297, 302–3, 417–18). Hutcheson (1755, vol. 2: 72–3) also has a hint of something like the idea, though conceived of more as a secular process through time. But this general idea of competition and the scale of accumulation determining (indeed reducing) rates of return in general over time – rather than merely regulating particular rates of profit relative to the general level of profit rates – has also a more considerable pedigree than just Hutcheson and Hume (see Tucker 1960: 7–73).

61 In relation to commodity prices, in previous sections above 'market imbalance' was employed to refer strictly to situations of $Q \neq D^*$ (see n. 10). Smith only once refers to 'effectual demand' for labour (*WN*: 76).

62 For some other instances in the English literature, see Fortrey (1673: 239), Sheridan (1677: 159, 198), North (1691: 518, 522) and Davenant (1695: 19). From among many which could be offered, Bowley (1963; or 1973: 64–90, a revised version of the same) and Hutchison (1988, *passim*) are good examples of reading marginalism back into this kind of early modern economic literature. They discuss also other instances from that literature, of what in fact are expressions of the common sense law of markets rather than incipient marginalism. Recall also the crucial analytical point made in section 3.4.1: the rising normal or long-period supply-price associated with marginalist commodity supply functions, so far from being a common sense concept, depends upon an elaborate (and highly disputable) theory of functional income distribution (the marginal productivity theory). The attempt to coherently formulate that theory took many decades of hard intellectual work, from the late nineteenth century forward. There is no trace of it to be found anywhere before the nineteenth century. (That latter-day programme was and remains grounded also upon the idea of autonomous individual preferences which are unobservable, as well as the marginal productivity theory of distribution. On both these issues, see the Epilogue. The problematic status of autonomous preferences is also touched upon in sec. 3.6.) Bowley (1963: 135–9) tacitly acknowledges the difficulty which the absence of any such marginal productivity theory poses for marginalist interpretations of early modern price analysis, by supposing that its absence is a reflection of the persistence of traditional socio-economic arrangements in which distribution is customarily determined. She admits also its absence from Cantillon and Smith. It may be added that Locke's (1698: 327–44) labour theory of value is not about exchange-value at all, though it has sometimes been mistaken for that. It is about use-value, with a view to a theory of property-right.

63 One is tempted to go one step further and say that there *is* no normal cost in the absence of systematic competitive forces. But in pre-modern societies, it is possible for a notion of normal cost-price to be operative, based on customary determination

of exchange-values, remunerations and costs. This is taken up further in section 3.5.6. Recall, incidentally, that competition as Smith understands it is constrained by customary norms, notably, subsistence prices as a regulator of money wages. See section 3.4.3, together with the discussion of taxes on wages in section 4.4.2.

64 This is what the anonymous writer of 1821, whose comment on the matter forms the epigraph to this chapter, so clearly grasped. O'Brien and Darnell (1982: 83–107) provide quite compelling grounds for concluding that Henry Brougham is the author.

65 To be sure, Locke (e.g. 1696: 71–2, 164–6) speaks of 'natural Value', but only to refer to the quantity-and-vent determined market price, absent of 'the prescription of Law' (cf. n. 71 below). He also speaks of 'Intrinsick value', but unlike Cantillon (more on this below), to refer to use-value more or less objectively understood: the 'fitness' of a thing 'to supply the Necessities or serve the Conveniencies of human Life'; for example, the physical quality of corn, 'musty and smutty' versus 'clean and sweet' (Locke 1696: 66–7).

66 We emphasize 'explanatory' because of the older, pre-modern notion of normal or natural cost-price as a benchmark for actual transactions (indicated in n. 63 above). But it is rather more an *assumption*, understood as a conventional outcome, and employed as a normative criterion for a concept of just exchange. Furthermore, the notion of an objective 'natural' value as centre of gravity of actual prices, in particular instances, does appear earlier than Petty; for example: the '*Natural Exchange*' rate between commodity currencies, in accordance with their silver content, as 'that *Cynosure* [i.e. pole star] or *Center*, whereunto all *Exchanges* have their naturall propension' (Misselden 1623: 97). And it is surely not accidental that this conception, limited to the exchange-ratio of just two particular and very special commodities, should arise – prior to the general conception – in relation to the parity between two commodity currencies of different conventional denomination (and no doubt likewise for other relatively sophisticated asset markets). On the one hand, the prominence of profit-seeking arbitrageurs in the trading of currencies, even in the seventeenth century, renders very visible the resulting competitive pressure upon price behaviour: their profit-seeking (or loss-avoiding) activity has the effect of *making* an integrated market with respect to the exchange of currencies. On the other hand, the zero-profitable-arbitrage condition entailed by that parity is very transparent: the exchange rate between two national currencies, which equalizes the quantities of silver, of identical quality, embodied in them. Certainly this condition is more compellingly obvious than the parities entailed by normal money (silver or gold) prices of produced commodities in general, which require comparison of monetary production costs and rates of remuneration between different production activities.

67 On wage relativities and the land theory of value, see Cantillon (1755 [1931]: 19–43, 115). The role of entrepreneurship in Cantillon's system, as a kind of risk-bearing quasi-labour, introduces complications into this pricing formula, since a certain kind of profit, as well as interest on borrowed funds, can then also enter into prices. Whether this amounts to an incipient theory of profits on capital is a somewhat contentious issue we put aside here, except to say that we would reject this conjecture (see Cantillon 1755 [1931]: 39–57; Prendergast 1991; Aspromourgos 1996: 82–3, 117–19). The character and significance of the Petty–Cantillon intellectual developments are considered in considerable detail in the latter work, especially Chapters 2 to 6, and with regard to Cantillon's theory of value, also Aspromourgos (1997).

68 See, for example, Steuart (1767: 159–61, 189). For a detailed treatment of these developments, see Chapters 7 to 9 of Aspromourgos (1996), and on Quesnay's price theory, Vaggi (1987c: 58–93) and the primary Quesnay texts referred to there. Boisguilbert makes extensive use of the language of 'proportion' in his economic analysis, and not only in relation to prices (Faccarello 1999: 103–41; and 179, n. 2 for a conjecture as to the genesis of this language use). But this involves also a notion of a necessary price, rather vaguely related to cost, and including a kind of profit compo-

nent (e.g. Boisguilbert 1707 [2000]:16, 19–20, 23, 27, 29, 50). Verri (1771 [1986]: 12–19, 39–41) likewise employs a notion of price or price changes as the result of the proportion between numbers of sellers and buyers, and a concept of a common or 'ordinary price'; but the determinants of the latter are even less explicit than is the case in Boisguilbert. There is a *concept* of normal price, but no account of its determination. It may be added that Steuart (1767: 117) uses the term effectual demand; but it is not defined by reference to normal price, in the manner of Smith. All of these early theories are subject to the problem of circularity, raised in section 3.4.3. There it found expression in terms of normal money wages, which enter into the determination of normal commodity prices, being themselves a function of at least some normal commodity prices (those for commodities which form part of normal real wages). More generally, the problem applies whenever any commodity inputs enter into production costs, indirectly or directly (see n. 94 below).

69 Most strikingly, by the following concise statement:

> Two types of value may be distinguished: fundamental value and exchange value. The fundamental value is what the things costs to him who sells it, that is, the raw material cost, the interest of the advances, the wages of labour and industry. The exchange value is the price which the buyer agrees upon with the seller. The fundamental value is fairly stable and changes less frequently than the exchange value. The latter is ruled by supply and demand, it varies with needs, and often a single event suffices to produce very considerable and very sudden fluctuations. It is not in any essential proportion to the fundamental value, but it has a tendency to approach it continually, and can never move far away from it permanently. It is obvious that it cannot remain below it for a long time; for, as soon as a commodity can be sold only at a loss, its production is discontinued until the resulting scarcity has again raised it to a price above its fundamental value. The price can similarly not be much above the fundamental value for any length of time, for this high price, implying high profits, would call forth the commodity and generate lively competition among the sellers. Now the natural effect of this competition would be to lower the price until it again approaches the fundamental value.
>
> (Groenewegen 1977c [1767]: 120n)

Notice the use of Quesnay's language ('fundamental' value), but with Turgot including profits as an element of this normal price. For the interpretation in general of this, the most advanced economic theorist before Smith, see Groenewegen (1982; esp. 323–4 with respect to price theory) and other essays pertaining to Turgot, reprinted in Groenewegen (2002a).

There is one particular Turgot manuscript, on 'Value and Money' (Groenewegen 1977c [1769]: 133–48), which has been interpreted as evidence for his taking a subjective approach to explaining prices (e.g. Kauder 1953: 645–7; and rather more carefully, Sewall 1901: 96–107). This work contemplates the determination of exchange-rates between commodities, based on individuals' estimates of their relative worth. In this analysis there is effectively no role for production, and hence no reference to fundamental value, so that it must be regarded as an attempt to more deeply consider the determination of market prices ('exchange value' in the quotation above), in the *absence* of the competitive pressures from the supply side, which draw market prices towards normal price, as beautifully summarized in the quotation above. Note also that the value and money manuscript is incomplete.

70 We follow quite conventional use of these historical categories (see, for example, the *OED*): 'medieval' thought as the European thought of the Middle Ages, from the fifth century (the fall of the Western Roman Empire, 476) to the fifteenth century (the fall of Constantinople, 1453); 'Scholasticism' as running from about the ninth century to the fifteenth century, with the twelfth and thirteenth centuries being the period of greatest intellectual activity, and Thomas Aquinas (d. 1274) commonly treated as the

highpoint; 'ancient' history as the history of the civilizations of the Mediterranean and Near East, before the fall of the Western Roman Empire. The Middle Ages also may be more narrowly understood as beginning with the end of what has traditionally been regarded as 'the Dark Ages' (*c.* 1000). Along with ancient Greek philosophy and Roman law, the other intellectual tradition informing Scholastic social thought is, of course, Patristic thought: the doctrines of the theological writers (in particular, the 'Church Fathers') who made Christian orthodoxy over the first six or seven centuries CE.

71 Cf. Sewall (1901: 36). Friedman (1980) has some kinship with this interpretation, but is more focused on the $p^j$ as a mechanism for minimizing bargaining costs, in the absence of competition, rather than as an institution for regulating bargaining power. Wood (2002: 133, 143, 147) notes that common or 'current' market price in medieval thought came to be known as the natural price. The conventionalism of the $p^j$ as market price is evident also in the widely held medieval view that justice in exchange is consistent with a band of prices ranging from half, to one and a half times, a benchmark price, a view which also may be read as allowing a degree of moral and legal latitude to bargaining power, though the moral latitude could be more restricted than the legal (Chafuen 2003: 86). This minus-50–plus-50 per cent rule is, one supposes, logically consistent with either a cost-price conception of the $p^j$ or a common-estimate-as-such conception; i.e. in the latter case, without reference to cost.

72 Here, there appears a diagram, supposed as representing the relations between these four elements.

73 Editorial footnotes are attached to some of these sentences. An alternative translation of the last sentences gives a more emphatic sense of the incommensurability of objects, resolved in exchange by the standard of 'need':

> Currency … by making things commensurate as a measure does, equalizes them; for there would be no association without exchange, no exchange without equality, no equality without commensurability. And so, though things so different *cannot become commensurate in reality*, they can become commensurate enough *in relation to our needs*.
>
> (Irwin 1985: 131; emphasis added)

This is pertinent to our argument immediately below.

74 Apostle (1975: 362) explains *χρήσιμον* ('useful', or 'instrumental') as '[t]hat which exists or becomes for the sake of something else and not for its own sake, like a spoon or money. Thus the enjoyment of music, being an end in itself, is good but not useful.' One of the instances of this that Apostle (1975: 5) cites points again to Aristotle's notion of legitimate use, and acquisition, being governed, and limited, by need: 'the life of a money-maker … is one of tension; and clearly the good sought is not wealth, for wealth is instrumental and is sought for the sake of something else'. Similarly in the *Politics*, as against unlimited accumulation of money, 'medicine, and the arts generally, recognize and practice a limit to the means they use to attain their ends, since the end itself constitutes a limit', the ultimate limit being legitimate need in the service of good household management (Barker 1946: 25; also 9–10). Barker (1946: 155, n. 3) translates *ta chrēsima* as 'practical utility'. Aristotle's distinction between 'production' and 'action' is in the same spirit (Barker 1946: 10; Apostle 1975: 104). Apostle (1975: 281) offers the following interpretation of that distinction:

> In producing, one produces something, a product, e.g., a chair or a house, and this is for the sake of something else, e.g., sitting or living comfortably; but in *acting*, like behaving properly at a party, there is no product but only the *action* itself which is performed for its own sake.

The example of music above is perhaps better than that of party behaviour!

75 That hierarchy, one supposes, can have two distinct dimensions: one in which needs

are ranked from the most pressing to the least vital; and one in which they are ranked from the most noble, down to the most banal. It may be added that, for our argument concerning heterogeneous use-values, there is no need to deny that use-values understood in such an 'objective' sense, in part, are conditioned by history, customs, social norms, modes of socio-economic life, and so on, whether or not they were understood as such by Aristotle and others (cf. Schefold 1999: 133). Schefold (1999: 122–3) also comments on the error of retrospectively identifying use-value in pre-modern (and classical) economics with 'utility' or 'total utility', and his view is at least consistent with our interpretation of use-values as heterogeneous. But in contrast to our conjecture of a hierarchy of needs as the means, in this framework, of rendering use-values commensurate in exchange, Schefold (1999: 126–7) suggests rather 'virtue' as the Aristotelian standard. This is fair enough, but reconcilable with our view: in the hierarchy of human needs or purposes, virtue is the ultimate civic purpose for Aristotle. In perhaps the same spirit as our interpretation of need in Aristotle, Kaye (1998: 98, n. 96) comments on its role in relation to medieval price analysis (with particular reference to Aquinas): 'need as the basis of market price was conceived as "common need" and as such was as much an objective consideration as the cost factors of labor and expense'. But we must dispute the suggestion that need could be 'as much' an objective consideration as cost (see immediately below).

76 Meikle (1995: 25–6, 190), and also Theocarakis (2006: 11, 18, 46), point out that at the end of the exchange discussion, Aristotle in effect admits that he cannot resolve the supposed equality in exchange. On Aristotle and exchange in general, Meikle (1995) is undoubtedly the most important and careful singular study, and the analysis of Vivenza (2001: 144–58) is also much to be recommended. Meikle's (1995: 85–6; also 183–4, 190) interpretation of Aristotelian use-value accords with ours:

> use value and exchange value fall on different sides of the Greek distinction between nature and convention, *phusis* and *nomos*. Use value is natural and belongs to *phusis*, because the usefulness of a product is explained by the natural properties in virtue of which it serves the purpose for which it was made.

With regard to needs versus wants versus demands, Vivenza (2001: 146, n. 55, 152–70) provides firm grounds for 'need' being the pertinent concept for Aristotle, to be understood in an 'objective' sense (cf. Meikle 1995: 28–42). Need in turn, Vivenza (2001: 148) suggests, is to be interpreted in a non-individualistic manner. Aristotle refers

> to *community* of exchange (*koinonia*) .... Within a community of this sort, citizens follow different occupations according to the needs of the group as a whole, and they exchange the produce of their work amongst themselves so as to supply the wants of the whole rather than those of individuals. Exchange takes place, in other words, between people with different occupations and with reciprocal, interdependent needs.

This is convincing; but still, it does not add any sense to the notion of equality in exchange. The notion of need as referring to the needs of the civic collective (the *polis*) is, however, a means of resolving any tension between the two distinct possible hierarchies of need suggested in n. 75 above. Vivenza's interpretation is confirmed by the view of Barker (1946: 33, n. 2): 'the essence of the art of household management [*oikonomia*] is ... in the last resort, moral, and not 'economic', in the modern sense of that word'. And speaking of ancient *oikonomia* in general:

> Such economic theory, subordinated as it is to political theory, which in turn is subordinated to (or, perhaps one should rather say, is the crown of) ethics, admits of no isolation of the economic motive, and of no abstraction of economic facts as a separate branch of inquiry. It is a theory of the ways in which households and

> cities can properly use the means at their disposal for the better living of a good life.
>
> (Barker 1946: lvi; cf. 1–8, 33–4, 37)

In an important paper aimed at explaining the apparent discrepancy between Aristotle's slight economic analysis, and his achievement and standing with respect to a great range of other sciences, Finley (1970: 33–44) arrives at the same kind of conclusion: the key *Nicomachean Ethics* and *Politics* texts are neither good nor bad economics; they are not *economic* analysis at all, and involve no notion of a determinate price theory. Cf. Meikle (1995: 81–5, 196–8) for a somewhat more nuanced view along the same lines.

77 By regular markets we mean deep markets, in which individuals are able to observe multiple transactions between buyers and sellers. That is to say, regular markets entail conditions under which individual transactions are not segmented from each other, but are integrated into a singular system of price behaviour. This implies a 'soft' notion of competition: the willingness of agents to compare transactions or offer-prices, and respond to the comparison. However, this is well short of thorough-going capitalist competition: the latter entails a tendency towards one price; but that tendency, somewhat mechanically represented by the LOOP, does not entail capitalist competition.

78 Nevertheless, one may still wonder how much a world of Smithian competition, even with all exchanges occurring at natural prices, would have satisfied Scholastics that a separate $p^j$ standard was superfluous. It is even questionable on Smith's own terms. While $p^n$ clearly has normative significance for him – it is in general a price he would prefer to prevail in exchange – there is this inherent difficulty with characterizing it as $p^j$ as such. The multiplicity of possible natural wage rates (see sec. 3.4.3, esp. n. 59), and the fact that in Smith's account, the particular natural wage which prevails depends upon ethically arbitrary circumstances (e.g. the rate of capital accumulation), tells strongly against the plausibility of such a characterization. The particular natural commodity price which prevails is as arbitrary as the particular levels of the natural wage rates which enter into its determination. Natural prices can be compatible with a bare minimum labour subsistence. Bowley (1973: 127–32) argues for an identification of Smithian $p^n$ and Scholastic $p^j$. Young (1997a: 107–27) also favours a stronger kinship between the two concepts than is justifiable; though in the end, at p. 122, the argument is more for Smithian $p^n$ as a *substitute* for Scholastic $p^j$. See also the acute commentary on Young (1995) by Salter (1997), and Young's (1997b) response.

79 See O'Donnell (1990: 201, 211). For the critique of Dobb, see especially Chapter 10, but also Chapter 7, and considerable references to Dobb elsewhere in the book. Dobb's approach bears some superficial resemblance to Karl Marx's notion of exoteric and esoteric aspects of Smith's economics, but is really not at all the same. O'Donnell (1990: 142–70) also comprehensively examines Marx's view of Smith, and detailed references to Marx's texts relating to Smith may be found there. A strange sin of omission is that the theory of rents is barely touched upon by O'Donnell (1990: 99–100, 182–3). A couple of sins of commission are indicated in Chapter 4 (n. 92), in relation to the concept of surplus.

80 More generally, see Vivenza's (2001: 143–4, 150, 155–7) acute rebuttal of reading marginalism into Aristotle; for example:

> [v]alue-in-use in Aristotle is not . . . to be understood in terms so much of subjective utility, as of the requirements of the self-sufficient *polis* in all its constituent parts. Once again, Aristotle was considering not the individual, but rather the citizen, the well-known, typically Greek figure of the 'political animal'.

Soudek (1952: 46, 73) is another example of marginalist misreading: Aristotle 'anticipated by more than two thousand years Jevons' theory of exchange'; the latter's 'theory of exchange ... in spirit and form, in premise and conclusion, provides the most amazing parallelism to Aristotle's doctrine in the history of economic thought'. It is rather Soudek's claim which is amazing. Sewall (1901: 1–4, 17, n. 2: cf. 27–8) rather loosely identifies Aristotle's notion of need with 'demand' and 'utility', but is more careful when explaining this language in relation to perhaps the most illustrious of the Aristotelians: 'the utility here referred to [in Aquinas] is usefulness in relation to an objective end'. Theocarakis (2006) provides an interpretation of the relation between the *Nicomachean Ethics* treatment of price and later schools of thought, via consideration of a range of figures representative of Scholasticism, mercantilism, natural law philosophy, the Enlightenment and marginalist economics (plus Marx).

81 See Book V, Chapter I on prices in Pufendorf (1688), translated in Oldfather and Oldfather (1934: 675–98), which reads like a summary of the Scholastic themes on the subject. An abridged version of the Chapter is translated in Carr (1994: 191–6).

82 This is melodrama, in the strict sense, of 'a dramatic piece characterized by sensational incident and violent appeals to the emotions, but with a happy ending' (*OED*) – where the happy ending for Kauder is, of course, the eventual rise of marginalism. Chafuen (2003) is another instance of the attempt to impute the latter-day subjective theory of value to pre-modern thought. Hollander (1973: 134–5; also 1965, quoted below), notwithstanding his false view of Smith's relation to marginalist theory, rejects the proposition that it is anticipated in ancient or medieval thought. Theocarakis (2006: 19, 24, 27, 45) draws attention to notions of subjective demand in Scholastic and mercantilist thought, in the sense of a role for more or less arbitrary human desires, but is careful to make clear that these do not amount to a theory of value along marginalist lines. Sewall (1901: 32–77, 119–21) interprets a number of early modern (sixteenth- and seventeenth-century) writers as incipient marginalists, but does not make this mistake with respect to earlier thought.

83 In the definition of natural price at *WN* (72–3), there is a somewhat oblique suggestion that profit partly is a remuneration to ensure the subsistence of the supplier of capital in production. Something like the same idea is more clearly expressed in *LJA*:

> if any trade is overprofitable all throng into it till they bring it to the naturall price, that is, the maintenance of the person and the recompence of the risque he runs; that is, what is sufficient to maintain the person *according to his rank and station*.
> (*LJA*: 363; emphasis added)

This is reminiscent of Hucheson's comment here, but perhaps even more, Cantillon's (1755 [1931]: 19–23, 31–43, 47–57) more systematic notion of multiple customary subsistences, depending upon socio-economic rank, as part of the explanation for wage relativities and for entrepreneurial quasi-wages, as elements of normal cost. Hutcheson's statement is more narrowly focused on mercantile profits. As indicated below, elements along these lines are to be found in medieval literature as well.

84 Notice the reference to 'ordinary profit', the same language as Smith; and also the attributing of scarcity to 'accident[s]', making clear enough that Hutcheson is thinking of scarcity merely in terms of abnormal supply shortfalls, not marginalist scarcity (cf. sec. 3.2.2). Hutchison (1988: 98) gives just this kind of marginalist misreading to similar articulations in Pufendorf. Hutcheson (1755, vol. 2: 58) also uses the expression 'quantity in proportion to the demand', but with no conception of effectual demand associated with normal price, along the lines of Smith. Thweatt (1983: 287–8, 291) traces the quantity-and-demand language to John Law (1705), and documents also Steuart's use of 'supply' (as a noun) and 'demand' together.

85 Hutchison (1988: 97–8) seizes upon a very similar statement by Pufendorf:

> The foundation of price *in itself* is the aptitude of a thing or action, by which it can *either* mediately or immediately contribute something to the necessity of

human life, or to making it more advantageous and pleasant. This is the reason why in ordinary speech things of no use are said to be of no value ....

Hutchison cites this as a quotation from Pufendorf (1672). In fact, Hutchison quotes Oldfather and Oldfather (1934, citing p. 675; cf. Hutchison 1988: 423), which is a translation of Pufendorf (1688), a much revised edition (see Seidler 1994: 23). Hutchison also misquotes the text. (The words we have emphasized above are omitted from his quotation.) He also cites the wrong page. (It is at p. 676.)

Combined with Pufendorf comments on the subjectivity of at least some elements of demand, Hutchison thinks he has a precursor of marginalism. This is to draw a ridiculously long bow. Pufendorf here is to be read in the same manner as Hutcheson: use-value's foundational role is as a prerequisite to exchange-value – including, for example, merely ornamental uses leading to a positive demand for diamonds – though Pufendorf certainly also has recourse to variants of something like SAD to explain prices. Hutcheson (1755, vol. 2: 54) also acknowledges subjective elements behind demand; but this places him no more in the marginalist tradition than Pufendorf. (The same of course is true as well of Smith.) Unsurprisingly, given his treatment of Pufendorf, Hutchison (1988: 194–5) thinks it *does* place Hutcheson in that tradition. Hutchison (1988: 97–8) even proposes that Pufendorf's apparently applying the idea of the foundation of value to the labour which produces commodities, as well as the commodities themselves (referring to the same Pufendorf quotation as above), points towards the marginalist theory of factor pricing. But it is just the same prerequisite notion referred back a step: if the things that some kind of labour produces are not demanded, then the labour will not be demanded either, and therefore will be incapable of having exchange-value. In fact, Pufendorf is probably not even referring the prerequisite notion back a step: he is rather thinking of artisan-labour, which is not sold at all, just the artisan's product or services, so that the sale of the product or service, and the sale of the labour, are virtually one and the same thing. The same identification of labour and product is implicit in Smith's *LJ* articulations of natural price, in terms of only labour cost (see p. 67 and n. 2 above).

86 Obviously, for any commodity to be produced under competitive conditions, in any quantity (allowing sufficient time for supply and capacity to adjust, in pursuit of normal remunerations), it must have a commensurate $D^*$, which presupposes a 'use' in some sense. Smith, like his teacher, Hutcheson, is emphatic: 'a thing of no use ... brought into the market will give no price, as no one demands it' (*LJA*: 358).

87 Cf. Kubin (1998: 244); Vivenza (2001: 153, 156). The heterogeneity of use-value is not for Smith the problem it is for Aristotle, because Smith does not seek to connect use-value or need with exchange-value. In passing discussion of Smith in relation to Aristotle, Meikle (1995: 48, 102–03, 111, 183, 187, 191) does not recognize their degree of kinship with regard to use-value, or is at least ambivalent about it. Smith's distinguishing between the 'utility' (explicitly identified with 'useful[ness]') and the 'beauty' of the precious metals, as distinct determinants of the demand for those metals, was mentioned in passing above (sec. 3.2.1; *WN*: 189–91). This clearly is to conceive of 'utility' differently from the latter-day marginalist sense: in the latter context, a contrast with 'beauty' would be meaningless. It confirms that utility and use-value are being deployed in the sense of Aristotelian use-value (cf. n. 55 above). Hence also, the claim made by Douglas (1928: 78; emphasis added), repeated so often since as to be a cliché, presumptuously imposes a completely alien interpretive framework upon the text: 'The main reason why Smith and those who followed him abandoned utility as a determinant of value was, *of course*, because they were comparing the total utilities yielded by varying types of objects rather than their marginal utilities'. Smith's use-value is not some supposed homogeneous substance, 'utility', in the manner of nineteenth-century marginalism.

88 See Hamouda and Price (1997: 206–7) for a pertinent criticism of $p^j$ as a solution to

the distributional problem. Langholm (1992: 45) regards Courçon's early thirteenth-century *Summa* as probably the first text in the medieval theological tradition, in which 'the cost and market criteria of just pricing appear together'.

89 With regard to commodity monopolies, Chafuen (2003: 82–3) points out another aspect of medieval thought indicating recourse to cost considerations: some Scholastics advocated a legally prescribed cost-plus price in instances of monopoly. This implies a notion of cost, plus profit of some kind, as the price which prevails under competition in some loose sense: 'many buyers and sellers', perhaps a notion of freedom of entry to the supply side of the market.

90 But cost can vary too, including as a result of differences or changes in natural scarcities. It may be added that the elements of cost and risk here serve to confirm how much the views of Grotius, Pufendorf and Hutcheson were grounded in medieval thought (cf. Sewall 1901: 18–19).

91 Footnotes are attached to some of the sentences in this Langholm quotation. An important element of the medieval intellectual achievement was the rediscovery and development of 'the monumental compilations of Justinian', the sixth-century Byzantine emperor,

> who ordered a codification of the texts of classical jurisprudence (Digest) and of the imperial legislation (Code) theoretically in force. A manual for the use of students (Institutes) and a collection intended for new laws (Novellae) later completed this work, significantly designated by the name of *Corpus iuris civilis*.
>
> Inoperative in the 'barbarian' West, Justinian's compilations were exhumed there only during the first decades of the 12th c. in Italy ... and soon occupied an autonomous place in the nascent universities [throughout Europe]. Teaching was based on the gloss, whose object was the literal explanation of Justinian's text ....
>
> (Krynen 2000)

Some terms in this quotation have asterisks attached to them, denoting that they also have entries in this encyclopedia.

The recourse to rather ad hoc jumbling together of SAD and cost elements in explaining exchange-value is well illustrated also in Conradus Summenhart's sixteenth-century enumeration of factors influencing price, more a 'shopping list' than a theory: abundance or superabundance of merchandise; accidental phenomena (such as plagues); ability and capacity of producers; usefulness of the good; the poverty of the region where the good is produced; scarcity; *complacibilitas* (desirability); and the counsel of righteous men (Chafuen 2003: 82). Readers may decide for themselves, which among these factors might reasonably be interpreted as 'cost'.

92 The same problem of multiple meanings applies to the term 'utility', though this is hardly an everyday term. In the twentieth century, marginalism found a way to dispense with recourse to utility understood as an invisible and homogeneous substance, by instead merely positing individually idiosyncratic 'preferences', conceived of as essentially arbitrary as to their content, but constrained to a certain logical structure: for example, imposing consistency and completeness upon preferences, though also imposing rather more substantive conditions, such as that 'more is preferred to less'. The superiority of Smith's treatment of the role of demand in competitive price theory applies as much to such later versions of the marginalist theory, articulated in terms of preference orderings, as it does to the earlier versions which had recourse to utility as a supposed measurable substance (see sec. 3.6).

93 The notion that distribution, even under competitive conditions, is partly governed by social conventions is by no means obsolete, even in contemporary circumstances (see the Epilogue, section 4). Recall also, that even with production methods taken as given, the determination of cost properly must deal with the interdependence of costs and prices, due to the presence of produced commodity inputs, an issue not adequately dealt with in eighteenth-century economic literature. See sections 3.6 (esp. n.

94), 4.3.3 and 4.3.5, which also deal with the determination of the profitability of capital, an issue mentioned immediately below.

94 To grasp the nature of the solution, putting aside joint production, suppose $k$ price equations showing normal prices of $k$ commodities ($p''_1, p''_2, \ldots, p''_k$), expressed in terms of a conventional unit of account; say, shillings and pence) equal to normal costs of production for each commodity. Assuming also homogeneous labour, these equations contain $k$ price variables, plus the money wage per unit of labour input ($w$) and 'the' rate of profit on capital ($r$) – putting aside scarce resources (and hence rents), and ignoring the (normal) profit differentials Smith considers in *WN*, Book I, Chapter x. Thus, taking production methods as given, there are $k$ equations and $k + 2$ variables. One of the commodities must represent Smith's commodity money (silver or gold); so it may be made the numeraire, by adding an equation making its price unity. If the given normal real wage per unit of labour is the consumption bundle ($c_1, c_2, \ldots, c_k$), then a further equation is added: $w$ equals $p''_1c_1 + p''_2c_2 + \ldots + p''_kc_k$. There are hence $k + 2$ equations for determining the $k + 2$ variables. The determination of normal prices is explored further in sections 4.3.3 and 4.3.5, which utilize some simple illustrative cases of these kinds of models and their solutions for normal prices. The major sources of these modern theoretical developments are indicated in n. 95 below.

95 For a concise history of these developments, from classical economics through to the late-twentieth century, see Kurz and Salvadori (1995: 1–20, 379–426), together with the 'historical notes' at the end of each chapter of that book. For the development of Sraffa's system see Garegnani (2005). The most important modern expressions of the tradition of objective theories of price – building on various theoretical developments in economic analysis subsequent to Smith, and employing all the sophistication which modern mathematical methods make possible – are von Neumann (1937), Sraffa (1960) and at least the young Leontief (1928). On all these matters and the relations between them, see Kurz and Salvadori (1993 – Kurz and Salvadori 1995: 403–14 is a concise version of the same argument), Kurz and Salvadori (2005), Kurz (2006b) and Kurz and Salvadori (2006).

96 Note also the impossibility in general of deriving conventional aggregate, market demand functions from the marginalist characterization of individuals' preferences, due to the interdependence of aggregated demands, relative commodity prices and income distribution (Kirman 1989, 2006: 257–68, 275–6; Keen 2001: 39–53). (On the endogeneity of preferences in general, see the valuable contribution by Bowles 1998.) Laibman (2004: 285–9) argues that the latter-day conventional 'market demand curve' is compatible with the classical conception of market price convergence (also taking for granted that market price may be conceived of as uniform at any point in time). Whether or not such functions are compatible with classical convergence is of course a different question from whether or not they are necessary or useful to that process. Smith (1951: 244, 257) correctly points out that Smith's $D^*$ refers to a singular quantity, but then argues that this must be intended as a point on a 'demand schedule'.

97 Hollander (1975: 318–19) attaches 'considerable importance' to evidence of substitutability in consumption in *WN*; but this is not synonymous with a role for demand functions in determining normal prices. Of course, *indirect* influence of demand upon $p''$, via possible influence of normal supply ($= D^*$) upon production methods (through division of labour and scarce natural resources), or even upon normal remunerations, is unobjectionable (cf. Hollander 1975: 315, 320, 323). This argument is reproduced from Hollander (1973: 133–43; in particular, 138–9 and 135, 140, 143).

98 On these issues see the various papers in Caminati and Petri (1990), with contributions by M. Caminati, L. Boggio, P. Flaschel, B. Schefold, W. Semmler, G. Duménil and D. Lévy, P. Garegnani and others. Smith's reduction of the costs of material inputs – raw materials, intermediate goods, machines and so on – to wages, profit and

rent (*WN*: 65–9) perhaps contributed to his failure to adequately appreciate the dependence of costs upon prices (see sec. 4.3.5). On the other hand, he excludes any influence of outputs upon effectual demand, in the convergence dynamics, by explicit supposition.

## 4 Production and capital accumulation

1 Apart from the list of Contents, where it appears in the titles of each of the first three chapters.

2 *WN* (13–36). Similarly systematic discussions occur in *LJA* (340–52, 355–6); *LJB* (489–94); *edWN* (562–74). There are also two Smith MS fragments on division of labour, published together with *LJ* and *edWN* in Meek *et al.* (1978a: 582–6), referred to here as *fA* and *fB* respectively. An interpretation of the relation between the latter five documents and *WN* is provided by Campbell and Skinner (1976: 19–24; also Ross 1995: 276–8), and most fully, by Meek and Skinner (1973). Meek *et al.* (1978b: 561) conjecture that all five date from the 1760s, deferring to the argument of Meek and Skinner (1973). On the lectures, see as well Ross (1995: 122–7), in particular, for the conjecture that '*LJ*(B) is a better guide to what Smith wrote ... *LJ*(A) ... is the better guide to Smith's delivery of the lectures' (123). The extant manuscript of *LJA* is incomplete, probably due to the existence of a seventh (yet undiscovered) manuscript volume, originally accompanying the six extant volumes. It is probable, given their length, that these lecture notes derived from a shorthand transcription taken during the actual lectures (Meek *et al.* 1978b: 11–13).

3 *WN* (15–21); *LJA* (342–7, 350–1); *LJB* (490–2); *edWN* (565–70). The connection between labour specialization and productivity, generally also with explicit reference to the role of machinery, is further made at *WN* (82, 104, 181, 260–1, 277, 343, 676, 680–1, 748).

4 But compare this suggestion of unintended consequence, with the motivation of productivity gain offered in the previous chapter (*WN*: 15, quoted immediately above). This is not a contradiction, since *WN:* 25 refers to 'not *originally*', and to '*general* opulence' (rather than individual gain), but the individuals' intentions are not far from the allegedly unintended social outcome (see also Chapter 5, n. 15). The concept of opulence is examined in section 5.1.

5 In *LJ* he does so inquire:

> If we should enquire into the principle in the human mind on which this disposition of trucking is founded, it is clearly the naturall inclination every one has to persuade.... Men always endeavour to persuade others to be of their opinion even when the matter is of no consequence to them.... [T]his is altogether the practise of every man in the most ordinary affairs.
>
> (*LJA*: 352; and similarly, at *LJB*: 493–4)

At *TMS* (336) 'the desire of persuading' is suggested as 'the instinct upon which is founded the faculty of speech'; the uniquely human faculty, 'speech is the great instrument of ambition'. Henderson and Samuels (2004) exhaustively examine Smith's treatment of the origins of division of labour, as well as much pertinent secondary literature. At one point, in the context of analysing slavery, Smith notes another natural propensity which may overrule the bargaining propensity: '[t]he love of domination and authority over others,... rather than be[ing] obliged to persuade others to bargain' (*LJA*: 192). Elsewhere he comments on the low moral status of trade:

> [T]hat principle in the mind which prompts to truck, barter, and exchange, tho' it is the great foundation of arts, commerce, and the division of labour, yet it is not marked with any thing amiable. To perform any thing, or to give any thing,

> without a reward is always generous and noble, but to barter one thing for another is mean.
>
> (*LJB*: 527)

The propensity to exchange requires no moral encouragement.

6 It is noteworthy that Pownall (1776: 338–9), while contesting Smith's speculations concerning the ultimate source of division of labour, concedes that the issue is separable from political economy proper: 'for the doctrine contained in the second chapter of your first book, seems only noted *en passant*, but is no where, either in the course of your Analysis, used, nor applied in the subsequent explications'. Force (2003: 201–2; also 124–31, 261–2) argues, unconvincingly, that the propensity to barter is for Smith a more fundamental factor in economic behaviour than the desire for material self-betterment (cf. sec. 4.3.2, esp. n. 50). In any case, Force (2003: 127) acknowledges also that 'an analytical work such as ... [*WN*] does not need to concern itself with first principles' with regard to 'the origin of commerce'. The political economy has an integrity independent of that issue.

7 The *WN* editors (30, n. 14) point out the striking fact that extent of the market does not figure in the *edWN* analysis of division of labour. Combined with a duplication between *edWN* (574) and the beginning of *fA* (582), and the fact that *fA* proceeds to consider extent of the market in relation to division of labour, this suggests the speculation that the two fragments, *fA* and *fB*, were extensions written subsequent to *edWN* (Meek and Skinner 1973: 1103–6). The key finding from the reconstruction of the development of Smith's views on division of labour by Meek and Skinner (1973: esp. 1102–3) is that the significance of extent of the market appears to have emerged in his mind during 1763. Note in addition, that in *WN* Smith speaks occasionally also of 'narrowness' of markets (see Chapter 3, note 11).

8 Allyn Young (1928: esp. 532–3, 535, 536–7) puts a case for just such a mutual causation, though in doing so, he has recourse to a tendency of the economy towards full utilization of resources along marginalist theoretical lines (see esp. pp. 540–2). Young states his position most bluntly at the conclusion (though without actually imputing this view to Smith): 'the division of labour depends upon the extent of the market, but the extent of the market also depends upon the division of labour' (p. 539). However, when he presses himself to nominate the leading factor in such processes, Young (p. 536) comments:

> is there any other factor which has a better claim to that rôle than the persisting search for markets? No other hypothesis so well unites economic history and economic theory. The Industrial Revolution of the eighteenth century has come to be generally regarded, not as a cataclysm brought about by certain inspired improvements in industrial technique, but as a series of changes related in an orderly way to prior changes in industrial organisation and to the enlargement of markets.

Smith's 'theorem' concerning division of labour and extent of the market is 'one of the most illuminating and fruitful generalisations which can be found anywhere in the whole literature of economics' (p. 529). Later, Young's idea of mutual and cumulative causation was taken up in a Keynesian framework, wherein a leading role for demand sits more comfortably than it does in the marginalist framework, notably by Nicholas Kaldor (e.g. 1972). Richardson's (1975) analysis also is very much in the spirit of Young, and see Lowe (1975: 420–2). For a broad overview of post-Smithian developments with respect to division of labour, see Groenewegen (1987b: 902–05).

9 See *WN* (14, 20–1); *LJA* (346, 351); *LJB* (492, 526); *edWN* (569–70). (See also *WN*: 282: 'The improved dexterity of a workman may be considered in the same light as a machine or instrument of trade which facilitates and abridges labour'.) Notice here at least a tension between the supposed role of workers in innovation, and the comment

at *WN* (782; quoted immediately above), that the stupefied worker 'has no occasion ... to exercise his invention'. Any apparent contradiction perhaps can be resolved by supposing that the scope for worker inventiveness declines as the division of labour develops: at *WN* (783) Smith contrasts the situation in 'barbarous societies', where 'every man' is able 'to invent expedients for removing difficulties' (cf. Rosenberg 1965). On the other hand, the examples Smith gives of worker inventiveness are wide-ranging, even down to a 'miserable slave' (*edWN*: 569), though also largely concerning the distant past – and in the case of agriculture, division of labour is not so extensive (cf. *WN*: 782, ed. note 47). (Contrariwise on slaves, at *WN*: 684 the reader is told: 'Slaves ... are very seldom inventive; and all the most important improvements, either in machinery, or in the arrangement and distribution of work which facilitate and abridge labour, have been the discoveries of freemen'. Cf. Rosenberg 1965: 130–1) It is an upside of the more limited scope for division of labour in agriculture, that agricultural workers are less stupefied than urban workers (*WN*: 143–4; *LJB*: 539). The *WN* editors (21, n. 20) draw attention to Smith's arguments elsewhere, that technical progress over time involves also simplification of machines (*EPS*: 66; *LRB*: 13, 223–4). The *LRB* text involves also an analogy between the progressive simplification of machines and of languages. The notion of specialization damaging workers does not appear in *LJA*.

10 Smith's educational proposals for addressing the ill consequences of the division of labour for workers, pragmatic and functional in character, are discussed in section 4.1.2.

11 Other, passing references to division of labour occur at *WN* (329, 376, 379, 492, 499, 504 – and in relation to the military (which requires 'the wisdom of the state'), at 697; cf. *LJB*: 411, 542). In addition, references to division of labour at *WN* (276–7) and *LJB* (521–2, 527) are discussed at the opening of section 4.3. There is no mention of it in *TMS*, *EPS*, *LRB* or *Corr*.

12 The *WN* editors indicate most of these texts, in various notes to Book I, Chapters I–III. Others could be considered (e.g. Beccaria, Ferguson, Millar, Josiah Tucker). Rashid (1998: 16–18, 25–7) considers most of these and others, as possible sources of Smith's views, in some cases, not so convincingly. (Nevertheless, the case of Ernst Ludwig Carl, cited by Rashid, is intriguing: see Viner 1965: 107–9; Hutchison 1988: 156–63.) Perrotta's (2004: 175–6) judgement on pre-modern and modern notions prior to Smith, supported by numerous detailed references, is sounder (though he perhaps gives too much credit to Ferguson; see *Corr*: 13n–14n):

> Up to and including Mandeville, the authors who deal with the division of labour among nations and among professions ... are less interested – with the exception of Petty, as usual – in identifying an increase in productivity as the aim of the division of labour.... It is this element that distinguishes the modern concept of the division of labour from the old one.

Marx's (1967, vol. 1: 336–68) analysis of division of labour includes incidental discussion of a wide range of literature on the subject, both before and after Smith. For an account of the likely sources of Smith's famous pin-making illustration of productivity growth from division of labour (*WN*: 14–15; *LJA*: 341–2; *LJB*: 490; *edWN*: 564–8), see Peaucelle (2006), which is a substantial advance beyond earlier conjectures on this matter. Groenewegen (1998: 219) indicates also that the article on 'Art' in the *Encyclopédie* details the benefits of technical division of labour as increased skill, better product quality, saving of time and materials, and invention. This is very similar to the elements of Turgot's account. The 'Part II' of Mandeville's *Fable of the Bees*, from which the division of labour commentary comes, first appeared in December 1728, though dated 1729 (Kaye 1924, vol. 1: xxxv–xxxvi). The first part was first published under that title in 1714, with an earlier variant first appearing in 1705 (Kaye 1924, vol. 1: xxxiii).

13 Progress, in the sense that we now use the term, entails a normative standard by which change can be judged as improvement. For some suggested dimensions of human progress in general, arising in the historical development of the notion, see Bury (1955: 7, 19, 22, 65–6 – and 220–1 for a comment on Smith; cf. Forbes 1954; Brown 1988: 57–9, 83). Spadafora (1990: 253–320) provides an account of the generally moderate and qualified notions of human progress in eighteenth-century Scottish thought in general (see also his comments on Bury: pp. 3–7, 381–2). For the absence from pre-modern thought of a concept of material progress in particular, see Perrotta's (2004: 16–18, 40–1, 49–50) thoughtful conclusions. (The normative sense of progress, it may be noted, is not how Smith generally uses the term: see Chapter 5, n. 5.) The normative standard is straightforward in the case of technical progress and Smithian opulence: rising labour productivity and increasing consumption per capita. With regard to the social division of labour, Aquinas, as usual, is a good example of the persistence of Greek ideas in medieval thought. Hosseini (1998) suggests some evidence for the significance of division of labour in Greek-inspired Islamic philosophy, and the transmission of this back to Western Scholasticism; but there is nothing of a dynamic specialization/productivity nexus in the literature considered there. The suggestion of a possible influence, direct or indirect, from Islamic thought to Smith is entirely fanciful.

14 Hence Smith comments:

> Is this improvement in the circumstances of the lower ranks of the people to be regarded as an advantage or as an inconveniency to the society? ... It is but equity ... that they who feed, cloath and lodge the whole body of the people, should have such a share of the produce of their own labour as to be themselves tolerably well fed, cloathed and lodged.
>
> (*WN*: 96; cf. *edWN*: 563–4)

This is considered more fully in section 5.1.1.

15 One may suggest here a distinction between what may be called the technical division of labour and the social division of labour. The former refers to distinct labour activities in the production of commodities or goods; the latter, to that dimension of the division of socio-economic activities and functions which imbues it with distinctions of social status and rank (cf. Groenewegen 1987b: 901). While conceptually distinct, to the extent that economic power and socio-political power go hand in hand, explanation and justification of one and of the other easily become intertwined. The naturalization of the social order and associated social hierarchy becomes the naturalization of economic activities and functions. Vincent-Lancrin (2003) deploys a different distinction, between social and 'organisational' division of labour in Smith, but goes too far in reading a theory of the firm into Smith.

16 Force (2003: 126–31) plausibly argues that Smith's idea derives from Rousseau, and also describes it as 'subversive' (cf. Pack 2000: 51, 55). The *WN* editors (28, n. 11) note that Harris (1757: 15) ascribes the division of labour to natural individual differences. To the extent that the figures between Petty and Smith noted above lack a notion of ongoing productivity growth, and/or naturalize the division of labour, they are perhaps closer to Plato than Smith. Vincent-Lancrin (2003: 215) comments: 'For Hutcheson, as for the ancient Greek philosophers ... division of labour and society are consubstantial; their purpose is more to show how it reflects a harmonious order of things than to show how the phenomenon originates.'

17 Vivenza (2001: 129–30) also points out that Plato's account is focused on social division of labour, rather than technical division of labour, though it must be said, ultimately the two aspects merge into each other. It is Xenophon who offers something more along the lines of technical division of labour, linking it, like Petty, and Smith a little (*WN*: 31–2), to large cities (Vivenza 2001: 130, 135–7). As mentioned above in relation to Petty, to the extent that transportation of commodities is difficult and

costly, large cities become a kind of proxy for extent of the market; and to the extent that this constraint on the market was less binding in 1776 than earlier, the significance of city populousness for division of labour declines (cf. *WN*: 31–6). Thus Harris (1757: 17, 22) writes that when 'the whole community is ... linked together in one general commerce', 'a large country becomes in effect as one great city', and comments on the disadvantages of 'small and unconnected societies'. Foley (1974), incidentally, makes no reference to Petty, though discussing the possible influence of other modern writers on Smith.

18 Smith sees extension of division of labour, paradoxically, as actually militating against education of the young (*LJB*: 539–40; also *WN*: 784–5).

19 There are many interpretations of Smith's *WN*, Book V view of the adverse consequences of labour specialization. West (1964) argues that it contradicts the *WN*, Book I treatment of division of labour. There is some tension between the two (see n. 9 above), but against West, Rosenberg (1965) ably argues for the absence of contradiction, partly via an appreciation of the role of historical change in Smith's view of the character of invention (cf. West 1975, a distinctly more moderate view than that put in 1964). West (1996) is yet a further, and wider, restatement of his position, to which Pack (2000) is a convincing response, which also draws out the kinship between Rousseau and Smith on this and other matters. See also Lamb (1973), which is primarily a critique of West (1969), Groenewegen (1977a: 391–4) and Winch (1978: 80–87, 103–120). More than most, the latter takes seriously the decay of martial spirit that Smith associates with division of labour.

20 All such references, for just Books I and II (apart from a few explicitly discussed below), are at *WN* (6–7, 11–12, 41, 73, 83, 86–7, 89, 91, 106, 187–8, 192, 232, 258, 279, 281–3, 285, 342, 346, 349–50, 352, 358, 361, 366).

21 The many such references need not be cited here. There are no references of any kind to 'revenue', either in *EPS* or *LRB*; there are two in *TMS*, discussed below.

22 The first two components are 'clean<n>ess' and 'ease or security', the latter in turn dividing into 'security ... against fires, or other such accidents' and providing 'against any injuries that may be done ... to the inhabitants'. The first, together with the first part of the second, are too 'trifling' to be a part of jurisprudence. The second part of the second belongs to the subject of justice (*LJA*: 5–6). Hence 'justice' and 'police' are not, strictly speaking, mutually exclusive objects of the science of jurisprudence. Compare also this *LJA* definition of police with a further description of political economy in passing, at *WN* (748): 'cheapness of consumption and ... encouragement ... to production' as 'precisely the two effects which it is the great business of political œconomy to promote'.

23 See, for example, *WN* (6, 290–2, 337, 339, 345, 364, 440–1, 447–9, 451, 455–6, 489, 608, 637, 675–6, 823, 844, 881, 929). Smith's use of the 'revenue' and 'wealth' identity is discussed in section 2.2.1. Recalling Smith's identification of wealth and national product which was also examined there, the equality of revenue and annual produce immediately follows. The qualification, *real* revenue, expresses Smith's intention to go beyond nominal incomes, to the physical product or consumption which lies behind them (see especially *WN*: 290–2).

24 By this is meant systems of production, or economies, in which the methods in use for producing commodities requires at least one of those commodities, directly or indirectly, as input for the production of all produced commodities. That is to say, there is at least one 'basic' commodity in the sense of Sraffa (1960: 8), all other commodities being non-basics. The social economy theorized in Smith's political economy entails circular production in this sense: if at least some labour is directly or indirectly required in the production of all commodities, and there is at least one produced commodity entering the subsistence consumption requirements of labour, then these two suppositions together suffice to make the production system circular.

25 That is, the 'value added', as we would now say. In fact, Smith uses this language himself; for example, in the immediate context here:

> As soon as stock has accumulated in the hands of particular persons, some of them will naturally employ it in setting to work industrious people, whom they will supply with materials and subsistence, in order to make a profit by the sale of their work, or by what their labour adds to the value of the materials.
>
> (*WN*: 65–6; also 455)

26 Smith also on a small number of occasions employs 'neat' and variants in the (connected) sense of tidy, well-proportioned or clear (*EPS*: 184, 248; *LRB*: 25–6, 33, 40; *LJA*: 343).

27 It might also appear to identify net revenue with consumption, but that is not actually the case. The latter generally will be less than net revenue, but may also be greater (see sec. 4.3).

28 Concerning gross and net revenue, see also the whole passage of argument continuing on to p. 295, and with regard to capital and revenue, *WN* (332–40). There are a further nine references to net and/or gross revenue by Smith, all of which refer to phenomena below the level of the economic system as a whole (*WN*: 487–8, 727n, 750, 753, 852, 882, 885, 896–7; *Corr*: 289–90).

29 Recall the generic core of Smith's constitutive definition, quoted more fully at the beginning of this section: 'neat revenue, what remains *free* ... after deducting the expence of maintaining ... capital' (*WN*: 286; emphasis added). At *WN* (823) Smith discusses agricultural revenue, without use of 'gross' or 'net', but in a manner illustrative of the generic notion of net revenue as that which is free for disposal, after restoring inputs used up (in particular, seed input).

30 Social norms as to how labour may be used (e.g. restrictions on how humans may be combined with machines) are also embedded in production methods, so that a purely 'engineering' concept of efficient production is not really adequate for economic theory.

31 We say 'roughly speaking' because of two potential complexities in particular. First, it is quite possible and viable for the gross output of a commodity to be less than the aggregate input of the same commodity across the entire production system, so that the surplus of this particular commodity is negative. That is to say, the production of a non-negative surplus of every commodity is not strictly necessary. Only a weaker viability condition is required: that the production system is capable in principle of at least self-replacement of its inputs (Sraffa 1960: 5n). The use of particular commodities can decline over time, even disappear. In such circumstances the aggregate, system-wide input quantities of some commodities can exceed the same commodities' outputs, for some time periods, in entirely viable systems.

Second, there is the issue of non-renewable or non-producible 'primary' inputs, which are thereby not also produced outputs. The aggregate quantity of any such input used up in a production cycle cannot in any degree be offset by output of the same commodity, so that it will appear as a negative element of the surplus. The content of the surplus as specified for any time period should fully account for the changes in the stocks of all the various commodities and assets used and/or produced, between the end of the previous time period and the end of the time period under consideration. Hence a quantity of any non-renewable resource used up in production, or in direct consumption, in any time period should appear as a negative quantity within the set of quantities of the various resources making up the surplus of that time period. This is a far more significant sense of negative components in the surplus than the first complexity noted above (cf. Chapter 3, n. 50). It is precisely the problem of non-renewable resource depletion. (Renewable resources are depletable also.) A simple instance of how a non-produced but renewable input may be treated is incorporated in the illustrative model directly below, in the treatment of land. For the wider issues of circular production systems and non-reproducible resources, see Schefold (1985), Kurz and Salvadori (1995: 340–1, 351–74), Steedman *et al.* (2001) and Kurz (2006a). Gilibert (1998) provides an analytically elegant summary of circular or reproduction systems in the history of economic theory.

32 In effect, it is being treated as an indestructible non-produced primary input. In fact, many forms of land use do not leave the land unchanged (cf. Kurz 2006a: 286).

33 The preceding two paragraphs closely follow Aspromourgos (2005: 2–4). It may be added that the commodity specification of surplus is capable of greater generality than the labour specification, since under conditions of joint production, necessary and surplus outputs are still distinguishable, whereas necessary and surplus labour may not to be.

34 All quotations in this paragraph are from the *OED* ('gross', 'neat'). 'Net' (under various spellings) was also in English use from the fourteenth century, for the senses of 'neat' relating to purity, and in the narrower technical sense, from the fifteenth century (*OED*: 'net'). The *OED* definition for the narrower sense captures its quantitative character: 'Of an amount, weight, etc.: free from, or not subject to, any (further) deduction; remaining after all necessary deductions have been made'.

35 An interpretation of Petty's surplus models, and his applications of the idea, as well as Cantillon's theory, is provided in Aspromourgos (1996: 22–46, 74–85). Aspromourgos (2005: 12–14; also 2000: 55–60, 68) details Petty's quantitative treatments of social surplus, including some important unpublished instances in manuscripts held by the British Library. For the lack of equivalence between the town/country and manufacture/agriculture distinctions, see Aspromourgos (1996: 80). Eltis's (2000: xxviii–xxx) suggestion that a concept of 'surplus-generation' can be found, before Petty, in the thought of Ibn Khaldūn (1332–1406), is fanciful. Or alternatively, one may say that it rests upon a much weaker notion of surplus than is appropriate for inquiry into the lineage of the theory. Sentiments along the following lines do not constitute a theory of social surplus: In Khaldūn, Eltis says,

> it is private economic activity associated with the acquisition of property which generates the potential surplus which finances government. Where government becomes unduly large and expensive in relation to private productive activity, output declines until 'the cities lie in ruins'.

People were complaining about taxes and their supposed deleterious consequences long before Khaldūn, and long before the theory of surplus.

36 Three successive versions (or 'editions') of the *Tableau* are reproduced in Kuczynski and Meek (1972), with English translations. To refer to the value of the net product or surplus, Quesnay commonly speaks of 'revenue' (*revenu*) as such (rather than net revenue) – literally, the genuine return – in contrast to expenditure or (capital) advances (Kuczynski and Meek 1972: *passim*). The sense of national 'revenue' as social net revenue is conveyed in one of his pre-*Tableau* articles:

> Wealth which is regenerated and which restores the expenses which have been incurred in the production of the revenue ought not to be regarded as new wealth, since it returns only the costs or expenses advanced .... Thus two-thirds of the harvest forms no part of the profit which is yielded by this harvest.... The annual wealth which constitutes the nation's revenue consists of the products which, after all expenses have been deducted, form the profits which are drawn from landed property.
>
> (Meek 1962: 103–4)

In remark no. 8 in the 'First Edition' of the *Tableau*, Quesnay explicitly uses the phrase 'net revenue' (*revenu net*): 'the advances of the farmers are sufficient to enable the expenses of cultivation to reproduce at least 100 per cent; ... if the advances are not sufficient, the expenses of cultivation are higher and produce little net revenue'

(Meek 1962: 112). The French text with English translation is in Kuczynski and Meek (1972: App. A). The same remark also appears in the 'Second' and 'Third' editions (and also numbered '8'), in very similar terms, but with 'net product' (*produit net*) replacing 'net revenue' (Kuczynski and Meek 1972: at pp. 4 and 6 of those two editions, respectively).

Meek (1962) did much to clarify the character and significance of Quesnay's economics, and subsequently, Vaggi (1987a, 1987b, 1987c). Steuart was considerably influenced by the French literature, including Cantillon, and utilizes the surplus conception in his *Inquiry* (1767). Aspromourgos (1996: 103–16, 126–53) considers Quesnay and Steuart in relation to the Petty–Cantillon heritage. Boss (1990: 15–62) provides an interpretation of what she calls 'surplus and transfer' theories from Petty to Smith, but from a standpoint unhelpful for taking those ideas seriously enough, on their own terms. The following sentiments are indicative: the 'heady simplicity' of the 'Smithian "productive/unproductive" dichotomy ... still seduce[s] the uninitiated'; '[s]erious difficulties of input-output logic and ultimately of relevance attend' the Quesnay, Smith and Marx 'theories of surplus-generation and its non-equivalent transfer beyond a narrowly-defined productive domain' (Boss 1990: 3, 9). In section 4.3 we provide a more satisfying alternative resolution of Smith's treatment of productive labour. See also the thoughtful account of circular production systems in Gilibert (1998; esp. pp. 114–15 on closed versus open systems).

37 The background assumption to all this is that agricultural commodities constitute the staples of labour consumption. Hence the concept of a vertically integrated wage-goods sector is the coherent reconstruction of such a notion of a self-subsistent subsystem within a larger economy (see n. 62 below).

38 For Smith's views on pure profits as a surplus, see section 4.4.2, and for the meaning of 'pure profits', n. 87 below. Turgot, like Quesnay, commonly speaks of 'revenue' as such, to convey net revenue or net return; but see, for example, Turgot (1769–70 [1977]: 88) and Groenewegen (1977c [1759]: 27–8) for explicit recourse to 'net revenue'. In ignoring his inconsistency concerning whether production of the surplus extends beyond agriculture, and net revenue extends beyond rents gross of taxes, Aspromourgos (1996: 155) is rather too generous to Turgot. The idea that the interest component of profit rates is in some sense a necessary cost of production and so not to be included in the social surplus or net revenue is elegantly stated by Turgot in Groenewegen (1977c [1767]: 123; cf. 125, and Turgot 1769–70 [1977]: 71).

39 For Petty's formulation of political arithmetic, its character and significance, and its relation to King's analysis see Aspromourgos (1996: 39–49, 57–60, 162–4; 2001: 79–83). It was intended by Petty to be much more than just national accounting; but in that limited domain, King (1696) is a substantial advance on Petty's efforts. Apart from a concept of accumulation as the difference between income and expenditure, King (1696: 30–5, 49–56) does also give a decomposition of national income into rents and the incomes derived from 'Trade arts & Labour', and estimates tax shares. (Recall that the Physiocratic doctrine, strictly construed, makes the surplus equivalent in value to land-rents gross of tax revenues.) Along with Yamey (1987) on double-entry, for early instances in the accounting literature of net income or profit, see de Roover (1956 [1974]: 147–9) and Lee (1977: 85). It may be added that the application of an accounting notion of net income to the balance of the revenue and expenditure of the Crown or the State is not yet the concept of a national or social net revenue. It is also an instance of the net revenue of an entity below the level of society as a whole, albeit a particularly important one.

40 To be more precise, the equivalence between net revenue and surplus product applies to any closed economic system. That is to say, it applies to a system which involves no economically relevant relations with entities outside itself. Hence it doesn't strictly apply to a national economy, or society, which trades commodities for use as necessary inputs with parties external to it, just as it does not apply to a subnational entity

which purchases inputs from others in the nation and sells others in the nation outputs which are used as inputs. With such international economic interrelations, the equivalence of net revenue and surplus product can only properly be applied to the resulting closed global economic system as a whole. Strictly speaking, production systems which deplete non-renewable natural resources are not closed systems either (cf. n. 31 above).

41 Smith seems here to ignore that the owner of stock which is employed as capital may be providing necessary labour input to production as well, so that his or her consumption is to some extent a form of capital as self-investment – a possibility made explicit elsewhere (e.g. *WN*: 83, 86, 362–3, 365). It is also made explicit in the introduction to Book II, that the prior provision of consumption to workers, to tide them over the production cycle, may be self-provision as well as provision by others. Filling out a little further the quotation from *WN* (276–7) above: 'A stock of goods ... must be stored up *somewhere ... either in his own possession or in that of some other person*' (emphasis added). It is the prior stock of commodities which is necessary, not a master/labourer contract or exchange as such. However, Smith observes further on that the 'greater part of the labouring poor in all countries' possess so little stock that their revenue derives from their 'labour only' (*WN*: 279; also 83).

42 Nevertheless, certainly it is not easy to reconcile this fundamental defining characteristic with Smith's inclusion of money used in circulation as part of capital. This just points to the inappropriateness of this inclusion (discussed also in sec. 4.2.1), even upon his own terms. In *WN*, Book V (940–3) Smith rather betrays himself on this issue. Discussing the manner in which the North American colonists have substituted paper for commodity money, thereby enabling an augmentation of their (other) capital, he more than once refers to the former as 'dead stock' and the latter as 'active and productive stock'. The contradiction between capital as value-adding stock, and money as a component of capital, is perhaps even more bluntly evident in an earlier passage: 'The gold and silver money which circulates in any country ... is ... all dead stock. It is a very valuable part of the capital of the country, which produces nothing to the country' (*WN*: 320–1; cf. 292–6). A similar argument can be found at *LJA* (377–80) and *LJB* (503–4). It may be noted also that stock held in the form of inventories is explicitly treated as part of capital, which must therefore also return profit (*WN*: 529–31).

43 Smith a few times uses this phrase, in the same sense as here, to convey physical capital (*WN*: 11, 110, 373, 848, 927–8), but also occasionally to refer to financial capital.

44 Also *WN* (66–7, 68–9, 73, 83, 280, 292, 296, 307, 320, *passim* Book II, Chapter III, 351, 361–3, 471, 674, 887, 927). There is some ambivalence in *WN* concerning the status of employers' incomes or their consumption, as part of capital. Hence at *WN* (361) a 'workman' (it is not clear if he also employs other labour, probably not) is treated as if his own consumption is not part of his capital:

> If a poor workman was obliged to purchase a month's or six months provisions at a time, a great part of the stock which he employs as a capital in the instruments of his trade, or in the furniture in his shop, and which yields him a revenue, he would be forced to place in that part of his stock which is reserved for immediate consumption, and which yields him no revenue. Nothing can be more convenient for such a person than to be able to purchase his subsistence from day to day, or even from hour to hour as he wants it. He is thereby enabled to employ almost his whole stock as a capital. He is thus enabled to furnish work to a greater value ....

Then, at the following page, in the context of discussing a fourfold division of productive activities, Smith argues:

> The persons whose capitals are employed in any of those four ways are

> themselves productive labourers. Their labour, when properly directed, fixes and realizes itself in the subject or vendible commodity upon which it is bestowed, and generally adds to its price the value at least of their own maintenance and consumption.
>
> (*WN*: 362; also 363, 365, 674)

This ambivalence may be read partly as reflecting the potential for a real ambiguity in the objective character of employers' economic activities in general (though it also is connected with Smith's inclusion of subsistence consumption as part of net revenue). Are they self-employed workers who also employ other workers? If so, their wages (but not the profits on any capital they advance) are properly capital, if they are engaged in 'productive' activities. If instead they act only as owners of stock or in an entrepreneurial role, then their incomes are not properly wages. The incomes of employers engaged in two or all of these three distinct activities should then be regarded as consisting of conceptually and functionally distinct wages and profits. Submerged within profits there is a distinction, not often explicit, between ownership of capital and entrepreneurship (see sec. 4.4.2). (Somewhat relatedly, Smith is explicit that capital embodied in the acquisition of labour skills must be replaced along with the normal profit rate, so that the skilled versus 'common' labour wage differential is a reflection of that: *WN*: 118–19.) The scope for intersection between the three sets of people who (along with entrepreneurs) make up the fundamental classes of Smith's socio-economic system – the porousness of the borders – is particularly explicit in the following (cf. Chapter 5, n. 10):

> [A]lmost the whole capital of every country is annually distributed among the inferior ranks of people, as the wages of productive labour. Secondly, a great part of the revenue arising from both the rent of land and the profits of stock, is annually distributed among the same rank, in the wages and maintenance of menial servants, and other unproductive labourers. Thirdly, some part of the profits of stock belongs to *the same rank*, as a revenue arising from the employment of their small capitals. The amount of the profits annually made by small shopkeepers, tradesmen, and retailers of all kinds, is every where very considerable, and makes a very considerable portion of the annual produce. Fourthly, and lastly, some part *even of the rent of land belongs to the same rank*; a considerable part to those who are somewhat below the middling rank, and a small part even to the lowest rank; common labourers sometimes possessing in property an acre or two of land.
>
> (*WN*: 887; emphasis added)

But elsewhere Smith asserts, as an empirical fact, that self-employed workmen are 'not very frequent', making up less than five percent of the European workforce (*WN*: 83). At another point, he allows the possibility that 'even the common workman, if his wages are considerable, may … contribute … towards maintaining … unproductive labourers' – by employing 'a menial servant', or going to 'a play or a puppet-show', or paying taxes; but again, the possibility is qualified in practice: such unproductive employment can be financed by 'his spare revenue only, of which productive labourers have seldom a great deal' (*WN*: 333).

45 Attached here is a footnote by Smith, concerning '[s]ome French authors of great learning and ingenuity' who have used those terms differently and improperly. He is referring to the Physiocratic notion, limiting productiveness to agricultural labour, systematically repudiated by Smith in Book IV, Chapter IX (esp. on productive labour, pp. 664, 666–70, 672–6, 678): 'The capital error of this system … seems to lie in its representing the class of artificers, manufacturers and merchants, as altogether barren and unproductive' (*WN*: 674). (Smith's use of 'capital' here is presumably an unintentional pun!) Hereafter in this chapter $L^p$ and $L^u$ are used to denoted productive

labour and unproductive labour respectively, signifying the concepts themselves, and in some contexts, actual quantities of productive and unproductive labour.

46 Notice that taken literally, this last clause excludes unproductive output from the national product, and hence also excludes it from growth.

47 The three-revenues notion of Book II, Chapters I–II – and likewise earlier, in the price theory (Book I, Chapters VI–VII in particular) – is here replaced with a two-revenues formulation (also, for example, at *WN*: 335, 927–8). The two approaches to income are reconciled by wages of $L^p$ being here partly placed under 'capital' replacement, and profits and rents being treated as the only sources of funding an *increase* of total $L^p$, together with $L^u$. That is to say, the possibility of wage-earners employing labour has been put aside.

48 Smith includes 'misconduct', along with prodigality, as a cause of capital diminution (*WN*: 340–3). It is concerned with investments which are, in principle, productive activities, but fail to cover their costs, due to poor judgement.

49 On saving, dissaving and accumulation, including at the national or system level, see also the remainder of this chapter (*WN*: 338–49, dissaving being explicitly considered at 339–40, 342, 344), as well as *WN* (292, 333, 411, 457–8, 497–8 (comparing the balance of national output and consumption with the balance of foreign trade; also on this, *WN*: 490–1, 505–6), 611–2). Hence at one point, speaking of the unproductive labour employed in the apparatus of State, Smith continues:

> When multiplied ... to an unnecessary number, they may in a particular year consume so great a share of this [annual] produce, as not to leave a sufficiency for maintaining the productive labourers, who should reproduce it next year. The next year's produce, therefore, will be less than that of the foregoing, and if the same disorder should continue, that of the third year will be still less than that of the second. Those unproductive hands, who should be maintained by a part only of the spare revenue of the people, may consume so great a share of their whole revenue, and thereby oblige so great a number to encroach upon their capitals, upon the funds destined for the maintenance of productive labour, that all the frugality and good conduct of individuals may not be able to compensate the waste and degradation of produce occasioned by this violent and forced encroachment.
> (*WN*: 342)

*WN* (439) refers to 'consumable capital'; capital in the form of wages is 'consumed' (*WN*: 341), but also therefore could be consumed by unproductive uses. The connection between productive labour (albeit here referred to as 'useful labour'), capital accumulation and saving is elegantly summed up at *WN* (677).

50 The concept and language of bettering one's condition appears twice further in this chapter (*WN*: 343, 345), and also at *TMS* (50); *WN* (99, 405, 540, 674). See also editorial notes 22 and 29–30 at *WN* (338, 340), concerning connections between *TMS* and *WN* on this matter. The phrase is not to be found in *LJ*. This desire to better one's condition is not, as such, to be identified with unfettered selfishness (cf. Chapter 3, n. 20). Note also that at the end of Book II, Chapter III (346–9) Smith as well endorses durable luxury consumption over less durable luxury consumption, as better favouring opulence and frugality. Force (2003: 42–3, 124–6, 131–4, 245–6) goes too far in arguing that Smith identifies material self-betterment with 'vanity' as such, and with a self-delusive indefinite postponement of consumption. (Brown 1994: 7, 208–15 has some kinship with this view.) It is one thing to say that Smith is contemptuous of the vanities of the rich (see, for example, *TMS*: 50; quoted in Chapter 5, n. 28); it is quite another to suggest that he similarly disdains individuals' prudent or long-sighted pursuit of material comfort as such. Smith's characterization in *TMS* of the 'virtue' of 'prudence', though it is not the highest virtue (*TMS*: 216, 296–8, 303–5), epitomizes the savers who drive accumulation in *WN*, as the *TMS* editors also point out (*TMS*: 212–17; Raphael and Macfie 1976b: 8–9, 18). (Cf. *TMS*: 189–90, 237–62, on the

'virtue' of 'self-command', which informs economic behaviour, but in its widest sense, comes to assume for Smith a primary and pervasive role in all of virtue: Raphael and Macfie 1976b: 6.) Hence for Smith, to the extent that prudence is a virtue, 'self-love can ... be the motive of a virtuous action' (*TMS*: 304; also 309, 312–13):

> CONCERN for our own happiness recommends to us the virtue of prudence: concern for that of other people, the virtues of justice and beneficence; of which, the one restrains us from hurting, the other prompts us to promote that happiness [of others].... [T]he first of those three virtues is originally recommended to us by our selfish, the other two by our benevolent affections.
>
> (*TMS*: 262)

51 Also pertinent here is Smith's inclusion of the labour skills acquired via education as an element of fixed capital (*WN*: 282; cf. 118–19). Since education is evidently a service, this further qualifies the notion of services as unproductive. And to the extent that education is provided by the State, which Smith himself favours (*WN*: 758–88), this also compromises the idea that all government activity is unproductive.

52 It may be added, returning to the notion of circulating money as part of capital, that Smith would have done better to treat that money, like government, as useful and necessary to production, but not capital (see n. 42). Money is more like $L^u$ than it is like the other components of capital.

53 Notwithstanding this, in the chapter appraising the Physiocrats, Smith refers to their labelling artificers, manufacturers and merchants 'barren or unproductive' as a 'humiliating appellation' (*WN*: 664), but perhaps this is a rhetorical flourish in the context of his critique. In the 'Introduction and Plan' of *WN* (11), useful and productive labour are identified (see also *WN*: 677, quoted in n. 49 above). This is not his precise view.

54 Notwithstanding this diagnosis, Smith has a valid point with respect to the ability of an economic system to accumulate services, as against physical commodities. For example, the services from a transport network do indeed perish in performance. How then are transport services able to be accumulated? The production *capacity* of transport services is able to be accumulated via expansion of the *physical* infrastructure for the service provision (the number of trucks available and so on). Electricity is a good example of a non-storable commodity employed as capital, but electricity-generating capacity also can be accumulated. Indeed, the non-storability of electricity is the reason why its production capacity with respect to average demand has to be relatively high, in order to satisfy peak demands.

One may conjecture also that Smith thought, as a matter of contingent, contemporaneous fact, rather than of principle, that services were generally not capital goods, or consumption goods of productive labour in particular, and generalized this contingent fact to almost a point of principle. Campbell and Skinner (1976: 30) and Skinner (1996: 165) equate Smith's $L^u$ with service-producing labour, apparently without noticing the problem thereby created for the status of transportation and distribution services. The analysis by Vianello (1999: 175–8) is close to our view. He points out also (p. 177), that at *WN* (333) Smith allows for unproductive services which are vendible (quoted in n. 44 above: the 'play or ... puppet-show'). With regard to menial servants as the archetype of unproductive labour for Smith, see also his historical argument for how the rise of commercial society has diminished the numbers of such 'menial servants' and idle 'retainers', replacing 'servile dependency' with 'liberty and security' (*WN*: 412–22).

55 Our referring to the second commodity as a 'machine' should not obscure the fact that from an analytical standpoint it is, in modern terms, only circulating capital. Smith's concern with the maintenance or replacement of fixed capital is therefore not formally incorporated in this illustrative system. As against Smith's way of distinguishing

fixed from circulating capital, the more pertinent distinction is that the former is not entirely used up in the production cycle; it remains still a usable input to production beyond that discrete time period. (This, *contra* Smith, makes seed corn input an element of circulating capital.) The distinction thereby becomes ultimately relative, relative to the length of the time period specified for analysis. In general of course, a fixed capital item so understood (e.g. a genuine machine) will be altered in its economically relevant characteristics by the production process, most usually, deteriorated in some manner, so that it will re-enter production in the next period as a different kind of machine, strictly speaking. Depreciation allowances or amortization are precisely designed to account for such deterioration of relatively long-lived production inputs.

56 The relation between the modelling of production here, and the modelling employed in section 4.2.2 to provide a benchmark conceptualization of 'surplus', is that here:

1 land use in production is ignored;
2 a third commodity, or class of commodities ('silk'), is included;
3 constant returns to scale are assumed, thereby putting aside Smith's concern with both increasing returns and natural scarcities (see secs. 3.4.1, 4.1.1);
4 neither corn nor manufacture uses direct corn input (only indirect corn input, via labour consumption).

In addition, since market prices, and the difference between market prices and normal prices, are not being treated here, the superscripting of price variables employed in Chapter 3 to distinguish market and natural prices ($p^m{}_i$, $p^n$) is dispensed with. Note also, that while 'silk' is here being employed to clarify Smith's $L^p/L^u$ distinction, it could also be used to represent his commodity or commodity-linked money (as against a pure fiat currency). We could then call it 'silver' rather than silk. The equations would then express the wages and prices in terms of this silver money. Since Smith would have been better off excluding the money stock from capital (n. 42, n. 52 above), the difference between silk and silver, at this level of abstraction, is not really so great.

57 The required restriction is:

$$(1 - cl_C)(1 - a_{MM}) - cl_M a_{MC} > 0$$

together with $c < 1/l_C$, $a_{MM} < 1$. This has a direct and compelling economic interpretation: the production methods in use must be capable of producing a surplus or net product over and above the inputs used up in an annual production cycle, including in this, the necessary (or above-subsistence) consumption of the workforce, associated with the given real wage per worker – otherwise positive profits with positive prices are not possible. To see this, impose the following inequalities, with at least one satisfied as a strict inequality; i.e. impose a positive net product or surplus:

$$Q_C \geq c(l_C Q_C + l_M Q_M)$$
$$Q_M \geq a_{MC} Q_C + a_{MM} Q_M$$

where $Q_C$, $Q_M$ are the annual gross outputs produced. This entails the above restriction. Hence this restriction parallels also the inequalities expressing the production of a surplus, employed in the illustrative model used to clarify the concept of surplus in section 4.2.2.

58 Our conceptualization of the social surplus (sec. 4.2.2) was articulated in terms of an economic system 'reproducing' itself in physical (commodity) terms: in circular production systems, viable production is *re*production. Smith also quite a number of times uses this term and variants thereof, but generally to convey merely the sense of labour producing value added in excess of its wages or consumption, rather than to characterize physical replacement of inputs used up, including labour consumption

(with or without a commodity surplus): 'an additional stock of materials, tools, and provisions, in order to maintain and employ an additional number of industrious people, who re-produce, with a profit, *the value of* their annual consumption' (*WN*: 294; emphasis added; also 295, 338–9, 341–2, 350, 363–4, 376, 513, 666, 668, 674–5, 678, 924). To that extent, his notion of reproduction involves the same imprecision as his definition of $L^u$. The use of the term at *WN* (342; quoted in n. 49 above) comes closer to the sense of physical reproduction; and also:

> The country supplies the town with the means of subsistence, and the materials of manufacture. The town repays this supply by sending back a part of the manufactured produce to the inhabitants of the country. The town, in which there neither is nor can be any reproduction of substances, may very properly be said to gain its whole wealth and subsistence from the country.
>
> (*WN*: 376; consider also the uses at 666, 678)

Some of the instances of the term at *WN* (339) and at *WN* (363–4) are quoted at pp. 169 and 178, respectively. Neither the term nor variants appear anywhere else in Smith's texts, save for one non-economic reference (*EPS*: 117).

59 This proportion refers only to the aggregate value of corn and machine output, not the silk output. Recall that Smith, strictly speaking, excludes unproductive activities and outputs from national product (n. 46 above).

60 This is what is happening when, given a viable value of $Q_{s(t+1)}$ derived from the third equation, the first two equations do not generate a unique and economically meaningful solution for $Q_{c(t+1)}$, $Q_{M(t+1)}$. Those equations should then be reinterpreted as weak inequalities showing two sets of feasible corn and machine outputs from utilization of the corn and machine stocks respectively, one feasible set for the stock of corn, one for the stock of machines. The lack of a unique solution for the two equations is equivalent to one of those two feasible sets being a subset of the other.

61 In the limit, steady-state growth conditions could be imposed: the outputs of all commodities growing at a uniform rate, with capital stocks perfectly adjusted to commodity demands, continuously through time. To give an example of such a steady-state solution, make the simplifying assumption that net profits are entirely expended on net investment. Then the following kind of steady-state system would emerge:

$$Q_{c(t+1)} = Q_{c(t)}(1+g) = c(l_c Q_{c(t+1)} + l_M Q_{M(t+1)})(1+g)$$

$$Q_{M(t+1)} = Q_{M(t)}(1+g) = (a_{MC} Q_{c(t+1)} + a_{MM} Q_{M(t+1)})(1+g)$$

Since there is no consumption out of profits, silk production disappears. The two equations serve to determine the steady-state growth rate ($g$) and the associated ratio between corn and machine outputs. In fact, $g$ will equal the solution for the profit rate embedded in the price equations of section 4.3.3. (Notice the similarity between the corn and machine price equations there – when taken together with $w = p_c c$ – and the output equations here.) The assumption here, that all profits are devoted to accumulation, has the effect that the rate of net capital accumulation equals the ratio of profits to capital. But whether in such a simplified or in a more general formulation, it is not necessary to place such a mechanical and rigid steady-state straightjacket on Smith's analysis. The tendency for market prices to be drawn towards normal prices requires neither a tendency to steady-state growth, nor that actual utilization rates of the capital stock be at desired levels (see Ciccone 1986: 21–32).

62 The equations for normal prices now are:

$$(p_c a_{cc} + w l_c)(1+r) = p_c \qquad 1 > c l_c + a_{cc} > 0$$

$$(p_c a_{cs} + w l_s)(1+r) = p_s$$

$$w = p_c c$$

$$p_c = 1$$

The rate of profit is fully determined by the production conditions of corn, together with the real wage. (A more general formulation of this idea is provided by Garegnani 1984: 313–20 or 1987: 568–72, determining the rate of profit by reference to the vertically integrated wage-goods sector of an economy.) The gross profit rate $(1 + r)$ is the reciprocal of the capital-to-gross-output ratio in corn production. A further point may be noted here: the growth equation might be read as entailing that growth is also a positive function of $r$; but Smith rather vigorously argues at one point that high profit rates discourage saving, both directly, with respect to the profit recipients themselves, and also by a demonstration effect (*WN*: 612–13). Eltis (1975; reproduced revised in Eltis 1984: 68–105) provides a careful, more general formal model of Smith's growth theory, incorporating growth of labour productivity and real wages, as well as the possibility of a stationary end-state to the growth dynamics (cf. Chapter 3, n. 50). However, the problem of demand sufficiency is very lightly passed over by Eltis (1975: 432; cf. Waterman 2001: 28–9, 39–40).

63 The presence of $p_s/p_c$ in the equation for $L^p/L^u$ is due to its reflecting the ratio of the commodity capital-output ratios:

$$(a_{cs} + cl_s)/(a_{cc} + cl_c) = p_s/p_c$$

The quantities of labour employed per unit of capital devoted to production of the capital good and the luxury consumption good are respectively,

$$[l_c/(a_{cc} + cl_c)],\ [l_s/(a_{cs} + cl_s)]$$

Hence the ratio between labour per unit of capital devoted to production of capital, and labour per unit of capital devoted to production of luxury consumption, is given by $(l_c/l_s)(p_s/p_c)$. Notice that if the labour theory of value holds (see Chapter 3, n. 56), $a_{cc}/l_c$ equals $a_{cs}/l_s$: the quantity of labour employed per unit of capital devoted to production of capital and the quantity of labour employed per unit of capital devoted to production of luxury consumption are identical, so that $(l_c/l_s)(p_s/p_c)$ reduces to unity and $L^p/L^u$ reduces to $\sigma/(1 - \sigma)$. It may be noted also that the trade-off between growth and surplus consumption is not so compelling if output-capital ratios are more flexible than is entailed by fixed input-output coefficients, notably, due to unutilized capacity in the capital stock as the normal situation (Garegnani and Palumbo 1998).

64 All other references to economic senses of 'capital' or variants (the plural is often used), incidental or not directly pertinent to our fundamental purposes here, for just Books I and II of *WN*, are at (4–5, 7, 11, 108–10, 112, 125, 129, 174, 182, 266, 350–53, 355–8, 360–75). (These pages do not include Book II, Chapters I–III.) Some of these refer to forms of financial capital, true also of some of the references to capital beyond Books I and II of *WN*. In addition, the discussion of capital and revenue at *WN* (286–92) has been sufficiently treated in section 4.2.1. The last two Chapters of Book II, Chapters IV and V (*WN*: 350–75), concern financial capital in the form of lending and borrowing for the acquisition or rental of stock or capital, including payment of wages; and supposed systematic differences in labour intensities of production, or value added per worker, across different sectors (agriculture, manufacture, wholesaling, and so on). (Jeck 1994 provides a plausible rationalization of Smith's views in relation to the latter issue.) There are five uses of 'capital' or variants in *TMS*, two in *EPS*, four in *LRB* and two in *Corr*, none of them economic senses. There are also some non-economic uses of the term in *WN* (capital cities; capital in the sense of major or primary). All other references to $L^p$ beyond Book II, Chapter III, which are of a character incidental to our purposes, are at (4, 351–2, 600, 602, 607–9, 611–12, 629, 633, 897). No references to $L^p$ or $L^u$ appear in any of the other five volumes of Smith texts in the Glasgow Edition.

65 Any reader inclined to object to this notion of conceptual or logical time, and the associated concept of dated labour, should realize that the approximation is a pure deduction from the normal price equation for production in a *single*, say the current, time period: the latter cannot be acceptable and the former unacceptable. The meaning of the equivalence is that the solution from the single-period price equation is approximately the result that would occur if we imagine the machine having been produced with present and past direct and indirect input, by the same production method as that currently in use (and with the current $r$ continuously prevailing). Hence this exercise in fact points to why past, obsolete production methods, no longer in use or no longer the dominant methods in use, are *irrelevant* to the current normal price.

66 So long as the system is capable of producing a surplus (n. 57 above), the quadratic equation in $(1 + r)$ entailed by the $p_{cw}$ equation will yield one and only one economically meaningful solution for $r$, and that solution will be a negative function of $c$ (see Kurz and Salvadori 1995: 63–9). The given real wage cannot be independent of technology; the historically-minded Smith would have no resistance to affirming this proposition. Hence the note 57 restriction required for an economically meaningful solution for $r$ should be interpreted as a restriction binding the feasible values of $c$, in relation to the production methods in use: $c$ must be so constrained as to ensure that labour consumption does not exhaust the entire net product – or entire surplus, if labour enjoys above-subsistence consumption – so that the profit share can be positive. (There are as well restrictions on technology independent of $c$.) These formal treatments of the problem are not grasped by Smith at such a level; they are offered here as a way of clarifying the logic and limitations of his conception of normal prices. Distribution and classical normal prices – or in much used latter-day terms, 'long-period' prices – in circular production systems, have received extensive formal analysis in recent decades, following the lead of Sraffa (1960). For a survey of the literature, see Aspromourgos (2004).

67 One is tentative because the evidence for the extent of Smith's intuition on this matter is rather slight, at one page of the Book I, Chapter VI component-parts-of-price discussion (though it extends to somewhat more than just the text quoted here from that page). The price of every commodity, the reader is told, in general 'finally' resolves into wages, profit and rent. Smith continues:

> In the price of corn, for example, one part pays the rent of the landlord, another pays the wages ... of the labourers and labouring cattle employed in producing it, and the third pays the profit of the farmer.... A fourth part, it may perhaps be thought, is necessary for replacing the stock of the farmer, or for compensating the wear and tear of his labouring cattle, and other instruments of husbandry. But it must be considered that the price of any instrument of husbandry, such as a labouring horse, is itself made up of the same three parts; the rent of the land upon which he is reared, the labour of tending and rearing him, and the profits of the farmer who advances both the rent of this land, and the wages of this labour [but what of the equivalent here, of the earlier 'fourth part' – stock and instruments?]. Though the price of the corn, therefore, may pay the price as well as the maintenance of the horse, the whole price still resolves itself either immediately or ultimately into the same three parts of rent, labour and profit.
>
> (*WN*: (68)

O'Donnell (1990: 85, 111–17, 219) takes a quite emphatic view that Smith did not grasp the reduction notion.

68 Smith does discuss situations of rising real wages and simultaneously falling profit rates (notably, Book I, Chapter IX), but the association seems a *contingent* outcome. The intensification of competition between capitals may at one and the same time cause real wages to be bid up and profit rates reduced, but via separate forces. In dis-

cussing these kinds of situations he twice uses the telling phrase 'at both ends', which points to the essential separability of the two phenomena in his conception:

> As capitals increase in any country, the profits which can be made by employing them necessarily diminish. It becomes gradually more and more difficult to find within the country a profitable method of employing any new capital. There arises in consequence a competition between different capitals, the owner of one endeavouring to get possession of that employment which is occupied by another. But upon most occasions he can hope to justle that other out of this employment, by no other means but by dealing upon more reasonable terms. He must not only sell what he deals in somewhat cheaper, but in order to get it to sell, he must sometimes too buy it dearer. The demand for productive labour, by the increase of the funds which are destined for maintaining it, grows every day greater and greater. Labourers easily find employment, but the owners of capitals find it difficult to get labourers to employ. Their competition raises the wages of labour, and sinks the profits of stock.... [T]he profits which can be made by the use of a capital are in this manner diminished, as it were, at both ends ....
>
> (*WN*: 352–3; also 110–11)

If Smith understood the functional relation between rates of wages and profits, two separate arguments – one explaining the fall of profits, the other explaining the rise of wages – would not be required. On the other hand, he does enunciate the idea of a minimum and maximum ordinary rate of profit, the latter associated with a minimum subsistence wage and zero rents (*WN*: 113). Marx (e.g. 1968: 106, 165–6, 216–35) much discusses Smith's failure to adequately grasp the constraint binding rates of wages and profits together.

69 Remember also that the reduction to dated wages and profits is only approximate: as one goes 'backwards', to logically earlier and earlier time periods, the required quantities of produced commodity inputs become smaller and smaller, but never vanish (as Marx 1963: 133, 138 recognized in relation to Smith's theory). This also is an expression of the simultaneity of normal price and normal cost determination. As Sraffa (1960: 94) indicates, for produced inputs to vanish in the Smithian reduction exercise requires that commodities ultimately can be produced by means of labour and unimproved natural resources alone, without need of produced commodity inputs. The existence of produced commodities as part of necessary labour consumption by itself suffices to contradict this supposition: it requires that labourers can live on unimproved natural resources. Nevertheless, if one considers the reduction-of-price issue in parallel with Smith's commentaries on accumulation of stock, it seems more than possible that he would assent to the proposition that in *historical* time, in early states of human society, initial accumulation of stock occurred in something like this manner, by acquisition and production from nature, without use of produced stock. To the extent that production in general, and division of labour in particular, presuppose stock, in both the notion of the price reduction and the issue of growth there is implied an original production of commodities or stock, without input of produced commodities or stock. (Whether Smith perceives this parallel is not clear.) This point with regard to production and division of labour, is strikingly expressed in a sketch of the causes of the slow progress of opulence:

> it is easier for a nation ... to raise itself from a moderate degree of wealth to the highest opulence, than to acquire this moderate degree of wealth .... The extreme difficulty of beginning accumulation and the many accidents to which it is exposed.
>
> (*edWN*: 579)

This problem of original accumulation is more considerably discussed in *LJB* (521–2). There is no parallel text in *LJA*, but this absence is probably due to the equivalent *LJA* lectures being in that part of the *LJA* manuscript which is no longer extant (see Meek *et al.* 1978b: 13, 26–7 with n. 40, 42 at pp. 31–2). This conjecture is supported by Smith's comment there, that in treating opulence he intends to consider, among other factors, '[t]he causes of the slow progress of opulence, and the causes which retarded it' (*LJA*: 353). In any case, the proposition that production and employment presuppose stock *is* in *LJA*, as well as elsewhere in *LJB*, as indicated in section 4.3.1. No such similarly explicit commentary on original accumulation, to that in *LJB*, is quite to be found in *WN*, but it is strongly implied in the transition from the 'rude [human] state' to society with division of labour. This is evident, for example, in the opening paragraphs of *WN*, Book II:

> In that rude state of society ... [e]very man endeavours to supply by his own industry his own occasional wants as they occur. *When he is hungry, he goes to the forest to hunt; when his coat is worn out, he cloaths himself with the skin of the first large animal he kills: and when his hut begins to go to ruin, he repairs it, as well as he can, with the trees and the turf that are nearest it.*
>
> But when the division of labour has once been thoroughly introduced ... [a] stock of goods ... must be stored up ....
>
> (*WN*: 276; emphasis added)

All this makes clear enough Smith's conscious belief that at some early point(s) in history, human labour, unaided by any prior produced commodities, produced commodities entirely out of materials appropriated from the natural environment. In any case, this historical fact does not undercut the significance of circular production for the theory of prices and distribution 'now'.

70 Hence elsewhere Smith comments:

> antiently, during the prevalency of the feudal government, a very small portion of the produce [of land] was sufficient to replace the capital employed in cultivation. It consisted commonly in a few wretched cattle, maintained altogether by the spontaneous produce of uncultivated land, and which might, therefore, be considered as a part of that spontaneous produce.
>
> (*WN*: 334)

Until the seventeenth and eighteenth centuries 'cattle' was widely applied to a variety of farm animals, but then came progressively to be confined only to bovine animals (*OED*: 'cattle').

71 Aspromourgos (1996: 116–23) systematically discusses the contrast between the salience of capital in Quesnay's system and the uneasy and shadowy half-presence of capital in Cantillon's economics approximately a quarter century earlier. Quesnay's capital theory, which incorporates a distinction between fixed and circulating capital advances (*avances primitives*, *avances annuelles*), also enables him to develop a theory of economic growth. The role of rates of return on alternative investments in Turgot's economics is evident enough in the account of his price theory given in section 3.5.2.

72 Aspromourgos (1996: 122–3) comments on the Vaggi interpretation. Vaggi (1987b: 25, 27–8) provides a summary statement of the interpretation, in relation to the logic of prices, profits and accumulation – not so much in the *Tableau*, as in Quesnay's earlier writings. The distinction between Quesnay's *bon prix* and *prix fondamental* (the latter, a notion of cost-price), and its significance for accumulation, is also summarized there. For an intimation, in the *Tableau*, of this function of prices and profits in relation to accumulation, see Kuczynski and Meek (1972: 9–11, '3rd edn'), especially the Quesnay notes accompanying the main text.

73 See the very last sentences of section 4.3.1 (cf. Chapter 2, n. 32). Also noteworthy in this context is that the term 'reproduction', which Quesnay aptly employs to characterize the circular conception of production with a surplus (*la reproduction*, and vari-

ants), does not appear in *LJ*, nor the concept. See note 58 above, for the uses of 'reproduction' in *WN*. On Smith's probable French debts with respect to both capital theory and circulation, see also Skinner (1996: 137–41; cf. Campbell and Skinner 1976: 28–32). One may further recall the absence from *LJ* of the very term 'political economy' (sec. 2.1.5).

74 The last sentence here alludes to the larger issue of Cannan's downplaying the influence on Smith of the Physiocrats in general and Turgot in particular, systematically criticized at Viner (1965: 128–33). Gherity (1993: 255–6, 268–70) discusses the Lundberg argument also, in the context of an unconvincing authorship claim.

75 Fisher (1896) is a critical account of concepts of capital from Turgot forward, focused on the question of coherent stock/flow distinctions. It is mainly of interest because by a significant figure in the rise of marginalism. A follow-up article (Fisher 1897) deals extensively with capital in relation to property rights, including 'human capital' (p. 212; Fisher's inverted commas). The closing sentences of the latter are indicative of the attitude informing the two articles: 'The conception of marginal utility has borne rich fruit. The distinctions between productive and unproductive labour and between "capital and other wealth" have borne little or none' (Fisher 1897: 213).

76 Recall also the point made at the end of section 4.3.4, that Smith's productive versus unproductive distinction is really about the *uses* to which commodities are put, not the qualitative characteristics which define any particular kind of commodity. If $L^p$ is coherently understood – as labour employed with capital goods, to produce further capital goods – then whether, say, a unit of corn, and the labour which produced it, are 'productive' or not depends upon the destination of that corn after it is produced. If it goes to employing labour in the production of more corn, it is productive; if it goes to the consumption of a landowner, it is unproductive.

77 There is an extensive literature on the history of ideas concerning luxury, from antiquity to modernity; e.g. Sekora (1977), Berry (1994), Perrotta (2004) and Wahnbaeck (2004). Of these, Perrotta provides the most comprehensive and deepest overview of the subject in Western thought in its entirety. Berry's (1994: 152–73) treatment of Smith's views on luxury is greatly compromised by taking no heed of his theory of growth and the role of $L^p$. Winch (1996; esp. 59–80) provides an account of Smith's position, in the context of the eighteenth-century luxury debates, which better reflects its subtlety and complexity. The pre-modern opposition to luxury connects with the antipathy to accumulation of money or excessive material goods (cf. sec. 2.2.2). It almost goes without saying that this is not about *capital* accumulation in the sense of Smith. Nor is the mercantilist economic argument against luxuries, because they are imports, which is with a view to *favouring* accumulation of money via balance of foreign payments surpluses.

78 It is variants of this idea that Berry (1994: 101–25) examines in terms of the early modern 'de-moralisation' of luxury. (Cf. Perrotta 2004: 225–34, for a fuller and more balanced account of pro- and anti-luxury views in this period.) It is an idea also to be found in Smith, most saliently, in 'the desire of bettering our condition' as the primary psychological driver of economic behaviour (sec. 4.3.2, esp. n. 50). But in Smith, it is accompanied by a substantial theory of the causal connections running from the human desires to the economic dynamics and outcomes. In any case, this idea is not an economic argument for luxury, since of itself, it provides no justification for either the luxury or the human desire for it. It may be emphasized that the general idea of desire for luxury or comfort providing the impetus to economic development is not synonymous with the much more specific and concrete claim, that production (and hence also consumption) of luxuries are necessary, in some considerable measure, in order to provide an adequate or desirable level of employment in society.

79 Gilibert (2001: 116) observes in relation to the term 'production', that 'until the end of the 18th century, [it] was used in its narrow etymological sense (from the Latin *producere*, to bring forth) of giving birth to new material objects, and was therefore

confined to the fruits of the earth'. This would be something of an overstatement, at least if applied to English use, but there is certainly a tendency to this sort of 'agricultural bias', so to speak. The following examples are quite representative of the variety of uses of 'productive': 'his tears ... having water'd the productive earth' (1672); 'He is not made productive of his kind ... but by coition with a Female' (1701); 'Corn hath not risen in proportion to other Commodities, because by a new-fashioned Industry the same Quantity of Ground is more productive than it was' (1734); 'Salted cod ... was ... productive of the scurvy' (1748; *OED*: 'productive'). The agricultural orientation is more pronounced for 'produce' (noun) and 'production'; but it is by no means the exclusive orientation in those cases either, in the eighteenth century and earlier.

80 Compare these conclusions with the growth formalization of section 4.3.4, which makes the further simplification of putting aside land-rents. See Aspromourgos (1996: 22–41, 74–80, 103–25) for an account of the content of surplus labour activities in Petty and Cantillon, and the activities they favour for the employment of surplus labour. This shows that there is a certain conception of accumulation already in Petty and Cantillon: accumulation of durable goods, including some attention to produced means of production; but the latter aspect does not amount to much. For Quesnay's conceptualization, see, for example, Kuczynski and Meek (1972: i–v, '3rd edn'). Quesnay in fact speaks of productive versus sterile *expenditure* (*les dépenses productives, les dépenses stériles*), and productive versus sterile expenditure *classes*. This expenditure formulation is by no means conceptually inferior to Smith's focus on labour. (Cf. the section 4.2.2 discussion of how surplus-producing activities may be thought of, equivalently, in either commodity terms or labour terms; and the section 4.3.4 observations concerning Smith's idea of productive stock.) For Turgot's conceptualization, see the *Réflexions* (1769–70 [1977]: 45–6, 49–50). Like Quesnay, he speaks of the 'productive' class versus the 'sterile' class (also described as 'stipendiary' or 'barren'), as well as the 'disposable' class (the landowners). For their economic arguments against luxury and in favour of accumulation or thrift, see Kuczynski and Meek (1972: xi, 12–14, '3rd edn') and Turgot (1769–70 [1977]: 84–5). Smith implicitly acknowledges the Physiocratic origin of the $L^p$ concept (n. 45 above). Recall also that surplus-producing labour should not be identified with value-adding labour as such (secs. 4.3.2, 4.3.3).

81 Even if he had used a surplus notion systematically in the treatment of net revenue, it would only be similar, and could not be identical, to the Physiocratic notion – because the productiveness of manufacture and other activities in Smith's political economy means that production of the surplus is not limited to agriculture.

82 Certainly Smith's two propositions, that division of labour depends on market demand growth, and that at the same time division of labour presupposes stock, also require some reconciliation of (capital) supply and (output) demand; for example, perhaps by supposing that demand growth induces supplies of stock. It may be added that, contemporaneous with Smith, Steuart (1767) conveys a strong sense of demand as the autonomous element in economic development.

83 There is one intimation of something close to the same idea in *LJB* (520). There is no similar statement to this in *LJA*, but again, probably due to the parallel text of *LJA* being no longer extant (see n. 69 above).

A word of explanation may be added concerning saving/investment balance, to indicate its equivalence to the balance of aggregate output demand and supply. In a closed system the value of the aggregate output of the economic system is identically equal to its aggregate income. Suppose the entire aggregate income accrues to the 'household sector', which divides it between consumption expenditure and saving. The 'production sector' undertakes investment expenditure. Balance between aggregate demand and aggregate supply requires that consumption plus investment equals the value of output. Since the latter is identically equal to aggregate income, this is equivalent to saving equalling investment. Properly understood, all these magnitudes should refer to planned values.

84 Smith's frequent identification of produce with 'what comes to the same thing', the *prices* of produce or outputs, is in one sense harmless, as a form of accounting identity; but it is also symptomatic of his largely ignoring problems pertaining to the successful realization of output in (sufficiently profitable) sales, at the level of the system as a whole. The identification using this phrase occurs at *WN* (22, 67, 69, 160, 237, 253, 264–5, 276, 330, 409, 419, 449, 457, 535, 588, 670, 672, 686, 837, 847, 865, 897). It is not to be found in *LJ*, but there are intimations of it (e.g. *LJA*: 343, 352; and *edWN*: 566). The most striking systematic expression by Smith of a notion of output sales as demand-constrained is, of course, division of labour being limited by extent of the market. A further, related point may be added here. In Chapter 3 we spoke of normal price as the 'anchor' for market price dynamics. With regard to the problem of growth dynamics, it should be noted that the anchor is actually a given normal-price, effectual-demand *combination*. It was argued in section 3.4.1 that normal price can retain its significance as an anchor when effectual demands are allowed to change, though the associated possible changes in normal prices are highly contingent. But there is in Smith no theory of changes in effectual demands over time, and their relation to the evolution of production capacities and aggregate incomes. This is partly an expression of the same lack of an account of saving/investment coordination.

85 Notwithstanding Smith's notion of a mechanism whereby labour supply and population adapt to labour demand or accumulation, Stirati (1994: 53–5) convincingly argues that his account of differing natural wage rates as between expanding, contracting and stationary economies entails persistent labour demand/supply imbalance. The persistence of low wages in stationary and contracting economies requires *persistent* excess labour supply pressure, in turn acting upon bargaining power. Similarly, the persistence of relatively high wages in expanding economies requires persistent excess labour demand pressure. Hence in the relevant passages of argument, Smith speaks of '*constant* scarcity of employment', labour demand falling '[*e*]*very* year', '*continual* complaint of the scarcity of hands' (*WN*: 88–90; emphasis added). Stirati (1994: 95–101) is thereby also able to explode the interpretations of Smith on wages and unemployment offered by Hollander (1973: 157–8) and Samuelson (1978: 1417–22), involving an equilibrium wage associated with equality of workforce and employment growth. To the extent that the growth scenarios involved in these multiple natural wage outcomes are long-lived phenomena, the population adaptation mechanism must be regarded as a *very*-long-run mechanism, or perhaps a mere tendency (though likely to impact with greater force and speed in a contractionary scenario). The idea of labour supply adapting to labour demand via population change no doubt was inspired by Cantillon (1755 [1931]: 23–85), who is mentioned in the wages chapter (*WN*: 85). It may be added that while this mechanism suggests demand-led growth, strictly speaking it is consistent with the saving-is-spending doctrine: one need only contemplate the von Neumann (1937) model to see that.

In section 3.4.3 we came to the conclusion that, with regard to the operation of competition, there is a less than complete analogy between the behaviour of commodity prices and of wages. Stirati (1994: 85) makes the same inference, most particularly, on the basis of the natural wage being a function of persistent labour demand/supply imbalance, dynamically understood. The key point in relation to unemployment is that the adjustment of aggregate labour supply to aggregate labour demand, via the population adaptation mechanism, cannot be of anything like the same rapidity as the adjustment of commodity production to demand. There is therefore ample scope for the general level of normal wage rates to change. (The speed of adjustment of particular labour supplies to particular demands, below the level of aggregate labour demand/supply, of course would generally be much more considerable.) All the issues considered here in relation to growth dynamics and demand/supply coordination indicate that one cannot so easily impute to Smith a 'supply-side' growth theory, as suggested, for example, by Omori (2003: 115–16) and Tanaka (2003: 142–3). The former also too readily reads into the Smith/Steuart contrast a variant of the latter-day marginalist distinction between long-run (supply-side) and short-run (demand-side) approaches to explaining activity levels and growth.

86 Vianello (1999: 174–5) offers an alternative resolution of the issue, by supposing that Smith is treating the annual production cycle as if it includes each and every successive stage in the production of a final commodity. (These successive stages are equivalent to the conceptual stages of dated labour employed in section 4.3.5, to clarify Smith's reduction of prices to remuneration for inputs.) Under this circumstance, all commodity inputs are produced in that same time period – no stocks of commodity inputs are inherited from past production, at the beginning of the time period – so that the gross produce and the net produce coincide. This certainly is a logically and conceptually consistent solution to the apparent infelicity of Smith's net revenue concept, but it would be very difficult to textually justify that he actually had this in mind. O'Donnell (1990: 38) takes the same view.

87 The interest component here can be either actual or notional. That is to say, it is applicable whether or not the capital is borrowed: it represents 'pure profits' (under competitive conditions), so to speak, net of profit paid for entrepreneurial functions, such as risk-bearing and organizing the production process. The quantum of this pure profit in any particular activity therefore would be determined by reference to the rate of interest as the opportunity cost of capital (whether or not capital is borrowed), together with the value of capital advanced (see also n. 92 below). Smith never uses the actual term *entrepreneur*, but quite frequently makes reference to 'undertakers' (though only in *WN*).

88 Smith says 'somewhat higher', as he goes on to explain, because he is speaking in proportional terms. For *given* money prices of subsistence goods, introduction of a 20 per cent income tax on wages requires a 25 per cent increase in wages, in order to preserve their purchasing power; a 25 per cent tax requires a 33 per cent wage increase; and so on.

89 He also comments here that this may not apply to wages of employees of the State ('offices'), which are 'not ... regulated by the free competition of the market'. The systematic treatment of wage relativities, under five heads, is at *WN* (116–27). There is some important kinship between the factors explaining entrepreneurial incomes and those explaining wage relativities: 'risk and trouble' on the one hand (*WN*: 847–8); 'disagreeableness ... [and] probability or improbability of success' on the other (*WN*: 116–17). Note also that Smith is quite emphatic that wage relativities are independent of variations in the overall level of real wages, the latter due to the strength of labour demand growth (*WN*: 80, 158–9).

90 The higher commodity prices would then feed back upon money wages, to the extent that those higher-priced commodities include the workers' subsistence goods. This might appear to point to an endless spiral of prices adjusting to wages and vice versa, but a determinate solution for prices and distribution can be derived, so long as one can posit a coherent set of equations linking money wages, profits and normal prices. By way of illustration, take the very simple system of note 62 above, with a uniform tax rate ($t$) imposed upon wages. The two price equations are unchanged and the same numeraire may be chosen (the fourth equation in n. 62). The wage equation becomes:

$$w(1-t) = p_c c \quad 1 > t > 0$$

This will generate a different solution for $r$ (lower), and for $p_c$, $p_s$. For any initial value of $w$, the introduction of a tax on wages, or increases in such a tax, cause determinate and finite increases in $w$, $p_c$ and $p_s$.

This, however, is not how Smith treats the incidence of taxes on wages. There is a peculiar asymmetry in his conception of the incidence of direct taxes on wages versus direct taxes on profits. The different outcomes are reconciled by way of his peculiar (and unsatisfactory) theory of the rate of profit, gross of direct taxation, being determined by 'competition of capitals' (sec. 3.1.2). A tax on wages leads to higher gross wages, in order to preserve the after-tax real wage, and with *r* unchanged, the incidence of the tax is forward-shifted into commodity prices (falling on surplus consumption) and/or backward-shifted onto rents (*WN*: 864–7). (Smith's view with respect to taxes on 'necessary' labour consumption goods is the same as for direct taxes on wages: see *WN*: 871, discussed immediately below.) A tax on profits cannot be forward-shifted via a higher *r* gross of taxation, since gross *r* similarly remains unchanged, and since the component of profit associated with entrepreneurial returns is treated as a necessary cost, the incidence is on pure profits or interest (*WN*: 847–8). Note also that if non-necessary labour consumption goods can be taxed without causing compensating wage increases (discussed directly below), then why could not also some measure of direct taxation of wages lead to no compensating wage increases?

91 Smith twice defines necessaries in the space of a single page: 'not only the commodities which are indispensably necessary for the support of life, but whatever the custom of the country renders it indecent for creditable people, even of the lowest order, to be without'; 'not only those things which nature, but those things which the established rules of decency have rendered necessary to the lowest rank of people' (*WN*: 869–70). He adds after the latter: 'All other things, I call luxuries' (evidently here ignoring capital goods other than those consumed by labourers). Gram (1998), in a thoughtful account of the social character of subsistence and wider consumption in Smith's thought (especially in *TMS*), rightly distinguishes between 'conveniencies' and 'luxuries', connecting the earlier Latin form, *convenientia*, with notions of propriety and decency. Walsh (2000: 14–17; 2003: 363–9) elaborates Gram's theme further, in relation to the notion of socio-economic 'reproduction' in Smith and others.

92 The pure profits will be realized partly as interest payments, to the extent that capital is borrowed. To be consistent, the pure profit component is only the interest payments net of any components for risk-bearing by lenders, the 'pure' interest, one may analogously say. With regard to wages, not all the elements of wage differentials can be regarded as surplus, in particular, to the extent that they reflect the costs of skills acquisition and risk, but also perhaps aspects of the other three factors offered to explain wage differentials. Recall also his more sceptical view of the wages of State employees (n. 89 above). O'Donnell's (1990: 27–52) account of Smith's notion of surplus suffers from two defects: a too rigid identification of wages with subsistence, thereby denying or overlooking the evidence of wages sharing in the surplus; and an unjustifiable dismissal of Smith's distinction between pure and entrepreneurial profits (see also pp. 91, 101, 104–6, 110, 212). Blaug (1987: 439) affirms that 'creation and disposition of surplus output ... – a theory of the reproducibility of economic systems in the making – ... captures much of the drift of [*WN*]'.

93 With regard to Leontief, consider the opening sentence (following a four-page introduction) of his modern, empirical application of the classical approach to production, a contribution of immense importance to the applied analysis of human production and consumption: 'The statistical study presented in the following pages may be best defined as an attempt to construct, on the basis of available statistical materials, a *Tableau Économique* of the United States for 1919 and 1929' (Leontief 1941: 9). Leontief (1936: 105) opens with virtually the same sentence. The book also has a Quesnay epigraph (p. 2).

## 5 Opulence and policy

1 Smith's apparent separation of political economy from jurisprudence here might seem to tell against the conclusion in section 2.1.1, that political economy is a branch of

jurisprudence. But in response to the same apparent separation in the final paragraph of *TMS* the editors note: 'he is evidently distinguishing between general principles of justice and detailed laws and institutions for giving effect to those principles' (*TMS*: 341–2, n. 8). That is to say, Smith is distinguishing 'police, revenue, and arms' from the (fundamental) *theory* of jurisprudence, not from jurisprudence as such (cf. *LJA*: 5–6, 331; *LJB*: 486).

2 Note, however, two qualifications which immediately follow. First, as labour productivity rises, 'it produces ... a much greater quantity of work than in proportion to the superiority of its reward': real wages rise less than proportionally to the rise in output per worker. Second, Smith observes that therefore rich countries generally will not lose markets to poor countries, unless due to the former pursuing inappropriate policy, one effect of which could be to increase 'the price of labour to an unnatural height, far beyond what the opulence of the society could of its own accord have raised it to' (similarly, at *LJA*: 343–4). Opulence is identified with 'plenty' also at *LJA* (6, 340, 356); opulence, plenty and 'abundance' are coupled together and identified with 'cheapness of goods of all sorts' at *LJA* (333; also 343; *LJB*: 487, 491, 503–4); and opulence is identified with high real wages in particular (*LJA*: 350).

3 Recall also that division of labour itself presupposes accumulation of stock; and from the historical standpoint, accumulation as a condition of opulence includes original accumulation (Chapter 4, n. 69). The role of accumulation or saving in relation to opulence is also explicit in *LJA* (393–4); *LJB* (513–14); *edWN* (578).

4 The role of 'peace' is further illustrated in a Smith historical commentary on ancient Rome (*LJA*: 235). At first glance the comment there that opulence follows from development of the arts might seem to contradict the *LRB* (137) statement that opulence is a prerequisite; but the latter concerns *fine* arts. Notice also that the administration of justice need only be 'tolerable', not perfect. This resonates with Smith's non- or anti-utopian attitude, discussed in section 5.3.2. As to security of property rights in general, he elsewhere argues that the historical impetus for the rise of government is the protection of material possessions, rather than the protection of life (*WN*: 709–10, 715; *LJA*: 16, 202–9, 228; *LJB*: 404–7). The point is stated most bluntly at *LJB* (404) – '[t]ill there be property there can be no government, the very end of which is to secure wealth, and to defend the rich from the poor'. (Concerning the legitimacy of this, see *LJA*: 338; *LJB*: 489.) A rather full statement of the significance of secure property rights for economic development occurs at *WN* (910); for example:

> Commerce and manufactures can seldom flourish long in any state which does not enjoy a regular administration of justice, in which people do not feel themselves secure in the possession of their property, in which the faith of contracts is not supported by law ....

5 'Progress' is sometimes, but by no means universally, used by Smith as an intrinsically normative term, to refer to a desirable course of events. Unless the term was being employed in a value-neutral manner, his frequent references to 'the progress of improvement' would be nonsensical (*WN*: 4, 165, 193–4, 234–5, 237–8, 241–2, 244, 246–7, 253, 259–60, 334, 697, 707–8, 786; *EPS*: 187). (Most of these are from the *WN*, Book I, Chapter XI discussion of agricultural development.) The same applies with regard to the phrases 'progress of ... decay' (*EPS*: 128) and 'progress of despotism' (*WN*: 729). In these kinds of contexts the term conveys just a neutral notion of temporal development. Elsewhere, a sense of desirable development is clearly intended (e.g. *WN*: 933; *LRB*: 181; *LJA*: 231; *edWN*: 576; *Corr*: 310). Smith once uses 'progressive state' as a synonym for the growth economy, in a manner evocative of general opulence (*WN*: 99).

6 And in general, beyond the property rights issue, government restrictions upon and regulation of economic life, including undesirable tax systems, are the political culprit in retarding growth and opulence. In *WN*, these matters are systematically discussed

in the short Book III, a mere fifty pages (also 145). As noted earlier (Chapter 4, n. 69), the subject of the slow progress of opulence is absent from the *LJA* manuscript, but almost certainly because it was discussed in that part of the text no longer extant. In some respects, the treatment of the subject in *LJB* (521–38) is richer than that in *WN*.

7 All further references to opulence and variants thereof, incidental to our fundamental purposes here, occur at *WN* (111, 190, 205, 347, 366, 376–7, 379, 381, 406, 711, 810, 813–14, 902); *LJA* (182, 185, 341, 353, 382); *LJB* (419, 443, 452–3, 467, 475); *edWN* (564, 574); *Corr* (241). The most intriguing of these concern the suggestion that slaves are worse treated in opulent than in poor countries (*LJA*: 182, 185; *LJB*: 452–3; cf. *WN*: 587). A good number of the rest do not concern nations or peoples in general, and in particular, refer rather to opulent individuals. Neither the term nor any variants of it are to be found in *TMS*.

8 Notice that Locke also connects the contrast to differential labour productivity:

> There cannot be a clearer demonstration of any thing, than several Nations of the *Americans* are of this, who are rich in Land, and poor in all the Comforts of Life; whom Nature having furnished as liberally as any other people, with the materials of Plenty, *i.e.* a fruitful Soil, apt to produce in abundance, what might serve for food, rayment, and delight; yet for want of improving it by labour, have not one hundredth part of the Conveniencies we enjoy: And a King of a large fruitful Territory there feeds, lodges, and is clad worse than a day Labourer in *England*.
>
> (Locke 1698: 338–9)

Smith owned the 1728 fifth edition of Locke's book (Mizuta 2000: 151). Notice also that Smith's comparisons of the consumption or income of a European prince, a European labourer, and a chief of a 'savage' nation, are entirely consistent with the proportion between a European prince's real income and that of the European peasant exceeding the proportion between an African king's income and that of one of his 'savages'. That is to say, it is entirely consistent with greater inequality of income distribution in commercial society. Consider the articulation of the trickle-down idea at the very beginning of *WN*, in the 'Introduction and Plan of the Work':

> Among civilized and thriving nations … though a great number of people do not labour at all, many of whom consume the produce of ten times, frequently of a hundred times more labour than the greater part of those who work; yet the produce of the whole labour of the society is so great, that all are often abundantly supplied, and a workman, even of the lowest and poorest order, if he is frugal and industrious, may enjoy a greater share of the necessaries and conveniences of life than it is possible for any savage to acquire.
>
> (*WN*: 10)

Hont and Ignatieff (1983a: 42) draw attention to the Lockiean formulation appearing also in Martyn (1701: 72–3). Larrère (2001b: 1073) connects it with Mandeville's (1733) 'contrast between the poor and egalitarian beehive and the corrupt and prosperous one'.

9 The argument at *LJB* (453–4; paralleled at *LJA*: 194–6), concerning the rich man who feeds 1,000 via his luxury consumption but 'eats or wears no more than the rest', also has close kinship with the intent behind trickle-down. The conclusion drawn at *LJA* (195) is notable: 'a people who are all on an equality will necessarily be very poor'. A similar but more famous passage of argument than these appears in *TMS* (184–5; quoted in sec. 5.2.6) – more famous, because involving the one instance of the invisible hand metaphor in that work. There is a subtle difference between the *LJA* (195) contention, and the drift of the parallel *LJA*, *LJB*, *TMS* arguments (cited above) concerning the capacity of the stomachs of the rich being no greater than that of the poor. The former justifies inequality; the latter propose that beneath the appearance of

inequality there is in fact a substantial equality. At *LJA* (196–8) Smith argues that something akin to trickle-down was obstructed in ancient societies, due to the institution of slavery (also slightly mentioned at *LJB*: 453–4).

10 Meek and Skinner (1973: 1108n) comment on the omission from *WN* of the rather stronger adverse views on inequality Smith expresses in the other manuscripts quoted here. With regard to the language of 'class' demarcations, Smith commonly uses the term 'class', to refer to socio-economic divisions and groups (e.g. *WN*: 90–1, 266, 295, 664–76 in relation to Physiocratic analysis; *LJA*: 232–3, 375; *LJB*: 410), as well as 'ranks' and 'orders'. However, in many instances 'class' conveys just the sense of a particular group of people (e.g. a particular category of artisans). In any case, the use of that language does not do violence to his socio-economic conception. The fundamental, *functional* class demarcation in Smith's political economy is tripartite: between proprietors of land, stock or capital; entrepreneurs or 'undertakers'; and labourers or workers (cf. Chapter 4, n. 44). (There is of course a further division for the theory of functional distribution, between land and capital ownership, with land-rents and pure profits determined by different principles. Also, Smith commonly collapses entrepreneurship with capital ownership, silently; but see sec. 4.4.2, further to entrepreneurship, functional distribution, and the concept of pure profits.) He nowhere uses the terms 'worker(s)', with one exception, or 'working class', but frequently uses 'workmen' and 'workman'. The one exception is at *LJA* (369), but the term is there employed to refer to a particular labour skill.

11 Boisguilbert provides an interesting case from earlier French literature. He employs notions of 'general' and 'public opulence' (*opulence générale*, *opulence publique*) as a normative standard for analysis, defined in terms of consumption, though rather vaguely articulated: the opulence of an individual is associated with 'abundant enjoyment of every necessity and pleasurable want'; 'general opulence', 'enjoyment and … consumption of goods', associated with 'a country replete with the necessaries and conveniences of life' (Boisguilbert 1707 [2000]: 2, 7–8; also 1, 38–9, 51–2, 54–6; see I.N.E.D. 1966: 978, 994–5, 1010–11 for the French phrases). But whether this is intended to extend down to the lowest classes does not seem so clear (cf. Faccarello 1999: 66–72). In Turgot's *Réflexions*, labourers' wages are said merely to tend towards the value of 'subsistence', due to competition among labourers; though at one point exceptions to this are allowed (Turgot 1769–70 [1977]: 45–6, 49, 65). The possibility of such exceptions is reinforced in later writings, though some of this is merely about temporary deviations, and in *both* directions (Groenewegen 1977c [1767]: 126–7, 131–2; [1770]: 167–8, 170, 175–9; both written after the *Réflexions*). In any case, there is no advocacy of high or rising consumption for all.

12 Further to this, see section 5.1.1 more generally. *WN* (22), quoted there, speaks of how plenty 'diffuses' through all the social ranks. Consider also the commentary on 'that emulation which runs through all the different ranks of men' at *TMS* (50), explicitly connected with 'bettering our condition' (quoted more fully, n. 28 below); and recall the analytical point concerning hysteresis at Chapter 3, n. 59. In the context of defining 'necessaries' in *WN* (870; see Chapter 4, n. 91), Smith illustrates changing customary necessary consumption: 'The Greeks and Romans lived … very comfortably, though they had no linen. But in the present times … a creditable day-labourer would be ashamed to appear in publick without a linen shirt ….'

13 Actually, a very substantial statement also occurs at *WN* (606), referring to 'the natural system of perfect liberty and justice', in the context of discussing the British monopoly of its colonies' trade. Because of its significance for Smith's views on the relation between theory and policy, discussion of this is left to section 5.3.2.

14 There are some references to a 'system of liberty' in *LJ*, but related more to political constitution than economic system (*LJA*: 264, 269–71; *LJB*: 421–2). Nothing resembling the system-of-liberty phrase appears in *TMS*, *EPS*, *LRB* or *Corr*.

15 This passage of argument leads into the one *WN* instance of the 'invisible hand'

metaphor, which appears three pages later (see *WN*: 454–6). Apart from this instance, and the one instance in *TMS* (184–5; quoted in sec. 5.2.6), Smith also has recourse to 'the invisible hand of Jupiter' in the 'History of Astronomy' (*EPS*: 49). Provocatively, but rather convincingly up to a point, Rothschild (2001: 116–56) has argued that the significance Smith attaches to the invisible hand has been greatly exaggerated. (In the process, she provides a comprehensive account of the history of ideas concerning Smith's original idea.) Two qualifications are in order. At core, the invisible-hand metaphor expresses a notion of unintended system-consequences of individuals' behaviours, where those system-effects are usually socially beneficial, though they need not be so in all cases. While two or three explicit invisible-hand references are not suggestive of an important role for the notion in Smith's self-understanding, the concept of unintended social consequences appears much more frequently, as Fleischacker has argued (Hanley *et al.* 2004: 144–7). (See, for example, the *WN* (417–22) historical argument concerning political power ceded away as a result of economic forces; *WN* (630), concerning the natural distribution of stock as that which is most advantageous to society; *WN* (707–8), on the profound consequences for history and civilization of 'a mere accident', the invention of gunpowder; and *WN* (800–6), on the decline in the temporal power of the clergy, due to economic development.) Second, Smith more than once appeals to 'invisible chains' of causal explanation in the 'History of Astronomy' (esp. *EPS*: 45–6, 48). (The invisible hand of Jupiter is really an instance of this, albeit involving spurious explanation.) One can say that for Smith, political economy, similarly, grasps and reveals that which is invisible to the individual participants in society, qua individuals: the macro-consequences of individual behaviour, including the feedbacks of such systematic forces upon individual behaviours. (Rothschild greatly exaggerates the case against this kind of interpretation.)

The explicit instance of the metaphor in *WN* is indeed of rather slight significance: each individual producer pursues maximum individual output, and so (implicitly, by simple aggregation), society's output is maximized. No one is aiming at maximization of the social product, but the outcome is hardly very hidden. (This is not a criticism of Smith: he is just providing some rhetorical flourish.) Similarly, the proposition that opulence is an unintended consequence of individuals' pursuing division of labour with the aim of increased individual productivity (sec. 4.1.1, esp. n. 4) is not very remarkable. No individual is intending *general* opulence, but it is hardly a deep insight that general opulence *might* result. (The causal connection here is rather more tenuous than mere simple summation, which would only get one to higher social product and higher product per capita, not necessarily to generalized higher consumption per capital: see pp. 207–9.) In fact, the convergence of market prices towards natural price is a more profound case of unintended beneficial system-consequences, though Smith does not in that analysis use such language (but comes close to doing so at *WN*: 630). With regard to feedbacks, individuals' pursuit of material self-betterment generates competition as a system-consequence, and also technical innovation to improve productivity; but competition in turn *drives* innovation (e.g. *WN*: 748; quoted sec. 3.4.1; cf. Kurz 2008: 273–4). (The manner in which competition disciplines individual producer behaviour is also exemplified by *WN*: 163–4, quoted in section 3.1.2, and in Smith's jousting analogy, also discussed there.) Morals and manners are also partly endogenous to commercial society (n. 21 below). But Smith certainly does not regard orderly commercial society as a system spontaneously generated out of human nature (cf. Vaughn 1987; Rothschild 2001: 146–53; Smith 2006: 1–14, 68–84). The *slow* progress of opulence in history alone indicates that (sec. 5.1.1), however natural the human traits which provide the impetus to opulence are supposed to be.

16 With regard to natural balance, see *WN* (499, 504, 523, 604); *LJA* (365–6); *LJB* (498); *edWN* (575, 578). Beyond these, naturalness is also applied to the balance of foreign

trade and to saving (the balance of consumption and production). For natural course see *WN* (116, 239, 247–8, 372, 378, 380, 401, 422, 457, 803); *LJA* (265, 351, 365–6); *LJB* (499). Smith also uses a natural 'channel' metaphor (*WN*: (506, 897–8). 'Natural course' is used in non-economic contexts as well (*TMS*: 168; *EPS*: 44, 50; *LRB*: 66; *Corr*: 383). For natural distribution see *TMS* (167–8); *WN* (3, 11, 13, 499, 504, 630–2, 673). That particular phrase is not primarily used in relation to functional income distribution (rather, for example, distribution of stock); but of course, insofar as natural balance is associated with market prices approximating natural prices, natural income distribution is implied. Smith's notion of history as expressing the working out of nature (in particular, human nature) – though not necessarily with compelling or overwhelming force – also connects with these formulations of a natural norm for economic society (e.g. *WN*: 345, 802; *LRB*: 203; *LJB*: 407). In other words, the norm is also, to some extent at least, the actual tendency of history. These naturalized notions, especially 'natural balance', are somewhat evocative of the 'economy of nature', discussed in section 2.3.4.

17 All further references to liberty or variants thereof (but not including 'liberal' and variants), incidental to our fundamental purposes here, for just *WN*, are at (9, 20, 24, 50, 90, 200, 327, 345, 388, 434, 534, 537, 542, 584, 577–8, 586, 606, 610, 614, 660, 700, 706–7, 735, 747, 787, 794, 796, 799, 803, 826, 912, 936). It should be added that there is a very considerable amount of material in *LJ* concerning individual liberties and the political and legal means to secure them, considered historically. Rothschild (2001: 223) makes a good point in emphasizing a certain seamlessness of freedom for Smith: 'the distinctness of "economic freedom" – the sense in which there is a special, innocuous kind of freedom [limited to commerce] ... – was an innovation of the 1790s'. For Rothschild (2001: 58, 70, 218–19) this gives a sharper edge to the meaning of the post-Smithian development of political economy as a distinct science: its 'depoliticization' so to speak (cf. n. 22 below).

18 We have left aside all references to 'free' (including variants) which are without any socio-political or economic significance, though this involves contestable judgement in some instances. Also left aside are the extensive discussions of freedom, punishment and law in *LJ*, as well as freedom and slavery (which includes some considerations of free government). For use of free trade and variants, just in *WN*, see (145, 398, 400, 433, 435, 449, 462, 464–5, 469, 471–2, 474–5, 492, 497, 502–3, 525–7, 532, 534, 538–9, 576, 580, 595, 598, 606, 608 (trade 'in its natural and free state'), 617, 632, 639, 650, 672, 680, 734, 736, 738, 755, 786 (interesting for making some education a requirement for entering trades), 901, 904, 935, 944; see also *Corr*: 240–4, 271, 381). Though they are not detailed here, both the idea and the language of free trade are to be found also in *LJ* and *edWN*. *WN* (853) and *LJB* (531) comment on certain forms of taxation as inimical to a free country. All further, rather trivial, references to 'free' and variants, of an economic kind in *WN*, are at (62, 98–9, 154, 183, 187, 248, 250, 286, 388–9, 391, 403, 405, 424, 434, 459–61, 467, 469, 494, 519, 522, 535, 537, 542, 552, 557, 571–2, 578, 610, 622, 655–7, 659, 675, 730, 733, 735, 777, 798, 833, 850, 857, 875, 881, 884, 925–6, 937, 950). Two uses of the phrase, free to choose, have been noted in the previous paragraph. In relation to the conduct of 'factions', see also the considerations on the role of the nobility (*LJA*: 157, 288–9; *LJB*: 444).

19 The assertion that these are the aims of 'every' government points to the manner in which Smith's theory and analysis are at one and the same time normative and thoroughly empirical: in one way or another all governments pursue these objectives; how well (and how well, even in terms of their own purposes) can be judged on the basis of a Smithian social science constituted by sound descriptive theory and correct normative standards.

20 Notice the inclusion of the opulence of *other* countries in the aims of police. This points to Smith's repudiation of mercantilism – in particular, his repudiation of the notion of international commerce as a zero-sum game.

21 This introductory statement is expanded upon with regard to police at *LJA* (331–3; and the parallel texts for *LJB* are at: 397–401, 486–7). One notable element there is an argument for how commercial society leads to more independent workers, and by thus reducing dependency, also reduces criminality and the need for 'police' (in a narrower sense, of laws, crime prevention and law enforcement, with respect to personal injury in particular): 'The establishment of commerce and manufactures, which brings about … independencey, is the best police for preventing crimes' (*LJB*: 486–7; also *LJA*: 332–3). This points to the fact that the relationship between morals or manners and commerce for Smith is not *just* one-way – not just that commercial society presupposes a certain standard of moral behaviour. Commerce can feed back upon morals or manners as well, and for the better. (Incidentally, the dependent workers who are here so much led to criminality, are typified by 'menial servants' or 'retainers', the species of labour which dominates Smith's perception of unproductive activities: see sec. 4.3.2.) *LJB* (538–9) provides another instance of commerce shaping manners: self-interest in the framework of commercial society leads to 'probity and punctuality', with a view to building good reputation in contracting and exchange. With regard to external defence, it may be noted that Smith sees a kind of historical near-inevitability to the growth of public debt in commercial societies (though it is not thereby rendered desirable) – in particular, to fund extraordinary expenditures associated with war (*WN*: 907–11).

22 While Smith nowhere refers to 'political science', at least three of Smith's contemporaries categorized his political economy project in terms of political science. William Robertson writes to Smith in 1776, referring to his political economy as one of the 'parts' of 'political science' (*Corr*: 192; more fully quoted in the epigraph to this chapter). A few years later James Dunbar (1780: 297, as quoted in Mizuta 2000: 84) refers to *WN* as 'a work which will, probably, in future times, be referred to in political science as the first just and systematical account that has appeared in any language, of the principles of public [e]conomy, and the phœnomena of commercial states'. The same year, William Eden (1780: 101, as quoted in Mizuta 2000: 85) writes of 'Adam Smith, whom political science may reckon a great benafactor [*sic*; the error is Mizuta's]'. Somewhat later still, Stewart (1811: 310–11) writes:

> in physics, where our progress depends on an immense collection of facts, and on a combination of the accidental lights daily struck out in the innumerable walks of observation and experiment; and in politics, where the materials of our theories are equally scattered, and are collected and arranged with still greater difficulty, the means of communication afforded by the [printing] press have, in the course of two centuries, accelerated the progress of the human mind, far beyond what the most sanguine hopes of our predecessors could have imagined.… It is evident … that the most important branch of political science is that which has for its object to ascertain the philosophical principles of jurisprudence; or (as Mr Smith expresses it) to ascertain 'the general principles which ought to run through and be the foundation of the laws of all nations*.' … To direct the policy of nations with respect to one most important class of its laws, those which form its system of political economy, is the great aim of Mr Smith's *Inquiry*.

In note *, Stewart cites the concluding paragraph of *TMS*. See also the reactions to *WN* of Hugh Blair and Thomas Pownall (*Corr*: 188–9, 337), and the title of Ferguson (1792). Phillipson (1987: 497), following Winch (1983b: 512–13; though he refers only to teaching), asserts that 'Stewart was the first academic to detach the study of political economy from that of the theory of government and to treat each as a distinct branch of political science'; but Smith himself articulates political economy as a distinct 'branch' of a larger political science (*WN*: 428, 678–9; both quoted at the opening of sec. 2.1.1; see also Larrère 2001b: 1071–2 on this issue). Winch (1978; see p. 13) is a very valuable systematic account of Smith's political thought, as distinct from – and in a sense, wider than – his political economy (see also Forbes 1975: 186).

23 With regard to the fundamental demarcations of the modern social sciences, we have here, in particular, left out anthropology, as well as history and historiography. The latter is considered in section 5.3.3, in the context of the relation of historiography to political economy – the second of the two 'intriguing' questions raised in the introductory paragraphs of this chapter. (Historiography was defined there as the study, writing and interpretation or theorizing of history.) Smith's historical writing includes a significant dimension of what would now be described as a kind of anthropology.

Any attempt to determine precise modern definitions of the several social sciences, such as to constitute mutually exclusive domains of inquiry, confirms the considerable arbitrariness of the demarcations. Social anthropology has been defined as '[t]he study of the entire range of cultures and societies in the world, although originally the discipline tended to concentrate on non-Western and so-called primitive societies' (Scott and Marshall 2005: 603); 'the description and explanation of similarities and differences among human ethnic groups ... serves to distinguish it [anthropology] from the other social sciences' (Greenberg 1968: 305). With regard to political science, Easton (1968: 283) observes that two distinct criteria for 'isolating the subject matter of political science' have emerged since the mid-nineteenth century:

> The one has sought to define political life in terms of the institutions through which it is expressed; the other has turned to the activities or behavior of which institutions are the particular historical forms. Under the first set, political science has been described ... as the study either of governmental (or political) institutions or of the state. Under the second set, which did not gain widespread acceptance until well into the twentieth century, it has been characterized as the study either of power of or decision making.

Colman (2006: 617) defines psychology as:

> The study of the nature, functions, and phenomena of behaviour and mental experience. The etymology of the word ... implies that it is simply the study of the mind, but much of modern psychology focuses on behaviour rather than the mind, and some aspects of psychology have little to do with the mind.

Sociology, as 'a special science', is construed as 'the study of social aggregates and groups in their institutional organization, of institutions and their organization, and of the causes and consequences of changes in institutions and social organization' (Reiss 1968: 1).

The latter-day status of jurisprudence as a project straddling philosophy, social science, and the inner logic of systems of legal thought or law, is evident in Cowan's (1968: 332) distinction between philosophical, sociological and analytical jurisprudence (see Martin and Law 2006: 299, for the same tripartite distinction, differently articulated). Laslett and Cummings (2006: 654) conceive of the history of political philosophy as 'the succession of notions about the actual and proper organization of people into collectivities and the discussion of those notions ...; the persistent preoccupation ... has been the definition of justice and of the attitude and arrangements that should create and perpetuate justice'. (See also Reeve 2003b: 419; both point as well to the descriptive dimension of the project.) The modern meaning of 'economics', and its relation to Smith's political economy, is taken up in the Epilogue (see also Chapter 1, n. 9; Chapter 2, n. 19).

24 All other references to 'policy' and 'police', or variants thereof (but not including 'politics' and variants), often referring to specific policies, are at *TMS* (63, 185–6); *WN* (3, 11, 171, 199, 216, 256, 264–5, 514, 547, 549, 573, 575–6, 580, 584, 586, 588–91, 636–7, 657, 670, 672, 727, 820, 832, 843, 891); *LJA* (54, 139, 150, 167, 192, 215, 238, 240, 362, 375); *LJB* (442, 497, 506, 512, 514, 528–30, 544, 550); *edWN*

(567); *Corr* (139, referring to the title of a French book, 243, 384). One further commentary on policy at *WN* (538–43), which concerns 'second-best' policy (our term), is discussed in n. 48 below, in the context of the relation between theory and policy. There is also an important discussion of policy at *TMS* (234), pertinent to the same issue, considered in section 5.3.2 as well. Apart from this and the passing reference to 'civil policy' noted above, the only other significant reference to policy or police in *TMS* is an apparent separation of 'police' from 'justice' at *TMS* (341–2), the very end of that work. This, together with the related statement at *TMS* (3), has been discussed in the introduction to this chapter (especially n. 1). Neither term is anywhere to be found in *EPS* or *LRB*. Brown (1994: 6, 143–60, 168–70) unconvincingly seeks to draw a sharp distinction between Smith's sense of police in *LJ* and in *WN*, where in the latter, it is alleged to have an entirely negative connotation. Related to this, she denies that 'political economy', as defined by Smith, can serve to describe his own project in *WN*.

25 To be clear, the implications of liberty versus discrimination for the scale and allocation of society's capital stock is the substance of his narrowly *economic* argument against discrimination. But the regulation he opposes is not just about commodities and capital allocation. In wider terms than the substantive economics of accumulation and growth, economic liberty, for example, is also about the freedom to seek work where and of a kind one wishes. And of course, liberty has an even larger human and political dimension as well.

26 Infant industry arguments support more or less temporary protection to enable the establishment and development of particular domestic industries, in the face of competition from already well established foreign industries producing the same or similar commodities. In effect, infant industry arguments are about policy influencing the relative costs of domestic versus foreign industry. Just as Smith denies the possibility of policy favourably influencing the private capital stock, so he is, in *WN*, averse to the use of policy to induce internationally competitive industries. Nevertheless, the only two references to competition in *Corr* are interesting in this context. The first indicates that Ireland has kind of infant industry impediments to successfully competing in manufacture with English product in England, even if allowed to; but there is no suggestion there of favouring protection to develop Irish industry (*Corr*: 243; late 1779). On the other hand, the second argues for using a duty on Dutch herring – though this is offered *in place of* import prohibition – as partial protection, and with a view to encouraging British herring production to rise to the quality of the Dutch product (*Corr*: 245; early 1780).

27 See the entire context at *WN* (604–7); and compare the treatment of industrial dislocation from trade liberalization at *WN* (468–72). (The policy gradualism evinced in both these cases is discussed in section 5.3.2.) There, Smith rather forcefully puts the view that dislocated workers and capital will fairly easily transfer to other activities:

> The stock … will still remain in the country to employ an equal number of people in some other way. *The capital of the country remaining the same*, the demand for labour will likewise be the same, or very nearly the same, though it may be exerted in different places and for different occupations.
>
> (*WN*: 470; emphasis added)

But he nevertheless concludes that a sudden and substantial removal of protection can render the capital of an 'undertaker of a great manufacture' redundant:

> That part of his capital which had usually been employed in purchasing materials and in paying his workmen, might, without much difficulty, perhaps, find another employment. But that part of it which was fixed in workhouses, and in the instruments of trade, could scarce be disposed of without considerable loss.
>
> (*WN*: 471)

In relation to the issue of causation between demand and supply (and between investment and saving in particular), raised in section 4.4.1 and discussed again immediately below, this is to assert a kind of supply-side answer, in this particular context. Destruction of capital stock is also allowed for by Smith in relation to failed industrial projects and bad loans (*WN*: 340–1, 357).

28 Smith has a certain Stoic disdain for conventional material desires:

> it is chiefly from ... regard to the sentiments of mankind, that we pursue riches and avoid poverty. For to what purpose is all the toil and bustle of this world? what is the end of avarice and ambition, of the pursuit of wealth, of power, and preheminence? ... From whence ... arises that emulation which runs through all the different ranks of men, and what are the advantages which we propose by that great purpose of human life which we call bettering our condition? To be observed, to be attended to, to be taken notice of .... It is the vanity, not the ease, or the pleasure, which interests us.
>
> (*TMS*: 50; cf. 181–3; see also Chapter 3, n. 25)

> With the greater part of rich people, the chief enjoyment of riches consists in the parade of riches ....
>
> (*WN*: 190)

> These four distinctions of colour, form, variety or rarity, and imitation seem to be the foundation of all the minute and, to more thoughtfull persons, frivolous distinctions and preferenc<e>s in things otherwise equall, which give in the pursuit more distress and uneasieness to mankind than all the others ... [a]nd whose prosecution leads men into customs ... which have no relation to convenience and are often conterary to the ends proposed to be supplied by those things, which make us dress and eat and lodge in a way not always adapted to ease, health and conveniency, and warmth.
>
> (*LJA*: 336–7; also *LJB*: 488)

His advocacy of allowing individual preferences free expression in market society is therefore not to be imputed to any latter-day liberal notion of the sanctity or worthiness of those preferences. Rather, it follows from a conviction that *in general* the preferences of government as to the composition of national expenditure and output will not be superior, even if capable of successful imposition. I say 'in general' because of his willingness to allow exceptions, discussed immediately below. On individual economic choices and State policy, see also n. 55 below.

29 There is also an argument for placing duties on imports to compensate for domestic taxes on the same commodities, domestically produced (*WN*: 465–7); but this is to ensure *non*-discriminatory fiscal treatment of domestic and foreign suppliers. That argument is followed by consideration of the desirability of policy retaliation in response to other countries' discriminatory policies, and the possible undesirability of suddenly re-establishing free international trade (*WN*: 467–72). This and important related texts pertaining to policy pragmatism – qualifying the appropriateness of implementing the system of perfect liberty – are discussed in section 5.3.2.

30 Recall also that the imperative of external defence overrides natural liberty, when the two come into conflict (sec. 5.1.1). For Viner's *WN* citations, we provide references to the Glasgow edition, since he of course cites an earlier edition. Viner also details further instances of Smith's support for discriminatory taxation, intended to alter behaviour (see n. 31 below). His endorsement of laws obliging payment of wages in money, incidentally, occurs in the context of his striking statement, that when legislatures make laws regulating employer/employee relations, it is 'always' the former from whom they take counsel (quoted Chapter 3, n. 21). Smith continues: 'When the regulation, therefore, is in favour of the workmen, it is always just and equitable' (*WN*: 157–8). With respect to Skinner's account, see in particular the details at p. 186.

With regard to some of these not really being exceptions to non-intervention or non-discrimination, Smith's endorsement of a tax on exportation of wool (*WN*: 653–4), for example, is couched in terms of the inescapability of taxation as such, together with broad equity considerations:

> Every different order of citizens is bound to contribute to the support of the sovereign or commonwealth.... It is scarce possible to devise a tax [such as that on wool exportation] which could produce any considerable revenue to the sovereign, and at the same time occasion so little inconveniency to any body.
>
> (*WN*: 654)

The support for bounties on exportation of corn (*WN*: 539–40), also mentioned by Skinner, is an instance of policy pragmatism rather than an in principle exception to perfect liberty (see n. 48 below). Others refer to the legal infrastructure of a free commerce – legal enforcement of property rights and contracts. Likewise with respect to Viner (1928: 146, 150), Smith's tentative willingness to 'regulate the price of the first necessary of life' ('bread') is in the context of 'an exclusive corporation', and explicitly ruled out if there is 'competition'; and his endorsement of compulsory registration of real estate mortgages is merely about facilitating secure contracts (*WN*: 158, 863). Interestingly, in the lectures on jurisprudence Smith argues that in earlier stages of human economic history, before commercial society, monopolies of trades were 'all most necessary', for reasons rather analogous to infant industry arguments (*LJA*: 85–6; *LJB*: 472; cf. n. 26 above).

31 This is the Kames statement verbatim: 'Because many vices that poison a nation, arise from inequality of riches; I propose it as a fourth rule, to remedy that inequality as much as possible, by relieving the poor, and burdening the rich.' He goes on to illustrate this principle, by way of explicitly progressive taxes on windows, deer-parks and pleasure grounds (Home 1774: 476–7). Smith's endorsement of progressive taxation is not noted by Skinner (1996: 183–208). He does however draw attention to *WN* (725), where Smith, in a similar sentiment, endorses a differential transport toll on luxuries (Skinner 1996: 190):

> When the toll upon carriages of luxury, upon coaches, post-chaises, &c. is made somewhat higher in proportion to their weight, than upon carriages of necessary use, such as carts, waggons, &c. the indolence and vanity of the rich is made to contribute in a very easy manner to the relief of the poor, by rendering cheaper the transportation of heavy goods to all the different parts of the country.

The considerable number of instances of Smith endorsing discriminatory taxation, which Viner (1928: 151–3) notes, can be read as belonging to the same genus as progressive taxation – with the latter a particular case of discrimination, with respect to income level. (The instances Viner cites are at *WN*: 831–2, 844, 852–3, 883–4, 891.) Skinner (1996: 184–6) draws attention also to a further element of Smith's view of policy: even implementation of the perfect policy regime, if practicable, would not be a once-and-for-all undertaking: there is a need for ongoing consideration of practices that, though once appropriate, may have become obsolete. This brings a historical dimension to policy analysis as well. Partly related to this, Rosenberg (1960) highlights the importance of institutional design as a *WN* theme (cf. Evensky 2005: 262–4).

32 Campbell and Skinner (1976: 53–4) judge Smith to have overstated the case on this matter. See also his strong support for liberty of labour to shift to foreign countries (*WN*: 659–60). On a separate issue, but one of perhaps more general pertinence, it is interesting that at one point Smith treats misbehaviours resulting from one particular bad policy regime – that governing the activities of the East India Company – as natural and due to the regime, rather than reflecting on the particular persons involved:

> It is the system of government, the situation in which they are placed, that I mean to censure; not the character of those who have acted in it. They acted as their situation naturally directed, and they who have clamoured the loudest against them would, probably, not have acted better themselves.
>
> (*WN*: 641; cf. 752)

33 Hereafter, in the remainder of section 5.2, liberty and freedom are generally treated as synonyms. Matravers (2005: 315) notes, in particular, the distinction between freedom as 'the *ability* of people to act', and liberty in the sense that a political or judicial system 'gives people *permission* to do something'. This accords with Isaiah Berlin's (1958) distinction between two concepts of liberty: 'negative liberty, focusing on the absence of interference by others, and positive liberty, focusing on an agent's capacity to [undertake an action or achieve a state]' (Reeve 2003a: 206). In these terms, Smithian liberty, certainly in the economic dimension, is negative freedom, a consequence of his narrow conception of justice (cf. n. 56 below), though one can see elements of positive liberty in Smith as well (Fleischacker 2004: 234–5, 309, n. 9).

34 One may question, a little, the *OED* definition of liberty of conscience, as to whether in early use it conveys a notion of freedom to *publicly* profess or exercise a religion, or commonly only a liberty of belief. In the latter sense, it could be just a notion of *privacy* (though that is no trivial thing), rather than a right to publicly display a religious conviction or practice, in contradiction to the established church. The *OED* qualifies the definition of press liberty, by reference to legal liability for publication of matter which is libellous, criminal or otherwise causes a wrong to some person.

35 Tierney (1995) makes a case for the constructive role of the medieval Church and medieval Christian thought in the development of ideas of limited government – including notions of consent as the ground of political legitimacy – arising particularly out of the duality of spiritual and temporal power, as well as developments within the Church around questions of papal power. Skinner (1978, vol. 1: 49–65) gives a positive and quite fundamental role to Scholastic thought in the evolution of Renaissance political thought, against earlier views. Bouwsma (1995: 213–17) presents Machiavelli as a kind of culmination of Florentine republicanism, albeit in a decidedly 'realist' form. (See also further important works discussed there, notably, those of J.G.A. Pocock.) Davis (1995) as a whole is a valuable collection of essays on the prehistory of modern ideas of political freedom – the constitution and distribution of political power as well as negative liberty. See also n. 38 below, concerning Smith's views on the development of liberties in medieval towns.

36 On Hobbes and Locke, see Faulkner (2003: 319–22). One element of the modern intellectual history of liberty, certainly evident in Hobbes, is an aspiration to free politics from the intervention of religion, to ensure the integrity of the State against religion-based claims to higher authority; another element, in the opposite direction, is an aspiration to protect religious belief from the intervention of the State (Laslett and Cummings 2006: 661–3). (Both these aspects are alluded to in the Berlin quotation above.) Particularly with the advent of the Reformation, and the associated proliferation of diverse Christian beliefs, the latter element may be understood as the modern rise of religious toleration and individual 'conscience' (cf. Tierney 1995: 96–8; Bouwsma 1995: 230–3). It was also a response to the Wars of Religion. The role of conflict around the status of religious authority and its relation to political power in the development of ideas pertaining to political liberty is well explored in Skinner (1978: vol. 1, 12–22; vol. 2, *passim*) – in the context of the Reformation and counter-reformation, as well as earlier. With regard to protecting the State from the intervention of religion, along with Hobbes, Laslett and Cummings mention Richard Hooker and Jean Bodin.

37 'Personal liberty', as defined by Forbes to characterize the primary objective of Smith's politics, is not a subset of political liberty in the sense of the distribution of

political power (the degree of democracy). This is so, not only because absolute government (e.g. a form of monarchy) may be compatible with personal liberty so understood. A majority-rule system is also compatible with an absence of personal liberty, and not only for minorities: a majority can vote away its own liberties as well. The references to systems of liberty in *LJ*, indicated in n. 14 above, well illustrate the personal liberty notion in Smith: 'security in person ... [and] estate'; 'a perfect security to liberty and property' (*LJA*: 264; *LJB*: 422). But it may be emphasized that this personal liberty is as much 'political', politically constituted, as the distribution of political power. The 'Civilians' in the Forbes quotation refers to the tradition of Roman civil law, which does indeed have strong kinship with Smith's primary conception of political liberty as personal security. But Forbes's imputing to Cropsey an interpretation of Smith as favouring a *democratic* polity goes too far: Cropsey (1957: 65–9) sees Smith's alleged 'republicanism' as decidedly aristocratic. Fleischacker (2004: 161–73), partly differing with Haakonnsen (1981), criticizes Smith for failing to provide a natural or rational basis for precise rules of justice, resulting also in a too imprecise content for liberty. In a similar spirit to Fleischacker, Cremaschi (1989: 92–5, 100–2) locates Smithian justice and liberty (personal liberty in the sense of Forbes) in the natural law tradition, but in a weaker form than the traditional rationalistic natural law, being precariously (i.e. unconvincingly) grounded in natural sentiments.

Distinct from, and somewhat in opposition to, interpretations of Smith's politics in terms of the natural law or natural jurisprudence tradition, there have been attempts to place him in the tradition of civic humanism. Hont and Ignatieff (1983b) is devoted to this issue, with regard to Scottish Enlightenment political economy as a whole – on Smith, see especially Phillipson (1983). Winch's (1983a: 256, 262–9) scepticism concerning the weight that can be attached to this element in Smith is convincing (also Fleischacker 2004: 246–9). This is not to say that there is no such element in Smith: his views on the debilitating impact of division of labour on labourers' intellectual and moral qualities are a trace of something like a civic humanist concern, which is at the same time, an element of concern for 'positive' freedom (sec. 4.1; n. 33 above; *WN*: 781–8). Skinner (1996: 205–6) comments on this, in terms of Renaissance civic humanism as a revival of the classical concept of citizenship (the conditions for individuals' fitness for civic participation), drawing attention also to Thomas Hill Green's distinction between negative and positive freedom, prior to Berlin (cf. Laslett and Cummings 2006: 668–9).

38 More than one commentator has remarked on the oddness of Smith's claim that Hume was 'the only writer' who had drawn a connection from commerce to liberty (*WN*: 412), since it was a theme pursued by a number of the Scottish Enlightenment writers, including Steuart: see the long editorial note at *WN* (412); also Forbes (1975: 193, 200) and Skinner (1996: 255–6). It was noted in Chapter 2 (n. 42) that the economic writings of Locke and North constitute probably the most consistent or 'principled' economic liberalism in the seventeenth-century English literature. Magnusson (1994: 101–3) warns that the fairly common recourse to 'free trade' language in that literature – for example, Malynes (1622), Misselden (1622, 1623) – does not convey the later general sense of the notion, but was specifically in opposition to 'the regulated companies' (e.g. the East India Company). Perrotta (2004: 205–10) also repudiates reading too much economic liberalism into the English and French literature before Smith. Faccarello makes strong claims for Boisguilbert's economic liberalism, and he may have had some influence on the Physiocrats in this regard (Faccarello 1999: 145–7; Groenewegen 2002a: 115–19).

At a deeper level, Mandeville's notion of the social utility of self-regarding behaviour provided an important new defence for negative economic liberty, and evidently informed Smith's thinking (Rosenberg 1987: 298; *WN*: 454n). Teichgraeber (1986) traces the lineage of Smith's economic liberalism in relation to Grotius,

Hutcheson and Hume. Smith himself (*WN*: 397–405) discusses the origins of actual economic and wider freedoms in Europe, arising out of the liberties granted to 'Free-traders' in medieval towns, particularly with respect to taxation. (Cf. the *OED* illustrations of 'free trade' and variants in sec. 5.2.4.) This led to 'a sort of independent republicks' (401; also 403–4, on the Italian city-states); here also those terms 'security and independency' are used (402, 405), which connect closely with liberty and freedom for Smith (sec. 5.2.1). North (1995) provides a latter-day interpretation of the interplay of polity and economy, and 'belief structure' and institutions, in what he regards as the unique and contingent Western history of the course of economic growth and political freedoms – an account that has considerable kinship with Smith's views. The emphasis on the evolution of belief structure is the least Smithian element.

39 See both the *OED* 'police' and 'policy' entries, for discussion of the early uses of the two terms as synonyms. 'Policy' also carried the senses of 'contrivance', 'stratagem', 'politic or expedient behaviour', 'shrewdness, sagacity', together with a range of uses related to 'polish and refinement' (*OED*: 'policy'). 'Policy' shares essentially the same etymology as 'police', except that the senses of the former related to refinement 'appear to be due to association with classical Latin *polītus* – as in the English, 'polite' (see *OED*: 'policy'; also for the Middle French term *policie*). But this latter sense is not unconnected with the other senses of police and policy, insofar as order, organization and civilization are linked. This linkage is evident in uses of police and policy, as well as in early uses of 'polity', which was also used as a synonym for police or policy (*OED*: 'polity'). Emsley (1983: 2) comments: 'within the tradition of Roman law the word "police" gradually acquired the meaning of internal administration, welfare, protection and surveillance'.

40 The concept of police (*polizei*) also played a considerable role in German social thought. Tribe (1984) considers its significance in relation to cameralism and the reception of *WN* in Germany (cf. sec. 2.1.6). See also Tribe (1980) and his associated translation of an article by Franz-Ludwig Knemeyer (1980; the original German article is in Brunner *et al.* 1978: 875–97). Knemeyer provides a very detailed account of the range of German meanings of the term and their evolution from the fifteenth to the nineteenth century. They are not so different from the French meanings, however different the institutions and practices. *Polizei* in these accounts appears as centred upon internal public order. Stauffer (1960: 240) discusses Linnaeus's use, in the context of his economy-of-nature notion, also of 'police of nature', to characterize mechanisms of species population balance. Hence, writing of insects, Linnaeus comments: 'each of them has its proper business assigned to it in the oeconomy and police of nature'. Stauffer notes, in relation to Linnaeus's *Politia Naturae* (1760), that '[p]olitia can be translated either as polity or as police, and this ambiguity also appears in the contents of this essay'. See also Rausing (2003: 179, 186).

41 With regard to police and arbitrary power, by way of contrast with English and British constitutional theory from Locke forwards, Rogers (1899: 124) observes of French and German thought concerning police: 'these continental writers were absolutists … they treated constitutional details as administrative … [they] blended legislative and executive duties [until Montesquieu in France and until the nineteenth century in Germany and Prussia]'. This is somewhat evident in the *OED* definitions of French uses of *police*, given above, where legislation and administration are hardly separated. (Sharpe 1994: 578 comments: the 'paramilitary overtones [of the "Parisian model"], together with the supposed French dependence on undercover agents and informers, rendered it unacceptable to English observers'.) Rogers (1899: 124) defines police, up to the eighteenth century, in the most general terms, as 'the internal regulations by a government; or in a secondary sense, the instruments by which or the purposes for which such regulations were enforced' – and traces the subsequent progressive narrowing in its meaning, with particular reference to England and France

(Rogers 1899: 124–8). He also sketches the history of English police practice from the thirteenth century, which eventually included, by the eighteenth century, highway maintenance, slaughter of diseased animals, fire prevention, imposition of rates, wage-fixing, administration of apprenticeships, price-fixing with respect to bread, and inspection of bakers' weights and measures (Rogers 1899: 125–6). Andrew (1989: 6–7, 98, 108, 168, 188, 197–202) examines eighteenth-century English notions of police in relation to private charity. The sense of 'refinement' is included in this policing (cf. n. 39 above), as rather literally, 'polishing' society (Andrew 1989: 6).

42 Raphael and Macfie (1976b: 14–15); and see the editorial commentary at *TMS* (397). Raphael and Macfie (1976b: 14) misprint Pouilly's title as '*Sentiments*' – as does Ross (1995: 159–60), who suggests how Hume may have drawn the book to Smith's attention. In a 1756 letter published in the *Edinburgh Review* Smith refers to Pouilly's Book as 'the Theory of agreeable sentiments' (*EPS*: 250).

43 Cf. *TMS* (342, ed. n. 9). There is a further parallel text to the *TMS* (341) statement in a short manuscript fragment – probably of a Smith lecture, and probably written before 1759 (see *TMS*: 395–6) – published in an appendix of the Glasgow Edition *TMS*:

> the Magistrates in all Governments that have acquired considerable Authority employs the power of the commonwealth to enforce the practice of Justice .... The magistrate promises to hear all complaints of injustice, to enquire diligently into the circumstances alledged upon both Sides, and to give that redress which to any impartial person shall appear to be just and equitable. Hence the origin of ... [t]he Rules by which the magistrate[s] in [all] <each> countries *actually* regu[l]lates all his discisions of this kind .... The Rules by which it is most suitable to the *natural* principles of Justice, or to the *Analogy* of those Sentiments upon which our Sense of it is founded that such descisions [*sic*] *should be* regulated, const[-?]<i>tute what is called Natural Jurisprudence, or the Theory of the general principles of Law. they make a very important part of the Theory of moral Sentiments.
>
> (*TMS*: 389; emphasis added)

Notice that here Smith writes of natural jurisprudence as a part of moral philosophy. (The square and angle brackets in the quotation represent revisions in the original manuscript: see *TMS*: 388.) The context of this statement is the manner in which criminal and civil law can and should embody natural judgements of justice, which the 'impartial' spectator of Smith's moral philosophy would make, with regard to punishment and other redress for injury (hence the reference to 'analogy'). The sense is of natural jurisprudence as derivative from the ethical theory, rather than being literally a branch of the latter – though one should not be overly preoccupied with merely semantic distinctions as to whether jurisprudence is a subset of moral philosophy broadly conceived, or intersects with it, or is merely dependent upon it. The jurisprudence is certainly logically dependent upon the ethics (see also pp. 219–22). Furthermore, the point of the reference to jurisprudence in the *TMS* advertisement, and of the associated reference in the concluding paragraph of *TMS*, was that the theory of jurisprudence was a *further* intellectual project, which Smith had yet to complete or place into print. The same (and other) unfinished business is mentioned in a 1785 letter, in terms of 'a sort of theory and History of Law and Government' (*Corr*: 287).

44 There is also one further reference to theory in *EPS*, in the essay on 'the Imitative Arts', where '[t]he theory of tune' is characterized as the great bulk of the subject matter of 'theoretical treatises' on music, and described as 'an extensive and an abstruse science' (*EPS*: 212). *Corr* (269) refers to the theory of music as well. Further references to 'theory' which are merely references to *TMS* by title occur at *TMS* (3); *LJA* (100); *LJB* (401); *Corr* (122, 255, 281, 286, 293, 310, 319). The one reference to theory in *LRB* (175) is discussed in section 5.3.2. The only other instances are a use

of 'Theory of Moral Sentiments', in the generic sense, in a *TMS* section subtitle (*TMS*: 8, 265), and a reference to Berkeley's *New Theory of Vision* (*EPS*: 148).

45 Smith's commendation of Machiavelli is noteworthy in this context:

> The different courts of Italy at that time piqued themselves greatly on a refined and subtle politicks; nothing could then be a greater reproach to a man of genius than that he was of an open and undesigning character. But these politicks he [Machiavelli] seems to have altogether despised and has therefore given little attention to them or represented them as of no great moment. He is to be commended above most modern writers on one account, as he does not seem to favour any one party more than another and therefore is generally very candid ....
>
> (*LRB*: 114–15)

At *WN* (945) Smith speaks of 'the great scramble of faction and ambition' at the centre of politics. See also *WN* (468, 471) on politicians, both quoted below.

46 The *TMS* (231–4) text is from Part VI of *TMS* (212–64), which first appeared only in the sixth edition of 1790, the last edition prior to Smith's death. Significance could be imputed to this: to the extent that it is interpreted as mere conservatism, its emergence only at the end of his life could allow the conclusion that it is an expression of the conservatism of old age. Raphael and Macfie (1976b: 18–19) discuss and dispute this kind of view, as put by Walther Eckstein in the introduction to his 1926 German edition of *TMS*. Further against this, the political moderation it expresses is amply supported by other Smith texts (see below). Ross (1995: 391–4) conjectures that the American and French revolutions may both have provided degrees of stimulus for that passage of argument (as well as the 1688 English Revolution), but not in a purely negative sense, in terms of encouraging an increased conservatism in Smith. Stewart (1811: 317–19) also comments a little on Smith's views as to the relation between theory and practice (cf. Winch 1978: 24–7, 170–2). Rothschild (2001: 52–71; a somewhat expanded version of Rothschild 1992) provides a wider rebuttal of the conservative representation of Smith's thought (Stewart is a key culprit). One may add that Smith's political moderateness goes hand in hand with a certain 'detachment' from political partisanship or advocacy, to which Winch (1978: 25–7, 71, 182–3) draws attention; both connect also with a degree of ambivalence, pessimism or realism, concerning commercial society. On the notion of 'spirit of system' in French Enlightenment thought, see Riskin (2003).

47 The same conviction, and also with a medical metaphor, is expressed in Book II, Chapter III, in the context of the role of parsimony and prodigality in relation to capital accumulation. Following an account of how excessive State unproductive activity may cause even the aggregate capital stock to contract (quoted Chapter 4, n. 49), Smith adds:

> [private] frugality and good conduct, however, is upon most occasions ... sufficient to compensate, not only the private prodigality and misconduct of individuals, but the publick extravagance of government. The uniform, constant, and uninterrupted effort of every man to better his condition, the principle from which publick and national, as well as private opulence is originally derived, is frequently powerful enough to maintain the natural progress of things toward improvement, in spite both of the extravagance of government, and of the greatest errors of administration. Like the unknown principle of animal life, it frequently restores health and vigour to the constitution, in spite, not only of the disease, but of the absurd prescriptions of the doctor.
>
> (*WN*: 342–3; also 345, 540)

A rather similar sentiment and biological analogy is expressed also in Smith's critique of foreign trade restrictions, though in this instance, politico-economic bodies appear somewhat less robust (*WN*: 466–7). Elsewhere he comments, with similar mild optimism, on two minor Danish colonies under the control of a private trade monopoly (*WN*: 570). See also the discussion of 'the science of man', nature and history in section 2.3.3. Griswold (1999: 301–10) provides an interpretation of Smith's politics as 'a sort of anti-utopian utopianism' (p. 308). Though articulated somewhat differently, Winch (1983b), following Haakonssen (1981: 79–82, 89–93, 152), takes a very similar view to ours, concerning the relation between theory and practice in Smith, concluding: 'The systematic understanding ... at which the philosopher aimed was different from the knowledge required by the man of action' (p. 510). Haakonssen's (1981: 79) distinction, paralleling ours between theory and practice, is in terms of 'system' versus 'contextual' knowledge. The two articulations are brought closer together by conceiving of the issue in terms of a distinction between theoretical knowledge and practical *judgement*.

48 Three chapters further on, Smith is expounding the benefits of 'the liberal system of free exportation and free importation' as the best means of preventing dearth and famine, but nevertheless concedes particular cases in which this would not be so: 'The very bad policy of one country may ... render it in some measure dangerous and imprudent to establish what would otherwise be the best policy in another.' Prejudice is the culprit here too:

> The laws concerning corn may every where be compared to the laws concerning religion. The people feel themselves so much interested in what relates either to their subsistence in this life, or to their happiness in a life to come, that government must yield to their prejudices, and, in order to preserve the publick tranquillity, establish that system which they approve of. It is upon this account, perhaps, that we so seldom find a reasonable system established with regard to either of those two capital objects.
>
> (*WN*: 538–9)

To be sure, at *WN* (471) Smith makes 'private interests' the greater culprit; but for the theory/practice issue, 'prejudices' point to historically specific aspects of practice. The pursuit of material interests is a natural and more or less universal phenomenon confronting legislators.

With regard to the law pertaining to corn exportation in general, Smith concludes the chapter:

> With all its imperfections ... we may perhaps say of it what was said of the laws of Solon, that, though not the best in itself, it is the best which the interests, prejudices, and temper of the times would admit of. It may perhaps in due time prepare the way for a better.
>
> (*WN*: 543)

Ross (1995: 355) indicates that this last statement was added in the second edition of *WN*, to soften Smith's first edition criticism of a policy instituted by his friend, Edmund Burke, who himself had responded to Smith's criticism by appealing to practice versus theory! (Frequent references to Smith's 'theory', sometimes with a certain disdain *vis-à-vis* 'practice', occur in Pownall 1776: 339–41, 345, 347–8, 364, 369, 373.) Hont and Ignatieff (1983a: 13–26) show how the question of the treatment of 'grain' – as the staple of subsistence consumption – was central to eighteenth-century debates around liberty versus police regulation of trade (including the contributions of the Physiocrats in France), with Smith very much at the liberty end of the spectrum. (Steuart is the most notable advocate of regulation with respect to subsistence in the English literature.) The example of Solon, incidentally, also occurs at *TMS*: 233. 'Oceana' and 'Utopia' are references to Harrington (1656) and More (1516; the first English translation is More 1551). For a 'case study' of theory versus practice in Smith's own life, not altogether favourable to him, see Campbell and Ross (1982).

49 Earlier, Skinner (1996: 179) strikes a rather different tone: 'the [nineteenth-century]

classical orthodoxy made it possible to think of economics as quite separate from ethics and history, thus obscuring Smith's true purpose'.

50 Most notably, *WN* (689–95, 709–23); *LJA* (14–16, 200–44;) *LJB* (404–17, 459–60). (At *LJB*: 494, the analysis of 'the slow progress of opulence' is placed under the subject of the 'history of commerce'.) For background in relation to the widespread use of this kind of approach in the eighteenth century, see *WN* (689, ed. n. 2). Campbell and Skinner (1976: 50–60) provide a subsection on 'Smith's use of History' in *WN*, which also considers the relation between his use of actual history and conjectural history. There are also valuable and systematic reflections on Smith and historiography in Skinner (1996: 13–15, 18, 20–21, 26, 72–3, 76–105), and the chapter at pp. 76–105 ('Historical Theory') provides a guide to key secondary literature. See further, Winch (1978: 56–69, 76–80; 1983a: 257–64), Raphael (1985: 85–95) and Griswold (1999: 349–54) – the latter, providing a thoughtful reflection on nature versus history and convention in Smith's thought in general. The conjectural method is applied not only to economic development. A 1761 essay on '*Considerations Concerning the First Formation of Languages*...' employs that method, as well as actual history – and his 1751 dissertation (no longer extant) for his Glasgow professorship was evidently on a related theme (see Bryce 1983: 23–7; Schreyer 1989: 159–72; also Smith 1755, his first publication; cf. *Corr*: 87–8). The method is evident also in *EPS* (Raphael and Skinner 1980: 1–7, 11–12), as well as *LRB*.

51 The advertisement with which the sixth edition of *TMS* was prefaced, discussed in section 5.3.2, carries a similar admission of unlikely completion, with regard to a part of this ambition. Notice how the theory and history of jurisprudence are explicitly distinguished in the quotation from *Corr* (286–7; cf. *TMS*: 340–2; *LJA*: 5–6) – as also in the case of philosophy elsewhere (*EPS*: 46; quoted sec. 5.3.1). Smith also uses 'philosophical history' at *EPS* (46). He thus only uses it twice; but it perhaps may be regarded as his term for that which Stewart named theoretical history (cf. Ross 1995: xix–xx, 89–90). Incidentally, in relation to Smith's reference to Hume as the most illustrious historian of the age, noted in the previous paragraph above, the *WN* editors misstate the source of Smith's quotation of Hume there (*WN*: 790–1): it's from Hume (1778, vol. 4: 30–1), not volume 3. Mizuta (2000: 127) repeats the error. The quoted text is in pre-1776 editions of the *History* as well.

52 The appearance of greater determinacy in modern economics, wherein 'theory' exhibits so much more expansive reach, is commonly an illusion. The modern mass academic enterprise in a marginalist framework produces a huge multiplication of *models*, not an expansion of the domain of determinate *theory*. A pretence of determinacy is achieved by constructing models on special and to that extent ultimately ad hoc assumptions, so that the contingency and indeterminacy shifts to the problem of which among a multiplicity of special models is the appropriate one.

53 His descriptive, theoretical objective for political economy – explaining distribution and growth – seems entirely sound. It is certainly more attractive than the latter-day ambition (or pretence), which originates from Wicksteed and Robbins, for economics to be a generic science of human choices as such (cf. p. 26, esp. n. 19). I have elsewhere suggested a modern definition of economic science along classical lines: 'economics is the study of how societies organize the production and distribution of the means of human sustenance and larger consumption' (Aspromourgos 2002). In its original classical manifestation and form, economics is, and it should still be, a science of the material reproduction of human societies.

54 See also the further comment of Keynes (1936: 374): 'there ... is justification for significant inequalities of incomes and wealth, but not for such large disparities as exist to-day.... [I]t is not necessary ... that the game should be played for such high stakes as at present.' One may ask, for example, is a one percentage point differential income or wealth tax on the rich, relative to the poor, legitimate or is it theft; what of a twenty-five percentage point differential tax; a seventy-five percentage point differ-

ential; what of such rates of taxation applied to inheritances rather than income or wealth? Nowhere in Smith is there to be found a basis for drawing a line between legitimate taxation (recall again, the support for progressive taxation) and illegitimate expropriation of individuals' material possessions. (It is possible to make a virtue of Smith's lack of any substantial and definite principles or rules of just material distribution: Lindgren 1973: 78–83, 131–2; Griswold 1999: 249–56.) That it is for him an issue of prudence and moderation in practice, rather than a matter of principle, is suggested by the following:

> It is in Britain alone that any consent of the people [to taxation] is required, and God knows it is but a very figurative metaphoricall consent which is given here.... No doubt the raising of a very exorbitant tax ... the half or even the fifth of the wealth of the nation, would, as well as any other gross abuse of power, justify resistance in the people. But where this power is exerted with moderation, tho perhaps it is not done with the greatest propriety as it is in no country whatever, and tho not even a figurative consent is requir'd, yet they never think they ought to resist tho they may claim the liberty of remonstrating against it. – Government was established to defend the property of the subjects, but if it come to be of a contrary tendency, yet they must agree to give up a little of their right. You must agree to repose a certain trust in them [i.e., governments], tho if they absolutely break thro it, resistance is to be made *if the consequences of it be not worse than the thing itself.*
>
> (*LJA*: 323–4; emphasis added; also *LJB*: 435; cf. n. 4 above)

Notice the example of intolerable tax rates: even 20 per cent, of 'wealth' (probably income is intended). In any case, whatever the justice of inheritance (or income) taxation from Smith's standpoint, there are no obvious economic ill consequences of, for example, inheritance taxation with the resulting revenues applied to transfer payments in aid of widows and orphans. The impact upon accumulation is a priori most uncertain; and such taxation causes no obstructions to market prices tending towards natural prices. The notion that smaller government or minimizing the public sector contributes to higher growth, and perhaps general opulence, for Smith proceeds from the characterization of public sector activities as unproductive in the Smithian sense (e.g. *WN*: 342). But this need not be so – e.g. public health and education services as elements of conventional subsistence or human capital accumulation. As a matter of fact, Smith does not completely exclude this possibility (see pp. 167–8, esp. n. 51). Furthermore, taxation may be realized in transfer payments (e.g. welfare) rather than government expenditures. Recall also, in relation to taxation of profit income, Smith's view that high profit rates discourage saving (Chapter 4, n. 62), which also tells against any adverse impact of taxation upon accumulation – even if one accepts the flawed idea of saving determining accumulation.

55 Few now really doubt that individual preferences with respect to consumption, backed by ability and willingness to pay, generally should be allowed free expression in the market. Taxes and subsidies, income support, social security, welfare policies, and other more direct regulation to change the terms upon which individual choices are made – e.g. with a view to externalities, guaranteed minimum consumption over the life cycle, public health and workplace safety – are very little aimed at overriding individual consumer preferences or choices. (Policy interventions to address externalities – e.g. greenhouse gas emissions – are not an overriding of consumer choices, but rather, an attempt to confront producer and consumer choices with their genuine opportunity costs.) To be sure, there is argument around these issues, including where they concern individual consumer choice (e.g. over regulation of non-medical use of drugs). It is publicly accepted that production is for consumers not producers. (Public policy designed to influence consumer *preferences*, rather than mere choices – via education campaigns or public advertising – is probably also of marginal significance;

but in any case, it is persuasion, not coercion. Education, as such, of course is partly about transforming people, and hence their preferences, at the deepest levels.)

The greatest point of contention (and systematic Left–Right argument) is about the free expression of *producer* choices, not consumer choices – the terms upon which production occurs with a view to consumer demand. There is at least one fundamental reason for this, evident in Smith's political economy: the pursuit of profits under conditions of systematically unequal bargaining power between individual workers and individual employers makes the terms upon which the labour contract is settled in general of a different significance to the terms of all other contracts. And the special character of that which is being traded in the labour contract means that both the wage and the other conditions under which work is performed arguably warrant unique forms of regulation, asymmetric with commodities in the usual sense of the term. It also should not be overlooked that 'consumers' and 'producers' are not mutually exclusive groups.

56 The lengthy accounts of property rights in *LJ* are not in any respect about the legitimacy, in developed commercial society, of the distribution of rights to material possessions as such; rather, they take as given an *initial* distribution of property, and inquire as to legitimate modes of *transfer* of that property (most notably, *LJA*: 13–92; *LJB*: 459–75). (Smith's position may be compared with Hume on the arbitrariness of property rights: Hume 1739–40: 501–16; Miller 1985: 482; cf. 498.) Hont and Ignatieff (1983a; esp. 24–6, 42–3) show how Smith seeks to reconcile commercial society (and the associated inequality) with justice, but with the latter understood in a very limited sense with respect to material distribution: meeting the 'needs' of the labouring classes. (The implications for any such notion of distributive justice, of those needs being creatures of history, as Smith freely acknowledges, are not considered by them.) Young (2005: esp. 98n, 116–17) seeks to demonstrate that Smith's economics incorporates a concern for 'distributive equity', this being left undefined, but evidently intended also in a very slight sense. The narrowness of Smith's notion of justice is very evident in *TMS*: 'justice is, upon most occasions, but a negative virtue, and only hinders us from hurting our neighbour' (*TMS*: 82; also 86, 175–6, 327, 329–30, 340–2; 166–8, 269–70 touch upon distributive justice). Justice in a very real sense is '*laissez-faire*': people are literally to leave each other alone (cf. Castelot 1896; Riskin 2003: 54). Vivenza (2001: 198–202) provides a compelling argument for the absence in Smith's thought of any binding notion of justice – as opposed to voluntary benevolence or charity – in relation to material distribution. See also in this regard the repudiation of Hont and Ignatieff (1983a) by Raphael (2001: 114), and as well, Salter (1997: 681–3; 2000). As to unemployment, while Smith supposes a very long-run mechanism or tendency for population change and the associated growth of labour supply to be endogenous to capital accumulation and the associated growth of employment, unemployment of considerable persistence is acknowledged in the mechanism of natural wage determination (see Chapter 4, n. 85).

57 Viner's (1928: 142) interpretation of Smith's general attitude to the scope of policy, in the context of his pragmatism with respect to natural liberty versus intervention, is akin to this (cf. Coase 1976: 545; Rosenberg 1979: 25–9):

> Even when Smith was prepared to admit that the system of natural liberty would not serve the public welfare with optimum effectiveness, he did not feel driven necessarily to the conclusion that government intervention was preferable to laissez faire. The evils of unrestrained selfishness might be better than the evils of incompetent and corrupt government.

But in a delicate balance, Viner (1928: 154) also rightly concludes:

> [Smith] saw a wide and elastic range of activity for government, and he was prepared to extend it even farther if government, by improving its standards of com-

> petence, honesty, and public spirit, showed itself entitled to wider responsibilities. … [I]t was the interests of the general masses that he wished above all to promote, in an age when even philosophers rarely condescended to deal sympathetically with their needs. He had little trust in the competence or good faith of government. He knew who controlled it, and whose purposes they tried to serve ….

Smith's general attitude is due to government failure (possibly remediable), as well as market success.

58 Winch (1978; esp. 1–27, 70, 86, 141–2, 165) presents his study of Smith in opposition to interpretations which treat him as a foil for evaluating the theory of economic liberalism or of liberal capitalism, whether from the Right or the Left. Winch's essay in this respect is a useful antidote to anachronistic interpretations in the secondary literature (also evident, as we have shown in Chapter 3 especially, in relation to narrower aspects of Smith's economic analysis). The point should not be pushed too far however: the fundamental socio-economic structure which Smith theorizes in relation to commercial society or the system of liberty is far from being discontinuous or incommensurable with subsequent liberal capitalism to the present day. There is greater discontinuity with respect to political constitutions.

## Epilogue

1 Reflecting on the history and prospects of game theory, Rubinstein (2004: 634–5) notes 'the fundamental difficulty of predicting behavior in the social sciences, where prediction itself is part of the game and forecasters are themselves players'; and further: 'When we teach game theory we may be affecting the way people think and behave in economic and strategic interactions. Is it impossible that the study of game theoretical considerations in economics makes people more manipulative or more selfish?'

2 It is instructive even though the authors' use of the phrase 'academic Left' to describe their target is ill-conceived. They themselves admit to discomfort with that phrase:

> When we use the phrase *academic left* we do *not* refer merely to academics with left-wing political views. There are plenty of such people with whom we have no quarrel. There are countless academics who do excellent and penetrating work … from a left-wing viewpoint. There are countless left-wing scientists – although we are stodgy enough to insist that there is no such thing as left-wing science.
>
> (Gross and Levitt 1998: 9; also 2–3, 27–37, 252; see also Wolin 2004)

3 The argument of the foregoing paragraphs is more fully laid out in Aspromourgos (2009). Contemplating the thesis of C.P. Snow's *Two Cultures* (1959), James (2007: 117) comments:

> Science lives in a perpetual present, and must always discard its own past as it advances.… The humanities do not advance in that sense: they accumulate, and the past is always retained. The two forms of knowledge thus have fundamentally different kinds of history. A scientist can revisit scientific history at his choice. A humanist has no choice: he must revisit the history of the humanities all the time, because it is always alive, and can't be superseded.

From this standpoint, our view here is that social science simultaneously shares in the character of the humanities and the character of the natural sciences. This is the sense in which the epigraph to this Epilogue is offered, and emphatically not as a repudiation of the use of mathematics in economic analysis. The qualitative differences between the social and natural sciences are not about the applicability of mathematical methods. The relation between natural science and economic science, in turn derivative from notions of the relation between nature and society, is the central theme, considered historically, in the essays collected in Mirowski (1994). See Turner and Roth (2003) for an overview of themes in the philosophy of social science literature over the last century, and further to the status of social science *vis-à-vis* natural science, Mazlish (2007: 9, 22–4, 215–28, 232).

The discussion in each of the following four sections here broadly parallels the issues of Chapters 2 to 5, respectively.

4 Hence this intellectual development has not primarily involved economics being synthesized with other social sciences, or learning anything from them; it has primarily been about the other social sciences becoming like economics. It may be added that even to the extent that game theory can allow for endogenous preferences, in the sense of the interpersonal formation of norms of conduct, this does not allow the conclusion that marginalist theory can cope with non-autonomous preferences in explaining the core subject matter of the discipline: prices, distribution and activity levels (cf. Kirman 2006: 268–74). Stocking (1975: 86–7) offers some interesting observations on how Scottish moral philosophy – as the most self-conscious among the intellectual elements contributory to pioneering the modern construction of a comprehensive social science – was transformed in the course of the nineteenth century into the several social sciences. Winch (1978: 6, 184–7) is partly motivated by a similar interest, which finds a more considerable realization in his later interpretation of the emergence of political economy as a distinct science (Winch 1996).

5 It is of course ultimately not sensible to ask what Smith would think of modern economics. One may recall in this context the cautionary message in Roy Harrod's (1974: 8–9) comment: 'It would be most inappropriate for me to stand up here and tell you what Keynes would have thought. Goodness knows he would have thought of something much cleverer than I can think of.'

6 Of course, as against given production methods, in Smith's economics technical progress and labour productivity growth are systematic phenomena. Under such conditions it will be the growth of real wages and change in profitability which are functionally bound together. The functional relation between rates of real wages and rates of profit with given production methods is illustrated in section 4.3 (esp. n. 66). For a thorough treatment of the subject as such, see Kurz and Salvadori (1995). This work also provides a formal diagnosis of the impossibility, in general, of deriving well-defined, conventionally shaped demand functions for factors of production in the presence of heterogeneous capital goods, even under conditions of multiple production methods (Kurz and Salvadori 1995: 427–67).

7 See his treatment of taxation of labour subsistence consumption, with profit rates taken as given, where the incidence of tax is upon rents and other consumption, discussed in section 4.4.2.

8 This conclusion should not be read as *necessarily* repudiating all use of an assumption of substitutability in consumption. For the purpose of analysing specific and particular issues, or for ad hoc models, such an assumption may or may not be useful. That is a matter for judgement in each specific and particular instance. It is for the purposes of the general theory of economic organization that the supposition of autonomous preferences (a much stronger supposition than mere substitutability) should be repudiated.

9 Whether or not any of these are better privately produced – and if so, whether or not with government funding support – goes to questions of technical efficiency and income distribution. Insofar as it is a mechanism of redistribution, the public sector is a very important site upon which conflicts over distribution of the surplus are worked out. Smith himself points out the role of education in the formation of labour skills, with those skills explicitly regarded as an element of 'capital' (Chapter 4, n. 51).

# References

(Names of publishers are not provided for works printed before 1800.)


Almenar, S. and Llombart, V. (2001) 'Spanish Societies, Academies and Economic Debating Societies', in M.M. Augello and M.E.L. Guidi (eds) *The Spread of Political Economy and the Professionalisation of Economists: Economic Societies in Europe, America and Japan in the Nineteenth Century*, London: Routledge.

Andrew, D.T. (1989) *Philanthropy and Police: London Charity in the Eighteenth Century*, Princeton, NJ: Princeton University Press.

[Anonymous] (1821) *Observations on Certain Verbal Disputes in Political Economy, Particularly Relating to Value, and to Demand and Supply*, London: Hunter.

Apostle, H.G. (ed.) (1975) *Aristotle. The Nicomachean Ethics: Translated with Commentaries and Glossary*, Dordrecht: Reidel.

Appleby, J.O. (1978) *Economic Thought and Ideology in Seventeenth-Century England*, Princeton, NJ: Princeton University Press.

Aspromourgos, T. (1996) *On the Origins of Classical Economics: Distribution and Value from William Petty to Adam Smith*, London: Routledge.

—— (1997) 'Cantillon on Real Wages and Employment: a Rational Reconstruction of the Significance of Land Utilization', *European Journal of the History of Economic Thought*, 4: 417–43.

—— (2000) 'New Light on the Economics of William Petty (1623–1687): some Findings from Previously Undisclosed Manuscripts', *Contributions to Political Economy*, 19: 53–70.

—— (2001) 'The Mind of the Oeconomist: an Overview of the "Petty Papers" Archive', *History of Economic Ideas*, 9 (no. 1): 39–101.

—— (2002) 'Defining "Economics" Inclusively', *Post-Autistic Economics Review*, no. 17.

—— (2004) 'Sraffian Research Programmes and Unorthodox Economics', *Review of Political Economy*, 16: 179–206.

—— (2005) 'The Invention of the Concept of Social Surplus: Petty in the Hartlib Circle', *European Journal of the History of Economic Thought*, 12: 1–24.

—— (2007) 'Adam Smith's Treatment of Market Prices and Their Relation to "Supply" and "Demand"', *History of Economic Ideas*, 15 (no. 3): 27–57.

—— (2009) 'Economic Science and the Left: Thoughts on Sraffa's Equations and the Efficacy of Organized Labor', in F.S. Lee and J. Bekken (eds) *Radical Economics and Labor: Essays Inspired by the IWW Centennial*, London and New York, NY: Routledge.

Bacon, F. (1605) *The Tvvoo Bookes of Francis Bacon. Of the Proficience and Aduance-*

*ment of Learning, Diuine and Humane*, London; repr. in T. Case (ed.) (1906) *The Advancement of Learning and New Atlantis*, London: Oxford University Press (reset 1951).

Baier, A.C. (1991) *A Progress of Sentiments: Reflections on Hume's* Treatise, Cambridge, MA: Harvard University Press.

Baldwin, J.W. (1959) 'The Medieval Theories of the Just Price: Romanists, Canonists, and Theologians in the Twelfth and Thirteenth Centuries', *Transactions of the American Philosophical Society*, 49: 1–92.

Banzhaf, H.S. (2000) 'Productive Nature and the Net Product: Quesnay's Economies Animal and Political', *History of Political Economy*, 32: 517–51.

Barker, E. (1934) 'Stoicism', in E.R.A. Seligman and A. Johnson (eds) *Encyclopaedia of the Social Sciences*, vol. 14, New York, NY: Macmillan.

—— (ed.) (1946) *The Politics of Aristotle: Translated with an Introduction, Notes and Appendixes*, Oxford: Clarendon.

Bate, W.J. (1978) *Samuel Johnson*, London: Chatto & Windus.

Becker, J.F. (1961) 'Adam Smith's Theory of Social Science', *Southern Economic Journal*, 28: 13–21.

Berlin, I. (1958) *Two Concepts of Liberty: an Inaugural Lecture Delivered before the University of Oxford on 31 October 1958*, Oxford: Clarendon; repr. in I. Berlin (1969) *Four Essays on Liberty*, Oxford: Oxford University Press.

—— (2005) 'Liberty', in T. Honderich (ed.) *The Oxford Companion to Philosophy*, 2nd edn, Oxford: Oxford University Press.

Bernholz, P. (2001) 'Political Parties and Paper Money Inflation in Sweden during the 18th Century', *Kyklos*, 54: 207–12.

Berry, C.J. (1994) *The Idea of Luxury: a Conceptual and Historical Investigation*, Cambridge: Cambridge University Press.

Blaug, M. (1962) *Economic Theory in Retrospect*, Homewood, IL: Irwin.

—— (1987) 'Classical Economics', in J. Eatwell, M. Milgate and P. Newman (eds) *The New Palgrave: a Dictionary of Economics*, vol. 1, London: Macmillan.

—— (1999) 'Misunderstanding Classical Economics: the Sraffian Interpretation of the Surplus Approach', *History of Political Economy*, 31: 213–36.

Bloom, A. (1968) *The Republic of Plato: Translated with Notes and An Interpretive Essay*, New York, NY: Basic Books.

Boas, G. (1973) 'Nature', in P.P. Wiener (ed.) *Dictionary of the History of Ideas: Studies of Selected Pivotal Ideas*, vol. 3, New York, NY: Charles Scribner's.

Boisguilbert, P. le P.S. de (1707) *Dissertation de la Nature des Richesses, de l'Argent et des Tributes*...; trans. P.D. Groenewegen (from the I.N.E.D. 1966 edn) (2000) *A Treatise on the Nature of Wealth, Money, and Taxation in which the Mistaken Views which are Fashionable in the World with Regard to These Three Subjects are Laid Bare*, Reprints of Economic Classics, no. 10 (series 2), Sydney: Centre for the Study of the History of Economic Thought, University of Sydney.

Bonar, J. (1893) *Philosophy and Political Economy in Some of Their Historical Relations*, London: Swan Sonnenschein.

—— (1922) *Philosophy and Political Economy in Some of Their Historical Relations*, 3rd edn, London: George Allen & Unwin.

Boss, H. (1990) *Theories of Surplus and Transfer: Parasites and Producers in Economic Thought*, Boston, MA: Unwin Hyman.

Boudon, R. (2004) *The Poverty of Relativism*, Oxford: Bardwell.

Bouwsma, W.J. (1995) 'Liberty in the Renaissance and Reformation', in R.W. Davis (ed.) *The Origins of Modern Freedom in the West*, Stanford, CA: Stanford University Press.

Bowles, S. (1998) 'Endogenous Preferences: the Cultural Consequences of Markets and other Economic Institutions', *Journal of Economic Literature*, 36: 75–111.

Bowley, M. (1963) 'Some Seventeenth Century Contributions to the Theory of Value', *Economica*, 30: 122–39.

—— (1973) *Studies in the History of Economic Theory Before 1870*, London: Macmillan.

—— (1975) 'Some Aspects of the Treatment of Capital in *The Wealth of Nations*', in A.S. Skinner and T. Wilson (eds) *Essays on Adam Smith*, Oxford: Clarendon.

Brewer, A. (1995) 'Rent and Profit in the *Wealth of Nations*', *Scottish Journal of Political Economy*, 42: 183–200.

Bridel, P. (1987) 'Montchrétien, Antoyne de', in J. Eatwell, M. Milgate and P. Newman (eds) *The New Palgrave: a Dictionary of Political Economy*, vol. 3, London: Macmillan.

Brown, M. (1988) *Adam Smith's Economics: Its Place in the Development of Economic Thought*, London: Croom Helm.

Brown, V. (1994) *Adam Smith's Discourse: Canonicity, Commerce and Conscience*, London: Routledge.

Bruni, L. and Porta, P.L. (2003) '*Economia Civile* and *Pubblica Felicità* in the Italian Enlightenment', in M. Schabas and N. De Marchi (eds) *Oeconomies in the Age of Newton* (Annual Supplement to *History of Political Economy*, vol. 35), Durham, NC: Duke University Press.

Bruni, L. and Zamagni, S. (2004) *Economia Civile: Efficienza, Equità, Felicità Pubblica*, Bologna: Il Mulino.

Brunner, O., Conze, W. and Koselleck, R. (eds) (1978) *Geschichtliche Grundbegriffe: Historisches Lexikon zur politisch-sozialen Sprache in Deutschland*, vol. 4, Stuttgart: Klett-Cotta.

Bryce, J.C. (1983) 'Introduction', in J.C. Bryce (ed.) *Adam Smith. Lectures on Rhetoric and Belles Lettres* (Glasgow Edition of the Works and Correspondence of Adam Smith, vol. 4), Oxford: Clarendon.

Bury, J.B. (1955) *The Idea of Progress: An Inquiry into its Origin and Growth*, New York, NY: Dover (1st edn 1920).

Caminati, M. and Petri, F. (eds) (1990) *Convergence to Long-Period Positions: Proceedings of a Workshop, Political Economy: Studies in the Surplus Approach*, 6: 5–359.

Campbell, R.H. and Skinner, A.S. (1976) 'General Introduction', in R.H. Campbell, A.S. Skinner and W.B. Todd (eds) *Adam Smith. An Inquiry into the Nature and Causes of the Wealth of Nations*, 2 vols (Glasgow Edition of the Works and Correspondence of Adam Smith, vol. 2), Oxford: Clarendon.

Campbell, T.D. and Ross, I.S. (1982) 'The Theory and Practice of the Wise and Virtuous Man: Reflections on Adam Smith's Response to Hume's Deathbed Wish', *Studies in Eighteenth-Century Culture*, 11: 65–74.

Cannan, E. (1894) 'Capital', in R.H.I. Palgrave (ed.) *Dictionary of Political Economy*, vol. 1, London: Macmillan.

—— (1904) 'Editor's Introduction', in E. Cannan (ed.) *An Inquiry Into the Nature and Causes of the Wealth of Nations by Adam Smith*, 2 vols, London: Methuen.

—— (1921) 'Early History of the Term Capital', *Quarterly Journal of Economics*, 35: 469–81.

[Cantillon, R.] (1755) *Essai sur la Nature du Commerce en Général. Traduit de*

*l'Anglois*, London; repr. in H. Higgs (1931) *Essai sur la Nature du Commerce en Général by Richard Cantillon: Edited with an English Translation and Other Material*, London: Frank Cass.
Carpenter, K.E. (2002) *The Dissemination of the* Wealth of Nations *in French and in France, 1776–1843*, New York, NY: Bibliographical Society of America.
Carr, C.L. (ed.) (1994) *The Political Writings of Samuel Pufendorf*, trans. M.J. Seidler, Oxford: Oxford University Press.
Castelot, E. (1896) 'Laissez-Faire, Laissez-Passer, History of the Maxim', in R.H.I. Palgrave (ed.) *Dictionary of Political Economy*, vol. 2, London: Macmillan; repr. in J. Eatwell, M. Milgate and P. Newman (eds) (1987) *The New Palgrave: a Dictionary of Economics*, vol. 3, London: Macmillan.
Chafuen, A.A. (2003) *Faith and Liberty: the Economic Thought of the Late Scholastics*, 2nd edn, Lanham, MD: Lexington Books.
Charles, L. (2005) [Review of Schabas and De Marchi (2003)], *History of Economic Ideas*, 13 (no. 3): 143–5.
[Child, J.] (1668) *Brief Observations Concerning Trade, and Interest of Money*, London.
Ciccone, R. (1986) 'Accumulation and Capacity Utilization: some Critical Considerations on Joan Robinson's Theory of Distribution', *Political Economy: Studies in the Surplus Approach*, 2: 17–36.
—— (1999) 'Classical and Neoclassical Short-Run Prices: a Comparative Analysis of Their Intended Empirical Content', in G. Mongiovi and F. Petri (eds) *Value, Distribution and Capital: Essays in Honour of Pierangelo Garegnani*, London: Routledge.
Clark, H.C. (2004) [Review of Carpenter (2002)], *Adam Smith Review*, 1: 175–80.
Clark, J. (2004) 'Light Sources – Paris, Washington, London: Departure Points for the Modern World', *Times Literary Supplement*, 12 November: 3–4.
Coase, R.H. (1976) 'Adam Smith's View of Man', *Journal of Law and Economics*, 19: 529–46.
Coats, A.W. (1958) 'Changing Attitudes to Labour in the Mid-Eighteenth Century', *Economic History Review* (2nd Series), 11: 35–51.
Cockburn, H. (1856) *Memorials of His Time*, Edinburgh: Adam & Charles Black.
Coleman, D.C. (ed.) (1969) *Revisions in Mercantilism*, London: Methuen.
Colman, A.M. (2006) *A Dictionary of Psychology*, 2nd edn, Oxford: Oxford University Press.
Corbier, M. (2005) 'Luxury', in H. Cancik and H. Schneider (eds) *Brill's New Pauly Encyclopaedia of the Ancient World*, vol. 7, Leiden: Brill.
Cowan, T.A. (1968) 'Jurisprudence', in D.L. Sills (ed.) *International Encyclopedia of the Social Sciences*, vol. 8, New York, NY: Macmillan & the Free Press.
Cremaschi, S. (1989) 'Adam Smith: Skeptical Newtonianism, Disenchanted Republicanism, and the Birth of Social Science', in M. Dascal and O. Gruengard (eds) *Knowledge and Politics: Case Studies in the Relationship between Epistemology and Political Philosophy*, Boulder, CO: Westview.
—— (2002) 'Metaphors in the *Wealth of Nations*' in S. Boehm, C. Gehrke, H.D. Kurz and R. Sturn (eds) *Is There Progress in Economics? Knowledge, Truth and the History of Economic Thought*, Cheltenham: Elgar.
Crocker, L.G. (1959) *An Age of Crisis: Man and World in Eighteenth Century French Thought*, Baltimore, MD: Johns Hopkins Press.
Cropsey, J. (1957) *Polity and Economy: an Interpretation of the Principles of Adam Smith*, The Hague: Martinus Nijhoff.
Davenant, C. (1695) 'A Memorial Concerning the Coyn of England…', in A.P. Usher

(ed.) (1942) *Two Manuscripts by Charles Davenant*, Baltimore, MD: Johns Hopkins Press.
Davies, B. (1998) 'Thomas Aquinas', in J. Marenbon (ed.) *Medieval Philosophy* (Routledge History of Philosophy, vol. 3), London: Routledge.
Davis, R.W. (ed.) (1995) *The Origins of Modern Freedom in the West*, Stanford, CA: Stanford University Press.
De-Juan, O. and Monsalve, F. (2006) 'Morally Ruled Behaviour: the Neglected Contribution of Scholasticism', *European Journal of the History of Economic Thought*, 13: 99–112.
Dobb, M. (1973) *Theories of Value and Distribution Since Adam Smith: Ideology and Economic Theory*, Cambridge: Cambridge University Press.
Douglas, P.H. (1928) 'Smith's Theory of Value and Distribution', in J.M. Clark *et al.*, *Adam Smith, 1776–1926: Lectures to Commemorate the Sesquicentennial of the Publication of 'The Wealth of Nations'*, Chicago, IL: University of Chicago Press.
Dryden, J. (1667) *Annus Mirabilis: the Year of Wonders, 1666…*, London.
—— (1701) *The Works of Mr. John Dryden. The Third Volume. Consisting of the Author's Original Poems and Translations…*, London.
—— (1760) *The Miscellaneous Works of John Dryden, Esq: Containing all his Original Poems, Tales, and Translations…*, 4 vols, London.
Dunbar, J. (1780) *Essays on the History of Mankind in Rude and Cultivated Ages*, London.
Easton, D. (1968) 'Political Science', in D.L. Sills (ed.) *International Encyclopedia of the Social Sciences*, vol. 12, New York, NY: Macmillan & the Free Press.
Eatwell, J. (1987) 'Natural and Normal Conditions', in J. Eatwell, M. Milgate and P. Newman (eds) *The New Palgrave: a Dictionary of Economics*, vol. 3, London: Macmillan.
Eatwell, J. and Milgate, M. (eds) (1983) *Keynes's Economics and the Theory of Value and Distribution*, London: Duckworth.
Eden, W. (1780) *Four Letters to the Earl of Carlisle…*, 3rd edn, London.
Eltis, W.A. (1975) 'Adam Smith's Theory of Economic Growth', in A.S. Skinner and T. Wilson (eds) *Essays on Adam Smith*, Oxford: Clarendon.
—— (1984) *The Classical Theory of Economic Growth*, London: Macmillan.
—— (2000) 'The Classical School of Economics: an Overview. Introduction to the Second Edition', in W.A. Eltis, *The Classical Theory of Economic Growth*, 2nd edn, London: Palgrave.
—— (2004) 'Emma Rothschild on Economic Sentiments: and the True Adam Smith', *European Journal of the History of Economic Thought*, 11: 147–59.
Emsley, C. (1983) *Policing and Its Context 1750–1870*, London: Macmillan.
Evensky, J. (2005) *Adam Smith's Moral Philosophy: a Historical and Contemporary Perspective on Markets, Law, Ethics, and Culture*, Cambridge: Cambridge University Press.
Faccarello, G. (1999) *The Foundations of* Laissez-faire*: the Economics of Pierre de Boisguilbert*, London: Routledge.
—— (2005) 'A Tale of Two Traditions: Pierre Force's *Self-Interest before Adam Smith*', *European Journal of the History of Economic Thought*, 12: 701–12.
Farge, A. (2001) 'Police', in M. Delon (ed.) *Encyclopedia of the Enlightenment*, vol. 2, Chicago, IL: Fitzroy Dearborn (French edn 1997).
Faulkner, R.K. (2003) 'Political Philosophy', in A.C. Kors (ed.) *Encyclopedia of the Enlightenment*, vol. 3, Oxford: Oxford University Press.

Ferguson, A. (1767) *An Essay on the History of Civil Society*, Edinburgh.
—— (1773) *An Essay on the History of Civil Society*, 4th edn, London and Edinburgh.
—— (1792) *Principles of Moral and Political Science; Being Chiefly a Retrospect of Lectures Delivered in the College of Edinburgh*, 2 vols, Edinburgh.
Finley, M.I. (1970) 'Aristotle and Economic Analysis', *Past and Present*, no. 47: 3–25; as repr. in M.I. Finley (ed.) (1974) *Studies in Ancient Society*, London: Routledge & Kegan Paul.
—— (1992) *The Ancient Economy*, London: Penguin (1st edn 1973).
Fisher, I. (1896) 'What is Capital?', *Economic Journal*, 6: 509–34.
—— (1897) 'Senses of "Capital"', *Economic Journal*, 7: 199–213.
Fitzgibbons, A. (1995) *Adam Smith's System of Liberty, Wealth, and Virtue: the Moral and Political Foundations of* The Wealth of Nations, Oxford: Clarendon.
Fleischacker, S. (2004) *On Adam Smith's* Wealth of Nations*: a Philosophical Companion*, Princeton, NJ: Princeton University Press.
Foley, V. (1974) 'The Division of Labor in Plato and Smith', *History of Political Economy*, 6: 220–42.
—— (1975) 'Smith and the Greeks: a Reply to Professor McNulty's Comments', *History of Political Economy*, 7: 379–89.
Forbes, D. (1954) '"Scientific" Whiggism: Adam Smith and John Millar', *Cambridge Journal*, 7: 643–70.
—— (1975) 'Sceptical Whiggism, Commerce, and Liberty', in A.S. Skinner and T. Wilson (eds) *Essays on Adam Smith*, Oxford: Clarendon.
Force, P. (2003) *Self-Interest Before Adam Smith: a Genealogy of Economic Science*, Cambridge: Cambridge University Press.
Fortrey, S. (1673) *Englands Interest and Improvement*..., London; as repr. in J.R. McCulloch (ed.) (1856) *A Select Collection of Early English Tracts on Commerce*..., London: Political Economy Club (facsimile Cambridge: Cambridge University Press, 1952).
Fox-Genovese, E. (1976) *The Origins of Physiocracy: Economic Revolution and Social Order in Eighteenth-Century France*, Ithaca, NY: Cornell University Press.
Friedman, D.D. (1980) 'In Defense of Thomas Aquinas and the Just Price', *History of Political Economy*, 12: 234–42.
Furniss, E.S. (1920) *The Position of the Laborer in a System of Nationalism: a Study in the Labor Theories of the Later English Mercantilists*, Boston, MA: Houghton Mifflin.
Garegnani, P. (1978–9) 'Notes on Consumption, Investment and Effective Demand', *Cambridge Journal of Economics*, 2: 335–53 and 3: 63–82.
—— (1983) 'The Classical Theory of Wages and the Role of Demand Schedules in the Determination of Relative Prices', *American Economic Review*, 73 (Papers and Proceedings): 309–13.
—— (1984) 'Value and Distribution in the Classical Economists and Marx', *Oxford Economic Papers*, 36: 291–325.
—— (1987) 'Surplus Approach to Value and Distribution', in J. Eatwell, M. Milgate and P. Newman (eds) *The New Palgrave: a Dictionary of Economics*, vol. 4, London: Macmillan.
—— (1988) 'Capital and Effective Demand', in A. Barrère (ed.) *The Foundations of Keynesian Analysis*, London: Macmillan.
—— (2002) 'Misunderstanding Classical Economics? A Reply to Blaug', *History of Political Economy*, 34: 241–54.
—— (2005) 'On a Turning Point in Sraffa's Theoretical and Interpretive Position in the Late 1920s', *European Journal of the History of Economic Thought*, 12: 453–92.

Garegnani, P. and Palumbo, A. (1998) 'Accumulation of Capital', in H.D. Kurz and N. Salvadori (eds) *The Elgar Companion to Classical Economics*, vol. 1, Cheltenham: Elgar.

Gherity, J.A. (1993) 'An Early Publication by Adam Smith', *History of Political Economy*, 25: 241–82.

Ghiselin, M.T. (1974) *The Economy of Nature and the Evolution of Sex*, Berkeley, CA: University of California Press.

Gilibert, G. (1987) 'Revenue, Gross and Net', in J. Eatwell, M. Milgate and P. Newman (eds) *The New Palgrave: a Dictionary of Economics*, vol. 4, London: Macmillan.

—— (1998) 'Circular Flow', in H.D. Kurz and N. Salvadori (eds) *The Elgar Companion to Classical Economics*, vol. 1, Cheltenham: Elgar.

—— (2001) [Review of Groenewegen (2000)], *Contributions to Political Economy*, 20: 113–17.

Gram, H. (1998) 'Necessaries, Conveniencies and Luxuries', in H.D. Kurz and N. Salvadori (eds) *The Elgar Companion to Classical Economics*, vol. 2, Cheltenham: Elgar.

Grampp, W.D. (1952) 'The Liberal Elements in English Mercantilism', *Quarterly Journal of Economics*, 66: 465–501.

—— (1965) 'The Mercantilists as Liberals', in W.D. Grampp, *Economic Liberalism*, vol. 1, New York, NY: Random House.

Greenberg, J.H. (1968) 'Anthropology: the Field' in D.L. Sills (ed.) *International Encyclopedia of the Social Sciences*, vol. 1, New York, NY: Macmillan & the Free Press.

Grice-Hutchinson, M. (1978) *Early Economic Thought in Spain 1177–1740*, London: George Allen & Unwin.

Griswold, Jr., C.L. (1999) *Adam Smith and the Virtues of Enlightenment*, Cambridge: Cambridge University Press.

—— (2006) 'On the Incompleteness of Adam Smith's System', *Adam Smith Review*, 2: 181–6.

Groenewegen, P.D. (1971) 'A Re-interpretation of Turgot's Theory of Capital and Interest', *Economic Journal*, 81: 327–40; as repr. in P.D. Groenewegen (2002) *Eighteenth-Century Economics: Turgot, Beccaria and Smith and their Contemporaries*, London: Routledge.

—— (1973) 'A Note on the Origin of the Phrase, "Supply and Demand"', *Economic Journal*, 83: 505–9.

—— (1977a) 'Adam Smith and the Division of Labour: a Bicentenary Estimate', *Australian Economic Papers*, 16: 161–74; as repr. in P.D. Groenewegen (2002) *Eighteenth-Century Economics: Turgot, Beccaria and Smith and their Contemporaries*, London: Routledge.

—— (1977b) 'Introduction', in P.D. Groenewegen (ed.) *The Economics of A.R.J. Turgot*, The Hague: Martinus Nijhoff.

—— (ed.) (1977c) *The Economics of A.R.J. Turgot*, The Hague: Martinus Nijhof.

—— (1982) 'Turgot: Forerunner of Neo-classical Economics?', *Kenzei Kenkyu*, 33: 119–33; repr. in P.D. Groenewegen (2002) *Eighteenth-Century Economics: Turgot, Beccaria and Smith and their Contemporaries*, London: Routledge.

—— (1983) 'Turgot, Beccaria and Smith', in P.D. Groenewegen and J. Halevi (eds) *Italian Economics Past and Present*, Sydney: Frederick May Foundation for Italian Studies; repr. in P.D. Groenewegen (2002) *Eighteenth-Century Economics: Turgot, Beccaria and Smith and their Contemporaries*, London: Routledge.

—— (ed.) (1986) *Pietro Verri 1771. Reflections on Political Economy*, trans. B. McGilvray (from the 1781 edn), Reprints of Economic Classics no. 4 (series 2), Sydney: Department of Economics, University of Sydney.

—— (1987a) 'Beccaria, Cesare Bonsana, Marchese di', in J. Eatwell, M. Milgate and P. Newman (eds) *The New Palgrave: a Dictionary of Economics*, vol. 1, London: Macmillan.
—— (1987b) 'Division of Labour', in J. Eatwell, M. Milgate and P. Newman (eds) *The New Palgrave: a Dictionary of Economics*, vol. 1, London: Macmillan.
—— (1987c) '"Political Economy" and "Economics"', in J. Eatwell, M. Milgate and P. Newman (eds) *The New Palgrave: a Dictionary of Economics*, vol. 3, London: Macmillan.
—— (1987d) 'Reflections on Pietro Verri's Political Economy', *Storia del Pensiero Economico*, no. 15: 3–10; repr. in P.D. Groenewegen (2002) *Eighteenth-Century Economics: Turgot, Beccaria and Smith and their Contemporaries*, London: Routledge.
—— (1987e) '"Supply and Demand"', in J. Eatwell, M. Milgate and P. Newman (eds) *The New Palgrave: a Dictionary of Economics*, vol. 4, London: Macmillan.
—— (1993) 'Marshall on Ricardo', in M. Baranzini and G.C. Harcourt (eds) *The Dynamics of the Wealth of Nations: Growth, Distribution and Structural Change. Essays in Honour of Luigi Pasinetti*, Macmillan: London; repr. in P.D. Groenewegen (2003) *Classics and Moderns in Economics: Essays on Nineteenth- and Twentieth-Century Economic Thought*, vol. 2, London: Routledge.
—— (1998) 'Division of Labour', in H.D. Kurz and N. Salvadori (eds) *The Elgar Companion to Classical Economics*, vol. 1, Cheltenham: Elgar.
—— (ed.) (2000) *Pierre le Pesant Sieur de Boisguilbert. A Treatise on the Nature of Wealth, Money, and Taxation*, Reprints of Economic Classics, no. 10 (series 2), Sydney: Centre for the Study of the History of Economic Thought, University of Sydney.
—— (2002a) *Eighteenth-Century Economics: Turgot, Beccaria and Smith and their Contemporaries*, London: Routledge.
—— (2002b) 'Thoughts on the Emergence of Economics as a Science', in P.D. Groenewegen, *Eighteenth-Century Economics: Turgot, Beccaria and Smith and their Contemporaries*, London: Routledge.
Gross, P.R. and Levitt, N. (1998) *Higher Superstition: the Academic Left and its Quarrels with Science*, 2nd edn, Baltimore, MD: Johns Hopkins University Press.
Guidi, M.E.L. (1994) '"Economy" and "Political Economy" in Italian Dictionaries and Encyclopedias (1729–1861)', in M. Albertone and A. Masoero (eds) *Political Economy and National Realities*, Torino: Foundazione Luigi Einaudi.
Haakonssen, K. (1981) *The Science of a Legislator: the Natural Jurisprudence of David Hume and Adam Smith*, Cambridge: Cambridge University Press.
Haakonssen, K. and Winch, D. (2006) 'The Legacy of Adam Smith', in K. Haakonssen (ed.) *The Cambridge Companion to Adam Smith*, Cambridge: Cambridge University Press.
Hacking, I. (2006) 'Making Up People', *London Review of Books*, 28 (no. 16): 23–6.
Hallie, P.P. (1967) 'Stoicism', in P. Edwards (ed.) *The Encyclopedia of Philosophy*, vol. 8, New York, NY: Macmillan & The Free Press.
Hamouda, O.F. and Price, B.B. (1997) 'The Justice of the Just Price', *European Journal of the History of Economic Thought*, 4: 191–216.
Hanley, R.P., Darwall, S., Werhane, P.H., Fleischacker, S. and Rothschild, E. (2004) 'Symposium on Emma Rothschild's *Economic Sentiments*', *Adam Smith Review*, 1: 125–64.
Harrington, J. (1656) *The Common-Wealth of Oceana*, London.
[Harris, J.] (1757) *An Essay upon Money and Coins. Part I. The Theories of Commerce, Money, and Exchanges*, London.

Harrod, R.F. (1974) 'Keynes's Theory and Its Applications', in D.E. Moggridge (ed.) *Keynes: Aspects of the Man and his Work*, London: Macmillan.

Hatfield, H.R. (1926) 'The Earliest Use in English of the Term Capital', *Quarterly Journal of Economics*, 40: 547–8.

—— (1934) 'The Early Use of "Capital" ', *Quarterly Journal of Economics*, 49: 162–3.

von Hayek, F.A. (1944) *The Road to Serfdom*, London: Routledge & Kegan Paul.

Heckscher, E.F. (1955) *Mercantilism*, 2 vols, London: George Allen & Unwin (ed. E.F. Söderlund; 1st English edn 1935; 1st Swedish edn 1931).

Heilbroner, R.L. (1973) 'The Paradox of Progess: Decline and Decay in *The Wealth of Nations*', *Journal of the History of Ideas*, 34: 243–62; repr. in A.S. Skinner and T. Wilson (eds) (1975) *Essays on Adam Smith*, Oxford: Clarendon.

Heise, P.A. (1995) 'Stoicism in the *EPS*: the Foundation of Adam Smith's Moral Philosophy', in I.H. Rima (ed.) *The Classical Tradition in Economic Thought* (*Perspectives on the History of Economic Thought*, vol. 11), Aldershot: Elgar.

Henderson, W. (2004) 'A Very Cautious, or a Very Polite, Dr Smith? Hedging in the *Wealth of Nations*', *Adam Smith Review*, 1: 60–81; repr. revised in W. Henderson (2006) *Evaluating Adam Smith: Creating the Wealth of Nations*, London: Routledge.

Henderson, W. and Samuels, W.J. (2004) 'The Etiology of Adam Smith's Division of Labour: Alternative Accounts and Smith's Methodology Applied to Them', in W.J. Samuels, W. Henderson, K.D. Johnson and M. Johnson, *Essays on the History of Economics*, London: Routledge.

Henry, D.P. (2006) 'Medieval Philosophy', in D.M. Borchert (ed.) *Encyclopedia of Philosophy*, 2nd edn, vol. 6, Detroit, MI: Thomson Gale.

Hepburn, R.W. (2006) 'Nature, Philosophical Ideas of', in D.M. Borchert (ed.) *Encyclopedia of Philosophy*, 2nd edn, vol. 6, Detroit, MI: Thomson Gale.

Herlihy, D. (1958) 'Discussion [of de Roover (1958)]', *Journal of Economic History*, 18: 437–8.

Hirschman, A.O. (1977) *The Passions and the Interests: Political Arguments for Capitalism before its Triumph*, Princeton, NJ: Princeton University Press.

Hobbes, T. (1651) *Leviathan or the Matter, Forme and Power of a Commonwealth Ecclesiasticall and Civil*, London; ed. M. Oakeshott, Oxford: Blackwell (n. d.).

Hollander, S. (1965) 'On the Interpretation of the Just Price', *Kyklos*, 18: 615–34.

—— (1973) *The Economics of Adam Smith*, Toronto: University of Toronto Press.

—— (1975) 'On the Role of Utility and Demand in *The Wealth of Nations*', in A.S. Skinner and T. Wilson (eds) *Essays on Adam Smith*, Oxford: Clarendon.

[Home, H. (Lord Kames)] (1774) *Sketches of the History of Man*, vol. 1, Edinburgh.

Hont, I. and Ignatieff, M. (1983a) 'Needs and Justice in the *Wealth of Nations*: an Introductory Essay', in I. Hont and M. Ignatieff (eds) *Wealth and Virtue: the Shaping of Political Economy in the Scottish Enlightenment*, Cambridge: Cambridge University Press.

—— (eds) (1983b) *Wealth and Virtue: the Shaping of Political Economy in the Scottish Enlightenment*, Cambridge: Cambridge University Press.

Hosseini, H. (1998) 'Seeking the Roots of Adam Smith's Division of Labor in Medieval Persia', *History of Political Economy*, 30: 653–81.

HROnline (2002) *The Hartlib Papers: a Complete Text and Image Database of the Papers of Samuel Hartlib (c. 1600–1662) held in Sheffield University Library, Sheffield, UK*, Sheffield: Humanities Research Institute, University of Sheffield.

Hume, D. (1739–40) *A Treatise of Human Nature: being an Attempt to Introduce the Experimental Method of Reasoning into Moral Subjects*, London; as repr. in L.A.

Selby-Bigge (ed.) (1888) *A Treatise of Human Nature by David Hume. Reprinted from the Original Edition in Three Volumes*..., Oxford: Clarendon.

—— (1778) *The History of England, from the Invasion of Julius Cæsar to the Revolution in 1688*..., 8 vols, London (1st edn 1762).

Hutcheson, F. (1747) *A Short Introduction to Moral Philosophy, in Three Books; Containing the Elements of Ethicks and the Law of Nature*, Glasgow.

—— (1755) *A System of Moral Philosophy, in Three Books*..., 2 vols, London.

Hutchison, T.W. (1988) *Before Adam Smith: the Emergence of Political Economy, 1662–1776*, Oxford: Blackwell.

I.N.E.D. (1966) *Pierre de Boisguilbert ou la Naissance de l'Économie Politique*, 2 vols, Paris: L'Institut National D'Études Démographiques.

Inwood, B. (2006) 'Stoicism', in D.M. Borchert (ed.) *Encyclopedia of Philosophy*, 2nd edn, vol. 9, Detroit, MI: Thomson Gale.

Irwin, T. (ed.) (1985) *Aristotle. Nicomachean Ethics*, Indianapolis, IN: Hackett.

James, C. (2007) *Cultural Amnesia: Notes in the Margin of my Time*, London: Pan Macmillan.

Jardine, N. (2007) 'World Before Word', *Times Literary Supplement*, 14 September: 10–11.

Jeck, A. (1994) 'The Macrostructure of Adam Smith's Theoretical System: a Reconstruction', *European Journal of the History of Economic Thought*, 1: 551–76.

Jevons, W.S. (1871) *The Theory of Political Economy*, London: Macmillan.

Johnson, S. (1752) *The Rambler*, vol. 6 (no. 202): 235–42.

—— (1755) *A Dictionary of the English Language: in which the Words are Deduced from their Originals, and Illustrated in their Different Significations*..., 2 vols, London.

—— (1771) *The Rambler*, 8th edn, 4 vols, London.

Jones, P. (1989) 'Introduction', in P. Jones (ed.) *The 'Science of Man' in the Scottish Enlightenment: Hume, Reid and their Contemporaries*, Edinburgh: Edinburgh University Press.

Kaldor, N. (1972) 'The Irrelevance of Equilibrium Economics', *Economic Journal*, 82: 1237–55.

Kauder, E. (1953) 'Genesis of the Marginal Utility Theory: from Aristotle to the End of the Eighteenth Century', *Economic Journal*, 63: 638–50.

Kaye, F.B. (ed.) (1924) *The Fable of the Bees: or, Private Vices, Publick Benefits. by Bernard Mandeville. With a Commentary, Critical, Historical, and Explanatory*, 2 vols, Oxford: Clarendon.

Kaye, J. (1998) *Economy and Nature in the Fourteenth Century: Money, Market Exchange, and the Emergence of Scientific Thought*, Cambridge: Cambridge University Press.

Keen, S. (2001) *Debunking Economics: the Naked Emperor of the Social Sciences*, New York, NY: Zed Books.

Keynes, J.M. (1933) *Essays in Biography*, London: Macmillan.

—— (1936) *The General Theory of Employment, Interest and Money*, London: Macmillan.

King, G. (1696) 'Natural and Politicall Observations and Conclusions. upon the State & Condition of England', British Library, Harleian MSS 1898; as repr. in G.E. Barnett (ed.) (1936) *Two Tracts by Gregory King*, Baltimore, MD: Johns Hopkins Press.

King, J.E. (1948) 'The Origin of the Term "Political Economy"', *Journal of Modern History*, 20: 230–1.

Kirman, A. (1989) 'The Intrinsic Limits of Modern Economic Theory: the Emperor has no Clothes', *Economic Journal*, 99 (Conference Supplement): 126–39.

—— (2006) 'Demand Theory and General Equilibrium: from Explanation to Introspection, a Journey down the Wrong Road', in P. Mirowski and D.W. Hands (eds) *Agreement on Demand: Consumer Theory in the Twentieth Century* (Annual Supplement to *History of Political Economy*, vol. 38), Durham, NC: Duke University Press.

Knemeyer, F.-L. (1980) 'Polizei', *Economy and Society*, 9: 172–96 (trans. K. Tribe).

Koerner, L. (1996) 'Purposes of Linnaean Travel: a Preliminary Research Report', in D.P. Miller and P.H. Reill (eds) *Visions of Empire: Voyages, Botany, and Representations of Nature*, Cambridge: Cambridge University Press.

—— (1999) *Linnaeus: Nature and Nation*, Cambridge, MA: Harvard University Press.

Kramnick, I. (1995) 'Introduction', in I. Kramnick (ed.) *The Portable Enlightenment Reader*, London: Penguin.

Krynen, J. (2000) 'Roman Law', in A. Vauchez (ed.) *Encyclopedia of the Middle Ages*, ed. in conjunction with B. Dobson and M. Lapidge, vol. 2, Cambridge: James Clarke & Co. (trans. A. Walford; French edn 1997).

Kubin, I. (1998) 'Effectual Demand' in H.D. Kurz and N. Salvadori (eds) *The Elgar Companion to Classical Economics*, vol. 1, Cheltenham: Elgar.

Kuczynski, M. and Meek, R.L. (eds) (1972) *Quesnay's* Tableau Économique*: Edited, with New Material, Translations and Notes*, London: Macmillan and New York, NY: Kelley.

Kurz, H.D. (1990) *Capital, Distribution and Effective Demand: Studies in the 'Classical' Approach to Economic Theory*, Cambridge: Polity.

—— (2006a) 'Goods and Bads: Sundry Observations on Joint Production, Waste Disposal, and Renewable and Exhaustible Resources', *Progress in Industrial Ecology*, 3: 280–301.

—— (2006b) 'The Agents of Production are the Commodities Themselves: on the Classical Theory of Production, Distribution and Value', *Structural Change and Economic Dynamics*, 17: 1–26.

—— (2008) 'Innovation and Profits: Schumpeter and the Classical Heritage', *Journal of Economic Behavior & Organization*, 67: 263–78.

Kurz, H.D. and Salvadori, N. (1993) 'Von Neumann's Growth Model and the "Classical" Tradition', *European Journal of the History of Economic Thought*, 1: 129–60.

—— (1995) *Theory of Production: a Long-Period Analysis*, Cambridge: Cambridge University Press.

—— (2002) 'Mark Blaug on the "Sraffian Interpretation of the Surplus Approach"', *History of Political Economy*, 34: 225–36.

—— (2003) 'Understanding "Classical" Economics: a Reply to Mark Blaug', in H.D. Kurz and N. Salvadori, *Classical Economics and Modern Theory: Studies in Long-Period Analysis*, London: Routledge.

—— (2005) 'Representing the Production and Circulation of Commodities in Material Terms: on Sraffa's Objectivism', *Review of Political Economy*, 17: 413–41.

—— (2006) 'Input-Output Analysis from a Wider Perspective: a Comparison of the Early Works of Leontief and Sraffa', *Economic Systems Research*, 18: 373–90.

Lai, C.-C. (1989) 'Adam Smith and Yen Fu: Western Economics in Chinese Perspective', *Journal of European Economic History*, 18: 371–82; repr. in C.-C. Lai (ed.) (2000) *Adam Smith Across Nations: Translations and Receptions of* The Wealth of Nations, Oxford: Oxford University Press.

Laibman, D. (2004) 'Is There a Classical Theory of Supply and Demand?', in G. Argyrous,

M. Forstater and G. Mongiovi (eds) *Growth, Distribution, and Effective Demand: Alternatives to Economic Orthodoxy*, Armonk, NY: Sharpe.

Lamb, R. (1973) 'Adam Smith's Concept of Alienation', *Oxford Economic Papers*, 25: 275–85.

Langholm, O. (1983) *Wealth and Money in the Aristotelian Tradition: a Study in Scholastic Economic Sources*, Bergen: Universitetsforlaget.

—— (1987) 'Scholastic Economics', in S.T. Lowry (ed.) *Pre-Classical Economic Thought: from the Greeks to the Scottish Enlightenment*, Boston, MA: Kluwer.

—— (1992) *Economics in the Medieval Schools: Wealth, Exchange, Value, Money and Usury According to the Paris Theological Tradition 1200–1350*, Leiden: Brill.

Larrère, C. (2001a) 'Nature', in M. Delon (ed.) *Encyclopedia of the Enlightenment*, vol. 2, Chicago, IL: Fitzroy Dearborn (French edn 1997).

—— (2001b) 'Political Economy', in M. Delon (ed.) *Encyclopedia of the Enlightenment*, vol. 2, Chicago, IL: Fitzroy Dearborn (French edn 1997).

Larsen, R.M. (1977) 'Adam Smith's Theory of Market Prices', *Indian Economic Journal*, 24: 219–35.

Laslett, P. and Cummings, P.W. (2006) 'Political Philosophy, History of', in D.M. Borchert (ed.) *Encyclopedia of Philosophy*, 2nd edn, vol. 7, Detroit, MI: Thomson Gale.

[Law, J.] (1705) *Money and Trade Considered, With a Proposal for Supplying the Nation with Money*, Edinburgh.

Lee, G.A. (1977) 'The Coming of Age of Double Entry: the Giovanni Farolfi Ledger of 1299–1300', *Accounting Historians Journal*, 4: 79–95.

Lempiäinen, T. (1994) 'Botanical Exploration by the Academy of Turku (Finland) in the 17th Century (to the Beginning of the 18th Century)', *Botanical Journal of Scotland*, 46: 581–8.

Leontief, W.W. (1928) 'Die Wirtschaft als Kreislauf', *Archiv für Sozialwissenschaft und Sozialpolitik*, 60: 577–623 [trans. as (1991) 'The Economy as a Circular Flow', *Structural Change and Economic Dynamics*, 2: 181–212].

—— (1936) 'Quantitative Input and Output Relations in the Economic System of the United States', *Review of Economic Statistics*, 18: 105–25.

—— (1941) *The Structure of American Economy, 1919–1929: an Empirical Application of Equilibrium Analysis*, Cambridge, MA: Harvard University Press.

Levy, D.M. (1999) 'Katallactic Rationality: Exploring the Links between Co-operation and Language', *American Journal of Economics and* Sociology, 58: 729–47; as repr. in D.M. Levy (2001) *How the Dismal Science Got Its Name: Classical Economics and the Ur-Text of Racial Politics*, Ann Arbor, MI: University of Michigan Press.

Lewis, C.S. (1960) *Studies in Words*, Cambridge: Cambridge University Press.

Lieberman, D. (2006) 'Adam Smith on Justice, Rights, and Law', in K. Haakonssen (ed.) *The Cambridge Companion to Adam Smith*, Cambridge: Cambridge University Press.

Lindgren, J.R. (1969) 'Adam Smith's Theory of Inquiry', *Journal of Political Economy*, 77: 897–915.

—— (1973) *The Social Philosophy of Adam Smith*, The Hague: Martinus Nijhoff.

Locke, J. (1696) *Some Considerations of the Consequences of the Lowering of Interest, and Raising the Value of Money…*, 2nd edn, in J. Locke, *Several Papers Relating to Money, Interest and Trade, &c.…*, London (1st edn 1691).

[——] (1698) *Two Treatises of Government…*, London (1st edn 1690; ed. P. Laslett, New York, NY: New American Library, 1965).

Lovejoy, A.O. (1927) '"Nature" as Aesthetic Norm', *Modern Language Notes*, 42:

444–50; repr. in A.O. Lovejoy (1948) *Essays in the History of Ideas*, Baltimore, MD: Johns Hopkins.

Lovejoy, A.O. and Boas, G. (1935) *Primitivism and Related Ideas in Antiquity*, Baltimore, MD: Johns Hopkins.

Lowe, A. (1975) 'Adam Smith's System of Equilibrium Growth', in A.S. Skinner and T. Wilson (eds) *Essays on Adam Smith*, Oxford: Clarendon.

Lowry, S. Todd (1987) 'The Greek Heritage in Economic Thought', in S.T. Lowry (ed.) *Pre-Classical Economic Thought: from the Greeks to the Scottish Enlightenment*, Boston, MA: Kluwer.

—— (2003) 'Ancient and Medieval Economics', in W.J. Samuels, J.E. Biddle and J.B. Davis (eds) *A Companion to the History of Economic Thought*, Oxford: Blackwell.

Lundberg, I.C. (1964) *Turgot's Unknown Translator: the* Réflexions *and Adam Smith*, The Hague: Martinus Nijhoff.

Lunghini, G. (1998) 'Political Economy and Economics', in H.D. Kurz and N. Salvadori (eds) *The Elgar Companion to Classical Economics*, vol. 2, Cheltenham: Elgar.

McLain, J.J. (1977) *The Economic Writings of Du Pont de Nemours*, Newark, NJ: University of Delaware Press and London: Associated University Presses.

McNally, D. (1988) *Political Economy and the Rise of Capitalism: a Reinterpretation*, Berkeley, CA: University of California Press.

McNamara, P. (2004) [Review of Vivenza (2001)], *Adam Smith Review*, 1: 182–5.

McNulty, P.J. (1967) 'A Note on the History of Perfect Competition', *Journal of Political Economy*, 75: 395–9.

—— (1975) 'A Note on the Division of Labor in Plato and Smith', *History of Political Economy*, 7: 372–8.

Magnusson, L. (ed.) (1993) *Mercantilist Economics*, Boston, MA: Kluwer.

—— (1994) *Mercantilism: the Shaping of an Economic Language*, London: Routledge.

Malthus, T.R. (1827) *Definitions in Political Economy*…, London: John Murray.

Malynes, G. (1622) *The Maintenance of Free Trade*…, London.

—— (1623) *The Center of the Circle of Commerce*…, London.

[Mandeville, B.] (1733) *The Fable of the Bees. Part II*, 2nd edn, London (1st edn 1729).

Marchant, E.C. and Todd, O.J. (eds) (1923) *Xenophon in Seven Volumes*, vol. IV (*Memorabilia, Oeconomicus, Symposium* and *Apology*), London: Heinemann.

Marenbon, J. (1998) 'Boethius: from Antiquity to the Middle Ages' in J. Marenbon (ed.) *Medieval Philosophy* (Routledge History of Philosophy, vol. 3), London: Routledge.

Marshall, A. (1890) *Principles of Economics*, London: Macmillan.

Martin, E.A. and Law, J. (eds) (2006) *A Dictionary of Law*, 6th edn, Oxford: Oxford University Press.

[Martyn, H.] (1701) *Considerations Upon the East-India Trade*, London.

Marx, K. (1963) *Theories of Surplus-Value: Volume IV of* Capital, Part I, Moscow: Progress Publishers (ed. S. Ryazanskaya; trans. E. Burns).

—— (1967) *Capital: a Critique of Political Economy*, 3 vols, New York, NY: International Publishers (1st German edns 1867, 1885, 1894, respectively).

—— (1968) *Theories of Surplus-Value: Volume IV of* Capital, Part II, Moscow: Progress Publishers (ed. S. Ryazanskaya).

Matravers, D. (2005) 'Freedom and Liberty', in T. Honderich (ed.) *The Oxford Companion to Philosophy*, 2nd edn, Oxford: Oxford University Press.

de Mayerne-Turquet, L. (1611) *La Monarchie Aristodémocratique, ou le Gouvernement Composé et Meslé des Trois Formes de Légitimes Républiques*, Paris.

Mazlish, B. (2007) *The Uncertain Sciences*, New Brunswick, NJ: Transaction.

Meek, R.L. (1951) 'Physiocracy and the Early Theories of Under-Consumption', *Economica*, 18: 229–69; as repr. in R.L. Meek (1962) *The Economics of Physiocracy: Essays and Translations*, London: George Allen & Unwin.

—— (1962) *The Economics of Physiocracy: Essays and Translations*, London: George Allen & Unwin.

Meek, R.L., Raphael, D.D. and Stein, P.G. (eds) (1978a) *Adam Smith. Lectures on Jurisprudence* (Glasgow Edition of the Works and Correspondence of Adam Smith, vol. 5), Oxford: Clarendon.

—— (1978b) 'Introduction', in R.L. Meek, D.D. Raphael and P.G. Stein (eds) *Adam Smith. Lectures on Jurisprudence* (Glasgow Edition of the Works and Correspondence of Adam Smith, vol. 5), Oxford: Clarendon.

Meek, R.L. and Skinner, A.S. (1973) 'The Development of Adam Smith's Ideas on the Division of Labour', *Economic Journal*, 83: 1094–116.

Mehta, P.B. (2006) 'Self-Interest and Other Interests', in K. Haakonssen (ed.) *The Cambridge Companion to Adam Smith*, Cambridge: Cambridge University Press.

Meikle, S. (1995) *Aristotle's Economic Thought*, Clarendon: Oxford.

Menger, C. (1871) *Grundsätze der Volkswirtschaftslehre*, Vienna: Braumüller.

Merton, R.K. (1993) *On the Shoulders of Giants: a Shandean Postscript. The Post-Italianate Edition*, Chicago, IL: University of Chicago Press (1st edn 1965).

Merton, R.K. and Barber, E. (2004) *The Travels and Adventures of Serendipity: a Study in Sociological Semantics and the Sociology of Science*, Princeton, NJ: Princeton University Press (Italian edn 2002).

Miller, E.F. (ed.) (1985) *David Hume. Essays: Moral, Political, and Literary*, Indianapolis, IN: Liberty Classics.

Mirowski, P. (ed.) (1994) *Natural Images in Economic Thought: 'Markets Read in Tooth and Claw'*, Cambridge: Cambridge University Press.

Misselden, E. (1622) *Free Trade. or, the Meanes to Make Trade Florish*. . ., London.

—— (1623) *The Circle of Commerce. or the Ballance of Trade, in Defence of Free Trade* . . ., London.

Mizuta, H. (ed.) (2000) *Adam Smith's Library: a Catalogue*, Oxford: Clarendon.

Moggridge, D. (ed.) (1980) *Activities 1940–1946. Shaping the Post-War World: Employment and Commodities* (The Collected Writings of John Maynard Keynes, vol. 27), London: Macmillan (for the Royal Economic Society).

de Montchrétien, A. (1615) *Traicté de l'Œconomie Politique*. . ., Rouen.

Montes, L. (2003a) '*Das Adam Smith Problem*: its Origins, the Stages of the Current Debate, and one Implication for our Understanding of Sympathy', *Journal of the History of Economic Thought*, 25: 63–90.

—— (2003b) 'Smith and Newton: some Methodological Issues Concerning General Equilibrium Theory', *Cambridge Journal of Economics*, 27: 723–47.

—— (2004) *Adam Smith in Context: a Critical Reassessment of some Central Components of his Thought*, Basingstoke: Palgrave Macmillan.

Montesquieu, C.-L. de Secondat (1748) *De l'Esprit des Loix*. . ., Geneva; trans. A.M. Cohler, B.C. Miller and H.S. Stone (eds) (1989) *Montesquieu. The Spirit of the Laws*, Cambridge: Cambridge University Press.

Moore, F.G. (1927) *De Officio Hominis et Civis Juxta Legem Naturalem Libri Duo by Samuel von Pufendorf*, vol. 2 (*The Translation* [of Pufendorf (1688)]), New York, NY: Oxford University Press.

More, T. (1516) *De Optimo Reipvblicae Statv Deqve Noua Insula Vtopia*. . ., Louvain.

—— (1551) *A Fruteful, and Pleasaunt Worke of the Beste State of a Publyque Weale, and of the Newe Yle Called Vtopia*…, London (trans. R. Robynson).

Morgan, K. (2002) 'Mercantilism and the British Empire, 1688–1815', in D. Winch and P.K. O'Brien (eds) *The Political Economy of British Historical Experience, 1688–1914*, Oxford: Oxford University Press.

Mossner, E.C. and Ross, I.S. (eds) (1987) *The Correspondence of Adam Smith*, 2nd edn, Oxford: Clarendon (Glasgow Edition of the Works and Correspondence of Adam Smith, vol. 6), Oxford: Clarendon.

Müller-Wille, S. (2003) 'Nature as a Marketplace: the Political Economy of Linnaean Botany', in M. Schabas and N. De Marchi (eds) *Oeconomies in the Age of Newton* (Annual Supplement to *History of Political Economy*, vol. 35), Durham, NC: Duke University Press.

Mun, T. (1664) *England's Treasure by Forraign Trade. Or, the Ballance of our Forraign Trade is the Rule of our Treasure*, London.

Mundy, J.H. (1995) 'Medieval Urban Liberty', in R.W. Davis (ed.) *The Origins of Modern Freedom in the West*, Stanford, CA: Stanford University Press.

Murphy, A.E. (1986) *Richard Cantillon: Entrepreneur and Economist*, Clarendon: Oxford.

Naldi, N. (2003) 'Labour Employed in Production and Labour Commanded: a Ricardian Conjecture', *Cambridge Journal of Economics*, 27: 547–62.

von Neumann, J. (1937) 'Über ein Ökonomisches Gleichungssystem und eine Verallgemeinerung des Brouwerschen Fixpunktsatzes', *Ergebnisse eines Mathematischen Kolloquiums*, 8: 73–83 [trans. as (1945–6) 'A Model of General Economic Equilibrium', *Review of Economic Studies*, 13: 1–9].

Newton, I. (1687) *Philosophiæ Naturalis Principia Mathematica*, London.

Norman, R.J. (2005) 'Freedom, Political', in T. Honderich (ed.) *The Oxford Companion to Philosophy*, 2nd edn, Oxford: Oxford University Press.

[North, D.] (1691) *Discourses Upon Trade*…, London; as repr. in J.R. McCulloch (ed.) (1856) *A Select Collection of Early English Tracts on Commerce*…, London: Political Economy Club (facsimile Cambridge: Cambridge University Press, 1952).

North, D.C. (1995) 'The Paradox of the West', in R.W. Davis (ed.) *The Origins of Modern Freedom in the West*, Stanford, CA: Stanford University Press.

Nozick, R. (1974) *Anarchy, State, and Utopia*, New York, NY: Basic Books.

O'Brien, D.P. and Darnell, A.C. (1982) *Authorship Puzzles in the History of Economics: a Statistical Approach*, London: Macmillan.

O'Donnell, R. (1990) *Adam Smith's Theory of Value and Distribution: a Reappraisal*, New York, NY: St. Martin's.

Oldfather, C.H. and Oldfather, W.A. (1934) *De Jure Naturae et Gentium Libri Octo by Samuel Pufendorf*, vol. 2 (*The Translation of the Edition of 1688*), Oxford: Clarendon.

Omori, I. (2003) 'The "Scottish Triangle" in the Shaping of Political Economy: David Hume, Sir James Steuart, and Adam Smith', in T. Sakamoto and H. Tanaka (eds) *The Rise of Political Economy in the Scottish Enlightenment*, London: Routledge.

Ostwald, M. (1995) 'Freedom and the Greeks', in R.W. Davis (ed.) *The Origins of Modern Freedom in the West*, Stanford, CA: Stanford University Press.

Pack, S.J. (1995) 'Adam Smith's Unnaturally Natural (Yet Naturally Unnatural) Use of the Word "Natural"', in I.H. Rima (ed.) *The Classical Tradition in Economic Thought* (*Perspectives on the History of Economic Thought*, vol. 11), Aldershot: Elgar.

—— (2000) 'The Rousseau–Smith Connection: Towards an Understanding of Professor West's "Splenetic Smith"', *History of Economic Ideas*, 8 (no. 2): 35–62.

Park, K. and Daston, L. (eds) (2006) *Early Modern Science* (The Cambridge History of Science, vol. 3), Cambridge: Cambridge University Press.

Pasinetti, L.L. (2001) 'Continuity and Change in Sraffa's Thought: an Archival Excursus', in T. Cozzi and R. Marchionatti (eds) *Piero Sraffa's Political Economy: a Centenary Estimate*, London: Routledge.

Peaucelle, J.-L. (2006) 'Adam Smith's Use of Multiple References for His Pin Making Example', *European Journal of the History of Economic Thought*, 13: 489–512.

Perrotta, C. (2004) *Consumption as an Investment: I. The Fear of Goods from Hesiod to Adam Smith*, London: Routledge (trans. J. McMullin).

[Petty, W.] (1647) *The Advice of W.P. to Mr. Samuel Hartlib. For the Advancement of Some Particular Parts of Learning*, London.

[——] (1662) *A Treatise of Taxes & Contributions*..., London; as repr. in C.H. Hull (ed.) (1899) *The Economic Writings of Sir William Petty*..., vol. 1, Cambridge: Cambridge University Press.

—— (1683a) *Another Essay in Political Arithmetick*..., London; as repr. in C.H. Hull (ed.) (1899) *The Economic Writings of Sir William Petty*..., vol. 2, Cambridge: Cambridge University Press.

[——] (1683b) *Observations upon the Dublin-Bills of Mortality*..., London; as repr. in C.H. Hull (ed.) (1899) *The Economic Writings of Sir William Petty*..., vol. 2, Cambridge: Cambridge University Press.

—— (1690) *Political Arithmetick*..., London; as repr. in C.H. Hull (ed.) (1899) *The Economic Writings of Sir William Petty*..., vol. 1, Cambridge: Cambridge University Press.

—— (1691a) *The Political Anatomy of Ireland*..., London; as repr. in C.H. Hull (ed.) (1899) *The Economic Writings of Sir William Petty*..., vol. 1, Cambridge: Cambridge University Press.

—— (1691b) *Verbum Sapienti*; as repr. in C.H. Hull (ed.) (1899) *The Economic Writings of Sir William Petty*..., vol. 1, Cambridge: Cambridge University Press.

Phillipson, N. (1983) 'Adam Smith as Civic Moralist', in I. Hont and M. Ignatieff (eds) *Wealth and Virtue: the Shaping of Political Economy in the Scottish Enlightenment*, Cambridge: Cambridge University Press.

—— (1987) 'Stewart, Dugald (1753–1828)', in J. Eatwell, M. Milgate and P. Newman (eds) *The New Palgrave: a Dictionary of Economics*, vol. 4, London: Macmillan.

—— (2001) 'Scotland', in M. Delon (ed.) *Encyclopedia of the Enlightenment*, vol. 2, Chicago, IL: Fitzroy Dearborn (French edn 1997).

Pivetti, M. (1991) *An Essay on Money and Distribution*, New York, NY: St. Martin's Press.

Pomeroy, S.B. (1994) *Xenophon.* Oeconomicus*: a Social and Historical Commentary, with a New English Translation*, Oxford: Clarendon.

Porta, P.L. and Scazzieri, R. (2002) 'Pietro Verri's Political Economy: Commercial Society, Civil Society, and the Science of the Legislator', *History of Political Economy*, 34: 83–110.

Pownall, T. (1776) *A Letter from Governor Pownall to Adam Smith*..., London; as repr. in E.C. Mossner and I.S. Ross (eds) (1977) *The Correspondence of Adam Smith* (Glasgow Edition of the Works and Correspondence of Adam Smith, vol. 6), Oxford: Clarendon.

Prendergast, R. (1991) 'Cantillon and the Emergence of the Theory of Profit', *History of Political Economy*, 23: 419–29.

Pufendorf, S. (1672) *De Jure Naturæ et Gentium*..., Lund.

—— (1682) *De Officio Hominis & Civis…*, Cambridge (1st edn 1673); repr. in *De Officio Hominis et Civis Juxta Legem Naturalem Libri Duo by Samuel von Pufendorf*, vol. 1 (*The Photographic Reproduction of the Edition of 1682*), with an Introduction by W. Schücking, New York, NY: Oxford University Press (1927).

—— (1688) *De Jure Naturæ et Gentium…*, Amsterdam (1st edn 1672); repr. in *De Jure Naturae et Gentium Libri Octo by Samuel Pufendorf*, vol. 1 (*The Photographic Reproduction of the Edition of 1688*), with an Introduction by W. Simons, Oxford: Clarendon (1934).

Puro, E. (1992) 'Uses of the Term "Natural" in Adam Smith's *Wealth of Nations*', in W.J. Samuels (ed.) *Research in the History of Economic Thought and Methodology*, vol. 9, Greenwood, CT: JAI Press.

Raaflaub, K. (2003) 'Freedom in the Ancient World', in S. Hornblower and A. Spawforth (eds) *The Oxford Classical Dictionary*, rev. 3rd edn, Oxford: Oxford University Press.

Rae, J. (1895) *Life of Adam Smith*, London: Macmillan.

Raphael, D.D. (1985) *Adam Smith* (Past Masters Series), Oxford: Oxford University Press; as repr. in D.D. Raphael, D. Winch and R. Skidelsky (1997) *Three Great Economists: Smith, Malthus, Keynes*, Oxford: Oxford University Press.

—— (2001) *Concepts of Justice*, Oxford: Clarendon.

Raphael, D.D. and Macfie, A.L. (eds) (1976a) *Adam Smith. The Theory of Moral Sentiments* (Glasgow Edition of the Works and Correspondence of Adam Smith, vol. 1), Oxford: Clarendon.

—— (1976b) 'Introduction', in D.D. Raphael and A.L. Macfie (eds) *Adam Smith. The Theory of Moral Sentiments* (Glasgow Edition of the Works and Correspondence of Adam Smith, vol. 1), Oxford: Clarendon.

Raphael, D.D. and Skinner, A.S. (1980) 'General Introduction', in W.P.D. Wightman and J.B. Bryce (eds) *Adam Smith. Essays on Philosophical Subjects…* (Glasgow Edition of the Works and Correspondence of Adam Smith, vol. 3), Oxford: Clarendon.

Rashid, S. (1998) *The Myth of Adam Smith*, Cheltenham: Elgar.

Rausing, L. (2003) 'Underwriting the Oeconomy: Linnaeus on Nature and Mind', in M. Schabas and N. De Marchi (eds) *Oeconomies in the Age of Newton* (Annual Supplement to *History of Political Economy*, vol. 35), Durham, NC: Duke University Press.

Redman, D.A. (1997) *The Rise of Political Economy as a Science: Methodology and the Classical Economists*, Cambridge, MA: MIT Press.

Reeve, A. (2003a) 'Freedom', in I. McLean and A. McMillan (eds) *The Concise Oxford Dictionary of Politics*, 2nd edn, Oxford: Oxford University Press.

—— (2003b) 'Political Philosophy', in I. McLean and A. McMillan (eds) *The Concise Oxford Dictionary of Politics*, 2nd edn, Oxford: Oxford University Press.

Reill, P.H. (ed.) (1996) *Encyclopedia of the Enlightenment* (principal author E.J. Wilson), New York, NY: Facts on File Inc.

Reiss, Jr., A.J. (1968) 'Sociology: the Field', in D.L. Sills (ed.) *International Encyclopedia of the Social Sciences*, vol. 15, New York, NY: Macmillan & the Free Press.

Richards, R.D. (1926) 'Early History of the Term Capital', *Quarterly Journal of Economics*, 40: 329–38.

Richardson, G.B. (1975) 'Adam Smith on Competition and Increasing Returns', in A.S. Skinner and T. Wilson (eds) *Essays on Adam Smith*, Oxford: Clarendon.

Riskin, J. (2003) 'The "Spirit of System" and the Fortunes of Physiocracy', in M. Schabas and N. De Marchi (eds) *Oeconomies in the Age of Newton* (Annual Supplement to *History of Political Economy*, vol. 35), Durham, NC: Duke University Press.

Robbins, L. (1935) *An Essay on the Nature and Significance of Economic Science*, 2nd edn, London: Macmillan.

Robertson, H.M. and Taylor, W.L. (1957) 'Adam Smith's Approach to the Theory of Value', *Economic Journal*, 67: 181–98.

Robertson, J. (2005) *The Case for the Enlightenment: Scotland and Naples 1680–1760*, Cambridge: Cambridge University Press.

Rogers, J.D. (1899) 'Police', in R.H.I. Palgrave (ed.) *Dictionary of Political Economy*, vol. 3, London: Macmillan.

Roll, E. (1961) *A History of Economic Thought*, 2nd edn, London: Faber and Faber.

Roncaglia, A. (1988) 'William Petty and the Conceptual Framework for the Analysis of Economic Development', in K.J. Arrow (ed.) *The Balance between Industry and Agriculture in Economic Development*, vol. 1: *Basic Issues*, London: Macmillan.

—— (2005) *The Wealth of Ideas: a History of Economic Thought*, Cambridge: Cambridge University Press.

de Roover, R. (1956) 'The Development of Accounting Prior to Luca Pacioli According to the Account-Books of Medieval Merchants', in A.C. Littleton and B.S. Yamey (eds) *Studies in the History of Accounting*, Homewood, IL: Irwin; as repr. in J. Kirshner (ed.) (1974) *Business, Banking, and Economic Thought in Late Medieval and Early Modern Europe: Selected Studies of Raymond de Roover*, Chicago, IL: University of Chicago Press.

—— (1958) 'The Concept of the Just Price: Theory and Economic Policy', *Journal of Economic History*, 18: 418–34.

Rosenberg, N. (1960) 'Some Institutional Aspects of the *Wealth of Nations*', *Journal of Political Economy*, 68: 557–70.

—— (1965) 'Adam Smith on the Division of Labour: Two Views or One?', *Economica*, 32: 127–39.

—— (1968) 'Adam Smith, Consumer Tastes, and Economic Growth', *Journal of Political Economy*, 76: 361–74.

—— (1979) 'Adam Smith and Laissez-Faire Revisited', in G.P. O'Driscoll, Jr. (ed.) *Adam Smith and Modern Political Economy: bicentennial essays on* The Wealth of Nations, Ames, IA: Iowa State University Press.

—— (1987) 'Mandeville, Bernard', in J. Eatwell, M. Milgate and P. Newman (eds) *The New Palgrave: a Dictionary of Economics*, vol. 3, London: Macmillan.

Ross, I.S. (1995) *The Life of Adam Smith*, Oxford: Clarendon.

—— (2006) 'Reply to Charles Griswold "On the Incompleteness of Adam Smith's System"', *Adam Smith Review*, 2: 187–91.

Rothschild, E. (1992) 'Adam Smith and Conservative Economics', *Economic History Review*, 45: 74–96.

—— (2001) *Economic Sentiments: Adam Smith, Condorcet, and the Enlightenment*, Cambridge, MA: Harvard University Press.

Rothschild, E. and Sen, A. (2006) 'Adam Smith's Economics', in K. Haakonssen (ed.) *The Cambridge Companion to Adam Smith*, Cambridge: Cambridge University Press.

Rubinstein, A. (2004) 'Afterword', in J. von Neumann and O. Morgenstern, *Theory of Games and Economic Behaviour* (Sixtieth-Anniversary Edition), Princeton, NJ: Princeton University Press.

Ruse, M. (2005) 'Nature', in T. Honderich (ed.) *The Oxford Companion to Philosophy*, 2nd edn, Oxford: Oxford University Press.

Russell, R. (1755) *The Oeconomy of Nature in Acute and Chronical Diseases of the Glands*, London.

Salter, J. (1997) 'Justice and Price: Comment on Jeffrey T. Young', *History of Political Economy*, 29: 675–84.

—— (2000) 'Adam Smith: Justice and Due Shares', *Economics and Philosophy*, 16: 139–46.

Samuelson, P.A. (1978) 'The Canonical Classical Model of Political Economy', *Journal of Economic Literature*, 16: 1415–34.

Say, J.-B. (1880) *A Treatise on Political Economy, or the Production, Distribution, and Consumption of Wealth*, Philadelphia, PA: Claxton, Remsen & Haffelfinger (trans. C.R. Prinsep, with additional trans. C.C. Biddle; 1st French edn 1803).

Schabas, M. (2003) 'Adam Smith's Debts to Nature', in M. Schabas and N. De Marchi (eds) *Oeconomies in the Age of Newton* (Annual Supplement to *History of Political Economy*, vol. 35), Durham, NC: Duke University Press.

—— (2005) *The Natural Origins of Economics*, Chicago, IL: University of Chicago Press.

Schabas, M. and De Marchi, N. (eds) (2003) *Oeconomies in the Age of Newton* (Annual Supplement to *History of Political Economy*, vol. 35), Durham, NC: Duke University Press.

Schefold, B. (1985) 'Ecological Problems as a Challenge to Classical and Keynesian Economics', *Metroeconomica*, 37: 21–61; repr. in B. Schefold (1997) *Normal Prices, Technical Change and Accumulation*, London: Macmillan.

—— (1999) 'Use Value and the "Commercial Knowledge of Commodities": Reflections on Aristotle, Savary and the Classics', in G. Mongiovi and F. Petri (eds) *Value, Distribution and Capital: Essays in Honour of Pierangelo Garegnagni*, London: Routledge.

Schreyer, R. (1989) '"Pray What Language did Your Wild Couple Speak, When First They Met?" – Language and the Science of Man in the Scottish Enlightenment', in P. Jones (ed.) *The 'Science of Man' in the Scottish Enlightenment: Hume, Reid and their Contemporaries*, Edinburgh: Edinburgh University Press.

Schumpeter, J.A. (1954) *History of Economic Analysis* (ed. E.B. Schumpeter), New York, NY: Oxford University Press.

Scott, J. and Marshall, G. (2005) *A Dictionary of Sociology*, 3rd edn, Oxford: Oxford University Press.

Scott, W.R. (1937) *Adam Smith as Student and Professor*..., Glasgow: Jackson.

Screpanti, E. and Zamagni, S. (2005) *An Outline of the History of Economic Thought: Second Edition Revised and Expanded*, Oxford: Oxford University Press (trans. D. Field and L. Kirby).

Seabright, P. (2004) *The Company of Strangers: a Natural History of Economic Life*, Princeton, NJ: Princeton University Press.

Seidler, M.J. (1994) 'Translator's Introduction', in C.L. Carr (ed.) *The Political Writings of Samuel Pufendorf*, trans. M.J. Seidler, Oxford: Oxford University Press.

Sekora, J. (1977) *Luxury: the Concept in Western Thought, Eden to Smollet*, Baltimore, MD: Johns Hopkins University Press.

Sewall, H.R. (1901) 'The Theory of Value Before Adam Smith', *Publications of the American Economic Association*, 3rd Series, vol. 2 (no. 3).

Sharpe, J.A. (1994) 'Police', in J. Black and R. Porter (eds) *A Dictionary of Eighteenth-Century World History*, Oxford: Blackwell.

[Sheridan, T.] (1677) *A Discourse on the Rise and Power of Parliaments*..., London; as repr. in S. Bannister (ed.) (1870) *Some Revelations in Irish History; or, Old Elements of Creed and Class Conciliation in Ireland*, London: Longmans, Green, Reader and Dyer.

Simpson, D.P. (1968) *Cassell's New Latin-English, English-Latin Dictionary*, 5th edn, London: Cassell.

Sippel, R. (1997) 'An Experiment on the Pure Theory of Consumer's Behaviour', *Economic Journal*, 107: 1431–44.
Skinner, A.S. (1996) *A System of Social Science: Papers Relating to Adam Smith*, 2nd edn, Oxford: Clarendon.
Skinner, Q. (1978) *The Foundations of Modern Political Thought*, 2 vols, Cambridge: Cambridge University Press.
[Smith, A.] (1755) [Review of Johnson (1755)], *Edinburgh Review*, no. 1: 61–73; repr. in W.P.D. Wightman, J.C. Bryce and I.S. Ross (eds) (1980) *Adam Smith. Essays on Philosophical Subjects* (Glasgow Edition of the Works and Correspondence of Adam Smith, vol. 3), Oxford: Clarendon.
—— (1761) 'Considerations Concerning the First Formation of Languages, &c. &c.', in *The Philological Miscellany*..., London; repr. (from the 1790 edn) in J.C. Bryce (ed.) (1983) *Adam Smith. Lectures on Rhetoric and Belles Lettres* (Glasgow Edition of the Works and Correspondence of Adam Smith, vol. 4), Oxford: Clarendon.
—— *For further Smith references, see the Note on Citation Practice at pp. xviii–xix.*
Smith, C. (2006) *Adam Smith's Political Philosophy: the Invisible Hand and Spontaneous Order*, London: Routledge.
Smith, V.E. (1951) 'The Classicists' Use of "Demand"', *Journal of Political Economy*, 59: 242–57.
Snow, C.P. (1959) *The Two Cultures and the Scientific Revolution: the Rede Lecture, 1959*, Cambridge: Cambridge University Press.
Soudek, J. (1952) 'Aristotle's Theory of Exchange: an Inquiry into the Origin of Economic Analysis', *Proceedings of the American Philosophical Society*, 96: 45–75.
Spadafora, D. (1990) *The Idea of Progress in Eighteenth-Century Britain*, New Haven, CT: Yale University Press.
Sraffa, P. (1960) *Production of Commodities by Means of Commodities: Prelude to a Critique of Economic Theory*, Cambridge: Cambridge University Press.
Stauffer, R.C. (1960) 'Ecology in the Long Manuscript Version of Darwin's *Origin of Species* and Linnaeus' *Oeconomy of Nature*', *Proceedings of the American Philosophical Society*, 104: 235–41.
Steedman, I. *et al.* (2001) 'Exhaustible Natural Resources and Sraffian Analysis: ... a symposium', *Metroeconomica*, 52: 239–328 (with contributions by C. Bidard, G. Erreygers, E. Hosoda, H.D. Kurz, N. Salvadori, C. Lager, S. Parrinello and B. Schefold).
Steuart, J. (1767) *An Inquiry into the Principles of Political Oeconomy: being an Essay on the Science of Domestic Policy in Free Nations*..., 2 vols, London; in A.S. Skinner (ed.) (1966) *Sir James Steuart. An Inquiry into the Principles of Political Oeconomy*, 2 vols, Edinburgh: Oliver & Boyd.
Stewart, D. (1811) 'Account of the Life and Writings of Adam Smith, LL.D.' in D. Stewart, *Biographical Memoirs of Adam Smith, LL.D. of William Robertson, D.D. and of Thomas Reid, D.D.*..., Edinburgh: Creech, Bell and Bradfute *et al.* (1st edn, 1794); as repr. in W.P.D. Wightman, J.C. Bryce and I.S. Ross (eds) (1980) *Adam Smith. Essays on Philosophical Subjects* (Glasgow Edition of the Works and Correspondence of Adam Smith, vol. 3), Oxford: Clarendon.
Stirati, A. (1994) *The Theory of Wages in Classical Economics: a Study of Adam Smith, David Ricardo and their Contemporaries*, Aldershot: Elgar (trans. J. Hall; Italian edn 1991).
Stocking, Jr., G.W. (1975) 'Scotland as the Model of Mankind: Lord Kames' Philosophical View of Civilization', in T.H.H. Thoresen (ed.) *Towards a Science of Man: Essays in the History of Anthropology*, The Hague: Mouton.

Stroud, B. (1977) *Hume*, London: Routledge & Kegan Paul.

Sylos-Labini, P. (1976) 'Competition: the Product Markets', in T. Wilson and A.S. Skinner (eds) *The Market and the State: Essays in Honour of Adam Smith*, Oxford: Clarendon.

Tanaka, S. (2003) 'The Main Themes and Structure of Moral Philosophy and the Formation of Political Economy in Adam Smith', in T. Sakamoto and H. Tanaka (eds) *The Rise of Political Economy in the Scottish Enlightenment*, London: Routledge.

Teichgraeber, R.F. (1986) *'Free Trade' and Moral Philosophy: Rethinking the Sources of Adam Smith's* Wealth of Nations, Durham, NC: Duke University Press.

Theocarakis, N.J. (2006) '*Nicomachean Ethics* in Political Economy: the Trajectory of the Problem of Value', *History of Economic Ideas*, 14 (no. 1): 9–53.

Thompson, W. (2004) *Postmodernism and History*, Basingstoke: Palgrave Macmillan.

Thweatt, W.O. (1983) 'Origins of the Terminology "Supply and Demand"', *Scottish Journal of Political Economy*, 30: 287–94.

Tierney, B. (1995) 'Freedom and the Medieval Church', in R.W. Davis (ed.) *The Origins of Modern Freedom in the West*, Stanford, CA: Stanford University Press.

Tobin, J. (1992) 'The Invisible Hand in Modern Macroeconomics', in M. Fry (ed.) *Adam Smith's Legacy: his Place in the Development of Modern Economics*, London: Routledge.

Tribe, K. (1980) 'Introduction to Knemeyer', *Economy and Society*, 9: 168–71.

—— (1984) 'Cameralism and the Science of Government', *Journal of Modern History*, 56: 263–84.

—— (1988) *Governing Economy: the Reformation of German Economic Discourse 1750–1840*, Cambridge: Cambridge University Press.

—— (1995) *Strategies of Economic Order: German Economic Discourse, 1750–1950*, Cambridge: Cambridge University Press.

Tucker, G.S.L. (1960) *Progress and Profits in British Economic Thought 1650–1850*, Cambridge: Cambridge University Press.

Turgot, A.R.J. (1769–70) *Réflexions sur la Formation et la Distribution des Richesses*, in *Éphémérides du Citoyen*, Paris, November 1769, December 1769, January 1770 [in 3 instalments]; trans. P.D. Groenewegen (from the 1788 edn) (1977) *Reflections on the Formation and Distribution of Wealth*, in P.D. Groenewegen (ed.) *The Economics of A.R.J. Turgot*, The Hague: Martinus Nijhoff.

Turner, S.P. and Roth, P.A. (2003) 'Introduction. Ghosts and the Machine: Issues of Agency, Rationality, and Scientific Methodology in Contemporary Philosophy of Social Science', in S.P. Turner and P.A. Roth (eds) *The Blackwell Guide to the Philosophy of the Social Sciences*, Oxford: Blackwell.

Vaggi, G. (1987a) 'Physiocrats', in J. Eatwell, M. Milgate and P. Newman (eds) *The New Palgrave: a Dictionary of Economics*, vol. 3, London: Macmillan.

—— (1987b) 'Quesnay, François', in J. Eatwell, M. Milgate and P. Newman (eds) *The New Palgrave: a Dictionary of Economics*, vol. 4, London: Macmillan.

—— (1987c) *The Economics of François Quesnay*, London: Macmillan.

Vanderlint, J. (1734) *Money Answers All Things*..., London.

Vassilakis, S. (1987) 'Increasing Returns to Scale', in J. Eatwell, M. Milgate and P. Newman (eds) *The New Palgrave: a Dictionary of Economics*, vol. 2, London: Macmillan.

Vaughn, K.I. (1987) 'Invisible Hand', in J. Eatwell, M. Milgate and P. Newman (eds) *The New Palgrave: a Dictionary of Economics*, vol. 2, London: Macmillan.

Verri, P. (1771) *Meditazioni sulla Economia Politica*, Livorno; trans. B. McGilvray

(from the 1781 edn), in P.D. Groenewegen (ed.) (1986) *Pietro Verri 1771. Reflections on Political Economy*, Reprints of Economic Classics no. 4 (series 2), Sydney: Department of Economics, University of Sydney.
Veyne, P. (1990) *Bread and Circuses: Historical Sociology and Political Pluralism*, London: Allen Lane (abridged O. Murray; trans. B. Pearce; French edn 1976).
Vianello, F. (1989) 'Natural (or Normal) Prices: Some Pointers', *Political Economy: Studies in the Surplus Approach*, 5: 89–105.
—— (1999) 'Social Accounting with Adam Smith', in G. Mongiovi and F. Petri (eds) *Value, Distribution and Capital: Essays in Honour of Pierangelo Garegnani*, London: Routledge.
Vincent-Lancrin, S. (2003) 'Adam Smith and the Division of Labour: is There a Difference between Organisation and Market?', *Cambridge Journal of Economics*, 27: 209–24.
Viner, J. (1927) 'Adam Smith and Laissez Faire', *Journal of Political Economy*, 35: 198–232.
—— (1928) 'Adam Smith and Laissez Faire', in J.M. Clark *et al.*, *Adam Smith, 1776–1926: Lectures to Commemorate the Sesquicentennial of the Publication of 'The Wealth of Nations'*, Chicago, IL: University of Chicago Press.
—— (1948) 'Power versus Plenty as Objectives of Foreign Policy in the Seventeenth and Eighteenth Centuries', *World Politics*, 1: 1–29; repr. in D.C. Coleman (ed.) (1969) *Revisions in Mercantilism*, London: Methuen.
—— (1955) *Studies in the Theory of International Trade*, London: George Allen & Unwin (1st edn 1937).
—— (1965) 'Introduction: Guide to John Rae's *Life of Adam Smith*', in *Life of Adam Smith by John Rae [1895], with an Introduction: "Guide to John Rae's* Life of Adam Smith*" by Jacob Viner*, New York, NY: Kelley.
Vivenza, G. (2001) *Adam Smith and the Classics: the Classical Heritage in Adam Smith's Thought*, Oxford: Oxford University Press (trans. C. Cheesman and N. Gelder; Italian edn 1984).
—— (2005) 'The Agent, the Actor, and the Spectator: Adam Smith's Metaphors in Recent Literature', *History of Economic Ideas*, 13 (no. 1): 37–56.
Vyverberg, H. (1989) *Human Nature, Cultural Diversity, and the French Enlightenment*, Oxford: Oxford University Press.
Wahnbaeck, T. (2004) *Luxury and Public Happiness: Political Economy in the Italian Enlightenment*, Clarendon: Oxford.
Walras, L. (1874) *Éléments d'Économie Politique Pure*, Lausanne: Corbaz.
Walsh, V. (2000) 'Smith After Sen', *Review of Political Economy*, 12: 5–25.
—— (2003) 'Sen After Putnam', *Review of Political Economy*, 15: 315–94.
Waterman, A.M.C. (2001) 'Notes Towards an Un-canonical, Pre-classical Model of Political Oeconomy', in E.L. Forget and S. Peart (eds) *Reflections on the Classical Canon in Economics: Essays in Honor of Samuel Hollander*, London: Routledge.
—— (2003) 'Mathematical Modeling as an Exegetical Tool: Rational Reconstruction', in W.J. Samuels, J.E. Biddle and J.B. Davis (eds) *A Companion to the History of Economic Thought*, Oxford: Blackwell.
West, E.G. (1964) 'Adam Smith's Two Views on the Division of Labour', *Economica*, 31: 23–32.
—— (1969) 'The Political Economy of Alienation: Karl Marx and Adam Smith', *Oxford Economic Papers*, 21: 1–23.
—— (1975) 'Adam Smith and Alienation: Wealth Increases, Men Decay?', in A.S. Skinner and T. Wilson (eds) *Essays on Adam Smith*, Oxford: Clarendon.

—— (1996) 'Adam Smith on the Cultural Effects of Specialization: Splenetics versus Economics', *History of Political Economy*, 28: 83–105.
White, M.V. (1987) 'Robinson Crusoe', in J. Eatwell, M. Milgate and P. Newman (eds) *The New Palgrave: a Dictionary of Economics*, vol. 4, London: Macmillan.
Wightman, W.P.D. (1980) 'Introduction[s]', in W.P.D. Wightman, J.C. Bryce and I.S. Ross (eds) *Adam Smith. Essays on Philosophical Subjects* (Glasgow Edition of the Works and Correspondence of Adam Smith, vol. 3), Oxford: Clarendon.
Willig, R.D. (1987) 'Contestable Markets', in J. Eatwell, M. Milgate and P. Newman (eds) *The New Palgrave: a Dictionary of Economics*, vol. 1, London: Macmillan.
Wilson, G.W. (1975) 'The Economics of the Just Price', *History of Political Economy*, 7: 56–74.
Winch, D. (1971) *The Emergence of Economics as a Science 1750–1870*, London: Collins.
—— (1978) *Adam Smith's Politics: an Essay in Historiographic Revision*, Cambridge: Cambridge University Press.
—— (1983a) 'Adam Smith's "Enduring Particular Result": a Political and Cosmopolitan Perspective', in I. Hont and M. Ignatieff (eds) *Wealth and Virtue: the Shaping of Political Economy in the Scottish Enlightenment*, Cambridge: Cambridge University Press.
—— (1983b) 'Science and the Legislator: Adam Smith and After', *Economic Journal*, 93: 501–20.
—— (1996) *Riches and Poverty: an Intellectual History of Political Economy in Britain, 1750–1834*, Cambridge: Cambridge University Press.
—— (1997) 'Adam Smith's Problems and Ours', *Scottish Journal of Political Economy*, 44: 384–402.
—— (2002) 'Introduction', in D. Winch and P.K. O'Brien (eds) *The Political Economy of British Historical Experience, 1688–1914*, Oxford: Oxford University Press.
Wolin, R. (2004) *The Seduction of Unreason: the Intellectual Romance with Fascism from Nietzsche to Postmodernism*, Princeton, NJ: Princeton University Press.
Wood, D. (2002) *Medieval Economic Thought*, Cambridge: Cambridge University Press.
Wood, P.B. (1996) 'The Science of Man', in N. Jardine, J.A. Secord and E.C. Spary (eds) *Cultures of Natural History*, Cambridge: Cambridge University Press.
Worster, D. (1994) *Nature's Economy: a History of Ecological Ideas*, 2nd edn, Cambridge: Cambridge University Press.
Yamey, B.S. (1987) 'Double-Entry Bookkeeping', in J. Eatwell, M. Milgate and P. Newman (eds) *The New Palgrave: a Dictionary of Economics*, vol. 1, London: Macmillan.
Young, A.A. (1928) 'Increasing Returns and Economic Progress', *Economic Journal*, 38: 527–42.
Young, J.T. (1995) 'Natural Jurisprudence and the Theory of Value in Adam Smith', *History of Political Economy*, 27: 755–73.
—— (1997a) *Economics as a Moral Science: the Political Economy of Adam Smith*, Cheltenham: Elgar.
—— (1997b) 'Justice and Price: Reply to John Salter', *History of Political Economy*, 29: 685–9.
—— (2005) 'Unintended Order and Intervention: Adam Smith's Theory of the Role of the State', in S.G. Medema and P. Boettke (eds) *The Role of Government in the History of Economic Thought*, Durham, NC: Duke University Press.

# Index

Note: Page numbers in bold type, e.g. **115–18**, indicate detailed discussion of the topic.